"*When Workers Shot Back* is a revelatory .... violence by workers in American hist. ....g a crucial historical and social legacy of the American labor movement."
–*Immanuel Ness, author of* Southern Insurgency: The Coming of the Global Working Class (*Pluto*), *Professor, Brooklyn College, City University of New York*

"Ovetz shows us how to answer the question of when and why have workers taken up arms, providing us with an essential methodology for thinking through our own situations, past and future."
–*Harry Cleaver, author of* Reading Capital Politically *and* Rupturing the Dialectic (*AK Press*)

"The ticking time bomb of revolt is percolating just beneath the surface of this surprisingly fragile social order. When it finally detonates, as it inevitably will, Ovetz's book will be prescient. I'd recommend getting acquainted with it and its enormous implications well before that imminent explosion."
–*Chris Carlsson, author of* Nowtopia (*AK Press*) *and co-director of Shaping San Francisco, Foundsf.org*

"An indispensable book for understanding the violent nature of the capital-labor relationship during the late 19th and early 20th century."
–*Andrew Kolin, Professor, Hilbert College, author of* Political Economy of Labor Repression in the United States (*Lexington Books*)

When Workers Shot Back

Historical Materialism Book Series

The Historical Materialism Book Series is a major publishing initiative of the radical left. The capitalist crisis of the twenty-first century has been met by a resurgence of interest in critical Marxist theory. At the same time, the publishing institutions committed to Marxism have contracted markedly since the high point of the 1970s. The Historical Materialism Book Series is dedicated to addressing this situation by making available important works of Marxist theory. The aim of the series is to publish important theoretical contributions as the basis for vigorous intellectual debate and exchange on the left.

The peer-reviewed series publishes original monographs, translated texts, and reprints of classics across the bounds of academic disciplinary agendas and across the divisions of the left. The series is particularly concerned to encourage the internationalization of Marxist debate and aims to translate significant studies from beyond the English-speaking world.

For a full list of titles in the Historical Materialism Book Series
available in paperback from Haymarket Books, visit:
https://www.haymarketbooks.org/series_collections/1-historical-materialism

When Workers Shot Back

Class Conflict from 1877 to 1921

Robert Ovetz

Haymarket Books
Chicago, IL

First published in 2018 by Brill Academic Publishers, The Netherlands
© 2018 Koninklijke Brill NV, Leiden, The Netherlands

Published in paperback in 2019 by
Haymarket Books
P.O. Box 180165
Chicago, IL 60618
773-583-7884
www.haymarketbooks.org

ISBN: 978-1-64259-059-3

Distributed to the trade in the US through Consortium Book Sales and
Distribution (www.cbsd.com) and internationally through Ingram
Publisher Services International (www.ingramcontent.com).

This book was published with the generous support of Lannan
Foundation and Wallace Action Fund.

Special discounts are available for bulk purchases by organizations and
institutions. Please call 773-583-7884 or email info@haymarketbooks.org
for more information.

Cover design by Jamie Kerry and Ragina Johnson.

Printed in the United States.

10 9 8 7 6 5 4 3 2 1

Library of Congress Cataloging-in-Publication data is available.

Contents

List of Figures and Tables

Figure

Tables

Introduction

If I fall by the hand of such, I shall fall the victim of the noblest of causes, that of maintaining the just rights of my country. I aspire to the honest ambition of meriting the appellation of the preserver of my country, equally with the Chiefs among *you*, whom, from acting on such principles, you have exalted to the highest pitch of glory. And if, after every peaceable mode of obtaining a redress of grievances proved fruitless, a recourse to arms to obtain it be a mark of the savage, and not of the soldier, what savages must the Americans be, and how much undeserved applause have your Cincinnatus, your Fabius, obtained.

HOBOI-HILI MIKO (ALEXANDER MCGILLIVRAY), 1787[1]

• • •

As the domination and arrogance of the ruling class increased, the capacity of the lower classes to resist, within the limits of law and constitution, decreased. Every avenue, in fact, was blocked by corruption. Juries, courts, legislatures, congresses, they were as if they were not. The people were walled in by impassable barriers. Nothing was left them but the primal, brute instincts of the animal man, and upon these they fell back, and the Brotherhood of Destruction arose.

IGNATIUS DONNELLY, 1890[2]

•
• •
•

In July 1877, as the remaining troops were pulled out of the South and Reconstruction brought to a premature end, railroad workers went on strike, shutting down nearly the entire country for about two weeks. The strike opened up nearly a half century of violent class conflict, an 'uncivil war' between capital and labour. The railroad workers, unemployed workers, and their supporters soon responded to the use of state and local militias with rocks, sticks, fire

---

1   Creek leader Hoboi-Hili Miko's (also known as Alexander McGillivray) letter to James White, superintendent of the Creek Indians appointed by Congress, 8 April 1787.

2   Donnelly 1960 [1890], pp. 95–6.

and guns. As they would do time and again in the coming decades, workers shot back in the face of the combined repressive force of capital and government. The 1877 railroad strike set the pattern for class conflict over the next half century: with little or no political space in which to organise and present grievances for redress, workers and their supporters took up arms in self-defence and to pursue their interests. By the 1940s, such armed class warfare became rare, and since the 1970s has become virtually non-existent. It would be foolhardy to mistake the lack of overt violence in class struggle today for its disappearance; there are many present parallels with the socio-economic and political conditions that dominated the era explored here. Today's corporate domination of the two party duopoly, elite control of the political process, the widening chasm of income and wealth inequality, and suppression of dissent are ominous precursors to the tactical use of violence. As Creek leader Hoboi-Hili Miko observed in 1787, after all efforts at peaceful redress of grievances are ignored, co-opted, blocked, diffused, deflected, or repressed, the dissident will become an armed revolutionary. Nearly a century later, Ignatius Donnelly wrote a novel warning of the explosive outcome made inevitable when all avenues of peaceful change are blocked. In the class struggle, workers will shoot back.

Trajectory of Violence

While much studied, the violence that characterised this half century of class conflict has rarely been examined other than from historical[3] or moralistic[4] perspectives, which serve to either document or judge.

A third, less common approach to analysing class struggle focuses on the self-organisation of workers in order to situate class struggle within the existing class composition.[5] Nearly half of this book deals with the 1877 and 1894 railroad strikes, as they illustrate an organisational and strategic transition in class struggle. But rather than understanding such experimentation as an

---

3 Bernstein 1960; Boyer and Morais 1955; Brecher 1972; Burbank 1966; Foner 1947, 1965, 1973, 1977; Gage 2009; Green 2015; Haring 1983; Lens 1973; Shoup 2010; Smith 2006; Stromquist 1993; Yolen 1936; and Zinn 2013.

4 Adamic 1931; Adams 1966; Bellesiles 2010; Bimba 1950; Grant 1915; Ross and Taft 1969; Sandine 2009; and Taft 1966.

5 Alquati nd; Bell and Cleaver 2002; Bologna 1976; Cleaver 1979, 1989, 1992, 2016; Glaberman 1965, 1973, 1984, 1991; Glaberman and Rawick 1977; Holloway 2005; Lindsey 1942; Montgomery 1974, 1977, 1980, 1989; Ramirez 1978; Rawick 1969; Silver 2003; Stone 1973; Tilly and Tilly 1998; Tronti 1962; and Watson 1971.

'attempt to impose some order on a chaotic and deteriorating labor market that undermined their wages and the rules that governed their work', these strikes demonstrated the potential for a perpetually disruptive working-class to trigger a systemic crisis of capitalism.[6] That these strikes were resolved through the lenses of wages and control is a manifestation of the search for new mechanisms of discipline to harness and manage class struggle.

While this later class composition approach has greatly influenced my thinking, it lacks the essential element of how workers' self-organisation within the context of the existing class composition shapes their tactics and strategy. For this reason, I propose a 'trajectory theory of political violence', which does two things. First, it seeks to explore both the tactics and strategies workers use to self-organise in order to recompose working-class power in light of the existing composition of capital. Second, it examines how capital designs its tactics and strategies in response in order to restore its class power.

Variably portrayed as the rationalisation of the labour process, consolidation of capital, government regulation, collective bargaining, and arbitration, each descriptor reflects capital's groping for a strategy of restoring control. The focus on the 1877 and 1894 railroad strikes is intentional. As Shelton Stromquist observed,

> Rationalization of the railroad labor process ultimately came through the intervention of the federal government and the consolidation of the industry. But it was the persistence and growth of railroad labor conflict during the last three decades of the nineteenth century that fueled the search for a systemic corporate labor policy.[7]

Beginning this book with a focus on the 1877 and 1894 railroad strikes is intentional. I have taken up Stromquist's call for a 'study of the evolving patterns of strike activity that would link and help make sense of the individual episodes' in order to analyse how these strikes drove development in the railroad industry as demonstrated through industrial work, class composition, and the relations between workers and capital.[8] I seek to widen the focus of Stromquist's project even further, recognising each of the discussed strikes as currents in a cycle of class struggle and the transformation of class composition that lasted nearly half a century.

---

6 Stromquist 1993, p. xvi.

7 Ibid.

8 Ibid., p. 25.

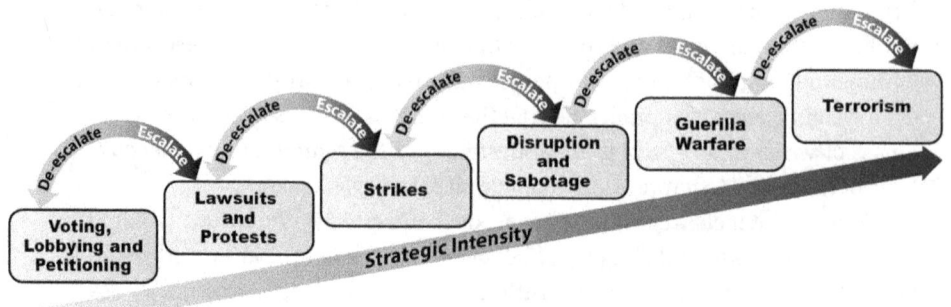

FIGURE 1   *Trajectory of political violence*

My examination of class composition seeks to understand why workers were more likely to shoot back – under what conditions were workers engaged in class struggle likely to become violent? To answer this question, violence will be explored through the lenses of tactics and strategy. In the face of repression and with widespread mass support, workers and their allies move along what I call a 'trajectory of political violence'. As shown in Figure 1, the trajectory begins at the point of accepted and legal political activity, escalating in force and tension until workers and their allies begin to deploy varying types of violence to achieve objectives. With all avenues of redress for their grievances blocked, unions virtually prohibited, organising criminalised, and collective bargaining and arbitration resisted, workers quickly move along the trajectory, deploying tactics of striking on the job, sabotage, strikes, and eventually armed struggle for the dual purposes of self-defence in an offensive war of manoeuvre to realise their objectives.

In an attempt to explain why insurgents use political violence, I have decided to ask why workers resorted to political violence in their struggles with industry, business, and the state between 1877 and 1921. In this study of nearly a half century of relentless class warfare I have asked two questions. First, when do workers escalate their tactics to use political violence to achieve their objectives? Second, did the use of political violence succeed in helping workers achieve part or all of their objectives?

To answer these questions, I test the trajectory theory by using it to analyse the conflicts of the period from 1877 to 1921. In testing trajectory theory, my objective is to not only retroactively understand why and when violence was used tactically in class struggle, but also to identify the determinant factors that increase the likelihood of its use. My hope is that in re-examining the historical record of a past period of violence in class struggle, we may be able to understand and analyse the determinant factors in the study of class struggle today.

While this approach could be potentially subject to misuse, my aim is to anchor it in a study of class composition, so as to understand when violence is more likely to occur and why it becomes a poor substitute for the absence of a recomposed working-class power.

The premise of trajectory theory is that in a struggle between capital and workers (interchangeably referred to as elites and insurgents, respectively), each side will deploy the appropriate tactics to engage their adversary based on their reading of the level of their own, and their opponents', power (or class composition), their level of support from the rest of the population, the existing opportunity to make gains, and the benefits and costs of deploying tactics of greater intensity. Trajectory theory contests the notion that political violence is a form of 'madness of the crowd', or a desperate, random, spontaneous, or undirected act. Rather, because tactical violence takes many forms – from sabotage and strikes to revolution and terrorism – its use and escalation depends on power, support, opportunities, gains, and costs to those that deploy the tactic.

Violence as Ideology and Psychology

While the literature on the political use of violence is bulging at the seams, the theoretical literature on the political use of violence in class conflict is far less developed. Since the urban rebellions and uprisings of the 1960s, almost no work has been done to understand when working-class insurgents resort to violence. The little that does exist suffers from the theoretical paralysis of the burgeoning cottage industry of anti-terrorism, plagued by flawed theories of violence as theological, ideological, or moralistically driven. Fuelled by exorbitant funding from governments and inter-governmental organisations in the perpetual war on terrorism, the field is far too vast to be explored here.

The anodyne days of thinking about violence in working-class struggle occurred between the first Russian Revolution of 1905 and the twilight of global colonialism. Spurred by the literary dramatisation of anarchism and the Russian Revolution in Joseph Conrad's The Secret Agent and Jack London's The Assassination Bureau, Ltd,[9] a debate raged in the decades between V.I. Lenin and Frantz Fanon that is mostly forgotten today, relegated to the margins of anarchism and armed insurgent groups. The role of violence as a political tactic of the working-class suffered from the ideological remnants of Lenin's unsophisticated labelling of violence as 'terrorism' in sectarian tirades against the

---

9   Conrad 1907; and London and Fish 1963.

Bolshevik's tenuous Social Revolutionary allies. In 1905, Lenin distanced himself from terrorism as a tactic wielded by a vanguard elite, only to later advocate for its use against the Bolsheviks' class enemies during the 1917 revolution. He advocated that tactical terrorism was not separate from the mass movement, but grew organically from it. 'Its strength was the strength of the revolutionary movement of the people ... *That* terrorism was due, not to disappointment in the strength of the mass movement, but, on the contrary, to unshakable faith in its strength ...'.[10] Lenin's point was that the use of tactical violence could not be a substitute for the strength of the working-class, but his analysis was opportunistic. Because the 1905 revolution was defeated, Lenin could effectively denounce the use of terrorism by other revolutionary groups when the working-class was weak as premature, and later as 'infantile'.[11]

Lenin's analysis of tactical violence is slim but remains influential, if hypocritical. After October 1917, he began to advocate its use in light of the Bolsheviks' relatively small size and limited mass support – exactly the conditions in which he had denounced his adversaries on the left for doing so twelve years earlier. While Lenin is credited as a key theorist of revolutionary terrorism, he really had little to say about it. His polemical commentaries lack a clear articulation of its tactical and strategic deployment. There is no subtlety concerning its use at certain moments when the balance of power shifts, or of whether it is to disrupt and destabilise or to advance and seize space. If Lenin argued that violence grew out of the mass movement, he seemed incapable of understanding how and why violence was deployed. Calling political violence 'terrorism' also muddied the waters and illustrated a lack of understanding of how tactical violence was tied to specific class strategies and objectives. Though a self-described 'communist', Lenin's theory of violence hints at but offers no class analysis. Rather, Lenin's reputation as a theorist of revolutionary terrorism has been exaggerated far beyond its scope because the Bolsheviks were one of the first to deploy it in order to actually seize state power and control of the economy.

The lasting impact of the Russian Revolution made armed struggle a legitimate strategy for contesting and seizing power. The Bolshevik use of armed struggle was increasingly emulated globally by independence movements, nationalists, anti-colonialists, and the left in the networks of European colonies and home countries across the globe. The next half century was perhaps the longest sustained period of global revolutionary activity in two millennia of

---

10   Lenin 1905, p. 161.
11   Lenin 1920.

human history. As anti-colonial movements escalated along the trajectory of political conflict by deploying armed struggle and terrorism, colonial militaries staggered to meet the challenge of a shift from a war of attrition to a war of manoeuvre against non-state actors, in what today are called 'small wars'.[12]

Though the scope of this critically important debate is far beyond the focus of this book, and was lacking a class analysis, the posthumous debate between Frantz Fanon and Hannah Arendt[13] addressed key themes of the role of political violence used by insurgents. After Fanon had died, Arendt took issue with the psychological basis of his theory of the role of political violence in insurgencies. For Fanon, 'violence is a cleansing force' that frees the colonised (he called them 'natives') from the violence and resulting inferiority, fear, inaction, and despair of colonialism.[14] In this way, Fanon saw that violence was used to wipe away blockages that impeded the revolutionary consciousness of the colonised. Because colonialism 'is violence in its natural state and will only yield when confronted with greater violence', Fanon observed that violence would be necessary to contest and defeat the greater power and violence of the colonist and end colonialism.[15] All failed efforts by the colonised middle class for redress of grievances demonstrated the truth in the National Liberation Front's (Front de Libération Nationale) assertion that France 'will only yield when there is a knife at its throat'. The colonised, seeing all ways to peaceful resolution of their suffering blocked and repressed, will respond by escalating their tactics, using violence in proportion to the violence deployed by the coloniser, resulting in a spiral of conflict towards 'a point of no return'.[16]

Fanon's presumption that violence becomes a tactic of the oppressed when all other avenues were closed was confirmed by the historical record. It is no accident that his works and the film *The Battle of Algiers*,[17] which is based on his theory, have been used by the u.s. military as counter-insurgency training materials. Fanon viewed the role of violence as one tactic among many, and warned that it is more likely to be used when the insurgent is dehumanised and denied access to existing political spaces in order to fight for political power according to the normative rules of politics. In this way, Fanon peered into Lenin's mass to uncover the conditions of the insurgency when violence is deployed. But, like Lenin, Fanon added further confusion by hinging the use of

---

12   Boyd 1987.
13   Fanon 1963; and Arendt 1971.
14   Fanon 1963, p. 94.
15   Ibid., pp. 61, 70 and 80.
16   Ibid., pp. 88–9.
17   Pontecorvo 1966.

violence as a tactic on the psychological predisposition of the insurgent, rather than the composition of class forces.

If Fanon attributed the use of violence to the psychology of the oppressed, Herbert Marcuse, writing about the revolts of the 1960s, entirely disconnected tactics from the balance of power. Portraying it as a desperate act of last resort, Marcuse wrote that 'as long as the opposition does not have the social force of a new general interest, the problem of violence is primarily a problem of tactics'.[18] Mistaking the lack of mass support as a rationale for resorting to the tactics of violence was to prove a tragic strategic blunder, as many left wing armed insurgencies formed out of the mass movements of the time to speed up the revolutionary conditions. Not only did these armed groups mistake strategy for tactics, they also cut themselves off from the mass movements that birthed them, and helped to undermine them, by substituting a clandestine tactic for the recomposition of working-class power.[19]

What few realise is that Fanon's influence on armed insurgencies such as the Black Panthers was parallel to his influence on social scientists tasked with theorising a new strategy for urban counter-insurgency. Over the next decade, several federal commissions, congressional investigations, and private foundations delved into the causes of political violence in the aftermath of Malcolm X's assassination, waves of urban revolts and riots between 1963–8, and the rise of armed struggle groups at home alongside the counter-insurgencies being fought abroad. What emerged from these exhaustive investigations has dominated the thinking of social scientists and the anti-terrorism industry to this day. So-called 'relative deprivation' theory covertly drew on Fanon's ideas to argue that political violence is a tool deployed by the urban masses (read: people of colour in poor neighbourhoods) in response to frustrated attempts to share in the promises of affluent capitalist America.[20] The theory of political violence has not progressed very far since Le Bon's 'psychology of the crowd' in which the faceless mass of automatons are swept up in a contagion of fury and violence.[21]

Relative deprivation theory argued that individuals and groups will revolt when they perceive that they have been denied their share of society's afflu-

---

18   Marcuse 1967.

19   D'Arcy also observes that clandestine armed struggle, in contrast to a citizen's militia for self-defence, presents itself as a 'self-appointed counter-elite' that usurps authority over a mass movement and replicates the same dynamics of power the movement seeks to struggle against. See D'Arcy 2014, pp. 179–81.

20   Davies 1970; Feierabend, Feierabend and Gurr 1972; Gurr 1972 and 1989; Kerner Commission 1968; Rubenstein 1970 and 1989; Skolnick 1969; and United States Senate 1974.

21   Le Bon 1896, pp. 1–35.

ence and are locked out from access to the polity, generating emotional turmoil that leads them to commit irrational violence.[22] The theory gained prominence in its explanation of the urban insurgencies of the mid-1960s that transformed into armed struggle groups such as the Black Panthers, Weather Underground, Brown Berets, Young Lords, White Panthers, the Symbionese Liberation Army, and the Black Liberation Army. While relative deprivation theory has lost its explanatory power and has withdrawn from the academic spotlight, its undue influence over counter-insurgency theory in the age of an endless war on terrorism continues under the guise of 'winning hearts and minds', and in the deployment of democratisation and NGO-led development as a weapon. Few disputed this social science consensus that eventually informed the decades-long legislative, police, and military counter-insurgency that underlies what Michelle Alexander today calls the 'new Jim Crow'.[23]

Arendt not only equated the contrapuntal violence of states and insurgents, but inextricably linked violence to the struggle over state power. For Arendt, states that lose authority, legitimacy, and obedience increasingly resort to the use of violence or terror. States resort to terror because they lack the numbers and, thus, the power. But this dynamic feeds back on itself as the lack of power continues to require the resort to terror, which further erodes power and ultimately erupts into a revolutionary situation:

> Where commands are no longer obeyed, the means of violence are of no use; and the question of this obedience is not decided by the command-obedience relation but by opinion, and, of course, by the number of those who share it. Everything depends on the power behind the violence. The sudden dramatic breakdown of power that ushers in revolutions reveals in a flash how civil obedience to laws, to rulers, to institutions – is but the outward manifestation of support and consent.[24]

Arendt put the tactical violence of insurgents in counter-point to the violence of state power while remaining doubtful about existing theories of revolutionary violence. 'Textbook instructions on "how to make a revolution" in a step-by-

---

22   While 'polity' ordinarily implies the institutions of politics including governmental and extra-governmental institutions, Tilly's use of the term can be understood more broadly as the political processes in which contending forces, including workers and capital, struggle for power.

23   Alexander 2010.

24   Arendt 1971, pp. 48 and 49.

step progression from dissent to conspiracy, from resistance to armed uprising, are all based on the mistaken notion that revolutions are "made"'.[25] She simultaneously refuted both Fanon and relative deprivation theory for essentialising violence as an automatic response of the oppressed. 'Violence is neither beastly nor irrational', Arendt posited.

> Under such conditions [concentration camps], not rage and violence, but their conspicuous absence is the clearest sign of dehumanization. Rage is by no means an automatic reaction to misery and suffering as such; no one reacts with rage to an incurable disease or to an earthquake or, for that matter, to social conditions that seem to be unchangeable.[26]

Rather, Arendt agreed with Fanon's notion that violence is a tactic deployed when reform is impossible. Insurgents that deploy violence must be sensitive to the legitimacy of their grievances and the terror arrayed against them while using non-violent tactics to prevent their redress. Arendt acknowledged the tactic of violence while dismissing its objective as incompatible with state power and governance: 'violence can be justifiable, but it will never be legitimate'.[27] For Arendt, violence is justifiable when the political system is closed to insurgents' pursuit of peaceful redress. 'Violence does not promote causes, neither history nor revolution, neither progress nor reaction; but it can serve to dramatize grievances and bring them to public attention'.[28] In this way, Arendt argued that violence cannot be the end goal or objective, transforming the irrationality of violence into the rational, a means through which to achieve a short-term goal.[29] As D'Arcy similarly argues, the use of militancy, including political violence, can be a legitimate tactic if it serves the objectives of democracy and social justice by bringing attention to unmet grievances.[30]

While much has been written about political violence as a weapon in anti-colonial struggle between the Russian Revolution and the 1970s, it remained primarily framed as an ideological rather than tactical premise: whether or not to use it, rather than when, how, and by whom. What Lenin, Fanon, and Marcuse all missed is that political violence can be explained by social conditions, not individual consciousness. Since we still live in a capitalist class society, it

---

25   Ibid., p. 48.
26   Ibid., p. 63.
27   Ibid., p. 52.
28   Ibid., p. 79.
29   Ibid., pp. 66 and 80.
30   D'Arcy 2013.

is necessary to look at the struggle of class relations to find the source of violence. According to Tilly and Tilly, 'The formulation tells us where to look for explanations and their confirmation: not in the abstractly conceived interest or motivation of an average individual worker, but in the social relations and culture laid down by previous interactions of work and contention'.[31]

In contrast, military counter-insurgency theory has made great strides in addressing the question of violence as a tactic. As Lawrence Freedman documents in his exhaustive book *Strategy*, after the Russian Revolution and during the anti-colonial movement, military strategists shifted their focus so as to understand when insurgents resort to violence as a tactic in order to learn how to counter it.[32]

John Boyd was one of the foremost military strategists articulating a 'conceptual spiral' in which insurgents deploy guerrilla warfare to 'disintegrate existing regime's [sic] ability to govern'.[33] The aim of a 'war of manoeuvre', according to Boyd, was to apply the strategy to the military in order to 'generate many non-cooperative centres of gravity, as well as disorient, disrupt, or overload those that adversary depends upon [sic], in order to magnify friction, shatter cohesion, produce paralysis, and bring about his collapse'.[34] In his wide-ranging historical overviews of evolving strategies of armed violence by the military and insurgents alike, Boyd's theoretical work illustrates how the military has come closer to conceptualising the tactical and strategic role of violence by insurgents than anything by Lenin, Fanon, and other theorists of revolutionary armed struggle during the bulk of the twentieth century.

Theory of Contention: Steps in the Spiral Staircase

What is widely missing from both the anti-colonial and military theories of political violence is a nuanced conceptualisation of how, when, why, and by whom violence is used to achieve a political objective. Their approaches are roundly ahistorical, attempting to construct a grand unifying theory without providing the theoretical tools to examine the political conditions under which violence is ultimately deployed as one tactic among others.

---

31 Tilly and Tilly 1998, p. 237.

32 Freedman 2013.

33 Boyd 1986 and 1987. Boyd achieved substantial influence in military strategic thinking as a mid-level US Air Force officer without publishing a book. His highly influential works are in the form of slideshows in which text was written as phrases not sentences.

34 Boyd 1986 and 1987.

Existing theories of political violence suffer from what I call the 'origination fallacy'. In other words, without an analysis of the conditions in which violence is deployed by insurgents, the appearance of violence is perceived to be the starting point of the insurgency. In reality, violence often appears as a tactic in later stages of a mature insurgency after it has already churned through a repertoire of other tactics of escalating intensity. By perceiving insurgents to have launched their campaigns with violence, methodically understanding when and why they choose to use violence becomes moot, if not impossible. As a result, violence becomes conflated as ideologically, rather than tactically driven – and studying when and why violence is used becomes further conflated, seeking to justify its existence rather than explaining it.

Avoiding the origination fallacy makes it necessary to analyse the political conditions in which violence is used. For this we can turn to the sociologist Tilly's 'theory of contention', which guided his study of French peasant uprisings and the French Revolution.[35] Tilly examined the political conditions and changing mode of production under which insurgents operate in order to surmise when insurgents deploy violence as a tactic from a 'repertoire of contention'. He insightfully explored how insurgents will study the conditions in which they struggle, their level of mass support, and the balance of power between 'contenders' to decide on which tactic to deploy.

The period from 1877 to 1921 was an exceptionally tumultuous and bloody time in American history, not merely because capital resorted to political violence in an attempt to assert its dominance, but because its power was being contested while the balance of power shifted dramatically. Workers had found vulnerable links in the industrial production process, distribution, and the movement of capital and goods. They were willing to use all available means to disrupt individual companies, entire industries, and even the entire country during wartime as leverage to have their demands met. Emerging from immigrant and indigenous mutual aid and cultural organisation, the working-class was able to parlay its new power into new forms of organisation to expand mass support and new tactics to assert their power. These tactics spanned a continuum of force from constitutionally protected rights to assemble, speak and petition to coordinated military assaults by worker armies. In a spiralling of action and reaction between workers and capital, an escalation of tactics from pressure to threats and ultimately political violence took place in an environment in which legal political action was blocked, repressed, or co-opted. In

---

35   Tilly 1977, 1978, 1989, 2003, and Tilly and Tilly 1998.

order to defeat the insurgencies and diffuse their potential to launch new insurgencies in the future, capital itself underwent a reorganisation and introduced new forms of social control both inside and outside of the workplace.

As insurgents present demands for redress of grievances, they must take into consideration the factors of support, threats, and opportunities to achieve gains. When the political system is closed while elites manoeuvre so as to block insurgent access to the available political space, the latter must escalate their tactics in order to pursue their objectives. The question is: what kind of tactics will they use to carry on their struggle? What causes political violence to take so many different forms? These questions present what Tilly describes as the 'problem of explaining variation in the character and social organization of violence'.[36] What occurs, and when, can only be answered by addressing the great variation in political conditions, balance of power, and the sometimes rapid shifts from one form of political violence to another.

> The point is not to establish general laws for all sorts of violence but rather to identify crucial causal processes: those that operate similarly in the short run across a wide range of circumstances yet produce dramatically different forms of collective violence depending on their settings, combinations, and sequences.[37]

Identifying the complex causal factors that produce political violence in class struggle is the objective of this book. The trajectory theory of violence is based on a careful examination of tactics and strategy in the context of the available political space, balance of class power, and class composition. Each step along the trajectory is the *tactic*, and movement to a higher intensity tactic is determined by the *strategy* to achieve the *objective*. The relationship between tactics and strategy is elusive, especially on the left, even while it has been conceptually mastered by the theoreticians of war.[38] The legendary British intelligence agent Thomas E. Lawrence, i.e. 'Lawrence of Arabia', succinctly linked tactics to strategy while working with the Arab guerrillas who harassed and blunted the superior Turkish army during WWI. He wrote:

> the task was to analyze the process, both from the point of view of strategy, aim in war, the synoptic regard which sees everything by the

---

36 Tilly 2003, p. 13.
37 Ibid., p. 23.
38 The one exception is Sharp 2005.

standard of the whole, and from the point of view called tactics, the means toward the strategic end, the steps in the staircase.[39]

Gene Sharp, the pre-eminent theorist of tactics and strategies of non-violent struggle, fills in the crucial elements of tactics and strategy missing in Tilly. He explains that 'tactics describe how particular methods of action are applied, or how particular groups of resisters shall act in a specific situation'.[40] In contrast, strategy is

> the conception of how best to achieve objectives in a conflict (violent or nonviolent). Strategy is concerned with whether, when, or how to fight, and how to achieve maximum effectiveness in order to gain certain ends. Strategy is the plan for the practical distribution, adaptation, and application of the available means to attain certain objectives.[41]

By understanding the interplay between tactics and strategy, trajectory theory can also help analyse when insurgents use a strategy of tension in which each new tactic is chosen with the intent of gradually ratcheting up the tension that provides leverage to achieve one's objectives. In this way, as the intensity of tactics rises and falls in relation to strategy, political conditions, opportunity and costs, Lawrence's staircase could be better described as a *spiral* staircase.

The categories of tactics along the trajectory allow us to distinguish between types of tactical violence, the conditions under which they are likely to be used, and whether elites or insurgents use them (although our focus here is on the latter). Tilly explains that they

> result from an interaction between challengers and other groups. In the terms we have been using here, they result from the interplay of interests, organization, and mobilization, on one side, and of repression/facilitation, power, and opportunity/threat, on the other.[42]

This interplay of contestation to counter-contestation to response to counter-contestation can spiral about one another infinitely in a *danse macabre* until one contender is defeated, disbands, disarms, de-escalates or both sides disarm,

---

39   Lawrence 1929.
40   Sharp 2005, p. 459.
41   Sharp, 2003, p. 21.
42   Tilly 1978, p. 138.

de-escalate, and negotiate. Each preparation for the deployment of tactical escalation signals movement along the tactical trajectory of violence.

The use of Tilly's calculus of contestation for elites and insurgents to move along the trajectory of political violence also raises issues of splits, pairing, or switching. Insurgents may not exclusively deploy a single tactic but put several into the terrain of struggle at the same time. Facing a rising threat of repression and costs, insurgents may open negotiations to pursue de-escalation and disarming while also holding the level of tactical escalation, or even increasing its intensity. In this way, insurgents may simultaneously deploy tactics at different points along the trajectory. Doing so offers them the leverage of ramping up the intensity of tactics if they are perceived to be weak at the negotiating table, or if their offer to negotiate is spurned entirely. Insurgents will sometimes be willing to unilaterally de-escalate to negotiate if elites also exhibit the willingness to do so according to an absolute gains strategy.

When the threat of repression and costs are extremely high, and offers of negotiation need to be tested, insurgents may replicate a parallel 'above ground' organisation while continuing 'underground' tactical escalation. In such cases the amoebic split-off is subordinate to the underground challengers. This pairing of de-escalation and escalation may also create a split in the insurgency as the above ground group gains recognition, authority, concessions, and is integrated into the elite coalition, while the underground group continues to mobilise and escalate.

If insurgents demobilise and de-escalate in order to obtain concessions, reforms, compromises, and access to the polity, they risk abandoning the disruptive tactics that made them effective in the first place. For this reason insurgents face the Sisyphean task of attempting to move an insurgency forward as tempting concessions appear from behind and storm clouds of repression mass on the horizon.

Cycles of Struggle

Unfortunately Tilly only gets us part of the way, as, like the anti-colonial and military theorists, he lacks a class analysis. Although his theory of contention operates in the context of the relations of production, he did not provide a class analysis of the struggle between capital and workers.

To understand how the composition of class forces shapes the decisions about which tactic to deploy from the workers' repertoire of contention, we must draw upon autonomist marxists like Alquati, Bologna, Cleaver, Glaberman, Holloway, and Tronti. Cleaver identified the necessity of a 'strategic deciphering ... which helps to clarify and develop working class struggle' from the perspective of the working-class.[43] Workers study what the autonomist marxists call the class composition to decide what tactics to deploy, which shapes the outcomes of their struggle. By fusing Tilly's theory of contention to autonomist marxist theory of class composition, my trajectory theory illuminates why class conflict between 1877 and 1921 was frequently characterised by violent armed struggle, as well as the conditions, factors, and balance of power that can confidently assess not only its use but also the potential responses to it.

Trajectory theory tells us that the use of tactical violence was neither a start nor an end point during these four decades of class struggle. Rather, as Arendt asserts, violence was used tactically as a means to overcome blockages, to counter threats of diffusion and co-optation, to exploit the weakness of elite power, and to achieve short-term goals. Faced with a closed political system dominated by elites, judicial, police and military repression, and efforts to deflect, divert, and co-opt their struggles, workers escalated their tactics to deploy violence to achieve their objectives. This book offers an alternative perspective to labor historians, political scientists, and sociologists who found the use of political violence by workers who had not articulated an explicit class consciousness or theory of revolution or socialism to be pursuing economistic and conservative objectives.[44] Self-organised workers whose efforts to unionise had faced violent repression leapfrogged over these impediments to attempt to disrupt capital accumulation in order to achieve their objectives. When they were successful in doing so, it was because they had successfully managed to recompose their class power, providing them with the necessary leverage to extract concessions. In cases where they were defeated, it was because the new composition of capital had tilted the balance of class forces against them.[45]

This book will apply the trajectory theory to five phases of class struggle during this period. Rather than seeking to uncover new historical documentation of these insurgencies, although some previously unused primary documents are used, this book seeks to use the existing documentation to rethink why

---

43   Cleaver 1979, p. 10.

44   The lack of class, revolutionary, or socialist consciousness is the dominant current running through many of the works of this era. See Adamic 1931; Bernstein 1960; Bimba 1950; Boyer and Morais 1955; Brecher 1972; Burbank 1966; Foner 1947, 1965, 1973, and 1977; Grant 1915; Green 2015; Lens 1973; Smith 2006; Yolen 1936; Ross and Taft 1969; Stromquist 1993; and Taft 1966.

45   Among the accounts of class struggle during this era that embrace this approach see Davis 1975; Harring 1983; Montgomery 1974, 1977, 1980, and 1989; Ramirez 1978; Savage 1985; Smith n.d.; and Stone 1973.

workers were more likely to deploy violence as a tactic. In doing so, this book will not be episodic, focusing only on the 'big strikes'; rather, it will explore the context in which these strikes were waged. The key element in understanding why and when workers deployed certain tactics hinges upon the composition of class forces at the time.

For this reason, strikes are situated in phases of struggle in which the conditions both leading up to and following the strike are recounted. This is intended to help illustrate how they fit into the cycles of class struggle and the give and take between capital and workers over this half century. These cycles can be seen as points in which the recomposition of working-class power tilted the balance of power towards the workers, who were then able to extract tremendous gains from capital and the state. At other points, a new composition of capital was deployed to defeat working-class insurgents and increase control and domination on the shop floor and throughout society.

This book is not intended to posit a theory of revolution, but to convey that revolution is something hammered out in the interplay of the composition of class forces. For this reason, a discussion of whether this was a period of civil war or revolution will be avoided, although an 'uncivil war' would seem to be more appropriate, considering the high level of force and violence common at the time. Rather, the interplay between capital and workers will be explored in order to answer the question of what role tactical violence played in achieving or failing to achieve concessions, reforms, and other objectives. The ebb and flow between repression and reform throughout this period can be best explained by the changing tactics deployed by workers according to the existing composition of class forces. The rising intensity of tactics so destabilised the accumulation of capital that the arrival of the Great Depression, itself an outcome of class conflict, ushered in a wide-ranging revision of the social contract between capital, the state, and workers that we now know as the New Deal. While this book ends a decade earlier, these cycles of struggle are essential for understanding the basis for the New Deal, and what may characterise other efforts to fundamentally revise the social contract and alter the balance of class forces or entirely rupture it. In order to understand what provoked the New Deal, this book will explore five cycles of class struggle between the 1877 Railroad Strike and the decade long Redneck Miner's War in West Virginia that ebbed in 1921.

1877 Railroad Strike

At about the same time the remaining US troops were being pulled out of the South and sent West to fight Native Americans, railroad workers in Baltimore and West Virginia refused to run their trains, sparking a nearly nationwide strike. Within days, workers spread the word of the strike across many railroad lines and dozens of states, shutting down much of the country and the economy. The strike was launched and spread without a union, as an earlier effort to form the Trainmen's Union (TU) was infiltrated by agents hired by the railroad companies and smashed. Drawing on the budding connections of the Trainmen's Union, much reduced membership of the craft unions, and the regional linkages from working on the railroads, the workers circulated their struggle, not only across vast distances and to other lines, but also throughout local communities suffering from high levels of unemployment and poverty due to ongoing depression.

Local police and local and state militias were unreliable, defected to the crowds, or were overwhelmed by strikers and their supporters. With few sympathetic local officials, workers and their supporters organised self-defence patrols, engaged in hit-and-run street battles, and sabotaged rail lines, roundhouses, and other equipment. Ultimately, the workers lacked an organisational capacity to coordinate the disparate points of action. Federal judges issued injunctions to protect bankrupt railroad companies, obtained federal troops to deploy against the strikers and the supporters, and managed to force the trains back into motion. The intervention of federal troops transformed the insurrection from a struggle against the widely unpopular railroad companies into one against the federal government with the memory of the Civil War still fresh in many people's minds.

The 1877 strike is evidence that, despite a lack of unions, workers and their supporters self-organised in the midst of one of the worst depressions of the later nineteenth century. The symbiotic bonds between the railroad companies and government, the end of Reconstruction, and the shrinking of the US Army with the end of the Civil War had left many workers alienated and shut out from a political system that was locked under plutocratic control. As the political system became increasingly closed to them, politics became illegitimate. Workers had little option for addressing their grievances or expecting their demands to lead to effective change. With their fledgling union crushed, workers expanded their struggles with the railroad company to the broader community which blamed unbridled financial speculation for the crash that was sparked several years earlier by reckless financial speculation by the railroads. The strike had widespread support in the streets of local communities because it expressed simmering unresolved class tensions.

In contrast to the working-class recomposing its own power, the railroad companies were disorganised, engaged in bitter competition with one another, lacked sufficient investment capital to weather the shutdown, and were dependent on government even as it had few effective local, state, and federal government institutions to rely on. Making matters worse, the existing composition of capital had manufactured a critical vulnerability: the railroads. Although fragmented into many competing systems, the railroads brought workers together in the centralised train depots that provided ideal chokepoints at which they could disrupt the entire capitalist economy.

Although the federal courts had begun intervening to protect bankrupt roads from their creditors, the companies had never expected to need to call upon government to intervene on their behalf against their own workers. The 1877 strike would forever change that. The insurrection ushered in a reorganisation and municipalisation of police, state militias were reorganised into the National Guard by Congress, Congress funded and expanded the US Army, and the railroads began to rapidly consolidate, financed by new types of investment capital, to meet the threat of a newly recomposed working-class. Capital embraced an expanded role of government in managing class conflict, relying on court injunctions, police, National Guard, and the military to repress workers and break strikes. New technologies such as the telegraph, telephone and police wagon, new principles of management, innovative policing strategies, and counter-insurgency tactics used in the Indian Wars thoroughly transformed state power into a more effective weapon in the class struggle. These new technologies and strategies were evidence of a new composition of capital that emerged out of the strike in order to meet the threat posed by the strike to decompose the power of the working-class and prevent the potential for disruption. The 1877 strike ushered in a new composition of capital that would be deployed effectively in the 1894 railroad strike, and provided a model emulated in the mining, manufacturing, steel, transport, and finance sectors until World War I.

1894 Railroad Strike

After several smaller strikes during yet another devastating depression, workers at Pullman Palace Car Company not only struck, but managed to quickly circulate their strike across much of the country. What made this possible was the American Railway Union's (ARU) vote to boycott any train pulling a Pullman car. This was no re-enactment of the 1877 strike. The ARU demonstrated how workers had recomposed their power through their efforts in the preceding few years to devise new organisational and strategic innovations. The ARU was organised according to the principles of industrial unionism opening it to membership of all railroad workers regardless of their employer, workplace, skill or craft although not race. The ARU provided a crucial organisational infrastructure for circulating and coordinating the strike to all of its affiliated locals that was missing in 1877. Driven by the membership, the ARU leadership used the telegraph to coordinate a masterful war of manoeuvre for about a week in which workers struck capital from numerous points, probing and penetrating its weaknesses to great advantage. Simultaneously, the boycott provided a strategy for spreading the disruption across corporate and geographical boundaries. Workers had closely studied the new composition of capital that emerged in response to the 1877 strike and devised a new means to meet that challenge.

The increasing consolidation of railroads only amplified their vulnerability to disruption. The railroad was the internet of the late nineteenth century, through which much of the economy ran under the control of a few highly integrated corporations. By paralysing virtually the entire rail system, the ARU threatened to disrupt the accumulation of capital nationwide. The response by the railroad companies was not merely expanded use of court injunctions, local police, private agents, the National Guard, and US Army. The railroad companies relied on their interdependence to coordinate their response to the strike. Chicago-based lines coordinated their efforts to break the ARU through their recently formed General Managers Association (GMA), which used its connections in government by bringing it to bear on the ARU. The GMA was indistinguishable from the federal courts and the US Attorney General which were deployed to repress the strike. US troops were called out to move the trains and the courts enjoined and arrested the ARU top leadership, thereby cutting the lines of communication that made it possible to coordinate the strike across the country.

Facing an unusually well-coordinated railroad industry response to the strike, the ARU membership quickly escalated its tactics by circulating the strike. It escalated into a general strike in New York, and nearly did so in Chicago, until AFL President Samuel Gompers threatened to throw any AFL local out of the federation if its members joined the strike. The AFL's position was bolstered by the Railroad Brotherhoods craft unions, some of which released their members to scab the ARU. The AFL exercised what would become the most prominent role of unions in a capitalist economy: disciplining workers and harnessing, managing, and even blunting class struggle. With the AFL tamping down on its membership, few sympathetic local and state elected officials, and facing direct federal military intervention to break the strike, ARU strikers and their supporters took up arms and carried out sabotage in self-defence to maintain their leverage, and to attempt to expand their power.

Much like the 1877 strike, capital and workers deployed ever more forceful tactics to meet the challenge of their adversary. The strike, mostly without violence or property damage during its first few days, spiralled in a *danse macabre* in which each side deployed ever more force and soon armed violence to hold or extend their position. Despite the defeat of the strike, workers demonstrated their capacity to self-organise across an entire industry, and the strategic need to circulate their struggle beyond it in order to disrupt the accumulation of capital.

Iron Workers Bombing Campaign

The new composition of capital that emerged after the 1877 railroad strike transformed the mining, manufacturing, steel, transit, and banking sectors. Capital consolidation was financed by new financial investment strategies, holding companies, and corporate debt. These new financial strategies made it possible not only for larger companies to drive out smaller and weaker competitors, but also to centrally coordinate production, distribution, and consumption across a single industry as well as all related sectors.

Such horizontal and vertical industry consolidation was much celebrated in 1900, when J.P. Morgan famously created the first $1 billion corporation by taking over a significant minority of the coal, steel, mining, and bridge-building industries and fusing them into US Steel. US Steel illustrated the strategic value of capital consolidation. The railroads were the backbone of the economy, but railroads need coal, iron, and steel just as coal, iron, and steel need each other. US Steel provided an organisational capacity for the integration of recently distinct sectors of industrial capital.

By making explicit what had long been implicit, US Steel also provided a strategic capacity to counter the growing threat of organised steel and mineworkers that had been disrupting their respective national industries, but had not yet succeeded in circulating their struggles beyond their sectors. US Steel demonstrated the strategy of using a holding company to deflect and diffuse class conflict across subsidiaries in and across entire industrial sectors while providing the necessary capital and political influence to weather storms. Capital had introduced a new composition that was quickly muting the strategic advantage of industrial unionism in a single industrial sector.

The consolidation of the coal and steel industries had ramifications for the iron fabrication and assembly industry which consumed its products. Seemingly overnight, us Steel had become the dominant corporate power by gaining control of several of the largest companies. Despite a contract that covered workers in some us Steel shops and departments, the International Association of Bridge and Structural Iron Workers (IABSIW) was unable to attain its long sought-after objective of an industry-wide contract. us Steel refused to allow further organising of unorganised workers and blunted several limited strikes by using its new integrated corporate management structure to shift work to unaffected shops.

The IABSIW met the blockage presented by us Steel's refusal to expand collective bargaining by rapidly escalating its tactics. Rather than attempt to expand their strike to other related sectors due to long-brewing hostilities with other unions, and lacking mass support or local sympathetic elected officials, the IABSIW launched a campaign of sabotage operated by a small secret cell. For several years it covertly financed a group of saboteurs travelling the country to carry out attacks that captured headlines and tightened the commitment of their members to the struggle, but created little power, leverage, or even monetary damage.

The industry organised itself through the National Erectors' Association (NEA) to infiltrate and provoke much of the ironworkers' sabotage campaign. Infiltrated by an *agent provocateur* paid by a private agent who would later head up the early precursor of the FBI, the ironworkers' cell and other unidentified provocateurs dramatically escalated the bombing campaign in terms of targets, lethality, and property damage. Demonstrating Arendt's dictum that the 'loss of power becomes a temptation to substitute violence for power ... and that violence itself results in impotence',[46] the ironworkers' sabotage campaign was exposed, its cell members prosecuted, convicted, and sentenced to prison, and the union wrecked for a time. The combined power of the new composition of capital and the state affirmed Arendt's supposition that 'Violence can always destroy power; out of the barrel of a gun grows the most effective command, resulting in the most instant and perfect obedience. What never can grow out of it is power'.[47] Ironically, although nearly bankrupted by the financially draining civil and criminal trials, the union's membership stepped up to finance the union, while its membership soon grew.

Nevertheless, lacking mass support, the sabotage campaign was bound to fail. But the campaign provided further stimulus for expanding state power into

---

46   Arendt 1971, p. 54.

47   Ibid., p. 53.

the economy. No longer was government expected to merely intervene once the crisis had erupted, but a new federal domestic intelligence and police agency was organised to meet and pre-empt the emerging threat. The new Bureau of Investigations, soon to become the Federal Bureau of Investigations (FBI), became a device to gather intelligence about potential and emerging threats to capital and use it to counter the threat by disrupting, blocking, diffusing, deflecting, or suppressing it before it could disrupt the economy. The founding of the FBI made another vital contribution to the existing composition of capital. As the FBI eclipsed widely hated private police, such as the Pinkertons, it transferred the costs and responsibility for fighting the class struggle from the owners of capital to the public financed by taxes on incomes paid primarily by workers. By absorbing the tactics and strategies of the widely hated and reviled private police into government police, power became the shank at the tip of the pilum. Federally coordinated counter-insurgency as a strategy for conducting the class struggle had now arrived.

WWI Wildcat Strikes

The rapid WWI build up gave workers in critical war industries powerful leverage. They resisted the AFL president Gompers's wartime no strike pledge, pro-war propaganda, and the appeal to nationalism, to disrupt production and make significant gains. Women workers had just successfully struck against Taylorist rationalisation and bonus schemes and for an eight-hour day in the Northeast. Male manufacturing workers soon followed by circulating the struggle to the arms manufacturing sector. While the IWW was disrupting critical mining and timber sectors in the West, arms workers defied their own unions to extract wage and hour concessions, compelling the federal government to intervene in the struggles and arbitrate temporary settlements.

Prompted by the new cycle of class struggle, the federal government established several wartime planning and labour arbitration bodies that used arbitration in order to minimise disruption of war production. Although the arbitration decisions often forced many companies to grant significant concessions to their workers during the war, the arbitration boards refused to grant recognition of plant level unions or enshrine collective bargaining rights. The arbitration boards issued rulings that drove a wedge between capital and the state during the war, serving as a trial run for a new federal role in using arbitration and collective bargaining to discipline and manage the class struggle.

Without union backing, the wildcat strikers managed to operate inside of what Boyd called capital and the state's 'observation-orientation-decision-action time cycle or loop (O-O-D-A loop)'.[48] As workers discovered short sharp strikes could create enough leverage to bring in a federal arbitration board and extract concessions without a contract, they were under no legal obligation to avoid further disruption. The arms workers had learned that earlier gains could be used as a launching pad to push for more gains and generalise them throughout the industry.

Rapid tactical escalation had the effect of raising wages while reducing both working hours (absolute value) and productivity (relative value). But lacking sufficient mass support beyond their local New England communities, mostly limited to the arms industry, and arrayed against the united front of capital, government, and their own AFL unions, the wildcat strikers met a storm of repression once the wartime emergency passed. Once WWI ended, capital and the federal government abrogated the wartime arbitration awards and unleashed a post-war Red Scare under the direction of the Bureau of Investigations to persecute the militant strike leaders, anarchists, the IWW, and socialists. The fledgling experiment with federally sanctioned arbitration demonstrated the dangers and limits of relying on the intervention of the federal government in the class struggle.

The wartime wildcat strikes were effective, but lacking a recomposition of working-class power, they proved to be pyrrhic victories. Their disruptive impact was dampened by arbitration settlements that proved to be fleeting emergency measures. Although some wildcat strikes resulted in effective shop floor organisations of militant workers, their leadership was swept up in the post-war Red Scare and their power broken.

If the role of the AFL in helping to break the 1894 strike demonstrated the role of unions in disciplining class struggle, bringing the AFL into government wartime planning demonstrated the potential for harnessing organised labour to the capital accumulation process as a bulwark against disruptive and unruly workers. Capital and the state learned important lessons about how to use arbitration in a crisis to trade control over work, higher productivity, and stability on the shop floor and throughout industry for higher wages. The lesson is that the Keynesian wage-productivity deal was born not from the much-heralded New Deal, but rather from the wildcat strikes during WWI.

---

48   Boyd 1987.

Seattle General Strike

The end of WWI brought about a reversal of wartime gains. As government contracts ended, unemployment skyrocketed, wages were ratcheted downward, and employers abrogated contracts and concessions forced upon them by workers. Wartime propaganda was transformed in the aftermath of the Russian Revolution and the Bolshevik seizure of power, the emergence of two communist parties in the US, and the pre-war threat of the IWW, into the Red Scare. Empowered by the wartime 1917 Espionage Act, 1918 Sedition Act, and numerous state criminal syndicalism laws, thousands of IWW members, militant and left wing workers, anarchist, immigrant radicals, union organisers, and elected and rank and file Socialist Party members were persecuted, driven out of their jobs and elected offices, arrested en masse, prosecuted, imprisoned, and deported. One of the exceptions to the wholesale combined repressive force of capital and the state was in Seattle, where port workers refused to work ships carrying arms for Russian counter-revolutionaries. With sanction from the leftist Central Labor Council, the boycott quickly turned into a city-wide general strike across manufacturing, services, street vendors, and transit that did not just shut down the city, but provided the means for the workers to take over and run it.

To launch the general strike, the port workers bypassed the established bargaining and grievance procedures, as well as most of their union leadership. Perhaps unexpectedly, their support was not merely in the form of petitions, marches and pickets but was inspired by news of Russian workers seizing their own workplaces to self-manage them democratically as soviets. For several days, workers, their families, and supporters turned a shutdown on the ports into a take over the city. The Central Labor Council set up self-management committees that, for the course of several days, coordinated essential services and organised self-defence for the democratic assemblies that ran them.

The general strikers escalated their tactics to immediately realise their objective of democratic control of the economy by seizing control of the city and running it themselves rather than engaging with those who controlled and owned it. In this way, the workers were engaged in a war of manoeuvre in which they attacked at multiple points of vulnerability to generate, as Boyd described, 'many non-cooperative centers of gravity' to 'disorient, disrupt or overload [sic] those that adversary depends upon'.[49] Rather than bring about the city's collapse, the workers transformed it by taking over the means of production and reorganising them to serve human needs. With the elite backed mayor

---

49   Ibid.

massing volunteer vigilantes and the National Guard, the Central Labor Council fragmented, and some affiliated unions called for ending the general strike out of fear of armed repression. The Seattle general strike demonstrated that workers could escalate their tactics to take over the work they already do, reorganise it themselves, and thus avoid violent confrontation that erupts in a direct contest over power at the point of production and reproduction. The thorough recomposition of working-class power in the area provided a rare illustration of how the escalation of tactics can transform leverage into control while avoiding armed conflict.

West Virginia Mine War

Organising the miners ran into the greatest opposition in West Virginia, and for good reason. The state was dominated by a plutocratic coal corporate elite, which used its economic and political power to repress nearly every nascent effort to organise. After a decade of organising efforts being met by the repressive apparatus arrayed against them, in the early 1920s the miners used their mass support to again escalate their tactics. They armed themselves both in self-defence in preparation for the inevitable repressive response, but also so as to launch their own strikes on critical mining infrastructure.

Despite having a few sympathetic local officials in several western counties, the miners were on their own. With limited resources from the national United Mineworkers of America (UMWA), they struggled to organise miners in the western sector of West Virginia. Miners in the UMWA state district deployed a strategy of pairing above and underground tactics. Once mines began to be organised, the coal companies forced the miners out of the mines and their families out of the company houses in which they lived. The UMWA organised tent camps for the displaced miners and their families, which quickly became base camps for self-defence against deadly armed assault on the miners' camps by hired agents, local and state police, and the assassination of a popular miner turned sheriff. The lack of influence in the state government and deadly repression demonstrated that all avenues to peaceful resolution to the strike were blocked.

The miners' camps became the centre for launching a hit and run sabotage campaign against the mine companies and ultimately fed into a Miners' Army identified by the wearing of red bandanas on necks and arms. Over the course of several pitched battles against the national UMWA leadership, and an array of police, National Guard, and even US Army troops dropping bombs on them, the miners reigned over several counties.

Unfortunately, the Miners' Army was unable to effectively circulate their struggle beyond the western counties of West Virginia. Despite widespread national media attention and mass support, the miners' escalation of tactics led them down the same road as the ironworkers' bombing campaign. Their ability to expand and circulate the struggle beyond West Virginia was blocked not only by the hostility of the senior UMWA leadership but also by the composition of coal capital and US Steel, the absentee owner of several significant mines. A remnant of the settlement following the 1898–1901 coal strike, the coal industry had emulated US Steel's strategy in the iron sector by signing an industry-wide contract with the UMWA that was limited to the anthracite fields of the neighbouring states while explicitly carving out the bituminous West Virginia mines. The UMWA was unwilling to circulate the West Virginia miners' struggle in order to protect their contract and diffused the effort to expand it into an industry-wide general strike. Escalating the strike into a mine war confined to a single sub-sector in a single region in a single state was insufficient to overcome the existing composition of capital. The coal companies had successfully manufactured conflicts between factions of workers in the same union which blocked the ability of the miners to expand their support and recompose their class power in order to disrupt the entire industry.

Class Composition

These six peaks in the cycle of working-class struggle hold many lessons for understanding why class conflict fails, extracts concessions, stimulates institutional and legal reform, and provides the conditions for an insurgency. Studying the class composition that underlies any class conflict is crucial for understanding these eventual outcomes. It provides a set of analytical tools to effectively assess the conditions in which workers struggle in order to deploy the appropriate tactics that can serve their strategy and move them closer to achieving their objectives. This is what lies at the heart of the class analysis of this book.

Although the autonomist marxist school has extended Marx's analysis of class composition, there are few case studies that apply the concepts to the details. There are several possible explanations for this dearth of case studies. First, it is extremely complex to thoroughly explore class composition. Class composition is not fixed or limited. One has to examine not only the dynamic movements of two classes and the state, but also their sub-groups, across borders, time and space both independently of and in response to one another. Class composition is an ever-shifting dynamic of relationships not merely between capital and workers but also between the capital and the state, coalitions of allies, organisational and management strategies. It is further complicated by developments in the technological, managerial, and social and behavioural sciences that can be applied to production to manage conflicts in the workplace in order to dampen their disruptive impact. The existing capital composition may make it vulnerable to attack and disruption requiring a shift in allies, corporate structure and a transformation in the role of government in the economy. The data is also woefully incomplete, inconsistent, contradictory, and obfuscated by the complexities of capitalism such as changes in owner-ship, the appearance and disappearance of corporations, the creation of new state agencies, the secrecy of corporations and their advocacy groups, and the absence or presence of unreliable data. Working-class struggle is also notori-ously difficult to study due to the anonymity of workers engaged in dangerous and risky struggle, the perils of disclosing sensitive information about tactics and strategy, and the euphemistic language of academia, capital, and the state in describing and documenting it.

On the flip side, working-class recomposition is also a function of the organ-isational dynamic both on and off the shop floor, the ubiquity of its support through the local community, its ability to circulate the struggle beyond cor-porate, legal and geographical barriers, to adapt to new challenges and setbacks and bypass new technological and managerial prerogatives that undermine workers' cooperation and power in the workplace. To the degree that a new composition of capital blocks, co-opts, diffuses, deflects, or represses the tac-tics and strategy of insurgent workers, their power is decomposed and previous gains are lost or transformed into new means of control, discipline and power over them.

This book is motivated by the need to explore the relationship between tac-tical violence and the relations of power in terms of both the economy and the character of the state. As Tilly observed, 'Let us not assume automatically that any social policy reducing violence is a good thing in itself ... [P]olitical regimes differ in the levels and kinds of violence they generate; in choosing political regimes, to some extent we also choose among varieties of violence'.[50] The level of intensity that characterised class struggle from 1877 to the 1920s not only informs our understanding of the character of the state, it also provides insight into other social movements for political change, reform and revolu-tion. Because the Progressive and New Deal era reforms followed this cycle of struggle, it also informs the policies, conflicts, and tensions still present today nearly a century later.

---

50   Tilly 2003, p. 9.

These six peaks in the cycle of struggle are not meant to be archetypal, comprehensive, or exceptional. There are certainly other important struggles – such as the 1886 eight-hour day strikes and the 1898–1901 coal strike, among others – missing here. These six are the focus of this book because they managed to deploy a strategy of tension to disrupt the accumulation of capital in the dominant industrial sectors of the era, covering vast geographical areas. In doing so they illustrate a range of possible outcomes along the tactical trajectory of violence in class struggle. This cycle is itself a case study of how the class composition can set the tempo for the *danse macabre* of class conflict that can spiral off into destructive violent struggle or a peaceful takeover and democratic reorganisation of the economy and society. The outcome of class struggle was unknown during this era and it remains so today.

Notes on Research

This book has been a long-time labour of love. One of the reasons it has taken so long to write is that I was either busy teaching or looking for teaching work. In this way, my academic work appears analogous in many ways to the contingent and insecure workers whose struggles are explored here. As a full-time part-time professor, I frequently teach as many as eight classes at three to five colleges and universities on both a quarter and semester across four counties. As a result, my only time to work on this book was during the economic crisis (during which my teaching load fell so dramatically that my pay was just enough to cover my rent), on weekends and holidays, and during the summer and winter breaks.

These working conditions are shared by more than 70 percent of all faculty in higher education. In addition to my family life, these working conditions make it extremely difficult to conduct research, to visit and spend time at important archives, and to write and rewrite. While I have received generous travel grants from the institutions where I have taught, I was not allowed to apply for research support until 2016, too late to help with this book. Until I started teaching at a university, I also lacked online access to the more extensive editions of vital academic databases unavailable at community colleges. Also, as an adjunct I do not benefit from actively engaging in research, writing, and publishing, since most of my evaluations offer no credit and no reference to any of these scholarly pursuits (often they have to be added as an auxiliary attachment). Such scholarly pursuits are even actively and passively discouraged in the community colleges. Although it has not yet been acknowledged, I suspect that these working conditions are having a significant detrimental

impact on scholarly research that may not come to light for years and genera-
tions to come.

None of this is to excuse any inadequacies, absences, oversights, or mistakes
in the book. It is intended to demonstrate that academia is a terrain of class
struggle in which academic workers are losing – badly.

One comment I received on my proposal to publishers was that this book
is neither sufficiently historical nor academic. This, however, misses the mark.
Aside from unearthing Luke Grant's unpublished (censored?) 1915 report on
violence in labour conflicts and the dusting off of long forgotten government
commission investigations into several of the strikes analysed in this book, I
never intended to write a book of original history. There are far too many excellent historical works on these strikes already. While the historical record has
been well mined, it probably could use another once over to vacuum up what
remains undiscovered or overlooked. I am not a historian and do not intend
this book to be a work of history. This is a book of theory.

There were two motivations for me to write this book. One is the inadequate
analysis of why violence has been used tactically by insurgents, which I discovered while preparing for and teaching a course on understanding terrorism.
After decades of a growing global cottage industry jammed full of research,
books, reports, commissions, films, journal articles, and encyclopaedias about
terrorism, an analysis explaining how and why violence is deployed by insurgents is glaringly absent.

The other was that, of the historical accounts of political violence used by
dissidents, rebels, strikers, revolutionaries, and protestors in American history,
nearly all of them focused on recording the events while steering clear of analysing why and when it was used and by whom. The reasons for this are painfully obvious: working in this field is bound to result in the study of political
violence being confused for its endorsement.

It is assumed, as discussed earlier in this introduction, that violence is used
by those with ideological, psychological, or theological motivations. The few
analyses over the past century of the use of political violence as a tactic, along
the lines of the one found in this book, take us a few steps along the way, but
only a couple of them see violence as one tactic among many, and few assess
its use by workers in class struggle.

This book is intended to revisit the longer, virtually uninterrupted, period
of bloody violence in American history, 1877 to 1921. While it is not intended
to be a thorough historical account, I do provide a substantial amount of historical detail of each cycle of struggle in order to provide my analysis of why
violence was used in them. This seems unavoidable for two reasons. First, few
Americans, including myself until just a decade ago, know anything about this

period or the specific events that gripped the nation at the time. Secondly, since I am analysing the tactics, strategies and objectives of these struggles, it seems necessary to provide the reader with the essential details required to follow my analysis.

While this book, blemishes and all, is entirely my own responsibility, it would have been impossible without the unwavering support, encouragement, and friendship of Manny N. who embraced my book, then still in extremely rough draft, from the moment I told him about it. I am also deeply indebted to my mentor Harry C. and colleagues Cynthia K. and John M. for reading and giving feedback on the prospectus and a few early draft chapters. I am forever grateful to the editorial board of the Brill Historical Materialism Book Series who agreed to publish my book and to Danny H. for helping me bring it to completion. The Wisconsin State Historical Library, Catherine P. of the San Francisco State University Labor Archives and Research Center, and librarians from the Library of Congress provided invaluable help in tracking down the Luke Grant report that had been missing for a century. Lisa W. designed the figure in this introduction, Simon M. and Calin V.P. proofread the final versions of the manuscript.

Finally, I owe boundless thanks to my daughter Nisa who has put up with many years of me reading or disappearing for endless hours to research and write this book and filling up the house with books. She has taught me to remember to ask, 'Have you considered the lowly worm?'

PART 1

The 1877 Railroad Strike

∵

Suppressing a Volcano: The 1877 Railroad Strike

The *laborer* is the author of all greatness and wealth. Without labor there would be no government, or no leading class, or nothing to preserve.

President U.S. GRANT, 16 June 1877[1]

• • •

Am I mistaken in thinking that we are drawing near the time when we must decide to limit and control great wealth, corporations, and the like, or resort to a strong military government? Is this the urgent question? ... Shall the railroads govern the country, or shall the people govern the railroads? Shall the interest of railroad kings be chiefly regarded, or shall the interest of the people be paramount? ... government policy should be to prevent the accumulation of vast fortunes; and monopolies, so dangerous in control, should be held firmly in the grip of the people.

President RUTHERFORD B. HAYES, 26 March 1886[2]

• • •

Since last week the country has been at the mercy of the mob, and on the whole the mob has behaved rather better than the country. The shameful truth is now clear, that the government is utterly helpless and powerless in the face of an unarmed rebellion of foreign workingmen, mostly Irish. There is nowhere any firm nucleus of authority – nothing to fall back on as a last resort. The Army has been destroyed by the dirty politicians, and the State militia is utterly inefficient. Any hour the mob chooses, it can destroy any city in the country – that is the simple truth. Fortunately, so far, it has not cared to destroy any but railway property.

JOHN HAY, 24 July 1877[3]

• • •

---

1 President Grant, 16 June 1877.
2 President Hayes, 26 March 1886.
3 Former Assistant Secretary of State Hay, 24 July 1877, p. 2.

> It [the public power] grows stronger, however, in proportion as class ant-
> agonisms within the state become more acute, and as adjacent states
> become larger and more populous. We have only to look at our present-
> day Europe, where class struggle and rivalry in conquest have tuned up
> the public power to such a pitch that it threatens to swallow the whole of
> society and even the state.
>
> FREDERICK ENGELS, 1884[4]

∴

The year 1877 was not merely the year the country abandoned Reconstruction and embraced Jim Crow apartheid at the highest levels of government –
the 1877 railroad strike shook the nation's confidence in American capitalism.
For elites, government, and the media, 1877 announced the arrival of the violent 'mob'. From another view, 1877 was the calling card of the arrival of the
self-organised industrial workers willing to escalate the intensity of their tactics to achieve their objectives.[5] Lacking all access to government to address
their grievances, and blocked from organising a union and bargaining with the
owners of capital, workers and their allies shut down much of the rail system
throughout the country. Lacking coordination, the strike erupted into sniping, sabotage, and scattered attacks against the companies and state militias
in order to wring out concessions. In St. Louis and East St. Louis, the strike
went further as workers across the cities shut down all industry and became
renown in the press of the time as America's 'Paris Commune'. The 1877 strike
is a remarkable illustration of the industrial working-class's potent power to
self-organise and disrupt the entire economy without any apparent leadership,
unions or otherwise, as unions and strikes were effectively illegal throughout
the country.

Just as remarkable as the 1877 railroad strike was its aftermath. The 10-day
strike involving an estimated 80,000 railroad workers and 500,000 other workers made it evident just how ungovernable the industrial working-class could
be.[6] The workers' ability to quickly disrupt the national economy transformed
the 1877 strike, whereby it crossed the line from a struggle at the point of pro-

---

4   Engels 1884, p. 158.
5   Sandine 2009.
6   Bellesiles 2010, p. 176.

duction to an insurgency. While there is no precise data on the extensiveness of the strike, it was estimated that 'of the nation's 75,000 miles of track, about two-thirds lay in areas affected directly by the strike; and that on these roads, most freight train and some passenger trains had stopped running'.[7]

Self-organised workers, despite lacking formal organisation or leadership, managed to paralyse the entire economy for about nine days and were willing to take up arms and take over cities to achieve their objectives. As a result, it had a profound influence over the organisation of work, industrial and financial capital, policing, and military force. Announcing a newly recomposed working-class, the insurgency provoked a new composition of capital in an attempt to contain it. A newly reorganised capitalist class sought to compose a new power over work, the relations of production, and the state. Facing the mortal threat of an unrestrained working-class, work began to be reorganised by introducing industrial organisation. Corporations were reorganised and integrated both within and across industrial sectors in order to better meet the threat. Judicial, police, and military state powers were redesigned to more deeply entrench them in regulating and controlling production and the working-class. To do that, the role of government in the economy would need to be further expanded in order to rely on state power to keep the balance of power tilted in its advantage.

The Backbone of the Economy

For about ten days in 1877, much of the country was paralysed by a railroad strike that began in a small town in West Virginia, the same state that opens and closes the cycle of class struggle in this book. In a single day it spread not only throughout the railroad industry but into the mines, canals, and industrial shops, reaching its apex in the complete takeover of several cities by the strikers. From its start on 18 July until 24 July the *New York World* estimated that more than 80,000 railroad workers and more than 500,000 other workers had struck, shutting down thousands of businesses directly and indirectly dependent on the railroads. By 25 July all the main railroad lines and some Canadian lines were affected or struck.[8] When the strike ended between 27–28 July, it took a combined force of possibly tens of thousands police, state militia, armed

---

7   Bruce 1959, p. 271.
8   Foner 1977, p. 189.

vigilantes, special agents, and, for the first time, the deployment of the US Army to smash the nationwide strike.

To understand the instabilities and ruptures provoked by Reconstruction it is crucial to study the 1877 railroad strike in detail by examining the changing composition of capital to meet the threat of the rapidly urbanising working-class. At the beginning of the nineteenth century, only 11 percent of the population were small craft workers and traders, 61 percent were farmers, and 28 percent were slaves.[9] By 1877, this was changing dramatically. Slavery was gone, a growing number of workers were moving from farming to industrial work. One-third of the country lived in urban areas and farming had fallen to 40 percent of the workforce and 19 percent of GDP compared to 30 percent for manufacturing and mining. While the acreage being farmed had grown rapidly as a result of colonial conquest and the Homestead Act, it attracted less capital than manufacturing.[10]

The massive internal migration from the countryside to the burgeoning cities reflected not merely a demographic shift but a fundamental transformation in the quality of life. Once self-sufficient, workers were not dependent on selling their labour for whatever they could get. Social relations, community cohesion, and the very cycle of life were ripped asunder. 'All human barriers to the perpetual continuation of production had to be eliminated. The human being and the rhythms of his or her life had to be subordinated more than ever to those of the machines'.[11] The breaking down of rural life made it possible to reorganise the population as an industrial working-class. Edward Markham's 1899 poem 'The Man with the Hoe' reflected this conflict and tension, issuing this warning to the exploiters of rural and industrial labour:

> O masters, lords and rulers in all lands
> How will the Future reckon with this Man?
> How answer his brute question in that hour
> When whirlwinds of rebellion shake all shores?
> How will it be with kingdoms and with kings –
> With those who shaped him to the thing he is –
> When this dumb Terror shall rise to judge the world.
> After the silence of the centuries?[12]

---

9   Levine 1977, p. 98.
10   Bruce 1959, p. 69; and White, n.d.
11   Levine 1977, p. 101.
12   Markham 1899.

The large number of people moving from the rural agricultural to the urban industrial regions was a significant source of worry. The large urban population was living in destitution and was becoming increasingly militant since the start of the 1873 depression. Many craft workers were out of work, sold their tools to survive, were deeply in debt, and transformed into waged workers. The central target of their grievances were the coal and railroad companies that were the beneficiaries of the first great expansion of the state and federal governments into the economy to help the owners of capital acquire vast land holdings to complete the Trans-Pacific railroad in service to the Union in the Civil War. The 1863 Homestead Act gave impetus to the US Army to genocidally expropriate Native American lands and hand them over either directly or indirectly to the emerging railroad companies. Although many of the initial land grants went to individuals and families who intended or claimed to be planning to settle and farm their claims, most of their lands soon found their way into property of the railroads. America's greatest land redistribution programme began with the violent enclosure of Native lands and ended with most of the lands in the possession of the great industrial trusts.

The historical irony of this great struggle was not lost on W.E.B. DuBois. He noted the role racism played in the Indian Wars, the end of Reconstruction, and the defeat of the white agricultural and industrial working-class. The defeat of the plains Native Americans to turn their lands over to the railroads set the stage for the defeat of the black working-class with the end of Reconstruction and of the industrial white working-class by the same corporations.[13] It was no historical coincidence that after being forced off their lands the Nez Perce were engaged in a mobile war of resistance at the same time as railroad strikers launched their own. Despite the expropriation of massive Western lands, Northern capitalists resisted redistribution for fear of the example it would establish. DuBois wrote:

> To the organised industry of the North, capital in machines was sacred ... They did not wish to set an example of confiscation before a nation victimized by monopoly; and they were bitterly opposed to giving capital to workers and redistributing wealth by public taxation.[14]

As a result, much of the redistributed land went indirectly into the hands of the railroads through various schemes and outright subsidies. Land grants to the

---

13   DuBois 1935.
14   Ibid., p. 368.

railroads were stunning in their magnitude. They included one-quarter of the states of Minnesota and Washington; one-fifth of the states of Wisconsin, Iowa, Kansas, North Dakota, and Montana; one-seventh of Nebraska; one-eighth of California; and one-ninth of Louisiana. The railroad's rapid expansion westward also brought a great migratory flow of people to settle in those areas. The percentage of the population living west of the Mississippi River grew a stunning 50 percent, from 18 to 27 percent, in the two decades following 1870.[15] The movement of land into the hands of the railroads, the relocation of people as their workers and customers, and the demand for industrial goods from the expansion of the railroads drove their annual output to 2 percent between 1870 and 1910, exceeding the annual growth rate of 1.5 percent for the entire economy.[16]

As Stromquist observed, 'the railroads directed the settlement process west of the Mississippi'. They settled new towns in locations that would be profitably dependent on the railroads for their connections to the rest of the country. By manipulating the supply of land they also controlled the price and determined the taxes they would pay on it. In effect, the railroads became local and state elites and in the process generated much of the cross-class community animosity that erupted in support of the strikers both in sentiment and in the streets.[17]

The Baltimore & Ohio (B&O), the first modern road completed in 1830, provides an illustrative example of the massive expansion of the railroads. In 1860, the company owned 30,625 miles of track, and added another 33,000 miles between 1867–73. By 1890 it owned 167,191 miles, and 200,000 miles by 1900.[18]

The B&O's growth was hardly exceptional. While total investment in the 1850s was $927 million to build about 20,000 miles of track, in 1877 alone, the 79,000 miles of track laid by 50 companies that year was valued at $5 billion, $2.26 billion of which was financed by debt.[19] In 1900, investment grew further to between $9.1 to $15.9 billion due to watered stock, undervalued securities, and exaggerated prices. In 1884 one estimate put the actual value at 50 percent of its published value.[20] Government investment and nurturance of the railroad industry ensured that state and federal governments would be compelled

---

15   Stromquist 1993, p. 9.

16   Ibid., p. 10.

17   Ibid., p. 17.

18   Lens 1973, pp. 35–6.

19   This exceeded the $2.1 billion of federal debt. See Bellesiles 2010, p. 146.

20   Stromquist 1993, p. 11.

TABLE 1   *US rail system 1850–1900*

Miles of track

1850	9k miles of track
1860	30k miles
1865	35k miles
1877	79k miles
1886	136k miles
1890	167k miles
1900	194 k miles

PAINTER 1987, P. 38
Note: Stromquist gives comparative
figures for different years (see Stromquist 1993, p. 7).

to intervene on behalf of the owners of capital when threatened by their workers. The railroads were deemed 'too big to fail'.

The railroads grew increasingly vulnerable to disruption by workers as the
number of workers rose and the capital composition declined in the 1870s
and 1880s. Railroad labour growth was 5 percent between 1870–1910 compared
to 3.25 in manufacturing. During this time, railroad employment more than
doubled from 9 to 20 percent of all employment in manufacturing.[21]

Railroad expansion (see Table 1) drove a new composition of capital in
related industries such as steel. The new Bessemer steel-making process resulted in the construction of large steel plants in the 1870s and '80s, so that 80
percent of all Bessemer steel was consumed primarily by the railroad industry.
This in turn triggered the industrialisation of steel, the growth of industrial steel
worker organising, and the consolidation of the industry into the US Steel con-
glomerate in 1901 (see Chapter 7).

The 1873–9 depression wrecked the railroad companies, reduced track expansion, and decimated the railroad brotherhood craft unions which used the
rapid growth in the demand for skilled labour to raise wages and improve
labour costs, mostly by avoiding strikes. The crisis began with the meltdown
of Jay Cooke's Northern Pacific Railroad in early September. Within a month,
banks had lost about 23 percent of their reserves, and as much as one-third of

---

21   See Ibid., p. 14.

the value of most railroad companies had evaporated by October. In the next few months, national banks were going under, 5,000 businesses had gone bankrupt – wiping out about $229 million in debts – and bank deposits dropped by $100 million. The number of railroad bond defaults grew from $400 million at the start of 1874 to eventually 40 percent of all bonds valued about $789 million. The roads continued to pay dividends of between 6 and 10 percent while continuing to cut wages by as much as half.[22] This pattern was repeated in the following crises in 1883 and 1893.

The number of miles of new track had declined to only 6,000 miles laid between 1873–7, a 50 percent decline, wiping out about half a million railroad jobs in the first year alone. The emerging industrial working-class was made vulnerable by the glut of desperate unemployed workers which drove down wages and made work insecure, short, and subject to exploitative conditions. It is estimated that there were between 3 to 5 million unemployed workers by 1875, two-fifths with no more than 6 or 7 months of work per year, and wages cut by as much as 55 percent. About 80 percent of the labour force was either unemployed or underemployed in 1878.[23] Many Americans were suffering terribly. As Philip Taft observed, 'it would appear that the long depression of the 1870's accompanied by widespread idleness and privation, was the dominant cause' of the 1877 railroad strike and revolt.[24]

The 1877 strike was hardly spontaneous or unexpected: in an attempt to counteract the impact of the depression, railroad workers organised and struck during the early 1870s. The 1877 strikes threatened industrial capital because they created a bottleneck that threatened to choke the accelerating expansion of the railroads and depress further track expansion.

The strike by workers on 18 lines, including the Pennsylvania Railroad, between November 1873 and July 1874 'foreshadowed the violent outburst three years later. For one thing, they revealed that although the railroad workers were mostly without trade union organization or experience, they had the power to disrupt traffic on many roads'.[25] Many of the disruption and sabotage tactics later common in the 1877 strike, such as removing coupling pins and brakes, tearing up tracks, making trains only run backwards, cutting telegraph wires, as well as shooting strikebreakers, were used.[26]

---

22   Belhesiles 2010, pp. 3–6 and 146.

23   Foner 1977, pp. 15–20 and 439; and Lloyd 2009, p. 177.

24   Taft 1966, p. 128.

25   Case 2105, p. 484; Gutman 1976, p. 295; and Foner 1977, p. 21.

26   Gutman 1976, pp. 299–306.

The 1873–4 strike demonstrated that railroad workers had begun exploring new tactics and strategies in an effort to recompose their power to confront the new industrial composition of capital emerging during the crisis. The largest railroad union at that time, Brotherhood of Locomotive Engineers (BLE), was torn by agitation by militant rank and file to support their calls for strikes. Facing opposition by the leadership, members joined with fireman in a wildcat strike on 26 December 1873, when 3,000 workers carried out the largest strike to date in US history affecting many cities in the west and midwest.[27] Other strikes followed in 1873–4, gaining widespread support from non-union workers, middle class, and other sectors of the population in smaller towns rather than large cities, which may explain why the 1877 railroad strike began in a small town in Maryland and West Virginia.[28] These strikes also signalled concerns about the dependability of the militia to break strikes as Indiana and Ohio troops resisted service and publicly sympathised with the strikers.[29] The Lackawanna County sheriff even gave up his posse's weapons to the strikers and intercepted 200 private police sent by the company.[30] A petition signed by many local elites protested Governor Hartranft's attempt to send the militia. The many local embers of the strike were eventually snuffed out by the use of private police, militia armed by cannons, martial law, and strikebreaking by BLE members.[31]

It was during these tumultuous struggles inside the union that engineer Peter Arthur was elected as the BLE's new Grand Chief Engineer as a militant challenger to the existing Grand Chief. Pushed by the rank and file to call strikes, the BLE struck to reverse a wage cut on the Central of New Jersey in October 1876. In December 1876, the BLE shut down all the railroads west of Montreal on the Grand Trunk Railway of Canada, turned back scabs and won the strike, reinstatement of strikers, and reimbursement for expenses. However, the BLE lost strikes against Charles Francis Adams II's Boston & Maine in February 1877 and Franklin Gowen's Philadelphia & Reading in April 1877. Arthur used these defeats as justification to ban unauthorised strikes, refuse to cooperate with other workers, and pledge to common cause with the companies by

---

27   Ibid., pp. 296–7 and 302–3.
28   Ibid., pp. 299–300; and Foner 1977, p. 201.
29   The Indiana militia was then led by future president Benjamin Harrison, who also participated in the prosecution of the strike leaders (see Burbank 1966, p. 39).
30   Gutman 1976, pp. 308–10.
31   In February 1874 the Grand Chief Engineer was ousted by the membership and replaced with Peter Arthur who would continue his predecessor's policies in 1877 (Gutman 1976, p. 318).

preventing thirteen potential strikes in 1876 alone.[32] Arthur took the BLE to its conservative opposition to strikes just as states passed laws making it a crime for an engineer to leave his train at any place other than its destination.[33]

As the size and economic power of the railroads grew rapidly, disruption of the rail system provided the workers immense disruptive power and leverage.[34] Gutman saw that workers' mobilised mass support allowed them to disrupt the train system in a manner that 'temporarily, at least, weakened the power of the employers and created additional obstacles for them to surmount'.[35] The 1873–7 strikes were a trial run for July 1877.

While the depression might have provided a spark for the strike, it did not provide an impetus for successful union organisation. As a result of massive lay-offs, the failures of business, and the contraction of the national economy, the already minuscule number of workers who belonged to labour unions dropped from 300,000 to about 50,000. About 20 of the existing 30 national unions disappeared.[36] Unions played virtually no role in the 1877 strike because they existed under conditions which made it nearly impossible for them to operate.

One of the starkest examples of such repressive conditions were the Pennsylvania coal mines, where corporate consolidation was proceeding apace with the railroads. The 1877 strike began less than a month after the first so-called Molly Maguire was hung on 21 June 1877. The same repressed grievances of the coal miners were felt by railroad workers who increasingly worked for the same companies whose connection was disguised by their formal status as 'independent' subsidiaries, a forebear to the holding company or trust that would come to dominate the economy by the end of the century. Trusts began to take on new prominence as a strategic response to the organised working-class by allowing the new composition of capital to shift production away from disrupted subsidiaries or sectors, thereby diluting the disruptive power of the strike. It also provided new sources of capital to invest in new technology to shift the division of labour as a means to reimpose control over unruly workers.

The railroads were not immune to the economic collapse triggered by the speculative investments of a railroad magnate. Share prices dropped between 1876–7. In 1876, 76 railroads were already in bankruptcy or foreclosure and

---

32   Foner 1977, pp. 24 and 27.

33   Lloyd 2009, p. 179.

34   As an example of the rapid growth of the railroad workforce, the Pennsylvania Railroad had about 18,000 workers, not including clerks, in 1870. By 1891, this grew to a total of 110,000 workers. In 1880, there were about 419,000 workers in total, nearly doubling to about 800,000 in 1890 (Gutman 1976, p. 296; and White, n.d.).

35   Gutman 1976, p. 319.

36   Lens 1973, p. 34.

placed under federal receivership. Federal receivership was a newly devised strategy in which a bankrupt company was placed under the authority of a federal court which oversaw its management by an appointed administrator.[37] Appointed by the court, the administrator put the power and protection of the federal government at the service of the company and shielded it from account-ability under the law. The railroad companies used receiverships to both attack workers and liquidate corporate assets for their investors. Companies used receivership similarly to bankruptcy today to fire employees, break contracts and other agreements, lower labour costs, and shield themselves from compet-itors.

By 1876, operating expenses per mile were 20 percent lower as a result of wage cuts and other reorganisational tactics while carriers paid normal or higher dividends to their shareholders.[38] The lower wages and increased pro-ductivity as a result of the depression led the *Commercial and Financial Chron-icle* to report that 'this year [1877] also labor is under control for the first time since the war'.[39] The newly emerging industrial corporation demonstrated that it would increasingly rely on the state to devise new tactics for containing insubordinate workers.

The extent of that control was apparently overestimated. Although the 1877 'Railroad Men's War' was 'an unplanned upsurge',[40] it was not unorganised. The self-organised nature of the strike wasn't merely the result of the near absence of labour unions; rather it occurred despite them. The existing train brother-hoods were highly fragmented by craft, didn't coordinate with one another, negotiated separate labour agreements, and were universally opposed to any strikes or disruptions.

Since so many roads were under receivership, organising legally without run-ning afoul of federal law was virtually impossible. If they were to act at all workers had to study and adapt to the conditions in which they found them-selves. Understanding that the railroads were being integrated into a national industrial system, even if on paper it appeared to be controlled by a fragmented multitude of railroad companies, would provide new tactical openings. While there is no evidence in the historical record of workers carrying out such an analysis, their tactics demonstrated some recognition of the ability to use the integrated rail system to their own advantage. The ability to spread the strike so quickly and widely across the Atlantic coast and Midwest was actualised by

37   Bruce 1959, pp. 33–4.
38   Lens 1973, p. 39.
39   Foner 1977, p. 462.
40   Lens 1973, p. 34.

railroad workers and their supporters using the very transportation and communication technology of the railroads to circulate their struggle.

This chapter is not intended to be an exhaustive historical account of the
strike, but it is useful to examine a small sampling of all the confrontations,
riots, clashes and battles taking place between workers and capital. In contrast
to the assumption of the unplanned and spontaneous character implied by
such terms, this chapter will explore the tactical significance of these actions
as scattered attacks, sniping, sabotage, and disruption along the tactical trajectory. What can be gleaned from these local aspects of the general strike is how
workers self-organised locally using their own communication networks, tactics, and strategies to expand mass support for the strike, sometimes prompted
local officials to intervene on their behalf, caused splits in the ranks of militias sent to break the strike, and escalated or de-escalated their tactics based
on their own assessment of the conditions of their contestation. Through it all,
these workers organised without any formal union organisational apparatus.
Despite their willingness to escalate their tactics, the strike was ultimately lost
due to the absence of a means to coordinate the decentralised insurgency and
achieve their objectives.

The 10 Days that Shook the Nineteenth Century

The strike actually began on a second attempt. When the brotherhoods didn't
oppose a recent wage cut on the Pennsylvania Railroad, the Baltimore & Ohio
(B&O), and other lines, members and workers self-organised their own secret
union open to all craft workers. The Trainmen's Union's (TU) first meeting was
organised by Pittsburgh, Fort Wayne & Chicago workers at Dietrich's Hall in
Allegheny City across the river from Pittsburgh on 2 June 1877 in the same state
in which the recent prosecution of the Molly Maguires had recently occurred.[41]
One of their fundamental principles was that they promised not to scab on
one another, 'in short, unity of capital would be met at last by unity of labor'.[42]
Twenty-five-year-old Robert Ammon was its founder and 'Grand Organizer',
travelling the rails and organising thousands of workers on other lines to take
action.[43]

---

41   The Pittsburgh, Fort Wayne & Chicago Railway and several other railroads were subsidi-
       aries of the Pennsylvania Railroad Company. (See Senate and House of Representatives of
       the Commonwealth of Pennsylvania 1878, p. 2).
42   Bruce 1959, p. 59.
43   Bellesiles 2010, pp. 147 and 332–3.

A diverse group of workers attempted to meet with Pennsylvania Railroad President Tom Scott in late May to ask him to rescind the planned 10 percent wage cut, and left satisfied with his pledge to do so when the economy rebounded. What the workers didn't know at the time was that the company had paid an 8 percent dividend on higher profits from the previous year, from which it had set aside an additional $1.5 million in reserve.[44]

Unsatisfied with the effort of the committee, a diverse group of brakemen and other railroad workers started self-organising in Allegheny City, Pennsylvania and formed the TU on 2 June. The TU was open to railroad workers of all skill levels working on grand trunk lines of the Baltimore and Ohio, Pittsburgh, Fort Wayne & Chicago, Erie, and Atlantic and Great Western who were obliged to swear an oath to join.[45] Ammon was the Grand Organizer of the first lodge organising workers all along the B&O railroad even into Martinsburg. The TU issued a general strike for 27 June. Forty organisers were sent out from Pittsburgh to organise the strike by word of mouth on these lines on 24 June, expecting the telegraph lines to be cut. When some members began to oppose the strike at a planning meeting on 25 June and only 200 men showed up in Pittsburgh on the 27th, the strike fell apart. At least two provocateurs took a westbound train spreading the false rumour that the strike had been called off, and since the railroads had interrupted telegraph services, these could not be countermanded.[46]

Although it was new, the TU was preceded by recent efforts of railroad workers to organise new kinds of brotherhoods that embraced strikes and cooperation with other workers. For example, in 1873 the Brakemen's Brotherhood (BB) – formed in Hornellsville, New York – played a key role in the strikes of the 1870s. The BB was an early form of industrial unionism among railroad workers, reportedly organised throughout the West, Southwest, and Florida in late 1875, and included engineers, trackmen, and shopmen as members.[47]

The historical record about the TU after this date is inconclusive. The TU stopped meeting and its leaders were caught by surprise when the strike began,

---

44   Senate and House of Representatives of the Commonwealth of Pennsylvania 1878, pp. 2 and 683; and Lloyd 2009, p. 179.

45   Senate and House of Representatives of the Commonwealth of Pennsylvania 1878, pp. 671 and 684.

46   Foner 1977, p. 31. Foner's account differs from the Pennsylvania state legislature's investigation that found that the TU called off the strike two days earlier when it was revealed that a spy had reported plans for the strike to the railroads. (See Senate and House of Representatives of the Commonwealth of Pennsylvania 1878, pp. 3–4, 671–2, and 684).

47   Stromquist 1993, pp. 51–3.

although the network put into place by the union likely helped to circulate news and information among strikers. In a few cities such as Hornellsville and Pittsburgh, TU members began meeting again to organise the strike locally. However, Ammon claimed that although the TU still continued, it stopped meeting in Pittsburgh and did not plan any further strikes. There is little in the historical record showing that the TU continued to operate as a national union except for telegraphs between Barney Donahue in Hornellsville and Ammon in Pittsburgh.[48] During its brief existence the union appears to have been quickly infused with informants, failing to function as a coordinating body almost from its start.[49] Despite the emasculated TU, some railroad workers had gotten its message and appear to have waited for an opportune grievance to take action. It is very likely that the workers in these cities continued using the foundation of the TU to continue to self-organise across the otherwise rigid divides of skill, status, and wage.[50] In Erie, Pennsylvania, for example, self-organised workers identified themselves as a 'Committee of Firemen, Brakemen and Citizens' in a letter to President Hayes, informing him that the Lake Shore Railway was purposefully blocking the mails.[51]

Ammon was clearly a master strategist, if an ineffective leader. In forming the first TU lodge he understood the need to bring all of the workers on several key lines together into a single union and organised workers along each entire line. These tactics illustrated that Ammon and the TU's strategy was to disrupt the entire regional railroad system in order to extract concessions. In his testimony to the legislative committee investigating the strike, Ammon contradicted himself on several issues, perhaps in order to protect himself and/or to avoid unnecessarily exposing others to prosecution and persecution. For example, he claims that he did not think the workers in Martinsburg would strike because their talk about striking 'was all wind'. Ammon also testified

---

48 The primary record of the TU's effort is Ammon's testimony to the Pennsylvania State Legislature's Committee to Investigate the Railroad Riots. Whether some continued to organise in secret or joined the Knights of Labor we cannot be sure. (See Stromquist 1993, pp. 53–4, and 291; and Senate and House of Representatives of the Commonwealth of Pennsylvania 1878, pp. 672–4).

49 Lens 1973, p. 42.

50 Of course, we can only read such conclusions from the strike itself, which was reported to have widespread participation by many skilled, semi-skilled, and unskilled, as well as waged and unwaged workers who otherwise rarely cooperated or were prevented from doing so by the brotherhoods' leadership, chauvinism, status hierarchy, racism and sexism. (See Self Negation n.d., pp. 13–14).

51 Burbank 1966, p. 59.

that he did not plan and was unaware of the second strike. Although he could have been telling the truth, in which case he did not direct a strike that was organised from below, he could have lied or the strikers could have had a contingency plan in place to activate the network in case something went wrong with the first attempt. Ammon did confirm that the strikers had secret signals with which to communicate with one another. Either way, it is impossible to know for sure.[52]

The debate over how the strike was launched and spread continues to this day. Calling it spontaneous, as most historical accounts of the strike do, is too simple and leaves many unanswered questions about how workers managed to organise, even during a great depression, without any above ground organisation or coordination, and in the face of repression. Major-General Winfield Scott Hancock perceived that any leadership that did exist was not really in charge. As he wrote to Secretary McCrary, the TU did not expect to start the strike until October, 'but certain events precipitated matters and the leaders were made to follow'.[53]

Once the TU's centralised and hierarchical leadership was exposed and suppressed, much of the membership fell into disarray, although some apparently continued to self-organise.[54] While the strike may have lacked a distinct centralised organisation and leadership, the strikers were not unorganised. Ammon testified that workers from at least five roads and mill and glass factory workers were cooperating and Pittsburgh was established as the strike centre. While the TU was re-activated in a few places, nearly all the workers self-organised locally and selected their own leadership – something hinted at, in the record of the strike in Pennsylvania for example, but has yet to be identified.[55] This may explain the apparently well-coordinated acts of sabotage and disruption although there is no evidence of formal efforts to continue coordinating regionally or nationally.

Because the depression and repressive conditions made it extremely risky to publicly organise, we can really only speculate as to how the strike spread. Without a union or coordinating body, relative isolated geography of many of the key strike areas, lack of national media, and the control of the telegraph by

---

52   Senate and House of Representatives of the Commonwealth of Pennsylvania 1878, pp. 684–5 and 687.

53   See, for example, Bruce 1959; Burbank 1966, p. 8, p. 225; Foner 1977, pp. 31–2; and Lloyd 2009, p. 182.

54   Self Negation n.d., p. 15.

55   Senate and House of Representatives of the Commonwealth of Pennsylvania 1878, pp. 9–13 and 686.

the railroads, the fact of the strike was a feat in itself. The tactics and strategies deployed to achieve a near nationwide shutdown have yet to be completely explored.

An early flash point for the 1877 strike was on Franklin Gowen's Philadelphia & Reading Railroad. Gowen was buying up much of the Schuylkill county coalfields and with it extending his influence over the regional lines. Although he signed a written contract with the miners in 1870 and set up a benefits system in 1875, these were delay tactics to give his company time to mobilise its forces to smash the miners' union. Emerging as a secret workers' self-defence organisation, the mythical Molly Maguire miners carried out armed assaults and sabotage of the mines in Pennsylvania. Gowen spent $4 million to crush the Workers Benevolence Association and terrorise the miners and their supporters in order to block them from circulating their struggle from his mines to his lines. Of the miners prosecuted for six murders committed between the mid-1860s and 1875, only three of the murders were labour related. In all, ten miners and organisers were executed.[56]

The effect of Gowen's bloody repression evaporated quite fast. In early March 1877, a committee of engineers and firemen petitioned Philadelphia & Reading Railroad president Gowen for a 20 percent raise, but they did not threaten a strike.[57] Although the brotherhoods conceded to the cuts, and one-half of the engineers struck on 14 April 1877, the line was back running at full capacity within a week.

Although the workers did not know it at the time, the railroad companies had been meeting over the previous months to coordinate a simultaneous wage cut across the industry in order to devise a new cooperative strategy to avoid further disruption of their operations.[58] The potential for disruption grew with the interconnected rail and depot systems which provided an opportunity for workers to spread their strike against the wage cut quickly across the systems, companies, 12 major cities and regions. Whether intended or not, the workers' tactic took advantage of the newly emerging composition of railroad capital which helped it spread along the rail system and across many separate companies.

Fearing further possible disruptions, in May and June 1877 the four largest eastbound trunk lines in Chicago had negotiated a pooling agreement as a tactic to meet the threat of strikes which helped them continue shipping

---

56   Bruce, 1959, pp. 38–9. Sean Connery also performed in a film portraying the Molly
        Maguires and their struggle. (Molly Maguires 1970)

57   Bruce 1959, p. 37.

58   Ibid., p. 34.

anthracite coal during the April strike. The agreement heralded a new model of cross-industry coordination leading the *Commercial and Financial Chronicle* to prematurely comment that 'this year [1877] ... labor is under control for the first time since the war'.[59] At this time they arranged to begin cutting wages one at a time on the condition that the other three in the pool would cover one another's losses in case of a strike. This pooling agreement was a tactic devised by an industry going through rapid centralisation and consolidation with the expectation that labour would soon be doing the same. Such reorganisation illustrated how capital continually reorganises in response to disobedient workers in expectation of further conflict.

With the pooling agreement in place, the lines began to roll out their next round of wage cuts. In June 1877, the Pennsylvania Railroad announced another plan to cut wages by 20 percent and a day later the Lackawanna railroad announced a 10 percent cut. Rather than fight the new round of wage cuts, the brotherhoods accepted them and did not issue a strike call. This prompted workers to form the TU.

Baltimore and Martinsburg

The initial spark for the strike began almost simultaneously on the B&O between Camden Junction, a switching point near Baltimore, Maryland, and Martinsburg, West Virginia (population 8,000). Although the B&O settled the 1876 strike promising no more cuts, it announced it was paying the usual dividend of 10 percent on 15 July, making yet another 10 percent wage cut on 16 July, and introducing the so-called 'double header' that dangerously doubled the number of cars per train, in effect cutting the number of workers per train by half.[60] This policy had the effect of doubling output for not only 10 percent lower pay, but also presumably half as many workers.

On the B&O line at Camden Junction, two miles from Baltimore, workers had suffered work reductions of 50 percent and average wage cuts of 30 percent. The strike began as crowds of workers, women, and the unemployed, of

---

59 Foner 1977, p. 29.
60 Double headers made railroad work even deadlier than it already was. In 1888–9, for example, the railroads had 704,000 workers of whom 20,000 were injured and 2,000 killed, a rate of injury of 1 in 35 workers and 1 in 357 killed. The plight of industrial workers was not just limited to the deadly and dangerous conditions on the job but amplified by the atrocious conditions in the growing urban industrial centres, where half the children of Chicago died by age 5 (Bruce 1959, p. 234; and Painter 1987, p. 39). The Pennsylvania Railroad started using double headers on freight trains in Pittsburgh beginning on 19 July. (Senate and House of Representatives of the Commonwealth of Pennsylvania 1878, p. 4).

which there were many due to the long depression, met the state militia with a shower of stones. Tensions were already running high in the city, as the box- and can-makers were already on strike. The strike quickly spread throughout Baltimore when 700 carmakers and other small strikes by other line workers erupted.[61]

The Maryland state militia members were suspected of being sympathetic to the strikers and unreliable. Governor John Carroll feared only few militia would respond to the emergency ringing of the city bells. He turned out to be right. The militia opened fire at a parade of thousands of strike supporters who quickly arrived, killing 10 or 11 and injuring 20 to 40 people. However, between one-half and two-thirds of the 120 troops who left the armoury to attack the crowd returned. The rest had dropped out, changed to civilian clothes, and faded away.[62] The dissipation of the militia force left the militia command- ers, Governor Carroll, Mayor Ferdinand Latrobe (also a B&O shareholder), the Board of Police Commissioners and various railroad officials, including a B&O Vice President, trapped in the depot by a now enraged crowd of about 15,000 people, who attacked the station and telegraph office, wrecked the building, tore up tracks, burned some passenger coaches, and cut hoses to prevent fire- men from putting out the fire. Fighting to reopen part of the line raged for three days and the strike ended after 16 days. The governor called President Hayes, requesting that he send the US Army to intervene. The people reportedly seized the depot, set it and the lumberyard and petroleum cars on fire and scared off the firemen.[63] By the time 500 US troops and Marines under the command of Major-General Hancock had arrived, the fires were out and the crowd had dwindled in size and anger. What most concerned the governor and the rail- road company was that there were no trains running east of the Ohio River. The arrival of the troops soon achieved the objective of getting the B&O pas- senger trains running again, although they were not immediately able to run freight.

President Rutherford Hayes was clearly struggling with the proper role of the military to address domestic issues. Two months earlier, he had written in his diary that 'My policy is trust, peace, and to put aside the bayonet'.[64] Perhaps the President had earlier feared further enraging the strikers and their supporters by inserting US troops, or considered the constitutional limits to using the US

---

61   Foner 1977, pp. 33 and 46.

62   Bruce 1959, p. 112; and Foner 1977, p. 47.

63   Bruce 1959, pp. 109–10; Brecher 1972, pp. 20–1; and Foner 1977, p. 48.

64   Lens 1973, p. 43.

Army for domestic purposes as a sop to the South. According to the record, their proper use and who would command them were issues of debate in his cabinet meetings for the rest of the month. His hesitation was clearly directed at the South, where he promised to end Reconstruction and pull out the few remaining troops, not the workers.

Eventually there were 1,200–2,000 state militia in or near the city. B&O refused to negotiate and fired the strikers, which stopped all freight from moving. On 26 July the strikers made a proposal for a new wage scale and minimum wage, lay-overs, and time and a half on Sundays, as well as other proposed changes to working conditions. In a later negotiation B&O conceded two demands but refused to reverse the 10 percent wage cut.[65]

The strike also started in Martinsburg when a crowd started blocking trains on 16 July. Another crowd composed of black and white boatmen, coal miners, and railroad workers soon blocked and decoupled a train leaving Martinsburg carrying railroad officials, reporters and 50 US troops. In Keyser, West Virginia, black and white railroad workers met together and voted to join the strike, and miners had blocked trains carrying troops and wrecked freights.[66] Although the mayor ordered the arrest of the strike leaders, the town's support for the strike prevented his order from being enacted and a street battle erupted. The strike almost immediately spread all along the line. Speaking at Tompkins Square, New York City rally, *Labor Standard* editor J.P. McDonnell said that 'It was a grand sight to see in West Virginia, white and colored men standing together ... Hereafter there shall be no north, no south, no east, no west, only the land of labor and the workingmen must own and possess it'.[67] This was only a small sampling of the kind of interracial working-class cooperation that DuBois had hoped for but found wanting.

Although one striker was shot and later died, the press reported calm, the B&O requested local, state and federal police and military force to put down the insurgency and restore control over the unruly workers. But much like in Maryland, elites were divided on whether to intervene and state forces were undependable. A Howard County judge prohibited police from operating outside the city limits. In response the B&O turned to the West Virginia governor to send in militia despite the lack of evidence of casualties or property damage. The Beverly Light Guards sent in to Martinsburg by the governor were unable to obtain enough volunteers to run the trains out because most of them were rail-

65   Foner 1977, pp. 50–2.

66   Bruce 1959, p. 97.

67   See Foner 1977, p. 122.

road workers if not strikers and were dismissed by their commanding officer. Unable to return home, some of the disbanded militia reportedly attended a fund-raising dance for strikers at Grafton.[68]

With the militia on the side of the strikers, the governor then commissioned police as special railway constables. Despite a militia colonel's report that 'the rioters are largely cooperated with by civilians', the Governor also wrote President Hayes on 18 July about 'unlawful combinations and domestic violence now existing at Martinsburg and at other points along the line of the Baltimore and Ohio railroad' and asked for 200–300 US Army troops.[69] He had not yet declared a state of emergency in Martinsburg, nor had he placed it under martial law. B&O's president also wrote Hayes of the 'gravest consequences' from 'measures of economy' implemented across the country's railroads. 'Labor was about to rise up in a form too gigantic for any one state to contain', he feared.[70]

The first federal troops to arrive in Martinsburg from Baltimore were under the command of a colonel of the Second US Artillery. Incredibly, the regiment's fund had just lost money invested in railroads bonds and had not been paid for seven months. Now they were ordered to defend the interests of a corporation operating in an industry that just cost them a substantial loss in assets. Despite the killings by the militia and US troops, the media was on the side of military force. The *Brooklyn Daily Eagle* wrote on 19 July that it wasn't pleasant to see 'men being mowed down by soldiers, but it will be a much worse spectacle for the country to have a mob triumphant in a state like West Virginia than to have the life blown out of men who refuse to recognize the right of every American to control his own labor and his own property'.[71]

The arrival of 300 US troops in the area had little immediate effect on the strike. The available forces were too small and met defiant mass support for the strikers, ignoring the president's proclamation to disperse. Six men and two women armed with clubs met a coal train guarded by 18 soldiers and three armed men. Although the insurgents moved aside when guns were pointed at them, an engineer had jumped off, stranding the train.[72] A second train was

---

68   After this betrayal the West Virginia state militia were temporarily reorganised and then abolished. In his study of the Cleveland militias, Isaac found that the working-class militias were widely disbanded after 1877. In their place socially connected elites formed, funded and armed their own militias and successfully lobbied for the militias to be reorganised into the National Guard. (Isaac 2002; and Bruce 1959, p. 79).

69   Bruce 1959, pp. 85–6.

70   Ibid., p. 85; and Foner 1977, pp. 34–6 and 38.

71   See Foner 1977, p. 104.

72   Ibid., p. 43.

later met by 100 armed strikers, including local strike leader Dick Zepp. Also onboard was Zepp's brother who had just joined the crew of armed scabs.

Although Brecher observed that 1877 'marks the first great American mass strike, a movement that was viewed at the time as a violent rebellion', he did not examine why insurgents deployed violence and the tactical role it played in the struggle.[73] In the early days of the strike, workers had mobilised sufficient mass support to up the ante with the company, knowing that its support reduced the risks and increased their opportunities to realise their objectives. With the state and federal governments coming to the aid of the B&O, the workers escalated their tactics to armed disruption of the rail lines in order to defend the strike and threatened continued escalation. Emboldened by the spread of the strike to hundreds of canal workers and miners who marched in support, a manifesto of workers issued in Westernport, Maryland, on 20 July warned the B&O to restore the earlier wages. Reduced to starvation, the workers warned that if the company did not meet their demands soon,

> the officials will hazard their lives and endanger their property, for we shall run their trains and locomotives into the river; we shall blow up their bridges; we shall tear up their railroads; we shall consume their shops with fire and ravage their hotels with desperation.[74]

The use of US troops against the strikers was a tactical escalation by elites. President Hayes was the first to use US troops domestically against strikers in peacetime on a national scale.[75] At a time of both Reconstruction and the Indian Wars, use of US troops was quite common. Between 1865–77 US troops were used domestically 25 times, all but once in the South. When President Hayes sent troops to West Virginia, the US Army was down to only about 25,000 men, all but a few out West fighting Native Americans, because Congress had recently adjourned without reauthorising funding, leaving the army without enough money to make payroll. The army was so broke that the B&O provided

---

73   Brecher 1972, pp. 13, 16, and 35.

74   Foner 1977, pp. 44–5.

75   Although President Andrew Jackson sent troops to break a strike on the Chesapeake and Ohio canal in 1834 as a favour to his friend who was the president of the company, Foner observed that 'the Great Strike of 1877 was the first instance in which the regular army entered into a labor disturbance on a national scale' (Foner 1977, p. 40). While President Hayes sent in US troops on a case by case basis, most of the troops were placed under the command of the state governor who requested them.

the troop train and then billed the federal government for its services.[76] Hayes's deployment established a new precedent. US troops were used to break strikes twice as often as all other uses to address civil disorder by 1959.

Using US troops to break a strike cemented the identity of interest between the federal government and the railroads. This is no better illustrated than by what occurred during the debacle of the disputed 1876 presidential election in which the fortunes of the two frontrunners – Democrat Samuel Tilden and Republican Hayes – were decided by backdoor dealings in the House of Representatives. Although Hayes was chosen in exchange for the Republicans' promise to withdraw the few remaining troops in the South and abandon its black allies and Reconstruction policies, it was a railroad executive who clinched the deal. Pennsylvania Railroad President Scott managed to intervene to get enough Southern congressmen to support Hayes in exchange for supporting the formation of the Texas & Pacific Railway. Republican candidate Hayes was informed by telegram that he had been selected president on 2 March 1877 while riding to Washington DC in one of the Pennsylvania Railroad President Scott's private rail cars.[77]

Pittsburgh to Philadelphia

The strike almost immediately spread to Pennsylvania, New York, New Jersey, Ohio, Illinois, Missouri, and California as workers spread the news by word of mouth along the lines and in the depots. Its rapid spread led Hayes's secretary of war and general commanding the troops to both call the strike 'an insurrection' to justify sending more US troops to Maryland and Pennsylvania.[78] On Wednesday 25 July, President Hayes and his cabinet drafted a declaration of war that

---

76   Foner 1977, pp. 41–2.

77   President Hayes had a complex personal history both with railroad corporations and the tragedy of the horrendous conditions of both railroad work and travel. Just before the 1877 strike erupted on 17 July, President Hayes's cousin Mary Birchard was killed in the Ashtabula Ohio railroad disaster when an iron truss bridge collapsed under a railroad, killing 159 people. Demonstrating how accidents of history seem so incredibly aligned, she was buried on 18 July 1877, just a day after the strike began. Although President Hayes advocated for regulating the railroads in the early 1870s, he no longer did so by 1875 when he listed his occupation in the Fremont, Ohio directory as 'capitalist' (Bruce 1959, pp. 87–8). Just a year earlier, in 1876, then-Governor Hayes had called out the militia to crush the coal miners' strike (Foner 1977, p. 15; and Bruce 1959, pp. 49 and 89).

78   Elites and militiamen in Pennsylvania reportedly opposed Governor John Hartranft's request that the federal government send in troops against the Erie strikers (Foner 1977, p. 24).

declared the rioters 'levying war against the US', which was not issued as the strike appeared to have ended by that time. Hayes's efforts began the process of establishing exactly when the federal government could intervene under the constitution and law during a strike when local and state authorities were unable to restore order. Among the areas of constitution and law available to President Hayes was Article IV, Section 4 of the US Constitution, Sections 1984 and 1989 of Act of June 18, 1878, Revised Statutes of the US, Sections 5297–5299, and the Revised Statutes of the US Section 3999.[79] Federal intervention spoke to the merging of the interests between capital and the state which would be further articulated during the 1894 strike.

The strike enveloped most of the main trunk lines across the Middle Atlantic and Midwest. By 24 July, about 100,000 workers were on strike on the Erie, New York Central, the Delaware, Lackawanna & Western Railroad, the Canada Southern operating in Ohio, Pennsylvania, and New York States, and the Chicago and St. Louis. The strike was most disruptive in Baltimore, Philadelphia, Pittsburgh, Buffalo, Cleveland, Toledo, Columbus, Cincinnati, Louisville, Indianapolis, Chicago, St. Louis, Kansas City, and Omaha, but also impacted New York City and Albany, Little Rock, New Orleans, and Galveston, and reached as far West as San Francisco. 'About two-thirds of the country's total rail mileage lay within the strike-affected area, and in those zones strikers halted most freight trains and delayed many passenger and mail trains'.[80] Ross and Taft assert that 'each strike was independent of those on other roads, each having a local cause particularly its own ... there was a sort of epidemic of strikes running through the laboring classes of the country ...'.[81] Describing the strike as an 'epidemic' of local independent strikes with their own local causes is too simple.[82] It overlooks the rapid integration of the local and regional railroad systems into a national system that was increasingly coming under the direct cooperative coordination of competing rail companies. By staggering the wage cuts, the companies made the grievances appear to be locally specific, although they were in fact industry-wide.

Another centre of armed struggle was in Pennsylvania. When the Pennsylvania Railroad attempted to introduce doubleheader trains on 19 July, brakemen and flagmen walked out on strike and took control of the switches in Pittsburgh.[83] When a crew was finally recruited to take out a train, the strikers, led

79   Bruce 1959, p. 279; United States Senate 1903, pp. 5–12.
80   Ross and Taft 1969, pp. 4–5.
81   Ibid., p. 5.
82   Senate and House of Representatives of the Commonwealth of Pennsylvania 1878, p. 46.
83   Foner 1977, p. 57.

by Andrew Hice, threw coupling pins and other objects at the workers. A crowd immediately blocked 94 freight trains and about 900 cars while it allowed passenger trains to travel. Distinguishing between the types of rail traffic was a tactic in the war of manoeuvre to divide potential allies of the rail companies by attempting to reduce the disruption to people, and to continue mustering public support for the strike which reportedly had wide support across the city's working-class.

Illustrating the self-organised character of the strike and the lack of coordination, the TU organiser Ammon was fired from his job as a freight brakeman on the Pittsburgh, Fort Wayne and Chicago railroad and left the area to take a job soon after their strike call had failed. However, on 18 July he received a telegram informing him that the strike had taken off and asking him to return. When Ammon arrived the next day he was met by a group of brakemen and conductors but he went home and went to bed, refusing to leave his house with them. Ammon claimed that he did not trust some of the men who came to his house who he considered scabs for their earlier efforts to disrupt the TU from within. The next morning he appeared to have changed his mind, went to the trains and jumped on the engine and defied the police by refusing to get down.[84]

The strike appears to have been started without the knowledge of the Pittsburgh TU's president Samuel Muckle, who had been fired for his union organising in June. He slept in late on 19 July and learned about the strike at noon, reportedly commenting 'Impossible!' He rushed to Twenty-eighth Street where the trains were being blocked and tried to get his former co-workers to go home. The TU was re-activated and quickly rented Phoenix Hall. There a strikers' committee called for an end to the doubleheaders, a return to the pre-June pay scale, no blacklist, and the abolition of pay grades. The committee passed a resolution for 'all working men to make common cause with their brethren on the railroad'.[85] On Friday, the Pittsburgh freight engineers and B&O freight workers joined the strike.

Disruption was paired with negotiation by making several attempts to settle the strike. The next day, 20 July, the TU sent a committee to negotiate with Pennsylvania Railroad superintendent Robert Pitcairn to reverse the wage cut, end the double headers, and rehire the strikers fired the previous day. However,

---

84   Senate and House of Representatives of the Commonwealth of Pennsylvania 1878, pp. 661–3.

85   Bruce 1959, pp. 125–6. Ammon referred to Muckle as 'showing the white feather' for betraying the strike by scabbing on his fellow strikers and attempting to get a job with the railroad again. (See Senate and House of Representatives of the Commonwealth of Pennsylvania 1878, p. 680).

Pitcairn refused to negotiate with them or city businessmen who encouraged the company to respond to the grievances. According to Ammon, 'we tried everything with reference to avoiding a strike'.[86]

Pittsburgh's city government had gone broke in June and was unable to borrow any money due to restrictions in the state constitution. Ironically, the city had laid off half of the police force only a few days before the strike began and, as a result, the city only had 11 officers, only nine of whom worked during the day due to a shortage of funding. With the city police only able to spare nine patrolmen, the company had to pay the city to recruit ten more. As the strikers' support grew, the mayor refused the company's further request for 50 more, sending only five or six policemen. A third request, this time for 150 policemen, went unheeded as the mayor went home to care for his wife. The mayor also rejected a further request to call in the local 'national guard'.[87] In total, the mayor sent 29 men. According to the state legislature's investigative committee, 'there does not appear to have been any serious attempt made by the mayor or police to assist in quelling the riots'.[88] There was also little effort to serve warrants for the arrest of strike organisers. On 20 and 21 July warrants had been issued twice for the arrest of 15 to 20 strike organisers but never served because none of them were located or arrested. Sheriff Fife was unsuccessful in raising the necessary posse to serve the arrest warrants and had to give up on the effort.[89] As the committee reported, those opposed to the strike were 'so few as to be of no use in controlling or directing public sentiment'. The strikers' widespread support in the city clearly dissuaded the mayor and sheriff from intervening at the request of the railroad. The near universal local support for the strike was but one illustration of conditions all over the country. As the committee reported, 'no strike had ever before taken place under such favorable circumstances to make trouble … never before was the laboring class of the whole country so ready to join in a move of that kind'.[90]

---

86   Senate and House of Representatives of the Commonwealth of Pennsylvania 1878, p. 674.

87   The legislature's investigative committee refers to the militia as the 'national guard' and that term is used here. Although the national guard was not formally established by congressional legislation until after the strike, some states like Pennsylvania had formed their own national guard while sometimes maintaining the militia alongside them. (Ibid).

88   Ibid., pp. 5–6.

89   Ibid., pp. 9–10.

90   Ibid., pp. 45–6.

After the sheriff tried to get the strikers and their supporters to return home, he gave up and went home himself. When a company official went to locate the sheriff, he was missing. Although he turned up later, the sheriff made no effort to organise a posse, and instead telegraphed the governor for the national guard to be sent in and also the Adjutant General James Latta, because the governor was out of the state riding on a Pennsylvania Railroad train to Wyoming.[91] The sheriff's telegram requested Adjutant General Latta call out the national guard to suppress a 'riot' that had not happened. The Adjutant General was given power to assume the authority as chief executive officer of the state in his absence if a disturbance arose, effectively putting the entire state under martial law and probably bypassing the state's constitutional order of succession. With local authorities understaffed and unwilling to intervene, elites divided and disorganised, the delayed military response gave the advantage to the strikers.

Despite the company's influence over the governor, as in Baltimore, the Pennsylvania state national guard also proved unreliable. Adjutant General Latta directed Pittsburgh national guard commander Major General Alfred Pearson to send in his troops. After colonels under General Pearson's command could not muster their men, General Pearson telegraphed Adjutant General Latta suggesting he muster the Philadelphia national guard instead. General Pearson's heart was not in it, as he admitted that 'The sympathy of the people, the sympathy of the troops, my own sympathy, was with the strikers proper'. His troops were composed of mostly local workers who either refused to muster when called, or could not be depended upon to carry out orders to suppress the strikers and their supporters who were friends and family. The troops were reported to have left their weapons stacked, cavorted with the crowds, and had to be withdrawn.[92]

Adjutant General Latta telegraphed Major General Brinton commanding him to move his troops to Pittsburgh. On 21 July, 600 Major General Brinton's Philadelphia national guard troops departed for Pittsburgh and picked up Gatling guns and ammunition in Harrisburg.[93] A Pennsylvania Railroad executive and the sheriff led the national guard assault on the depot with loaded weapons and fixed bayonets which they used to stab some people in the crowd. Unprepared for the challenge, the national guard, armed with at least two artillery pieces and a Gatling gun, opened fire on the angry crowd throwing coal. The

---

91   Ibid., pp. 6–7; and Foner 1977, pp. 57–8.

92   Senate and House of Representatives of the Commonwealth of Pennsylvania 1878, pp. 8–9; and Lloyd 2009, p. 183.

93   Foner 1977, pp. 59–60.

national guard shot at both those who had taken cover by the railcars and onlookers on the hill. They fired into the crowd killing at least 22 (including a woman and three small children), and maiming or wounding between 29 to 70 more, some crushed by the crowd. A few more were killed by troops over the next two days. A grand jury later denounced the national guard for acts of 'murder'. Pittsburgh national guard men – many of whom had dropped their weapons, gone home, or joined the crowds – were in the crowd, and one was killed.[94]

Despite Major General Brinton's claim that he ordered his men not to fire on the crowd, he did give them permission to defend themselves if threatened. Although officers ordered firing to cease, they claimed that no order to fire had been given. Major General Brinton was not present at the scene because he was at the Pennsylvania Railroad's office conferring with the company at the time.[95]

The Philadelphia national guard were ordered to disband by General Brown and the few remaining marched out through the crowd without incident. The Philadelphia national guard made it to the roundhouse where it was trapped, besieged by a growing hostile crowd. 'At the news of the slaughter at Twenty-eighth Street the whole city went mad'.[96] Many more workers struck their workplaces and headed to the scene of the slaughter. Marchers assembled in processions with bands and colours, shutting down factories still in operation, jammed the streets, and looted the national guard armoury and stores for guns and ammunition. The workers and their supporters used their new arms to besiege the national guard in the roundhouse, intercepted their food deliveries sent by Pennsylvania Railroad President Scott, set fire to railroad property, and stopped fire engines from responding to the fire on railroad property although they allowed the crews to fight fires on other nearby property. Strikers and their supporters destroyed every car on the tracks leading from the roundhouse to Twenty-third Street after looting the contents.

According to local accounts, the crowd had full control of the city. Their power so overwhelmed the national guard that local elected officials effectively abandoned their duties. The mayor refused to either send in the police or

---

94 Although inquests were carried out by the coroner on 22 people, the state legislature's investigative committee gives these figures as a low count because many in the crowd were probably taken away to be cared for by friends, families, and allies and never reported to the coroner. See Senate and House of Representatives of the Commonwealth of Pennsylvania 1878, pp. 8–12; and Bruce 1959, pp. 145–7.

95 Senate and House of Representatives of the Commonwealth of Pennsylvania 1878, pp. 10–11.

96 Foner 1977, p. 63.

face the crowd. The strikers took control of the city by demonstrating an ability to rapidly reorganise and a willingness to escalate their tactics in light of the opportunities of rapidly growing mass support and the abrogation of power by elites. A significant number of women were reportedly among those engaged in street fighting, sabotage, and looting.[97]

In another effort to pair their tactics, the strikers and their supporters organised a public mass meeting and selected a negotiating committee of five. A man who addressed the crowd, urging people to return home and give the negotiating committee 24 hours to negotiate, was ignored. The insurgents had no intention of de-mobilising but rather sought to take advantage of their leverage to extract concessions.

The insurgents continued their assault. Six coke cars were set on fire and crashed into derailed cars setting oil cars on fire, the sand house was set on fire, and the crowd cut the firehoses and hauled in a cannon, threatening the firemen not to put out the fire. The crowd reportedly also had in its possession a field piece that it attempted to fire on the roundhouse on 22 July, but General Brinton's men fired on them, killing as many as 11.[98] Eventually, crowds managed to shove burning cars toward the roundhouse, setting an entire block of lumberyard and shanties on fire. Fearing the roundhouse too would be set aflame, the Philadelphia militia abandoned the roundhouse. Although they brought along the Gatling guns, the national guard dismantled and left behind their heavy guns and soaked the powder to keep it from being used by the crowds.[99] The troops reached the arsenal and then proceeded over the bridge and out of town back to Philadelphia, defeated by apparently well-organised insurgents.

The national guard commanders realised that the crowd proved to be well-organised, armed, and on the offensive. On their slow march out of town the Philadelphia national guard was pursued by snipers shooting at them from behind. Snipers led by an unidentified man known in legend as 'Pat the Avenger' pursued the national guard along parallel streets to which they returned fire with their Gatling guns. The national guard reported being shot at by Pittsburgh policemen from the porch of the police station. Three troops were killed and four wounded on the retreat out of town.[100] A national guard

97　　Lloyd 2009, p. 183.
98　　Senate and House of Representatives of the Commonwealth of Pennsylvania 1878, pp. 12–13.
99　　Ibid., pp. 13–14; and Bruce 1959, pp. 157–8 and 165–7.
100　Senate and House of Representatives of the Commonwealth of Pennsylvania 1878, p. 14.

regiment was ordered to be disbanded by its general while he was in the crowd speaking with people. The mayor attempted to speak to the crowd outside a depot but was picked up, crowd surfed and dumped on the street. Adjutant General Latta refused to reassemble his troops and wandered about town with other state officials watching the crowd in command of the city. In the meantime, the sheriff hid in his office and General Brinton met up with his troops outside of town and refused to order their return to Pittsburgh.[101]

The Philadelphia national guard was in disarray and quarrelling among themselves. A colonel warned a general that 'you can place little dependence on the troops of your division; some have thrown down their arms, and others have left, and I fear the situation very much'. Little did this colonel realise he could also put little faith in the general to whom he was writing who had confidentially written at the time of his sympathy for the strikers' demand for higher pay.[102] As his national guard was deteriorating, he fled the command centre at the depot, gave up his command to another general, and never returned.

Elites were disorganised and divided and their authority, credibility, legitimacy, and control was crumbling before the insurgency.

> Thus, on that day and in that place, law had no force. City authorities were feeble in numbers and spirit. The county's chief officer cowered at his desk. State troops were disaffected or dispersed. The Federal government lacked official grounds for action. Like a staked out pig, the Pittsburgh yards of the great corporation lay waiting in the sun for the tiger to spring.[103]

Despite forming a 60-man Committee of Safety composed of some strikers among the professionals and businessmen, the mayor's group was easily disarmed by the crowds and returned to drop their weapons at City Hall.[104]

Neither arms nor an effort at compromise proved immediately successful. The mayor's peacemaking committee went to the Pennsylvania Railroad offices across the Allegheny River to ask for token concessions to end the strike, but the company refused to concede anything. The company preferred to end the strike by force of arms. Although elites tried to meet to form a committee of safety, they were in disarray with the mayor refusing to act, the sheriff having run away

---

101   Ibid., p. 15; and Bruce 1959, p. 169.

102   Bruce 1959, pp. 143–4.

103   Ibid., p. 171.

104   Ibid., p. 177.

to hide, and no one to lead them.[105] Elites soon raised about $15,000 to recruit a posse armed with axe handles, and old muskets without ammunition. But after a day, many resigned. It wasn't until later that the mayor rehired many of the laid off police for a new larger committee of safety and armed them with weapons from the Allegheny Arsenal.

For the next several days, the workers ran the city and redistributed goods from cars to the residents of the city. The fire had spread a couple of miles to the city limits destroying 39 Pennsylvania Railroad buildings. The fire spread rapidly because the crowd prevented the firemen from protecting the company's property, cutting their firehose and threatening them, while the police refused to protect them. When 50 US troops marched in from Columbus they reported passing about two miles of smoking ruins, including 1,600 mostly freight cars, 126 locomotives and 2,152 burned Pullman, postal, refrigerator, express, and stock cars. Strung together, the wreckage would have stretched 11.5 miles, and it later required 1,200 cars to haul all the scrap to Altoona. A total of 79 railroad buildings, including the Union Depot and grain elevators, were burned.[106]

Estimates of the damage in Pittsburgh ranged from $2–10 million depending on whether the value of the freight is included. The Pennsylvania Railroad later sued Allegheny County for $4.1 million for damage to its property from the fighting and was awarded $3 million. However, an Allegheny county committee formed to adjust claims settled 169 claims for only $160,000. Another $200,000 in claims were unresolved, and stolen property valued at $60,000 was recovered. In all, the county appears to have calculated the losses at much less, one-seventh of the total, than it was forced to pay by the court.[107]

The coroner reported 22 people killed. Of those, three were railroad workers and four were members of the Philadelphia national guard, although three of the national guard were workers. However, 10 years later the *Pittsburgh Post* reported that more were killed and buried but never reported. Although 75 people were arrested for looting, the Deputy Mayor Butler released most of them. One uniformed policeman was reportedly helping loot the rail cars.[108]

---

105   Senate and House of Representatives of the Commonwealth of Pennsylvania 1878, p. 16.

106   Ibid., pp. 18–19; and Bruce 1959, p. 180.

107   Ibid., pp. 18–19; Lindsey 1942, p. 7; and Foner 1977, pp. 64–6.

108   Ibid., pp. 15–16. The strike has been memorialised around Pittsburgh by the Howling Mob Society which has erected historical markers all over the city. The markers can be seen at http://www.howlingmobsociety.org. (See also Bruce 1959, p. 180).

What has been ignored in both Foner and Bruce's historical accounts of the insurgency in Pittsburgh was the prominent role of women in the street battles. According to the legislative committee investigation, 'a large number of women were in the crowd at Twenty-eighth street' on 20 and 21 July. These women were 'worse than the men, used viler epithets, and more indecent language, and did everything in their power to influence and excite the mob to resistance'. The role of women was complex and contradictory at best as women reportedly arrived serving the men tea and coffee and left carrying looted goods.

The *Chicago Inter-Ocean* called the fighting in Pittsburgh 'America's First Great Revolution'. The *New York Times* bemoaned 'God help us, if these are the rewards of freedom'.[109] By 23 July, things had settled down but the strike had already been spread by a marching brigade that closed all the mills in the area including a steel and tube works. Explaining the justification for escalating their tactics, the railroad strikers issued a statement outlining how they had made an effort to negotiate but were rebuffed. They laid the cause for the resulting violence on the Pennsylvania Railroad which had rejected calls by local elites and the media calls to arbitrate.

To gain mass public support, the railroad strikers informed the public in the newspaper that they had been trying to meet with the company to negotiate before the outbreak but it never answered them. The strikers warned that they were willing to escalate their tactics if they were ignored. On 20 July the BLE made two additional efforts to negotiate but were refused by the company. It again asked for the wage cuts to be rescinded, new job classifications removed so that all workers would be paid equally, double headers abolished, among other demands.

The company had preferred to up the ante and rely on the national guard to crush the strike. But their confidence in state power to decompose working-class power was misplaced. Elites were divided and their national guard was run through with solidarity for the insurgency. Memories of the lethal repression of the Pennsylvania Molly Maguire miners was likely still fresh and much of the population carried a hatred for the railroad companies.

It is worth quoting the legislature's investigative committee at length as it captured the deep hostility towards the company that translated into mass support for the strikers and the insurgents.

> From the first commencement of the strike, the strikers had the active sympathy of a large portion of the people of Pittsburgh. The citizens had

---

109   Foner 1977, p. 66.

a bitter feeling against the Pennsylvania Railroad Company on account of, as they believed, an unjust discrimination by the railroad company against them in freight rates, which made it very difficult for their manufacturers to compete successfully with manufacturers further west, and this feeling had existed and been intensified for years, and pervaded all classes. A large portion of the people also believed that the railroad company was not dealing fairly by its men in making the last reduction in wages, and the tradesmen with whom the trainmen dealt also had a direct sympathy with the men in this reduction, for its results would affect their pockets. The large class of laborers in the different mills, manufactories, mines, and other industries in Pittsburgh and vicinity, were also strongly in sympathy with the railroad strikers, considering the cause of the railroad men their cause, as their wages had also been reduced for the same causes as were those of the railroad men, and they were not only willing but anxious to make a common fight against the corporations.[110]

The strike spread to other industries during these two days of armed struggle. Workers at National Tube Works at McKeesport struck and about 1,000 men marched around town in a band spreading the strike to a rolling mill, car works, and planning mill, effectively turning the railroad strike into a city-wide general strike. The McKeesport strikers demanded $1.50 per day for labourers and a 25 cent raise for all workers, even boys. Those who struck included planning and tin mill workers at Carnegie's Edgar Thomson Steel Works, miners at Jones and Laughlin, and the pipe works at Evans, Dalzell and Company. A mill strike was even settled within a few hours with a raise for the workers.

Although local elites, the media, local and state officials, and the railroad companies portrayed the strike as a direct threat to the government, corporations were clearly the target of the insurrection. That conflict between the strikers and government occurred was only in response to their intervention on behalf of the companies. A West Chester national guard reflected this when he explained that of 'all the strikers I could get my hands on and I could find but one spirit and one purpose among them: that they were justified in resorting to any means to break down the power of the corporations'.[111] The *Scranton Republican* echoed this sentiment when it warned that 'the popular heart is sound. It is full of warning to the corporations to adopt a wiser and kindlier

---

110   Senate and House of Representatives of the Commonwealth of Pennsylvania 1878, p. 18.
111   Bruce 1959, p. 183.

policy in their dealings with their employees'.[112] The *Pittsburgh Globe* called it 'The Lexington of the Labor Conflict at Hand' and the *Critic* warned 'there is tyranny in this country worse than anything ever known in Russia ... Capital has raised itself on the ruins of labor. The laboring class cannot, will not stand for this longer. The war cry has been raised ... the principle that freed our nation from tyranny will free labor from domestic aggression'.[113] As Bruce observed,

> the stress of riot exposed a growing fear of powerful corporations ... In 1877 these fears centered on railroad corporations, for the age of the great industrial corporation had scarcely begun (only three of these being capitalized at more than a million dollars).[114]

The battle of Pittsburgh provided a spark that fanned the strike across the state and westward. In a bit of hyperbole, one account described

> The Pittsburgh holocaust had meanwhile acted on the nation like a hot coal in a barrel of firecrackers. On Monday and Tuesday, July 23 and 24, nerves crackled, tempers smoked and glowed, violence burst forth in a score of cities from the Middle Atlantic States to the Mississippi Valley.[115]

Fearing the growing power and range of the strike, all ten divisions of the militia were called out in Pennsylvania on Sunday, 870 officers and 9,000 men in all. In Lebanon, one company and part of another mutinied and marched through town. The US Army troops sent to the state occupied the Eastern Pennsylvania mining region while 100,000 men went out on strike. The lives of the strikers and their families were so dire that they were reduced to subsisting on potatoes and berries.[116]

When the strike arrived in Scranton the mayor was unable to muster any special police and national guard. In response, a Citizens' Corps was organised by the Lackawanna Iron & Coal Company, attacking striking miners and killing six.

Interpretations of how workers seized and ran the line in Allegheny differ. Brecher portrays the workers taking over and running the railroads and town.

---

112   Demonstrating that crisis is the mother of necessity, the first Sunday newspaper edition appeared as an 'extra' to report on the strike in Pittsburgh (Bruce 1959, pp. 159 and 161).

113   See in Bruce 1959, p. 164.

114   Bruce 1959, p. 162.

115   Ibid., p. 184.

116   Foner 1977, p. 76.

In contrast, Bruce and Foner seem to concur with the legislature's investigative committee which described local authorities lining up with the strikers to form a peculiar coalition between strike organiser Ammon, the railroad company and the mayor to protect the railroad from strike supporters. By dramatically referring to Ammon as 'Boss' Ammon, it is clear that the committee conclusively placed the workers in command if not entirely in control of the city.[117]

When the strike began in Pittsburgh, Mayor Phillips obtained 500 guns from the Secretary of War and used them to arm a local posse who guarded two bridges with two cannons loaded with shrapnel to cut off possible support from Pittsburgh into the city. Ammon reportedly recruited other railroad workers who moved ten miles of cars out of the city to keep them away from this expected invasion of 'outside' strikers. The workers took over the rail yard, strung the cars, ran passenger and freight cars with armed guards, operated the telegraph which at that time was also owned and managed by the railroads along whose track system it ran, and kept out crowds with police protection. They brought the cars back once things quieted down. In exchange for their cooperation the mayor offered to refrain from calling in the national guard and used police to keep the bars closed. For four or five days Ammon successfully ran one division of a great railroad, the Pittsburgh division of the Pittsburgh, Fort Wayne, and Chicago Railroad Company, until 24 July, with about 400 strikers and other supporters.[118]

The workers did not merely run the railroad; they began to take up arms and prepare themselves for the inevitable repression. They received donated or looted arms and food to protect themselves against local elites and the national guard that might try to enter Pittsburgh. When the strikers learned that a division of the Pennsylvania national guard was on its way, they dug trenches and barriers one mile outside of town and guarded them with guns. On 21 July Ammon sent the men from their posts to guard the freight trains

---

117 It is unclear how involved the company and local elites were or whether they were powerless to stop the workers. Allegheny was an early illustration of an effort to turn the strike from a tactic of disruption into a strategy of transition, or what would later come to be called worker control in which 'economic management and political power had in effect been taken over by the strikers' (Brecher 1972, p. 27; see also Senate and House of Representatives of the Commonwealth of Pennsylvania 1878, pp. 21–3; Bruce 1959, pp. 184–5; and Foner 1977, p. 68). This was not the only example of workers taking over and running the trains. Workers in East St. Louis and on an unnamed railroad in Ohio also did so (see Burbank 1966, p. 64).

118 Senate and House of Representatives of the Commonwealth of Pennsylvania 1878, pp. 22, and 664–5.

again.[119] Ammon provided conflicting testimony to the legislative committee. While he reported that he was willing to resist with arms any effort by soldiers to disperse the strikers to get the trains running again, he later assured the committee that he would not have allowed arms or violence to be used against government authorities to prevent the trains from running. He also insisted that the arms were only intended to 'keep off the mob, or the tramps ...'. While he made the point that self-defence by armed force was justified if arms were used against the strikers because 'we thought we had some rights that the railroad men were bound to respect, but they did not seem to respect them', his contradictory testimony makes it unclear as to how he would have responded if soldiers did attempt to force the train to run again. Nevertheless, Ammon also claimed that the destruction of Pennsylvania Railroad property was likely supported by many in the community including local businessmen, the newspapers, and other workers who widely despised the company and sympathised with the strikers.[120]

On 22 July Ammon took over the dispatchers' office under the authority of a general manager of the Pittsburgh, Fort Wayne, and Chicago railroad. During that time he assured safe passage for the return trip of the governor along the entire Pittsburgh, Fort Wayne, and Chicago road to Pennsylvania on 24 July. However, 24 July turned out to be the end of Ammon's short reign as 'Boss'. Working with the governor, company, and the mayor, Ammon told the strikers on 24 July to bring the cars back, turn the railroad back over to the company, and return to work. But strikers he supposedly commanded quickly resisted his call to end the strike and their control of the railroad and the city, and shouted him down as a traitor. They were also upset at Ammon for allowing a coal train to depart with a shipment of coal. Ammon soon resigned and went home. Cut off from his base of support he was later arrested but never tried. So was the end of the 25-year-old founder of the TU, who was both despised and feared by the legislature's investigative committee for keeping 'the passenger trains running regularly without accident on such a railroad' as a 'dictator' of the 'mob'.[121]

---

119   Bruce 1959, pp. 184–5; Brecher 1972, p. 27; and Foner 1977, p. 68.

120   Senate and House of Representatives of the Commonwealth of Pennsylvania 1878, pp. 670, 681, and 688–9.

121   Ibid., pp. 23, 679, and 681. After his short stint as founder of the TU and then four or five days running Allegheny City, Ammon had a surprising turn in his life, becoming a Wall Street lawyer, serving a prison sentence in Sing Sing in 1904 for financial crimes. (See Burbank 1966, p. 203). Considering that he had worked as a representative of four Chicago insurance companies before working on the railroads, it may not have been so surprising after

The legislature's committee investigation raises questions about whether Ammon led or followed the workers, and whether he was removed as their leader when he tried to lead. After all, Ammon's record as the founder and chief TU organiser was spotty, calling a strike that he did not initially support once it had occurred. He also assured the legislative committee that he would not have interfered with the railroads if the company could find scabs willing to run the trains.[122] But the committee report adds more questions about his supposed dictatorial command. The report describes him as

> a king so long as he led in the direction the crowd wished to go; when he undertook to put on the brakes and get them to reason about their situation, and ran counter to their opinions, he was dethroned with as little ceremony or compunction as one school boy shows in knocking the hat of another ... in politics, society, or with the mob, the leader must go in the direction his followers would have him go, or he is replaced for one more subservient.[123]

Aside from the questions of why a 'mob' could be so organised as to select and 'dethrone' a leader, let alone run a large railroad, the opposition to Ammon's leadership this second time (the first being to launch the strike without him) demonstrates how the strike was self-organised and run from below. Workers whose names are possibly lost to history devised their own tactics and strategies to achieve their objectives and resisted being diffused, steered, or de-escalated by their own 'leaders', local elites, or military repression. We may never know Ammon's actual motivation for calling a strike he stopped supporting and then placing himself in charge of a local part of the strike that he tried to end – without achieving any of the strikers' demands – after only a few days. Most startling is that Ammon was so quick to give up their leverage of complete control of the city without wringing out any concessions. Whether Ammon made these decisions because of his lack of experience, due to fear of the costs from continued escalation of the strike, to ingratiate himself with elites, or because he was collaborating with elites, we will never know. Since Ammon served three months in prison for refusing to name the people, some of whom were 'prominent citizens', who provided arms and money to the strikers and

---

all. (See Senate and House of Representatives of the Commonwealth of Pennsylvania 1878, pp. 684–5).

122   Ibid., p. 665.

123   Ibid., p. 23.

their supporters, it is unlikely he was a collaborator.[124] Nevertheless, Ammon's reversal weakened the strike and the railroad was running again in a few days.

In the meantime, the strike continued to spread to mill, glass, machine, and carpentry workers in Allegheny City and every major town in the state including Johnstown, where some men were shot. The main Pennsylvania Railroad line from Pittsburgh to Philadelphia was shut down. Ammon reported that they also had support from workers on the B&O, Lake Shore, and Michigan Southern railroads. Two national guard trains passing through Pittsburgh were attacked and when some surrendered the crowd fed them and offered to return them home to Philadelphia. On their way home the national guard were fed again in Harrisburg. Similarly, four militia companies called out to Newark, Ohio were fed by strikers and local businesspeople and caroused with strikers.[125]

Turning the strike into an armed insurgency triggered alarms in nearby Washington D.C. President Hayes's cabinet discussed using Article IV, Section 4, declaring the state of Pennsylvania in a state of insurrection and ordered US troops to guard Washington DC. Newspaper headlines, including those in *The Nation*,[126] literally screamed that Pennsylvania was under the control of communist insurgents. Since the 1871, Paris Commune had posed an existential threat to the crown heads of Europe earlier that decade, the term 'communism' had come into parlance as a derogatory term to describe any form of working-class organisation, action, or strike.

The state was certainly in a state of insurrection. The strike was circulating rapidly, workers were escalating their tactics to armed struggle, and the national guard was fracturing. The strike also spread to Altoona, where the debris from Pittsburgh was hauled and dumped. Strikers and their supporters locked the train in the roundhouse and captured troops sent to get it out. The troops eventually dropped their arms, mingled with the crowd, and went home. In Harrisburg, strikers guarding railroad property and the Philadelphia national guard fleeing Pittsburgh were greeted by whites and blacks to whom they gave up their guns, which the strikers deposited at City Hall. In Philadelphia, police attacked crowds including two Workingmen's Party meetings, killing an 18-year-old. Escalating their tactics, the strikers and their supporters set oil and freight cars on fire. The mayor asked for US troops and 125 marines arrived from

---

124 Although he repeatedly refused to name names, he did provide details as to the arms they received. (See Ibid., pp. 668–9).

125 Foner 1977, pp. 69–70; and Senate and House of Representatives of the Commonwealth of Pennsylvania 1878, p. 686.

126 This is the same *Nation* magazine considered to be on the 'progressive' left today.

Baltimore which were soon accompanied by 500 troops under the command of Major-General Hancock. The mayor also formed an armed Committee of Safety. Within days there were 1,400 armed police, 400 armed firemen, 700 US Army, 125 marines, 2,000 special police, and another 500 vigilantes from the Veterans Corps.[127]

In Reading, workers struck against Gowen's Philadelphia & Reading Railroad and Iron & Coal Company. They had widespread support throughout the area because of the popular hatred of Gowen for his role in the executions of the Molly McGuire miners. A popular saying in the city went:

> There's an army of strikers
> Determined you'll see
> Who will fight corporations
> Till the Country is free.[128]

The railroad strikers were soon joined by a wave of miners striking in sympathy throughout Western Pennsylvania in Allentown, where they stoned police, laid off miners in Shamokin who were shot at by a posse, and thousands more in the Scranton area.[129]

As soon as the strike began, a crowd stormed the new depot, tore up tracks, jammed switches, and derailed a car. The strikers and their supporters burned one of two railroad cars and the Lebanon Valley bridge, and blocked the Schuylkill and Union canals.[130]

The crowd was hardly cowed by the violence, and burst into the Reading Rifles armoury and took unloaded weapons. Although the sheriff issued a proclamation ordering people to stay in their homes, he did not make an effort to form a posse. The mayor was absent and no official other than the police chief took any action against the strikers and their supporters.[131]

The Easton Grays militia and six other companies of the 4th National Guard Regiment commanded by Major General William Bolton were sent to the area on 22 July by command of Adjutant General Latta. At the request of the Reading Railroad Company general manager J.E. Wootten, General Bolton sent General Reeder to Reading. When General Reeder's troops arrived on 23 July they

---

127   Bruce 1959, pp. 186–7 and 198.

128   Filipelli 1972.

129   Lloyd 2009, p. 185.

130   Senate and House of Representatives of the Commonwealth of Pennsylvania 1878, p. 26.

131   Ibid.

found the city occupied by the Coal and Iron Police. His troops were directed to release a train under control of the crowd when they were bombarded with brickbats and other objects and a couple of pistol shots. The troops began firing on the crowd, killing 11, including five policemen and a *Reading Post* reporter, and wounding 50 more including seven policemen.[132]

The 16th regiment sent to reinforce General Reeder the next day broke ranks and openly supported the strikers and shared their ammunition with them. These troops reportedly threatened to shoot at the Easton Grays if they fired on the crowd at the Pennsylvania St. as two companies of another regiment attempted to escort a train out of the depot. General Reeder marched his troops out of town to Allentown and refused to return to Reading. According to the legislative committee investigation,

> company I mutinied and refused to return, and disbanded in dishonor by the general. He afterward issued an order to disband companies C, D, E, and H, of the Sixteenth regiment, subject to the approval of the Governor, for general insubordination and mutinous conduct while under orders.[133]

These national guard troops were replaced by the 1st US Artillery. The tracks were repaired by the Coal and Iron Police who also rounded up suspects around town. One possible reason for the fracturing of loyalties among the national guard was that the Eastern Grays were already infamous to locals for having guarded four suspected Molly Maguire defendants armed with 26 muskets as they were hanged in Mauch Chunk. The members of the Reading national guard that refused to shoot strikers were fired by the governor and their employers.[134]

The battle in Reading illustrated how workers were forced to rapidly escalate their tactics in response to local conditions. Gowen's Philadelphia & Reading Railroad's hegemonic domination of local and state government and willingness to hang strikers foreclosed any expectation that grievances could be presented let alone responded to. On 22 July, the *Reading Daily Eagle* put it quite succinctly when it warned that

---

132 Ibid., pp. 26–7.

133 Ibid., pp. 27–8 and 35.

134 Ibid., p. 26; Bruce 1959, pp. 191–3 and 194; Lens 1973, p. 10; and Foner 1977, p. 204.

> The corporations have the law on their side. They own the Legislatures.
> They retain the ablest lawyers. They control most of the newspapers and
> manufacture public opinion. And if the laborers protest in the only way
> that is left to them to assert their manhood, and contend for the rights of
> human nature and American citizenship, they are branded as rioters, met
> by force of arms, provoked to violence, and then shot dead.[135]

No better explanation of the trajectory of violence can be found in observations
of the strike.

During the strike some of the Philadelphia & Reading Railroad's property
was seized by strikers and their supporters. Although the Reading Rifles militia
reported for duty, it refused to fire upon workingmen. In the meantime, a police
force was ambushed and five were shot and injured. The Pennsylvania national
guard was sent in and opened fire randomly on the crowd, killing 10 and wounding 40. The sheriff claimed to not know the guard was called in; apparently,
Gowan's Philadelphia & Reading Railroad had gone over the authority of the
local government to request them. The railroad refused to negotiate, expecting
troops to break the strike.[136]

In Scranton, workers met with the superintendent of the Delaware, Lackawanna and Western Railroad to warn him that they would strike and prevent
all trains but a mail car from leaving. As there were only ten police remaining in
the city, the company received no help from the mayor here as well. The strike
spread to the Lackawanna Iron and Coal Company the next day when 6–8,000
people met in the Round woods to organise and form a negotiating committee. The miners planned to allow the mines to be flooded, which prompted the
mayor to organise a posse of special police – a measure opposed by a vote of
the city council, which refused to pay for them. The mayor met with the negotiating committee, and together they announced that they would return to work
faced with the armed posse.

Again, the strike prompted efforts to expand it into a city-wide insurgency.
About 8,000 people met outside the city at the silk works on 1 August and
decided to march into town in search of the mayor while sending flying squadrons into shops and factories along the line of march, calling out workers to join
them. When the strikers found the mayor, they beat him with clubs and sticks
and bombarded the special police, who fired at the marchers, reportedly killing
three of the organisers. The mayor and his private police prevented further

---

135   Foner 1977, p. 71.
136   Ibid., pp. 72–3.

gatherings until troops arrived the next day. The legislative committee investigating the strike explicitly attributed the uprising to the many Molly Maguires
who fled repression in Schuylkill country for the Scranton area.[137]

Surprisingly, the legislative committee investigating the strike took issue
with the use of the militia and national guard, in the absence of the governor
who had left for a family vacation to California on 16 July. The committee found
that the mayor of Pittsburgh and Allegheny county sheriff had both called in
troops before they had fully used their own local powers to respond to the
strikers and their supporters. Demonstrating either that local government officials had ceded control to the strikers and supporters or refused to act against
them, the military officers had acted unilaterally without being directed by civil
government, effectively placing these two areas under military rule.[138]

It is apparent that while a large majority of the troops followed orders, many
did not. Along with local government officials, the military lost control of their
own troops as well. As the committee warned 'this guard cannot be always
relied upon to do its full duty in case of troubles at home, requiring the intervention of the military', due to being ordered to shoot at friends, neighbours, and
fellow workers in violation of their own norms and values. Not surprisingly, the
large number of national guard who defied orders to suppress the strike was
sufficient to prompt a reorganisation of the state militias and national guard
following the strike (see Chapter 3).[139]

Faced with the collapse of local authority and the national guard, the governor again called upon President Hayes for troops, but was initially refused.
On 27 July, the railroad provided a train to move in 3,000 US troops and 6,000
state militia armed with Gatling guns. The arrival of US troops succeeded in
breaking the strike and reopening the line by 30 July. The troops were kept in
the area in order to send them into the mining districts to break the spreading
general strike there.

---

137   Senate and House of Representatives of the Commonwealth of Pennsylvania 1878, pp. 28–
9.
138   Ibid., p. 31.
139   The committee attributed the defiance of orders by national guardsmen to many being
'foreigners ... imbued with the spirit of foreign communism', without any evidence. It also
denounced labour 'demagogues' for stirring up unnecessary and non-existent class conflict between capital and workers. Ibid., pp. 32, 34, and 36–8.

Coast to Coast: From New York to Texas and California

The strike spread to New York, where a similar pattern emerged. Strikers and their supporters were stopping trains and removing the scab crews on the Lake Shore line in the direction of Buffalo. When one group was shot at by militia, killing between six to nine people, the workers smashed the car and set it on fire. Another train heading into New York City was similarly blocked and the guards driven away. Parading strikers spread the strike across Buffalo between yards, mills, factories and canal works, shutting them down with pick handles and brickbats. Similar actions took place in West Albany as strikers and their supporters drove away rail yard workers who hadn't joined the strike.

As in many hot spots, railroad workers crossed craft lines to join the strike and circulate the struggle. Desertions by members of the railroad brotherhoods further fractured the elite coalition and gave evidence of the growing mass support for the strikers, which gave them impetus to continue their tactical escalation. While such divisions fed the growing circulation of the insurgency to new regions, without coordination the strike was vulnerable.

The historical accounts of the strike have retained the perception that the strike was leaderless, adrift, and unorganised. Bruce observed that 'From Albany westward, New York Central trainmen fell rapidly into line with the shopmen. They had no over-all leadership'.[140] In West Albany a striking machinist claimed there were 'No leaders, no head and no concerted action'.[141] This is the inescapable outcome of an over-reliance on government documents, personal records of elites, and media accounts. As long as archives, diaries, and personal affects of strikers continue to be missing from the historical record, this is bound to indefinitely remain the dominant view.[142]

The anonymous machinist had hit upon the paradox of the strike. It seemed to erupt without a plan, leadership, or organisational form, which made it a powerful threat. The strike did not necessarily require leadership or a central organisation, but without a means to coordinate many disparate local actions,

---

140   Bruce 1959, p. 202.

141   Ibid.

142   Absent the memoirs of striking workers we have the press, some of which were sympathetic to workers although most were controlled by elites, and the personal records and biographies of elites. For example, Burbank drew on interviews with two members of the executive committee of the St. Louis general strike, one of which was conducted while he was in jail after the headquarters was raided. The other is the memoir of Albert Warren Kelsey, a member of the St. Louis elite, who despite his repeated hyperbole provided unconfirmed reporting on the behind the scenes efforts of fellow elites to organise the repressive counter-attack. (See Burbank 1966, pp. 43–7 and 171).

especially with few trains running to carry the news across various locales, and the railroads shutting down the telegraph (the two key means of communications workers used to circulate the strike) the strike was vulnerable to dissipation and deflection in the case of local settlements, or a slow grinding defeat by military force.

Nevertheless, as the strike spread, workers similarly escalated their tactics as mass support grew. The Erie Railroad was in receivership in 1877 and issued a 10 percent wage cut that year. In June, Barney Donahue and other workers began meeting and 50 strikers were selected to negotiate with the receiver. When they asked for the cut to be reversed they were not only refused but fired by the receiver on 1 July. The committee continued its efforts to peacefully resolve the strike by making a detailed settlement proposal including their reinstatement, lower rents, better company housing, and a new wage scale among other demands. In case they were unable to settle they set the strike to begin on 19 July. After their second attempt to settle was rejected, they struck on 20 July, as workers removed and hid the coupling pins preventing any more trains from leaving the key junction of Hornellsville, New York. Because liquor was banned by the strike committees, the *New York Times* reported that public drunkenness disappeared during the strike in Hornellsville. The sheriff initially sent to break up the strike sent home his deputies when he found them well behaved and meeting about temperance.[143]

The governor acceded to the company's request and sent in militia from Rochester and Emira. Almost immediately, discipline in the ranks of the militia began to crack, with some members of the New York militia going over to the side of the strikers. One officer made clear on which side they stood when he remarked that 'We may be militiamen, but we are workmen first'.[144] Many knew the strikers and allowed them to block train departures while allowing mail cars to proceed. Female strike supporters soaped the tracks to prevent attempts to push out the trains.[145] All three attempts to move the trains on 22 July failed and the company gave up. The governor soon declared martial law, though not a single shot was fired.

When the company tried to bring in a trainload of militia on 23 July, the strikers tore up the tracks ahead of the train and eventually pulled the spikes and plates off the rails, causing the train to collapse to the ground. Later that day, the company invited striker leader Donahue to negotiate in an attempt

---

143   Foner 1977, pp. 79–81; and Stromquist 1993, p. 23.
144   Foner 1977, p. 469.
145   Ibid., p. 83.

to flush out the anonymous leadership. On the way home to Hornellsville, Donahue was arrested and charged with contempt of court based on a sworn warrant from the receiver. The next day the company made small concessions, refused to address the contempt charge, attempted to divide the strikers by only offering to rescind the pay cut for trainmen, and left it up to the receiver to decide whether to reinstate the 50 fired strikers. The divide and conquer strategy failed. That evening the strikers met and voted to reject the settlement. When local businessmen and lawyers pleaded for the strikers to accept the offer, they returned a third time to negotiate but the company would not budge from their earlier offer.

Elites flexed a show of military force during the 25 July Workingmen's Party solidarity rally attended by 20,000 strikers and supporters in Tompkins Square, New York City. Using the telegraph line connecting the arsenals, two militia divisions were able to be called out and police leave was cancelled. The militia mounted two Gatling guns at Pine and Wall Streets, 75 volunteers were assigned to guard the US Subtreasury building, 800 police assigned to the rally, 1,000 sailors and marines were put on alert, and about 8,000 rifles and 1,200 clubs made available.[146] New York City elites were ready for class war.

With the forces of repression mounting and the company refusing to negotiate any further, the strikers soon accepted the company's last offer and ended the strike the next day. Despite losing the strike it was the first concession made by capital, followed soon after by the Union Pacific Railroad line.[147] Conceding the strike may have been the turning point in the insurgency. It gave the companies an example of how making a minor concession could stall the momentum of the spreading strike and sever it in a significant region of the country.

The New York Central still refused to run any trains, and the governor and mayor of Buffalo organised a militia of Civil War veteran vigilantes, state militia, police, special police, and deputy sheriffs. On 10 May the state legislature had passed a law criminalising the blocking of trains or damage of railroad property with a 10 year sentence and $1,000 fine. The governor offered a $500 bounty for those who violated it. The militia killed 8 on the New York Central and Lake Shore line strikes. The day after a strike meeting on 24 July, strike leaders were arrested. Two strikers went to Cornelius Vanderbilt on 26 July to negotiate but he refused to discuss the wage cut. They approached the mayor and other elites but they never followed through on their offer to address their grievances to Vanderbilt. The engineers had scabbed and the strike was given up with a vague

146   Ibid., p. 119; and Harring 1983, p. 107.
147   Foner 1977, pp. 85–9.

understanding that he offered to rescind the wage cut and increase the strikers' wages if they went back to work. Although they accepted the settlement offer and went back to work the workers reported not getting either. When pressed later, Vanderbilt claimed to have given away $100,000 to strikers and unemployed as charity and refused to admit he conceded to the demand to rescind the pay cut.[148]

The *Elmira Daily Advertiser* opposed the agreement even though the trains were running again because 'It is because the mob, for a consideration, has given its consent that business may be resumed. It is a recognition of the idea that the mob is co-ordinate in authority over the railroad with the officers and directors'.[149] All existing tactics to reimpose subordination had been defeated. Despite the settlements, the workers were momentarily still in control.

Although the militia and federal troops played little role in the state, the Mayflower Navy vessel was stationed near the Pine and Wall Street entrances, armed with two Gatling guns to protect the US Customs House and Subtreasury which held $100 million in gold and cash. The strikers may not have known just how close they were to cutting a key artery of US capitalism.

As the strike spread out west to Ohio, the Lake Shore line joined Vanderbilt's New York Central line by revoking the 10 percent pay cut. Although the Cincinnati, Hamilton & Dayton Line and the Dayton Short Line also rescinded the pay cut the workers continued to stay out until other strikers won elsewhere. As a result, the strike disrupted Ohio in several places. In Zanesville, a crowd shut down nearly every factory until a citizens' patrol was organised. In Toledo, the strike received the public blessing of the Police Commissioner who told strikers 'You are not slaves, gentlemen, and I am glad to see you assert your manhood'.[150] At the meeting a group called for a general strike and the next day formulated demands for a $1.50 a day minimum wage for labourers and $2.50–3.50 for skilled workers. The day after they marched four abreast through the manufacturing district closing down shops that didn't agree to it. It was short-lived, however, since the sheriff assembled a posse the next day and arrested the leaders. A street battle was nearly unleashed in Neward, Ohio by 600 miners who sought to drive a militia which had been recently used against them during their strike out of town until they were stopped by rail strikers.

Despite the Louisville, Cincinnati & Lexington Railroad rescinding the wage cut as a result of earlier negotiations in Louisville, its workers struck in Cin-

---

148   Ibid., pp. 92–4.
149   Ibid., p. 89.
150   Bruce 1959, p. 207.

cinnati on 23 July. That day workers and their supporters paraded on the tracks, blocking switches, pulling spikes, and blocking passengers from taking the trains. Brakemen and firemen on the Pittsburgh, Cincinnati, St. Louis & Chicago Railroad struck in Columbus, Ohio and were joined by the local BLE chapter. Thousands of mill workers walked out in solidarity the next day. Workers also struck the Cleveland, Columbus, Cincinnati & Indianapolis Railroad and the Cincinnati, Hamilton & Dayton line and won reversals of the wage cuts.[151]

Toledo, Ohio was shut down by a general strike on 23 and 24 July. Workers set up a Committee of Safety and initially had support from the city police commissioner and militia commander, extracting a wage increase from local factories. However, local elites deputised 400 police and used them with the militia to crush the strike.[152]

The Cincinnati Workingmen's Party came late to the strike with some ambivalence about supporting the strikers in the streets. The German section of the Workingmen's Party had organised two rallies and the party held a general assembly announcing its support for the strikers. Addressing the assembly, the mayor warned them against using violence.[153] Also speaking was Peter Clark, a local school principal and new black member of the Workingmen's Party, who denounced the autocratic power of the railroad companies and advocated for government ownership of the railroad and socialism. Clark observed that all attempts to address grievances peacefully are blocked by capital's control of the state.

> The door of justice seemed shut in their faces. They have no representation on the Board of Directors. Every State has laws punishing conspiracy, punishing riot and unlawful assemblages, but no State has laws providing for the examination and redress of grievances of which these men complain. The whole force of the state and National Governments may be invoked by the railroad managers, but the laborer has nothing.[154]

He knew of what he spoke. After first expressing sympathy for the strike and promising not to ask the governor for militia, the mayor soon returned with 125 police and arrested the leaders. The mayor proceeded to swear in special police and stationed guards in the yards with the order to shoot anyone trying

---

151   Lloyd 2009, p. 186.

152   Ibid., p. 187.

153   Bruce 1959, p. 231.

154   Clark 1877; and Foner 1977, pp. 130–2.

to interfere with the trains.[155] Despite the repression, the Workingmen's Party continued to play a similar moderating role as it did in St. Louis and Louisville and the strike was lost.

By Tuesday 24 July, the strike had spread not only West to Ohio, Indiana, Illinois, Michigan, and Iowa but also South and West to Kentucky, Missouri, Texas, and California before ending on 25 July in Detroit, nine days later. The strike began as a universal shutdown of the national rail system. Although it overlooked the impact of the strike as far west as California, according to *Harper's*, 'On the morning of the 25th the strike had reached its height, when hardly a road was running, from the Hudson to the Mississippi, and from Canada to Virginia'.[156] The strike didn't affect much of the South or the Northeast except for New York City, Buffalo, and Albany. With the strike threatening, the Georgia Central line told a grievance committee it would put off the cut scheduled for 1 September through November. As the strike spread, it skipped over into other sectors, in some cases crossing the divides of race and gender.

The strike lasted about a week in Texas, beginning with the strike on the Texas & Pacific in Marshall on 24 July and ending on 30 July when the company agreed to concede back pay. In a rare showing of cross-racial worker alliances, the rail strike spread to other sectors when black longshoremen in Galveston struck and won equal pay with whites. On 27 July, the day the strike was broken in Chicago and St. Louis, hundreds of black and a few Irish workers struck in Galveston against a pay cut and for $2 a day. They had marched down the Strand and called construction, tracklayers and others to join them, eventually closing down the majority of businesses in the city. White workers joined the strike the next day. One black striker was shot by police and rumours about black strikers being attacked by armed men swirled. By 31 July the majority of businesses consented to return their daily wage to $2. Just as those workers settled, black washerwomen struck for $9 per week.[157]

When workers in Louisville called a strike demanding the July cut be rescinded and the workers be given a raise, Louisville, Cincinnati & Lexington Railroad sent a committee to negotiate. Using race as a tactic to carve cleavages among the workers, the railroad agreed to rescind the cut and restored wages to what they were on 1 July, but only for white workers. Black sewer workers took advantage of the momentum from the railroad strike to launch their own. In a show of cross-racial worker solidarity, black and white workers marched

155   Foner 1977, pp. 133–4.
156   *UE News* 2002.
157   Foner 1977, pp. 197–9.

on the waterworks project. Workers there joined them on the march to the centre of the city where they shouted down the mayor and headed for the railroad depot armed with stones which they used against street lamps, mansion windows, and the railroad. With their newly arrived mass support, the strikers marched to the depot and pulled up in front of the Louisville & Nashville Railroad (L&N) president's house and attacked it with rocks and bricks. Having succeeded in shutting down most of the city's factories and shops, another city-wide general strike loomed. The next day, the company president offered a 5 percent raise but only for workers on the L&N line. Although workers were guarding the property of two railroad lines, the governor called in 700 militia troops, composed of many elites, who attacked the strikers, wounding several. In a quirk of history, future Supreme Court justice Louis Brandeis, who had just graduated from Harvard Law School, responded to the call with his brother by joining the militia, although he never fired a shot. The strikers had no support from the newly organised Workingmen's Party, which opposed the strike. The party even went so far as to suggest that 'the ballot-box is the medium between us and capital'.[158]

The strike reached California in the form of protest rallies in San Francisco, Oakland, San Jose, Sacramento, and San Diego, calling for solidarity with the strikers rather than strikes. The rallies in San Francisco were quickly hijacked and redirected into anti-Chinese violence and elite paramilitary mobilisation.[159] As in much of the rest of the country, California was deep in depression, had just experienced a winter-long drought, crop failures, cattle die offs, and massive mining devaluation. The downturn was devastating, reducing commercial traffic on the San Francisco docks, which prompted lay-offs even as 20 percent were unemployed.[160] Seeing the situation spiralling out of control, the smaller Central Pacific Railroad of San Francisco rescinded the 10 percent wage cut and some shipping companies agreed to concessions.

About two-thirds of San Francisco workers were immigrants, the largest groups being Irish and Chinese. Attempting to organise solidarity action for the strike, the mostly immigrant based Workingmen's Party began holding rallies in open lots in downtown denouncing the railroad corporations and use of the military against strikes. During one rally, three people were shot and members in the crowd attempted to derail the event by making racist anti-Chinese calls. The Workingmen's Party may have been attempting to bring the strike to

158   Ibid., pp. 124, 126–7, and 129.
159   Miller 2008, pp. 164–87; Kazin 2008, pp. 136–63; and Shoup 2010, pp. 308–13.
160   Kazin 2008, p. 140.

California, but they were up against elites and their armed paramilitaries, who had their own plan to ensure that didn't happen.

Drawing on the momentum of recent anti-Chinese rallies led by the current mayor and governor, rival rallies by groups of anti-Chinese racists workers attacked businesses that employed immigrant Chinese workers and shops in Chinatown.[161] An anti-Chinese rally derailed the strike fervour into a carnival of hate and racist violence throughout the Chinese working-class neighbourhoods and businesses, setting fires, beating, and killing at least one Chinese worker. Several nights of anti-Chinese riots were led by Dennis Kearney, a member of a vigilante group funded by the Committee of Safety which met at the Chamber of Commerce.

Kearney's backers were a well-organised secretive group of San Francisco elites, some of whom had been the instigators of the bloody Committee of Vigilance coup in 1856, which removed working-class Irish politicians from local office by force.[162] By fanning racial hatred as a tactic of deflection and fragmentation, the Committee of Safety appears to have manufactured a race riot in order to justify a military suppression of the insurgency. It paid some members of the labour movement and Workingmen's Party of California to stir up some workers into attacking fellow Chinese workers instead of capital. Although he had been on the Committee of Safety's payroll Kearney now decided to go rogue and found himself opposed by his former allies.

The Committee of Safety coordinated the repression of the anti-Chinese rioters stirred up by Kearney. With 5,000 men armed with 10,000 guns from the nearby federal Benicia arsenal, and backed by 200 marines and three warships at Mare Island armed with howitzers and Gatling guns, the Committee of Safety once again took over the city and imposed martial law.[163] The Committee of Safety vigilantes engaged with rioters, killing at least five. 'The mob action directly and destructively attacked another sector of working people, diverting a critique of the capitalist system and actions of the capitalist class mainly into cultural/racial attacks directed against other workers'.[164] As Chris Carlsson

---

161   Kazin 2008, p. 141 and 145; and Shoup 2010, pp. 308–13.

162   Among the leading members of the Committee were names still prominent across San Francisco and the country including Levi Strauss, Claus Sprekels, Mayor Andrew Jackson Bryant, and William Tell Coleman, who chaired the group, and was supported by pronouncements from Archbishop Joseph Alemany. (See Kazin 2008, p. 147 and 149; and Shoup 2010, pp. 332–4).

163   Coleman also organised Union and Confederate veterans into a Veteran's Brigade with their own separate command. (See Kazin 2008, p. 150).

164   Shoup 2010, pp. 308–13 and 332–4.

concludes, 'class war was in the air, but an air choking on racism'.[165] That racism fragmented the working-class by turning the blame for their misery on workers more vulnerable and of a lower status than themselves, undermining the potential for circulating the strike to California.

The leader of the Workingmen's Party of California soon parlayed his new notoriety, mistakenly perceived as being anti-capitalist, into a meteorically short-lived rise to prominence, winning nearly every local elected office in San Francisco only to disappear by 1880.[166] The episode's influence proved to be lasting, prompting bi-partisan support, with Congress passing the 1882 Chinese Exclusion Act after the strike.

The Battle of Chicago

The strike nearly completely paralysed not just the railroads but the entire city of Chicago. On 23 July workers organised into multiple roving small groups to 'enforce and extend the strike' from factory to factory, blocking streetcars, wagons, and buggies. They shut down iron, boiler, nail, lumber, planning mills, brickyards, die, packinghouses, machine shops, stockyards, tanneries, stoneworks, factories, brickyards, lumberyards, distilleries, workshops, and construction sites. Insurgents forced the companies to sign an agreement increasing pay to $2 a day for the next 18 months. Lake vessel workman struck and soon other mills and industries had to shut down as the city began to be tied up and coke supplies were running out. Although the Northwestern line revoked its recent pay cut, in Chicago strikers and their supporters swept through the yards of the various lines in an attempt to keep freight from moving.

Insurgents recognised that force was needed to disrupt production and distribution in order to impose their demands on capital. These efforts to expand the strike demonstrated coordinated tactics and strategy, hardly the thoughtless behaviour of what Bruce called the 'invertebrate mob' and much of the media at the time referred to as 'rioters'.[167] According to Bruce, 'Every factory

---

165   Carlsson 1995.

166   In a stunning turn of events, one of San Francisco's most prominent elites, Charles De Young, publisher of the *San Francisco Chronicle*, shot the Workingmen's Party mayoral candidate Kalloch, who won re-election 10 days later. The following year Mayor Kalloch's son killed De Young. (Carlsson 1995).

167   Bruce 1959, p. 253.

from Chicago Avenue to North Avenue, stood idle'.[168] The Workingmen's Party entered the fray, calling for a general strike for the eight-hour day, a 20 percent wage increase, and the formation of an executive committee to run the strike. Crowds of men, women and children a few thousand strong were the force that spread the strike in its first few days without bloodshed. 'From the beginning, then, the Great Strike in Chicago was obviously more than just a railroad strike'.[169]

The peace was not to last long. The mayor had the city bells rung to call out 400 militia to their armouries. His strikebreaking force was soon composed of 200 veteran vigilantes, several thousand special mounted police paid for by local elites, and two US artillery companies. Gun stores restricted sales only to the wealthy in order to deprive insurgents of a necessary supply of arms.[170]

The mayor began implementing repressive measures that were a little carrot and a lot of stick. On 25 July the mayor's forces attacked a crowd with guns and clubs, creating a stampede which overturned the speakers' stand, killing three and wounding eight. The growing tensions ensured that the Chicago, Burlington & Quincy switchyards remained shut down. Locked out of the policy and enraged by their attempt to peacefully assemble in public, the strikers and their supporters escalated their tactics as it became apparent that elites were armed to suppress the strike. Launching scattered attacks, insurgents stoned railroad buildings, ditched engines and cars, halted street cars, and broke into a gun and hardware store to take what they were prohibited from buying. Yet another chapter of the Workingmen's Party of the United States opposed the strike, warning that 'any riotous action in our meetings will be immediately put down by us'.

As the *danse macabre* spiralled in intensity, the mayor petitioned the governor to request US troops from President Hayes, who sent the six companies stationed at nearby Rock Island that had just returned from the Dakotas where they had been fighting Native Americans. Here was the stark accuracy of DuBois's lamentation of the failure to circulate the struggle across racial lines. The failure of the white working-class to take the side of the Plains Indians cemented their own repression by the same troops months later.

Those attending a 'citizens' meeting organised by elites were sworn in as special police, elected their own officers from the abundant bankers, merchants, and lawyers, and were armed with army muskets. These vigilante groups were

---

168   Bruce 1959, pp. 50 and 240–4.

169   Foner 1977, pp. 144–6.

170   Ibid., p. 148.

formed in at least half of the city wards. In all, there were more than 20,000 armed men, including 450 police and 2,000 reservists, arrayed against the strikers. In an early recognition of the role of the welfare state in diffusing class conflict, the city also frantically borrowed $500,000 to restart public works projects that had been stalled for four years.[171]

Despite the arms race, few elites demonstrated a willingness to defend their class interests with arms. Only 12 businessmen of the 1,200 member Board of Trade answered the mayor's call to join a citizens' guard. Of the 12 that showed up five were messenger boys. When the mayor sounded the bells to call out the militia, few showed up. The 'generals and colonels were very thick with a liberal sprinkling of majors and captains' according to the *Chicago Times*, circumstances perhaps parodied by L. Frank Baum's Royal Army of Oz in *Ozma of Oz*, which consisted of 26 officers and one private.[172] Eventually, a rich businessman paid the costs for the mayor to assemble several hundred special police, eventually expanding the force to 5,000 armed men. If armed men could not be found for hire, they were forced to serve. The companies deputised their remaining employees and organised them into armed companies. As happened elsewhere, Civil War veterans organised vigilante patrols preceding the formation of the American Legion in 1915 and its frequent intervention to break strikes.

Once it was finally organised, this force of mercenaries and scabs was deployed against the strikers and their supporters who had locked down the city in a general strike. Joined by police, these forces violently attacked any organised workers they could find. They shot at a crowd at the Chicago, Burlington & Quincy switchyards that was enforcing the strike closures, killing between nine to eleven people, including a switchman. Police invaded Turner Hall during a meeting of striking cabinetmakers, opened fire and killed one and wounded several others. Throughout the battle people countered with guns, sticks, and stones and not only refused to disperse but were joined by people heading to the scene of the street fight to join in. Although a sergeant and another officer were later found guilty of provoking a 'criminal riot', they were only fined 6 cents each by the judge.[173]

President Hayes pulled out the last troops enforcing Reconstruction in the South to join the counter-insurgency in Chicago. Newly arrived US cavalry commanded by General Sheridan killed and wounded an unknown number of

---

171   Ibid., pp. 141–2 and 149–51.
172   Baum 1907.
173   Bruce 1959, pp. 50 and 240–4; and Foner 1977, p. 156.

strikers and supporters.[174] At the time of the 1877 strike there were only 3,140 US Army troops stationed East of the Mississippi River. As DuBois observed, the same US troops that were pulled out of the South, thereby abandoning black workers, were deployed against striking, mostly white, workers in the North. The failure to sufficiently circulate the insurgency to black workers in the South made the defeat of mostly white workers in the North inevitable. As Bellesiles put it, 'in 1877, Southern whites accepted union and Northern whites accepted racism'.[175]

The arrival of the US troops eroded the credibility and legitimacy of the state and federal governments by making it apparent that access to the polity for redress of workers' grievances against industry was closed. This encouraged the strikers and their supporters to further escalate their tactics. The next day dozens of crowds continued to enforce the strike across the city. One crowd formed at a viaduct over several railroad lines near the lumber district and began cutting telegraph wires and stopping streetcars. Unfortunately, cutting telegraph lines hampered the ability of the workers to coordinate and circulate the strike, the equivalent to flipping a kill switch on cell phone service today. A running battle with police resulted in six deaths. In all, an estimated 18 people were killed. US troops joined in by firing two ten pound guns at the strikers, perhaps one of the few cases of heavy artillery being used against US citizens with the exception of the Civil War period.

Demonstrating a sophisticated means of self-organisation, when the police and troops broke up the large crowds they re-emerged in smaller groups. They used guerrilla warfare by fighting on the run and using the urban space and local mass support to their strategic advantage. According to newspaper accounts,

> smaller groups and crowds of working people continued the battle, skirmishing, fighting on the run, charging and retreating, coalescing into crowds and fragmenting into small groups, using the friendly neighborhoods and the homes of sympathetic women as protection for the ongoing struggle. The crowds fought on through the afternoon, using the alleys, streets, rooftops, fields, and narrow passageways of the area for safety.[176]

The spirit of cooperation 'showed the effect of the Great Strike in eradicating ethnic differences among the workers'.[177] Several thousand Irish packing-

174   *UE News* June 2002.
175   Bellesiles 2010, p. 57.
176   Foner 1977, p. 155.
177   Ibid., p. 153.

house workers armed with butcher knives were met by cheering Czech workers marching across the city to enforce the strike and forced employers to raise wages. Gender differences were also dissolving in the strike. The *Times* estimated that 20 percent of the strikers and their supporters were women. The *Chicago Inter-Ocean* generated national attention with their report of 'Bohemian Amazons' whose 'Brawny, sunburnt arms brandished clubs. Knotty hands held rocks and sticks and wooden blocks'. A fence around one plant was 'carried off by the petticoated plunderers' and other similar portrayals of the powerful women who helped enforce the strike.[178]

Ultimately, the mayor's extensive forces arrayed against the strikers and their supporters managed to arrest over 400 strikers and their supporters, enforce a ban on all meetings, and break the strike. Although the rail strike ended by 28 July, groups of butchers, rail, streetcar, stonecutters, lumber shovers, coopers, harness makers, iron moulders, cigar makers, switchmen, and ship carpenters continued their strikes, although they lacked the necessary leverage provided by mass support in the streets. As mass support dwindled, the risk of continued tactical escalation rose precipitously.[179]

Some members of the Chicago branch of the Workingmen's Party attempted to organise shows of support for the strikers but met fierce repression. Printer Albert Parsons, who would later be hanged as one of the Haymarket martyrs, spoke at a Workingmen's Party Chicago rally but repeated the party's call for calm restraint. The mayor sent in police cavalry armed with swords, killing 12 protesters. The Board of Trade organised a band of vigilantes armed with repeating rifles. Alongside federal troops, they attacked strikers, arrested Workingmen's Party leaders, and demolished the party's headquarters.

Despite its marginal role, the Chicago Workingmen's Party opportunistically attempted to translate the strike into political demands. Like the national party, it called for government ownership of the railroads, a telegraph system, and an eight-hour day. But such demands only made strategic sense if access to the polity existed and insiders stood to gain by forming a coalition with outsider groups in order to further their reform efforts. Dominated by Central European immigrants, such a coalition with the small Chicago Workingmen's Party offered few strategic advantages. Such coalitional politics as a strategy for deflecting the threat from insurgents was not even in the incubator stage.

With memory of the 1871 Paris Commune still so fresh in the minds of elites, such demands made the party a target for a nascent anti-communist backlash.

---

178   Ibid., pp. 153–4.
179   Ibid., pp. 155–6.

Despite its reformist platform, the party hardly played the role claimed by the notorious private agent Allen Pinkerton, who established himself by providing special agents to break the Chicago general strike. The Workingmen's Party neither launched nor led the strike. Rather, Parsons and the rest of the party leadership 'had tried to *restrain* the crowds, but had lost complete control of the workers'.[180] But it's unlikely the party could lose what it most likely never had.

It is estimated that 30 to 50 strikers and supporters were killed and about 100 wounded in street fighting in Chicago alone. This force of militarised repression broke the strike after several days and began moving freight under military guard.

The East St. Louis and St. Louis General Strike

The climax of the 1877 railroad strike were the general strikes in St. Louis and East St. Louis where for a few days workers shut down much of industry and the cities were controlled by executive strike committees. During 24–25 July, the first two days of the general strike, nothing but the US mail had moved in or out of St. Louis.[181] These two legendary general strikes remain little known today despite the fact that they were 'one of the first strikes anywhere in the world to paralyze a major industrial city; and without doubt was the first general strike of the modern, industrial movement in the United States ... The St. Louis strike deserves to be recognised as the first exercise in America of labor's ultimate weapon'.[182] These general strikes were the calling card of an emerging working-class that in the midst of a long depression self-organised itself and disrupted the entire capitalist economy.

The city had also been hit hard by the depression and experienced a number of bank failures on 10 July. The well-organised and ambitious new St. Louis Workingmen's Party (SLWP), which was mostly composed of Central European immigrant radicals, called for an immediate city-wide general strike, and although it did not spark the strike it soon found itself leading it. As Burbank observed, 'it is difficult to distinguish to what extent the Party *led* the move-

---

180 Parsons lost his job at a local newspaper for personally supporting the strike and soon become a well-known anarchist journalist, organiser, and Haymarket martyr. Ironically, Parson's brother was a Major General in the Texas cavalry during the Civil War. (Foner 1977, p. 156, italics in original).

181 Burbank 1966, p. 95.

182 Ibid., p. 55.

ment, and to what extent was *carried along* by it'.[183] Nevertheless, the strikers were well positioned; these two cities combined were second only to Chicago for rail traffic in the region. And the SLWP was ideally positioned to lead the insurrection in St. Louis because the unions had been so decimated by the depression that there was no longer a labour council or labour newspaper and the Knights of Labor had maybe a handful of members.

The Workingmen's Party of the United States was formed at a socialist unity meeting on 15–19 July 1876 in Philadelphia, attended by Adolph Strasser, Peter McGuire, and Otto Weydemeyer among others.[184] While its declaration of principles was silent on the question of race, it supported equality of rights for men and women. The party had four ethnic sections with about one-third of its estimated 3,000 members at its peak. Each section and chapter functioned autonomously of the executive committee in Chicago.

Although socialist the party played no role in initiating or spreading the strike in any of the cities where it was active, likely had no advance knowledge of it, and a minimal connection with railroad workers. Some sections of the party became active in the strike once it began, but 'in no city did the Workingmen's Party of the United States advocate armed insurrection, and everywhere its influence on the 1877 strikes was a moderating one'.[185]

The party tried to organise strike support in Philadelphia but Mayor Stokley banned all meetings and the Committee of Safety broke up a meeting, killing one worker. He often chaired stockholder meetings of the Philadelphia Railroad, in which the city was the biggest stockholder. The 1,000 page investigation into the strike by the Pennsylvania legislature didn't even mention the Workingmen's Party, repression or the death.[186]

The St. Louis party played a more influential role than in any other city. It provided a centralised leadership that made the general strike in St. Louis 'not a spontaneous movement of the "rabble"' as it was elsewhere, according

---

183   Ibid., p. 41.

184   Foner 1977, p. 110.

185   It should be noted that Foner frequently refers to the 1877 strike in the plural as 'strikes'. Foner, like the other historians of the 1877 strike, thought that the strike was spontaneous, disorganised, and lacked a leadership. He portrayed it as a series of dispersed strikes rather than a singular insurrection. 'It was, in short, a spontaneous uprising against oppression, without careful premeditation or organization'. (Ibid., pp. 113 and 122).

186   Foner suggests that the lack of any mention of the party illustrates that it played no role in the strike. However, this is arguing from silence since the investigators may have either inadvertently or intentionally ignored its role. (Ibid., p. 116).

to Burbank.[187] The SLWP played a moderating role by providing an organisational identity and coordinating structure through the party dominated executive committee. It 'brought the nation's first formal general strike of the new
industrial era – not the mob improvisation of other cities, but the deliberate
undertaking of an established organization'.[188]

Asserting that the working-class could take over and run St. Louis, several
members of the SLWP, of whom only one was actually a striker, formed a six
member executive committee to coordinate a general strike and run the day to
day functions of the city. To launch a general strike the workers first had to shut
down the city so that the committee could re-open and run it according to the
needs of the working-class.

To achieve that objective, workers from a number of shops and factories
appeared at the SLWP headquarters at Turner Hall demanding that it send
around marchers to shut down more workplaces. Led by black workers, SLWP
members, strikers and supporters paraded around the city with banners, fife,
and drums spreading the railroad strike and initially shutting down at least
60 factories and shops, including *St. Louis Dispatch* newsboys, levee boatmen,
and others. The next evening a larger procession of at least 10,000 people,
some reportedly carrying lathes and clubs on their shoulders, continued to
spread the strike, shutting down about 20 more shops. By Thursday 26 July,
the general strike was in effect. The executive committee was calling the shots,
meeting with local industrialists and the mayor, and providing guards for select
factories, allowing the US mail through, and arranging emergency medical services.[189]

The SLWP and its allies debated when and how to prepare for an escalation
of tactics, even the use of arms. Accounts from elites, the media and later by
party activists have provided conflicting details. One SLWP speaker claimed at
a rally that they had 7,000 guns available, but they never materialised. One East
St. Louis strike leader proposed workers organise into companies of 10–100 and

---

187 Burbank 1966, p. 168.
188 General strikes took place in several other cities including Kansas City and Toledo. Much
     like in Cincinnati and other cities where local officials initially expressed genuine or
     feigned support for the strike, Toledo's general strike had the apparent support of the
     mayor (who ordered no arrests), police commissioner, and the head of the local militia.
     Their support turned out to be a tactical deception because a few days later the Mayor
     swore in 400 special police and arrested the strike leaders, ending the strike. (Foner 1977,
     p. 159; and Bruce 1959, p. 274).
189 Roediger 1994, p. 87; and Burbank 1966, p. 43.

set up patrols to protect property and 'organise force to meet force' but he was not heeded. As a harbinger of the 1919 Seattle general strike, all accounts reported an entirely peaceful general strike with no reports of property damage or violence. The orderliness of the rally was confirmed by the *Globe-Democrat* and a sergeant in the US Signal Service in his wired report to Washington DC.[190]

The glimpses of bi-racial cooperation evidenced in Galveston and elsewhere was substantial in St. Louis. Observers reported significant cooperation between black and white strikers of several ethnicities, contributing to the rapid success of the general strike. At one rally when someone asked if they also supported the black boatmen on strike, the crowd shouted back 'Yes!'. When a black boatman rose to speak and asked the crowd 'Will you stand to us regardless of color?' the reply he received was 'We will!'. After the rally, beef cannery and black longshoremen struck.[191]

Over the course of the general strike processions of black and white workers departed from the rally to continue spreading the strike and began winning their demands. Committees were sent to cooper, foundry, bagging, flour mill, bakery, iron, steel, zinc, white lead, agricultural tool, wire, and chemical shops where workers walked out spreading the strike. On 26 July the strike was still spreading on the day the executive committee abrogated its leadership. As workers decided to spread the strike to the street cars, barbers went out on strike, and wagon makers, blacksmiths, and painters began meeting to consider joining the strike.

The marches were organised to shut down industries in several areas at once. At the rallies, workers organised themselves into groups that would march through different parts of the city to call workers out to join the strike and circulate the struggle. Such marches shut down industries in the west and southwest on 25 July and in the north and northwest on 26 July. One of the plants the marchers shut down on the twenty-sixth was a sugar refinery. The owner then petitioned the executive committee for permission to keep functioning and received about 150 men to guard it. The struggle to shut down the sugar refinery demonstrated the complexities of the general strike and the tensions between the self-organised strikers, their supporters and the leadership. Elites may have recognised the executive committee as the city's 'de facto authority' but the workers were resisting the executive committee's attempt to centralise and manage the strike. On 26 July, the same day the executive committee issued

---

190   See Foner 1977, pp. 171–2, 176, and 179.
191   Ibid., p. 173.

a proclamation that it would no longer hold any more marches, about 40 factories employing about 1,000 workers were still shut down, leaving no significant plant still operating.[192]

Among the committees were 300 black workers who entered plants in the southern areas of St. Louis, shutting off engine room fires and closing down buildings. The steamer Centennial was boarded by several hundred black and white workers who kept it from leaving for New Orleans until it raised the wages for its mostly black crew.[193] Few employers resisted and many conceded to demands to reverse recent wage cuts or increase wages.

In a substantial understatement, the New York Sun noted the cooperation between black and white workers in the strike was 'a novel feature of the times'.[194] More than just a novelty, it became a source of concern for elites, the local press, and several racist SLWP leaders alarmed by the significant role of black workers in the strike. Executive committee member and Workingmen's Party organiser Albert Currlin reportedly led a racist backlash among the executive committee by turning away hundreds of black workers from a strike meeting and later telling a reporter that he opposed their involvement in the general strike.[195]

In a tactical manoeuvre to dampen the momentum of the general strike by diverting it into the polity, the governor called the legislature into session with directions to pass child labour and eight-hour laws. One of those who spoke at the strike rally for the eight-hour day was J.J. McBride, a member of the state legislature, notorious racist, and labour organiser. At a rally in Carondelet SLWP

---

192   Burbank 1966, pp. 110–12.

193   Ibid., p. 71.

194   Foner 1977, pp. 176–7, and 181.

195   Burbank attributes Currlin's racism to opportunism which went too far, 'attempting to save his own neck and the necks of his associates'. Although his motivation cannot be justified, questions could be raised about his commitment. Currlin had a long convoluted history that brought him in and out of various radical movements during his lifetime. He had fled Germany in 1874 to avoid serving in the military, became a paid organiser of the Workingmen's Party's German section, and a Democratic Party newspaper writer after the strike. In the 1880s he moved to Chicago where he edited the infamous anarchist newspaper Arbeiter-Zeitung during the Haymarket era when he took over for August Spies, who had been arrested and would be hanged. His arrival in Chicago may have been due to his relationship with one of the Haymarket defendants Adolph Fischer whose brother William was a St. Louis general strike leader arrested with Currlin. He was a speaker at one of the funerals and translated one of Spies's books. He later moved to California where he owned several newspapers and died wealthy. (Roediger 1994, p. 88; and Burbank 1966, pp. 72 and 199–201).

member Harry Eastman raised a demand for jobs for all the unemployed but it does not appear to have been made by the executive committee.[196]

Just as the general strike was in effect, the executive committee set up by the SLWP began to equivocate. When a crowd marched to the building where the executive committee was meeting on the evening of Thursday 26 July, most of the executive committee members not only refused to go out to meet with the strikers to explain their actions but even asked the police to arrest those still massing. As news began to circulate that a Committee of Public Safety was formed in Mayor Henry Overstolz's office and arming itself in preparation to break the strike, the day before the general strike was even in effect, the strikers became alarmed. Some called for armed self-defence of the general strike. Some workers did begin to self-arm with tools of their trade a day earlier, as some showed up to the rally and march carrying brooms, clubs, irons, coupling pins, brake rods, and red signal flags.[197]

It is unclear whether the executive committee intended to or actually did attempt to arm a workers' militia. Although there were reports of a speaker at the 26 July rally describing a plan to organise a worker's militia, Irish Fenians raising money for one, and hundreds of guns being discovered at Schuler Hall, the reports were not credible. Although Burbank asserted the SLWP 'never advocated armed insurrection, and its influence in the 1877 strikes was everywhere a moderating one', he appears convinced that the executive committee did attempt to organise workers' militias on 27 July for the purpose of keeping order, such as the sugar refinery, not to defend or expand the strike. After the strike about 200 mostly German workers set up the 'Socialistic Workingmen's Protective Association' and began drilling with rifles.[198]

Inside, the executive committee debated and issued communiqués but neglected to take action, with a vocal minority vehemently against preparing self-defence measures. Before long, the police began to prevent marchers from shutting down additional factories and the tide began to turn. The general strike suddenly appeared rudderless as the executive committee cut itself off from the rank and file it had professed to lead but was now abandoning to the forces of repression.

With the city long on the verge of bankruptcy, the following day the sheriff managed to raise a 5,000 man posse under the command of the Commit-

---

196 Burbank 1966, p. 80.
197 Ibid., pp. 73–4 and 80.
198 Ibid., pp. 118–22, 130–1,172, and 190–1. Burbank gives credence to a newspaper interview with executive committee member Henry Allen, given while he was in jail, and admissions by Currlin.

tee of Public Safety. It was overwhelmingly composed of merchants, white-collar employees, and elites, and led by a judge and five ex-generals. The two former Civil War generals from the Union and Confederate sides illustrated how nationalism and shared ruling class interests trumped their prior factional interests.[199] The paramilitary posse was raised after elites grew to distrust Mayor Overstolz although he was present at their meetings. Their distrust may be linked to their ethnic hatred – Overstolz was German-American as were many of the SLWP leadership – and the fact that he met with a committee of the executive committee in an effort to negotiate.[200]

The posse was armed with about 3,000 rifles and Colt revolvers, including four brass cannons sent by Governor John Phelps from a state arsenal. After the federal government refused to grant their request for thousands more weapons, artillery and ammunition, local merchants raised $20,000 to arm 1,000 more vigilantes, the St. Louis Gun Club donated shotguns, and another 1,500 arms arrived from the state arsenal. Among the paramilitary force were merchants, lawyers, clerks, cashiers and local elites, all white and non-ethnic. As a test of strength, the mayor issued a proclamation ordering all businesses to reopen.[201] Although not requested by the governor, six companies of 400 US infantry with four Gatling guns under the command of Colonel Jefferson C. Davis arrived to join US troops already in East St. Louis.[202] Colonel Davis assured the city that they were there 'merely to protect government and public property' and not to break the strikes or run the trains and did not take part in the raid on the executive committee headquarters on 27 July.[203] Over the next few days the paramilitary forces organised an elaborate command structure. Companies were set up in the city wards, an emergency hospital established, and an artillery company was armed with two 12-pound cannons loaded with bags of nails as shrapnel.[204]

---

199   Roediger 1994, p. 89; and Burbank 1966, p. 51.
200   While it cannot be confirmed, Currlin told a newspaper reporter that the committee had done what the mayor ordered them to do. (Burbank 1966, p. 146).
201   Foner 1977, pp. 175 and 184; and Brecher 1972, p. 34.
202   His namesake is serendipitous on two levels. Not only was Jefferson Davis an appropriate name for someone redeploying US troops from occupying the former Confederate states in order to crush a strike, but Davis had commanded troops in the 1872–3 Modoc Indian War in northern California, thereby tying this deployment to help crush the multi-racial strike to the genocidal wars against California native peoples.
203   Burbank 1966, pp. 50 and 139.
204   Ibid., pp. 103 and 139–41.

Before the military force arrived the executive committee had already abrogated its leadership role. Strikers were looking for directions about tactics and strategy that were not forthcoming. It has been speculated that the executive committee became paralysed because it expected the mayor to help settle the strike and feared a bloodbath or the ascendance of a multi-racial insurgency. Whatever the reason, the leadership publicly conceded defeat both by refusing to lead the mobilised insurgents in self-defence and by de-escalating its tactics. As the forces of repression were gathering, on 26 July an executive committee issued another proclamation calling for the eight-hour day, asking the mayor to feed the strikers in order to avoid 'plunder, arson or violence', and conceding that it did not control the strike. To assist Mayor Overstolz 'in maintaining order and protecting property' (which it repeated twice) and 'avoid riot', it promised to hold no more large marches, meetings, or rallies.[205]

The executive committee stopped holding large marches and mass meetings despite the fact that the strike gained its greatest strength from large marches and mass meetings, by which the executive committee maintained its organic connection to and communication with the strikers and their allies. Although it cancelled plans for further rallies to mobilise strikers and marchers to keep industry shut down, the workers went ahead all the same. When a speaker at the rally on 25 July called for organising and arming the workers, the executive committee tried to have him arrested, perhaps to illustrate their ability to manage the struggle they had helped to unleash.[206] Whether this was an effort of the leadership to reduce the risks to themselves of the inevitable repression can only be speculated about. Whatever the reason for offering to de-escalate and demobilise, the leadership was contradicting their actions of the past few days and actually making the strike vulnerable to forces massing against them.

> While the Executive Committee was issuing proclamations and handbills affirming its devotion to peaceful activities and its abhorrence of violence in any form, powerful forces in the city, undeterred by any such scruples, were mobilizing to crush the strike by whatever means might be necessary.[207]

---

205   Ibid., pp. 101–12.

206   While Burbank identified executive committee member James McCarthy, a shoe worker, as the only proponent of self-arming, he raises questions about how accurately he was quoted by the newspapers and points out that there is no evidence that such a 'people's militia' was formed.

207   Foner 1977, p. 184.

De-escalation and de-mobilisation removed the leverage provided by mass support, which was crucial for continuing the general strike or escalating their tactics by seizing the means of production and mobilising to defend it. This raised the costs to the insurgency as elites were mobilising in the streets to crush the general strike.

There are several important factors for the executive committee's abandonment of the general strike it presumed to lead. The make-up of the strikers and their mass supporters differed significantly from the executive committee whose members' identities have never fully been revealed. Roediger found that about 40 percent of the 47 identifiable leaders were skilled workers, about 28 percent were professionals, white-collar workers or small merchants, and the remaining members were unskilled workers. Inversely, all nine top leaders of the executive committee were skilled workers, most of whom had experienced downward mobility from the trades, being a merchant or professional to waged labourer or unemployed. Among those local unions, widely decimated by the long depression, participating in the executive committee were furniture workers, iron moulders, and shoe workers. Notably, the lathers' union was opposed to the strike and many members joined the militia.[208]

Among the core leadership of the German dominated party Peter Lofgren spoke English fluently, had a college degree and was a teacher and lawyer. Joseph Glenn was one of the few labour organisers among them.[209] At least one man, known as Wilson, was black. James Cope was a member of the International Workingmen's Association (IWA), or the First International, founded by Karl Marx among others. Currlin was in attendance at the Philadelphia Congress the previous year, which founded the Workingmen's Party and dissolved the IAW.[210]

The leadership differed significantly from the rank and file of strikers and their supporters. Unskilled workers were about 62 percent of those arrested and

---

208 Burbank makes an important point that the apparently low documented participation of local unions in the executive committee was 'perhaps more indicative of the organizational weakness of all unions in 1877' (Burbank 1966, p. 57). But both Roediger and Burbank miss the main lesson that much of the general strike in St. Louis was self-organised from below and the rank and file of whom we know almost nothing used the executive committee to expand the strike into a general strike. (See also Burbank 1966, pp. 98–9).

209 Lofgren reverted to his earlier name Laurence Gronlund and published *The Cooperative Commonwealth, An Exposition of Modern Socialism* under that name in 1884. He later worked in the office of US Commissioner of Labor Carroll Wright. (See Ibid., pp. 195–7).

210 Ibid., pp. 17 and 33–5.

prosecuted. As many in the leadership were or had recently been high status skilled or educated workers, the leadership's class interests were more likely closer aligned to local elites than those they led. Such shared interests were reflected in their overtures to local merchants, use of strikers to guard property, efforts to bargain, warnings to strikers about using violence, and eventual abandonment of leadership to de-mobilise the strikers and their supporters.[211]

Racism among members of the executive committee and fear of the significant role of blacks in the strike were key factors in demobilising the strike. Blacks played a crucial leadership role early in the strike. Black rivermen joined the strike to help shut down the city, one of the early members of the executive committee that met with the mayor was black, and at least three black men worked with the executive committee, although blacks made up a small part of the parades and marches that travelled the city enforcing and spreading the strike.

Their vital role in making the strike was a key motivator for the executive committee seeking to end it. The executive committee began giving racist speeches about black and Chinese workers. Currlin, a SLWP executive committee member and leading Workingman's Party's spokesman, admitted as much in an interview with a local paper while out on bail. He claimed that all further rallies were cancelled to keep blacks out of the strike and to prevent the strike from becoming an uprising. He and other executive committee members met with the mayor to assure him the strikers would not resist when his forces arrived. It's likely that the leadership saw the racially integrated rank and file strikers and supporters as further evidence of a strike they neither launched nor controlled and soon preferred to shut down. While it was uncertain about what tactics to use and lacked a strategy to achieve a successful outcome for the general strike, it was clear in its repudiation of the very strikers it purported to lead.[212]

The issue of inter-racial and inter-ethnic cooperation among the strikers was at the centre of the storm. As Burbank observed, the SLWP 'found itself, overnight, at the head of an angry mass movement of the organised and unorganised, German and Irish, black and white alike – a responsibility which the party was perhaps not prepared to assume'. The controversy, Burbank added, is not that there were many black workers involved but 'the mere fact that they were there'.[213] If the rank and file workers' strategy of cooperation across the

211   Roediger 1994, pp. 96–7.
212   Burbank 1966, pp. 57 and 73.
213   Ibid., pp. 86–7 and 168.

barriers of race and ethnicity is what made the general strike so threatening, it is also what made the executive committee repudiate the strike it supposedly led.

On the evening of 26 July, about 2,000 strikers and supporters assembled for the daily rally in Lucas Market, but the executive committee did not show up. Many marched to the executive committee headquarters, recently moved from Turner Hall to Schuler's Hall, demanding coordinated action to defend against the approaching forces, continue to organise mass support, and spread the strike, but the leadership refused to meet them or issue any concrete steps.[214]

By 27 July, the strike was starting to lose force. Although marchers were still shutting down shops, the first passenger train arrived from the east and ships began to be loaded and unloaded. About 1,000 strikers and their supporters again marched on Schuler Hall to demand the executive committee disclose its plan for furthering the strike, but it had only planned a meeting of representatives of the city unions. When they entered the hall they found the executive committee in a meeting; when they finally addressed the crowd, Currlin told them that if the police came they would give up without a fight.

On 27 July, 600–700 paramilitaries and police approached the building armed with a cannon and launched several mounted attacks on the crowd with clubs and without firing a shot. The two former Union and Confederate generals refused to participate and the state militia and US troops were not involved.[215] The force easily entered the building and arrested 73 people still inside the building, including two local reporters, and marched them to the Committee of Public Safety's headquarters. Twenty-four of those arrested were released and the rest were jailed for the night without being charged. There was no warrant for their arrest. While only one of the executive committee members was arrested during the assault on their headquarters, all were arrested over the next two days. While arrested rank and file strikers and supporters were widely convicted and sentenced to the workhouse or jail all nine executive committee members were acquitted on a *nolle prosequi* verdict.[216] In the meantime, the mayor and governor both issued proclamations of martial law prohibiting public assemblies or interference with local industry. There were no clashes, no property destroyed, and no one was killed.

---

214   Burbank attributed part of the breakdown in communication between the executive committee and rank and file to being evicted by the Turners and having to relocate. (Ibid., p. 99).

215   The militia did occupy Carondelet where the executive committee collapsed. (Ibid., p. 150).

216   Bruce 1959, p. 282; Foner 1977, p. 186; and Roediger 1994, p. 104.

While it may have paralysed capital for a few days, the SLWP's equivocation about whether to continue escalating tactics resulted in its rapid defeat. There were several reasons why the strike failed. First, the SLWP focused on using the strike to push forward reforms rather than further escalate the general strike into one that ran the city instead of shutting it down. The leadership 'was watching a strike grow on very different lines from those with which it was comfortable'. This strike was determined by the objectives of its racially diverse and cross-gender rank and file. The leadership took steps to de-escalate and de-mobilise it.[217]

The focus on reform was characteristic of the origin and dominance of the executive committee by the Workingmen's Party. In the midst of an insurgency, it neither launched nor controlled the imperatives of the party as a mass-based membership organisation took precedence. At risk of losing credibility and thus its fortunes at the ballot box, the party placed its organisational interests and imperatives above the interests and objectives of the strikers. Piven and Cloward identify an impulse common to membership-based organisations: 'endeavoring to do what they cannot do, organizers fail to do what they can do'.[218] Party members sought to build the organisation even at the expense of the strike and thereby futilely tried to steer the strike to a close so it could enter the polity in the upcoming elections.

Lloyd argued that the executive committee's turn from leading a strike to advocating for legislative reform weakened the strike because 'Workers in St. Louis were nowhere near being ready to force Congress to act on a far-reaching political program that would require seizing railroad property and regulating labor and unemployment policy beyond anything contemplated in Washington to that point'.[219] But this misses the point in two ways. First, such reforms are not 'contemplated' in Washington until they have to be. The working-class cannot force Congress to act. Rather, its struggles disrupt the relations of production and create crisis conditions that give reformers an upper hand to push through reforms that respond to some of the demands and so encourage the leadership to de-mobilise and restore control. Second, the SLWP's demands proved prescient as they were ultimately implemented by the 1930s turn toward Keynesianism.

Roediger attributes the turn towards political reform to the shared class position and interests of the leadership and local elites. At the start of the strike, the

217   Roediger 1994, p. 102.
218   Piven and Cloward and 1977, p. xxi.
219   Lloyd 2009, pp. 189–90.

executive committee had already approached local merchants for their support and offered to guard various factories. While they were attempting to expand the coalition of support for the strike, the party's organisational interests of gaining funding and voters in the next election were also at work. Despite gaining legitimacy as a force to be dealt with as a result of the disruptive power of the strike, the party-dominated executive committee remained focused on extracting concessions and resources from elites rather than escalating the tactics that had proved successful in gaining previously impossible concessions to rescind the wage cuts and double headers. What the leadership failed to realise is that 'elites are not actually responding to the organizations; they are responding to the underlying force of insurgency'.[220]

The Workingmen's Party more than just lost contact with the people it had organised and led, as Foner and Roediger both suggest. The SLWP placed itself in the position of self-appointed leaders of the strike from the top down. Rather than facilitating the strikers' already existing efforts to self-organise the strike they had started themselves and transform it into a means of taking power, the SLWP attempted to channel and manage the strike, an insurgency 'not wholly subject to forces they controlled or understood', to achieve the objectives of the party.[221] Because all of the SLWP's demands were far removed from the shop floor, it detracted from and diffused the focus on the strike and diluted the very leverage that could be used to wring out these concessions. In this way it turned its initial strength into its ultimate weakness.

By refusing to continue leading what it had imposed itself on, the SLWP caused, if not accelerated, the defeat of the general strike. Instead of leading the workers to use their power to achieve the objectives of the strike, the leadership shifted to offering concessions and making appeals to elites for legislative reforms such as government ownership of the railroads and other industries, revoking bank charters, a public works programme, and an eight-hour law.[222] The executive committee demobilised in a futile effort to institutionalise its authority to achieve reforms through negotiations while lacking the leverage to ensure it could get any of them. Even the reforms they proposed were focused on the national and not the local level, perhaps to build the reputation of the national party rather than achieve redress of the grievances for which the workers were striking locally. In this way, the SLWP placed itself at the head of the general strike which it never successfully channelled into furthering its own

---

220   Piven and Cloward 1977, p. xxi.
221   Roediger 1994, p. 102.
222   Foner 1977, pp. 180–3; and Burbank 1966, p. 85.

separate organisational objectives. If the executive committee had no plan for achieving concrete gains, the elites certainly did.

Despite offering the means for coordinating the strike that was missing elsewhere, having a centralised leadership proved to be more a liability than an asset. The leadership was gathered in one place, undefended, and reportedly infiltrated by one or more collaborators. After several days of relying on the centralised leadership for direction, the strikers and their allies were unprepared to re-take the initiative when the leadership changed course in an undesirable direction, encouraging them to de-mobilise, de-escalate, and discontinue expanding its base of support at the very moment when they wanted to continue expanding it.

Although the executive committee tried to bring together the unions on 26 July, it was too late. It no longer coordinated the tactics that made the general strike, denounced participation by black workers, and was no longer communicating with the rank and file strikers and supporters. As Burbank insightfully observed, the executive committee seemed unable to coordinate all but a few unions that could maintain the momentum of the strike and 'negotiate with the employers and the city government some kind of settlement that would allow at least some of the gains of the strike to be retained and defended'.[223]

The SLWP's attempt to lead the general strike didn't fail because it failed to establish a 'centralized and responsibility leadership', as Burbank suggested.[224] Its efforts to put itself in charge made its organisational imperatives more important than helping to continue circulating the strike in the face of growing risk of repression. The executive committee lacked the strategy to either extract some local concessions and de-mobilise while the costs of doing so were low, or continue helping circulate a struggle it did not control in order to increase the opportunity for more than a few modest gains.

The executive committee's de-mobilisation and de-escalation raised the costs for those who continued to escalate their tactics and reduced the opportunities of those who demobilised to achieve any concessions. Elites used the pause to regroup and escalate their tactics in order to tilt the balance of power back in their favour, retake control of the city, and restart production. The strikers' de-mobilisation and de-escalation increased the opportunities and reduced the risks for capital to escalate its tactics and resort to political violence and repression.

---

223   Burbank 1966, p. 98.
224   Ibid., p. 98.

Ironically, if local elites had been willing to negotiate with the executive committee, it would have found an ally in disciplining the city's workers. It instead perceived an enemy to crush rather than an opportunity to gain an ally to help manage class struggle. By offering to demobilise and de-escalate the SLWP explicitly offered itself as an ally for capital to carry out this disciplinary function rather than an adversary to deepen the disruption. In its 25 July 'Proclamation', the executive committee had already offered to 'do all that lies in our power to aid the authorities in keeping order and preventing acts of violence, and will do our utmost to detect and bring to punishment all guilty parties', an offer echoed by the Cincinnati party.[225] Overall, the role of the Workingmen's Party in the strike was either to try to sabotage it in San Francisco, oppose it in Chicago and Louisville, or attempt to control and channel it by dampening further tactical escalation. Rather than wielding no influence, the presence of an active Workingmen's Party actually made de-escalation more likely, thereby raising the costs of continuing the strike.

The Workingmen's Party also played a central role in the East St. Louis strike where workers had begun meeting, issued resolutions in support of strikers in the east, and formed an executive committee with workers from as many as seven lines. They soon stopped all but select train traffic, took control of the depot as their headquarters, began to take over control of the city, appointed their own 'police', and attempted to negotiate a settlement.

There were several important differences with the St. Louis general strike. Most of the strike was centred in the railroad industry. Unlike in St. Louis, the strike had the support of at least two important local officials including a judge who spoke at an open air rally of strikers organised by the Workingmen's Party at the East St. Louis depot. At the rally a committee of five, including a black man named Wilson (his first name is unknown), were selected to negotiate with the mayor to ask that no US troops be requested, but they were rebuffed.[226] Since there were only 12 police, the mayor swore in strikers as special police to guard the railroad property. Local elites briefly recognised the executive committee as the local authority, asking for its help to guard a local sugar refinery and allow a meat packer and stockyard to operate. The mayor then approached the receiver of the St. Louis & Southeastern Railway Company to mediate but was refused. Ironically, the East St. Louis Mayor Bowman had been involved in revolutions in Germany or Austria as a boy and brought his revolutionary experience to his position as an elected official.[227] In response to the mayor's success

225   See Foner 1977, p. 102.

226   Foner 1977, pp. 164–7.

227   Bowman was murdered while in office under mysterious circumstances in front of his

in de-escalating the strike the Indianapolis and Missouri Pacific Railroad initially offered to rescind the wage cut and restore wages to what they were on 1 January but was overruled by the receiver who refused to allow any negotiation or compromise. The executive committee also wisely forbid any separate offers to settle out of fear that the strike would be divided and conquered. In preparation for efforts to divide and conquer the strikers and their supporters, the executive committees in both cities issued 'all or none rules' for settling the general strikes.

Because the St. Louis & Southeastern was also under court receivership as a result of its 1874 bankruptcy, the receiver likely perceived the company as protected by the federal courts and not compelled to negotiate, compromise, or concede anything. These protected railroads were an early example of being 'too big to fail' since they had the assets, power and protection of the federal government behind them.

When the strike appeared imminent, the receivers of both the St. Louis & Southeastern and the Indianapolis and Missouri Pacific Railroad requested US troops from the Hayes administration. The St. Louis & Southeastern receiver James Wilson wired Secretary of the Interior Carl Schurz, part owner of the St. Louis newspaper the *Westliche Post*, that 'The time has come when the President should stamp out mob now rampant ... The law can be found for it after order is restored'. Wilson had a vested interest in the road as its former director and vice president and was at that time engaged in a bond buy back. In response, Secretary of War McCrary sent six companies of the 23rd Infantry, about 300 men, from Fort Leavenworth, Kansas to protect the company from both the strikers and their presumably sympathetic revolutionary mayor despite General Pope of Fort Leavenworth reporting no danger of rioting.[228] The US troops were commanded by Colonel Davis and armed with two Gatling guns arrived that evening under orders 'not to quell the strikers or run the trains'. The receiver then got federal Judge Thomas Drummond, who had appointed Wilson the receiver, to send a US marshal to East St. Louis.[229] The mayor was reportedly organising a Committee of Public Safety posse and preparing an order for the strikers to return to work.

---

house in 1885. Two East St. Louis policemen were later charged with his murder but they were never tried. Although he was considered friendly to the railroad companies, it is suspected that they had him assassinated by the Pinkertons. (See Burbank 1966, p. 28; Bowman, John B. (1832–85), *Politicalgraveyard.com* and *New York Times*, 21 November 1885).

228   Foner 1977, pp. 164–5; and Burbank 1966, p. 91.

229   Ibid., p. 170.

The federal intervention to defend the two railroads then under receivership was a trial run for using the courts to expand the role of the state into the economy on behalf of capital to protect other railroads over the coming decades from the threat of striking workers. The receiver's call for federal troops and court protection proved incredibly profitable for the railroad. In early August, he resumed a deal for undervalued mortgage bonds which he cancelled at the onset of the strike.

Although the executive committee had taken control of several trains and the telegraph for their own use and were joined by workers in the car yards, packing houses, and stockyards, the East St. Louis executive committee soon demobilised. After 25 July, the executive committee ended all parades and meetings, although workers reportedly continued them, and focused solely on negotiations and guarding property. Roediger identified the failure in their negotiation strategy in the fact that 'the leverage in making such appeals lay in control over the alleged mob, control of which the Executive Committee increasingly abdicated'.[230]

On 27 July four members of the executive committee resigned over a dispute as to whether to compromise or hold the depot and cooperate with the St. Louis general strike. Although the executive committee soon abandoned the strike they may have been in haste. On 27 and 28 July workers stopped street cars, began acquiring arms, and blocked a train from leaving the depot while Governor Cullom was there. Several hundred striking miners arrived by train, some with arms, to support the strike but were disarmed and sent back home.[231]

An effective state military force that could suppress the strike was not available. The Illinois National Guard lacked military equipment and guardsmen from nearby Montgomery County had reportedly refused to serve against the strikers. Instead on 28 July between 350 and 1,000 US troops were sent to retake the depot, which was guarded by two strikers positioned there in cooperation with the mayor, who were arrested. Troops were also sent to retake the bridge.[232] The last strike action was on 29 July when many strikers were arrested and held in baggage cars for attempting to block freight trains. Although the strike was over, coal was in short supply and expensive, which slowed industry getting restarted.

---

230   Roediger 1994, p. 101.
231   Burbank 1966, pp. 158–9.
232   Ibid., pp. 153–4, and 157.

The St. Louis general strike was widely characterised in the press as America's first Paris Commune. As Painter observed, 'now, it seemed, a great new threat existed in the nation's very bosom, in the form of strikers and what were called the dangerous classes, who had figured so prominently in the crowds of Baltimore and Pittsburgh'.

> The strike awakened everyone to the existence of an intense, formless anger among the poor and working people that was too shocking to be consonant with the older ideal of an American society spared class conflict ... The strike gave notice that American society, long accustomed to seeing itself as exempt from the class struggles that rent Europe, no longer enjoyed this exemption.[233]

The threat posed by the working-class's willingness to escalate the intensity of its tactics brought down the rain of relentless denunciations in the press by elites and officials of all levels of government, the militias and the US Army. Hysterical language about the 'mob' was widely used by the press, especially after the 1871 Paris Commune, and was trained at every effort at political and economic reform. The 1871 Paris Commune lasted 73 days and created, among other objectives, free secular public education for girls, used vacant housing for the homeless, and worker takeovers and self-management of abandoned workshops. The Commune was a dire threat to the ruling class of Europe, which repressed it mercilessly. In the fighting, 870 Versailles troops were killed but between 20,000 to 25,000 Parisians were killed by the time the Commune was crushed. The aftermath of the 1848 Paris uprising was key to the successful repression of the 1871 Paris Commune. The narrow winding streets were rebuilt as large boulevards with radiating intersections to allow a freer movement of larger numbers of troops.

These lessons would not be lost on urban planners and reformers in the US after 1877. The spectre of communism in the US had been building with each effort at reform. *The Nation* magazine warned of the spectre of communism after the passage of the 1872 federal eight-hour law, which would not be enforced until the passage of the 1937 Fair Labor Standards Act. Over the coming decades fear of the 'mob' and strategies to control and suppress it would take centre stage. Among the most influential writers was nineteenth-century French psychologist Gustave Le Bon, whose work sought the means of con-

---

233   Painter 1987, pp. 21 and 24.

trolling and managing masses of people in reaction to the Paris Commune and movements for socialism, and continues to inform counter-insurgency and public relations today.[234]

But the 1877 strike was the effort of self-organised workers not communists, socialists or anarchists. Despite the organised participation of communists, socialists, and anarchists in Chicago and St. Louis, the communist *Labour Standard* reported that 'There was no concert of action at the start' by any organised group or party. The Workingmen's Party in Hoboken and Philadelphia had no prior information about any action. The group in Hoboken, demonstrating how little importance it gave to the strike at first, even postponed a planned mass meeting until September even though the B&O strike had begun the day earlier. The Workingmen's Party did not engage in any strike related activity until Sunday 22 July when it urged members to aid the strikers and along with its other chapters called for an eight-hour day and government ownership of the railroad and telegraph.

Its demand for government ownership of the railroad and telegraph was prescient. The party clearly understood how monopoly control over the nation's communication and transportation systems could be wielded as an instrument of ruling class power. In 1894, the railroad companies used their unregulated control of the telegraph system against the strikers by rerouting the American Railway Union's telegrams to their General Managers Association, which was working to crush the strike. The Workingmen's Party realised early that communications could be a tool in the class struggle, only their demand wrongly assumed government ownership would somehow neutralise its use in the event of class struggle.

The 1877 strike initially appeared to stir the winds of fortune for the organisation of a national labour and/or socialist party, as Karl Marx had hoped. At the October 1877 elections the St. Louis Workingmen's Party won five of the 15 school board seats. In the 1878 election two SLWP members were elected to the city House of Delegates. Two executive committee members also began publishing labour papers and Currlin became an editor for a socialist German daily newspaper.[235]

---

234 Le Bon 1896.

235 Currlin was a classic political opportunist. Before moving to Chicago and immersing himself in the anarchist movement as editor of the *Arbeiter-Zeitung*, Currlin endorsed the Republicans in the 1880 election after it adopted a few planks of the SLWP's platform. He then became a journalist for Secretary Schurz's anti-strike *Westliche Post* newspaper and a city water inspector. (See Burbank 1966, pp. 198–9).

Ultimately, the SLWP saw its first step towards the reforms it advocated when the state Bureau of Labor Statistics was established in 1879 and a St. Louis cigar makers' union leader was appointed by Governor Phelps as its Commissioner and a future co-founder of the American Federation of Labor as its Assistant Commissioner. Prompted by the 1877 strike, collecting data on the working-class and class struggle was the initial step towards co-opting the labour movement and managing class struggle.[236]

Workingmen's Parties were formed in a number of other cities and immediately began to field a plethora of labour backed candidates in local and state elections, resulting in a dramatic showing for Greenback-Labor Party in the national election the following year.[237] It elected members in elections in Milwaukee and gained significant votes in three other cities. On 6 August 1877, the Workingmen's Party won five of seven races for the state legislature in Louisville and more than half the vote. In December, the Workingmen's Party became the Socialist Labor Party, a predecessor of the Social Party of the early twentieth century. The *Martinsburg Independent* captured the translation of the demands of the 1877 strike into adversarial politics when it warned that 'the political striker has taken the place of the railroad striker'. In the autumn 1878 election the newly formed Greenback-Labor Party got 1 million votes and elected 14 can-

---

236   Roediger 1994, pp. 104–5; and Burbank 1966, pp. 190–2.

237   The influence on the strike in local Terra Haute party politics is worth noting in detail. In the May 1879 three-way race for City Clerk, Eugene Debs won as a Democrat, eschewing any identification as a labour candidate, and ironically beat the Greenback-Labor candidate Clifford Ross. Debs did the same in his re-election in 1881 and for the state legislature in 1884. Debs masterfully 'fashioned his victories from a multi-class cross-party alliance' that included Vandalia Railroad President Riley McKeen, who endorsed and donated to Debs's campaigns. McKeen also loaned Debs $1,000 to rebuild the lodge after 1877 and was one of a number of businessmen who guaranteed his bond when Debs became Secretary-Treasurer of the local in 1880. McKeen was presented two gifts in appreciation by the Brotherhood in 1880 and 1881 and sat in the place of honour at the 1882 Firemen's convention. Debs's brother was a leader in the McKeen Rifles militia. Vandalia was Terra Haute's largest employer and McKeen had called for US troops twice. The day after troops returned for the second time the workers called off the strike. Terra Haute railroad workers struck three more times by 1894. There were 19 strikes in all by non-railroad workers between 1881–94. Considering his prestigious position in the Brotherhood and relationship to local political power brokers, it is not surprising that Debs was opposed to the 1877 strike. Contrary to Salvatore's claim 'there is no record of his involvement', his opposition is 'involvement'. (Salvatore 1980, pp. 532 and 533–7).

didates to the US House. The Greenback-Labor Party later merged with several other unions, parties and farmer's movements to form the People's Party in the 1880s.[238]

Volcano under the Sidewalk

Ultimately, the 1877 strike caused a shudder that disrupted much of the country's economy. The nation's rail system and many factories, mines, and ports were shut down as the strike circulated among black and white, waged and unwaged, and male and female workers in multiple regions and industries. In fact, even after the rail strike had ended on about 29 July, it had spread to about 100,000 Pennsylvania and Illinois miners, many of whom extended their strike from May to 20 August, and black levee workers in New Orleans. The railroad strike unleashed a new cycle of class struggle, demonstrating that the working-class was an untamed explosive force, a 'volcano under the sidewalk', ready to unleash its fury in a moment's notice. Lacking its own organisation, such as political parties and unions, the working-class was unleashed and unmanageable. This time it was repressed at the barrel of an unsteady gun. Next time, the gun would again suffice until a leash could be found.

Whether the strike could be considered a series of local strikes or a national strike, it spread rapidly and amassed widespread support among different sectors of the working and middle classes as a symbol of the suffering and deprivation of the long depression and the railroads' exploitation of their misery. Bellesiles explained the significance of the strike despite the absence of any apparent coordinated organisation. The rapid spread of the strike portrayed a 'working class struggling to form some sort of common bond among workers based on their shared sufferings over the previous four years'.[239] The explosive power of those bonds prompted a range of responses by elites from reversing the cuts, reorganising the industry, and expanding the role of the state in expectation of the next insurrection.

Despite the eventual defeat of the St. Louis general strike, there were some limited victories, particularly on the wage cuts which were rescinded or delayed by some lines. The Cleveland, Columbus, Cincinnati & Indianapolis Railroad rescinded the 10 percent wage cut. The Indianapolis and Missouri Pacific Rail-

---

238   Bruce's suggestion that 'farmers had little interest in labor's woes' is belied by the record of the Farmer's Alliance and the People's Party that were formed in the coming decade and aligned their efforts with the Knights of Labor. (Bruce 1959, p. 318).

239   Bellesiles 2010, p. 153.

road also declared that it wished to rescind the cut and raise wages 25 percent, returning wages to 1876 levels, but was prevented from doing so by its receiver. According to Bruce, as the strike came to an end

> it had come close to success – closer, indeed, than the strikers knew. Even on the surface, signs had been encouraging early that week. Some roads – the Long Island, the Union Pacific, the Central Pacific, the Louisville Short Line and others – had narrowly forestalled a strike by rescinding their wage cuts. Other roads, such as the Missouri Pacific, the Chicago & North-western, the Louisville & Nashville, the Atchison, Topeka & Santa Fe, the Great Western, the Texas Central, had quickly conceded the strikers' demands. Beneath the surface, private correspondence reveals a near cave-in all along management's lines.[240]

The Chicago, Burlington & Quincy Line's Vice President and Treasurer estimated that yielding on the wage issue while it was still an ordinary strike would be cheaper than the expected property damage caused by an unruly insurrection. Some striking Pennsylvania miners were even rehired at a previous higher wage and there was a 10 percent increase in Wilkes-Barre, a clear reversal of the recent, hubris-driven repression of the Molly Maguires.[241] The St. Louis, Kansas City & Northern Railway offered to rescind the wage cut but a crowd sent by the East St. Louis strike committee kept both yards closed. Some roads gave raises of between 4 to 12 percent, full pay for July, and as much as $3,000 to those who didn't strike.

It is worth considering what 'victory' meant to the newly emerging industrial working-class in 1877. While these small victories appear to be materially inconsequential, the concessions managed to ease up the destitution of these workers and reverse the double headers in the midst of a several year long depression. The concessions were essentially a wash: workers kept their already low wages stagnant and resisted a doubling in productivity. Some of the brotherhoods gained renewed legitimacy in the eyes of the railroad companies, particularly Arthur's Brotherhood of Locomotive Engineers (BLE), which signed contracts raising wages and improved work rules with companies in the east and west. The BLE's relationship with local elites also prospered, with its locals even attempting to emulate them with conventions and balls attended by local dignitaries.[242] However, the shortage of skilled workers in the western states

---

240   Bruce 1959, p. 283.
241   Ibid., pp. 283 and 284; and Foner 1977, p. 191.
242   Stromquist 1993, p. 55.

soon led the companies to promote engineers from other classes of workers for lower pay, which undermined the BLE's power and provoked internal dissent among its members.[243]

There was a more intangible victory that far exceeded these limited tangible concessions. Transformed into a general strike for eight hours, banning child labour under 14, and with blacks and whites working together, workers demonstrated their ability to disrupt the accumulation of capital at the point of production, crossing geographical, corporate, craft and race lines, and devising and adapting new tactics and strategy. The strike also demonstrated what is possible by recomposing working-class power.

Between 1877 and 1894 railroad workers struck more frequently and had a higher rate of success than all striking industrial workers combined. There were 668 railroad strikes, nearly one per week, between 1881 and 1894. Forty eight percent of these strikes, 322, were by unskilled and mostly non-unionised workers who were 54 percent of all striking railroad workers. Until the founding of the American Railway Union in 1893, which included a large share of these striking unskilled workers, nearly all of the strikers were self-organised. Some regions were more turbulent than others, with about 10 percent of railroad workers in the west going on strike between 1885 and 1894.[244]

But what was important was not merely the number on strike but the leverage they wielded by their strategic location in the capitalist economy. As Stromquist observed, 'the interruptions in commerce and manufacturing that frequently accompanied railroad strikes made them particularly serious and brought to bear extraordinary pressures for their resolution'.[245]

But did the strike alter the balance of power and control over work between capital and workers? The circulation of the 1877 strike demonstrates the importance of understanding its strategic leverage in the context of the patterns of class struggle in order to understand changes in railroad work, class composition in the industry, relations between management and workers, and other factors. Understanding the 1877 strike in the context of this cycle of struggle can be seen as what Stromquist called one of several 'tremors of varying intensity that reflect shifts in the social geology of class relations'.[246]

Without the ability to turn several local strikes into a nationwide insurrection, the concessions would not have happened at all. The concessions were

---

243 Ibid., pp. 57–8.
244 Ibid., pp. 25, 27, 30, and 276–7.
245 Ibid., pp. 24–5.
246 Ibid., p. 25.

a response by a fragmented and disorganised railroad industry to the demonstrated power of workers to disrupt the means of production at will by escalating their tactics when mass support increased the opportunities and lowered the costs of doing so. *The Nation* magazine spoke to this fear when it wrote that 'the strikers may come out of the struggle with an appearance of victory' if companies conceded on wage demands or agreed to rehire strikers at any wage. 'It would be a national calamity, for it would be virtually the surrender to a body of laborers of the lowest grade of power, whenever they were discontented with their conditions, to block all the great highways in the country …'.[247] Inversely, Sidney Lens concluded that 'labor was too weak, and the combined forces of capital and the government too strong for the workers to prevail in the end'.[248]

But tactically, they were both wrong. The workers' minimal gains were possible only because they were too powerful to be ignored while lacking the capacity to take advantage of further tactical escalation. The use of the US Army, and about 45,000 state militia troops in 11 states, was the largest domestic counter-insurgency operation in US history. But military repression was bound to be temporary unless concessions could be used to forestall yet another upsurge long enough to devise a new composition of capital to prepare for the next insurgency.

It would be inaccurate to call the 1877 strike a 'railroad strike'. While sparked by the engineers, conductors, trainmen, and other railroad workers, the strike triggered an escalation of tactics across the industrial working-class in the mines, mills, ports, newspapers, and factories, to name but a few sectors to which the strike circulated. 'By now, the movement was no longer simply a railroad strike. With the battles between soldiers and crowds drawn from all sectors of the working population, it was increasingly perceived as a struggle

---

247 The reformer *Nation* magazine was not alone in its denunciation of the strike. The strike exposed rifts among elite reformers and brought class to the forefront of the pressing issues of the day. Suffrage leader Lucy Stone wrote in the *Women's Journal* that 'The insurrection must be suppressed, if it costs a hundred thousand lives and the destruction of every railroad in the country'. (See Foner 1977, pp. 192 and 265). Two years later historian Francis Parkman used the strike to oppose expanding suffrage.

'There are those who think that the suffrage would act as a safety-valve to political passions; but it has not so acted in the case of men. Dissatisfied masses, foiled of their purpose at the polls, are more apt to resort to force than if they had not already tried lawful means without success. The bloody riots of 1877 were the work of men in full enjoyment of the suffrage. It is to the dread of lead and steel that the friends of order must look in the last resort …' (Parkman 1879, p. 319).

248 Lens 1973, p. 53.

between workers as a whole and employers as a whole'. As Burbank put it, the strike was a time when 'the canaille turn on their masters, eager for one bite in return for many kicks'.[249]

---

249   Brecher 1972, p. 29; and Burbank 1966, p. 37.

CHAPTER 2

'We Shall Consume Their Shops with Fire': Working-Class Recomposition in the 1877 Railroad Strike

For the hour hath come, thou knowest it forsooth, for the
great, evil, long, slow mob-and-slave-insurrection: it extendeth and extendeth!
Now doth it provoke the lower classes, all benevolence and
petty giving; and the overrich may be on their guard!
FRIEDRICH NIETZSCHE, 1909[1]

∴

From the local self-organised committees during the 1877 strike to the American Railway Union in 1893–4, Shelton Stromquist observed that 'railroad workers experimented with a variety of organizational forms to assert their rights and to contend with the changing conditions of work in the industry'.[2] It was such experimentation that made the recomposition of working-class power possible and placed railroad strikes at the nexus of class conflict during the final three decades of the nineteenth century. Beginning with the 1877 railroad strike and continuing until the 1894 strike, railroad workers explored new tactics, strategy, and organisational forms to assert their power and exploit their leverage to achieve their objectives.

The rapidity by which the 1877 strike spread and escalated the trajectory of tactical violence of scattered attacks, sniping, street fights, sabotage, and a general strike illustrated how an insurgency with wide mass support is more likely to mobilise and escalate its tactics to take advantage of increased opportunities for gain and reduced risks of defeat. Workers who achieved an expanded base of mass support could be emboldened to escalate their tactics, expecting

---

1   Nietzsche 1909, p. 329.
2   Stromquist 1993, p. 48.

it to provide the prerequisite conditions to achieve gains. This in turn furthered working-class recomposition to the point of a revolutionary crisis when the potential for workers to take control of the means of production is present. To the degree that workers are able to recompose their power by expanding their mobilisation, organising, and mass support in the way described, they can expect the opportunity to achieve resolution of some or all of their grievances as long as they are either willing to de-mobilise or de-escalate, split, create an above-ground body to carry out negotiations, or pair negotiations with more intense tactics or switch between tactics as the opportunity to do so arises.

As the perception of achieving gains increases, this can have a further feed-back effect, attracting even more mass support and further circulating the strike which in turn furthers the perception of increased opportunity and declining risks. Tilly describes how three factors play a role in the rising intensity of mobilisation and conflict: when multiple parties are involved, timing of vulnerabilities and strengths, and the assessment of relative strength. 'The closer two antagonists come to equality, the greater incentives they both have to attack. And relative strength shifts speedily as a function of mobilization, de-mobilization, and coalition-formation'.[3]

The presence of large and continually growing mass support places workers on an equal terrain with capital and provides an incentive to escalate tactics. The paradox is that this can increase the opportunity for achieving gains or taking losses when costs are both high and rising and low and declining. At this sweet spot, rising opportunities to achieve the objectives of the insurgency far outweigh the rising costs. Insurgent workers' capacity to adequately assess the costs and opportunity to make gains will determine the tactics they deploy and when they escalate them. The task is incredibly complicated. As Tilly rightly warns, 'every analysis requires delicate threading through a web of reciprocal causation' for which there are multiple adversaries engaging in a dynamic, ever changing relationship. For this reason,

> any sound analysis must avoid imputing the fluctuations to changes in the conditions of a single collective actor – workers or others. The analysis must take into account a continuous stream of strategic interaction, much of which takes place outside of strikes.[4]

---

3   Tilly 1989, pp. 433–4.
4   Tilly 1989, p. 435.

The task is even further complicated when taking into account that the cycle of struggle does not stop at the company gates or national borders and is in no way frozen in a cross section of time.[5]

Strikers' Repertoire of Contention

Despite the plethora of writing on class conflict, political violence, and terrorism over more than a century, there is little work to inform how insurgents assess costs and opportunities. Tilly's theory of contention provides a means to understand just that. Collective action by elites and insurgents (who Tilly calls 'contenders')[6] are an outcome of factors that shape the choices they make from their tactical repertoire.[7] Tilly called the facilitation factors interest (I), organisation (O), mobilisation (M), and opportunity (O), or what here is referred to as IOMO.[8] Insurgents use a rational assessment of the access to the polity to present their grievances, possibility of redress, balance of power, level of mass support, costs, and opportunities to determine the most appropriate and effective tactic or combination of tactics to deploy, and the necessary level of force or intensity of the tactic. This assessment exists in a dynamic with the dominant contender (who are called elites here) which takes into account the same factors as well as the willingness and ability to deploy repressive tactics of rising

---

5 To make this analysis of class composition over a period of nearly half a century feasible it was unavoidable to limit it to a handful of industries in a single country.

6 Because 'contenders' implies equivalency where none exists and lacks specificity I have substituted elites and insurgents.

7 Tilly and Tilly explain that their choice of the word 'repertoire' derives from the symbolic interactionist use of performance and theatre to analyse collective action and social relationships:

'A continuous sequence of actions by which an actor makes a claim is a *performance*. All performances that characterize claim-making among a specified set of collective actors constitute that set's *repertoire of contention*. Most repertoires resemble the tunes known to a jazz ensemble rather than the strict scores of a military band: They encourage improvisation and combination within well-established patterns rather than precise repetition. Performances veer away from rote recitation because they form part of strategic interaction in which situations change continuously ... Familiarity greatly lowers the cost of mobilizing people and guiding them safely through the interaction ... performances build upon existing interpersonal networks and contracts, established rights and obligations, including those instilled in legal codes, always favor a limited range of interactions and subject many other possible interactions to penalties' (Tilly and Tilly 1998, pp. 239–40).

8 Tilly 1978, p. 7.

levels of intensity. At each step in the assessment, elites and insurgents must decide whether to continue to mobilise and expand mass support, escalate the intensity of tactics, or de-mobilise, de-escalate, and disarm in order to negotiate, compromise, and be co-opted, institutionalised, diffused, deflected, and integrated, or pair negotiations with their current tactics.

Carrying out such an assessment is certainly difficult. Because of the documentation process, such assessments by insurgents are necessarily lacking due to reasons of literacy, the lack of preservation of internal communications, the secrecy required by those conspiring to carry out illegal, political or violent acts, and the failure to attribute enough importance to their records to obtain the necessary assets to preserve them. For this reason they must be implied in a careful analysis of the historical record by reading through it to ascertain the implicit tactics and strategies. While elites more frequently leave a written record, these too are flawed by confidentiality, internal filtering, self-aggrandisement, and the problems of memory, particularly in autobiographical accounts written long after the events took place. For this reason, an assessment of tactics is necessarily a theoretical analysis of the existing historical texts.[9]

Tilly assumes that elites and insurgents operate according to the following decision matrix in which repression, power, collective action, and opportunity and threat dynamically interact:

1. Collective action costs something.
2. All contenders count costs.
3. Collective action brings benefits, in the form of collective goods.
4. Contenders continuously weigh expected costs against expected benefits.
5. Both costs and benefits are uncertain because:
   a. contenders have imperfect information about the current state of the polity; and
   b. all parties engage in strategic interaction.[10]

---

9   Lacking any access to research support and the excessive full-time plus teaching load of a part-time adjunct professor at three to five institutions, I have resolved to primarily rely on secondary sources and selected limited primary sources to conduct this theoretical analysis.

10   Tilly 1978, p. 99.

With these assumptions in mind he provides an analytical matrix by which to proceed with the assessment.

> The formalization would consist of mapping the interests of the participants, estimating the current state of opportunity and threat with respect to those interests, checking their mobilization levels, gauging their power positions, then seeing to what extent these variables accounted for the intensity and character of their collective action. One step back from that formalization we would find ourselves examining the prevailing pattern of repression and facilitation, the impact of the various groups' organization on their mobilization and on their interests, the effect of coalitions with other contenders on their current power positions, and so on.[11]

In practice, blocking access to the polity to present grievances allows elites to maintain existing coalitions and retain power. Such blockages generate intensified collective action by insurgents in the face of the rising threat as well as the rising opportunity to achieve gains by engaging in collective action. The rising intensity of the contention proportionally raises the threat of repression while simultaneously raising the opportunity for gains if the insurgency can create instability that evokes concessions or offers of compromise from elites or a crisis that shifts the balance of power to insurgents. For Tilly, the tactics elites and insurgents select from their repertoire is the product of the dynamic between whether it facilitates action that lowers costs or repression that raises the cost of continued collective action.[12]

In the 1877 railroad strike the cost of collective action was lower than the much higher cost of dangerous working conditions, pay, and the threat of the doubleheader and further pay cuts. This leads Stephens to argue that 'it is not safe to assume that the cost of unilateral defection – the cost of "staying put" when others act – is the always highest payoff. In 1877, the costs of unilateral inaction approached or exceeded the costs of unilateral action' although there is no guarantee of success.[13]

The costs were further lowered by the ineffectiveness of the forces of the police, defections from the militias to the side of the strikers, widespread mass

---

11   Tilly 1978, p. 227.
12   Ibid., p. 100.
13   Stephens 1995, p. 365.

support, and the size of the crowds that provided a 'dilution effect' that reduced the risks to any one person participating in the strike actions.[14]

Tactical escalation along what I call the trajectory of political violence appeared to move quickly during the 1877 strike. However, that would be a mistaken observation based on the origination fallacy. While only lasting about nine days, the strike arose after several years of attempts to bargain, strikes, and the violent suppression of the Pennsylvania Molly Maguire miners. The B&O workers who stepped off their trains in Baltimore and Martinsburg were not taking rash action. All their efforts had come to naught or the gallows. Even their attempt to organise the Trainsmen's Union (TU) was sabotaged by infiltrators from the start. Few elected officials were willing to remain neutral in the strike and even fewer were sympathetic. The immediate appearance of local and state militia and police provoked a mass outpouring of support for the strikers on the streets. When supporters were gunned down, support continued to swell even after small numbers of US troops were inserted leading to direct confrontations that appeared to observers as a revolutionary insurrection. Wherever the strike spread a similar outcome followed.

The tactical escalation along the trajectory of political violence occurred not out of desperation, but strength. With growing mass support and the willingness of strikers and their allies to take up arms to defend themselves, the strike manifested the growing opportunity to win the modest demands of the strikers for freezing wages and productivity. Support grew as elite coalitions fragmented, stumbled and crumbled. Primarily working-class militias disintegrated or went over to the strikers, local and state elected officials equivocated, and regrouping came with delay and a lack of arms. The evident breakdown and vulnerability of elite power reduced the expected costs of the insurgency, further emboldening strikers and their supporters to continue to circulate the strike and escalate their tactics.

Railroad workers managed to strike and transform the strike into an insurrection not only by circulating the struggle to sympathetic members of local communities but also by overcoming the divisions on the shop floor. To build their strength, workers most effectively self-organised when they could overcome divisions between skilled, semi-skilled, and unskilled, as well as between workers both inside and outside the brotherhoods that mostly worked to prevent or constrain strikes when they did occur. While the historical record of how such self-organisation took place at the level of person to person

14   Ibid., p. 360.

interactions, local informal organisations, and in the community has yet to be uncovered or was never recorded, we can see the impact of such self-organising at the macro level when strikers carried out apparently coordinated tandem acts of disruption and sabotage at strategically critical railroad junctions often supported by rapidly mobilised unemployed workers, small shopkeepers, women, and children in local communities. That these actions are of a similar type and took place at critical pressure points demonstrates that they were not random acts born of anger alone but tactics intended to create maximum disruption with minimum numbers of people.

The strike presented a threat not because of random anger, but rather because of the well-planned and executed tactics and strategies carried out by apparently self-organised workers who set aside their otherwise great divisions of status, skill, wage, and employment to cooperate and connect their grievances and circulate their struggles.

> Often the barriers between the different skilled running trades – the engineers, firemen, brakemen, and conductors – would collapse in such circumstances and many if not all workers in the 'running trades' would support each other, despite the strong stances of their various organizations against 'entangling alliances'. Sometimes this solidarity would extend even further, to encompass not only railroad workers outside the running trades – the laborers who laid and maintained the railroad tracks, the shopmen, the switchmen – but workers in different industries entirely and even members of the working class who were not, in fact, 'workers', such as the unemployed, housewives, and youths.[15]

There were reports of widespread participation of unwaged women workers and unemployed men, as well as cooperation between various ethnicities and races. Czech, German, and Irish waged and unwaged male and female workers cooperated in Chicago, and black and white workers who walked off the job in mutual expressions of solidarity in Memphis, Tennessee, New Orleans, Louisiana, Galveston, Texas, Cairo, Illinois, Louisville, Kentucky, Keyser, West Virginia and St. Louis, Missouri, for example, illustrated the threat of a recomposed working-class that was in the process of crossing the boundaries of the wage and job status to circulate their struggles. In East St. Louis women marched to the depot to support the strike.[16] As waged and unwaged workers openly

---

15   Self Negation n.d., p. 10.
16   Ibid., pp. 17–18; and Burbank 1966, p. 84.

cooperated, it stimulated others to perceive declining costs and rising opportunities to gain from joining the insurrection.

Elites similarly assess opportunities and costs in seeking to inflate the perception of cost to supporters during the mobilisation rather than later once the capacity for escalation is in place and the balance of power has shifted to the insurgents.

> From a government's point of view, raising the costs of mobilization is a more reliable repressive strategy than raising the costs of collective action alone. The anti-mobilization strategy neutralizes the actor as well as the action, and makes it less likely that the actor will be able to act rapidly when the government suddenly becomes vulnerable, a new coalition partner arises, or something else quickly shifts the probable costs and benefits of collective action. Raising the costs of collective action alters the pattern of effective demand from mobilized groups, while raising the costs of mobilization reduces demand across the board.[17]

The ability of elites to raise the costs of mobilisation was mixed. Organisers and leaders were fired, enjoined by courts, arrested, or attacked by hired agents as a means of signalling the threat of rising costs to supporters for joining the insurgency. However, the delays, weakness, and fragmentation of the reaction raised doubts about the level of risk of participating.

When police, militias, and the army first attacked strikers, mass support appeared to continue growing not merely out of anger at the government taking the side of the widely hated railroad companies and the atrocities being committed, but likely as a result of the military advantage held by the insurgents. In Baltimore and Pittsburgh, for example, troops and their leaders were penned down by snipers, trapped in burning buildings, and surrounded and overwhelmed by the apparently coordinated self-defence aided by deserters from the militias. As they fled the city, strikers and their supporters were emboldened that the costs of their escalation was declining.

The presence of substantial mass support made it more likely that insurgents will escalate intensity, even deploying tactical violence. Mass support raises the costs for capital and elites even when the costs of striking were high. If mass support is substantial and crosses lines of status, class, race and gender, the costs to capital from escalating its tactics to deploy various forms of political violence to suppress a strike bring potential costs in credibility, legit-

---

17   Tilly 1978, pp. 100–1.

imacy, sales, customers, strikebreakers, and guards. Non-strikers might march, boycott, refuse to break strikes (resulting in the frequent need to bring in strikebreakers from out of state), and provide funds and in kind support such as food, medical care, and legal aid. When the elite coalition fragments and its members go over to the side of the strikers, they will wield influence on public opinion through the press, lobby local and state elected government officials to remain neutral or support the strike, push legislative reform proposals, and provide money, buildings, land and other tangible property for offices, meeting spaces, and campsites. While in disarray, few elites supported the 1877 strike and were more likely to momentarily remain neutral or equivocate. Because of low participation of male workers in the polity, the political costs of repression were low.

The large number of unemployed workers was widely blamed on speculation by the railroad companies. This reduced the potential supply of local workers to serve as private agents or deputy marshals to break the strike. In one case employees were forced to serve by their employer as special deputies. Bringing in militias and recruiting strikebreakers and agents from another town took time and expense. Untrained and under attack, strikebreakers and armed guards were unsuccessful in getting the trains running. While not documented in the 1877 strike, strikebreakers were frequently of questionable character and motives, committing crimes of assault, murder, burglary, and other violence, such as during the 1894 railroad strike and the 1890s–1914 Colorado miner strikes, which further increased mass support for the strikers.

Generalising the strike throughout an entire shop allows strikers to overcome the craft and wage barrier in order to connect their shared grievances. Circulating the strike off the shop floor and into the community further allows them to connect to already existing struggles in other areas of society. For example, when strikers and their allies and supporters share related grievances over the company's plutocratic dominance of the local government and politics, price gouging, and control of housing and utilities such as in company towns, the strike can be generalised into an insurgency that confronts the existing political conditions and balance of power. When strikers successfully circulate the struggle to the broader community they could vastly expand their base of membership in the struggle and increase the opportunity to achieve their gains. Such a coalition can result in reducing the legitimacy of the existing relations of power, fragment elite coalitions, and increase the possibility of allying with reformers in the polity to launch negotiations and transform proposals into new laws and policy.

Several of the strikes examined in this book, even those that were defeated, resulted in the formation of investigative commissions. Their reports highlighted not only the reasonableness of many of the strikers' grievances but also the unacceptable level of repression, discrediting elites, and prompting the passage of new laws and regulations that hitherto had been blocked in order to remove the most insidious causes of the initial grievances. Such outcomes, if ultimately paper tigers, were largely absent when strikers lacked wide mass support or a significant disruptive impact. In 1877, the concessions offered by the railroad companies withdrawing the wage cuts and double headers were hardly new laws or policies but presaged such later reforms.

Mass support also raised the spectre of non-strikers taking the insurgency to other sectors of society. The workers' actions demonstrated that challenging elites was possible. The multi-racial cooperation in Galveston and St. Louis hinted at the power to be gained by rejecting racist divide and conquer strategies. Craft workers who defied their unions to join the strike provided the underpinnings of a newly emerging strategy of industrial unionism that made the 1894 railroad strike possible.

Prior cycles of struggle that achieved some level of gain had the additional lesson that challenges were not just possible but could also be successful. The 1877 strike opened a small but growing rupture in the polity that gave access to otherwise marginalised groups. The Workingmen's Party's modicum of success in local and state elections after the 1877 strike was followed by the growing success of the People's Party after the 1886 strike and Haymarket Square for the eight-hour work day. The populists eventually captured control of a number of Southern state governments, threatening to break the two party duopoly in place since 1866. They were followed in turn by the Socialist Party that made significant local gains in the first decade of the twentieth century following decades of class turmoil. The populist and socialist parties were mass movements that translated class grievances into demands for changes to the political system and economic policies to turn capital over to public control and ownership. During WWI, faced with disruption of war production, wildcat strikes compelled government-imposed arbitration awards frequently characterised by less work and more pay. The end of WWI also brought about votes for women and access for the unions to the political arena.

Local reformers could play their hand during strikes, advocating for policies that had previously failed to gain traction or support. Using an inside/outside strategy, these reformers frequently channelled dissent into the streets not merely to support the strike but to enhance the credibility and persuasiveness of their own grievances. Such reformers provided legal defence for fired and prosecuted strikers bringing their grievances to a regional and even national and international audience that provided further momentum for their efforts. Occasionally, they were swept into office by promising reforms that mostly never materialised – sometimes eventually wielding the reins of power against supporters that voted them into office.

Reformers could draw from the persistent threat of mobilisation, tactical escalation, disruption, and violence occurring in the background to restore stability. As Moore explains,

> the prospect of a peaceful and democratic resolution of serious social conflicts depends rather heavily on the capacity of dominant elements in the society to make those concessions that will split off segments of the discontented and break the force of the radical opposition. For those on top to be willing to make concessions they must be in a position that is strong enough so that concessions do not constitute a mortal blow to their privileges.[18]

The reforms strengthened the hands of the reformers already in the elite coalition, restoring the necessary stability for elites to regroup and shift power back in their favour. 'These leaders, too, ride to power on the back of the waves of anger, hope, and frustration'.[19]

The moment when elites are ready to make concessions presents the greatest opportunity for gains from continued tactical escalation. This is when the greatest risk of systemic rupture exists. In order to build the broadest mass of support so as to raise the opportunities from tactical escalation, workers must recompose their power across geography, industries, firms, sectors, gender, race and position in the production process. As this is occurring, the class struggle can be said to be generalising throughout society. At that time, we see strikes spread not merely across the entire point of production in a single location, firm or industry, but across other sectors of the national and global economy.

Here is the greatest weakness of the insurgency. While the insurgency spread to numerous localities and became generalised in a number of them, their success turned into defeat, as successfully spreading the strike to a new location necessarily resulted in shutting down the rail system that allowed them to communicate and spread the strike from one place to the other. Once the strike arrived at a new place, the insurgency became localised and cut off from the rest of the country. What appeared as a nationwide insurgency quickly became a series of uncoordinated scattered attacks against local elites who were coordinating their efforts through the White House. As the local strikers

---

18   Moore 1969, pp. 6–7.
19   Ibid., p. 7.

settled and went back to work, were overwhelmed by force of arms, or gave up, the insurgency quickly dwindled and the possibility of further rupturing and recomposition of the power of the working-class evaporated.

New Forms of Organisation

Workers' power is a factor of their ability to organise themselves, form alliances with other workers both inside and outside their immediate shop, industry sector, and even region, and build mass support in the community. Organising must occur at both levels simultaneously. To organise their own shop, workers must find ways to overcome not only gender, racial, and other divisions, but also distinctions based on location, skills, seniority, wages, status, and schedule. It is crucial that they articulate shared interests with other workers while overcoming ethnic, gender, and racial barriers of prejudice, patriarchy, language, privilege, customs, and values. To organise, they need to not only speak to and organise fellow workers with shared positions, conditions, and grievances but also speak to one another's class interests specific to their particular places in the hierarchy of power, privilege and status. To transform the strike into an insurgency, they must find allies in other shops, companies, industries, and sectors of society and devise ways to continue circulating the struggle to overcome internal class divisions of geographic space, boundaries, nationality, language, etc.

The process by which people with shared grievances are brought together to engage in political mobilisation are characterised by what Tilly calls cumulative and constructive factors. Cumulative (or better subjective) factors are those that cause social dislocations, fractures, stress, and cleavages that generate shared grievances among otherwise disparate people. When people affected by these social changes and conditions recognise a shared interest, they become willing to join together to form organisations and engage in collective action with common objectives. Constructive (or better structural) factors are the structural features of the economy and social institutions and processes that strategically bring people with shared interests and grievances together. Among these factors are the economic relations of production, division of labour, social networks, and political power and relationships.[20]

Overcoming internal class divisions is necessary, but not sufficient for engaging in collective action. Actions limited to a specific shop will have limited

---

20   Tilly 1989, p. 8.

objectives, and will rarely become an insurgency. To have what Beverly Silver calls 'workplace bargaining power' a local strike must be strategically situated to disrupt a critical industry.[21] While the strategy and objectives determine the tactics, the tactics and strategy determine the alliances that will provide mass support to achieve the objectives. For example, a strike by only white or skilled workers may not be sufficient to adequately disrupt production since the shop may still be able to operate without them. A single strike in a single department of a single shop will have little disruptive effect on the company and economy, and will lack the strategic leverage to force concessions in order to remove the strain. Such a strike cannot facilitate the cumulative and constructive factors. Even if they win, the former strikers will be forced to break the strike of fellow workers in other parts of the same shop if they sign a contract.

To promote constructive factors, an alliance with workers in other shops and companies will also prevent the slack in production being picked up by other subsidiaries or competitors, increasing production to fill demand and diluting the impact of the strike on the entire sector. Similarly, another shop may supply an alternative component that allows the struck shop to continue operating. Management may also be able to implement a new division of labour to continue operating with a reduced workforce. The lack of mass support will make it more likely that members of the local population will be recruited as strikebreakers. While the 1877 strike had significant mass support in the opening days that shut down much of the rail system, the greatest threat to the strike were the craft brotherhoods that refused to join it and released their members to strikebreak.

It is insufficient to strike a single industry. Striking a single shop or even the shops in a single region will not prevent the other points of production from increasing their output to compensate. Competitors may also rush an alternative product or technologies to market to take advantage of shortages of goods disrupted by the strike. The company may stockpile necessary supplies in an effort to outlast the strike. Production may be shifted to another location and redesigned to reduce vulnerability to disruption. While the railroad companies were unprepared to pursue any of these strategies in 1877, the new composition of capital put into place soon after (see Chapter 3) gave them the strategic advantage during the 1894 strike. This was the lesson learned by the miners in

---

21   Silver describes the strategy of 'workplace bargaining power' that 'accrues to workers who
         are enmeshed in tightly integrated production processes, where a localized work stoppage
         in a key node can cause disruptions on a much wider scale than the stoppage itself' (Silver
         2003, p. 13).

the lead up to the 1900–2 strike when they proposed organising all the workers in both the anthracite and bituminous fields and sought an alliance with workers on the railroads that moved the coal. Striking a single company may result in the proverbial cutting off of the nose to spite the face, not realising the company they are striking is actually a silent subsidiary, shadow investor, or shareholder in another that they aren't striking. This is one of the causes of the repeated defeats of the miners' strikes in the anthracite or bituminous fields between 1897 and 1914.

Even striking a single industry may fail to provide the crucial leverage to create sufficient systemic disruption to force elites to make concessions. After the introduction of the telephone and gas-powered truck, rail strikes lost their power to generate sufficient systemic disruption in the distribution of communications, goods, and people. That accounts for the less disruptive impact of the 1919 and 1922 railroad strikes compared to the 1877 and 1894 strikes. For one sector to succeed it is necessary to find leverage available in as many other related sectors as possible by circulating the struggle. By disrupting multiple sectors of the economy simultaneously, investors will lose the option to shift their assets elsewhere or make a technological fix and are likely to push for rapid settlement. The inescapability of this lesson is illustrated in the new composition of capital that emerged after 1877 (see Chapter 3). Capital consolidation both within the railroad and across related sectors gave it the assets, flexibility, and power to weather the 1894 railroad strikes and later coal and rail strikes discussed above.

Despite the mass support that raised the opportunity to gain from escalating tactics, the 1877 strikers were catastrophically incapable of addressing these strategic prerequisites because they lacked the means to coordinate the strike between the numerous localities dispersed across dozens of states and to continue circulating it to other related sectors. The strike did not usher in a recomposition of working-class power sufficient to both disrupt the accumulation of capital and fracture the emerging fusion between capital and the state. Although workers expanded their power in the ways described, they had not fully succeeded in sufficiently recomposing their power to confront the existing conditions and organisation of capital with whom they did battle.

The lack of capacity to coordinate action spurred a vibrant debate about the most effective means of organisation. According to Foner,

> Labor learned two fundamental lessons from the great strike: first, that future success would depend upon effective national organization along trade union and political lines. The role of local, state, and national governments in crushing the strike convinced workers that no reliance could

be placed on either of the major parties. Second, labor realised the executive committees set up during a struggle and scattered mass meetings were not enough. Strikers with hungry families to feed required swift relief payments. Hastily established committees could not meet this need. The railroad strike proved the necessity of strong unions with an adequate dues system to meet strike expenses.[22]

Yet, the lesson for labour would eclipse Foner's narrow assumption of the need for a revolutionary workers' party. The emerging debate was far broader, encompassing whether organising should follow the craft or new industrial model, whether it should be subordinated to a socialist party, and later whether there should be a formal union organisation that signs contracts or facilitates workers' exerting direct power on the shopfloor. Whatever the organisational question, it was of utmost importance to address the relationship of capital and the state in order to devise new ways to counter the repressive tactics they now faced.

The strike had caught the attention of Karl Marx, who wrote to Frederick Engels on 25 July 1877 about the potential for the recomposition of the black and white and rural and urban working-class as a political force.

> What do you think of the workers in the United States? This first eruption against the oligarchy of associated capital which has arisen since the Civil War will of course be put down, but it could quite well form the starting point for the establishment of a serious labor party in the United States. There are moreover two favorable circumstances. The policy of the new President will turn the Negroes into allies of the workers, and the large expropriations of land (especially fertile land) in favor of railway, mining, etc., companies will convert the farmers of the West, who are already very disenchanted, into allies of the workers. Thus a fine mess is in the offing over there, and transferring the centre of the International to the United States might, *post festum*, turn out to have been a peculiarly opportune move.[23]

Like DuBois decades later, Marx too saw the critical importance of a bi-racial alliance between black and white workers.[24] The populist uprising soon to fol-

---

22   Foner 1977, pp. 473–4.

23   Marx, 25 July 1877, p. 137.

24   DuBois 1935, pp. 353 and 359.

low proved Marx partially correct in forecasting a farmer-labour alliance, but like Foner his focus on the revolutionary workers' party as the answer to the organisational needs of the working-class was misplaced.

Many sought to answer the organisational question by organising more unions. In the face of federal intervention, the organisational imperative of survival made the craft unions even more cautious for fear of losing existing members and the dues they paid. The brotherhoods were beginning to become firmly entrenched among the skilled railroad workers at this time but had already hitched their railcars to the fortunes of capital. These unions not only opposed the strikes but actively sabotaged their efforts by prohibiting their members from acting in solidarity and contributing organisational resources such as communications infrastructure to help. The Grand Chief of the Order of Railway Conductors, which only had 1,100 members at the time, noted after the strike that it refused to offer any support to what it called 'unwise and desperate attempts to coerce their and our employers'.[25] Although he would later lead the American Railway Union during the 1894 railroad strike, Eugene Debs, then a top official of the Brotherhood of Locomotive Firemen, was also vehemently opposed to the strike. He told the 1877 Firemen's Indianapolis convention that he did not support the strike because it 'terrified the entire nation ... [and] signified anarchy and revolution'.

> Does the brotherhood encourage strikers? To this question we must emphatically answer, No, brothers. To disregard the laws which govern our land? To destroy the last vestige of order? To stain our hands with the crimson blood of our fellow beings? We again say, No, a thousand times No![26]

The 1877 strike provided an early glimpse into the institutional role that unions would begin to play at a much greater scale once it was recognised by capital

---

25   Bruce 1959, p. 224.
26   Ibid., p. 224. When Debs later argued for ending a strike by a coalition of engineers, firemen, and switchmen on the Chicago, Burlington & Quincy Railroad Company in 1888 he was reportedly shouted down and interrupted by the shouting firemen. The strike had been forced upon the brotherhood leadership by self organised workers who formed themselves into parallel committees inside the brotherhoods and were supported by the Knights of Labor. These self-organised workers attempted to form a 'systems federation' of the brotherhoods which laid the groundwork for the later ARU. The engineers killed the federation proposal by limiting cooperation to only the firemen. (See Stromquist 1993, pp. 70–2).

that the best defence against unruly workers was a contract with a union that could apply its organisational resources to discipline, demobilise, and diffuse self-organised workers tugging at their leashes. Ironically, the more effectively they played this role, the more the craft unions wrote their obituaries. As their work became deskilled, their pool of potential members shrank until they were perceived to no longer be an effective partner for industry.

In addition to giving impetus to socialist and labour parties, the strike also stimulated experimentation with new types of organising and unions. 'After the uprising of July, labor knew its strength; and gradually, painfully, it learned how to use it' and the type of organisation to realise it.[27] The dual threats of craft unionism and repression of organising above ground spurred the founding of the Knights of Labor, which held its first national convention in Reading, Pennsylvania on 1 January 1878. Despite initially operating as a secret workers' society, the Knights grew dramatically over the next eight years along with the formation of more city central labour bodies by socialists.[28]

The newly organised Knights of Labor began to gel as a national organisation and went public in 1882, although not initially as a union. The union went through an internal struggle over the most appropriate tactics and strategy to organise the working-class to face these new forces of production. The Knights had three wings. The craft workers faction, which accepted capitalism and sought compromise, eventually splitting off to merge into the new AFL. The second faction was that of founder Uriah Stephens and his successor Terence Powderly, who rejected strikes and sought to organise small-scale craft production and cooperatives and promote class harmony. The last rank and file faction sought to organise all the unorganised along what would become known as the industrial union model.[29]

Organising the Knights was an effort to meet the challenges of the tactics that defeated the 1877 strike. The Knights advocated for an eight-hour day, equal pay for men and women, labour arbitration, national currency, abolishing labour for children under 14, health and safety, a postal savings bank to replace private banking system, government ownership of the telephone, telegraph and railroads. While not a party, the Knights, ability to connect the political and economic conditions faced by workers put it ahead of its time.

As workers flocked to the organisation, invigorated by its broad vision of industrial democracy, its leadership resisted the pull towards the rank and file's

---

27   Bruce 1959, p. 318.
28   Foner 1978, p. 498.
29   Levine 1977, pp. 102–3.

effort to make it an industrial fighting force. Led by Scranton, Pennsylvania Mayor Terence Powderly, it initially opposed the use of strikes, instead embracing a populist agrarian democracy and land reform as solutions to the ills of industrial capitalism. Just like the Workingmen's Party, the national leadership of the Knights of Labor disavowed tactical escalation and disruption, seeing itself as a moderating force. The national leadership's refusal to embrace rank and file tactical escalation put it into conflict with industry-wide strikes of skilled, unskilled and day labourers that included both black and white workers organised by autonomously functioning local assemblies. These strikes changed the Knights from below, prompting it to organise workers by industry instead of skill or job type and regardless of gender and race, an early strategy that would become known as industrial unionism.

Some workers took yet another approach. Recognising the vulnerability of unarmed workers facing elite coordinated police, private agents, militia and the US Army, some militant German and other central European immigrant groups began preparations for further armed resistance. According to Adamic's sometimes whimsical history of strike violence,

> ... After the riots many commenced to gather in secret revolutionary meetings. The underdog movement was thus driven underground. Groups of workers even began to provide themselves with arms and to drill in the woods in preparation for the forthcoming final battles with capitalism – 'the Revolution' – in which they meant to meet the police and the soldiers with guns and bombs. The explosion of the Haymarket Bomb was but a few years in the future.[30]

These ethnic cells were joined by anarchists who also advocated for escalating tactics to include self-defence and scattered attacks, 'propaganda by the deed' that targeted the worst corporate offenders and struck at vulnerable sites of the capitalist economy. However, because these efforts were at best auxiliary to organised class struggle, they are not considered in this book.

While the strike may have been repressed and some of the wage cuts reversed or postponed, industrial peace was not at hand. Bruce observed that

> there was no peace. Reverberations followed, and sympathetic detonations. Then, after the dust settled and the debris was cleared away, came

---

30   Adamic 1931, p. 28.

the work of building anew. Meanwhile, fissures had been started and forces released, the ends of which were not to be seen by that generation.[31]

That was left for 40 years in the future.

Recomposing Working-Class Power

There is one question that has yet to be definitively answered: was the 1877 strike a failure? Workers might have gained little, but what they did achieve was impossible only 10 days earlier. Considering the refusal to negotiate, the dire conditions of the nearly four-year-old depression, they accomplished what was possible. Certainly the strike was perceived as more threatening by capital than the left and unions at the time or historians since.

'A Dismal Failure'?
Foner concluded that demanding – and achieving – a reversal of the wage cuts made the strike a failure.

> [At] no point did the workers have either the power or the leadership to have transformed the strikes into a revolutionary seizure of the economy or the state ... Judged purely as a strike movement against wage cuts, the great upheaval of 1877 had to be considered a dismal failure. In other respects too, the labor rebellion seemed to have ended in what could only be called a defeat for the workers.[32]

But this is far too simple. First, the demand was for reversing the cut and the doubling of productivity with double headers that was certain to make the work more deadly. While their objectives were hardly revolutionary, successfully resisting a cut in wages and maintaining the same level of productivity was no small feat. Their ability to realise their objectives was a reflection of their power, not their weakness. The use of tactical violence as a disruptive force to accomplish their objectives '[grew] from an impatience born of confidence and rising efficacy rather than the opposite ... it is not the weakness of the user

---

31   Bruce 1959, p. 292.
32   Foner 1977, pp. 11 and 204.

but the weakness of the target that accounts for violence'.[33] In the midst of a depression capital was weak.

Second, the railroad strike let a thousand flowers bloom. It provided the spark for numerous other struggles to be launched which, paired with the railroad strike, made many of them successful.

In a little more than a week, strikers accomplished a range of subtle but important tasks. In addition to winning their modest tangible gains, they overcame their destitute conditions to mobilise wide mass support, escalated their tactics to take advantage of opportunities and lower costs, experimented with multiracial and multi-ethnic alliances, spread the strike to additional geographical areas and railroad lines, took up arms in self-defence, and articulated their objectives and a political vision by taking over the running of St. Louis and three other cities.

Foner's analysis of the strike is typical. He saw it as economistic and non-revolutionary because it lacked a formal centralised leadership, party or union, and an identifiable class consciousness. Seeing the lack of a revolutionary organisation and programme, he saw a reformist movement. Such a view detracts from the immense importance of how a horizontally self-organised strike lacking a centrally organised leadership could disrupt nearly the entire national economy.

If the level of repression is an indicator of the level of the threat, then having to resort to deploying the US Army to suppress the strike speaks for itself. The institutional relations of power, coercion, and the normative system that typically channel or discourage protest had disintegrated. The level of the threat posed by the disruptive power of the strike and the spread of worker insubordination were reflected in the counter-attack: the new technological, legal, organisational, political, and tactical innovations to repress it and prepare for the next one. From another view, there was not merely one strike but many that grew out of local struggles, circulating across geographic, industrial, and racial divides. The strike defeated the wage cut and the new division of labour illustrated by the double header (e.g. measures in Marx's terms intended to increase absolute and relative surplus value) and discourage further investment in the industry in the short term. In response, the federal government reorganised the military and state militias, local and state governments revamped the police, and capital began integrating the railroads and concentrating ownership and control vertically across mining, iron and banking over the coming decades.

---

33   Gamson 1975, p. 81.

These tactical actions were convincing evidence of the power of the working-class to disrupt the process of capital accumulation in 1877 in the midst of the worst depression in US history.

Perhaps the most astute observation of the threat of the strike came from former President U.S. Grant who was near death at the time. Upon hearing that US troops had been sent against the strikers, Grant wrote on 26 August 1877 that both the Democratic and Republican press thought it

> horrible to keep US troops stationed in the Southern States, and when they were called upon to protect the lives of negroes – as much citizens under the Constitution as if their skins were white – the country was scarcely large enough to hold the sound of indignation belched forth by them for some years. Now, however, there is no hesitation about exhausting the whole power of the government to suppress a strike on the slightest intimation that danger threatens.[34]

The fortunes of the 1877 strike were indubitably intertwined with the fortunes of Reconstruction, itself a threat to capital. DuBois's observation that

> The South, after the war, presented the greatest opportunity for a real national labor movement which the nation ever saw or is likely to see for many decades. Yet the labor movement, with but few exceptions, never realised the situation. It never had the intelligence or knowledge, as a whole, to see in black slavery and Reconstruction, the kernel and meaning of the labor movement in the United States ... The labor leaders went into the labor war of 1877 having literally disarmed themselves of the power of universal suffrage. And thus in 1876, when Northern industry withdrew military support in the South and refused to support longer the dictatorship of labor, they did this without any opposition or any intelligent comprehension of what was happening on the part of the Northern white worker.[35]

DuBois's insight is that black and white workers missed a strategic opportunity to connect different cycles of the same struggle. The general strike launched by black workers against slave plantation capital spread north to mostly white workers targeting industrial capital. The defeat of the 1877 strike sealed the

---

34   Grant 2005, pp. 251–2.
35   DuBois 1935, pp. 353 and 359.

defeat of the largest slave strike in history that began during the Civil War and evolved into the forward thinking economic and political reforms in the South known as Reconstruction. During this brief period, black strikers managed to transform their class power into political emancipation and political reform. If Reconstruction brought Northern and Southern white capital together to oppose it, racism kept black and white workers apart defeating Reconstruction.

Activists and revolutionaries have long futilely sought the Holy Grail for precipitating such cycles of struggle. There is no formula for translating struggles from one place to another. What DuBois portrayed as the greatest strike in American history by slaves clearly circulated to miners, railroad and industrial workers in 1877 although the material details by which that may have been the case have yet to be uncovered by historical research. That the strike was initially launched in West Virginia, where the population broke off from Virginia, refusing to join the Confederacy, much like those in the recent Hollywood film *Free State of Jones*, deserves further investigation.

Working-Class Recomposition

To assess its potential power, workers closely study the organisation of capital both at the point of production and in the political space it occupies, controls or dominates. There are several key elements to this analysis necessary to any effort to recompose working-class power. It is necessary to identify the means of control, alienation, domination, and separation of workers. How is work organised, who does it, and what is the process of exploitation of waged and unwaged labour? What challenges are faced by the existing relations of production, division of labour, and technologies of work? Studying these material details informs a strategy to overcome the divisions among the working-class that block or prevent it from self-organising as a class. It also highlights the weakest links in the relations of production and reproduction onto which tactical leverage can be applied.

Understanding workers' power is interwoven with understanding capital's power. As Panzieri explains, 'The capitalistic social relationship is concealed within the technical demands of machinery', that is, understanding the tools of work can illuminate the relations of production and reproduction.[36] But inversely, the relations of production and reproduction also tell us about the organisation of society. Marx observed that

---

36   Panzieri 1976, p. 9.

The a-priori system on which the division of labour within the work-shop is regularly carried out, becomes in the division of labour within the society an a-posteriori, nature-imposed necessity, controlling the lawless caprice of the producers, and perceptible in the barometric fluctuation of the market prices.[37]

What appears to be 'natural' or objective can be read in the financial data, government reports, and historical record. Reading through the data allows us to provide what Cleaver calls an 'inversion of class perspective' to find local points of class struggle.[38] The inversion is extremely valuable when the first-hand accounts of workers are missing.

When these accounts are available, the answer to these questions can be found in 'the daily experience of people that shapes their grievances, establishes the measure of their demands, and points out the targets of their anger'. For Piven and Cloward, the 'institutional patterns shape mass movements by shaping the collectivity out of which protest can arise. Institutional life aggregates people or disperses them, molds group identities, and draws people into the settings within which collective action can erupt'.[39]

In these settings new social formations and collectivities form both on and off the shop floor. Workers engage in 'small scale actions' that test their strength and probe for elites' weaknesses. In time small-scale actions produce small-scale successes that provide experience in developing tactics and strategies, mobilising allies, and assessing costs and opportunities for further success by tactical escalation. Those who learn this art of class struggle emerge as organisers and leaders. As Tilly and Tilly explain,

> Small-scale struggles over such [grievance] issues occur all the time ... Workers initiate such contention chiefly when they can see that collective action has a chance of gaining them more in these regards, or at least losing them less, than existing inaction. Workers 'seeing' operates, of course, within the limits set by existing work mechanisms, preferred configurations, current threats/opportunities, available connecting net-workers, known means of coordination, plans for strategic interaction, disposable incentives, and shared definitions of possible action-outcome combinations. As with technological invention, innovation in conten-

---

37   Marx 1867b, p. 390.
38   Cleaver 1992.
39   Piven and Cloward 1978, pp. 20–1.

tion follows strongly path-dependent trajectories, referring repeatedly to accumulated, reinterpreted experiences in past and present.[40]

In 1877 organisers, whose names have mostly been lost to the historical record, did just that by drawing on the concentration of large numbers of workers to act where they found themselves on widely shared grievances both on and off the shop floor. In some places it was workers in the short-lived effort to launch the Trainmen's Union but in others it was workers brought together by shared grievances in their shops, on their lines, and in their communities.

Strikers implicitly recognised that abandoning engines on tracks in key points on the rail system would cause a backlog across entire regions and that replicating the backlog in enough key locations would shut down the entire national rail system, even if only a minority of workers were actively participating. Ironically, the workers who devised this strategy were almost immediately repressed and never had the chance to complete their strategic analysis before their fellow workers ran with it. Although the repression cost at least 100 strikers' and supporters' lives with countless hundreds of others injured by the military repression that followed, the initial attempt to repress the strike failed when working-class members of the local militias themselves mutinied. Unfortunately, stopping the rail system had the unintended effect of also choking off workers' ability to spread the strike by face to face communication and through the telegraph system that was cut by the railroad companies.[41]

As we will see in Chapters 4, 5, and 6, the defeat of the 1877 strike laid the foundation for the later defeat of the 1894 strike. The fusion of capital and the state begun in 1877 was combined with capital consolidation across the banking, mining, and rail sectors, accelerating after 1877 to provide a new composition of capital of which the strikers were not yet fully aware. At the time the average factory employed less than ten workers.[42] As the size of firms grew they brought more workers together under a single factory roof, into a single firm, onto a single rail line, and into a single industry. The previous cycles of struggle which peaked in 1877 prompted capital to also begin reorganising management and control over work in order to dampen the disruptive potential of large numbers of insubordinate industrial workers.

Despite their efforts to deploy a strategy of industrial union organising, in which all workers in a single shop, company, or industry are in the same union,

---

40   Tilly and Tilly 1998, p. 243.
41   Burbank 1966, p. 69.
42   Stromquist 1993, p. 5.

workers threatened but were unsuccessful in overcoming the existing composition of capital. It was not for the lack of effort. Between 1886–94 'non-economic' strikes outnumbered 'defensive' strikes by as much as three to one and exceeded 'offensive' and 'defensive' strikes in 1893–4.[43] 'Noneconomic', or what Montgomery calls 'control', strikes were struggles to resist efforts by management to undermine or weaken workers' authority and control over work rules, speed, productivity, and other characteristics of work.[44]

'Non-economic' strikes can be distinguished from offensive and defensive. Several strategic patterns emerged when railroad workers struck over non-economic grievances. Such strikes often preceded offensive wage strikes to use their prior success as a launching pad to further circulate and expand their struggle. One of the unrecognised outcomes of the 1877 strike was that railroad workers went on the offensive from 1881 to 1894 with offensive non-economic strikes outnumbering defensive strikes except for the two years 1886 and 1890. Offensive non-economic strikes more than tripled between 1892 and 1894.[45]

These occurred in the context of the brutal depression in which workers continued to escalate their tactics even while the chance of success declined.[46] The depression altered the fundamental objectives of these strikes which 'were not strikes over incremental control issues: they were contests over the fundamental relationship between labor and capital'.[47] It would be a mistake to assume these were defensive strikes reacting to the deteriorating conditions of the depression. Rather, class struggle triggered the crisis as railroad financiers sought to flee to safer financial speculation in the midst of the threat posed by the massive growth of industrial railroad workers using disruption to assert their demands. Continued strikes during the depression may have further lengthened the extent of the depression, which left 25 percent of the railroads seeking protection of the federal courts from their insurgent workers, hoping to gain time to impose a new composition of capital. It is thus not surprising that tactical escalation became increasingly offensive rather than defensive.

One illustration of the offensive character of the noneconomic strikes was the explosion of sympathy strikes between 1884–8 and in 1894 (see Table 2).

---

43   Stromquist 1993, pp. 34–5.

44   Montgomery 1974, p. 515; Montgomery 1979, pp. 94–8; and Stromquist 1993, p. 35.

45   Stromquist 1993, pp. 36–7.

46   Stromquist argues that such offensive non-economic strikes rose rapidly even while the success of all non-economic strikes fell dramatically, although no data is presented to support this. (Ibid., p. 36).

47   Ibid., p. 38.

TABLE 2   *Proportion of railroad*
            strikes involving
            sympathy strikes

1885	11 percent
1886	27 percent
1887	45 percent
1888	35 percent
1894	85 percent

STROMQUIST 1993, P. 38
Note: Stromquist noted that
the number between 1889–1893
was very low due in part to the
intransigence of the brotherhoods.

Sympathy strikes were the product of the workers' ability to circulate their struggle to new lines and geographical locations. Rather than retreat to defend against firings, wage cuts, and increased productivity demands, workers were using the momentum that had sent the industry into crisis to continue to expand their struggle to more workers and communities. Tapped into the hostile sentiment towards the railroads among workers and the middle class in their communities, railroad workers used their growing mass support and strategic leverage of disruption to strike more not less, even in the midst of several consecutive depressions. Stromquist attributes the decline in sympathy strikes between 1889–93 and the uptick again in 1894 to the workers' need to deploy a new industrial organisation with sufficient rank and file power to use the tactic to disrupt the entire national railroad system.[48]

Coupled with the growing frequency of sympathy strikes is a significant number of unsanctioned or wildcat strikes during this period. While the number of wildcat railroad strikes declined from 82 percent in 1881 to 47 percent in 1894, one cannot ignore the fact that it remained nearly half of all strikes during this period.[49] By definition, wildcat strikes are launched by self-organised workers who defy efforts by the union leadership to repress, diffuse, or limit a strike. Although Stromquist attributes the founding of the ARU to rising rank and file militancy within the railroad brotherhoods that pushed for these sympathy and wildcat strikes, the ARU leadership was not exempt from the same

---

48   Ibid., p. 39.
49   Ibid., pp. 40–1.

militancy.[50] Ultimately, as we will see in Chapter 4, the 1894 strikes were forced on Eugene Debs and the other leadership despite their persistent effort to avoid a sympathy strike with the Pullman Palace Car Company strikers. The persistence of sympathy and wildcat strikes spurred efforts to resolve strikes by voluntary arbitration soon after the 1894 strike and was mandated during WWI (see Chapter 8). Reformers acknowledged that without arbitration or collective bargaining, unions were insufficient to control and regulate workers and prevent strikes and other forms of disruption.

The high numbers of sympathy and wildcat strikes would seem to counter the commonly accepted premise in labour studies that strikes, whether sanctioned or wildcat, decline during a depression when workers are vulnerable to losing their jobs and risk not finding a new one. The evidence during the 1880s and 1890s appears to show that workers are more likely to engage in offensive strikes even when the risk of unemployment is high if they have substantial mass support, can bypass the efforts of union leadership to prevent them, and can successfully circulate their struggle.

In each cycle of struggle, workers study their own class composition and that of capital, and launch the appropriate offensive or defensive tactics. While their study may not be explicit, it can be read in the tactics and strategies they pursue. Upsurges in class conflict will commonly be followed by the reorganisation of work. Tilly and Tilly explain that

> Collective contention often results in deliberate, abrupt reorganizations of work and its personnel instead of the incremental, piecemeal, trial-and-error alterations that characterize most transformations: mass firings, new work rules, changes in wage schedules, introduction of novel labor process, and more.[51]

As Panzieri tells us: new tools, new social relations of capital.

These new 'innovations', promoted in the name of 'efficiency', 'best practices' and the like, shift the balance of power back to capital and over time workers reset and relaunch their struggles on a new terrain. As Silver observes,

> revolutions in the organization of production and social relations may disorganise some elements of the working class … But new agencies and

---

50   Ibid., p. 41.
51   Tilly and Tilly 1998, p. 253.

sites of conflict emerge along with new demands and forms of struggle, reflecting the shifting terrain on which labor-capital relations develop.[52]

New tactics and strategies emerge in response to workers' reading of the new terrain, conditions, and division of labour. As Tilly and Tilly observe, 'we should expect today's contention (its collective claims, strategic interaction, and deployment of incentives) likewise to alter in response to transformations of work mechanisms'.[53] For this reason, the dynamic between the recomposition of the working-class and capital's attempts to decompose it tells us that 'labor and labor movements are continually made and remade'.[54]

Insurgents do not blindly act at the point of production or go into the streets unless they have some way to assess the balance of class power, the level of mass support, and the costs and opportunities of mobilising and escalating their tactics. The ability to assess these factors determine the necessary tactic, or combination of tactics, and the appropriate level of intensity and force required to achieve their objectives. Such a tactical assessment is informed by the composition of capital and the recomposition of the working-class or the balance of power over the social relations which govern the organisation of work. It provides the analytical framework to evaluate why workers escalate their tactics.

It is common to assume that in capitalism the owners of capital have total control. Yet, common economic data on wages, unemployment, productivity, return on investment, and share of productivity returned as income can show fluctuations that reflect the shifting balance of power between capital and labour even when collective action appears to be absent or subdued. Reading these fluctuations can provide invaluable information that can form a tactical analysis, as well as identify vulnerabilities and opportunities to transform everyday forms of resistance, such as what the Industrial Workers of the World called 'striking on the job', in overt forms of mobilised action.[55]

Capital's counter-repertoire puts tactics at its deposal to decompose working-class power.[56] For example, when owners of capital have disproportionate power they can cut wages and force workers to work longer and more intensely. Capital can also alter the division of labour by introducing labour

---

52   Silver 2003, p. 19.
53   Tilly and Tilly 1998, p. 237.
54   Silver 2003, p. 19.
55   Chaplin 1933, p. 6.
56   Isaac 2002, p. 396.

saving technologies or work processes so that workers produce with the same or fewer hours of work. Another option is to transfer the work to a different set of workers over whom management has more control and power. Tilly and Tilly note this dynamic between capital and labour is driven by what they call 'contention'.

> Employers typically responded to major surges in strike activity by trying to substitute other labor for organised workers and other factors of production for labor in general; how well they succeeded in either regard depended in part on available technologies. But it also depended on the current power position of management and organised labor with respect to each other and the state ... far from driving the entire system, employers investments in new technologies and capital intensive production followed the rhythms of labor militancy with a lag for search and imposition of the new forms.[57]

The balance of power between capital and workers is a constant thread that runs throughout each case study in this book because it is the starting point for insurgents to mobilise for renewed action at a higher level of struggle, and the basis of capital's response. The outcome depends on not merely how workers identify the balance of power, but also their ability to shift it in their favour with appropriate and effective tactics and strategies to achieve their objectives.

For example, the balance of power between capital and workers is illustrated by the share of productivity that goes to capital as profits relative to labour as wages and benefits. Shifting most of the gains of productivity to the wealthy, as is well documented to have occurred since the 1970s, means capital has shifted power in its favour. Although workers may organise to demand higher wages and less work, they have been unable to achieve these goals due to the composition of capital that allows it to successfully deploy tactics such as global outsourcing, unemployment, firings, and automation of production or bringing in the state so as to translate its power on the shop floor into repressive political power in the streets.

The balance of power between capital and workers is a dance of give and take in which one side probes the other for points of weakness and continues to attack it until the other side becomes destabilised, fragments, compromises, concedes, withdraws, or escalates. In the language of military strategy this is

---

57   Tilly and Tilly 1998, p. 231.

called a 'war of manoeuvre'.[58] If the adversary manages to survive the attack, it studies the cause of its defeat and the weakness of its opponent in order to devise news forms of organisation, tactics, and strategy by which it can go back on the attack or prepare to repulse the next attack and turn defeat into a victory. The process of studying the conditions of the struggle and devising new forms of organisation, tactics and strategy can be said to be the process of formulating a new composition of class power.

An analysis of class composition flies in the face of the dominant view that workers *react* to the initiative and power of the owners of capital by organising and reacting. Understanding class composition provides another perspective on the cycles of conflict between capital and workers as the outcome of dance of action by workers against capital and reaction of capital to workers. Class composition theory examines class struggle as a dynamic spiral rather than back and forth on a linear plane. Such cycles stand out in the historical record of strikes collected by the US government during the 1880s to 1905 and 1916–20 discussed in Chapters 7 to 10. It can be argued that the increase in strike activity during this time period tells the story of the recomposition of working-class power just as the decline in strikes tells the story of the new composition of capital's power. This recomposition was not limited to the US but was a localised aspect in a global cycle of class struggle.[59]

In this way working-class recomposition flips the causal forces driving social reform. It is at the moment when the threat of rupture to capital is greatest that the great periods of reform – populist, progressive, and New Deal era – have occurred. Piven and Cloward hinge reform on disruption.

---

58   Boyd 1987.
59   Bologna identified three distinct global cycles of class struggle in the first two decades of the twentieth century:

'While in the periods 1904–06, 1911–13, and 1917–20, we face a highly unbalanced capital in advanced and backward areas, we witness an extremely homogeneous political class activity in all countries. Thus, we can speak of a series of international *cycles of struggle* beginning in the 1904–06 period. The specific traits of this first cycle are very clear, even if it is difficult to chronologically locate it. It is the mass strike resulting in violent and insurrectional actions. This is best exemplified in the US[.] Starting in 1901, a series of violent mass strikes shakes the whole US industrial structure. With its center, its class pole, located with the Rocky Mountain miners, these struggles spread primarily among steel, textile, and transportation workers, but, above all, construction workers. In 1905, at the peak of the cycle, while the Soviets were coming into being in Russia, in the US the International [sic] Workers of the World (IWW) was formed: the most radical proletarian organization ever in the U.S., the only revolutionary class organization before the rise of the Afro-American movement' (Bologna 1976, p. 72).

We ordinarily think of major legislation as taking form only through established electoral processes. We tend to overlook the force of crisis in precipitating legislative reform, partly because we lack a theoretical framework by which to understand the impact of major disruptions.[60]

Class composition provides us with a theoretical framework. It allows us to see a disobedient workforce is an unprofitable workforce and needs to not only be displaced or replaced but engineered out of existence by new technologies, management strategies, organisation of work, and social policies that not only deskill or make them obsolete but diffuse the challenge and redirect it in such a way as to restore the capital accumulation process. The new division of labour created by automation, deskilling, and outsourcing subdivides, rationalises, and redistributes the remaining work into its component parts. As an outcome of class struggle, as Noble observed, 'the ultimate viability of these technologies under the present mode of production depends, in the final analysis, upon the political and economic conditions that prevail and upon the relative strengths of the classes in their struggle over the control of production'.[61] The crisis leads both to a new division of labour and reform. The new division of labour is the foundation for a new composition to shift the balance of power back to capital. Corresponding social policies cushion the impact of downward pressure on wages and make work and social conditions more tolerable in order to dampen some of the fervour of grievances while opening limited political space into which they can be channelled.

This, however, is not the end of the story. If capital succeeds in decomposing the working-class's power in the last cycle of struggle, rupture is avoided or delayed and the cycle begins again. After some time workers will study the new relations of class power, the new division of labour, identify where their strengths lie, and learn from previous cycles of struggle to apply new forms of leverage to assert their power to disrupt production both on and off the shop floor. From there the dance begins again, albeit at another level. The assessment of which tactics to deploy is informed by the existing conditions and updated with new tactics and strategies to address the need to recompose working-class power. According to Bell and Cleaver,

> while it can be said that capital seeks a 'class composition,' i.e., a particular distribution of inter- and intra-class power which gives it sufficient

---

60   Piven and Cloward 1966.

61   Noble 1979, p. 40.

control over the working class to guarantee accumulation, it is also true that workers' struggles repeatedly undermine such control and thus rupture the efficacy (from capital's point of view) of such a class composition. Such a rupture occurs only to the degree that workers are able to *recompose* the structures and distribution of power among themselves in such a way as to achieve a change in their collective relations of power to their class enemy.[62]

Each cycle of struggle is a war of manoeuvre between the working-class and capital. As Bell and Cleaver explain,

thus the struggles which achieve such changes bring about a 'political recomposition' of the class relations – 'recomposition' of the intra-class structures of power and 'political' because that in turn changes the inter-class relations ... In response to such an overcoming of its structure of control, of some particular configurations of its mechanisms of domination, capital (i.e., the managers of production) must seek to 'decompose' the workers' newly constructed relations among themselves and create some new, controllable class composition. The introduction of new technologies, of new organizations of machinery and workers, if successful, results in the undermining of workers struggles and their reduction, once more, to the status of labor power. But whatever new 'class composition' is achieved, it only becomes the basis for further conflicts because the class antagonism can only be managed; it cannot be done away with. Thus, these three new concepts, one static and two dynamic, provide guides to the analysis of what have come to be called 'cycles of class struggle,' wherein the upswing in such a cycle involves a period of political recomposition by workers and the downswing, however much the workers win or lose, a process of class decomposition through which capital reestablishes sufficient control to continue its overall management of society.[63]

This tension between recomposition and decomposition mark out the moments of instability and what Cleaver calls the rupture of capital's dialectic which can either be harnessed, thereby restoring stability and generating vast new wealth, or managed so that tensions are diffused or rechannelled in ways

---

62   Bell and Cleaver 2002, pp. 50–1.
63   Ibid.

that allow just enough conflict while avoiding the possibility of disruption in order to restart accumulation.[64]

The interplay between capital and workers, Holloway suggests, is analogous to a dog straining on the leash held by its owner, always threatening to break free. Unless the leash is broken workers will remained harnessed to capital as the social relation relentlessly asserts itself.[65] 'The paradox of capitalism is that both workers and capital struggle constantly, in different ways, to liberate themselves from labour. There is, in the peculiar form of the antagonism between capital and work, a centrifugal one: the two poles of the antagonistic relation repel each other. There is a mutual repulsion between humanity and capital (obvious enough, but all-important).'[66]

The continual struggle between capital and workers shows itself in the disruption of the accumulation process. From the 1877 railroad strike to the West Virginia Mine Wars the interplay of capital composition and working-class decomposition and recomposition at each cycle of class struggle was at the same time a *danse macabre* in which workers escalated their tactics, threatening to rupture capital's dialectic.

Tilly's repertoire of contention cannot make sense without taking into account the material relation and struggle over class power in existing capitalist society. It shapes not only an interplay between the two distinct sets of interests, objectives, tactics, opportunities, and costs, but also the struggle of one to dominate the other. But herein lies the paradox. As Holloway notes, the objectives of capital and workers are in fundamental opposition: capital seeks to dominate workers while workers seek to break free of capital. The ultimate

---

64   Cleaver 2016, p. 77.

65   He writes:

'crisis comes not when owner and dog run in opposite directions, but when the unity of the relation asserts itself through the leash. Dog and owner may have forgotten about their attachment, but eventually it asserts itself, independently of their will. It is the same with capital: no matter how much labour and capital may wish to forget about their mutual relationship, eventually it asserts itself. Behind all the forms that the relationship may take lies the fact that capital is nothing but objectivized labour. The process of social disarticulation does not in itself constitute a crisis ... all that does not matter too much as long as the production of capital (that is, the objectivisation of doing) itself is not threatened. The dis-articulation of social relations means that the reproduction of capital depends on one particular type of social practice-the production of surplus value. It is when the dis-articulation of social relations threatens the production of surplus value (expressed through money as profit) that the underlying unity of social relations asserts itself' (Holloway 2002, p. 190).

66   Ibid.

objective of the class struggle for workers is to not merely shift the balance of power but to destroy it, rupture capital's dialectic and free themselves from being workers.[67]

This book proposes three corollaries using class composition theory. First, we find the greatest momentum for implementing reform during 'upswings' in class struggle when the working-class has recomposed its power and the greatest momentum for dismantling reforms during 'downswings' when the new composition of capital is successful in decomposing working-class power. This ebb and flow of class struggle is woven throughout the case studies in this book. During WWI the federal government imposed arbitrated settlements that raised wages and shortened work hours in response to workers' power to disrupt war production and revoked it after the war had ended once the costs of disruption fell.

The second corollary is that workers achieved their greatest gains by tactical escalation – even when using tactical violence – rather than de-escalation, demobilisation, and negotiation. In other words, peaceful change by negotiation without being paired with the threat of tactical escalation was insufficient in itself to achieve any gains for workers.

Lastly, the decomposition of workers' power allows concessionary reforms to be transformed into the means to discipline, manage, and suppress class conflict and harness it to the accumulation process. Since reform is the outcome of the failure of repression alone it cannot in itself be the objective of class struggle, but only a strategy that helps establish the next higher level of struggle. Reform is a grudging recognition that, as Cleaver suggested, the 'class antagonism ... cannot be done away with' but only managed. The rise of welfarism, mandatory arbitration, and union recognition gained during the half century of this book are capital's concessions to decades of working-class struggle that it could only manage but not completely defeat. It is a compelling lesson that was finally learned by the institutionalisation and legalisation of collective bargaining in the 1930s. But much as previous reforms conceded in victory have been transformed into defeat, this lesson has been mostly forgotten over the past four decades.

---

67   Ibid.

CHAPTER 3

Putting Out the Class on Fire: A New Capital Composition

If the 1877 strike announced the arrival of an unruly industrial working-class capable of launching an insurgency, it also marked a reorganisation of elite power in preparation for the next cycle of class struggle sure to follow. The strike made evident the urgent need to reorganise the elite coalitions and innovate the relationship between capital and the state. Before the strike, the state provided land, subsidies, and the military for Indian removal. After the strike, state power was extended to manage class conflict by expanding and reorganising the courts, police, militia, and military, and consolidating and integrating the disparate industrial sectors paralysed by the strike.[1]

For elites, the central focus was on how to shift that balance back in its favour by devising a new composition of capital to meet the challenge of working-class power. The *New York Times* observed that the 1877 strike demonstrated that

> the workmen have here and there compelled compliance with their demands, and in other instances they have attracted popular attention to their grievances, real or alleged, to an extent that will render future indifference impossible ... [T]he balance of gain is on the side of the workmen.[2]

The 1877 strike was a harbinger of the disruptive and destabilising power of a recomposed working-class power and a warning to elites that the outcome of class struggle was not foretold. Capital needed to regroup if it was going to meet the challenge of the next insurgency. As the country was gripped by sensationalist media warnings of the 'mob' and 'communists', a new composition of capital was formed to meet the challenge. Several new tactics first deployed in 1877 would be refined over the coming decades. They were intended to raise the costs and reduce the opportunities of achieving gains from mobilising and escalating tactics in an effort to decompose working-class power.

---

1 Stromquist makes a similar point that the instruments of capital-state innovation were driven by the need to 'contain and defuse industrial conflict'. (See Stromquist 1993, p. 24).

2 Bruce 1959, p. 301.

A New Composition of Capital

The 1877 strike prompted an existential threat captured by a letter from the Gatling Gun Company, manufacturers of the Gatling gun, possibly the deadliest weapon of its era, to the president of the Baltimore & Ohio railroad during a strike. The company recommended their weapon to deal with the 'recent riotous disturbances around the country'. Appealing to the higher level of productivity of their product, the letter promised that 'four or five men only are required to operate [a gun], and one Gatling ... can clear a street or block and keep it clear'. The company was offering a new tactic for doing what the police, sheriffs, elite vigilante groups and state militias couldn't for the first few weeks: clearing the streets of mass public support for the strikers.[3] The strikers were up against not merely the railroad and gun companies, but the dominant media of the day that had no qualms about advocating armed suppression of the strike. Although considered a left-leaning magazine today, at the time *The Nation* took the view that 'Common sense ... insists that it [the interference with property] be refuted with gunpowder'.[4]

The Gatling Gun Company and *The Nation* got their wish. The strike was bloody for strikers, bystanders, and supporters alike. Estimates of the number of strikers, supporters and others killed range from 30–50 people to the 97 people killed in just Baltimore, Chicago, Reading, and Pittsburgh, and at least 117 strikers, supporters and others killed in total. Among those killed were 13 people in Baltimore by a single militia regiment, 24 people in Pittsburgh, five in Philadelphia by the militia, and six strikers on Monday 23 July in Reading, Pennsylvania.[5] The true body count may never be known. Many in the crowds most likely dragged away the wounded to care for and bury them on their own, unwilling to report deaths or injuries for fear of arrest. What made the strike so bloody was the immediate willingness of the railroad corporations to apply the Molly Maguire strategy by sending in the local and state police, sheriffs, deputised gunmen, militias, and the US Army, Marines, and Navy. At least 45,000 troops were used in 11 states.

Both capital and the working-class took away acute lessons from the strike. Illinois militia General Bates's proposal that the US Army be enlarged and regiments quartered in key cities was prescient. Capitalists

---

3   Unionist.com 2015.

4   Lens 1973, p. 49.

5   Bellesiles 2010, p. 175; Lens 1973, pp. 33, 44–5, and 48–9; Foner 1977, p. 204; Painter 1987, pp. 16–17; Adamic 1931, p. 28; and Brecher 1972, p. 35.

saw the importance of a militia controlled by wealthy men, a larger standing army, and more and better armories. During the next few years the
militia in several states was centralized, more armories strategically built
and conspiracy laws enacted against trade unions.[6]

Understanding these preparations is critical to understanding the new composition of capital that emerged following the strike.

Sending in the Troops

The breakdown of discipline and loyalty among some of the state militias, local
elected officials, and local police and sheriffs made these unreliable forces of
repression. Eventually that task was accomplished over the course of eight days
at the request of nine governors with only 3,000 US troops.[7] From the arrival
of Col. French's 70 men in Martinsburg, West Virginia on 19 July 1877 until the
middle of August, US troops were deployed in the states of West Virginia, Maryland, Pennsylvania, Indiana, Illinois, and Missouri not merely to insure order
by their presence but as a symbol of federal authority. These troops primarily
protected property, and in the case of General Winfield Scott Hancock's men
consulting daily with railroad officials, carried out strikebreaking actions by
reopening railroads in West Virginia, Maryland, and Pennsylvania from 20 July
until August.

The army's contribution to strikebreaking was not so direct. By blurring
insurrection with a work stoppage, the government entered the conflict on the
side of capital, although the army reportedly did not kill a single striker. It didn't
have to. The US Army remained in some states until the end of August performing 'the most important part of their duty, strikebreaking'. By opening traffic in
six states, 'protecting non-striking train crews maintaining peace along the line
of traffic, in the rail yards and in train stations, the Army guaranteed management the kind of protection state and local governments could not give'.[8]

By calling for the insertion of US troops, local and state officials could appear
to avoid taking sides in the local conflict while reframing a strike against widely

---

6   Foner 1977, pp. 473–4; and Burbank 1966, p. 178.
7   Foner 1977, p. 192.
8   See Ibid., p. 193. Foner appears to have provided the wrong page numbers for this passage
    from Cooper's unpublished manuscript. He also provided the wrong first name of the author.
    (See Cooper 1980).

hated railroad companies into a seditious insurrection against the government. The appearance of neutrality was an attempt to prevent their local coalitions that put them into office from fragmenting over which side of the strike they stood on.

Introducing US troops into the strike would become a preferred tactic replicated for decades to come. It had the effect of appearing to workers that the 'neutral' federal government was intervening to somehow rectify the wrongs that triggered the strike. The arrival of US troops was interpreted to mean that the federal government would restore calm and introduce a truce in order to make itself available for strikers to present their grievances and to expect redress.

The appearance of troops also created a crisis of legitimacy for the strike. Wearing the uniform, to which many workers were loyal, having most likely recently served in the Civil War and Reconstruction, the US troops could not be opposed without appearing to make the strike a struggle not merely against capital but against the republic itself. Any further tactical escalation would bring the workers directly into confrontation with the federal government. Because local and state officials had lost credibility by their efforts to repress the strike, the federal government was considered more legitimate. This was evidenced by the willingness of supporters to engage in scattered attacks on local police and state militia which had the effect of further swelling their support.

Since many workers placed loyalty to their nation above their class interests, just the presence of federal troops was enough for workers to discontinue their picketing, street fighting, and even the strike itself. They expected that the federal government would play the role of a neutral arbiter and bring about a just resolution to their grievances. They were sorely disappointed.[9] Most had not yet realised that the relationship of the state to the economy was changing dramatically, even as it intervened to crush the strike.

On several occasions, scattered attacks on local and state police and militia attacks included US troops. The appearance of US troops with guns drawn and bayonets ran the risk of further inflaming the conflict. Pennsylvania Congressman Wright of Luzerne County warned how their appearance could be perceived to be to the advantage of the corporation.

> Troops were introduced into my district at the solicitation of the men who controlled the mines and the manufacturing establishments ... There was

---

9   Cooper 1977, pp. 183–7.

no necessity or occasion for it ... It only stirred up [the labor] element. And now, since that has been done, that element has shown its power and its strength, a power and strength that cannot be resisted, that will work its way out ... You cannot suppress a volcano.[10]

Overall, the presence of US troops deflected the focus and target of the strike from the widely discredited railroad companies onto the federal government. This had the effect of fragmenting the coalition of strike supporters who went into the streets against the companies, not the government. As supporters and strikers hesitated before US troops, they lost the momentum and struggled to continue attracting supporters, which was crucial to reducing the risk to their current tactics.

That calm following the arrival of US troops removed a crucial source of leverage the strikers had to win the struggle: a strategy of tension inflicted by armed resistance to the combined forces of capital and local and state governments. The strategy of tension that led to the insertion of US troops was lost once they arrived. As long as the strikers had mass support, such leverage raised the opportunities and reduced their risks. With US troops present, the inverse was the case – although there were a few instances of street fighting with US troops, the strikers de-escalated, expecting the arrival of US troops to bring justice and the opportunity to achieve their gains. They were willing to pay the cost of demobilising and de-escalating their tactics at just the moment when their escalation of tactics had won their first demands: that the wage cuts and double headers be rescinded.

While improvised, and lacking adequate resources and men, the Hayes administration had unknowingly created a new precedent for using US troops as a strikebreaking force that would continue for decades. Troops alone cannot break a strike. In 1877 they had learned that the potency of their presence was an effective tactic that could compel insurgents to demobilise and de-escalate just when they were most effective.

While they were deployed, the troops were put to use breaking other strikes. Some US troops stayed long past the end of the strike in July and extended their mandate to break strikes that had spread to other industrial sectors. Colonel Getty's men remained in Maryland and West Virginia until 25 August to help put down the coal miners and canal boatmen strikes. US troops also remained in Pennsylvania from 2 August until 30 October and aided National Guard pro-

---

10   See Bruce 1959, pp. 309–10.

tecting trains and mines and in enforcing martial law by banning public meetings and demonstrations. In both cases troops did not leave until strikers went back to work.[11]

The skeletal force available was a stark warning to Congress and the President that prompted a modernisation and expansion of US forces. It was immediately acknowledged that too few US troops were available to put down the strike; the US Army had a shortage of men and money as most of its troops were out West fighting the genocidal Indian Wars and some were returning from the last deployments in the South enforcing Reconstruction. In an effort to sabotage Reconstruction, Congress had refused to pass the Army Appropriations Act, so ironically the Army was not funded at the start of the new fiscal year on 1 July 1877, only days before the strike began. The timing of congressional intransigence could not have been worse. Congress's refusal to act prompted an offer from a group of bankers including J.P. Morgan and August Belmont (owners of a major urban street car line and later president of the National Civic Federation, which will be discussed in Chapter 7) to advance the funds to pay 955 of the officer's salaries.[12] The reason for Congress's intransigence was that the Democratic Party, dominated by Southern so-called 'white redeemers', had regained majority control and were punishing the Army for its short-lived military occupation of the former Confederacy during Congressional Reconstruction, which ended in a back room compromise to hand the presidency to Hayes only a few months earlier. The near breakdown in the Army's ability to put down the general strike prompted President Hayes to call a special session in October to pass the appropriations bill.

The crisis of the US military and the barely averted disaster during the strike were the outcomes of a catastrophic rupture in the elite coalition along racial lines. Elites had split over the Republican Party's half-hearted willingness to continue the policies of Reconstruction. Members of the Democratic Party set aside their shared class interests to paralyse the nation's armed forces in order to coerce the withdrawal of the last few thousand US troops in the Southern states. The split over race had left the capitalist economy nearly unguarded. When the strike erupted and spread to the South, class interests overtook those of racial supremacy to thwart the strikers' unintended exploitation of a serious vulnerability. The strike, particularly reports of black and white cooperation in the Galveston and St. Louis strikes, had the effect of removing the blockage for President Hayes to get the army funded. Here again DuBois's stark lesson about

---

11   Cooper 1977, pp. 183–6.
12   Bruce 1959, p. 88.

Reconstruction would continue to have ramifications for decades to come. The racism of white workers of the time blinded them to the strategic need to defend Reconstruction, thereby undercutting their ability to recompose their class power and costing them the strike and perhaps much more.

The collapse of local and state authority, and difficulties in rallying US troops, would spur not only the passage of the Army Appropriations Act but a wholesale rethinking and reorganisation of the local and state police, National Guard and US Army over the coming decades. The revamping of these forces realigned their *reason d'être* to confronting the growing menace of working-class conflict.[13]

Proposals to reform the US Army followed those that came after the 1871 Paris Commune. The editor of *The Nation* proposed doubling the size of the Army and the president of the Pennsylvania Railroad company called for stationing US troops at key points in large cities and business centres.[14] The National Guard Association, formed a year before the strike, had new impetus to lobby for passage of the Militia Act to set up a National Guard modelled after French *Garde Nationale*. Chicago and Cleveland businessmen, who formed a cavalry during the strike, reorganised themselves into five battalions of National Guard cavalry. By the end of the nineteenth century, all the states had formed a National Guard with officers mostly coming from the middle and upper classes. Local self-defence groups, often at the service of merchants and industrialists, continued to form and were eventually coordinated into a national network that operated alongside the paramilitary American Legion, which was chartered by Congress in 1919.[15] After 1877, elites in St. Louis reminded the working-class of their armed power by parading akin to the KKK in the Veiled Prophet Fair known today as the St. Louis Fair.[16]

State militias were also professionalised and reorganised into the National Guard with a clear chain of command stretching from the governor to the president. Fancy state militia uniforms were discontinued and many new armouries were built in or near more large cities in order to have resources strategically

---

13   Bruce was incorrect to claim that the 1877 strike did not result in an enlargement of the Army. According to Cooper, the 1877 strike was a strong impetus to the debates that led to the reorganisation and expansion of the size and role of the US Army history in the following decades. (Bruce 1959, p. 311).

14   Stephens 1995, p. 63.

15   Isaac 2002; and Painter 1987, pp. 21–2 and 376. Membership in the American Legion is limited to veterans even today, making it an official type of para-military force.

16   Aronoff 2015.

placed in preparation for the next strike or insurgency. Armoury buildings now included holes for gunners to avoid being trapped inside as the Philadelphia militia experienced in Pittsburgh.[17]

To Protect and Serve

The 1877 strike fundamentally transformed local and state policing. In the years following the strike, local and state police were widely reorganised. The lack of effective and reliable police prompted the reorganisation and profession-alisation of local police by making them not only municipal public employ-ees, but also a more potent force at the disposal of capital. Police work was Taylorised by establishing a clear chain of command, assigning patrolmen to rationalised beats, and introducing new technologies such as telegraph boxes and telephones (especially in the homes of the wealthy) to manage beat police, along with wagons to be used as weapons used to break up crowds and carry off arrestees. 'Police professionalization is properly understood as simply one small part of the total process of rationalization under advanced capitalism'.[18]

While police and militias emerged in the eighteenth to nineteenth centur-ies to manage slavery and put down slave rebellions, the police that exist today were redesigned in response to the class struggles of the 1870–90s. Throughout the 1840–1850s, there was a wave of inter- and intra-ethnic and racial riots pre-cipitated by the anti-Catholic Know Nothing Party's control over local cities and police departments, which they used to stoke ethnic and racial hatred and terrorise immigrant communities. Between 1830–65, there were 80 major riots affecting about 70 percent of cities with about 20,000 or more people. Although the riots stoked a wave of fear among the ruling class that the current police sys-tems were unprepared to control or repress a growing working-class, there was no firm consensus among the ruling class of the need to support and fund the police.[19]

As a result, to take just one example, cuts in the Chicago and Pittsburgh police during the depressions of the 1870s and 1890s left them incapable of

---

17   Bruce 1959, p. 311.

18   Harring 1983, p. 249.

19   One exception was Boston where police were organised into a full-time office of profes-sionals in 1837 after three riots and criticism from elites. It was not until they were placed under state control in 1885 that they were forced to protect property during strikes. (John-son 1976, p. 93).

defending property and elite neighbourhoods during the strikes. The 1877 strike resulted in a new emphasis on legitimising and expanding the police. Changes to policing coincided with the reorganisation of the militia into the National Guard. For example, in St. Louis, the police force was enlarged, a National Guard armoury was built, and the Lucas Market, where strikers had assembled, was demolished as part of the process of reorganising public space to facilitate the deployment of police and military force. There was a substantial growth in the size of forces, as much as sevenfold in some cities across the Great Lakes region. Because 'class struggle is at the core of the police function', its growth and reorganisation was intended to meet the need for changing tactics and strategy of class conflict.[20]

The industrialisation of policing corresponded to the prerogatives of industrial capital to control workers by preventing disruption and restoring control. 'As capitalism developed, individual capitalists' adaptations to the class struggle needed to be rationally organised and disciplined, a function beyond any individual capitalist but appropriate for the capitalist state'.[21] They did not exist to police the elite.[22]

The takeover of policing by local city and state governments socialised policing as a public function of government paid for by the public rather than elites alone. The industrialisation of policing, and its placement under the public authority of government, by which officers and constables were hired or appointed, made it more efficient and legitimate.[23] Between the 1880s–90s police departments were restructured with a new division of labour that mimicked the military. They obtained a centralised bureaucratic structure, standardised recruitment, training, professionalism, discipline, and specialised units. In the 1890s police began to be trained, their 12-hour workdays and 7-day workweeks, during which they slept at the station, were shortened and they received days off, pensions, and benefits.

The 1877 and 1886–7 strikes reinforced the emphasis on local police rather than militia. In Pittsburgh the defeat of the Philadelphia militia by the strikers and their supporters prompted elites to focus on improving the local police. There were several advantages to using police rather than militia for local

---

20   Harring concurs with Marx's (Marx 1887) observation that the state 'employed the police to accelerate the accumulation of capital by increasing the degree of exploitation of labour'. (Harring 1983, pp. 3–4, 33, 35; and Roediger 1994, p. 105).

21   Harring 1983, pp. 8, 13, 18, and 30–2.

22   Johnson 1976, p. 100.

23   Harring 1983, p. 10.

crowd control: they were more flexibly mobile because they didn't move in military formation, had experience with crowd control, operated under local political control, were locals familiar with the local terrain, worked full-time, and belonged to an institution that emphasised obedience and loyalty despite their recruitment from the working-class.[24]

Several critical new technologies made the police a more effective force for carrying out policies of social control in the rapidly growing cities. The police call box was invented in 1880 in Chicago, modelled after the fire alarm telegraph installed in the homes and businesses of the rich. It had three mechanisms to sign a simple short message – riot, robbery, send help – with the pull of a lever, an alarm bell that would ring each box to alert men on the beat to call in for a message (which was dropped early on), and two way conversation between the officer and switchboard. That call boxes were installed by the rich for $25 in 1881, the equivalent of two weeks, pay for a labourer, 'clearly shows the class basis of the innovation: the public police apparatus was merged with a private system of mobilizing officers', transforming every member of the elite thereby into a policeman. Police box systems were estimated to increase force productivity by the equivalent of 200 men at a reduced cost, a dramatic rise in constant capital that increased the production of surplus value.[25]

The mass produced telephone soon replaced the telegraph, beginning in 1880. While 10,385 messages were sent by telegraph in 1870, by 1880 363,080 messages were sent by telephone. Police now had the technological capacity to immediately coordinate policing city-wide rather than one beat at a time in sequential order.[26]

With city-wide coordination came the ability to rapidly move police in large groups using the light patrol wagon, modelled after the ambulance and fire wagons harnessed to horses and always ready to depart through the new automatic door opener.[27]

The combination of these new technologies and management of policing had a tremendous impact on controlling mass action. The signal system and patrol wagon now allowed a dozen or more officers to be put on the scene in a few minutes compared to an hour under the previous system of running about town to round up a force to march on the scene. Data on the impact in Buffalo between 1887–96 is one of exponential growth in calls, responses, and arrests by

---

24   Ibid., pp. 109–10.
25   Ibid., pp. 50–1 and 56.
26   Ibid., p. 52.
27   Ibid., p. 51.

increasing the number of wagons from one to seven. The patrol wagon became a symbol of intimidation and power, making unruly crowds give way at its approach. It allowed a small number of police to defeat immense crowds, which was not possible in earlier decades – Pittsburgh police estimated that a wagon had the impact of a dozen policemen. Wagons were used as weapons, slamming into crowds to break them up, make mass arrests, and take away large numbers of people.[28] Such technologies made policing a productive industry at the service of elites.

While the technologies and management of policing was used to control insurgent workers, they were also tools to control and discipline police labour. Police work was rationalised by placing call boxes at the beginning and end of each beat at which officers were required to call in according to a time motion study measuring how long it would take an officer to travel the area between them. The timing of the beat allowed management to know where the officer was and how productive they were, as well as preventing absence and suppressing shirking. The telephone made it possible to manage larger forces over wider geographical areas.[29]

The rationalisation of police work provided the means to manage the conflict over the transition of policing from contingent fee for service to industrial work. While strikes were extremely rare, sabotage was commonplace.[30] The telephone provided one way to overcome officers disrupting the entire line of call boxes wired in sequential order by leaving his phone off the hook. Police officers on the beat had different class interests than their commanders and the rank and file organised proto-union benevolent associations.[31] Police work

---

28   Ibid., pp. 53–5.

29   Ibid., pp. 58–60.

30   In addition to the 1919 Boston police strike, there were only two police mutinies in the 40-year period studied by Harring. They occurred in 1910 during the Columbus streetcar strike when 32 police and 23 specials (25 percent of the department) refused to ride streetcars to protect scabs and in 1913 during the Indianapolis streetcar strike when 29 police also refused to do the same. Facing heavily armed scabs, the Columbus workers dynamited the cars and car barn and faced four days of vigorous police anti-strike repression until the strike ended after three weeks. The police mutiny was also a job action protesting overwork and the mayor's veto of a bill establishing the 8-hour day for police. The mayor had little success recruiting volunteer specials and called out the National Guard. The mutiny undermined the use of the police to break the strike. (Ibid., pp. 137–9).

31   At the time of the 1919 Boston police strike, there were AFL affiliated police unions in 37 other cities. (Painter 1987, p. 369). These conflicting interests have been immortalised in countless cop shows and movies in which the rogue officer combats the bureaucratic man-

was no less a terrain of struggle and contradictions even as police were used to smash insurgent workers.[32]

An effective and efficiently managed police force provided a potent weapon for raising the costs of mobilising and striking. Police not only more effectively protected property, but also carried out the social control functions that intimidated and coerced burgeoning urban populations and which had the effect of dampening collective action. When class conflict emerged, the police could also be used to protect strikebreakers, break up meetings, marches, and pickets, keep workplaces open, deploy special agents to supplement their forces, and provided the bulk of the forces of repression.[33] As a branch of local government the police legitimated and sanctioned the official use of violence to protect capital that fuelled the tactical escalation, spiralling into armed conflict and often refocused away from capital and onto the police. Sympathetic local officials might delay their use of police but they rarely kept them on the sidelines.[34]

Reorganisation of the police alone failed to realise the necessary discipline and control that would prevent further insurgencies. Policing must be understood within a larger context of intra-class conflicts over tactics and strategy of class domination and control that was paired with the courts, military, welfarism, arbitration, and the new division of labour.

---

agement. But perhaps none compares to the goofy antics of Officer Dribble in the 1960s cartoon series *Top Cat* who frequently pairs up with the criminal gang of cats who live in an alley where his call box is located to cover for his long absences and foul ups as he struggles to get his 'man'. (*Top Cat* 1961–2; see also Harring 1983, p. 58).

32 Even today the 'blue code of silence' endemic in police departments could be seen as a means of solidarity among rank and file officers to avoid accountability in a struggle with management and city officials responsive to public complaints about excessive use of force, racial profiling, shootings and murders.

33 Many of these functions were adapted from those used by private police such as the Pinkertons. The company was the first to use fingerprints for identification, had highly mobile interconnected capability across jurisdictions that matched their corporate clients, and engaged in industrial espionage, infiltration of unions, protecting strikebreakers, and investigation of property crimes. They helped break 77 strikes between 1869–92. (Johnson 1976, pp. 96–7).

34 Toledo Mayors Jones and Whitlock were unique in that they did not allow local police to protect scabs and as a result the 1906 Pope-Toledo Motor Car Company strike resulted in an arbitrated settlement favourable to the workers. Otherwise, cases in which workers influenced let alone controlled police during strikes are rare. Police who appear sympathetic were quickly reassigned or disciplined. (Harring 1983, p. 136).

Class violence was not as well controlled by the police as the bourgeoisie originally expected or hoped that it might be, and this failure can be seen as one reason for the turn toward 'progressive' or 'reformist' methods of controlling the class struggle, now identified with the welfare state.[35]

As a result, the size of local and state government grew dramatically while shifting the costs to the working-class for education, training, public services, and policing. This necessitated new sources of tax revenue that corresponded with the establishment of the federal income tax in the Sixteenth Amendment.

The Pennsylvania Governor, who oversaw both the suppression of the Molly Maguire miners and the railroad strike, had just set up the Coal and Iron Police in summer 1877, amassing 100 men by June 1878. The Coal and Iron Police were used to replace local police in strikes where the latter might be too sympathetic to strikers. Portrayed in the film *The Molly Maguires*, the Coal and Iron Police were mercenaries on the state payroll whose only purpose was to protect mining companies and their capital from organised workers.[36]

Science of the Mob

To inform the new organisation of policing required new schools of academic thought. This development was prompted by the urgent need to study the 'mob' in order to control and manage it. The new academic disciplines of psychology and sociology gained a foothold in the dominant thinking of the time and provided a valuable service to capital by articulating a science of the mob. Theories of the mob centred on the threat in the growing US metropolises being populated by teeming hordes fleeing the slums of Europe. 'Bunched together in the great cities ... there one found what might be called "the mob-in-being"'.[37] Channelling Le Bon's portrayal of the mob, Bruce paints a picture of the ungovernable force of the working-class at mid-century. Repeatedly describing strikers and their supporters alternately as 'mobs', 'hostile mob', 'boys', and 'half drunk boys', he observed the strike through the lens of relative deprivation theory:

Whenever quitting time poured thousands into the streets, whenever warm weather emptied the tenements onto sidewalks and front stoops,

---

35   Ibid., pp. 253–4.
36   *The Molly Maguires* 1970.
37   Bruce 1959, p. 27.

there stood the mob, ready-made. Working on the minds of these people were the dishonesty and cynicism of politics, the injustice of law and courts, the weakness of law enforcement. They knew death as a daily acquaintance and violence as the normal response to frustration. They brooded on the oppression of labor, the arrogance of capital, the wild inequality of fortune, the misery of tenement life, the fear and hunger and degradation of hard times. The makings of a grand social bonfire were heaped high. Beneath them, like shavings, were scattered the tramps, bitter, desperate, standing to lose nothing but life and counting that small loss. And everywhere ran the volatile children and teen-agers, eager for excitement, full of dime-novel yarns, acting on pure impulse, ready like so much kerosene to take fire at the drop of a spark.[38]

As discussed in the Introduction, portraying insurgency as a psychological release for frustrated individuals would become the predominant school of thought explaining political violence following WWII. But in 1877, not only was the economy half way through a long depression that threw a huge proportion of the population into utter destitution, but the political space in which grievances could be presented for redress was widely understood to be closed to the common working man and woman. Not for the lack of trying to use the political process and negotiations with companies to address their grievances did protests quickly turn into strikes and insurgency. The working-class was faced with a tactical repertoire in which the possibility of peacefully organising and presenting their grievances was already blunted by the law or the costs of doing so. Blocked from presenting their demands, with little or no formal organisation, workers quickly escalated their tactics to shut down the railroads and disrupt the national economy, tactics which (as shown in Chapter 2) brought almost immediate concessions that were unimaginable only days earlier. Bruce himself identified the many instances in which the workers articulated and physically presented their demands and organised themselves and their supporters to both shut down the railroads, with whom they had unacknowledged grievances, and take up arms to protect themselves from wanton corporate and state violence. This was hardly the work of a riotous mob. These were the efforts of an organised and tactical disruptive protest.

Emerging from these new academic disciplines, and corporate sponsored welfarism two decades later, came the new academic discipline of industrial relations, the science of managing workers. Industrial relations begot human

---

38   Ibid., pp. 27, 103–4, and 109.

resources, which managed the recruitment, hiring, disciplining, and firing of
workers (now 'employees'), their integration into the corporate culture, and
the management of their grievances through collective bargaining, which by
the early twentieth century had become the Holy Grail of the labour movement. Collective bargaining, which was popular neither with capital nor with
the unions, emerged according to the logic of jurisprudence as arbitration. Seen
as the means of reconciling a contractual dispute between two parties, capital
and worker (singular), arbitration would later be seized upon when workers
threatened to disrupt the capital accumulation process to channel the threat
from the shop floor and streets to the negotiating table. A decade later, Congress
passed the Arbitration Act in 1888 providing for voluntary arbitration in railroad strikes, but it was never used. It would be the first of several laws extending
first voluntary and then mandatory arbitration and mandatory collective bargaining by Section 7(a) of the 1933 National Industrial Recovery Act and then
the 1935 National Labor Relations Act.

At the 31 July 1877 cabinet meeting, its last concerning the strike, as Senator Sherman and President Hayes discussed regulating the railroads, Secretary
of War McCrary interjected that 'The country is ready for an exertion of its
power' into the economy to regulate otherwise disruptive class conflict.[39] A
decade later, the 1887 Interstate Commerce Act was sold to the public as a
means for government to place its reins on the growing monopolies. During
the debates over the bill were proposed statutory arbitration, a National Bureau of Industry (which later became the Department of Commerce and Labor)
to gather information about the growing industrial working-class, limits on suffrage, a universal poll tax, and property, literacy and education requirements.
Modelled after the Black Codes and later Jim Crow laws that targeted blacks,
Asians, and Latinos, these measures were pointedly directed at the emerging
working-class menace.

The outcome of the 1877 strike revealed the fabric of the American republic,
exposing just how thin was the stated commitment of elites to representative
democracy. In the midst of a disruptive insurgency, opponents of democracy
appeared at the highest level of representative government. Among them was
Judge Gresham, who asserted that 'All honest, thoughtful men know that the
ballot must be restricted and I suppose that can be done only through blood ...
Democracy is now the enemy of law and order and society itself and as such
should be denounced'.[40] Gresham spoke for his fellow plutocratic elite that in

39   Ibid., p. 315.
40   Ibid., p. 317.

little more than a decade would see the spectacular rise of the People's Party sweep state elections throughout the South and Plains states, seize control of several states at the ballot box, and wield their pens against the monopolies and two party duopoly. The perception that America had an excess of democracy informed Judge Gresham for years to come. He was Secretary of State when President Grover Cleveland sent in the Army to break the 1894 Pullman railroad strike. Gresham's 1877 precedent would again be used to enjoin workers from interfering with a railroad under federal receivership.[41]

Hyperbole about the riotous mob that inflicted violence and property destruction to be tamed with a 'rifle diet' allowed the efforts of organised workers advocating for economic democracy to be reframed as a disorganised menace to government, order, and property. The theory of the mob provided a rationale for reorganising and professionalising the state militia into the National Guard, expanding and reorganising the us Army, and creating local riot and strike squads over the coming decades. The 1877 strike could not have come at a worse time and provided a shock to obstructionist Democrats who had been sabotaging the remnants of Reconstruction, weakening their ability to respond to the working-class insurgency. 'With the great upheaval now grown continental, the little United States Army had been spread disturbingly thin. Mexican rebels, Indian chiefs and railroad presidents seemed in league with striker and Communists to embarrass McCrary's overworked department'.[42]

The 1877 strike impressed the necessity for capitalist class unity that had been fractured since 1860. It provided the necessary language to deflect attention from the plutocratic erosion of democracy, the systemic instability of capitalism, and the tenuous elite coalition. Despite the dramatic license, from its first day the 1877 strike was portrayed by governors and railroad companies alike as not merely a struggle at the point of production but as an insurrection against the state itself, requiring federal military intervention. 'A labor dispute that could constitutionally qualify as an "insurrection" was something rather new under the American sun'.[43]

---

41   Ibid., p. 320.
42   Ibid., p. 277.
43   Ibid., p. 87.

Turning the Strike into Sedition

Federalising the strike as a threatened act of sedition was among the most effective labour law reform emerging from efforts to repress the strike. It not only provided the legal rationale to insert US troops to break it, but also deflected the focus on the strike from the railroad companies and local and state officials to the US government. More than 140 years later, federalising a strike is still a common tactic to raise the costs of action.[44]

Calls from the railroad companies, mayors, and governors to President Hayes to intervene provided the catalyst to devise a legal rationale to justify federal intervention. Federal intervention was necessary, the administration asserted, to put down sedition and prevent disruption of the mails. But it was several federal judges that provided the strongest reasoning: railroads in bankruptcy proceedings had the protection of the federal courts and thus the entirety of the federal government that could use injunctions, federal marshals, and US troops to shield them from disruption.

On Sunday 22 July, President Hayes met with five cabinet officers to consider Pennsylvania Railroad president Scott's telegrams requesting federal troops. 'Scott, it seemed, wanted a general showdown with labor; he wanted the United States government to fight for him; and he was now applying his formidable influence to that end'.[45] The cabinet was directed to brainstorm both legal and practical roles for the federal government to intervene in the strike.

The railroads were well represented by every member of the cabinet at the table. Among those cabinet officials were Secretary of State Evarts whose law firm had worked for Vanderbilt's Lake Shore railroad as recently as the previous Tuesday. Secretary of War McCrary was a close friend of General Dodge, the Chief Engineer on Scott's Texas and Pacific Railroad and a go-between for Scott and President Hayes during the disputed 1877 presidential election. Secretary of the Navy Thompson had been the long-time chief counsel for the Terre Haute & Indianapolis Railroad. Attorney General Devens and Secretary Evarts had been on a trip to the Pennsylvania coal regions paid for by the railroads and were passing through Baltimore on Scott's private car on the day the B&O strike began. The night before West Virginia Governor Mathews called President Hayes for troops, Devens and Evarts had been with Reading's General Manager Wootten in Gowen's private car.

---

44   The most recent federalised strikes are President Truman's takeover of the railroads in 1950 and steel in 1952, and President Reagan's infamous 1981 mass firing of about 11,000 air traffic controllers.

45   Bruce 1959, p. 217.

By the time the cabinet met, Pittsburgh was calm and there would be no further clashes in West Virginia or Maryland. Nevertheless, the next morning, Monday 23 July, the Navy deployed a twelve gun ship up to Alexandria and an eight gun ship to the Navy Yard, deployed 500 sailors for garrison duty, and sent for Major General Schofield from West Point to run the defences.

The cabinet had several very good reasons to worry. The federal military was in woeful shape because Congress had just refused to approve funding for the Army. It was also dangerously understaffed, especially at the arsenals, which were virtually unprotected, with only 20 to 40 men guarding three of them, one of which held 25,000 rifles and 1 million cartridges.[46] Considering numerous direct confrontations between workers and the militias, with at least one on an armoury, the fall of any of these arsenals would have vastly expanded the workers' advantages to withstand armed repression. The military presence was an expression of the cabinet's concern about the reported unreliability of state militias. At one meeting the cabinet even considered suspending *habeas corpus*, although that power is enumerated only to Congress under Article I, Section 9, Clause 2 of the US Constitution.

Protecting mail trains also became a rationale for sending in US troops. By shrewdly placing US mail on non-mail trains blocked by strikers, the railroads provided a justification for President Hayes to send troops to prevent strikers from interfering with the mails.[47] The railroads began refusing to run the mail lines, despite strikers publicly allowing them to travel, as a further pretext to justify federal intervention. Strikers in Erie wired President Hayes that the Lake Shore line was refusing to run separate mail and passenger trains. The next day, in an apparent attempt to justify federal intervention, Vanderbilt and Scott refused to run mail only trains, insisting to the US Postmaster General that US mail only be carried on passenger trains. Although in some locales strikers allowed some passenger trains through, it was not common.

The only known example of the federal government intervening to open the road for a supposed mail train was when strikers and their supporters had stopped a Chicago, Burlington & Quincy passenger train carrying US mail in Iowa. They were warned that all passenger trains carrying US mail were mail trains and it was illegal to interfere with them. Although some were prosecuted and convicted of interfering with the US mail and fined $40–100, it is unknown if any went to prison. While this legal tactic was apparently rare in 1877, it

---

46   Ibid., pp. 218–20.
47   Foner 1977, p. 196.

became a central tactic used to break the 1894 railroad strike by arresting and prosecuting strike leaders for violating federal injunctions issued to ostensibly protect mail trains.

Protecting bankrupt companies under federal receivership provided yet another justification for federal intervention. During the strike, Seventh US Circuit Court Judge Drummond ruled that any attempt to disrupt a railroad in federal receivership would be found in contempt of court. The ruling made clear that disobeying a judicial order was not limited to the person to whom it was specifically addressed but could be applied to a group, organisation, and even unions. The ruling turned the blanket injunction into a judicial ban on strikes that would play a prominent role in breaking the 1894 strike.

Using the federal courts was a new tactical innovation in strikebreaking. It placed all federal judicial and executive power at the disposal of bankrupt corporations. Striking a railroad under receivership brought contempt of court charges as well as US troops into the area to protect the road.

After a crowd stopped a train on the Indianapolis, Bloomington & Western line Judge Gresham of Indianapolis claimed the city was under mob rule and asked for the militia to be called out. With few locals willing to join the militia, Judge Gresham swore in US marshals, including future President Benjamin Harrison, and recommended that a Committee of Safety be formed. Two companies of 100 men under the command of a general were formed and armed with guns from the US arsenal. Following Judge Drummond's precedent, US District Judge Gresham requested President Hayes send in US troops to protect a railroad under receivership. Although no trains could move, Judge Gresham's claims of mob violence in Indianapolis were contradicted by reports that 50 strikers were guarding company property and all was quiet. Judge Gresham wired President Hayes for US troops to protect the court despite the fact that the US Signal Service in Indianapolis had wired President Hayes that there were no signs of violence threatening the railroad under federal receivership. While Hayes's cabinet first appeared to hesitate in sending troops to Judge Gresham out of fear of provoking the strikers, they eventually ignored the US Signal Service.

On 26 July President Hayes made soldiers from the Indianapolis arsenal available to him and ordered 200 more troops to move up from the South to Terre Haute, Eugene Debs's hometown. The US general in command of the Army detachment met with the strikers and warned them not to interfere with lines under receivership; fearing military intervention, the strikers let the trains through. Secretary of State Evarts ordered Marshal Spooner, who had earlier warned the strikers of the risk of contempt, to protect the roads under control of the courts. The next day, Spooner arrested the strike leaders and deployed troops throughout the area to open the lines, including the Vandalia line which was not under receivership.[48] The deployment of these troops persuaded the strikers to give up the strike without winning any of their demands.

This was the first time troops were sent to protect railroads under receivership, a 'precedent-setting decision that was to plague the labor movement for years to come'.[49] Troops had previously only been used during wartime, the Civil War, to protect US property, or by request of a governor to protect a republican form of government under Art. IV, Sect. 4 of the US Constitution and the Revised Statutes of the US, Sections 5298, 5299, most recently in the South during Reconstruction to control white racist terrorism.[50] The first and only prior time they were sent in to break a strike was in 1834 when President Jackson sent US troops to break a strike on the construction sites of the Chesapeake and Ohio Canal.

President Hayes reinterpreted not only Article IV, Sect. 4 of the US Constitution and the Article IV, Section 4 of the US Constitution, Sections 1984 and 1989 of Act of 18 June 1878, and Revised Statutes of the US, Sections 5297–5299, Revised Statutes of the US Section 3999, but also his Article II powers as Commander in Chief when Congress declares war under Article I, Section 8, Clause 11.[51] The president directly reinterpreted his war-making authority by putting governors and federal judges at the top of the military chain of command, giving them full discretion over the deployment, movement and even the withdrawal of the federal troops, at times over the protests of the commander in the field. This strategy allowed the governors, judges and the president and his cabinet to redefine the strike as an insurrection against the government rather than against the companies.[52] Although future administrations would no longer place the governor in the chain of command, the 1877 strike set a precedent by which US troops, and the soon to be reorganised National Guard under the command of the governor, would be deployed as capital's arsenal against organised workers.

---

48   Bruce 1959, pp. 287–9 and 290.

49   Foner 1977, pp. 193–5.

50   US troops were also used against the domestic population during the 1787 Shay's Rebellion, 1791 Whiskey Rebellion, during the centuries of war against Native Americans, and slave rebellions.

51   Bruce 1959, p. 279; United States Senate 1903, pp. 5–12.

52   Cooper 1977, p. 188.

Court Imposed Composition of Capital

The strike stripped bare the class nature of America's judicial system. Striking workers and their supporters experienced the class character of the state directly when local and state police, sheriffs, local and state militia, private agents, and US troops arrived to feed them the 'rifle diet' recommended by Pennsylvania Railroad's Scott. The use of the courts to break the strike illustrated their role in using government to impose a new composition of capital that could break the newly recomposed working-class.

While much attention has been given to the role of the courts in criminalising the strike on roads under receivership, court protection provided relief as much from the vestiges of competition as from the company's own workers. As Stromquist observed,

> court-supervised reorganization ... would salvage the investment by imposing cost-reduction measures and refinancing of debt. This process most often occurring during a depression, led to wage reductions, revisions of work rules, and the elimination of trade unions as impediments to further rationalization of the labor process. Lower operating costs produced improvements in earnings.[53]

Court supervision of failing railroads began during the 1873–8 depression when 89 of 364 railroad companies – 25 percent of the industry – were placed under court receivership. The common practice of appointing the existing manager of the company as the receiver frequently put many shareholders and workers at a disadvantage.[54] As we have seen in Chapters 1 and 2, the federal courts wielded the injunction to protect these railroads from strikes. This expanded with the 1886 Southwest strikes, where they were used to protect any railroad that crossed state lines under the Art. I, Section 8, Inter-state Commerce Clause of the US Constitution and to prevent secondary boycotts with the 1894 Pullman strike (see Chapters 4–6), and during the national coal strike and strikes in West Virginia between 1919 and 1921 with the help of the *1917 Hitchman Coal & Coke Co. v. Mitchell 245 US 229* precedent (see Chapter 10).

Court protected railroads continued to cooperate and even paid dividends on over-valued stock, thereby allowing them to continue to expand with the next upturn. 'Depression was absolutely integral to the process of railroad

---

53   Stromquist 1993, p. 14.

54   Ibid., pp. 18–19.

growth in the nineteenth century', Stromquist noted.[55] Once the courts could impose on the railroads what the companies were incapable of doing alone, the depression finished the job by imposing a new rationalisation of labour such as the double header, driving down wages, and shattering the unions.

And Justice for All?

Halls of justice painted green
Money talking
Power wolves beset your door
Hear them stalking
Soon you'll please their appetite
They devour
Hammer of justice crushes you
Overpower ...
Lady Justice has been raped
Truth assassin
Rolls of red tape seal your lips
Now you're done in
Their money tips her scales again
Make your deal
Just what is truth? I cannot tell
Cannot feel
       Metallica[56]

While the courts protected the railroad companies from the strike they didn't protect the strikers and their supporters from the violence used against them. Few were arrested for murdering or brutalising strikers and their supporters, and even fewer of those who were arrested were prosecuted for these crimes. Unlike the strikers and supporters who were prosecuted and sentenced to prison, such as in St. Louis, these defendants either escaped punishment entirely or received a slap on the wrist. Some of the most notable cases illustrate how the judicial system served the class interests of elites during and after the strike. The judicial record conclusively shows that 'the law's chief concern

---

55   Ibid., p. 14.
56   Metallica 1988.

was to punish rioters and strikers'.[57] Strikers and supporters received sentences of three months to six years and ten months, time in the workhouse, and fines ranging from $1,500–5,000.

There is no record of any militia commander being prosecuted for killing and injuring peaceful unarmed strikers and their supporters. There was an effort to hold the Philadelphia militia general and some of his men, known as the 'butchers of Pittsburgh', accountable for killing and injuring dozens of peaceful unarmed strikers and their supporters. However, the grand jury did not indict him, and the men put on trial for murder and manslaughter for a massacre in Scranton were acquitted by the jury.

In Chicago, Judge Drummond sentenced nine strikers to two to four months for contempt. He then arrived in Indianapolis to take over for Judge Gresham who had to recuse himself for having led the citizen's committee. Drummond oversaw the prosecution of 15 strikers on the Chicago & Indianapolis line entirely on testimony of company officials. Thirteen were found guilty and sentenced to one to six months in jail, although they served three months, and one was acquitted and another was released on a $5,000 bond. Drummond also charged several strikers with felonies for interfering with mail trains but they got off lightly because they were not convicted of criminal intent.[58] Judge Treat of the Southern District of Illinois sentenced 37 strikers to three months.

On 1 August, Judge Gresham had four leaders in Indianapolis arrested for contempt of court, the chief witness against them the head of the Vandalia line. They were each given sentences ranging from 30 days to six months. Although the strikers had de-escalated in the expectation of a peaceful resolution to their grievances, 'the strikers' vision of class harmony had not been able to survive the presence of federal troops'.[59]

Urbana strikers were convicted by Judge Treat in Springfield of criminal contempt for interfering with trains under receivership and sentenced to 90 days. Some of the East St. Louis strikers were also tried in Judge Treat's court but their charges were dropped. The prosecutor was Bluford Wilson, brother of James Wilson, the receiver of St. Louis & Southeastern who obtained federal

---

57   Bruce 1959, p. 307.

58   Foner 1977, pp. 195–6 and 206.

59   Indianapolis proved to be not only calm but even a centre of experimentation with cross-class cooperation and collective bargaining. Mayor Caven enlisted strikers as special police and set up a committee to hear workers' grievances, thereby coopting the strikers and short-circuiting the growing influence of the Workingmen's Party. (Ibid., pp. 99–101).

military aid to break the St. Louis general strike. Barney Donahue, leader of the Erie strikers, was convicted by Judge Jennings of conspiracy and sentenced to three months.

On 29 and 31 Judges Drummond, Treat and Jennings released a total of 61 convicted strikers on a $500 bond and banned them from interfering with property under the control of a federal court for one year. The hundreds arrested in Pittsburgh were tried before juries and given short workhouse sentences, although most were discharged in preliminary hearings. Of the 63 indicted in Reading only three were convicted and 13 of the 14 arrested for inciting a riot were acquitted, as was a fired engineer. The more than 60 arrested in Harrisburg were all fined.[60]

Although the St. Louis leadership was arrested along with many rank and file strikers and supporters, they were acquitted by the jury and suffered no lasting legal consequences. Although some cases were dismissed, some were fined and those who couldn't pay their fines were sentenced to short terms in the workhouse. The members of the St. Louis strike executive committee were held for $3,000 bail and two were released after they posted bail. At trial in mid-August, the prosecution asked for more time to locate witnesses; the court would not allow it and a *nolle prosequi* (a Latin term meaning that the case is dropped) was entered. A grand jury in October refused to recommend further prosecution because it doubted the constitutionality of the law used to prosecute them.[61] As we saw in Chapter 2, some of the leadership suffered no political consequences and the party did surprisingly well in the upcoming election.

These cases were the first use of the strike injunction backed up at gunpoint by the entire federal government. The judges used receivership as justification to issue injunctions that made the strike illegal under threat of imprisonment without due process and prosecution based on biased testimony. The combined efforts of Judges Drummond, Gresham, Treat, and Secretary Evarts had wide-ranging, long-term consequences for workers and unions.

> [Evarts] did not realise how extraordinary Thursday's decision had been, if not legally, then at least historically. It pulled the lanyard, of course, on management's biggest gun in the Midwest. But beyond that, the first round set a whole battery of such guns roaring down the decades, until the

---

60   Ibid., pp. 206–7.

61   Ibid., pp. 207–9; and Burbank 1966, pp. 186–7.

threat of contempt charges became one of the most formidable weapons organised labor had to face.[62]

With these rulings, capital was handed a potent legal weapon that effectively criminalised all strikes, picketing, boycotts, job action, and even worker organising.[63]

> The doctrine introduced by Drummond and his colleagues had turned all receivership orders into standing injunctions against strikes – indeed, the very language of such orders bore a close resemblance to the dread labor injunctions of later years. In such cases, strikers could now be swept up and deposited in jail without the inconvenience of jury trials. Companies not in receivership would have to get injunctions issued first in order to turn strikers into criminals, but the courts came to be admirably compliant and prompt in such cases.[64]

The wide-ranging ramifications of the tactical use of the courts remains with us today beyond the use of preemptive injunctions. Large-scale arrests depleted mass support and shifted the focus and energy to jail support, raising funds for attorneys, and conducting legal defence at trials which drained insurgents' efforts. Contempt charges were used to raid homes and offices, seize records, and preemptively arrest and deport strikers and their supporters.

By raising the costs of mobilising, such disruption provided a disincentive to organising, striking, and forming unions. It simultaneously provided impetus to those advocating for labour law reform and mandatory arbitration of labour disputes which channelled unions into de-escalating and demobilising in order to enter negotiations, avoiding the expected costs of escalating their tactics.

In 1870s many states passed Tramp Acts that made it a crime for those without work to travel across state lines, effectively attempting to criminalise the circulation of people and communication critical to insurgency. The growing criminalisation of tramping and vagrancy was not merely a means to control the large number of unemployed workers and their families during the

---

62   Bruce 1959, p. 289.

63   Court protection was an imperfect weapon in its infancy. Although the Erie line was in receivership, it did not intimidate the workers who struck, blocked passenger and freight cars, and demanded brakeman Barney Donahue and the dozen or so others fired for protesting the 1 July cut be rehired. The Erie was in the process of obtaining an injunction and had Governor Robinson, an Erie director, on its side. (Ibid., p. 100).

64   Ibid., p. 309.

depression. These laws were intended to cut off the flow of workers who would flood into strikes from other areas or states to provide mass support and would later impede the flow of the Industrial Armies in 1894 (see Chapter 4). Policing focused on repressing the most marginal among the working-class,

> one presumably prone to involvement in community class struggles. To the extent that vagrants and tramps were unemployed workers, they had an obvious stake in class struggles carried out in the form of popular strikes or other community actions.[65]

An example of this was Buffalo Chief of Police Morganstern who explained the sweep for tramps as follows:

> The idea is to get as many of these good for nothings as possible out of the way during the present difficulty [1892 railroad strike], as they are apt to hang around with the strikers and incite them, and possibly may do mischief themselves. Besides it reduces the crowds so that it is easier to distinguish the classes of citizens with whom the police and militia have to deal.[66]

During that strike, strikers (as well as scabs who refused to work as switchmen and joined the strike) were arrested, charged and jailed as tramps and vagrants.

There were different class uses for distinguishing between tramps/vagrants and workers. Capital could use the term to delegitimise strikes and jail strikers and brotherhood leaders could denounce the use of violence by workers in order to avoid responsibility. 'The characterization of militant workers as "tramps" probably had an element of truth in it, but it concealed the real issue: tramps were unemployed workers, and this use of the term criminalizes militant workers and delegitimates class struggle'. Ultimately, the arrests of workers as tramps and growing anti-tramps laws evidenced a threat to capital – a 'dangerous troublemaker in local labor relations'.[67] Jack London served 30 days in an Erie County jail as a tramp during the June–July 1894 Industrial Army marches. However, Roediger's study of the St. Louis and East St. Louis strike found no basis for the claim that the strikers were migrant workers or recent transplants.[68]

---

65   Harring 1983, pp. 201 and 223.
66   See *Buffalo Express*, 21 August 1892 in Harring 1983, p. 208.
67   Harring 1983, pp. 284 and 209.
68   Ibid., p. 210; and Roediger 1994, pp. 98–9.

Arrests for vagrancy and tramping increased in Toledo, for example, from
159 in 1892 to 357 in 1894. In Buffalo, there was a huge increase in arrests for
tramping from zero to 2,110 and a decline in vagrancy arrests from 3,170 to 1,750
between 1890 to 1891 when the state began subsidising the jail costs for tramping. Arrests for both evened out in 1894 at about 4,700 for each.[69]

Polish and Bohemian workers formed an Industrial Army under the leadership of 'Count' Joseph Rybakowski and made it from Chicago to Buffalo. Along
the way they were attacked, beaten, and arrested in Toledo. They were attacked
again by police in Buffalo who killed two, severely injured 20, and jailed 120 for
up to six months. In 1893 Polish workers in Buffalo had rioted for bread and
then 5,000 met to demand public works. The presence of the Army the following year reignited the mass movement when 500–800 marched on the offices
of the mayor and poor department demanding better relief and public works.
When the army stayed around to organise, the police attacked again, seriously
clubbing 10 people.[70]

The prosecution and imprisonment of strikers and their supporters following the 1877 strike reflected a new aspect of the criminalisation of working-class
social life but also working-class conflict.

> Various social groups in America, alert to the power of the legal sanction,
> have agitated for the inclusion of almost any kind of behavior which they
> find objectionable in the penal code. This agitation has met with con-
> siderable success. One classic example is the criminalization of various
> activities associated with labor organizing; another is the criminalization
> of non-victim behaviors, such as public drinking, consensual sexual activ-
> ities and drug use.[71]

Regulating Class Conflict

The federal Bureau of Labor and Labor Commissioner established in 1884 was
modelled on similar states agencies. While limited to merely collecting information about the conditions of industrial work and strikes, the data was used to
make the case that labour conflict was a growing threat to industrial stability.
While the US Labor Commissioner later began to offer mediation services to

69   Harring 1983, pp. 203 and 206.
70   Ibid., pp. 202 and 213–17.
71   Johnson 1976, p. 92.

bring together capital and labour at the bargaining table, it remained voluntary and unenforceable until WWI.

The exception was the 1898 Erdman Act which was passed following the 1877 and 1894 strikes, 'the seminal period during which the foundations of federal policy toward catastrophic strikes were laid'.[72] The Erdman Act was the first federal effort to apply the new fields of labour relations and human resources to the railroad industry. The Act established an arbitration process to hear labour disputes and made it illegal for workers to strike and the railroads to fire employees for being a member of a labour union during the arbitration process. The law effectively outlawed the 'yellow dog' contract, in which workers were forced to sign a pledge that they would not join a union as a condition of employment. According to Ross and Taft,

> There is no evidence that the riots of 1877 brought reforms in the handling of railroad disputes, which was the initial cause of the disturbances. They did demonstrate that the United States would not escape the trials and tribulations affecting other industrial nations, and that more attention must be given to the problems that industrial societies tend to generate. It was, however, more than a decade later that the first hesitant step was taken by the Federal Government to provide a method of adjusting labor disputes, a method that was never tried. Not until the Erdman Act of 1898 did the Federal Government provide a usable procedure for settling labour-management disputes on the railroads. An added provision guaranteeing railroad workers protection of the right to organise was declared unconstitutional by the U.S. Supreme Court when challenged by a carrier, *Adair v. United States*, 1908.[73]

Unknown prior to the 1877 strike, regulatory and welfarist policies in the railroad industry also gained new momentum. In addition to the formation of labour research bureaus and investigative commissions, regulatory agencies, corporate insurance schemes and state insurance programmes also began to appear. Among the earliest proponents of regulation and welfarism was Charles Francis Adams II, grandson of President John Quincy Adams, who proposed establishing the Massachusetts Board of Railroad Commissioners in 1869

---

72 Destler 1968, p. 413.

73 The case concerned Louisville and Nashville Railroad Company employee William Adair who had violated the law by firing a locomotive fireman who had joined a union. (Ross and Taft 1969, p. 5).

and became one of its first three members and leader. He advocated public investigations into labour disputes and jail and fines for workers who struck and boycotted lines experiencing strikes, and criminal punishment of workers who abandoned a train between stations or intimidated scabs.

Later the president of a small railroad company, Adams was no friend of organised workers or labour unions. His proposals were not meant to aid workers' efforts to organise, unionise, and strike but rather to expand the role of the state to regulate, control, manage, and normalise the class struggles that were disrupting the most important industry of the time. He proposed that the Brotherhood of Locomotive Engineers be broken up and that corporations establish life insurance and pension programmes to undercut the attractiveness of unions. After the Brotherhood of Locomotive Engineers lost the February 1877 strike on Adams's Boston & Maine due to police repression, seven states followed Adams and passed laws making it a crime for an engineer to abandon the train. Similar legislation was passed in five other states, but it would take decades for mandatory arbitration to trickle upward to the federal level during WWI.[74]

Some companies also began studying and experimenting with Adams's welfare programme ideas. Lehigh Valley set up a relief fund with matching contributions similar to unemployment insurance established by the 1935 Social Security Act. The Central Pacific opened a hospital for sick and injured workers, another welfarist programme that would be replicated in a modified form by the Kaiser Steel Corporation in the 1930–40s.[75] *Harper's Weekly* editor Curtis and *The Nation*'s Godkin formed the Civil Service Reform League in 1881 with the objective of removing the influence of local ethnic political machines which were voted into office in exchange for patronage and jobs for ethnic working-class voters.[76]

Since information and research about the working-class was needed to make these welfarist policies more effective in managing conflict, special commissions began to be established to hear testimony, gather data and research on the working-class and propose action, programmes, regulations, and other measures. Among the most prominent commissions was the 1883–4 Senate Committee on the Relations Between Labor and Capital which conducted an investigation and issued a five volume report in 1885. These new agencies and com-

---

74   Adams 1877; and Foner 1977, p. 26.
75   Today it is the Kaiser Permanente company.
76   Painter 1987, p. 32.

missions were aided by the academic disciplines of psychology, sociology, and management, while industrial relations provided staff and training, and corporate human relations departments provided expert testimony and reported on their own welfare schemes. In effect, these agencies and commissions carried out research that provided intelligence about the working-class that would inform the regulatory and welfarist policies. Such policies were advocated by reformers to lighten some of the deprivations that fed the grievances behind strikes and to create the appearance of access to the polity by marginalised workers in order to begin managing class conflict. Regulation was intended to further expand the state into the economy as much to regulate unruly workers as to rein in the most egregious corporate activities that provoked them.

Socialising the Costs

States began to take responsibility for damages and financial losses of companies affected by the strike, in effect providing a type of publicly financed risk insurance. This allowed the corporations to pass on the cost of disciplining the working-class to the workers themselves through taxes and debt. The direct cost of the 1877 strike was estimated by the *New York Journal of Commerce* to be $26.25 million. It is unclear how this estimate contributed to inflating B&O's property damage from $2.5–15 million. The true costs will probably never be known because some of the railroad companies managed to shift the costs to local, state and federal governments both directly and indirectly. The Pennsylvania Supreme Court ordered Allegheny County to pay Scott's Pennsylvania Railroad $2 million in damages for stolen and destroyed freight in Pittsburgh. The county eventually settled for $1.4 million plus interest in 1880 paid by floating a bond that was not paid off until 1906. To pay for the force of 4,925 men in Philadelphia used to protect the Pennsylvania Railroad, 35 local banks loaned the city $518.40 each, totalling $18,144, which the city repaid in October.[77]

The strike hammered the profitability of the railroads although it had little effect on the stock market as a whole. Railroad company dividends declined by $5.6 million in 1874–5, $6.2 million in 1875–6, and $9.5 million in 1876–7. No dividends were paid on any railroad in ten states in July 1877.[78] The

---

77   Foner 1977, p. 192.
78   Ibid., p. 20.

Pennsylvania line even missed dividends for August and November. In October 1877 Scott sold the Pennsylvania to Rockefeller. The Pittsburgh strikers had ironically contributed to the formation of the greatest monopoly of its day.

While the companies may have 'wildly overestimated' the costs of the strike, the monetary costs cannot be limited just to losses during the strike from disruptions in production, shipping, sales, and security.[79] The strike generated inestimable costs for decades to come to reorganise and expand the US Army, establish the National Guard, professionalise the police, implement welfare policies, set up new agencies and commissions, and to pay for other measures to regulate and manage class conflict. While never calculated, these costs – most of which were incurred by expanding the role of the state in regulating class conflict – are likely substantial.

Capital Consolidation

These are the costs of the new composition of capital to forcefully respond to and decompose the working-class power that made the 1877 strike. The railroad's entreaties to the federal courts, state governors and President Hayes to intervene may have been improvised emergency measures but they launched a new redesign of capital and the state. As separately managed companies operating in a political climate in which government was preferred limited and distant, each regional line was vulnerable to nationwide disruption by workers who did not recognise distinctions between owners of capital. Although the industry-wide negotiated wage cut demonstrated a capacity for railroad capital to coordinate, they were still highly competitive and vulnerable to disruptions in the coal mines on which they depended, such as by the Pennsylvania strikes over the last several years, which were renewed only a month later.

Capital, too, reassessed its tactics and strategy in the current climate. The wave of capital consolidation in the railroad, mining, steel, and banking and other sectors, typified by Rockefeller's buy-out of Scott, illustrated two developments taking place. First, vast amounts of capital would be needed to finance the consolidation within and across these industries. This was made possible by innovations in banking and the development of new forms of financing such as the so-called 'watered stock' and corporate bonds. The financialisation of industrial capital was a tactic devised to respond to the real threat of disruption wrought by the 1877 strike.

---

79   Bruce 1959, p. 299.

In a strange turn of fate, the financialisation of railroad capital is integrally connected to the labour organiser responsible for setting the 1877 strike in motion. Robert Ammon, the founder and Grand Organiser of the Trainmen's Union, became a Wall Street lawyer and went to prison for financial crimes. The man who helped lay the groundwork for the strike that prompted a new financial tool – one that financed the consolidation of railroad capital and its integration with related sectors – eventually became a wealthy Wall Street investor.[80]

Second, a new relationship between capital and the state to manage and, if necessary, repress working-class insurgency would necessitate a transformation and growth not merely in government authority, power, and responsibility but in the revenue to pay for it. This intensified the contentious debate over the tariff and the income tax between the two dominant parties over the next several decades. Ultimately, it was the shift from the tariff to the federal income tax with the ratification of the 16th amendment in 1913 that generated sufficient revenue to finance the expansion of policing, military and regulatory functions of government to meet the challenge of an increasingly disruptive working-class.[81]

The 1877 strike prompted efforts to develop a new means of raising capital to pay for corporate consolidation and transform the role of the state to regulate class relations. A century later, Hamilton's vision of a capitalist market supported by a strong central government was coming into view. The strike shattered a fundamental rationale for laissez-faire capitalism: that the state had little to no role to play in the economy. As *Harper's Magazine* succinctly put it after the 1877 strike, 'it is the business of the State, that is, of the people, to prevent disorder of the kind that we saw in the summer, by removing the discontent which is its cause'.[82] At last, the Hamiltonian argument won the day. The state was no longer limited to borrowing and coining money, enforcing contracts, establishing bankruptcy laws, regulating inter-state commerce, and setting up a well-armed and -funded militia and military in times of emergency. As the working-class threat came into focus, the emergency became permanent, requiring the fiscal means to maintain the expanded infrastructure to ensure its functioning. Police, military, prosecutorial, and penitentiary powers were becoming unquestioned, if not expensive, responsibilities of the state in market capitalism.

---

80   See Burbank 1966, p. 203.

81   The amendment became necessary after the 1895 Supreme Court ruling in *Pollock v. Farmers' Loan & Trust Company* struck down the income tax passed by Congress.

82   Bruce 1959, p. 314.

As Alquati explains,

> The present reorganization/recomposition of sectors (aerospace, research, automation of services, containers, etc.) corresponds to a new POLITICAL initiative by the collective capitalist patron to outflank the working-class internationally and for a fairly considerable length of time.
>
> This initiative is POLITICAL in that it aims to alter politically the composition and political terms of [sic] class relation, and so extricate itself from the crisis situation in which it has been placed by the class movements of struggle vis-à-vis wages in the preceding cycle of struggles.[83]

Working-Class Decomposition

Despite the threats, workers' efforts to cross divisions of craft-labourer, rural-urban, black-white, industrial sector, and corporate ownership continued over the coming decades. These efforts established the working-class as an ungovernable force, a volcano threatening to explode just beneath the surface of the sidewalk. The new tactics described earlier were critical features of the composition of capital that emerged in response to a newly recomposed working-class, raising the costs and reducing the opportunities of mobilising and insurgency.

Elites have at their disposal what could be called a 'repertoire of blockage', including tactics that range in the level of intensity from opening space in the polity to advocating or contesting elections, concessionary reforms, co-optation, absorption, diffusion, deflection, institutionalisation of insurgent leaders and organisations, dividing or eroding mass support, and repression. Each of these tactics in its repertoire serves to rupture working-class power by breaking its alliances, carving off leadership or allies, or forcibly destroying its base of power.

As Bell and Cleaver explain, the decomposition of working-class power proceeds to the degree that new relations of production and a division of labour successfully fragment the basis of workers' power. One of the most common tactics to achieve this is to encourage de-escalation to gain access to the polity in the expectation of delivering gains in the form of concessions and compromises through negotiation. As discussed in Chapter 2, elites will seek out organisations with which they can deal, such as the Workingmen's Party in the

---

83   Alquati n.d.

1877 strike, in order to redirect the strike into bargaining. As fortunes of the organisation become tied to access and resources, they attempt to de-escalate and demobilise the insurgency.

Reforms gained by previous cycles of struggle become the launching point for the next level of struggle. They may also be transformed into the tactics for dismantling bases of organisation and discouraging further mobilisation and escalation. When combined with threats or actual repression, insurgents may demobilise and de-escalate in the face of rising costs and declining opportunities. The craft unions and Workingmen's Parties in St. Louis and East St. Louis were not the only ones to do so in 1877. As we will see in the remaining chapters, recognition and legitimacy given to union leadership by elites to negotiate for prior gains has been repeatedly deployed to discourage further mobilisation and prevent further tactical escalation as the leadership sought to protect existing gains.

Two millennia ago, Indian political theorist Kautilya explained the tactic of conciliation by emphasising merit, mutual shared interests, or by offering inducements, awards, and honours. These made up two of his four tactics for dealing with conflict.[84] Kautilya ingeniously discovered that conciliation can have the effect of transforming prior success into the means of disempowerment.

Access to the negotiating table or the polity initiates what Rubenstein called the process of 'intra-group disaggregation' that foments fractures between the leadership and rank and file. When a group's intelligentsia and leadership are incorporated into 'existing structures of power and privilege', the remaining members of the group are offered symbolic inclusion in the national debate such as by serving on an agenda-setting committee, receiving funding, or being made the beneficiaries of funding resources for the organisation and membership.[85] Intra-group disaggregation would play a central role in the strategy of the welfarists during the strike wave of the first decade of the twentieth century that pursued the dual approach of negotiations with labour unions with the family wage, disability, unemployment, and other wage supplements, to dampen upward pressure on wages.

A unified elite coalition can effectively repress an insurgency or render its tactics impotent or ineffective. The normative order and economic and political system are vulnerable when elites are not unified, when they lack political will, are unable to forcefully respond to tactical escalation, and appear to lose

---

84   Kautilya 2000, pp. 91–2.

85   Rubenstein, nd, p. 17.

legitimacy, power, and stability. Piven and Cloward, for example, argue that elites are most likely to offer a conciliatory response when insurgents' disruptive actions provoke electoral instability.

> ... it is usually when unrest among the lower classes breaks out of the confines of electoral procedures that the poor may have some influence, for the instability and polarization they then threaten to create by their actions in the factories or in the streets may force some response from electoral leaders.[86]

The potential loss of members of the elite coalition and political resources (votes in exchange for patronage) are likely to cause realignments that open the coalition to new members that provide new opportunities and resources. This is especially the case when many of the aggrieved are excluded from the polity altogether.

The disruptions caused by the 1877 and 1894 strikes aggravated splits among elites over whether the appropriate tactical response should be repression, negotiations, conciliation, or welfarism. This disrupted the two party duopoly pushing both Democrats and Republicans to add new members to their party coalitions. Over the coming decades both parties agreed on repressing the IWW, socialists, and anarchists, while the Democrats absorbed the populists and then the AFL and the Republicans did the same with the Progressives by the end of WWI. If conciliation and reform become ends in themselves, it may restore stability by placating insurgents, absorbing its leaders, repressing them, or waiting it out.

In addition to identifying how insurgents are tactically able to force concessions, Piven and Cloward demonstrate how they also have a tactical value by fragmenting the power of insurgents that forced elites to concede. That an insurgency may provoke the very concessions that destroy it could be called the 'paradox of success'. When de-escalating to negotiate achieves gains, the focus shifts to institutionalising the gains by establishing formal membership-based or grant-funded organisations that advocate for and monitor the delivery of concessions. In the process, the leadership or organisations play a moderating role by expressing a willingness not merely to de-mobilise but even to reorganise themselves to make it possible to defend these gains. In the process the insurgent leaders become increasingly alienated from the movement as they begin to spend more time with their adversaries, learn to speak their language,

---

86   Cloward and Piven 1978, p. 15.

internalise their logic, language, and ways of dress, and become dependent on elites for funding and delivering promised concessions.

For example, in labour struggles the internalisation of the elites' language and logic by insurgent leaders happens subtly. To represent themselves, the rank and file establish a union as an institutional representative of the membership and choose or have self-selected for them the union leadership which uses the union's resources to enter into arbitration, negotiations, or collective bargaining. To facilitate negotiations, the rank and file are encouraged to 'cool it' unless management attempts a nefarious manoeuvre to which a limited action may be allowed.

The bargaining process has the effect of shifting the adversarial conflict to a pursuit of shared interests between capital and workers known today as 'interest-based bargaining', which accords to the principles of absolute gains theory. Once an agreement is initially reached, the union pursues negotiations so as to maintain and gradually expand existing gains at the lowest possible threat or cost and attempts to impose it on others in similar or related industries through a sector-wide agreement or what is more recently referred to as 'pattern-based bargaining'. Both approaches harness the politics of the possible to the fortunes of capital. Maintaining the gradual gains weds the leadership to the employer so that success in business can translate into success at the negotiating table. Inversely, concessions are imposed on the workers, rationalised by a myriad of reasons including minimising give backs, upholding the sanctity of the contract, and preserving the bargaining process when business is bad so that losses can be restored to the workers when the fortunes of capital improve. Any attempt by either side to mobilise is taken as an unprovoked escalation of tactics that may impede continued negotiations and is frowned upon by leaders on both sides and state and federal collective bargaining law as 'bargaining in bad faith'.

Once a settlement is reached, the union leadership and negotiators have obtained a specialised expertise and extensive detailed knowledge of the complex technicalities of the agreement not available to the rank and file. Organising parts ways from servicing the contract and bargaining so that where the former once made the latter possible, the inverse becomes true. Through a thousand myriad ways the leadership becomes intertwined with their former adversary.

The leadership becomes responsible for enforcing the contract by serving the membership. They ensure it is faithfully implemented and followed not only by management but also by their own members. In this way, collective bargaining and the grievance process, gradually almost imperceptibly transform insurgent leaders into auxiliaries of management policing adherence to the contract. As Glaberman explains, such a process results in 'the unions turned into their opposite, from representatives of the workers to an independent power that imposes its discipline over the workers in the period of state capitalism'.[87]

The union's resources soon shift from organising members and non-members to assert their power at the point of production to less adversarial and confrontational bargaining, negotiations and resolving grievances for contract violations and even partnering with management to lobby government for contracts, protectionist policies, subsidies, trade agreements, and new regulations. The struggle is gradually moved further away from the shop floor to pluralist mobilising of allies to ensure compliance with legal frameworks and to change state policies.

Cooperation between management and labour may lock in the initial concession until management finds the union no longer useful and seeks to break the contract, automate, relocate, go bankrupt, etc. Negotiations have succeeded in de-escalating tensions long enough to survive the initial disruption but the achieved gains do not increase the opportunities for workers to achieve further gains. Because these gains are achieved by de-mobilisation and de-escalation, the very leverage that provoked the initial concession is abandoned so as to institutionalise the gain. Piven and Cloward capture this process when they write that

> The more important point is that by endeavoring to do what they cannot do, organisers fail to do what they can do. During those brief periods in which people are roused to indignation, when they are prepared to defy the authorities to whom they ordinarily defer, during those brief moments when lower-class groups exert some force against the state, those who call themselves leaders do not usually escalate the momentum of the people's protests ... Organisers not only failed to seize the opportunity presented by the rise of unrest, they typically acted in ways that blunted or curbed the disruptive force which lower-class people were sometimes able to mobilize.[88]

A gradual emergence of mutual interests further highlights the paradox of success. Union representatives find shared mutual interests with employers in the mutual objective of ensuring the survival of the business and thus the jobs and

---

87   Glaberman 1975, p. 10. See also Zerzan 1999, pp. 185–198.
88   Piven and Cloward 1978, pp. xxi–xxii.

membership which serve to undermine the interests of the workers on whose behalf the concession was initially made. A complementariness emerges in which the union leadership needs negotiations to justify their existence and employers need union reps to keep their members disciplined, manageable, and productive. Using collective bargaining to defuse violence in strikes, as the Brotherhoods and then the AFL would do, had the effect of transforming unions into partners with capital in an effort to make workers more compliant and productive. As the number of wildcat strikes and the use of political violence rose during WWI, elites' willingness to allow unionisation declined precipitously after 1919 until the next great disruptions in West Virginia in the 1920s (see Chapter 10) and then Michigan in the 1930s. Collective bargaining succeeded in using unions to ensure that workers became more productive even as they failed to make them more docile. This symbiotic partnership between capital and unions existed until it was replaced in the 1970s.[89]

The point at which most thinking about social movements and insurgencies ends is the moment when they appear to have achieved sufficient political legitimacy to be invited to participate in either negotiations and/or the polity and achieved some concessions.[90] Insurgents now find their leaders seated at the table as stakeholders with the expectation that they will receive redress for a semblance of their grievances or concession of part of their objectives.

With few exceptions, social movement theorists have been wholly unable or unwilling to explain what follows because of its own institutional imperative to serve to stabilise the normative order.[91] Portraying disruption as deviant, criminal, or dysfunctional resonates with the need to dmonstrate sociology's value to elites, to obtain funding for the discipline and research, and to certify its scientific objectivity by avoiding any appearance of advocacy. Yet, in fact, by not peering beyond de-mobilisation and de-escalation to achieve concessions, it is taking the side of elites to defuse and deflect the disruptive power wielded by insurgents in order to smooth the way for the agenda of domination

---

89 Neoliberalism ushered in the use of financial liberalisation, austerity, automation, and outsourcing as new disciplinary tools to replace unions. (See Cleaver 1997 and 2016; and Harvey 2007).

90 For example, in his otherwise insightful examination of the tactics and strategy of contention in the modern black civil rights movement, McAdam (1999) ends his study just when the civil rights movement gains access to the Democratic Party coalition and before the movement further escalates into the Black Power movement.

91 The exceptions being Gamson 1975 and 2009; Tilly 1978 and 2003; and Piven and Cloward 1978.

and control. Sociology's study of social conflict and social movements is not to understand the basis for social change but to serve elites's need to suppress it.

To answer the critical question of how insurgents can avoid being defeated by the paradox of their own success that decomposes their own power, it is necessary to transcend sociological social movement theory. According to McAdam, the answer depends on the insurgents' ability to adapt and innovate in the face of new threats from *both* newly open and closed political spaces. 'To survive, however, a movement must be able to sustain the leverage generated by the use of such novel tactics. To do so requires further experimentation with non-institutionalized forms of protest'.[92] The key is to devise tactics that continue applying leverage to extract further concessions from elites that continue shifting power to insurgents.

This strategy is hardly new. Rosa Luxemburg wrote about the German Social Democratic Party seeking reform as a goal in itself (winning elections, entering government, etc.) rather than reform as a tactic to shift the balance of power to the workers in the process of recomposing their class power to the point of expanding the crisis of capital's power and provoking a revolutionary situation.[93] The ability and willingness to continue escalating tactics even while negotiating for further gains, what Tilly calls pairing or switching, is by no means easy or risk free.

Mass support may shrink if there is a perception that the insurgents' goals have been achieved, further demands are seen as excessive and destabilising, an expectation that de-escalation and negotiating will be sufficient to obtain further objectives, and if those who hold power regain credibility and appear to be reasonable and willing to negotiate differences. Continuing to advocate further tactical escalation may appear to be unreasonable and risky since elites may now be widely seen as conciliatory and sympathetic. If mass support dwindles, and insurgents can no longer effectively escalate their tactics (the very means that gave them leverage to force concessions), the opportunity for further gains or even holding on to whatever may have been gained so far declines rapidly. As we will discuss in Chapter 8, this was the case of the WWI wildcat strikers once the war ended. The cost to workers of continued tactical escalation and attempts to apply leverage rise rapidly. They may be channelled into the very political process they originally rebelled against, where little if any reform may be achieved with so much delay, equivocation, and redirection as to devolve into quiet defeat.

---

92   McAdam 1999, p. 164.

93   Luxemburg 1900.

Not continuing to mobilise, escalate tactics, and apply leverage may also subject insurgents to another kind of cost: repression. If insurgencies are not willing to allow themselves to be co-opted, they can expect to face repression and will be defeated if they do not continue organising mass support, escalating their tactics, and destabilising elites. At this juncture, the insurgency is faced with the decomposition of its power if it is unable to continue escalating its tactics and applying the leverage that will make further gains possible.

Insurgencies that begin to achieve some of their objectives may experience intra-group disaggregation and split over these very tactical issues. The leadership begins to gain status, power and legitimacy by engaging with elites and pushes for de-escalation and de-mobilisation to defend newfound recognition and existing gains. They will now assess a greater likelihood of success working inside the system rather than against it. They will split from those who advocate that the movement continue to escalate tactics and apply the leverage that made these gains possible to achieve more of their objectives. Both will soon find themselves facing one another across a great divide of power. The very question of whether to demobilise and de-escalate tactics may cause an insurgency to fragment, delay, hesitate, appear fragmented, lose credibility among supporters, and be defeated. This was evident by WWI when the AFL moved onto electoral terrain by beginning to endorse Congressional candidates and joining the war effort.

The dominant streams of social movement theory reduce insurgencies to pluralistic movements of interest groups contending for resources in order to achieve their political demands while ignoring the class relations that shape, constrain, and limit choices and opportunities.[94] Interest group pluralism implicitly assumes the necessity of de-escalation to achieve access to the polity to resolve grievances. As a result it is inherently conservative, because it assumes stability and preservation of the system as the utmost objective of political conflict. Tactics of disruption, tension, and even political violence, short of being a 'tactic of last resort', cannot be examined in isolation from the composition of the working-class carrying out its own struggle. When the working-class manages to recompose its power, it finds itself at its apex of power and in the position to escalate its tactics to achieve some of its objectives while continuing to escalate its tactics to realise ever more – even systemic – change.

In order to continue mobilising and escalating tactics it becomes necessary for insurgents to reject leadership and allies who demobilise and de-escalate

---

94   Piven and Cloward make a similar point referring to the institutional context rather than
      class relations (1978, pp. ix–40).

to not merely extract new concessions but to defend them. In such cases insurgents have perceived how negotiations merely offer access and an opportunity to 'be heard' rather than material control and power over assets, resources, and the system itself. Access itself gives elites power to define and legitimise the 'leaders' of the insurgency and thus divide and weaken them. As Tilly explains,

> [G]overnments also sometimes accept or reinforce boundaries separating challengers from polity members by bargaining out who belongs to them and who has the right to speak for challengers even while denying them routine access to governmental resources.[95]

Insurgents sit at a table made by others only to find themselves listed as the main course on the menu.

A New Capital Composition

To respond to insurgent workers, capital too studies the workers' tactics and strategies to identify weak points at which it can apply leverage, escalate repression to encourage supporters and insurgents to de-escalate and demobilise in the face of growing threats and costs. Working-class power is decomposed when capital achieves a new composition in both the relations of production and the balance of political power.

The workers' defeat results in a decomposition of their power when capital puts in place new relations of production to overcome further threats from workers' insurgencies. This establishes the contours of a new composition of capital. Alquati describes how this is achieved through a new division of labour, 'producing predominance of a new form of "job", vis. parcelized, assembly-line & series labor process controlled via decomposition and simplification of labour, extending to administration & services (Circulation)'.[96] Management may replace workers with children, lower-waged women and immigrant workers, move production to new locations, rationalise and deskill the work, lay off the workforce, replace them with strikebreakers, or introduce new technologies or procedures to increase their productivity and reduce reliance on labour. As we have seen, the 1877 railroad strike sped up the consolidation and standardisation of the railroad industry and its further integration

---

95   Tilly 2003, p. 29.
96   Alquati n.d.

into the vertical trusts which also controlled significant portions of the coal mining, banking and steel industries – all key inputs into the railroads.

The new capital composition is characterised by what Silver calls a 'techno-logical fix' (e.g. new division of labour), 'product fix' (e.g. move into new sectors of production), and 'financial fix' (e.g. move out of production and into finance and speculation) that seek to decompose working-class power.[97] What is commonly called 'disruption' and 'innovation' could rather be seen as a defensive reaction to class struggle.

The only thing missing during this time is a 'spatial fix' in which capital can flee the geographic constraints on its movement into global markets. The 1877 and the later 1894 (see Chapters 4 and 5) strikes were so threatening to the process of capital accumulation because of the centrality of transporta-tion systems at the time to move tangible goods, people, information, and even physical capital. As Silver observes,

> Thus, the source of their workplace bargaining power often is to be found less in the direct impact of their actions on their immediate (often public) employers and more on the upstream/downstream impact of the failure to deliver goods, services, and people to their destination. The 'relative fortunes of capitalists in different locations' are greatly impacted by the development of new transportation networks ... as well as by the disrup-tion of existing transportation networks, including disruptions caused by workers' struggles.[98]

The railroad tracks themselves also spotlighted the physical limitations and vulnerabilities of capital to disruption by a recomposed working-class. As long as capital was confined to moving on physical, linearly running steel rails, it was subject to disruption. The truck and interstate highways would provide a new fix to such disruption.

The new composition of capital alters the balance of political power by insti-tutionalising new means of force developed *in situ* during the conflict and reor-ganising the state so as to better serve its needs. Here too, after the 1877 strike,

---

97   See Silver 2003, pp. 39–40. As has been widely demonstrated, those constrictors have been eroded since the Bretton Woods agreement of 1944 as a result of the rise of neoliberalism. (Harvey 2007; and Cleaver 2016). What is less understood is how the emergence of the US onto the international arena as a colonial power in the late nineteenth century, especially accelerating during the era of 'gunboat diplomacy', marked the beginnings of an attempt to put into place such a spatial fix.

98   Silver 2003, p. 100.

railroad capital expanded the telegraph and introduced the telephone, over-hauled local and state police forces, brought the courts into labour disputes as a coercive arbiter, reshaped the role of the federal government in the eco-nomy, and reorganised the unreliable militias into the National Guard – all of which would reduce the effectiveness of workers' mobilisation and disruption anywhere in the system.

This process of devising a new composition of capital has the effect of decomposing the working-class's power that proved so threatening in the previ-ous cycle of struggle. This shift in the balance of power will likely persist or even worsen until workers yet again reassess the composition of capital, expand their mass support, and devise new tactics and organisational strategy to put into place a recomposition of working-class power that can overcome their disadvantage. These new tactics and strategies that characterise the new com-position of capital are difficult and take time to overcome. For railroad workers, it would take 17 long years.

PART 2

The 1894 Railroad Strike

∴

CHAPTER 4

The Nineties Dripped with Blood: The 1894 Railroad Strike[1]

It is understood that a strike is war; not necessarily a war of blood and bullets, but a war in the sense that it is a conflict between two contending interests or classes of interests.

EUGENE DEBS, 1895[2]

• • •

We cannot overlook the fact that at the present time the relations subsisting between capitalists and laborers are those of war.

GEORGE W. WALTS, Commissioner, California Bureau of Labor Statistics, 1891–2[3]

•   •
•

The years following the 1877 railroad strike were abuzz with efforts by both capital and the working-class to shift the balance of power. Elites devising a new composition of capital reorganised the police and military, articulated new legal doctrines, expanded the role of the state into the economy, consolidated industry, and transformed the division of labour on the shop floor. Workers, in turn, explored new tactics and strategies to recompose their own power. By 1886 the disruptive threat of class struggle was once again prevalent for all to see.

Class struggle re-emerged in 1886 with a central demand to shorten the workday to eight hours. In the midst of what would be decades of virtually uninterrupted depression, 'eight hours labour, eight hours recreation and eight hours rest' became a clarion call for a renewed cycle of struggle. This strategy added a new element of control over the length and intensity of work to the demand for higher wages. Eight years later the 1894 railroad strike shook the country

---

1   The phrase is adapted from a passage written by journalist Ida Tarbell. (Painter 1987, p. 72).
2   See Debs's testimony to the United States Strike Commission, 1895, p. 143.
3   Biennial Report of the Bureau of Labor Statistics of California 1891–2, p. 29.

yet again. The turbulent 1880s and 1890s demonstrated the disruptive power of the self-organised working-class but this time with a new strategy of industrial unionism that was designed to meet the new organisation of industrial capital.

Flush from a successful Knights of Labor (KoL) strike on the Gould line earlier in 1894, many railroad workers broke from the brotherhoods to form the American Railway Union (ARU). The rank and file members of the KoL defied the leadership's opposition to strikes by using the assemblies as a vehicle for self-organising. Earlier strikes on the Wabash Railroad in 1885 and the Great Southwest strike in 1886 carried their power over into the ARU.[4] The vertical struggle within the Knights of Labor and later the ARU between the self-organised workers and the leadership paralleled the struggle between workers and capital. While the organisations and their leadership sought to channel and manage class struggle to produce gains with minimal risk to the survival of the organisation, the membership tried 'to use the resources and established networks of the organization to further their struggle'.[5] When workers were able to use union resources and networks, they reduced the costs of escalating their tactics while substantially increasing the potential for gain while also placing the organisation at a great risk of potential repression.

In this way, both the unions and the shop were sites of struggle between self-organised workers. To the degree that unions were subsumed to the objectives of these workers they became targeted for repression by capital and the state. Ultimately, union leadership that showed a capacity to use the union to manage, diffuse, and deflect self-organisation demonstrated their potential usefulness for managing class struggle and found new legitimacy when they entered into collective bargaining and signed contracts that could be used to maintain discipline over their membership.

Initially opening the ARU membership to black and white skilled and unskilled railroad workers gave it a new strategic advantage. The move to the 'one big union' of the IWW was still decades away. While the ARU had moved part of the way towards meeting the challenge of an increasingly integrated and consolidated railroad industry, its later exclusionary racial policy demonstrated the limit of its attempt to recompose working-class power. While it overcame the barrier between craft worker and labourer and corporate ownership by organising all railroad workers into locals, it only organised workers in the single

---

4 Self Negation n.d., p. 26.

5 Ibid., p. 41.

industry. These two strategic limitations would limit their ability to build mass support, which substantially raised the costs of mobilising and reduced the opportunity to achieve gains when the membership escalated its tactics.

The escalation of tactics began almost immediately. Only one year after the ARU was formed its first convention received a contingent of striking workers from the Pullman Car Company. They asked the ARU delegates to call a solidarity strike to boycott all trains carrying a Pullman car which would shut down much of the country. By organising all white railroad workers regardless of job type and company, the ARU provided the organisational infrastructure and tactical leverage that made it possible to escalate the tactics of a strike from merely disrupting a local shop to bringing the entire system to a halt in 1877.

After successfully winning two strikes in previous months the ARU membership pushed the leadership to support their demands to escalate tactics by boycotting Pullman cars. Boycotting Pullman cars was an ingenious strategy devised by the ARU rank and file and pushed onto the leadership. Because nearly every rail line pulled Pullman cars, boycotting them provided increased leverage by disrupting not only the entire industry but also much of the national economy. The workers had read the signs of the last cycle of struggle in 1877 and coordinated new tactics and strategy to meet the new composition of capital by forming the ARU. Similarly, the industry too was ready, having used the lull to organise themselves through the General Managers Association (GMA) and strengthen their connections to allies in the federal courts and the White House in preparation for further insurgent organising.

Birth Pangs

The 1894 Pullman strike illustrated the multi-faceted ways in which railroad workers escalated their tactics, informed by their reading of the risks and opportunities. They bypassed the existing brotherhoods that exclusively organised skilled workers and used contracts to discipline them. The brotherhoods had a well-known record of compromise and participating in breaking strikes by non-members and low or unskilled fellow workers often in the same shops and on the same lines.

In contrast, the ARU was self-organised by workers who had fled the brotherhoods or were dual members. Since the ARU was open to railroad workers of all skill levels and lines regardless of skill, job classification, employer, region, or the existence of a contract, it allowed them to build a wider base of workers and mass support. Many of these organisers had learned from the tactics of the KoL in recent strikes and applied them with some innovations and missteps.

Perhaps the most important lesson they learned from their experience in the KoL was to strike first and then join the KoL after.[6] In this way, what Stromquist called 'strikers' unions' like the KoL and the ARU were built by the rank and file in the heat and fire of the strike. Strikers' unions were the product of prior accumulated experience in attempting to transform their brotherhoods and to form system federations of brotherhoods so they would cooperate across craft lines. Their efforts were 'guided by an explicit debate among railroad men over which form of industrial organization was most appropriate to their purposes'.[7]

In 1888, that debate led to action as self-organised engineers, firemen and switchmen within the brotherhoods forced their brotherhoods to call a strike on the Chicago, Burlington & Quincy railroad and then attempted to organise a systems federation to formalise their cross-craft cooperation (see also Chapter 2). In June 1889 officers of the Brotherhood of Railroad Trainmen (BRT), Switchmen's Mutual Aid Association (SMAA), and the Brotherhood of Locomotive Firemen (BLF, represented by Debs) met in Chicago and organised the Supreme Council of United Orders of Railway Employees (SCUORE) as a federation of organisations not, as was originally proposed, as a federation of classes. They excluded the Knights of Labor, which supported the original plan to organise a federation open to all railroad workers and decentralising power under the control of the rank and file, who could deploy it as a confrontational strikers' union. This vision contrasted sharply with SCUORE which was organised to preserve the authority and power of the brotherhoods' organisational leadership over their own particular members in order to prevent and control strikes by impeding them from circulating. In the new federation, the three brotherhoods' 'succeeded in only federating themselves' in order to channel the movement for federation from below. Two years after it formed, SCUORE imploded in Spring 1891 when trainmen members took jobs from the locked out switchmen on the Chicago & Northwestern and the Brotherhood of Railroad Trainmen were kicked off the council.[8] SCUORE preserved the imperatives of the organisation at the expense of the objectives of the workers.

A year earlier, in July 1890, Debs, G.W. Howard of the Brotherhood of Conductors, and Frank Sweeney of the switchmen and other representatives of the BLE, BRT, and the KoL met to form an industrial union. The strategy they pursued was best articulated by trainman and former member of the SCUORE L.W. Rogers, who drew upon the experience and model of the Knights. In 1892

---

6   See Selig Perlman in Stromquist 1993, p. 60.

7   Stromquist 1993, p. 60.

8   Ibid., pp. 72–5.

he laid out the vision for the new union as one that 'holds within its ranks every man on the road from the tie tamper to the engineer, conductor and dispatcher' and combines 'the whole working force of the corporation controlled at one time and united in common defense'.[9] Roger's idea informed the ARU constitution which explicitly embraced a federation of all workers rather than of organisations, which had failed miserably.[10]

Their efforts brought together 50 rank and file militants, representatives of the KoL, Debs, Howard, and Rogers to form the ARU, in June 1893. The railroad workers who formed the ARU first self-organised without a union and then formed the ARU to formalise their decentralised bottom-up approach. While they balked at abandoning the racism that was rampant among unions at the time, they sought to overcome the divisions of craft and skill, brotherhood organisational form, the contract, and efforts to channel the strike through established political channels and arbitration. In the face of mounting repression, they established the ARU, which would escalate tactics very quickly to a general strike characterised by scattered attacks, sabotage and street battles.

In little more than a year, the ARU made immense progress toward achieving its goal of opening its membership to all railroad workers (with the exception of blacks). A list of blacklisted ARU strikers assembled by the Northern Pacific Railroad shows that in 1894 the ARU was composed of a broad array of railroad workers, in most cases its membership of each craft exceeding the proportion of the entire railroad labour force in 1890. For example, among the highest ratios were those of firemen (300 percent higher), trainmen and shopmen (50 percent higher), and conductors (33 percent higher). The only group which was significantly underrepresented among the ARU membership were the section labourers who composed only one-seventh of their ratio in the entire labour force. The ARU membership was represented overwhelmingly by skilled workers of the so-called running trades, shopmen, and switchmen, and far underrepresented by sectionmen. This may have contributed to them losing the strike, as sectionmen, like shopmen and switchmen, do not travel with the trains. Since they make up 21 percent of all railroad workers, it may have dampened the support the strikers needed from local communities, but we cannot be sure of this. Since the ARU was crushed by the 1894 Pullman strike, it would not have time to address this imbalance.[11]

---

9   In Ibid., pp. 76–7.

10   ARU 1893, p. 5.

11   Stromquist 1993, p. 91. 'All other trades' were also underrepresented by about 44 percent.

The ARU was the next stage of organisational strategy devised by critical KoL assemblies, dissident brotherhood officials and rank and file members who built the ARU from their strike experiences. They came to the ARU through the tortuous routes of cross-class organising that led to strikes being defeated by not only the companies but also their own unions, which prevented them from circulating their efforts to other rail lines and other areas of the country. Reflecting on the lessons learned from the Chicago, Burlington & Quincy and other strikes of the past few years that provoked agitation for, first, a systems federation and, then, a union open to all members, Stromquist discerned that

> If defeats such as that on the Burlington pushed leaders of the brotherhoods toward caution and forbearance, they pushed many rank-and-file railroad workers who were faced with job competition and declining wages toward broader organization and more militant action ... [and] renewed their efforts to form a union of all railroad workers capable of prosecuting the struggle to its ultimate conclusion.[12]

It was the experience of earlier strikes led by the rank and file that resulted in the strike making the union.[13]

The 1886 Prelude

Within a decade, a range of events happened that would signal the recomposition of working-class power. In 1886, there were more than 200 percent more strikes, about 47 percent of which were wildcat strikes, and more than 60 percent more workers on strike than in the previous year.[14] There were three times as many strikes and workers on strike than during any year between 1881–4. Union membership had also exploded as a result of vigorous multi-racial industrial unionism of the KoL rank and file. Between 1884–6, union membership grew from 110,000 to 950,000.[15] In 1886, 350,000 were on strike nationwide with the KoL for an eight-hour day. With a still minuscule number of workers belonging to labour unions, these actions were testimony to workers' efforts to assert

---

12   Ibid., p. 79.
13   For this principle of union formation see Burns 2014.
14   Montgomery 1979, p. 20.
15   Smith 2006, p. xiv.

their demands but bypassing the existing unions and collective bargaining to directly disrupt production at the level of the shop floor to achieve their objectives.[16]

Although the newly formed AFL is credited by historians with calling for the general strike for an eight-hour day, the strike was sparked months earlier on 2 March when rank and file members of the KoL defied its president to launch a wildcat shopmen's strike. They struck Gould's Wabash, Missouri Pacific, and Union Pacific Railroad, part of his gigantic 15,000 mile system that stretched from St. Louis to the Pacific. As in 1877, the strike began in the South, this time in Texas, the birthplace of the Farmer's Alliance. After the KoL President Powderly twice attempted to call off the strike in a gesture to the uncooperative Gould, the workers ignored his directive to escalate their tactics, resulting in deadly battles in which 11 workers were killed.[17] With a mere 25,000 members, the AFL played a minuscule role in the strike.

Observing the growing railroad strike on 26 March 1886 now former President Hayes, who wielded the Army to break the 1877 railroad strike, questioned which class government would serve:

> Am I mistaken in thinking that we are drawing near the time when we must decide to limit and control great wealth, corporations, and the like, or resort to a strong military government? Is this the urgent question? ... Shall the railroads govern the country, or shall the people govern the railroads? Shall the interest of railroad kings be chiefly regarded, or shall the interest of the people be paramount? ... [G]overnment policy should be to prevent the accumulation of vast fortunes; and monopolies, so dangerous in control, should be held firmly in the grip of the people.[18]

Former President Hayes had a cause for concern. The railroads had grown exceptionally fast in size and power, nearly doubling between 1877 and 1886, following the 1877 strike he helped defeat.[19] The massive expansion of the railroads was financed by the rapid inflow of capital into industry. During the 1880s total capital investment grew by 150 percent, investment in manufacturing more than doubled from $2.8 billion to $6.5 billion, and the number of factory workers doubled.[20]

---

16   Montgomery 1974, p. 99; and Montgomery 1979, p. 95.
17   Painter 1987, pp. 43–4.
18   Hayes 1924.
19   Painter 1987, p. 38.
20   Lens 1973, p. 56; and Painter 1987, p. xxxiv.

This influx of new capital served several integrated functions. It financed consolidation of control of the industry and its integration with the related banking, coal, iron, and steel industries and the introduction of a new division of labour. As discussed in Chapter 3, consolidation was a tactic intended to restore labour discipline in order to rekindle the capital accumulation process. The tremendous growth in the size of industry in the intervening years is testament to the new composition of capital arranged following the disruptions of 1877. The 1894 strike only accelerated the process of consolidation. The consolidation of 85 percent of the industry into seven large companies had taken place between 1886 and 1893.[21] The class struggle had subsided but it had not been resolved. With this expansion came great vulnerability and the need for stability.

The centre of the 1886 eight-hour strike was Chicago where an estimated 25 percent of the 1 May strikers walked out. Tensions were high and both sides had been escalating their tactics during recent struggles, such as when Mayor Harrison had used the police against the street railcar strike. During the 1885 McCormick Reaper Works strike the company's request for more police protection was rejected by Mayor Harrison, who urged him to settle with the union which he was forced to do.[22] The next year when workers struck again against the new machinery and the permanent strikebreakers now given the eight-hour day the mayor sent in 600 police joined by Pinkertons, and the state militia armed with Gatling guns, to violently open the picket lines, killing at least two workers. This attack led August Spies and others to call for the Haymarket Square rally the next day (4 May) that led to the bombing, police massacre, hunt for radicals and frame ups and executions.

At the 4 May rally to protest the repression at Haymarket Square, a bomb was thrown when hundreds of police assaulted the remaining few hundred at the protest. In all, as a result of the police riot and the bomb, about 60 police were injured, eight were killed, and another 30 people were wounded. The eight so-called 'Haymarket martyrs' were prosecuted on trumped up charges for setting off a bomb that killed and injured police and members of the public at the protest. Seven were given the death sentence, one died in prison, four were executed, and the remaining three were eventually released by Governor Altgeld in 1893 after garnering widespread support for their cause, although not from the Knights' Powderly.

---

21   Stromquist 1993, p. 13.
22   Harring 1983, p. 113.

The country was once again threatened with tactical violence by the state, armed workers, and anarchists. On 2 May German workers heeded the *Arbeiter-Zeitung* 'To Arms!' poster and the Lehrund-Wehr Vereine's 1,000 members began training with rifles in secret halls and shooting in the woods on 2 May.[23]

Capital did not take the field with arms alone. As businesses became professionalised, linked by the telegraph, and consolidated under the trust, the new composition of capital provided the means to block, absorb, co-opt, deflect, and repress the newly emerging recomposition of working-class power. The tactics put into place following the 1877 strike came into use. Capital now had at its disposal a potent pairing of tactics of repression, co-optation and institutionalisation, including the injunction, arbitration, revamped police and military, new National Guard, and legislative measures such as immigration law, regulation, and welfarism to derail the re-emerging threat of disruption. Gage notes their long-lasting influence on class conflict.

> The strategies and principles forged in that moment proved to have enormous staying power, not only for Chicago but also for the nation as a whole. Over the next few decades, as the sort of violence first displayed at Haymarket evolved into a familiar fact of American life, the responses pioneered in 1886 – raids, speech laws, immigration restriction, police crackdowns – gained new currency.[24]

Capital's new tactical repertoire put strikers and their supporters at greater risk, thereby raising the costs of mobilising and escalation. Yet, by escalating the intensity of its tactics elites foreclosed the possibility of de-escalation frequently offered by union leaders. It also facilitated further in kind escalation of tactics by rank and file workers, which threatened instability, fragmenting of elite coalition, and systemic disruption. Thus began the *dance macabre*. It was unavoidable that

> ... an injunction was an act of war ... the injunction – which meant that labor leaders were arrested and held as 'prisoners of war' as soon as they began a strong movement against the employers – stirred in the working class more and more bitterness. Labor began to lose its illusions about the justice of the country's legal system. Labor's impulse to violence – to

---

23   Adamic 2008, p. 47.
24   Gage 2009, pp. 53–4.

dynamite, arson, and assassination – became stronger after each injunction, after the failure of each peaceable effort to better its conditions.[25]

The more elites resorted to state sanctioned violence in response to workers'
peaceful attempts at gaining redress for their grievances, the more likely it was
for workers to escalate their tactics as mass support builds, reducing the costs
and increasing the opportunities to achieve their objectives. As negotiations,
concessions, and arbitration were not allowed at the dance it was inevitable
that disruption would crash the gates.

Industrial Army of the Poor

The sheer scale of suffering caused by the 1893 depression prompted unemployed and destitute workers to self-organise in many major cities to demand
that government provide relief. In the midst of the harrowing depression, unions and the Socialist Labor Party (SLP), descendants of the Workingmen's Party
of the United States, organised marches in several cities to force the city councils to appropriate funds which they controlled for relief. In one city they succeeded in getting the city council to set up a short-lived works programme that
ended after a month.[26]

Little came from these efforts until 4 April 1894, when unemployed and
destitute workers self-organised into mobile protest encampments on commandeered trains. When 1,500 people calling themselves the Industrial Army
departed San Francisco, it inspired other Armies to form around the country.
The Industrial Army was portrayed from the start as a mobile Paris Commune,
a working-class army intent on invading Washington DC, the centre of American power. The movement got its first push from the mayor of San Francisco,
who paid ferry fares to Oakland and Sacramento for 600 people. The Industrial Army was soon led by SLP member 'General' Charles Kelly. A larger group
of 1,500–2,000 departed from Oakland on the Southern Pacific heading to Sacramento and then Utah, where they captured a new train outside Ogden. The
Industrial Army was popular, often receiving money, food, waived bridge tolls,
rail repairs, support and greetings from populists, unions, and the poor. They
received public support in western areas from the ARU, which was striking
against the Great Northern Railway the same month. Sometimes aid came from

---

25   Adamic 1931, p. 76.
26   Folsom 1991, pp. 152–3.

local officials and elites anxious to see them leave just as quickly as they had arrived. Although little is known about the many people who joined the Industrial Army, it became the training group for several notable radicals, including novelist Jack London and Wobbly William Haywood, who would go on to spread its passions elsewhere. London wrote about his travels with Kelly's Army by riverboat, receiving provisions from towns along the way. He also described the army having an internal authority and command structure.[27]

Among the now 4,500 strong Industrial Army that passed through Omaha and Council Bluffs, Nebraska on a commandeered train were two women who became known as 'Kelly's Angels'. One of the women, a journalist, was among 50 other women and 100 men who took a train in Washington, Iowa after marching across Iowa in parades with fife and drum. Kelly arrived in Washington DC on 12 July after leaving the Industrial Army in Wheeling, West Virginia where many were arrested. Only a few managed to reach their destination and join him in DC.[28]

The Industrial Armies were both an insurgency and a glimpse into an alternative future in the present. They bypassed taking power by setting up a parallel social system based on mutual aid that provided transportation and other necessities. As Folsom put it, Kelly's Army 'were creating a new society within the one from which they had been cast loose'. With cooks, a dentist, song and dance teams, glee clubs, local ministers, baseball teams, and carpenters that built flat boats for the Armies to traverse the Des Moines, Mississippi, Missouri, and Ohio rivers.[29] It provided a model for working people to organise themselves not just to protest the injustices but to shape a self-sufficient community to address unmet needs.

News of Kelly's Army spread like wildfire. Three weeks after Kelly's Army departed, another Industrial Army of about 500 led by Anna Smith left the San Francisco Bay Area. Although it is unknown how far they made it, most likely it wasn't very far. Another group of 600 to 700 left Los Angeles headed by Lewis Fry, a former soldier who organised them into drilled companies, giving validity to the nickname Industrial Army. This Industrial Army captured a train in Ontario, obtained generous food donations, and made it to El Paso, Texas where they seized another Southern Pacific train. Unfortunately, only a few made it to Washington DC. Another Industrial Army led by William Hogan departed Butte, Montana with passive help from a local marshal and a sheriff

---

27   London 1907.

28   Folsom 1991 pp. 156–9, and 167.

29   Ibid., p. 165.

deputy who appeared to be pursuing them with stalling tactics and by keeping a distance that made it unlikely they would block their path. On their arrival in Billings the deputy sheriff and his men opened fire and killed a local but were disarmed by the crowd and sped out of town. They took control of a train but were stopped outside Glendive, Montana by US troops armed with Gatling guns called out by President Cleveland to protect the bankrupt railroad under receivership. Hogan was arrested and sentenced to six months in jail but the army continued without him and traversed the Missouri River on flat boats. Ultimately, only a few made it to Washington, DC.[30]

The groups leaving Portland and California consolidated themselves into the Fifth Regiment United States Industrial Army. The Fifth Regiment took over and ran the railroad depot in Troutdale, including the sending and receiving of telegrams. Although they departed after being served with an injunction forbidding them from interfering with the railroad, the Fifth Regiment returned later and carried on running the depot. The marshal and Union Pacific Railroad left them an empty train with copies of the injunction on board, which they took. They were eventually captured. All 507 of those brought to court for violating the injunction were released by a judge with a warning. From there they continued commandeering trains.[31]

Although many historical accounts of this worker uprising label it is as Coxey's Army, most of the groups self-identified as autonomous Industrial Armies. The leader of the group that gave the movement its name was not actually destitute. Quite the opposite. Jacob Coxey owned a sand quarry, farm, and race horse breeding operation and was worth an estimated $200,000 in 1893. He and his family rode in splendour in a carriage and stayed in hotels while the army slept on the ground.

Coxey's name stuck because he was the most prominent of those who translated the grievances that sparked the Industrial Army insurrection into a concrete political programme. Coxey pursued his reform efforts for several more decades, thus giving him the staying power and influence to shape how the history of the movement was documented. Coxey had his own names for the group he led, one of the smallest but the best known, which he called a 'petition in boots' or the 'Commonweal of Christ'.

He specifically lobbied for his programme as the equivalent to a modern day non-governmental advocacy organisation. Coxey's plan was a mix of populism and Keynesianism including a minimum wage of $1.50 for eight hours and

---

30   Ibid., pp. 169–71 and 173–6.
31   Ibid., pp. 176–7.

$500 million to build and repair roads and schools funded by non-interest bearing bonds. The latter was a way to print paper money in order to increase the money supply inspired by similar populist proposals to expand the money supply with the subtreasury and silver proposals. Foreshadowing Keynesian works programmes during the Great Depression about 40 years later, 'the Industrial Armies had borrowed from the past and projected into the future one fundamental idea: Public works were essential in times of mass unemployment'.[32]

About 500 managed to arrive in Washington D.C. but Coxey and two other leaders were arrested and sentenced to 20 days in jail. Although it was widely reported in the news media, they were never able to formally present their petition to Congress. In all, more than 40 Industrial Armies started for Washington DC in 1894. Congress never acknowledged any of their ideas, made no concessions, and created no public works programmes in response to the movement.[33]

Lacking mass support, they never intended to escalate their tactics beyond a petition in boots. While they offered to negotiate, they lacked leverage and were defeated by a combination of indifference and repression with little risk to elites. The Industrial Army accomplished little other than months of media publicity. Negotiations never happened because they lacked resources that might attract allies among the elites who might gain from an alliance.[34] While they had a strong visual message and widespread mass support, as destitute workers and their families they were far removed from any strategic location in which they could carry out economic disruption.

The one tactic that proved effective for the Industrial Armies was seizing the railroads. But that was used only for transporting themselves to their destination, not to disrupt the economy. The ease with which they not only seized control of railroads, likely due to passive support from railroad workers, and the widespread active support they received around the country stoked fears of working-class rebellion. The primary government response to the Industrial Armies came from Attorney General Olney who devised new federal protections for the railroads in preparation for the next inevitable class conflict on the tracks. These new procedures would soon be deployed to break the nationwide Pullman strike and boycott.

The Industrial Army was a late nineteenth century mobile Occupy Wall Street movement converging on Washington DC, rattling the confidence of cap-

---

32   Ibid., pp. 185–6.
33   Ibid., pp. 169 and 180–5.
34   Piven and Cloward 1977, pp. 24–5.

ital to control the organisation and movement of the most destitute among the working-class. A key asset to this Industrial Army were the trains which groups seized almost at will to move their numbers across the country. Working-class rebellion seemed to be in the air. The Pullman strike became the trigger that unleashed the newly reorganised repressive power of capital and the state.

All Roads Lead to Chicago

Adam Smith, lauded as the philosopher of capitalism, was also lucid about the role of power in setting working conditions and wages and the struggle between capital and workers to determine them. As the struggle is asymmetrical, Smith recognised the inevitability of both capital and workers 'combining' to use force to impose their will, acknowledging that workers were in a disadvantageous position.

> What are the common wages of labour, depends everywhere upon the contract usually made between those two parties, whose interests are by no means the same. The workmen desire to get as much, the masters to give as little, as possible. The former are disposed to combine in order to raise, the latter in order to lower, the wages of labour ... It is not, however, difficult to foresee which of the two parties must, upon all ordinary occasions, have the advantage in the dispute, and force the other into a compliance with their terms. The masters, being fewer in number, can combine much more easily: and the law, besides, authorises, or at least does not prohibit, their combinations, while it prohibits those of the workmen. We have no acts of parliament against combining to lower the price of work, but many against combining to raise it. In all such disputes, the masters can hold out much longer. A landlord, a farmer, a master manufacturer, or merchant, though they did not employ a single workman, could generally live a year or two upon the stocks, which they have already acquired. Many workmen could not subsist a week, few could subsist a month, and scarce any a year, without employment. In the long run, the workman may be as necessary to his master as his master is to him; but the necessity is not so immediate.[35]

---

35   Smith 1776, p. 60.

As in 1877, the 1894 strikers, lacking parliamentary acts in their favour, were bound to mobilise to gain the mass support necessary to force their will on their ever more powerful adversary.

The role of the Pullman company in the strike was not merely a product of the boycott strategy. For decades, it was a corporate power in Chicago and a provider of luxury to the nation's elite. After he was assassinated in 1865, President Lincoln's body was shipped home to Springfield, Illinois on Pullman's exclusive 'Pioneer' sleeper. For the next several decades, US Presidents would continue to ride in luxury on many of the most powerful railroad lines in the county.[36] President Cleveland would come to express their deepest gratitude for its service.

The route from the end of black slavery to industrial wage slavery followed the tracks of the railroads system. During the Civil War the burgeoning railroad corporations helped win the war by transporting arms and men to and from battle. The Pullman car carrying the assassinated President just days after the cessation of war would 30 years later become the centre of another war, this time between capital and workers that would further reshape the role of government, law, and policy in class conflict.

This new role for government was a long time in coming. In 1877 soldiers were called up from the South where they had been defending the civil rights of former black slaves and the West where they had been suppressing Native Americans. In 1894 soldiers were again called up from the front at the end of the genocidal war on Native Americans to once again go to war against workers. In these intervening decades Civil War and the Indian War had been replaced by the class war. Monstrous railroad corporations yet again faced down a burgeoning and restless industrial working-class that stubbornly refused to stay down.

By 1894, the railroad industry was reorganised and better protected. There were more lines under federal receivership. During the crisis of 1893, 642 banks failed, 16,000 firms went bankrupt, and 220,500 miles of railways went into receivership.[37] According to ARU Vice President Howard, by 1894 the government already controlled 30 percent of the railroads under federal receivership. In light of the vast extent of federal control it would be but a small jump to outright federal ownership of the entire system. Even with the severe contraction of the railroads they still employed 850,000 workers.

Beginning in September 1893, all the railroads began to lower wages gradually one by one. The wage cuts and local issues of long hours, blacklists, mis-

---

36   Lindsey 1942, p. 22.

37   Josephson gives a lower number of 500 banks failing. (See Lindsey 1942, p. 12; Folsom 1991, p. 148; and Josephson 1934, p. 376).

treatment and persecution of ARU members combined to fuel the rapid spread of the boycott throughout the Midwest and West in July and August.[38]

The railroads continued to deploy federal receivership as a strategy to decompose the workers' power by imposing wage cuts and productivity increases. Because the companies could not be assured of getting these in a struggle with their workers they turned to the federal courts in order to obtain the protection of the federal government, which could pre-empt any response from the workers. The Northern Pacific Railroad receivers appointed J.W. Kendrick as the new general manager in 1893. Kendrick confided in a letter to receiver T.F. Oakes that the cycle of wage cuts provided the opportunity to revise its entire relationship with its workers, hammer down wages, change work rules, and make other long-desired changes. The company could now do this, Kendrick noted, because under receivership it had the 'power to invoke the protection of the forces of the US government for its property; all afford an opportunity that certainly should not be neglected'.[39] It then proceeded to obtain an injunction preventing the strike and prohibiting the brotherhood leaders from communicating with one another. The strike was broken and the unions conceded to the new lower wages in February 1894. The workers of the Northern Pacific Railroad were so furious that they nearly launched a wildcat sympathy strike during the ARU's April Great Northern strike but were dissuaded from doing so by Debs and Howard, who shared their assurance not to strike with Kendrick. Not surprisingly, when the ARU endorsed the Pullman boycott, many Northern Pacific workers flocked to the campaign.[40]

Federal court receivership was a key tactic in capital's repertoire for new strategies to respond to the recomposition of the working-class in the 1877 and 1886 strikes and the rise of the KoL and their populist allies pressing for regulation and government ownership of the railroads. The merging of rail lines, the integration of the railroads, coal, and banking sectors, and the introduction of a new division of labour had decomposed working-class power, preparing it for repeated disruption. That came in 1894 when railroad workers boycotted Pullman cars across the country in a sympathy strike to support several thousand Pullman workers labouring under authoritarian conditions, living, working, praying and schooling under the dictates of George Pullman.

The new composition of capital continued to successfully prevent the recomposition of workers' power. Debs insightfully grasped this when he wrote that

---

38   Lindsey 1942, p. 131.
39   In Stromquist 1993, pp. 87–9.
40   Ibid., pp. 88–9.

the strict trade organizations have served their purpose, the conditions have changed; there used to be hundreds of small railroads in operation, but they have been merged with and absorbed by the great corporations; there has been a consolidation of the interests of corporation, whereas the employees, on the other hand, have been dividing their forces in rival organizations.[41]

The continuation of yet another in a series of great depressions that wracked the country for more than half of the last third of the nineteenth century both contributed to weakening workers' leverage and dampening mobilisation, while providing a shared grievance that sparked a new cycle of struggle.

Pullman: A Case Study of Capital Composition

The Pullman company presented a formidable obstacle to the ARU. Understanding how Pullman was organised and the power it wielded is crucial for understanding the new composition of capital and the array of forces aligned against the strikers and their supporters. Just as the ARU presented a national organised threat to the railroad industry, Pullman exemplified how well organised and integrated capital had become since 1877.

No company represented authoritarian organisation of the economy better than Pullman, then based just outside of Chicago. Begun as a railcar company to take advantage of the expanding rail system after the Civil War, Pullman captured control of the burgeoning industry of luxury sleeper cars. By 1894 Pullman controlled sleeping car service on 75 percent, or 125,000 miles, of the US railways.[42] Thousands of craftsmen hand tooled and crafted each Pullman car into wonders of elegance, with sleek wood-panelled comfort. Pullman cars came with their own porters, waiters, and maids.

Pullman was capitalised at $1 million when the company was launched in 1867. The company's books showed it to be virtually unaffected by the depression of 1893, remaining profitable during 1893–4. The $15.9 million in capital stock and $28 million in assets it held in 1885 rose in 1894 to $36 million in capital and $62 million in assets. Even as the company was cutting wages and staff, it held $25 million in reserves in 1893. Its quarterly dividends were never less than 2 percent and as high as 8 percent in 1893–4. During 1893 undivided profits

---

41   See Debs in United States Strike Commission 1895, p. 153.

42   US Strike Commission 1895, p. xxi; and Lindsey 1942, p. 23.

were $26 million on which 8 percent was paid in dividends leaving $4 million in surplus. The 1894 payout in dividends remained 8 percent yielding a $2.3 million surplus. While the company remained profitable and paid dividends, the cost of wages fell $2.7 million to $7.2 million primarily as a result of a reduction in the workforce to 14,500 employees working 10- to 11-hour workdays by 1894.[43]

While the cost to ride a Pullman was steep, Pullman's workers paid the heaviest price of all in perpetual insecurity and low wages that put them in debt peonage to the authoritarian company. Pullman paid his workers poorly because he believed that he was paying them in other intangible ways. A Christian self-proclaimed social reformer, Pullman ran the Google of the late nineteenth century: he didn't merely employ workers to manufacture and serve elite customers on his cars, he also manufactured the workers and their families, socialising them according to his own vision of corporatopia. Workers were required to live in Pullman's town of which he was the sole owner. They rented Pullman-owned houses at inflated prices, prayed in churches run by the Pullman-employed ministers, sent their children to Pullman-owned schools, and even got water, gas, and sanitation (if their house had such amenities, since many did not) from Pullman's company at, of course, Pullman prices of 33 to 90 percent higher than in neighbouring communities. Pullman's town did not receive any services from the village of Hyde Park or later the City of Chicago when Hyde Park was annexed in 1889.[44]

Pullman was extremely well-connected to local and national elites, some of whom were to later split from the coalition supporting the company. The January 1883 dedication of the Pullman Arcade Theatre was attended by General Sheridan, who was instrumental in using the US Army to break strikes, and Judge Trumbull. Trumbull later defended Debs before the US Supreme Court for contempt of court charges brought against him during the 1894 strike.[45] While widely disliked in the Chicago area, Pullman's town was independent and thus insulated for a time from any pressure that could be brought to bear on local elected officials to intervene.

Analogous to free enterprise zones and corporate run charter cities of recent decades, Pullman's town was its own private government. The only locally elected officials were the school board members, but they were mostly all Pullman officials and the school grounds were owned by Pullman. The company

43 Lindsey 1942, pp. 24, 27–8, 100.
44 Ibid., pp. 67 and 92.
45 Ibid., p. 55.

also succeeded in frequently having its property tax assessments reduced to absurdly low amounts, a scheme denounced by Chicago Mayor Hopkins as 'one of the most glaring illustrations of corporate tax dodging in Chicago'. Mayor Hopkins knew of what he spoke, having started as first a labourer and then paymaster at Pullman in 1880.[46]

Another way in which Pullman kept the town outside the bounds of public government was by suppressing voter registration and voting. In 1884, only about 1,200 of the 8,500 adults in Pullman voted. The extremely low turnout was most likely due to voter intimidation, company distribution of ballots, firing employees who voted against Pullman's wishes, and heavy campaigning for Pullman's favoured parties. Ironically, although Pullman tried to engineer Cleveland's defeat in 1892 the now President Cleveland came to the company's aid to break the strike, demonstrating that shared class interests trumped political partisanship.[47]

Even when depression struck, orders collapsed and workers' hours were cut, rents, food prices, tithing, and the water bill continued unabated. Rents on company houses were estimated to be 20 to 33 percent higher than in neighbouring areas where workers were prohibited from living. As Pullman town was insulated from local elected government, workers had no access to the polity to address their grievances and seek redress. Because Pullman refused to meet any workers other than mid- and upper level management, negotiations with the company were not possible despite their best efforts. Despite having a union, Pullman ruled the shops and town with a heavy hand.

Even local elites had no pull in Pullman town. When outside elites intervened in attempts to seek reconciliation, they found themselves having to negotiate with Pullman about negotiating. Northwestern University economist and progressive reformer Richard Ely called Pullman's factory town a type of 'benevolent well-wishing feudalism' which dictated even the minutiae of everyday life. So complete was Pullman's heavy hand on all aspects of his town and expansive factory complex that during their study of life and work at Pullman, Professor Ely and his associates had great difficulty getting any of the residents to speak to them for fear of company spies. Professor Ely was joined by US Senator Sherman, who called Pullman and the Sugar Trusts 'the most outrageous monopolies of the day' in 1894.[48]

---

46   Ibid., pp. 77–9, 80, and 83.
47   Ibid., pp. 50 and 84.
48   Ibid., pp. 26 and 64.

State Circuit Judge Gibbons concurred with Ely's assessment of the lives of workers and their families in Pullman, observing that 'every municipal act is the act of a corporation'.[49] Although the company's corporate charter prohibited it from owning land, it evaded this by setting up the Pullman Land Association which sold all of its shares back to the Pullman Palace Car Company. The company's blatant evasion of the law continued for years until Illinois Attorney General Maloney successfully sued to force Pullman to divest itself of all real estate, which it eventually did after two five-year delays. By then the company was in the midst of a long decline.[50]

Pullman workers had been subjected to ongoing lay-offs, reduction in work hours, and five reductions in wages totalling 30 to 70 percent. The company used the depression to justify these cutbacks, starving its workers by taking much of their meagre pay to cover bills and rent or simply evicting them. It was under these conditions that the workers' 'grievances were fused into a spirit of violent resistance against a corporation which the employees had come to distrust, fear, and hate'. Although no incidents of overt violence were reported at Pullman during the strike, this resistance sought to disrupt the company's national operations.[51]

The Pullman workers had no access to local government, few elite allies, no political space to present their grievances, and no resources to bring to bear in their struggle. As a result, not only was there no cost to Pullman for continuing to escalate its tactics, but its opportunity to achieve its objectives only continued to rise. If the workers wanted to achieve their objectives, they were left with little option but to similarly escalate their tactics. Since a strike against Pullman alone was ineffective, they sought to disrupt it nationwide. When the GMA soon followed Pullman's policy of refusing to negotiate, the stage was set

---

49   Ibid., p. 85.

50   Soon after the strike had ended, Attorney General Maloney filed suit against Pullman for buying real estate and owning and developing a town in violation of its charter, demanding it be revoked. In October 1898, the Illinois Supreme Court overturned the lower court in a 4 to 3 decision against Pullman, sending it back to the circuit court. The circuit court ordered Pullman to cease all city operations within one year and sell lands not required for manufacturing within five years but was later granted an additional five-year extension. All of the lands were completely disposed of by October 1907 and the town sunk into disrepair and decay, the end of what the press eulogised as 'a travesty of feudalism'. (Ibid., pp. 342–4, 347, and 349). Soon after, Pullman town was annexed by the city of Chicago. The company continued to build sleeping cars until it shut down its manufacturing operations and laid off its remaining workers in the early 1980s, a tragic end detailed in the film *The Last Pullman*. (See Ibid., pp. 62 and 65).

51   Ibid., pp. 91 and 128.

for rounds of mutual tactical escalation by both capital and workers which the Strike Commission meekly denounced, declaring that

> The refusal of the General Managers' Association to recognize and deal with such a combination of labor as the American Railway Union seems arrogant and absurd when we consider its standing before the law, its assumptions, and its past and obviously contemplated future action.[52]

Pullman shut down its Detroit shop in September 1893, laying off 800 workers, or 20 percent of its workforce, cancelling pending orders and stopping car production. Pullman also imposed a universal reduction in piece wages and hourly rates averaging about 25 percent but as high as 41 percent. Time motion studies were used to set the new lower piecework rates which affected 2,800 workers, or two-thirds of its workforce. Because the company refused to negotiate, the workers didn't know about the cuts until they went into effect. The company rationalised the cuts as being necessitated by declining demand. However, the workers demonstrated that only the car shop was losing money because orders for new cars were cancelled or sold cheaply. The total savings in labour costs from the wage cut only amounted to $60,000 and there were no wage cuts for management. Layoffs had reduced the Chicago plant to only 1,100 employees, many working part-time and receiving net pay literally just pennies more than their rent and bills. The company paid its workers with two separate checks issued by the Pullman Loan and Savings Bank so as to skim off workers' debts before they could receive their pay. The company kept on hitting its employees even as they were down and continued falling.[53]

On 7 and 9 May 1894, the workers selected a committee of 46 men headed by Thomas Heathcoate to ask that the June 1893 rates be restored, but the company refused to negotiate and fired three of the men the next day. According to ARU Vice President Howard, the Pullman workers sent seven committees to Pullman in an attempt to negotiate during the course of the strike.[54]

The 1894 strike was not the first time Pullman workers organised, attempted to negotiate, and struck. In 1882, 1,000 workers struck over the cost of commuting to the plant. In March 1884, 150 men struck over a pay cut. Another wage cut in October 1885 led workers to organise and join the KoL. Workers joined the 1 May 1886 strike for an eight-hour day and asked for a 10 percent increase

---

52   US Strike Commission 1895, p. xxxi.

53   Lindsey 1942, pp. 96–8.

54   Ibid., pp. 103–4; US Strike Commission 1895, p. 7.

but they were defeated when the police showed up to help the company. There were other strikes in 1888, 1891, and most recently in December 1893, but most of these strikes were weakened by being limited to separate crafts and shops.[55] Assessing the outcome of their previous organising, Lindsey observed,

> The brusque and uncompromising attitude of George Pullman increased the determination of the workers to strike. All hope that their grievances would be harmoniously adjusted seemed completely shattered, and the only remaining alternative appeared to be self-help.[56]

Despite 12 years of agitation and strikes, the workday would not be lowered to nine hours until 1903.

Pullman responded to his increasingly organised workforce agitating for an improvement in their working conditions and wages by employing more immigrant workers, whom he sought to control and socialise in his model town to be obedient. Between 1884 to 1892, the proportion of foreign-born workers, mostly Northern and Western Europeans, increased from 51 to 72 percent.

Debs's ARU

After failing to achieve anything in the first two attempted meetings, the workers opted to escalate their tactics by turning to the newly formed ARU for support. As a national industrial, rather than craft, organisation of railroad workers, the ARU had the potential to use a boycott of all trains pulling Pullman cars as leverage to force the company to negotiate. By approaching the ARU for a boycott, Pullman workers sought to escalate their tactics by circulating their struggle throughout the industry.

The ARU was fresh off its first victory. Large numbers of trackmen were joining, and sometimes entire lodges moved over to the ARU. It attracted many unskilled or low skilled railroad workers. The ARU had organised 96 locals by mid-November 1893, 125 locals by 1 January 1894. It had 4,000 members in April 1894 mostly concentrated in the West and Southwest. When it met for its convention in summer 1894, it had exploded to 150,000 members in 453 locals.[57]

---

55   Lindsey 1942, pp. 28–9.
56   Ibid., p. 104.
57   Stromquist 1893, pp. 84–6.

Among those who joined were Great Northern Railway workers. Their brotherhood had recently accepted all three wage cuts without a fight. It seemed to be an opportune moment to launch an innovative new tactic of organising according to the industry rather than the craft. Unlike the brotherhood, which helped the company recruit strikebreakers, the ARU charter was predicated on local rank and file democracy. While it had national leadership, they could not call or end strikes, leaving that up to a vote by the members of each local. Although only a minority of Great Northern Railway workers were ARU members, an overwhelming number of workers went out on strike. The strike lasted 18 days and the company was forced to accept an arbitration decision and concede a $146,000 increase in monthly wages. No bloodshed or damage was reported.[58] The workers built the union by striking.

Workers rushed to join the ARU, which grew from their success, taking on and beating the infamous Jim Hill who owned the Great Northern Railway. By the time the Pullman strike had begun, the ARU's 150,000 members was more than all the brotherhoods combined and a bit less than the entire AFL. The switchmen, whose union had cancelled a planned strike in 1893, was its strongest faction.[59] Ironically, the Great Northern Railway was the only transcontinental railroad not affected by the July strike because it had no contract with Pullman and did not use its cars, as did most of the eastern lines.[60]

Much like with the KoL, from the moment it was founded the ARU was pulled between the needs and expectations of its rank and file members and its most prominent organisers. Almost immediately the ARU's constitution, which explicitly preferred to settle conflicts by avoiding strikes, lockouts, blacklists and boycotts, would be tested by the fire of necessity. Speaking to the 1894 Strike Commission, Vice President Howard, who had left his leadership position with a brotherhood to join the ARU, sought to assure capital of the ARU's principled opposition to strikes. Howard emphasised the disciplinary role of unions that could moderate the disruptive force of unruly workers.

> They can not help but say yes; and if the railroad officials would go into partnership with these organizations – organized men can be handled better than unorganised men – if employers would only do this they would find, after while, they could have everything their own way that was just and right, at least; and beyond that they should not care to go.[61]

---

58   Lindsey 1942, pp. 103 and 113.
59   Brecher 1972, pp. 98–9.
60   Lindsey 1942, p. 257.
61   US Strike Commission 1895, p. 31.

Howard correlated organisation with order, discipline, and stability, explicitly pursuing an absolute gains commonality of interests approach that would be articulated by elite reformers over the next several decades.

> Where I had to deal with the devil and wanted a show-down, if I did not know, to a dead moral certainty, I could crush him out of existence, I had enough sense to know that my only hope was to go into partnership with him, and that is the only thing any sensible man can do unless he wants to get turned down himself.[62]

Howard was hardly exaggerating. The ARU constitution explicitly stated that the primary objective of the union is labour peace and eschewed any tactical escalation beyond negotiations and cooperation:

> First. The protection of all members in all matters relating to wages and their rights as employees is the principal purpose of the organization. Railway employees are entitled to a voice in fixing wages and in determining conditions of employment. Fair wages and proper treatment must be the return for efficient service, faithfully performed. Such a policy insures harmonious relations and satisfactory results. The order, while pledged to conservative methods, will protect the humblest of its members in every right he can justly claim; but while the rights of members will be sacredly guarded, no intemperate demand or unreasonable propositions will be entertained. Corporations will not be permitted to treat the organization better than the organization will treat them. A high sense of honor must be the animating spirit, and evenhanded justice the end sought to be obtained. Thoroughly organised in every department, with a due regard for the right wherever found, it is confidently believed that all differences may be satisfactorily adjusted, that harmonious relations may be established and maintained, that the service may be incalculably improved, and that the necessity for strike and lockout, boycott and blacklist, alike disastrous to employer and employee and a perpetual menace to the welfare of the public, will forever disappear.[63]

The ARU pursued objectives far short of what they were portrayed as pursuing at the time. According to its constitution, the ARU was limited to using legislative reform to achieve the eight-hour day.

---

62   Ibid., p. 32.
63   Constitution of the American Railway Union 1893, p. 5.

Fifth. There will be a department designed to promote legislation in the interest of labor, that is to say, the enactment of laws by [sic] legislature and by congress having in view well-defined obligations of employers and employees, such as safety appliances for trains; apprentices in all departments not to be encouraged, and the influence of the unions used to suppress them; work for the inauguration of the eight hour day and the regulation and payment of wages, the rights of employees to be heard in courts when they have claims to be adjudicated. The enactment of employer's liability law and the restriction of Sunday work.[64]

While the constitution also sought to abolish what it called the 'wages system', an objective Debs repeated in testimony to the us Strike Commission, this would be hard to achieve given that it foresaw that 'the necessity for strikes and boycotts among railway employees will disappear' because strikes are 'hopeless' 'failures' that lead to 'defeat'. The ARU leadership likely advocated for public ownership of the railroads by government or the people as the means to reach these objectives.[65] The 'declaration of principles' in the ARU constitution was inconsistent and contradictory with the rank and file's strategy to form a strikers' union. To make matters worse, it was amended at the 1894 convention to limit membership to whites. The haphazard writing of the constitution was a factor of the union not surviving long enough to reconcile these problems.

The ARU constitution's tacit acceptance of workers' limited capacity to achieve their objectives by strikes placed Debs and Howard in a predicament of leading the ARU into a general strike armed with a single oar of compromise, negotiations, and conciliation. Because the leadership saw the ARU as an organisation that could moderate the disruptive force of the workers it is not surprising that they did their utmost to find a negotiated solution to the Pullman strikers. They sought to avoid a membership vote on the request for a Pullman boycott, thereby launching a general strike they most likely could neither lead nor control.

It should also be observed that historians see the 1894 Pullman strike as being led by Debs's ARU. What is overlooked is that workers first made the strike by self-organising at Pullman. The boycott was called by the ARU rank and file at the request of the Pullman strikers over the opposition of the ARU leadership. Once the boycott began, the number of strikers quickly far exceeded the number of ARU members because many craft workers wildcatted, bolting from their

---

64   Ibid., p. 7.
65   ARU 1893, p. 4; Debs in US Strike Commission 1894, pp. 129–80; and Stromquist 1993, p. 83.

conservative railway brotherhoods, some of whom were under contract with the railroad companies. As the streams turned into a tidal wave of walkouts, the strikers transformed the ARU into an organisational coordinator of their national effort, not its leader. Once it appeared that the strike was lost and the ARU appealed to call off the walkout, workers outside of Chicago continued to escalate their tactics into scattered attacks and sabotage even as Debs sat in prison for violating a court injunction for being unable to end the strike he did not start or really run.

The Boycott Becomes a Strike

Once the ARU learned of the planned Pullman strike in May, Debs asked Howard to try to prevent it. 'We concluded it would be best, if it was possible, to keep out of any trouble whatever, for the time being at least, and I was particularly anxious at that time to avoid any strike if it was possible to do so'.[66]

When it became apparent that the strike could not be prevented, Howard then proposed de-escalating tactics by limiting the boycott only to Pullman shops:

> You declared your action simply against the Pullman palace car sleepers and others owned by that company? – Ans. It was, I suppose, although I advised against it; my advice to the convention was not to do it; I advised that they merely declare the Pullman shops at St. Louis, Missouri and Ludlow, Kentucky, closed. I had organised the men at both those points myself, for I realised that if we could shut off Pullman's supplies his quota of cars would soon stop; I realised that if we merely took one sleeper off one of the roads we broke their quota of cars and they could not operate them; they would have to get wheels and other material to repair the cars, and if his shops at St. Louis were shut up, as well as the shops at Ludlow, that we could effect the desired end without involving the whole country; and I advised the convention to that effect, but they did not take my advice.[67]

The Pullman workers had voted unanimously on the third ballot on 10 May to strike but didn't set the date so that the locals could vote to ratify. ARU Vice

---

66   Lindsey 1942, p. 129.
67   US Strike Commission 1895, p. 17.

President Howard and the general secretary were present and warned against voting to strike. The strike began the next day when Pullman announced a lockout to begin at noon. However, by that time 3,000 Pullman workers had already walked out, leaving 300 to 600 remaining at work. However, these scabs were soon laid off and the shops closed until 2 August, which had the effect of reducing Pullman's inventory. Heathcoate was elected chairman of the central strike committee which held daily open meetings. The union organised 300 men to patrol the plant to protect the property and continued doing so until the military arrived on 4 July.[68]

Efforts to settle the strike continued unabated. The Civic Federation of Chicago tried twice to get the company to arbitrate but it refused. On 15 and 22 June, Pullman refused ARU's proposals to establish an arbitration committee. The company also ignored a proposal by the common council of Chicago to arbitrate. The proposal had been delivered by the mayors of Detroit and Chicago, who carried a telegram sent by the mayors of more than 50 large cities urging the strike be settled by arbitration. The ARU was not asking for arbitration at first but to just discuss whether there was something to arbitrate, but they refused.[69]

Representatives of ARU's 465 locals met in convention 9–26 June, one month after the Pullman strike began. At the convention a significant block of members made a motion for the boycott, but Debs refused to hear it. He asked for time to attempt to negotiate. Debs and Howard used two more committees in an attempt to delay the strike vote. On 15 June, a 12-man investigative committee, one half of whom were Pullman employees, was sent by the convention to negotiate with Pullman's Vice President. After he refused to negotiate, another six men were sent to meet with the Vice President again. When the investigative committee reported that he again refused to discuss or arbitrate anything, it recommended support for the strike and the motion was approved unanimously by representatives of ARU's 465 locals. On 26 June the boycott of all Pullman cars began immediately and Pullman workers in St. Louis, Missouri and Ludlow, Kentucky joined the strike until Pullman would consent to arbitration. The ARU voted to pass a small weekly dues assessment to provide funding to manage the strike. The convention also appointed three ARU members to notify Pullman of the ARU boycott and strike date but the VP yet again refused to discuss anything, bringing the number of failed attempts by the ARU to settle

---

68   Ibid., p. 130; and Lindsey 1942, pp. 122–3.
69   US Strike Commission 1895, p. 130.

the strike to five.[70] Each time the ARU had attempted to negotiate, it made it clear that it was not seeking recognition of the union as the Pullman's representatives.

Pullman's refusal to attempt conciliation, or respond to local elites who urged him to do so, fuelled the workers' desire to escalate their tactics in order to achieve their objectives. In some way, the ARU rank and file could not have hoped for more. Facing a widely hated adversary brought supporters to the side of the strike. But facing an adversary unwilling to compromise foreclosed the possibility that the ARU leadership could justify de-escalation to negotiate. Pullman was not someone they could talk with. This strike would be a winner takes all power struggle between the workers and capital.

Support soon flowed in to the Pullman strikers. Although Debs at first opposed the strike, he recognised that the workers 'are striking to avert slavery and degradation' and eventually lent it his leadership after the 26 June strike vote. The strikers received widespread support from all over Chicago, especially after the 27 May mass rally. Mayor Hopkins donated a room for medical care, 25,000 pounds of meat, 25,000 pounds of flour, and $1,500 to the strike fund. The *Chicago Times* was the only local press that supported the strikers.

Although the ARU convention had only declared a boycott, the members themselves took the initiative to escalate it into a strike in retaliation for the firing of workers who refused to handle Pullman cars. By the third day, the boycott and strike were widespread on five railroad lines. About 18,000 workers were on strike in the Chicago area, refusing to handle all railroad traffic. The strike had spread quickly to roads such as the Chicago, Rock Island and Pacific railroad, which were not included in the original boycott strategy. 'The movement in some respects was almost spontaneous, revealing on the part of many unions a willingness to strike that greatly surprised Eugene Debs'.[71] In these first few days, with telegrams of support coming in from the United Mine Workers of America and Knights of Labor, the strike briefly threatened to spread into other industrial sectors, although no other statements of support would follow.

The ARU was surprised by the number of workers whose local committees voted to join the boycott once it began. Out of the 850,000 railroad workers nationwide, an estimated 260,000 eventually joined the boycott, half of whom were not ARU members. All but one of the 26 roads out of Chicago were struck.

---

70   Lindsey 1942, pp. 129–31.

71   Ibid., p. 134.

Not surprisingly freight out of Chicago declined by 75–100 percent. Illinois US Senator Douglas had purposefully designed the transcontinental railroad in the 1850s so that all roads led to Chicago, something the industry most likely now regretted.

Since Chicago was a key nexus point in the national rail system, the ARU obtained a second strategic advantage. By almost entirely shutting down Chicago, the ARU could quickly cause nationwide disruption, amplifying the impact of even a minority of workers walking out. As a result, the boycott quickly transformed into a strike that spread to 27 states and territories.

With no access to the polity or possibility of negotiating a compromise, the membership forced the leadership to escalate its tactics. With growing mass support among railroad workers, the costs of escalation were low and the opportunity to achieve their objectives rose. However, broader mass support beyond the industry was critical to maintain the favourable ratio between costs and opportunity and to counter the industry's coordinated response through the GMA.

It should be emphasised that the tactical escalation was forced upon the ARU leadership from below. As the US Strike Commission found, the membership defied their leadership and revised the tactics, strategy and objectives of the union from below.

> It is undoubtedly true that the officers and directors of the American Railway Union did not want a strike at Pullman, and that they advised against it, (a) but the exaggerated idea of the power of the union, which induced the workmen at Pullman to join the order, led to their striking against this advice. Having struck, the union could do nothing less, upon the theory at its base, than support them.[72]

This is the key lesson of the 1894 strike: the existence of an organised national union, even one like the ARU based on the principle of industrial unionism, was not sufficient to ensure either that the strike could be called let alone won. While the membership had learned that organisation was needed to provide the necessary capacity to coordinate a general strike, organisational prerogatives could steer the leadership toward de-mobilisation and de-escalation in order to pursue conciliation. Without sufficient self-organisation by the rank and file that could overwhelm the leadership's organisation prerogatives, the

---

72   US Strike Commission 1895, p. xxvii.

leverage of a strike to confront the new composition of capital could not be realised. The rank and file had to confront not only an ever more powerful industry but also its own leadership.

The General Managers Association: Self-Defence for Capital

Pullman immediately opted to escalate rather than negotiate. It began hiring private guards, requesting US marshals be sent in, and reaching out to the rest of the industry for cooperation in his efforts to crush the strike. The company could not defeat the strike alone, especially once the ARU voted to ratify the nationwide boycott. For that it turned to the General Managers Association (GMA), an organisation of railroad companies that sought to coordinate their anti-strike actions alongside coordinating their rates in pools. The GMA was composed of nearly every road emanating out of Chicago. Its members had a combined value of $2 billion and employed about 25 percent of the national railroad workers.[73] In the GMA Pullman had a coordinated self-defence organisation for capital.

Much like the ARU, the GMA did not appear overnight, but after nearly two decades of efforts of railroad companies to find their shared class interest that would be served by cooperating to meet the threat of strikes. There had been sporadic efforts to establish lasting institutions for cooperation among the railroad companies after 1877. In 1886, after the KoL strike on Gould's line, Chicago railroad managers met for nearly ten days. Although they promised to cooperate, it failed to materialise and some companies made separate settlements to resolve strikes over the next several years.[74]

The GMA was officially formed in January 1893, the same month the ARU was established, to respond to the threatened strike by the Switchmen's Mutual Aid Association of North America. To counter strikes, the GMA organised two committees. One recruited scabs and the other coordinated anti-strike activities and relations with government officials. The organisation also provided insurance to any line facing a strike. The policy required that all GMA members share losses in revenues and increase in expenses according to a sliding scale as a result of a strike, a type of corporate socialism uncannily similar to Marx's principle of 'from each according to his ability, to each according to his needs!'[75]

---

73   Wright 1894, p. 34.
74   Stromquist 1993, pp. 249–50.
75   Marx 1875.

The total losses from the strike were hardly trivial, estimated by Bradstreet's to be about $80 million.[76]

A third committee functioned as a sort of collective bargaining committee for the companies to approve or reject changes to wages and work rules proposed by a company in response to worker demands. In the first few months of operation only eight of 19 requests were approved, and just one strike occurred. In this way the GMA functioned as a proto-state governing a federation of corporate members. Each member was obligated to comply with the GMA's mandate making the issue of wages on any line an issue for all the lines. These rules were an attempt to prevent any fractures in the industry coalition from forming if one member were to negotiate or settle with its workers. The GMA effectively extended Pullman's obstinate refusal to negotiate system-wide, leaving no possibility for the ARU to de-escalate in order to achieve any gains. The strike was immediately a zero sum game.

In January 1894, the GMA attempted to expand into a nationwide organisation. The rate-setting committee set a wage scale for each region of the entire US to which all members would be required to conform. Northern Pacific general manager Kendrick proposed a GMA for the entire country so 'all the conflicts with organised labor should be dealt with as a unit, that the companies so organised would be very much stronger than the men'.[77] The nationwide scale would have resulted in the railroads making massive wage cuts and lengthening the working day. It almost came to fruition except for the refusal of James Hill to include his Great Northern Railway in the plan. Thinking the Chicago based roads well prepared in the event of a strike, the GMA proceeded with a new system of wage rates for all its members for early 1894. As with other efforts in 1877 and preceding the 1894 strike, coordinated wage cuts actually had the opposite effect of bringing workers together by giving them a shared grievance that allowed them to overcome the wage hierarchy among and within employers and cross the company lines that divided workers from one another. With a shared provocation, the strike circulated, rapidly building support as it spread.

In standardising wages and working conditions, the GMA illustrated a newly emerging composition of railroad capital by which the Chicago-based railroad companies could coordinate their management and cooperate to defeat strikes. As Stromquist observed, this coordination was 'a new level of corporate collectivism [that] was ushered in by the Pullman boycott. It was the product of careful and systematic construction'.[78]

---

76   Wright 1894, p. 35.
77   Stromquist 1993, pp. 252–3.
78   Ibid., p. 256.

Far ahead of its time, the GMA's strategy was a key aspect of the new composition of capital in which a single organisational structure coordinated risk, profits, and losses for the entire sector of industry. Cooperation among banks and industry was a key element of the composition of capital after 1877. Bringing capital to a new higher level of organisation illustrated Marx's observation about the cooperative aspect of capitalism as a social system which socialises the output of productive labour.[79] As capital consolidates and expands, not only does it bring larger numbers of workers who share common experience, language, and grievances together in one place, but it also simultaneously amplifies the cooperation between different companies, industries, and groups of elites.

Such 'points of maximum massification', as Alquati calls them, are both a response to working-class recomposition and the starting point for a new composition of capital to attack it. They are the

> greatest direct combination of different moments of the anti-capitalist struggle. This generally occurs in the points of greatest physical concentration of different MASSIFIED MASSES of labour-power. But no less important is the utilization (strategic importance for the working class) of the integration of the capitalist circuit so that this accumulation of information is very dense within the international network of the large intentional capitalist groups.[80]

To understand the cycles of class struggle it is necessary to study the dynamic of class composition and explain it in terms of the specific historical changes taking place in technology, division of labour, flows of capital, movement of workers, productivity, regulations and other factors resulting from class struggle explored here.

> Concentration, massification are 'conditions', certainly, but do not themselves explain everything: historically, and from the standpoint of the working class, it is they themselves which have to be explained. That is, concentration, massification, integration must be seen as outcomes of the class struggle, which is then itself conducted, unified, homogenized precisely by these sectors.[81]

---

79   Marx 1858.
80   Alquati n.d., capitalisation in original.
81   Ibid.

Massification in turn created new vulnerabilities for capital by bringing together larger numbers of workers who were less divided by categories of skill, craft, wage, race, or work status.

> Workers who can easily disrupt production, impose large replacement costs by quitting, and put substantial capital at risk have great collection-action advantages over their fellows. So do those whose work, training, or nonwork connections give them more extensive internal communication.[82]

The socialisation of capital was accompanied by its continuing expansion which precipitated further opportunities for disruption. Expansion required the development, introduction, and management of extended integrated communications, information, supply, and transportation systems. Disruption in any one nexus could disrupt the entire system and other systems that relied on or were integrated with them. One reason for the nationwide impacts of the 1877 and 1894 railroad strikes was that all other commercial activities relied on the railroads and its telegraph system.

Most unions either did not recognise capital at the social level or steered clear of any attempt or appearance to confront it at the systemic level for fear of losing status as a potential reasonable bargaining partner and whatever limited access to elites they already had. IWW, formed a decade later, attacked capital's growing mobility and circulation strategically at the same time as it organised workers by capitalising on their existing contingency and mobility. For this reason the IWW emphasised organising workers in critical industries depending on global circumstances (mining and spruce timber during WWI for example) and newly emerging sources of vulnerability in the global supply chain. These were the flipside of the same strategy of mobility. As Bologna saw,

> the Wobblies' concern with transportation workers and longshoremen, their constant determination to strike at capital as an international market, their perceiving of the mobile proletariat – today employed, tomorrow unemployed – as a virus of social insubordination, as the agent of the 'social wildcat'.[83]

---

82   Tilly and Tilly 1998, p. 243.
83   Bologna 1976, p. 73.

Capital too adapted to workers' new tactics and strategies to make them their own. Debs cogently portrayed the cooperative combination of railroad capital into the GMA as a kind of sympathy strike borrowed from workers.[84] Although both monopolies and unions were banned under the 1890 Sherman Anti Trust Act, only unions faced the full wrath of the law. Companies were rapidly consolidating ownership through holding companies, mergers, interlocking directorates, pooling, and bank leveraged investments. Coordination among independent companies was a response to the recomposition of labour in which workers were organising across not only crafts, but companies, industries, wage scales and races into nationwide industrial unions. The advantages of combination among the railroad companies in the GMA were immediately apparent. The 1894 US Strike Commission observed that

> there is no longer any competitive demand among the 24 railroads at Chicago for switchmen. They have ceased competing with each other; they are no longer 24 separate and competing employers; they are virtually one. To be sure, this combination has not covered the whole field of labor supply as yet, but it is constantly advancing in that direction.[85]

Because cooperation among the companies was akin to boycotts and sympathy strikes by workers, it was apparent that capital studied and adapted workers' tactics to their own needs inversely to workers' efforts to do the same.[86]

GMA's anti-strike committee initially ran the Chicago industry's entire anti-strike operation, soon expanding nationwide. Its organisational capacity was impressive.

> Headquarters were established; agencies for hiring men opened; as the men arrived they were cared for and assigned to duty upon the different lines: a bureau was started to furnish information to the press; the lawyers of the different roads were called into conference and combination in legal and criminal proceedings; the general managers met daily to hear reports and to direct proceedings; constant communication was kept up with the civil and military authorities as to the movements and assignments of police, marshals, and troops, each road did what it could

---

84   Lindsey 1942, p. 222.

85   US Strike Commission 1895, p. xlviii.

86   The GMA was a model for other organisations providing mutual aid for capital to soon follow such as the National Association of Manufacturers in 1895 and the US Chamber of Commerce in 1912.

with its operating forces, but all the leadership, direction, and concentration of power, resources, and influence on the part of the railroads were centered in the General Managers' Association. That association stood for each and all of its 24 combined members, and all that they could command, in fighting and crushing the strike.[87]

This committee exploited the tactical use of federal receiverships innovated by Judge Gresham to issue injunctions to break the 1877 strike. Perhaps not so coincidentally, Judge Gresham had been appointed US Secretary of State, eventually signing the US Strike Commission report. The GMA called upon Attorney General Olney, a former railroad lawyer and member of the board of directors of three railroads who shared the GMA's objective to break the ARU, for federal cooperation.[88] Not surprisingly, Attorney General Olney appointed a member of the GMA's legal committee, who was also the general counsel for one of the struck railroads, as a special federal attorney for Chicago. The new special federal attorney vastly expanded court injunctions into nationwide blanket injunctions – what *The New York Times* aptly called a 'Gatling gun on paper'.[89]

Attorney General Olney used court receivership as a justification to convince President Cleveland to send federal troops without a request by a governor. Although a required step under Article IV, Section 4 of the US Constitution and Revised Statutes of the US, Sections 5298, 5299, a new precedent had been set by President Hayes in 1877 (see Chapter 1). This became a source of contention when Illinois Governor Altgeld protested against President Cleveland's order to send troops into Chicago without his request. Olney explicitly ignored the process by which local authorities sought the governor's request of federal troops, who in turn made his request to the president and bypassed the local and state governments altogether in response to requests by local federal judges or marshals. The Olney rule was a key part of a two-part strategy by which the federal government protected the struck railroads.

The second part to the strategy to justify federal intervention was Olney's premise that the federal government needed to protect the movement of the mails, interstate commerce, and critical military routes.[90] Olney's legal rationale had been originally used months earlier to stop the Industrial Armies from

---

87   US Strike Commission 1895, p. xliii.
88   Lindsey 1942, p. 148.
89   See Ibid., p. 161.
90   Cooper 1977, p. 187.

commandeering trains to make their way to Washington DC. Olney issued federal court injunctions and sent in a large number of US marshals and the Army to enforce them. Using these legal and punitive measures to stop the eastward movement of the Industrial Armies was redeployed as a tactic to crush the railroad strike in the summer. To get around local police who were sympathetic to the Coxeyite 'Commonwealers', Olney directed the marshals to appeal directly to President Cleveland for troops, which happened in 14 states.[91]

The legal strategy used against the Industrial Armies was useful to the GMA who had no difficulty getting Olney to assemble about 3,000 deputy US marshals to enforce federal court injunctions. Meanwhile, President Cleveland sent in Major-General Miles to reopen the struck railroad lines while leaving state and local police to restore order.[92]

The revolving door swung freely between the GMA, Cleveland administration, and the railroads. On 27 June, John Egan, former General Manager of the Chicago and Great Western railroad, was appointed by the GMA to coordinate all the anti-strike activity including taking requests for scabs and communicating with government officials. The key to Egan's management of the anti-strike effort was the GMA's media strategy to quickly shift the focus of the strike away from its members to an attack on government itself. This was accomplished by having the railroad lines file for injunctions against the strike as a disruption of the mails and interstate commerce, expecting the US district attorney to intervene.[93]

The GMA was sharply criticised by the US Strike Commission, which questioned its violation of the corporate charters of its member companies in pursuit of forming monopolistic industrial control.

> The commission questions whether any legal authority, statutory or otherwise, can be found to justify some of the features of the association which have come to light in this investigation. If we regard its practical workings rather than its professions as expressed in its constitution, the General Managers' Association has no more standing in law than the old Trunk Line Pool. It cannot incorporate, because railroad charters do not authorize roads to form corporations or associations to fix rates for ser-

---

91   Lindsey 1942, pp. 13–14.

92   Cooper 1977, pp. 188–9. In the 1880s to 1890s alone Major-General Miles also played a commanding role in the suppression of Geronimo and the Apache, the Lakota Sioux and the massacre at Wounded Knee. He also participated in the taking of Cuba and Puerto Rico from the Spanish. (US Army 2006).

93   Lindsey 1942, pp. 137–8 and 141.

vices and wages, nor to force their acceptance, nor to battle with strikers. It is a usurpation of power not granted. If such an association is necessary from a business or economic standpoint, the right to form and maintain it must come from the state that granted its charter. In theory, corporations are limited to the powers granted either directly or by clear inference. We do not think the power has been granted in either way in this case.[94]

The GMA's violation of corporate charter laws led the US Strike Commission to momentarily imagine the necessity of nationalising the railroad, a central tenet of the populist movement, and legalising unions as chartered organisations, an idea that would gain traction over the coming decade.

The association is an illustration of the persistent and shrewdly devised plans of corporations to overreach their limitations and to usurp indirectly powers and rights not contemplated in their charters and not obtainable from the people or their legislators. An extension of this association, as above suggested, and the proposed legalization of 'pooling' would result in an aggregation of power and capital dangerous to the people and their liberties as well as to employees and their rights. The question would then certainly arise as to which shall control, the government or the railroads, and the end would inevitably be government ownership. Unless ready for that result and all that it implies, the government must restrain corporations within the law, and prevent them from forming unlawful and dangerous combinations. At least, so long as railroads are thus permitted to combine to fix wages and for their joint protection, it would be rank injustice to deny the right of all labor upon railroads to unite for similar purposes.[95]

The Commission's strong denunciation spoke to growing fervour to regulate capital in order to instil stability between capital and workers. But it also more deeply engrained the urgency to completely rid itself of the charter laws, which was now possible since the Supreme Court's 1886 *Santa Clara County v. Southern Pacific R. Co.* ruling extended artificial personhood to corporations.[96]

The GMA represented more than the sum of its parts – it reflected the organisational new composition of capital that was not met by a newly recomposed

---

94   US Strike Commission 1895, pp. xxx–xxxi.
95   Ibid.
96   *Santa Clara County v. Southern Pacific R. Co.* 118 US 394 (1886).

working-class until the ARU appeared on the scene. By then, 'in pressing for the settlement of a dispute, the employees of a railroad were pitted against the united front of twenty-four powerful corporations'.[97]

But the ARU leadership was unwilling to deploy the tactics necessary to counter the threat of a new composition of capital and further the recomposition of working-class power. In his opening address at the ARU Convention on 12 June, Debs foresaw the day when the unity of workers would mean that 'such an army would be impregnable. The reign of justice would be inaugurated. The strike would be remanded to the relic chamber of the past'.[98] That day, as he would find out, had not yet arrived.

Calling in the Army against the 'Mob'

Unlike craft unions, which were premised on preserving the privileges of specialised skilled workers, industrial unions organised all the workers in each shop of every company in the entire industry. This provided a greater ability to disrupt the entire industry or even a significant portion of the economy. Organising everybody was intended to prevent small groups of craft workers carving out their own private deal and returning to work. In this way, craft unionism obstructed efforts to mobilise mass support and circulate the strike across shops, job categories, and wage hierarchies in geographically dispersed companies and industries. Because of Jim Crow colour bars these tracked closely with race. The GMA's aborted effort to standardise wages facilitated the removal of barriers to the circulation of struggle across the disparate crafts, skill levels, geography, and companies.

Unfortunately, the ARU succumbed to the dominant racism of the day when the June 1894 convention included a clause opening membership to employees 'born of white parents' in a close vote after an entire day of debate and Debs's opposition to the amendment. Before the change, the first constitution made membership open to 'all classes of railway employees' with no mention of race.[99]

The 1894 strike was a tactical dance between capital and workers, in which railroad companies attempted to devise new tactics in an effort to dismantle the newly recomposed power of the railroad workers. Their tactics encountered

---

97   Lindsey 1942, p. 119.
98   Ibid., p. 127.
99   Stromquist 1993, p. 81; and ARU 1893, pp. 12 and 20.

workers deploying ever more intense tactics. In this way, the level of tension continually rose as capital and workers swirled about one another. Without the possibility of a negotiated settlement that would send the workers back to work, the new strategy of industrial unionism necessitated an escalation of tactics to overcome the new composition of capital.

Immediately after it began, the strike spread peacefully across the country with no reports of violence or destruction of property until 3 July, when the *dance macabre* began. Debs's warning that 'the first shot fired by the regular soldiers at the mobs here will be the signal for a civil war' would prove to be prescient.[100] US Army troops were sent into Chicago on 3 July by President Cleveland under the Revised Statutes of the US, Sections 5298 and 5299 following reports that rail cars had been damaged at the Blue Island depot just outside Chicago, a sign that both capital and labour had begun escalating their tactics.[101] ARU VP Howard accused a *Chicago Tribune* employee of firing the first shot from a gun, after which the Army was called in.[102] Regardless of whether the damaged train-cars were a false flag operation to justify a call for military intervention, the resulting shortage of operable cars benefitted the companies. They could now claim that strikers had carried out sabotage, bring in the military to break the strike, and then collect on damages later and replace old worn capital with brand new. Federal intervention absorbed the costs of escalation while increasing its opportunity of success.

3 July is believed to have been explosive in other ways. According to the US Strike Commission, after 3 July the strike became an 'insurrection' by a 'mob', an upwelling of pent up hostility and anger. This framing device by elites and the press was identical to the portrayal of the 1877 strike. It shifted the supposed target of the strike from the widely hated railroads to the government in order to justify the use of US troops, a unilateral tactical escalation that dramatically raised the costs of the strike and reduced the opportunity to achieve its objectives.

The Strike Commission accepted the framing of the strike as a mob insurrection by curiously lumping together women, immigrants, and criminals.

---

100   Brecher 1972, pp. 104–5.

101   However, the President had actually violated these because a prior presidential proclamation was required by Section 5300 and was not made until 8 July. (See Hannon n.d., p. 22; and US Strike Commission 1895, p. 662).

102   US Strike Commission 1895, p. 19.

The mobs that took possession of railroad yards, tracks, and crossings after July 3, and that stoned, tipped over, burned, and destroyed cars and stole their contents, were, by general concurrence in the testimony, composed generally of hoodlums, women, a low class of foreigners, and recruits from the criminal classes. Few strikers were recognized or arrested in these mobs, which were without leadership, and seemed simply bent upon plunder and destruction. They gathered wherever opportunity offered for their dastardly work, and, as a rule, broke and melted away when force faced them.[103]

The reframing had begun even before the first injunction was issued. On 29 June, the *New York Times* prematurely wrote that the strike had 'assumed the proportions of the greatest battle between labor and capital that has ever been inaugurated in the United States'.[104] Even Lindsey's otherwise sympathetic account of the strike repeatedly refers to strikers and their supporters as mobs, hoodlums, tramps, criminals, half-grown boys, without leadership, engaging in purposeless, unpremeditated destruction after troops arrived.[105] The US Strike Commission targeted the growing population of immigrants for the violence, blaming it on 'mobs' which it defined as 'a certain class of objectionable foreigners, who are being precipitated upon us by unrestricted immigration'.[106] Despite the lack of credible evidence to support the colourful hyperbole, such assertions still hit upon a basic truth likely evident to many at that time: there was mass support for the workers' struggle against capital.

This framing device prefigured the crucial concept of relative deprivation theory that became dominant in the 1960s, as discussed in the introduction. It explains political violence as a consequence of emotional breakdown, frustration, disruptive events, or ruptures in social norms and hegemonic institutions. The US Strike Commission, established by the federal government, adopted the framework that the strike was an unstructured action of a faceless mass driven not by clearly articulated grievances but by a relentless rage bent on destruction and rebellion to legitimate the expanded governmental role in the economy. It provides gloss for gross violations of constitutional principles of separation of powers and federalist power sharing, applies a veneer of credibility for the emerging responsibility of the federal government for protecting property and

---

103   Ibid., pp. xlv–xlvi.
104   *New York Times* June 29, 1894, p. 1.
105   Lindsey 1942, see for example p. 205.
106   US Strike Commission 1895, p. xliii.

managing an unruly working-class, and retroactively justifies the use of military repression against what until 3 July were otherwise peaceful strikers.

This rationale was not merely a public relations stunt. It reflected another reality that a number of local and state officials felt capable of handling the strike locally for several reasons. Some local officials may have contradicted reports of an insurrectionary mob in order to maintain the appearance that they were in control, wait out the settlement of the strike, and not lose votes and support from labour unions and workers who put them in office. Before 3 July, reports of local conditions contradicted claims of an insurrectionary mob and local officials either refused, hesitated or did not need the state militia or federal troops.

Exaggerated claims about the mob provided the needed justification to bypass local and state officials and send in US troops. The language of a 'mob gone wild' implied that law and order had crumbled, local and state governments were no longer functioning or capable of requesting help, and the exclusive authority for preserving 'a republican form of government' against 'domestic violence' now lay in the hands of the US government.

It is no accident that one of the powers to intervene is found in the revised Statutes of the US Section 2118 that authorises the President to intervene against Native Americans. It is a short path from deploying the military to suppress Native American resistance to colonialism and genocide to an insurrection of railroad workers. The use of the military in both the 1877 and 1894 strikes deeply linked the workers' struggle against the railroad companies to the struggles of both blacks during Reconstruction and Native Americans. Revised Statutes of the US Sections 5297–5299 made the linkage clear by extending the President's authority to use the military to suppress 'as he may deem necessary for the suppression of such insurrection, domestic violence, or combination'. Revised Statues of the US Section 3995 further extended this authority to preventing obstruction of the US mail. It was extended by the 2 July 1890 Sherman Anti-Trust Act to 'every contract, combination in the form of trust or otherwise, or conspiracy in restraint of trade or commerce', which was soon used to criminalise unions and legitimise their repression.[107] That the struggle did not circulate effectively among these sectors of the working-class was the tragic

---

107   See Article IV, Section 4 of the US Constitution; and United States Senate 1903, pp. 6 and 9. The legislative record of the debate over the passage of the Sherman Anti-Trust Act clearly shows that the Congress intended to exclude unions from being subject to the prohibition. Revised Statute of the US Section 5577 even did the unprecedented by identifying 'the President as Commander in Chief', although no war was declared which explicitly violates the separation of powers principle of the US constitution. (See United States Senate 1903, p. 11).

consequence of racism that divided, deflected, and prevented the recomposition of working-class power.[108]

Federal law was also replete with specific carve outs to protect specific lines with federal military powers. For example, an Act of 1 July 1862 Sections 4 and 6 protected the railroad and telegraph line of the Union and Central Pacific Railway companies from the Missouri River to the Pacific Ocean for the use of the US mails and the military. An Act of 2 July 1864 Section 11 classified the Northern Pacific Railroad as a US mail route and 'military road'. Lastly, an Act of 27 July 1866 similarly protected the railroad and telegraph line of the Atlantic and Pacific Railroad from Missouri and Arkansas to the Pacific Coast and the Southern Pacific Railroad in California, including a line in San Francisco.[109]

The conflict over deploying troops to Chicago provided a case in point in the conflict that emerged between the federal and state governments over deploying US troops. Chicago Superintendent of Police Brennan reported little violence before 3 July. Mayor Hopkins concurred, reporting no troubles before 5 July. Between 5 and 8 July only a couple of dozen rail cars had been overturned, although seven people had been killed by police in some clashes. Hopkins asked Governor Altgeld on 5 July for four additional militia regiments to join the city's police force of 3,000 and about 500 more special police that were already on duty. Although the local police force was intended to intimidate the strikers, they did not escalate their tactics until the militia and US army arrived.[110]

The introduction of the militia began to provoke the strikers and their supporters. One deadly battle occurred on 7 July when a militia company attacked several thousand rock throwing strikers and their supporters with gunfire and rocks by a crowd on the Grand Trunk line at 49th and Loomis. The troops opened fire at will and charged with bayonets, killing four and wounding 20 including a few women. By the end of the strike the entire state force of about 2,000 was in the field. These state troops were withdrawn gradually by 6 August.

Much like Governor Altgeld, Mayor Hopkins's role in the strike illustrates the limits of the strikers' support from elected officials. In a republic, elected

---

108   Interestingly, tactical escalating of military power was specifically scripted in federal law so that 'Troops must never fire into a crowd unless ordered by their commanding officers, except that single selected sharpshooters may shoot down individual rioters who have fired upon or thrown missiles at the troops'. Troops are also given the discretion to escalate their use of force and violence but 'As a general rule the bayonet alone should be used against mixed crowds in the first stages of a revolt'. (Ibid., p. 12).

109   Ibid., p. 10.

110   Harring 1983, p. 119.

officials are in practice elected by a majority but theoretically represent every eligible voter regardless of whether or how they voted. They also serve the market regardless of their own beliefs. For this reason, Mayor Hopkins could have claimed to support the strike even while deploying thousands of police and troops against strikers and their supporters. The record of Hopkins's actions during the strike illustrates the limits even of a powerful local official short of quitting office and joining the strikers in the streets.[111] At best Hopkins was neutral on the strike; he did not entirely favour the strikers, but nor did he entirely favour the companies. He was also unwilling to allow the militia and police to be placed under the command of Major-General Miles although he was willing to cooperate with them.[112] It seems rather that Hopkins's actions were an attempt to assert order by wielding the baton when necessary while ensuring they were local and state, rather than federal, batons which he did not control.

Mayor Hopkins was in a tight spot. He had given material support and public sympathy to the Pullman workers' strike, which provided further justification for President Cleveland to bypass his local authority to send in US troops. Despite his earlier show of solidarity to the Pullman strikers, Hopkins still found himself having to carry out his responsibility in a position of government authority.

Attempting to balance these two irreconcilable loyalties, Hopkins twice accompanied a city council committee to meet Pullman who refused to arbitrate both times. One group that attempted to facilitate negotiations between the ARU and Pullman was a committee which included reformer Jane Addams, sent by the Civic Federation of Chicago which was unable to even initiate arbitration just on the issue of rents. Reconciliation by local elites was ineffective in light of Pullman's relative isolation from local elite coalitions of power and self-sufficiency in the delivery of public services.

Mayor Hopkins claimed that he neither requested nor was asked if US troops should be brought in. Once the troops had been in Chicago, Hopkins claimed he informed Major-General Nelson Miles on 16 July that they were no longer needed since the rail traffic had restarted, but backed off on the request. Instead, the mayor again attempted to arbitrate with the GMA but it asked him to return unanswered the union's letter effectively offering to capitulate.[113] At

---

111   The ARU had received support from the mayors of Havre, Great Falls, Butte, and Helen, Montana during the April 1894 Great Northern Railway strike. (Stromquist 1993, p. 86).

112   Lindsey 1942, p. 233.

113   US Strike Commission 1895, pp. 147, and 344–3.

best, Hopkins's actions were the best a strike could hope for: a neutral local official who was disinclined to put the full force of state violence at the disposal of capital.

Like Mayor Hopkins, Governor Altgeld walked the precarious line between capital and the working-class. The young governor was already under fire for pardoning three men convicted for the 1886 Haymarket events. Considered a 'friend of labour', Altgeld may have opposed the use of federal troops but he did not hesitate to wield the state militia to rein in the strike. He sent the militia to eight areas during the strike, including Mount Olive where the miners blocked the Chicago, Peoria, and St. Louis railroad from shipping coal. Once there the governor issued General Order No. 8 which included the unusual prohibition on the militia being used 'as custodians or guards of private property'. Altgeld was under pressure to keep the strike from circulating into the mines, especially following the 1893 strike in which 180,000 miners struck for eight weeks.[114] It was rare that instruments of the state force were deployed but explicitly prohibited from being used against the workers. Yet, this should not be overstated. The mere presence of police and state and federal troops can hardly be considered 'neutral' because their presence is intended to be intimidating. The presence of federal troops additionally forces workers to check their patriotism since opposing the Army is conflated with opposing the flag.

The first federal injunction was requested by the US district attorney in Chicago on behalf of the GMA and granted on 3 July, about seven weeks after the Pullman strike began. At this point, the railroads were at risk of losing the strike, which had tied up traffic across a huge swath of the country. Up to that point the companies had been unsuccessful in their efforts to obtain the full cooperation of Mayor Hopkins and Governor Altgeld to break the strike. GMA's Egan had admitted on 2 July that the railroads had been tied up by the strike and sought to instigate conditions that would accelerate federal intervention on the side of the railroads. It was time to up the ante.

The injunction not only facilitated the reframing of the conflict from a strike against the railroads to an insurrection against the government. It also tilted the advantage to the railroads by having the federal government take over the fight and the political and monetary costs.

> A vital part of the strategy of the association [GMA] was to draw the United States government into the struggle and then to make it appear that the battle was no longer between the workers and the railroads but

---

114   Lindsey 1942, pp. 14–15.

between the workers and the government ... Once the federal government interceded to enforce the injunctions it became a fight between the ARU and the federal government leaving the railroads out of it.[115]

It is likely that without the federal government absorbing the intangible and tangible costs of countering the strike, the railroads, many of which were already bankrupt, would have had to absorb the costs themselves. Lost customers, lower profits, and declining share prices and dividends would have provoked criticism from the financial press and shareholders, threatened to fracture their elite coalition, and made them toxic to elected officials, putting pressure on them to concede. The ability to pass security costs on to the local, state and federal government is one reason why share prices are commonly unaffected during a contentious strike. Since the professionalisation and reorganisation of the police, militia, and US military following the 1877 strike (see Chapter 3), these costs are passed from the corporations to government which further passes them primarily onto the very working-class taxpayers who would have otherwise benefitted from a successful outcome to the strike.

Socialising the costs of the strike is certain to erode some public support for the strikers from those who object to disruptions, delays, rising prices, and taxes as the cost of the strike, even if they support the grievances behind it. Such costs are aggravated by the strategy of using the injunction to shift the blame for the disruptions of service from the railroads, which refused to negotiate, to the workers. The spin encourages strike supporters to feel betrayed by an unpatriotic union which instigated a strike that inconveniences and punishes them.

The injunction provided cover for the railroads' other tactics to actually aggravate the service disruptions they attributed to the strike alone. The lines refused to accept freight, removed passenger trains from service, hooked up Pullman cars to trains claimed to be carrying US mail, put US mail on every outgoing train, and purposefully created insufferable delays for passengers. Although the delays were caused by a lack of crews, the GMA could now blame them on non-existent threats, dangers, and sabotage it attributed exclusively to the strikers and their supporters.[116]

The railroads' preferred solution to the problem they helped manufacture actually made things worse. Introducing US troops created the very circumstances that justified their presence by actually transforming the strike into an

---

115   Ibid., pp. 142 and 144.
116   Ibid., p. 144.

insurgency. Once 10,000 troops began arriving from the Stock Yards to Rock Island property on 4 July the battles escalated in earnest. Trains were overturned, stoned, and set on fire, switches were thrown, and signal lights were changed. That the first US troops would be deployed to the Rock Island Line, whose General Manager St. John also chaired the GMA, raised shouts of foul play. The overt deployment of the US Army on the side of the railroads, particularly those with the greatest power in the GMA, enraged the strikers and their supporters who quickly escalated their tactics in kind.

The introduction of the US Army further disrupted the rail system in Chicago. By 5 July, 13 of the 26 roads centred in Chicago were forced to cancel operations. Even with four companies of US infantry, the Rock Island Line was unable to resume operations on 4 July.

Workers and their supporters clashed with the 14,000 armed private agents, federal deputy marshals hired and paid by the railroads, state militia, and soldiers guarding the trains to get rail traffic flowing again. About 40 US troops and deputy marshals provided by the GMA guarded each train on at least five lines out of Chicago and were given permission to fire.[117] The trains were driven by strikebreakers recruited by the brotherhoods.

The attempt to take the trains out by force accelerated the growth of mass support for the strike, which began to circulate, triggering solidarity strikes throughout Chicago and threatening to continue spreading to other regions. On 30 June the Chicago Trades and Labor Assembly, representing unions with about 150,000 members, promised to strike in sympathy. The Chicago Building and Trades Council, representing unions with about 25,000 members, followed suit on 7 July, voting unanimously for a sympathy strike, and called for a nationwide general strike to follow. The next day a meeting of representatives from more than 100 Chicago unions set 10 July for a general strike if there was no settlement of the railroad strike, and appointed a committee to meet with Mayor Hopkins.

The blatant intervention of the US Army in Chicago on behalf of the railroads initially did what the strike had not yet accomplished: it stimulated tremendous mass support for the strike. This lowered the costs of escalating their tactics and provided the necessary opportunity to expand the strike to more workers in more industries and new areas in order to achieve their objectives.

Unfortunately, only about 25,000 workers joined the Chicago general strike, mostly members of the KoL. The general strike collapsed when Debs, local unions with contracts, and the AFL opposed it. Many unions refused to follow

---

117   Ibid., p. 210.

through because Debs and other ARU leaders had already been arrested on 10 July, fearing the strike was floundering and the costs of joining it were too high. One contributor to the costs of support was their own AFL. On 12 July AFL President Gompers came to Chicago and called a meeting of 24 unions which not only refused to back the strike, but called for strikers to return to work. Rubbing salt into the wound, Gompers donated just $1,000 for Debs's legal defence. Gompers proposed shifting the strategy from class struggle to voting, urging the workers to

> organise more generally, combine more closely, unite our forces, educate and prepare ourselves to protect our interests, and that we may go to the ballot box and cast our vote as American freemen united and determined to redeem this country from its present political and industrial misrule, to take it from the hands of the plutocratic wreckers and place it in the hands of the common people.[118]

As a result of the meeting, the Chicago Building and Trades Council was forced to call off their sympathy strike, prompting the *Chicago Tribune* to gloat that 'DEBS STRIKE DEAD. It is Dealt Two Mortal Blows by Labor, Federation Hits First, Trades Council Follows with a Crusher'.[119]

Several days earlier Mayor Hopkins's committee of aldermen had met with Pullman officials to see if the company would meet to decide if there was anything to arbitrate, but it refused yet another attempt at negotiations. The aldermen gave Pullman until 10 July to arbitrate. But Pullman, acting now through the GMA, which had assumed command over the anti-strike efforts, was in no mind to negotiate. It instead manoeuvred to have Debs arrested on 10 July and President Cleveland impose martial law.

Workers Shoot Back

Although the advantage shifted toward the railroad companies in Chicago with the arrival of US troops, this was hardly the case elsewhere around the country. As the strike spread to other lines and regions, the fighting in and around Chicago prompted strikers and their supporters elsewhere to similarly escalate

---

118   See Manning 1960, p. 35.

119   See Brecher 1972, pp. 110–11; and Lindsey 1942, pp. 222–5. Decades later Gompers recounted his decision as 'the biggest service that could have been performed to maintain the integrity of the Railroad Brotherhoods' (in Stromquist 1993, p. 264).

their tactics. The strike spread so rapidly and tactics escalated so intensely that the California Bureau of Labor Statistics observed that 'At the present time the relations subsisting between capitalists and labourers are those of war ...'.[120]

The 'labour war' had spread to dozens of states where workers endorsed the boycott. Before US troops arrived in Chicago on 5 July the boycott had been universally non-violent. Workers had selectively withdrawn their labour from any train that pulled a Pullman car. Since Pullman cars were used on about 75 percent of the national rail system, it had the effect of paralysing much of the national rail traffic. In effect, either by design or by the initiative of the rank and file, the boycott was transformed into a general railroad strike that disrupted much of the national economy.

After 5 July, railroad companies, local officials, and police took the use of US troops in Chicago against the strike as a cue to further escalate their tactics and move the trains by force. Across the country the rail system was gripped by a strategy of tension in which the tactical escalation of one side was countered by further escalation by the other. Efforts by police, private guards, vigilantes, and state militia to move trains by force provoked boycotters, now strikers, to further escalate their tactics. In countless locations, workers engaged in scattered attacks and street fighting with these forces and began to disable, disconnect, delay, sabotage, damage and destroy trains, tracks, and depots, as well as directly engage police, private guards, vigilantes, and state militia in a battle for control of the rail system.

The strike affected a total of 27 states and territories, disrupting many of the railroads operating in the east, north and south.[121] Fearing the growing power of the railroad workers and their supporters to disrupt the country, President Cleveland also sent US Army troops to North Dakota, Montana, Idaho, Colorado, Washington, Wyoming, California, and the territories of Utah and New Mexico.[122] Battles continued in many of the places where these troops were sent.

The scene of one of the most intense battles was in Trinidad, Colorado where US troops had been sent in on 1 July without consulting Governor Waite, a populist who had significant support from workers and unions. Governor Waite had earlier the same year ordered the dispersal of private company-employed deputies in a mining dispute, instead sending in troops to prevent a battle between strikers and local deputies. The governor's earlier actions appear to have con-

120   Biennial Report of the Bureau of Labor Statistics of California 1891–2, p. 29.
121   Lindsey 1942, p. 239.
122   Ross and Taft 1969, p. 8.

vinced President Cleveland that he was an unreliable ally and that US troops should be sent in without consulting with him. US troops arrested 48 strikers without a warrant and their presence 'allowed the US Marshal to enlist a private army to suppress alleged state troubles ... waging an active war in Colorado without any declaration thereof by the U.S. ... and utterly in violation of law'.[123]

Strikers received extensive mass support in some Western states, even from local law enforcement and several governors. Where local governments were unreliable or tacitly neutral, US marshals and strikebreakers had to be imported under state militia and US Army protection. These forces frequently faced widespread hostility upon their arrival. Troop trains were shot at or attempts made to derail them in Trinidad, Colorado, between San Francisco and Los Angeles, and in Bakersfield to name a few. Brigadier General Brooke explained in his final report 'The troops were met with a considerable degree of hostility' while on duty in the West.[124] The strike was so popular among local communities and so universal on the rail system that strikebreakers had to be transported in Nevada, Montana and California under the protection of bayonets, gun, and swords.

In California, the strike bordered on an insurrection in three geographic areas around Sacramento, the San Francisco Bay Area and Los Angeles. The boycott was so effective in California that court injunctions enforced by local police and US marshals were inadequate to break it. On 28 June, Oakland brakemen joined the boycott and were fired. The ARU responded by declaring a strike against the entire Southern Pacific Railroad. By 30 June, about 3,000 railroad workers were on strike in the greater Sacramento area. The drawbridge over the Sacramento River was pulled up.[125] In response, Governor Markham called out the state militia, eventually sending in 1,000 troops to Sacramento. Federal Marshal Baldwin, who had been disarmed by strikers the day before, swore in about 100 Sacramento businessmen as deputies. The Southern Pacific Railroad paid their salaries, housed the militia command centre and coordinated the effort to break the strike with local authorities.

On 10 July, US troops arriving in Sacramento on riverboats were shot at by armed strikers from across the Sacramento River, in defiance of ARU leader Knox who told them to disperse. Firing back, the soldiers killed a boy. Running armed battles continued for several more days until the troops proceeded to the Bay Area. Four soldiers and an engineer were killed and several wounded when spiked rails caused their train to derail. Knox and other ARU leaders were

123   Ross and Taft 1969, p. 12; and Brecher 1972, p. 106.
124   See Cooper 1977, p. 190.
125   Lindsey 1942, p. 250; *US v. Cassidy* 1895; and Shoup 2010, p. 398.

arrested, some charged with grand larceny for taking over trains to transport strikers and supporters to Sacramento.[126]

Public support for the strikers was widespread in the San Francisco Bay Area as well. Militia troops pulling a Gatling gun were attacked with bricks by strikers and their supporters as they were boarding a ferry in San Francisco for Oakland. When the troops arrived, the *San Francisco Call* reported that all the companies other than San Francisco's removed the rounds from their rifles, saying they wouldn't fight the strikers, and marched away from the crowd. One militia company was dismissed and members of another were court martialed.

In a reversal from the race hatred promulgated by the Workingmen's Party of California during the 1877 strike, Chinese, blacks and whites showed their support for the ARU strikers by wearing its distinctive white ribbons. ARU strikers and supporters 'all armed to the teeth' seized trains in Dunsmuir (North of Redding) and Truckee and headed for Sacramento. To counter the corporate and state forces assembling in Sacramento, armed companies were formed in Fresno, Los Angeles and San Francisco to support the strikers. The breakdown in militia discipline spread to Red Bluff, South of Redding, where a militia company was sent back to the armoury to disarm and go home because it was feared they supported the strikers.[127] The strike began circulating to other industries such as *Los Angeles Times* newsboys who walked out, prompting customers to cancel ads and subscriptions.

Strikers and their supporters also put non-violent resistance into action. On 4 July, about 50 people blocked tracks in Oakland and six laid down on the tracks stopping a train filled with scabs and militia troops from leaving. President Cleveland declared martial law in California and other Western states on 9 July. The protesters eventually took over the train pier connecting to San Francisco and disabled five engines. A military force of 542 militia and 370 sailors arrived from Mare Island Navy Yard on 11 and 12 July in Oakland. On 14 July Oakland strikers and their supporters again blockaded the tracks with timber. Two days later they were attacked by militia cavalry armed with sabres and bayonets and supported by the US Navy battalion and other infantrymen armed with Gatling and Hotchkiss guns. Although there were rumours that people had been killed by the troops none were found on the streets, although they may have already been removed. The navy and soldiers remained until mid- to late August to protect the Central Pacific railroad.[128]

---

126   Lindsey 1942, pp. 254–5; *US v. Cassidy* 1895; and Shoup 2010, p. 420.

127   Shoup 2010, pp. 402–3 and 407; *US v. Cassidy* 1895.

128   Lindsey 1942, p. 255; Shoup 2010, pp. 421–2; *US v. Cassidy* 1895.

The strike spread to Los Angeles as well. On 3 July, the US marshal was roughed up by a crowd that was disconnecting Pullman cars. The state militia that arrived the next day were sympathetic to the strikers and proved ineffective. Los Angeles US Attorney Denis feared there were 5,000 armed men in the area. Colonel Shafter reported that he feared men were secretly arming and preparing attacks on all trains pulling Pullman cars throughout California. However, on 8 July eastbound trains began to depart from Los Angeles with troops aboard without incident. From that time forward there were no more reports of trouble, although about 300 troops remained in the area until the middle of August.[129]

As a major rail junction, the strike in California disrupted several of the main systems throughout the West. The entire line between California and Nebraska, especially on the Central Pacific and Union Pacific lines, was disrupted. The President declared these lines a military necessity and deployed US troops to break the strike.[130]

The system connecting California to Ogden, Utah was also disrupted. Strikers controlled the rail yards and disconnected Pullman cars. The US marshal was powerless to act and was unable to make any arrests. Fires were set at the same time in seven different areas along the line causing more than $100,000 in damages. On 13 July nine militia companies were sent to open the line to Sacramento and repair two small bridges that had been burned in Carlin, Nevada.[131] The first train from Ogden arrived in San Francisco on 16 July.

In addition to Illinois, Colorado, California, Nevada and Utah, other significant battles and disruption occurred in Iowa, Oklahoma, Montana, New Mexico, Oregon, Missouri, and Indiana. As events in several other states illustrate, the strike was quickly becoming an armed insurgency in which strikers and their supporters disrupted the railroads and fought with troops sent to restore business operations. The tactics of the strikers varied across other Western states and the Midwest, from attempts to negotiate to scattered attacks and sabotage. The mass support and circulation of the strike allowed workers to escalate their tactics and counter the use of US troops. Armed self-defence became a tactic to maintain the disruption of the rail system, the key leverage the strikers had to achieve the objectives of the strike.

On rare occasions, strikers controlled the local area. City officials of Rawlins, Wyoming took the exceptional step to throw all the deputy marshals out of

---

129 Lindsey 1942, pp. 250–2.
130 Ibid., pp. 252–3.
131 Ibid., p. 253.

town. In other places strikers and their supporters established a parallel system of authority to preserve the shutdown, although the details of how they did so are yet to be thoroughly documented.

The Northern Pacific Railroad was struck on 26 June. The strike shut down nearly the entire line between St. Paul and Puget Sound and was strongest in North Dakota and Montana. Engines were ditched, property destroyed and a bridge burned on Hell Gate River. Like the Central Pacific railroad, this line was declared a military necessity. Since the line was subsidised by Congress the federal government called in US troops to keep it open and kept them there until September.

Lines that served Missouri were also struck. A bridge on the Atlantic and Pacific Railroad was burned. The Mobile and Ohio Railroad, which ran Pullman cars between St. Louis and New Orleans, offered to concede. The company informed Debs it would not run any Pullman cars until the strike was settled but the workers refused to return to work. The Cleveland, Cincinnati, Chicago and St. Louis railroad was struck in response to a 10 percent wage cut. Although the company didn't belong to the GMA or run Pullman cars it unsuccessfully attempted to negotiate with the ARU on 3 July. The company was playing both ends against the middle. The company was simultaneously requesting Attorney General Olney issue blanket injunctions for Indiana and Southern Illinois.[132] On 10 July, the Rock Island Line was attacked by striking miners with stones in Spring Valley, Illinois. The strikers were shot at by US troops who killed two and injured several others.

Hammond, Indiana experienced more than a week of clashes. On 29 June, strikers stopped, uncoupled, and sidetracked trains. The sheriff and US marshal were powerless to stop them and the governor wouldn't call for troops. Strikers and their supporters attacked scabs, derailed trains, stopped all train traffic, and seized a telegraph office on 7 July. Militia and US troops arrived on 8 July without the authority of the mayor. The troops' indiscriminate shooting of anyone on the tracks resulted in the killing of a man who was not a striker while he was looking for his son. A local judge issued a warrant for the arrest of the soldiers but it was never served.[133]

Bridges were blown up, trains derailed, and other acts of sabotage were deployed against the Rock Island Line in the Cherokee Nation of the Oklahoma Territory. Somebody sawed off the piling of a bridge and stuffed it with dynamite. The explosives blew up a train, destroying 13 freight cars and severely injur-

---

132   Ibid., pp. 241 and 258.
133   Ibid., pp. 259–60.

ing a few crew members.[134] At the Dubuque and Sioux City, Iowa junctions switches were spiked blocking the railroads. Six militia companies were called out to protect the rail lines.

The strike didn't effect much of the East because some of the lines had con-tracts with Pullman's two other competitors which spared them disruptions in service caused by the boycott. The strike was supported by the Boston Central Labor Union, New York City Central Labor Union, and the New York state AFL, although there was little for them to do but send messages of solidarity.

One of the greatest challenges the ARU faced came from the four largest brotherhoods which opposed the strike and threatened to kick out any mem-ber that joined it. Some of the brotherhoods were torn by splits in their own ranks, since many of their members were active participants in the strike. Arthur, grand chief of the Brotherhood of Locomotive Engineers, denounced the 400 engineers who struck on the Wabash Railroad and allowed other mem-bers to scab on them. Arthur wrote a letter to the GMA on 2 July, reassuring the companies that it could count on his members to stay at work, would not distinguish between union and non-union strikers, and supported the fir-ing of strikers. The Switchmen's union also supported expulsion of members who participated in the strike. Wilkinson, the grand master of the Brother-hood of Railroad Trainmen, also supported the GMA's efforts to break the strike, reporting that he disguised himself and took up arms to identify and suspend 20,000 men from the brotherhood for joining the strike. Even Powderly, who until recently had been the grand master of the Knights of Labor, opposed the strike, although the Knights joined the UMWA and ARU in the call for a general strike.[135]

The Recomposition of Class Power

By looking at the relationship between the 1877, 1886 and 1896 strikes it be-comes apparent that new organisations are outcomes of the lessons of previous cycles.

> The unions did not organise the strikes; the working class in the strikes and through the strikes organised the unions. The growth of successful

---

134   Ibid., p. 258.
135   Ibid., pp. 264–6; and Stromquist 1993, p. 259.

organizations always followed strike activity when some workers engaged in militant activities and others joined them.[136]

The industrial unionism of the ARU was the product of learning from the defeat in 1877 and the internal struggles inside the brotherhoods.

However, the ARU itself was wrought with the dangers of any organisation in which the prerogatives of the leadership to keep the organisation alive begin to diverge from those of the rank and file. As the ARU was very new, the rank and file was still dominant and the leadership mostly subservient to its collective will.

It is not surprising that the UMWA and Knights of Labor were unique among those who joined an alliance with the ARU. The ARU was not alone among national unions in conflict with the relatively new AFL. The AFL was not organised by a rank and file but by affiliate craft unions organised into a federation. Because the craft unions' leadership retained local autonomy and mostly ruled their members from the top down, they were an impediment to recomposing working-class power. The craft unions have mostly been described as flawed due to the narrow-minded strategy of only organising skilled white male workers and the arrogance of class social status that reinforced it. But this was inseparable from their efforts to retain the privileges they had carved out for themselves from their symbiotic relations with employers. As a result, few strikes or labour actions were allowed and in those rare occasions when it could move, the leadership harnessed the workers to prevent them from adequately circulating the struggle to all the workers in their shops let alone the entire city, industry, or the country. The leadership felt compelled to let out a bit of the leash on their unruly workers before they were crushed by conceding the strike or negotiating minor concessions to retain the contract and rein the leash back in. Because the craft union's fortunes were tied up with the employer's, a strike that cut into their profitability or didn't lead to settlement would result in unemployed workers, which reduced the membership rolls, dues, and the chance of the union surviving. When they fought, the craft unions did so for their organisational interests, not those of the workers or the working-class.

The ARU certainly didn't need an alliance with the AFL as long as its affiliates and their members were free to join the strike, bring their supporters, and help circulate the strike along the national rail system and into related industries and communities, transforming it into a general strike. But when the AFL refused to endorse a general strike, it also brought down the ham-

---

136   Rawick 1969, p. 27.

mer on all of its affiliates and members. While Gompers claimed to the US Strike Commission that the AFL leadership cannot call strikes, it certainly could direct them not to. Threatening affiliates, especially the much needed mighty Chicago Trades and Labor Assembly which threatened a general strike, and members with punishment for joining the strike and ordering wildcatters to return demonstrated the value of the AFL to capital. It could use the contract to impede the necessary recomposition of class power and manage class conflict.

It should also be observed that the 1894 Pullman strike is considered among historians as being led by Debs's ARU. What is overlooked is that workers first made the strike by self-organising at Pullman. The boycott was called by the ARU rank and file at the request of the Pullman strikers over the opposition of the ARU leadership. Once the boycott began, the number of strikers quickly far exceeded the number of ARU members because many craft workers wildcatted, bolting from their conservative railway brotherhoods, some of whom were under contract with the railroad companies. As the streams turned into a tidal wave of walkouts, the strikers transformed the ARU into an organisational coordinator of their national effort, not its leader. Once it appeared that the strike was lost and the ARU appealed to workers to call off the walkout, workers outside of Chicago continued to escalate their tactics into scattered attacks and sabotage, even as Debs sat in prison for violating a court injunction for being unable to end the strike he did not start or really run.

From Boycott to Insurgency

One of the more perplexing developments during the 1894 strike was that even after the ARU leadership was jailed, its records seized, and all communications ceased, the strikers and their supporters continued to escalate their tactics. While it is difficult to know what, if any, tactical and strategic planning happened in the many areas where the strike continued after this point, it was hardly chaotic or haphazard. The specific targets of the scattered attacks and sabotage that continued in many places for about another week demonstrate that insurgents made choices based on their own analysis of the existing conditions. These likely included, among others, the balance of power, level of mass support, available resources, potential opportunities, threats and costs, and how elites responded in the past to decide whether to continue mobilising and escalating or wind them down. 'We can gauge the importance of repertoires by comparing the successive choices of similar groups and by observing innovation and diffusion in the means of action'.[137]

---

137   Tilly 1978, pp. 153 and 155.

Absent a study of the micro-tactics of each point of struggle, the continuing mobilisation and escalation of tactics might appear 'contagious' or 'spontaneous', spreading without intention, plan, or reasoning. An alternative approach is to see such 'contagion' as the outcome of the availability of information that the costs and threats related to certain tactics have changed. In this way the struggle appears to ebb and flow in cycles as groups make their own independent assessment of costs, opportunities, tactics, strategy and objectives, other groups learn what is happening elsewhere and make their own assessment, and so on as the struggle circulates.

> The idea of a standard repertoire also provides insight into contagion and 'spontaneity' in collective action. It raises the possibility that when a particular form of riot or demonstration spreads rapidly, what diffuses is not the model of the behavior itself, but the information – correct or not – that the costs and benefits associated with the action have suddenly changed. The news that the authorities are (or are not) cracking down on demonstrators in city A filters rapidly to city B, and influences the estimates of potential demonstrators in city B as to the probable consequences of demonstrating.[138]

So what appears unplanned is actually intentionally worked out, just out of sight of adversaries, the press, or anyone who might be able to generate documentation to be discovered and mulled over by historians and analysts later. In the early days of telecommunications and mass literacy, much of what happened in everyday life was opaque, unrecorded, and lost to later discovery. Some of it may also have been intentionally avoiding the expected prying eyes that might put jobs, safety, and lives at risk if they were revealed. We can only read through the existing, mostly partisan accounts, to get at the ubiquitous means of working-class self-organisation.

Nevertheless, Tilly is uncertain as to why certain tactics still spread even when it is known that the costs are high and rising. For example, even after it became known that the sympathy strike had been broken and the American Railway Union leadership imprisoned, strikers in the West continued to escalate their tactics by taking over trains and engaging in armed confrontations with the strikebreakers, militias and the US Army.

---

138   Tilly notes, for example, that despite the rarity of sit down strikes in Italy in 1919, the following year 500,000 had deployed the tactic and US workers took it up in the 1930s as strikes were also taking off in the US and other places around the world at the same time. (Ibid., p. 158).

What Cleaver and other autonomist marxists call 'cycles of struggle' are not contagious, improvised, mechanistic, or spontaneous 'waves' but a product of the interconnections and relations among insurgents that circulate through folklore, music, migration, immigration, media, personal networks, and coordinated efforts. Insurgents rely on existing social networks and institutions and recruit those who have existing social attachments rather than isolated individuals.[139] The process of recruiting members to an insurgency should give pause to the notion of a spontaneous contagion. As Tilly recounts,

> events such as great peasant revolts do not ordinarily sweep up society's rootless, disorganised, leftover people, but draw in coherent but aggrieved groups of people who remain attached to each other and to their social settings.[140]

In 1877 and 1894 the strikes spread as much by way of the workers connected by the train tracks as by their existing social networks in the cities that were an outgrowth of the rural to urban migratory routes from the fields to industry.[141] While the railroads sped up the information flow, once they were shut down information kept flowing through the existing social networks built up over years and decades.

The opaqueness of cycles of struggle is reproduced in understanding the tactical choices of insurgents. Although the process of recruiting to a strike or insurgency and the tactics they choose from their repertoire may appear inexplicable to the outside observer, it is immediately obvious to the participants based on shared work, values, experiences, routines, organisation, accumulated experience, social and familial relations, and shared adversaries and grievances. Selection of tactics 'generally changes slowly, seems obvious and natural to the people involved. It resembles an elementary language: familiar as the day to its users, for all its possible quaintness or incomprehensibility to an outsider.'[142]

---

139   See Zibechi's excellent analysis of the factors in contemporary urban Bolivian working-class struggle. (Zibechi 2010).

140   Tilly 1978, p. 83.

141   Again Zibechi highlights the role of rural to urban networks and institutions in Bolivian class struggle. (Ibid).

142   Tilly 1978, p. 156.

Winning the Battle, Losing the Strike

Tactically, the success of the non-violent boycott tactic was its own worst enemy. Without any avenue to redress grievances, workers boycotting trains could expect to face private and state police power to force them to comply. Having achieved their objective of stopping rail traffic and attracting mass support both among an increasing number of fellow railroad workers and in a growing list of local communities, boycotters faced little cost and the promise of significant gains. This encouraged them to escalate their tactics first to circulate the strike and then to sabotage and armed conflict to keep the roads shut down. By refusing to negotiate, concede, or compromise, the combined force of the railroad companies and the government made it impossible for the strikers to de-escalate without total defeat, ensuring that they would not back down. The costs of doing so were too high and the expected gains too little or non-existent for the strikers.

Although deployed with great success, the boycott in itself was insufficient to achieve the objectives of the strike. By definition, a boycott is prompted by an unresolved grievance. The source of the grievance is avoided until it agrees to act to remove the cause of the dispute. In this case, resolution of the strike depended entirely on the ability to apply the necessary leverage to force Pullman to recognise the specific grievances of his workers and negotiate, which he adamantly refused to do. Once the GMA took over the anti-strike effort and passed it to the federal government, Pullman had become far removed from the focus of the strike.

The boycott tactic was successful but alone was insufficient to achieve the objectives of the strike. To succeed, the strike needed to escalate beyond the boycott, but that was impossible with the ARU leadership in jail and the line of communication to the central office shut down. The strike now lacked the coordination to escalate tactics by seizing control of the railroads or spreading the strike to allies in other industrial sectors in order to obtain additional leverage. The inability to do so validated Debs's assessment that the conditions were not yet prime for the strike, as the workers' recomposition had not yet been completed. With the breakdown of coordination, strikers and their supporters became isolated and focused on locally organising their efforts to sustain the strike. As a result, the 1894 strike followed the pattern of the 1877 strike as it turned into numerous local strikes that gradually wound down their use of scattered attacks, sabotage, and street battles. As these local efforts dissipated and the strike no longer circulated, the costs of continued mobilisation rose and the opportunity to achieve their objectives dropped. As a result, workers and their supporters demobilised and de-escalated until the strike was lost.

The 1894 strike also followed another pattern of the 1877 strike: in its aftermath, the AFL brotherhoods got a second look from the companies as possible allies in disciplining and controlling the recalcitrant workforce. By opposing the strike and disciplining members who joined it, the brotherhoods survived long enough to profit from the demise of the ARU. As Stromquist discerned,

> the brotherhoods found themselves the unexpected beneficiaries of the audacious aspirations of railroad industrial unionism. After the Pullman boycott and the inevitable recrimination that followed in its wake, railroad corporations were prepared to accept, and in fact sought, 'responsible' partners among the old and conservative brotherhoods of railroad labor as insurance against another episode of industrial unionism.[143]

The collapse of coordination once the ARU leadership was arrested and the telegrams ceased illustrated another significant limitation of the strike strategy. Placing responsibility for coordinating the strike in the hands of the ARU leadership who were centrally located in Chicago and dependent on the telegraph, a system owned and run by their adversary and which was rerouted to be intercepted by local authorities, made the strike extremely vulnerable to easy disruption. Any tactic such as arresting the leadership, cutting their access to the telegraph, or blockading them in their office would have destroyed the centralised command system on which the rank and file now depended to coordinate a strike they launched from below.

To their credit, while initially unsupportive of the strike, Debs, Howard and their aides followed the lead from below and unwaveringly led the strike. But as soon as they were incapacitated by the federal injunctions that shut down the command centre, the further coordinated escalation necessary to win the strike was impossible. Considering the leadership's principled opposition to the strike, let alone the insurgency that followed the arrival of US troops, even if they had not been arrested they would have been unlikely to support further necessary escalation. While the strategy of industrial unionism came from below, it still relied on centralised organisation to realise it, which was vulnerable to being overwhelmed by the combined forces of the companies, private gunmen, and local, state and federal judicial, police, and military power. The workers' boycott succeeded, but the rest of the working-class was not yet prepared to help them win the strike.

---

143   Stromquist 1993, pp. 98–9.

CHAPTER 5

Government by Injunction and Bayonet: Working-Class Recomposition in the 1894 Railroad Strike

If men could not do unlawful acts because violence might possibly or reasonably result, then the most innocent deeds might be crimes. To make men responsible for the remote consequences of their acts would be to destroy individual liberty and make men slaves.

CLARENCE DARROW, 1894[1]

• • •

Every act of destruction meets its response, sooner or later, in an act of creation.

EDUARDO GALEANO, 1971[2]

∴

Crushing the 1877 strike with the force of the US Army did not tamp down class conflict for long. By the mid-1880s, a new movement which imagined a life outside work emerged, calling for an eight-hour workday, eight hours of rest, and eight hours to enjoy life. From this idea grew the May 1886 strike, showing the first signs of a newly re-energised working-class, this time with tactics, strategy and a vision of the kind of life they wanted. All that was missing was the moment to test years of patient rebuilding of working-class power. That day arrived in 1894.

Beginning in the autocratic confines of the corporatist Pullman company town, the 1894 railroad strike disrupted much of the country for weeks. What made it possible in a very short period of time was the year-old American Railway Union (ARU), modelled after a provocative new idea of organising all workers into a single union regardless of skill, wage, location, employer, and, for a

---

1 Darrow 1894, p. 85.
2 Galeano 1971, p. 282.

short time, race. Providing the missing ingredient of coordination, the ARU rank and file turned a sympathy strike for the Pullman workers into first a strike and then an insurgency that was only tamped down by the combined force of consolidated capital, the judicial, police, and military power. The strike announced a new cycle of class struggle seized upon by reformers set on recognising unions, imposing arbitration and collective bargaining in order to manage what it could not entirely prevent or repress.

Gatling Gun on Paper

The railroads pursued a winner takes all strategy in the strike, refusing to negotiate, opting instead for a unilateral tactical escalation to bring about a forcible end to the strike. Unable to achieve that outcome on their own, the Chicago-based lines coordinated their efforts through the GMA, an organisation they established, which was politically well-connected with the White House. Their central organisation and elite coalition gave them the leverage to obtain tacit support from local and state authorities, federal marshals, and the federal courts in order to obtain police, militia, and military intervention. With its direct channel to Washington DC, the GMA could pretty much write their own injunctions to ostensibly protect the US mail and bankrupt railroads under federal receivership which were used in nearly 20 states.

Whether the GMA's strategy was preordained or crafted in the heat of circumstances, it quickly fell into place. Each of the GMA's steps ran parallel to one another, sometimes with little coordination, and in others they were unfurled in a matter of days. While the boycott remained uneventful, some mayors and governors resisted deploying police or militia to interfere with the workers.

The federal courts issued injunctions prohibiting the strikers from interfering with the mails, which prompted the railroads to put US mail on all the trains. The federal government then began issuing blanket injunctions which relieved the railroads of petitioning for individual restraining orders. Without naming the person or specific action being enjoined, the blanket injunctions were so all-encompassing that 'labor, wishing to strike or striking, found most of its customary avenues for redress of grievances closed'.[3] Attorney General Olney planned to blanket the country with omnibus injunctions, sometimes seeking them with little prompting from the railroads.[4] Although the blanket injunc-

---

3   Lindsey 1942, p. 156.
4   Ibid., p. 243.

tions were targeted at unknown parties, the use of company employees as deputy marshals allowed the railroads to identify, arrest and indict specific offenders.

The blanket injunction had just been developed by the Northern Pacific Railroad while under bankruptcy protection in April 1894 to protect it from the ARU's first strike.[5] In granting the injunction, Milwaukee Federal Circuit Court Judge Jenkins wrote that 'a strike is essentially a conspiracy to extort by violence'.[6]

The first move to federalise the anti-strike efforts came on 28 June, when the Chicago US Attorney Milchrist met with the GMA and promised to issue warrants to arrest those interfering with mail trains in Chicago. It was a solution in search of a problem. With the participation of Attorney General Olney, the GMA didn't merely federalise the issue, it wrote the legal policy enforcing it.[7] On 30 June, before there had been any serious disorder in the city, Olney appointed Edwin Walker, a railroad attorney, as Special US Attorney for Chicago to work with Milchrist without bothering to consult with Milchrist on the decision. Putting aside their rocky start, Milchrist and Walker applied for an injunction against the ARU for engaging in trust-like behaviour under the 1890 Sherman Anti-Trust Act. By doing so they turned the law into a weapon to be used against labour, an intention explicitly rejected by both Senator Sherman and the Senate at the time the Act was passed.[8]

---

5   Lindsey is incorrect that the blanket injunction had never been used before (Ibid., p. 156). A similar type of injunction was issued during the 1877 strike (see Chapters 1, 2, and 3).

6   Ibid., pp. 157–8.

7   In his 5 July 1894 letter to President Cleveland, one in a series of remarkable letters, Governor Altgeld dissected the dangers of the lack of oversight in the decision:
    'You say that troops were ordered into Illinois upon the demand of the Post Office Department and upon representations of the judicial officers of the United States that process of court could not be served, and upon proof that conspiracies existed ... All of these officers (post office officials) are appointed by the Executive. Most of them can be removed by him at will. They are not only obliged to do his bidding, but they are, in fact, a part of the Executive. If several of them can apply for troops, one alone can; so that under the law as you assume it to be, an Executive, through any one of his appointees, can apply to himself to have the military sent into any city or number of cities, and base his application on such representation or showing as he sees fit to make' (Altgeld 1915).

8   Senator Morgan's proposed amendment to the Sherman Anti-trust Act to apply it to unions was defeated. (US Strike Commission 1895, p. 202). Despite the legislative intent of the law, it was used against unions more frequently than corporations during its early years.

Although the head of the Chicago US mail service reported no piling up of US mail, Milchrist and Walker successfully obtained the first omnibus or blanket injunction issued in Chicago by federal judges Woods and Grosscup on 2 July. Judge Grosscup had just been appointed to the US District Court for Northern Illinois in 1892 as political payback for Pullman's large donation to President Harrison's failed re-election bid. The injunction covered 22 railroads and covered 'all other persons whatsoever who are not named herein'.[9] It threatened anyone interfering with interstate commerce and the mails with a conspiracy charge. The injunction was served on members and officials of the ARU in a huge dragnet. The injunction prevented strikers and the ARU from encouraging anyone to strike, attempt to prevent strikebreaking, and assisting, aiding, directing or committing an act prohibited by the injunction – effectively banning the strike. That day the *Chicago Times* got it right when it wrote that 'the object of the injunction is not so much to prevent interference with trains as to lay a foundation for calling out the United States troops ...'.[10] On 3 July, the *New York Times* described the blanket injunction as a 'Gatling gun on paper', an instrument that 'punishes an individual for doing a certain thing, and is equally merciless if he does not do it ...'.[11]

Blanket injunctions became the legal cover allowing the railroad companies to escalate their anti-strike tactics. These Gatling guns on paper were issued from Michigan to California just by request of a railroad. Judges issued them even for the minor charge of failure to obey, the first and sometimes only step leading to the deployment of US troops. The process by which injunctions were issued demonstrated the fusion of effort between the railroads and the federal government.

The opening shot that transformed the strike into an insurrection didn't come from a gun, but rather from one of the Gatling guns on paper. Local Chicago police sympathetic to the strike broke ranks and could not be depended upon to engage the strikers. Although police were ordered to assist the state militia, the familiar experience of the 1877 strike

> that policemen sympathized with strikers rather than with the corporations cannot be doubted, nor would it be surprising to find the same sentiment rife among the military. These forces are largely recruited from the laboring classes. Indeed, the danger is growing that in strike wars

9   Lindsey 1942, p. 193; and US Strike Commission 1895, p. 180.
10   Lindsey 1942, p. 164.
11   See Ibid., p. 161.

between corporations and employees, military duty will ultimately have to be done by others than volunteers from labor ranks.[12]

The lack of reliable police led the GMA to turn to the local US deputy marshals. Milchrist recommended that the US marshal be given 50 more deputies. By 1 July, the US marshal had more than 400 deputies.[13] On 2 July, the US marshal at Blue Island just outside Chicago read the blanket injunction to a crowd of about 2,000. The strikers and their supporters had been disrupting the Rock Island Line, ditched a mail train and several baggage cars, and were blocking all train movement. When the strikers and their supporters refused to disperse, US troops were called in and a clash erupted.

The deployment of US troops at Blue Island had ignited a firestorm across much of the country. Within the next two days US troops were active in Chicago, Los Angeles, Raton, New Mexico and Trinidad, Colorado.[14] By 5 July, US attorneys in 19 states and territories had been instructed to protect the movement of mail trains.

What constituted a mail train was in dispute because it was not clearly delineated in the law. Was a train a mail train if it pulled a designated mail car or carried a single envelope? Attorney General Olney attempted to resolve this issue when he ruled that any train, even with just one car with US mail in it, was a mail train. Considering the source of this ruling, it seemed intended to provide a tactical weapon to the companies rather than a neutral resolution to the question.[15]

The ARU offered to allow any train carrying US mail to run as long as they didn't have any Pullman cars attached.[16] But the railroads countered the ARU's concession by using Olney's definition of a 'mail car' by attaching a Pullman car to all possible trains since the US Post Office defined a train with *any* quantity or type of US mail as a mail train. Using mail trains was vital to the GMA's strategy not to draw the federal government into the fight as much as provide a legal rationale to do so.

The mail train issue worked in conjunction with the precedent established during the 1877 strike that the federal government may enjoin any attempt to disrupt a railroad under receivership. These types of injunctions were used nationwide. On 27 June, US circuit court judge Caldwell imposed an injunction

12   US Strike Commission 1895, p. xliv.
13   Lindsey 1942, p. 153.
14   Ibid., pp. 164–5, 175.
15   US Strike Commission 1895, p. 9.
16   Lindsey 1942, pp. 150–1.

prohibiting interference with the Santa Fe Railroad, which was under federal receivership. His injunction was later extended to the Illinois Circuit on 29 June by federal judge Woods. The Santa Fe Railroad was two to four months late in paying its workers and the site of serious clashes between La Junta, Colorado and Las Vegas, New Mexico. Earlier in the strike, US Attorney Hemingway initially refused to apply for an injunction because he thought that the lack of movement of the mail trains was due to a shortage of labour and not interference. Hemingway later changed his mind, requesting protection by the US marshal on 2 July. On the same day, an armed crowd disarmed 52 deputy marshals, cut the telegraph wires, and blocked all the trains heading into and out of Trinidad. That day US troops were sent to Trinidad from Fort Logan, Colorado to put down the insurrection.[17]

Insurrection was raging elsewhere on 2 July, as 500 ARU members and 300 miners struck in Raton, New Mexico. Although the sheriff warned the US marshal not to enter town, he was overruled and threatened with arrest by an associate justice of the state Supreme Court if he interfered. Unable to get the trains moving, and facing the strike spreading to the town hotel, the associate justice took the unprecedented step to order in state troops from Trinidad. The strikers evaded the associate justice and the militia by moving a few miles above Raton where they struck on 3 July. Suddenly 16 runaway train cars came crashing wildly into town where they lay blocking the tracks until the troops arrived to clear it. The militia was kept in the area throughout August.[18]

These were but a few instances in which strikers and their supporters escalated their tactic by attacking property. Such tactics were endemic. According to the US Strike Commission,

> The strikers' experience and training were to be seen in the spiking and misplacing of switches, removing rails, crippling of interlocking systems, the detaching, side tracking, and derailing of cars and engines, placing of coupling pins in engine machinery, blockading tracks with cars, and attempts to detach and run in mail cars.[19]

Such well-organised sabotage had thrown the rail system into disarray and threatened to spread the disruption to the entire economy.

---

17   Ibid., pp. 160 and 246–7.
18   Ibid., p. 248.
19   US Strike Commission 1895, p. xlv.

Not all the US attorneys agreed that injunctions were meant exclusively for the strikers. On 18 July, Los Angeles Special Federal Attorney Call reported to Attorney General Olney that something needed to be done about the Southern Pacific Railroad's monopoly, as they otherwise risked an outright rebellion. Stanford's Southern Pacific Railroad was also known to be conspiring with the two other lines entering San Francisco to set rates; together the three companies also controlled the ferry and streetcar lines. Near the end of the strike Los Angeles US Attorney Denis attempted to file an injunction against the Southern Pacific Railroad, but Attorney General Olney prevented him from doing so and the issue was dropped.[20]

These examples demonstrate Lindsey's point that the purpose of the omnibus injunction 'was designed not so much to protect property as to crush the strike'.[21] The impact on the striker was immediate. Debs and all the ARU officers along all the roads being struck were issued blanket injunctions on 3 July, prohibiting them from communicating with the rank and file and supporters. A newspaper publisher reported that the US marshal arrived in Indianapolis with blank injunctions on the B&O Railway Company which paid his expenses and provided the names to fill in the blanks.[22]

For Debs, the court injunctions played the central role in paralysing the strike. The injunctions made it impossible for him to coordinate the strike and the strikers to communicate with one another, spread the strike to other lines, geographic areas or industries, or recruit supporters. The injunctions and arrests for contempt of court sabotaged the Chicago ARU office's centralised communication system because all the union's telegrams were routed through there. As he explained to the US Strike Commission,

> It was not the soldiers that ended the strike; it was not the old brotherhoods that ended the strike; it was simply the United States courts that ended the strike ... [T]he strike was broken up by the Federal courts of the United States, and not by the Army, and not by any other power, but simply and solely by the action of the United States courts in restraining us from discharging our duties as officers and representatives of the employees.[23]

---

20 Lindsey 1942, pp. 159–60 and 249.
21 Ibid., p. 275.
22 US Strike Commission 1895, p. 665.
23 Debs 1895, p. 143.

Debs was being overly dramatic but he made a crucial point. Without the blanket federal injunction there would have been little justification for either arresting the leadership or sending in US troops under the pretence of contempt. But the injunction alone was insufficient to break the strike. Written to apply to almost anyone, anywhere, and at any time, the injunction was only a legal tactic that provided a pretext for sending in US troops, not to defuse the conflict but to protect the railroad companies from having to compromise, negotiate, settle, or even lose the strike. The blanket injunctions, followed in their wake by US troops, appear to have enraged the strikers and their supporters because they so obviously brought in the federal government and the US Army exclusively on the side of the railroads companies. The actions of the federal courts illustrated the existence of a coordinated partnership between the federal government and the railroad companies to paralyse the ARU and break the strike. No better evidence of this can be found than the ARU's attempt on 4 July to apply for an injunction to compel the Union Pacific Railroad to stop running Pullman cars in order to allow mail cars to run. The court did not grant the injunction. On 7 July the ARU headquarters in Chicago was raided and all their records taken. In a rare ruling against the railroads, the judge had them returned the next day because their seizure was not authorised.

However, the railroads' successful coalition building and insertion of the US Army presented the possibility of failure. Reliance on the federal government and the military made the railroads' vulnerability explicit: they were not powerful enough to win the strike on their own, let alone negotiate a favourable settlement for themselves. Drawing the US Army into the fight also eroded the legitimacy of the federal government, which was now seen by the population as unequivocally coming into the fight on the side of the railroads and against workers with legitimate unanswered grievances that were echoed in the widespread animosity towards the railroads. Lastly, unilateral tactical escalation to the use of the state force of violence triggered further tactical escalation by workers and their supporters spreading to new locations all over the country. It didn't lead to capitulation or immediate crushing defeat; instead it further raised the cost of crushing the strike in property damage, share prices, dividends, public spending on the armed forces, and political support. What had just been a boycott became a strike which became an armed insurgency that threatened to become something much more.

The railroads and the GMA were in a predicament – they needed a way to justify the use of military force to break the strike. The injunction became the key to explaining the presence of US troops, as appealing to local and state officials to send in more police and the state militia was ineffective. Local and state officials sympathetic to labour unions and working-class voters equivocated and delayed responding to requests for forces of order, which emboldened the 'mob' and raised the costs of their riots. When the militia was brought in, troops either mutinied or were ordered not to interfere with the mob. Without effective local protections, the companies turned to the federal courts for two measures. They received deputised private agents, e.g. 'deputy sheriffs', hired and paid by the railroads to ensure their loyalty and effectiveness protecting company property under federal receivership. The courts also granted injunctions against the ARU enjoining the leadership from communicating about the strike. When the ARU defied the court injunctions the companies could call on the Attorney General and President for protection.

Injunctions became the permit for federal intervention which caused the very problem it was premised to solve, an example of what is known as the cause and effect fallacy. Whether or not the claims of disorder by strikers and their supporters used to justify an injunction to bring in US troops were fabricated, their arrival on the scene was certain to provoke the strikers to more disorder thus retroactively justify the injunction. This was especially so when troops protected strikebreakers, forced strikers to drive trains, attacked strikers and their supporters, or otherwise tried to open up rail traffic by force of arms. Other times local police or private agents had already provoked strikers and their supporters prompting the governor called in the state militia. When the police and militia were ineffective in moving the trains, the arrival of the US Army to do so was clearly intended to turn the stalemate into defeat, leaving the strikers no other choice than to escalate their tactics to defend the strike.

Flaunting federal court injunctions protecting railroads under receivership successfully led to further escalation by the federal government. But arresting the other ARU leadership and inserting US troops were insufficient in themselves to end the strike, as it transformed the strike into countless locally focused armed conflicts. The President declared martial law in several places in order to bypass due process by pre-emptively arresting and imprisoning strikers in order to allow the railroads to begin operating. Escalating tactics to set aside the constitution during a strike became a precedent to be repeatedly deployed for decades to come. It convincingly put a spotlight on the limits to civil liberties in the class struggle and the fundamental class nature of the constitution.

The brutal naked force of martial law, or military occupation and rule, became the quickest route to tamping down the disruption. Deploying state violence raised the costs for both capital and workers. Capital risked further disruption to the accumulation process and further delays to restoring business. Workers faced greater risk of death, injury, blacklisting from employment, and destitution, which eviscerated any remaining opportunity to achieve even a minuscule part of their objectives.

Militarising the Strike

After the 1877 railroad strike, there had been a debate within the US Army about the appropriate constitutional authority to deploy US troops in a labour conflict. Violating a federal court injunction was interpreted to trigger the President's constitutional authority under Article IV, Section 4 of the US Constitution to

> guarantee in Every State in this Union a Republican Form of Government, and shall protect each of them from Invasion; and on Application of the Legislature, or of the Executive (when the Legislature cannot be convened) against domestic Violence.

The US Strike Commission found the President's power to send in troops under Article IV Section 4 of the US Constitution also articulated in federal statutory law under the Revised Statutes of the US, Sections 5298 and 5299.[24] The Commission argued that the President is not limited to a request by either the state legislature or governor or the presence of domestic violence but has a much more expansive mandate than previously assumed.

> United States troops were not sent into Illinois upon the application of the legislature, nor of the executive, against domestic violence; i.e., violence affecting the State and its government as such. The President ordered the troops to Chicago –
>
> (1) To protect federal property.
> (2) To prevent obstruction in the carrying of the mails.
> (3) To prevent interference with the interstate commerce; and
> (4) To enforce the decrees and mandates of the federal courts.[25]

The President's authority was also asserted under section 5298 of the Revised Statutes of the United States, which provides:

> Whenever, by reason of unlawful obstructions, combinations, or assemblages of persons, or rebellion against the authority of the Government

---

24 Section 5299 became law on 20 April 1871 and Section 5298 of the Revised Statutes of the United States, became law on 29 July 1891.

25 US Strike Commission 1895, pp. xx.

of the United States, it shall become impracticable, *in the judgment of the President*, to enforce, by the ordinary course of judicial proceedings, the laws of the United States within any State or Territory, it shall be lawful for the President to call forth the militia of any or all of the States, and to employ such parts of the land or naval forces of the United States as he may deem necessary to enforce the faithful execution of the laws of the United States, or to suppress such rebellion, in whatever State or Territory thereof the laws of the United States may be forcibly opposed, or the execution thereof forcibly obstructed.[26]

The US Strike Commission overlooked that section 5298 provides a vast array of justifications for doing so, ranging from 'unlawful obstructions, combinations, or assemblages of persons, or rebellion against the authority of the Government of the United States'. This may have well exceeded the President's Article IV powers and grossly allowed the violation of the 1st amendment free exercise, speech, assembly, and grievance clauses, the 5th amendment due process clause, and the 14th amendment equal protection clause.

The US Strike Commission also referenced section 5299, which allows that

Whenever insurrection, domestic violence, unlawful combinations, or conspiracies in any State so obstructs or hinders the execution of the laws thereof, and of the United States, as to deprive any portion or class of the people of such State of any of the rights, privileges, or immunities, or protection, named in the constitution and secured by the laws for the protection of such rights, privileges, or immunities, and the constituted authorities of such State are unable to protect, or, from any cause, fail in or refuse protection of the people in such rights, such facts shall be deemed a denial by such State of the equal protection of the laws to which they are entitled under the constitution of the United States; and in all such cases, or whenever any such insurrection, violence, unlawful combination, or conspiracy, opposes or obstructs the laws of the United States, or the due execution thereof, or impedes or obstructs the due course of justice under the same, it shall be lawful for the President, and it shall be his duty, to take such measures, by the employment of the militia or the land and naval forces of the United States, or of either, or by other means, as he may deem necessary, for the suppression of such insurrection, domestic violence, or combinations.[27]

---

26   Ibid., p. xx, italics added.
27   Ibid., p. xx.

In addition to the problems of unlimited discretion and suppression of civil liberties shared by 5298 the US Strike Commission was silent on two critical aspects of section 5299. First, the section refers to the privileges, immunities and protections of 'people', which the railroad corporations were not. Second, since section 5299 became law in 1871, it was clearly intended as a temporary emergency measure to protect the rights of freed blacks during Reconstruction against white Klan terrorism, the denial of their rights by recalcitrant local and state governments, and local and state governments against coups.

In short, the US Strike Commission read the federal statutes as providing for an open-ended presidential power to insert federal troops into a state even without a request from local and state officials or the presence of violence, merely because of the 'combination or assemblage of persons' exercising their First Amendment civil liberties. It conflated constitutionally-protected actions with insurrectionary and violent action that 'obstructs or hinders' the operation of federal law or 'deprive[s] any portion or class of the people of such State of any of the rights, privileges, or immunities, or protection' in order to justify the use of the US military.

Note the use of the word 'or' in the following clause in Section 5299. The president may use US troops either when such conditions exist 'or whenever any such insurrection, violence, unlawful combination, *or* conspiracy, opposes or obstructs the laws of the United States, or the due execution thereof, or impedes or obstructs the due course of justice under the same ...'. Section 5299 appears to have been intended to grant federal power to suppress white terrorist violence against blacks and several coups overthrowing elected local and state governments in the South during Reconstruction, especially in states controlled by Democrats. Used this way, the federal statute established a much lower standard by which a president may militarise the response to any domestic disturbance. However, the additional requirement that the 'constituted authorities' are 'unable', 'fail', or 'refuse' to protect the people were not met in Illinois since Governor Altgeld called out thousands of militia to protect the railroads' property and Mayor Hopkins did the same with thousands more police.

On 9 July, President Cleveland claimed 'it was impracticable to enforce federal law by the ordinary course of judicial procedure' in North Dakota, Montana, Idaho, Colorado, Washington, Wyoming, California, and the territories of Utah and New Mexico, sent in US troops, and imposed a 3 p.m. curfew the next day.

Soon after, the first trains departed the Stock Yards and the boycott was broken. At the time Cleveland sent troops into Chicago, there had been few reported disorders. The Chicago Superintendent of Police, sheriff and Governor

Altgeld had all reported no serious disturbances other than isolated acts of sabotage before troops arrived, and did not even request state militia of which there was already a large force in the city. The only thing really keeping the trains from moving was the lack of willing workers. At that time the state legislature was not in session and Governor Altgeld had not requested any US troops so they couldn't be called out under Article IV, Section 4. However, according to the US Strike Commission, President Cleveland didn't need it. He had the sole discretion to call out federal troops to suppress disorder under Sections 5298 and 5299.[28]

The US Strike Commission was strangely silent on the dangers of vastly expanded discretionary authority of the President to unilaterally make this determination without requiring any other input or requests by state governors. Governor Altgeld denounced the usurpation of local and state shared powers by the president as an act of 'violence to the constitution' that would destroy local self-government and place the country under 'military government'.[29]

When Major-General Miles of the Department of Missouri arrived on 5 July as the commander of the Chicago troops he reportedly went immediately to the GMA office to meet with Egan, Milchrist, and an Assistant US Marshal, although he denied having ever met with them.[30] The day Miles arrived he reported that troops were not necessary once they arrived. However, he used them to defend against what he perceived as lawlessness and the possibility that the US government could be paralysed if not overthrown. He would later claim that only federal troops saved the country 'from a serious rebellion'.[31] Miles's inquiry as to whether his troops could fire on those obstructing trains was denied. He was never given permission to impose law and order, which he insisted was the responsibility of local authorities.[32] In addition to his 1,936 troops, there were already 3,000 to 5,000 police and special deputies, 500 substitute police, and 250 special sheriff deputies guarding the 3,000 miles of railroad track in the city.

Governor Altgeld was not asked whether he would like US troops sent to Chicago and he didn't find out about them until they arrived. Governor Altgeld denounced the trampling of local government authority, protested the lack of civilian control over the troops (apparently unaware of the GMA's central role in managing their deployment), denounced their presence as illegal,

---

28   Lindsey 1842, p. 263; Ross and Taft 1969, p. 8; and see Manning 1960, pp. 39–40.
29   See Manning 1960, pp. 40–2.
30   US Strike Commission 1895, p. 339.
31   Brecher 1972, pp. 105 and 108.
32   Lindsey 1942, pp. 182–3, 205–6, and 213.

and demanded the troops be immediately removed in several letters to President Cleveland. Altgeld had already responded to disturbances elsewhere in the state according to his state constitutional authority. On 6 July, the Illinois Central Railroad reported that 48 of its cars were burned. A passenger train had been boarded, and the engine detached, causing it to run out of control along the track.[33]

Soon after this incident, Governor Altgeld ordered thousands of militia into Chicago, but this came after the arrival and deployment of US troops had already sparked the battles at Blue Island. Trying to balance the responsibilities of his office and the plight of the strikers, Altgeld ordered the militia to avoid bloodshed and keep their guns unloaded, and prohibited them from protecting private property, policies which incurred the wrath of the local media, the US Attorney, and Attorney General Olney. *The Nation* magazine joined the flurry of denunciations of Altgeld and three other governors who refused to use their state militias to break the strike by denouncing them as 'anarchists', an unlikely accusation as any.[34] Considering their cooperation with the GMA and the use of police and militia against the strikers over the next few days, Lindsey may be overstating Altgeld's and Hopkins's support for the strikers. Their stated support for the strikers could be better described as wavering and equivocating in order to delay making a decision that would cause inevitable loss of political support among the working-class for appearing to defend the much despised railroads.

Missouri Governor Stone and Colorado Governor Waite joined Illinois Governor Altgeld to protest the President's usurpation of local and state authority under the guise of protecting interstate commerce and the mails. Governor Waite denounced US deputy marshals who operated as if they were a 'private army' that 'is waging an active war in Colorado without any declaration thereof by the United States, or notice or knowledge thereof by the state authorities, and utterly in violation of law'.[35] Despite these governors' best efforts, there is no record that they succeeded in reining in Cleveland's use of the federal courts, marshals, or military. In fact, the opposite occurred, establishing a precedent that continues to this day.

Once in place, US troops hardly took a neutral position. Responding to reports that men were forced back to work by bayonet, even Major-General Miles admitted that 'there might be certain conditions under which that might

---

33   See Manning 1960, pp. 38–45; and Lindsey 1942, pp. 171–4, 185, 187–9, and 198.

34   Lindsey 1942, p. 262.

35   Ibid., pp. 168 and 262.

be done'.[36] The documentary evidence raises doubts about the truthfulness of Major-General Miles's claim to the US Strike Commission that he had had no contact with the GMA or Egan.[37] Commanding General Schofield consulted extensively with the GMA even seeking advice about troop movements. Major-General Miles met daily with GMA strike coordinator Egan. Major-General Miles appears to have plagiarised Egan's text in his memos, resisted pulling his troops out of Chicago on Egan's request, and hired spies to infiltrate and monitor strikers. There was no light between Miles and the GMA.

Whether or not Major-General Miles was coordinating with the GMA is a crucial historical issue. Unlike in 1877, in 1894 the US Army claimed to have maintained the chain of command instead of giving over command to the governors.[38] However, some commanding officers such as Miles inserted the railroad corporations into the chain of command by consulting and coordinating the use of US troops with them in order to implement Attorney General Olney's plan to break the strike.[39] This has been attributed to the membership of the US Army officer corps in the same elite power networks and a sharing of the same class perspective of the railroad corporation executives.[40] The shared hegemonic ideology of elites inside and outside the military is complemented by the institutional power relations that merged capital and the state. The expansion of the role of the state in the economy and the integration of capital and the state were critical tactics for decomposing working-class power.

The justification for sending in US troops was predicated on hysterical and fabricated media reports of riots, mobs, and sabotage disrupting the trains and threatening the functioning of local civilian government. When US troops arrived in areas where disturbances had been reported, they found none. What they did find was a strike in effect, which led to staff shortages and prevented the trains from being operated. The troops were sent to combat a strike that had successfully brought the railroads to a mostly calm standstill. The story many of the officials in charge had told had little basis in fact because the American

---

36   US Strike Commission 1895, p. 339.
37   Cooper 1977, pp. 191–2.
38   The opinion of the US Army Judge Advocate General explicitly explains that the military may not be directly summoned or put under the authority of either local and state officials or US marshals. He is silent about whether it may be put under the authority of private corporations. (Winthrop 1901, pp. 36–7).
39   For a detailed contrast of the two plans see Cooper 1977, p. 194.
40   Ibid., p. 194.

public would have been outraged to have learned the truth that US troops were sent to protect many bankrupt railroads against American workers with legitimate grievances.

Privatising State Policing Power

Once on the ground, the US troops supported state militias, US marshals, deputy marshals, and police, making arrests for violating court injunctions, dispersing strikers and their supporters, and guarding railroad property. The integrated role of each of these police and military forces blurred the line between capital and the state in both a figurative and literal sense. The railroad companies hired and paid the salaries of many men wielding government authority. The GMA is estimated to have hired and armed between 3,600 to 5,000 US deputy marshals who were simultaneously railroad company employees and federal law enforcement agents. To recruit these agents the GMA opened employment offices in six cities in four states at the cost of about $36,000.[41] Among these special agents were 20–30 detectives hired to carry out surveillance of the ARU and identify strikers.

The standards for the type of men to be hired to wield federal power were quite low. The press and local officials reported US deputy marshals being drunk and engaging in violence and looting. The US deputy marshals had all the force of government and none of the accountability.

> While operating the railroads they assumed and exercised unrestricted United States authority when so ordered by their employers, or whenever they regarded it as necessary. They were not under the direct control of any Government official while exercising authority.[42]

In effect, the federal government had privatised federal police and military power at the end of the nineteenth century, much earlier than previously thought.[43] By reassigning federal authority in the use of force to private cor-

---

41 Lindsey 1942, pp. 144 and 168.

42 US Strike Commission 1895, p. xliv.

43 This is an historical parallel to military contractors today in Afghanistan and Iraq hired to carry out fighting, counter-insurgency operations, and counter-intelligence, who are exempt from the US Uniform Code of Military Justice and the laws of the nation in which they are hired to operate.

porations, federal and state officials could retain some plausible deniability for
the abuses and violence that occurred during their watch.

The injunction proved to have many uses for escalating tactics and raising
the costs of the insurgency: not only did it redirect the target of the strike
from the railroads to the federal government, sever the leadership from the
rank and file, and allow the deployment of the combined firepower of the US
military against the strikers and their supporters. Most insidiously, the injunction carved out an exception to yet-to-be-tested constitutionally enshrined civil
liberties in times of class struggle. Here, the judiciary played a starring role in
dismantling the legal organisation of workers that made the strike possible.

Dismantling the ARU

As the national strike ended on 10 July, the dismantling and bankrupting of
the ARU as an organisation began. Here, the strategy was to tie up the leadership in two multi-faceted legal proceedings that would force the rank and file
to redirect their attention, resources, and supporters from the railroads to the
legal defence of the ARU leadership.

Bringing in Debs faced resistance. The GMA complained that Special US
Attorney Walker was unnecessarily delaying the arrest and contempt proceedings of Debs. One reason for this was that Walker informed Olney that the
defendants had not personally interfered with any trains and actually warned
against the use of violence and interfering with the mails.[44]

Since the facts would stand in the way of the truth, the grand jury was
impaneled the next day. The only witness was the manager of the Chicago Western Union where the ARU sent its 9,000 telegrams at a cost of $3,000. Judge
Grosscup threatened the witness with arrest unless he turned over the copies,
which he had initially refused to do as he considered them privileged communications. The danger of private corporations possessing the content of vast
communications is not a new issue.[45]

On 10 July, the grand jury promptly indicted four top ARU officials for criminal conspiracy to interfere with the US mail and interstate commerce. Debs
and the three others waived their $10,000 bail and spent six days in jail awaiting
the initial hearing.[46] The indictments asserted that the ARU had the authority

44 Lindsey 1942, p. 289.
45 This is most glaring at a time of the use of 'big data' obtained by private companies and
    used by the US government during the ongoing endless war on terrorism.
46 Papke 2008, p. 6.

to call out its locals on strike although its constitution gave that power exclusively to the locals. While they were in custody the ARU office was raided and all its files were seized. Among its files were Debs's private papers, which Judge Grosscup ordered be returned to him since their seizure had violated the subpoena. After a short time the case was eventually dropped.

Two weeks later, 69 people, including all of the officers and the entire board of directors of the ARU, were held in civil contempt for violating a court injunction and brought by federal Circuit Court judge Seaman. Many were dismissed, and very few were actually found guilty. But regardless of the outcome, the indictments 'served their purpose which was to spread fear and defeatism among the strikers' and tie them up in lengthy court cases as 'part of the strategy of the Department of Justice to undermine the morale of labor'.[47]

The contempt charge was for disobeying the 2 July US federal court injunction prohibiting the ARU from, among other things, 'compelling, or inducing by threats, intimidation, persuasion, force, or violence, railroad employees to refuse or fail to perform their duties'. Some of the indictments stated that men refused to turn switches and to get on and fire an engine, not just talk about taking such actions. Such acts were construed as being in contempt of court. In this way, the indictment turned *not working* into a defiance of a court injunction because it interfered with interstate commerce and the mails. Olney also portrayed the strike as an act of interference because it was a public nuisance. Lacking evidence to demonstrate contemptible *actions* the prosecution pursued contemptible *inaction* by using the blanket injunctions to criminalise workers for refusing to work. This was quite a sharp turn since Reconstruction when the federal government protected the rights of former slaves to refuse to be compelled to work under the 'freedom of contract' principle.

Here, the legal tactic ran aground on the shores of the legal strategy. If the blanket injunction could be used to disable the ARU as an organisation, it could not criminally punish workers for what they didn't do. Could refusal to act be subject to punishment? Prosecuting individual workers for striking was the equivalent of punishing them for exercising the very right of 'freedom of contract'. Since the principle was then the judicial weapon of choice presumably to protect workers from unlawful combinations, e.g. unions, this was a glaring hypocrisy at best.

Surprisingly, Clarence Darrow was hired as the ARU's lead defence attorney. The soon to be famous attorney left his position as counsel to the Chicago and Northwestern Railroad and the legal committee of the GMA to jump the track

---

47   Lindsey 1942, pp. 277–80.

to the ARU.[48] It would be a rigged legal battle: the initial hearing was before Judge Woods, who had helped write the injunction.

Cut off from the many strikers and supporters who had now been demobilised, the strike shifted to the legal terrain, which put the ARU at a huge disadvantage. Attempting to dispute the legality of the injunction, ARU attorney S.S. Gregory, the former president of the American Bar Association, argued in a defence brief that 'no more tyrannous and arbitrary government can be devised than the administration of criminal law by a single judge by means of injunction and proceedings in contempt'.[49]

Darrow questioned the absence of a single fact to prove the defendants or the union were connected with an unlawful action. Foreseeing a constitutional struggle over civil liberties that would come to the fore in the later WWI-era Debs sedition case among others, Darrow questioned 'If men could not do unlawful acts because violence might possibly or reasonably result, then the most innocent deeds might be crimes. To make men responsible for the remote consequences of their acts would be to destroy individual liberty and make men slaves'.[50] Darrow's thinking spoke to the trajectory of tactics. Making even non-violent tactics such as a strike illegal because those who deploy it might someday escalate their tactics illustrated, to paraphrase President John F. Kennedy's warning, that making peaceful change impossible makes violent change inevitable.[51]

After a long delay, on 14 December Judge Woods ruled that the defendants were guilty of conspiracy in restraint of interstate commerce. Debs was sentenced to six months in jail and the others to three months. Debs soon racked up his first loss at the US Supreme Court when it refused his request to be granted a writ of *habeas corpus*. The US Supreme Court issued a unanimous ruling on 27 May upholding Judge Wood's ruling. 'The injunction had received from the Supreme Court a legal sanctity such as it had never had before. It is little wonder that this decision, coming as it did close upon the heels of the income tax ruling, caused many people to view that high tribunal as an exalted servant of the vested interests'.[52]

---

48   Ibid., p. 287.
49   Ibid., p. 293.
50   Ibid., p. 294.
51   President Kennedy's passage was 'Those who make peaceful revolution impossible will make violent revolution inevitable'. (Kennedy 1962).
52   This is a reference to the US Supreme Court's ruling *Pollock v. Farmers' Loan & Trust Company*, 157 US 429 (1895) which struck down the Income Tax Act of 1894, a second attempt to put a federal income tax into place. (See also Lindsey 1942, pp. 292 and 299).

Denouncing the ruling as the 'judge being legislator, court and executioner', Governor Altgeld wrote on 2 June 1895 that

> ... The corrupt money power has its withering finger on every pulse in the land ... What, then, is the situation today? For over twenty years foreign and domestic capitalism has dominated. It sits in the White House and legislates in the capitol. Courts of justice are its ministers and legislatures are its lackeys.[53]

Of the 69 men indicted by the Chicago grand jury for conspiracy to interfere with the US mail, 45 were originally slated for prosecution. The number was later lowered to 20. The trail began on 24 January. US Attorney Walker served as a prosecutor even while still being employed as counsel to the Chicago, Milwaukee, and St. Paul railroad. Despite ARU attorney Gregory's objections to Walker's conflict of interest, the court declined to investigate. Workingmen were excluded from the jury, which was dominated by farmers angry about their losses due to the disruption of railroad service.[54]

Although Pullman was subpoenaed, he never appeared in court. Instead, his lawyer Robert Todd Lincoln, son of President Lincoln, worked out a back room deal with Judge Grosscup after the jury had been dismissed on 12 February. Pullman was excused from appearing due to illness when, according to Darrow, the jury leaned nearly unanimously towards dismissal.[55]

Just as the trial transformed Darrow from corporate attorney to advocate for the oppressed, the strike had further transformed Debs, who became devoted to the cause of socialism while in prison. Debs was met by 100,000 people when he was released from prison. Henry D. Lloyd, speaking at a rally at a local convention hall, called him 'the repudiator of contempt of court as a substitute for the constitution of the United States, and of Gatling guns as harmonizers of labor and capital; the first rebel against government by injunction'.[56] Maybe so, but one man alone does not a strike make. That the strike involved possibly hundreds of thousands of railroad workers and supporters at the time, the injunction was a symptom of their power, not their weakness. Without federal intervention, the railroad companies might have been beaten and the balance of power shifted a bit further towards the workers on the shop floor.

---

53 Lindsey 1942, p. 299.
54 Ibid., pp. 300–1.
55 Ibid., p. 303.
56 Ibid., p. 305.

On 2 August the ARU gave the locals permission to call off their strikes and all but the Santa Fe workers did so. In all, the Pullman workers had been on strike for about three months.[57] Once the strikers conceded, Pullman rehired workers on the same wage scale and rental costs. The workers that were allowed to return were escorted into the plants under guard by a regiment of the Illinois militia. By 24 August, 2,300 were at work, 550 of whom were new workers.[58]

With the strike over, the workers' remaining power to achieve their objectives evaporated. 'The real issue was one of power; it was understood that this in turn would determine the other questions of wages, working conditions, and the like'. This was a power diametrically opposed to power as Pullman saw it: 'the principle that a man should have the right to manage his own property'.[59]

For the workers, the means to assert this power by organising, mobilising support, and disrupting the industry and the national economy was now gone. Police and military power had prevented the strikers from further circulating their strike and building mass support which would have lowered their risks and increased their opportunity to achieve their objectives. The use of the police, military, and judicial power of the state had raised the workers' costs to escalate their tactics and circulate their struggle, forcing them to de-escalate by restricting the strike once again to only the Pullman workers. Without the boycott of Pullman cars on the national rail system, all ability to disrupt the accumulation process as leverage to force concessions was lost, and the strike reverted to a local struggle of workers of a single company in a few limited areas. State power had not defeated the strike so much as repressed the conditions that made it an insurgency. By doing so it constricted the scope – and most importantly the potential disruptive capacity – of the strike to Pullman alone.

The strike was defeated because the arrival of US troops ultimately blocked the workers from further escalating their tactics to match those of the railroad companies. Until this happened, both sides had been locked in a stalemate. Escalation by one elicited more or less an equivalent escalation in turn by the other. As the railroads coordinated their efforts through the GMA, the workers circulated their strike through the ARU. When the railroads expanded their coalition, the strikers reciprocated. When the ARU's allies threatened a general strike, the railroads called in the militia, US troops, and the AFL. As US troops

---

57   Not all the Pullman workers were still on strike. The Wilmington, Delaware plant never shut down because the ARU was weak there. The St. Louis plant was struck on 25 June and the one in Ludlow, Kentucky shut down on 3 July. Both reopened after two weeks. (Ibid., p. 269).

58   Ibid., p. 270.

59   Brecher 1942, p. 112.

attempted to disperse the strikers and their supporters at gunpoint with bayonets fixed, the workers took up arms and went on the offensive. But as scattered attacks, sabotage, and street battles escalated, the ability to coordinate them was impeded by the GMA and the federal government's dismantling of the ARU. Without the ability to communicate or coordinate among themselves or with existing or potential supporters, the strike could no longer escalate. The strikers had been tactically trumped.

Debs astutely understood this tactical imbalance, telling the US Strike Commission that

> We have no power of the Government behind us. We have no recognized influence in society on our side ... On the other side the corporations are in perfect alliance; they have all of the things that money can command, and that means a subsidized press ... The clergy almost steadily united in thundering their denunciations; then the courts, then the State militia, then the Federal troops; everything and all things on the side of the corporations.[60]

What he left out, of course, is that such an elite coalition was necessary to counter the strategically superior leverage the strikers held with their mass supporters: they could disrupt virtually the entire national railroad system and the capitalist economy by withdrawing their labour and blocking the trains from running.

Moderating Disruption

The ARU leadership also shares responsibility for helping put the brakes on the tactical escalation demanded by its own members when the conditions required it.

> They would not have been able to win the strike against a state power resolved to crush it without a complete change of approach. The union was committed to 'legal' and 'orderly' tactics, even while it was being destroyed by the forces of 'law and order' ...[61]

---

60   US Strike Commission 1895, p. 169.

61   Brecher 1972, p. 113.

In this way, the ARU leadership was in alignment with the AFL. Although workers in several locations began to escalate their tactics once the US troops were deployed on Blue Island, the ARU did not. 'Thus we are presented with the spectacle of Eugene Victor Debs ... trying to end the strike to prevent it from becoming an insurrection'.[62] The ARU, much like the Workingmen's Party during the 1877 general strike in St. Louis, played a moderating role to channel the strike away from escalating into an insurgency. At the moment when the tactic of disruption is most effective 'endeavoring to do what they cannot do, organisers fail to do what they can do'.[63] To Debs's credit, however, while he repeatedly attempted to avoid the boycott, once the rank and file overwhelmingly called for it, he appeared to be committed to seeing it to its conclusion.

The dominant thinking about strikes is if the workers had remained orderly, then the employers couldn't resort to the courts or call out the military. But this unquestioned assumption, which remains the dominant thinking, has it backwards. If tactics that cause disruption had not been deployed, there would have been no reason to resort to force to restore order. Therefore, refusing to escalate one's tactics or de-escalating can ensure a quick defeat because the leverage necessary to extract concessions is absent.

The assumption that non-disruptive tactics can achieve the objectives of a strike is to confuse the framing narrative with the actual relations of power. While avoiding disruption may seem to give strikers the moral high ground, because they do not control the media framing, the media may still portray disruption that doesn't exist – which is what happened in 1894. The military was called under the fabricated pretext that property damage and scattered battles were taking place, thereby generating it when the workers escalated their tactics in turn. The assumption also overlooks the leverage produced in the tactical interplay between elites and workers, which the latter can quickly lose when they do not escalate their tactics as elites do.

Lastly, it demonstrates the futility of offering to unilaterally de-escalate with the expectation that the other side will follow in kind. The dominant perspective, that de-escalation can lead to satisfactory concessions and compromise, is a rejection of the relative gains perspective, in which someone stands to gain more than their adversary in negotiations, in favour of absolute gains, in which all parties gain proportionally to one another. Because relative gains is based on the assumption of self-reliance, that no one can be expected to give up their

---

62   Ibid., p. 114.
63   Piven and Cloward 1977, p. xxi.

leverage if the other side cannot be trusted to do the same, conflict is likely to escalate. While labour relations today is dominated by absolute gains, this was only after enshrining the right to organise, form a union, and collectively bargain in law. Before then relativism dominated, making class conflict a zero sum game in which the conflict ended only when one side had a clear relative advantage. It could be argued that with the rise of absolute gains the strategic advantage has almost exclusively tilted in favour of capital.

In 1894 the ARU's offer to de-escalate was ignored by the GMA because it appeared as a sign of weakness. As the leadership made plans to de-escalate, the GMA was doing the opposite. Before the boycott was called, Debs and Howard attempted to prevent it by futilely attempting to meet and negotiate with Pullman as many as five times and several other times meeting with Mayor Hopkins in an effort to get him to intervene. Failing this, on 6 July, 'at the time when the strike was at its worst – at its zenith' according to Debs, the ARU board voted to offer to concede on the condition that the men be rehired without recognising the ARU.[64] In their unanswered message, the ARU leadership acknowledged their fear of the very success of their tactics which resulted in 'The existing troubles growing out of [the] Pullman strike having assumed continental proportions ...', and the clearly demonstrated disruption of the industry which they described as 'wide-spread business demoralization and distress'.[65]

Debs spoke to this while explaining the decision to concede defeat in his testimony to the US Strike Commission.

> When we became satisfied that things were assuming too serious a phase, and that a point had been reached when, in the interest of peace and to prevent riot and trouble, we must declare the strike off, we advised with those committees. We gave it out as our opinion to the men, through the committees, that the strike had better be declared off, if we could do so honorably. The men agreed, without a dissenting voice that I heard, from every source and from every road that they were willing to declare the strike off, if they were allowed simply to go back to work. It was in the crisis when everything was at stake, where possibly it might have eventuated in a revolution.[66]

---

64   US Strike Commission 1895, p. 145.
65   See Hannon n.d., p. 25.
66   US Strike Commission 1895, p. 146.

Considering his admission that he explicitly discouraged tactical escalation, it is unclear how exactly Debs thought he could achieve his goals to nationalise the railroads, abolish the wage system, and create what he called a 'cooperative commonwealth'.[67]

While the membership was explicitly calling for escalating the Pullman strike into a national boycott, the leadership was busy attempting to discipline the membership while removing the very leverage that would bring them to the negotiating table: the power of the strike. The workers had proven their ability to shut down the rail system and disrupt the entire economy in a couple of days. The numerous attempts of the ARU leadership to negotiate countered the apparent objectives of the rank and file, giving the GMA invaluable time to organise, arm deputy marshals, and recruit the federal government to join the fight.

By offering to de-escalate (end the strike) and lower the potential gain from mobilisation to zero (get their old jobs back at the same wage and without a recognised union), the ARU leadership actually emboldened the railroads to raise their potential gains (hire new workers at lower wages, fewer reliable hours, and without a union) by escalating their tactics (armed occupation of conflict areas, blacklists, and prosecutions). To use an old cliché, the companies 'smelled blood' when the ARU leadership offered to countermand its own membership and relinquish the leverage it had to negotiate a concession. Such an offer likely persuaded the GMA to assume that the gulf between the leadership and its base would widen further as it continued to escalate its tactics. The ARU leadership misread the conditions in which it contended for power because its offer to de-escalate encouraged the GMA to continue escalating. As the US Strike Commission observed, there was a 'determination of capital to crush the strike rather than to accept any peaceable solution through conciliation, arbitration, or otherwise'.[68]

---

67   Debs told the US Strike Commission:

'I do believe, however, that the Government ownership of the railroads and of all means of transportation and communication and all other productive forces which are in those monopolies should be taken hold of by the Government. I have heard a good many objections to the Government ownership of railroads, but, as has been tersely said to you, the question was whether the Government should own the railroads or the railroads own the Government. The Government of the United States practically operates a vast number of the railroads, but simply waits until they have been bankrupted and in the hands of a receiver, and then conducts them. If the Government can conduct a bankrupt railroad why should it not be in a position to conduct a railroad which has not yet been bankrupted?' (Ibid., p. 200).

68   Ibid., p. xix.

While in theory common sense tells us that de-escalating tactics can resolve a conflict, it is limited in practice to circumstances in which both parties agree to de-escalate in order to meet and negotiate. For this to occur both parties must be willing to adhere to the premises of absolute gains: trust, cooperation, and negotiations in which both parties stand to gain. However, to assume that unilateral de-escalation can achieve the same result, especially between elites and insurgents with different levels of power, misreads the conditions that shaped the conflict in the first place. Unilateral de-escalation may end the conflict but it creates a winner and a loser. In reality, no side will de-escalate during a struggle after much has been expended and suffered only to come to believe that they lost by doing so. Because unilateral de-escalation leaves in place or worsens the balance of power, further sparks of conflict are sure to reignite. The width of the power gulf at the conclusion of conflict and how each side perceives the costs and gains of further struggle will determine whether de-escalation and negotiations leads to a lasting peace or a tense truce.

In 1894, neither were to be. Continuing class conflict would engulf the industry over the next several decades. The 1917 nationalisation of the railroads and the 1919 and 1922 national strikes demonstrated that the workers were left dissatisfied with the persisting balance of power after the 1894 strike. The emergence of trucking, and disinvestment and dismantling of the national rail system that followed over the next few decades also made it apparent that capital was disenchanted with its outcome as well.

Despite this history, offering to either prevent further escalation or de-escalate in exchange for negotiations and concessions has become a virtue today among elites, the media, labour lawyers, social movement scholars, and the leaders of unions, advocacy groups, and protest movements. Such offers are most likely to occur when organisational leaders are disconnected from their members and supporters and have organisational prerogatives that conflict with the rank and file and the rest of the working-class. As Errico Malatesta warned,

> The entire [labour] movement boils down to a monotonous round inside a vicious circle. They [labour leaders] deal with the government and threaten and make concessions and enter into compromises ... but ultimately they take care that everything is done according to the law, quietly, and ending in blessed peace. That way they can hang on to the friendship or at any rate tolerance of the government and the bosses, their sway over the workers and their salaries.[69]

---

69 Malatesta 2014 [1902], p. 324.

Offers to prevent further escalation or de-escalate are also likely because the dominant underlying principle of absolute gains that inform interest-based bargaining, consensus decision-making, stakeholder negotiations, etc. guiding protests and strikes have either not been acknowledged, examined, or debated. The result is that the rank and file are locked out from making the most fundamental decisions about when and whether to demobilise and de-escalate and what to achieve from doing so. As a result, leaders offer to demobilise and de-escalate either prematurely before escalation has happened or when escalation has given the tactical leverage to the insurgents with which they may achieve their objectives. This can be seen in the greater number of strike threats than actual strikes in the US. Strike threats have become a symbolic tactic to settle a labour dispute, thereby avoiding the strike rather than actually having it. Without questioning the underlying assumption of the absolute gains perspective, conflict is reduced to a shadow-play with power in which nothing is gained because nothing is tried and only one side wins because it holds the advantage. When insurgent leaders pursue absolute gains, the outcome for elites is shaped by relative gains.

Estimating the Costs of Repression

The strike affected about two-thirds of the country, a significantly larger area than the 1877 strike. The total economic costs were estimated at a minimum of $80 million or the equivalent of about one-eighth of the total US government revenue of $1.1 billion that year.[70] The city of Chicago was left with a $400,000 bill for the militia and deputy marshals. The federal government spent a bit less, $375,000, nationwide. About one-third of that expense, around $125,000, was spent in Chicago on US deputy marshals.[71]

The Chicago railroads lost $5.36 million of which only about $700,000 was due to property losses such as to shipments and rolling stock.[72] Damage costs skyrocketed after the battle of Blue Island. On 6 July crowds caused $340,000 damage to railroad property, a huge increase from a previous daily average of only $4,000. One of the costliest incidents of property destruction was at

---

70 Ross and Taft wrote that an 'undetermined millions of dollars were lost in the rioting connected with this conflict'. (Ross and Taft 1969, p. 8).

71 Lindsey 1942, p. 168.

72 There was also a huge fire on 5 July at the World's Columbian Exposition at Jackson Park that destroyed seven structures and cost an untold amount in damages, although it is unclear if it was connected to the strike.

the Panhandle yards in South Chicago where a crowd of an estimated 6,000 people allegedly burned about 700 cars, many of which were unloaded, old and dilapidated, and certainly not Pullman cars. The rest of the losses were in earnings. Chicago railroad workers lost $1.4 million in wages and Pullman workers $350,000. The total wages lost nationwide is unknown.[73] The markets seemed to little notice the strike, as railroad stocks only declined by an average of 1.5 percent.

The question of damages deserves further discussion. There were no incidents of any damage to Pullman property, other than to the large windows in Pullman's house, which were smashed on 25 July. Because there were no Pullman cars located near the fires at the Panhandle yards, there were suspicions that it was a false flag operation to cast blame on the strikers and their supporters while eliminating devalued capital stock presumably reimbursed by insurance. There was evidence that Major-General Miles or the railroads employed agent provocateurs and private agents, whose interests lie in demonstrating a threat to justify their employment, to set the fires. US Commissioner of Labor and US Strike Commission Chair Wright claimed the railroads instigated the fires to provide a reason for federal troops to intervene. Chicago Superintendent of Police Brennan also suspected as much. It may be possible that the railroads did not request compensation from the city for its failure to provide adequate protection in order to avoid further investigations.[74] Questions should be raised about the validity of reports of property damage by the railroads and sensationalist press which was almost entirely lined up against the ARU. Although it will never be known who caused the damages and sabotage, the lack of any damage to the Pullman company property raises questions about whether strikers and their supporters actually used attacks on property as part of their tactical repertoire. There has been little study of damage that occurred in other places than Chicago.

The question of the tactical use of attacks on property by strikers and their supporters is inseparable from question of damage. There is no evidence that the ARU leadership were involved in, promoted, or condoned the clashes and sabotage that did occur. 'There is no evidence before the commission that the officers of the American Railway Union at any time participated in or advised intimidation, violence, or destruction of property'.[75] In contrast, there were reports of attempts by ARU members to dissuade crowds from engaging with

73   Lindsey 1942, pp. 335–6.
74   Ibid., pp. 210, 215, 216–17, and 233.
75   US Strike Commission 1895, pp. xliv–xlv.

police and troops and damaging property, even urging them to go home to prevent it from happening. The ARU even reported some suspects to local police,
but none were prosecuted. On 7 July, Debs warned that 'Those who engage in
force or violence are our real enemies' and urged they be arrested. It should be
recalled that the ARU had patrolled railroad property during the Great Northern Railway strike and were given shoot to kill orders.[76]

The lack of sabotage by the ARU and its use by the rank and file and strikers
are two interrelated but distinct events. While the ARU leadership was certainly interested in furthering the cause of the strike by de-escalating tactics
and appearing to be managing the strike so as to avoid any pretext to send in
further troops to restore law and order, there are numerous accounts of armed
clashes of police and troops with strikers and supporters. If the ARU discoun-
ted the use of armed resistance for defensive and offensive tactical purposes,
it is fairly certain that not all the strikers and their supporters did. Cut off from
communication with the Chicago office and facing armed troops, strikers and
supporters were intent on keeping the railroads from moving while protecting
themselves from being shot. Much of the property damage outside Chicago, it
should be recalled, was not wanton destruction but targeted scattered attacks
and sabotage of rail lines, bridges, and engines, tactical strikes meant to keep
the trains from moving. While the ARU leadership helped coordinate the boycott and resulting national strike it didn't start the strike or really control it.

If sabotage and scattered attacks were intended to defend the strike's
strength, its weakness was in failing to continue mobilising mass support in the
streets. There is little evidence that strikers held public assemblies, protests,
or rallies to gauge or organise public support. This is not surprising, as Debs
explicitly sought to avoid escalating the struggle into a revolution and feared it
spiralling out of the ARU leadership's control.

Much of the cost involved the arming and fielding of massive military force
in just Chicago. The US Strike Commission estimated that between 6 and 11 July
a total of 14,186 troops, deputy marshals, militia, deputy sheriffs, and police
were deployed in the city. Of that total about 4,000 were state militia, 5,000
deputy marshals, 250 extra deputy sheriffs, and 3,000 police. Of that total, 1,936
were US Army troops used from approximately 3–10 July in Chicago to protect the US mail service and federal buildings, and to execute the orders of
the United States courts.[77] For a month, 4,243 militia were deployed in more

---

76   Lindsey 1942, pp. 219–21.
77   The US Army troops remained in Chicago for 15 days. (US Strike Commission 1895, p. xix;
      and Lindsey 1942, pp. 182–3).

than 50 stations, costing Illinois about $250,000. US troops began leaving on 19 July although several thousand switchmen, engineers and firemen were still on strike. The precise total number of troops, police and deputies used nation-wide is unknown, although it is estimated that more than 16,000 US troops from bases in six of the eight military areas of the country were deployed.[78]

There is little firm documentation of the human costs of repressing the strike. It was estimated that about 34 people were killed, 515 arrested, and 71 indicted by the federal grand jury for obstructing the US mail. In Chicago, 13 were killed and 53 seriously wounded, although none of them by US troops. The Illinois state militia killed five and injured 16 and the rest were caused by marshals, accidents or unknown causes. Two people were also killed by Illinois Central railroad agents. The US Strike Commission provided the much lower figure that 12 people were killed in strike.[79]

These figures are imprecise and contradicted by different historical ac-counts. Considering the state of medicine at the time and the likely hesitation of the wounded to seek medical attention for fear of arrest, it is impossible to confidently know how many were wounded and how many of those died.[80]

The Strike Commission's estimates of the human costs of the police and military repression of the strike cannot be considered entirely credible. The list of interviewed witnesses is slim on strikers and non-strikers who were in the streets and the most complete data is limited to Chicago. The informa-tion presented by railroad executives and GMA officials is frequently unchal-lenged by the US Strike Commission members, sometimes disputed by other witnesses, and is unconfirmed. The US Strike Commission did not challenge Major-General Miles's claim that he never conferred with the GMA and Egan's failure to disclose he communicated with Miles to coordinate the anti-strike effort. Nor did it request they be indicted for perjury. Some of the most prom-inent protagonists in the strike are also glaringly absent. General Schofield, the commanding US Army General, Attorney General Olney, and federal judges Drummond and Gresham did not testify.

---

78   Lindsey 1942, pp. 199–200, 234, and 239.

79   The US Strike Commission reported that 71 people were indicted by federal grand jury for obstructing the US mail, but this overlooks the fact that only 20 people were actually brought to trial. (US Strike Commission, 1895, p. xviii). These 71 were out of a total of 190 arrests made in Chicago. (Ross and Taft 1969, p. 8; Lindsey 1942, pp. 213–16; and US Strike Commission 1895, p. xviii).

80   Lindsey 1942, pp. 207–10 and 215; Brecher 1972, pp. 105 and 108; and US Strike Commission 1895, p. xviii.

One of the most common explanations for why strikes became violent is that the strike is disorganised, undisciplined, lacks a strong leadership, and descends into a mob. The US Strike Commission reached the same conclusion, ironically attributing the cause to the ARU.

> The great inherent weakness of such organizations at present is that in contentions with employers these principles are forgotten and that strikes are often ordered in hasty and disorderly ways, and are frequently conducted with attendant violence and lawlessness.[81]

The US Strike Commission then commits a genetic fallacy, laying the blame on the ARU for not having a provision to punish or kick out any members who use violence. It did not apply the same standard to the GMA's corporate members, since there is no mention in the report about the violence used by the deputy marshals they hired and armed.

This was not merely a double standard. The US Strike Commission conveniently sidestepped the record of the ARU leadership attempting to prevent the strike and then later offering to give it up for an infinitesimal concession. The Strike Commission also assigned criminal culpability for actions the ARU did not control, plan or support thereby confirming Darrow's argument about the dangers of punishing one who takes non-violent actions that result in unconnected violent consequences they do not control.[82]

If, as Galeano once insightfully wrote, 'There is always, I believe, a close relationship between the intensity of the threat and the brutality of the response', then the timing, intensity and targets of the political violence used by the strikers and their supporters during the 1894 strike are an illustration of the threat they posed to not merely the railroad companies but the entire national system of industrial capitalism.[83] In order to understand the scope of the threat it is necessary to evaluate the composition of the industrial working-class at the time the Pullman strike began.

---

81   US Strike Commission 1895, pp. xxiv–xxv.
82   See epigraph, p. 252. Darrow 1894, p. 85.
83   Galeano 1971, p. 269.

The New Division of Labour

While the Pullman strike was over, the destitution and authoritarian domination of every aspect of the workers' and their families' lives remained. The boycott and strike spread rapidly around much of the country in response to both wage cuts and the deteriorating work conditions. The double header was widely hated because the same number of railroad workers now handled twice as many engines and cars. While the double header was an effort to increase productivity, or in class terms, relative surplus value, it was more importantly an attempt to introduce a new division of labour. The double-header reduced the number of required workers while introducing interchangeability, standardisation, and deskilling to railroad work. As railroad corporations became increasingly vertically integrated they began to standardise not only their freight rates, pay, and schedule but also track gauges and work procedures. In turn, standardisation across corporations, many of which were controlled by the same interlocking directorate, included standardising railroad work and making railroad workers interchangeable, which reduced the critical importance of skilled craftworkers.

Changes to the division of labour further socialised the production process and eroded the barriers among workers based on skill organised into the craft brotherhoods. Ironically, standardisation made the effort of industrial unionism pursued by the ARU that much more possible and the companies that much more vulnerable to a recomposed workforce capable of disruption.

While corporate consolidation and standardisation was a threat to the craft unions, it allowed rail workers to relate to one another across industrial sector, companies, and geography as well as job type. The expressions of solidarity from the UMWA and KoL early in the strike were strategically valuable because these workers were strategically located in related industries. The threat that the strike could further circulate to the coal mines would have allowed railroad workers and coal miners to connect their struggle across industrial barriers. The railroads were the communications and transport circulatory system of capitalism. Coal powered the railroads (and much of the industrial economy), which transported the coal and the telegraph line, the means of long distance communications by which the economy was managed. Shutting down the railroads could have disrupted the circulatory system and shutting down coal production would have starved it of fuel. Circulating the strike between these two industries would have dramatically lowered the costs and increased the opportunity of workers to achieve their objectives.

The potential linkage between the railroads and coal industries illustrates how the new composition of capital provided the means for recomposing working-class power. Consolidation of capital and the new division of labour, the tactical responses to the recomposition of the industrial working-class in 1877, made the threat of disruption more dangerous. The 1894 strike was an explosive insubordination to this new division of labour.

Self-Organisation

One of the great unanswered questions of the 1894 strike is how countless thousands of destitute workers managed to self-organise so rapidly and thoroughly across so many companies and across so many states in the middle of a depression. In 1877, workers most likely used the existing social networks to communicate among rural to urban migrant workers with links to their previous rural homes. They also used the depots to spread news by word of mouth and seized the telegraphs to send news about the strike. The 1894 strike was certainly a beneficiary of existing rural to urban social networks that were likely crafted in the recent successful Great Northern Railway and other smaller strikes.

One of the outcomes of strikes was the blacklist, a dreaded weapon of retaliation used against organisers and strikers. But the blacklist was also a push factor that sent workers on the road from place to place and line to line inadvertently circulating news of prior struggles and laying the foundation for new ones. As they moved they brought with them the accumulated lessons and knowledge of workers organising, archival knowledge of past struggles, and personal contacts on the next line or at the next depot. Studying these interlinkages would construct an anthropology of class struggle, as Peter Linebaugh and Marcus Rediker did for slaves and sailors who circulated their struggle through ships and ports in the decades preceding the American and Haitian revolutions.[84]

The evidence to support this observation is tenuous. Every striker blacklisted by a railroad contributed to dismantling a community of workers in one location but as they moved a new one was formed or reconfigured somewhere else. Class-conscious workers who suffered blacklisting changed their names and became itinerant migrant agitators. Like Dick Zepp, although he ended up on the opposite side in the class struggle in 1894, workers searching endlessly for work of any kind or duration 'moved on in an "agitational circuit" that fueled the growing movement for the industrial organization of railroad workers. The great Pullman boycott of 1894 was, therefore, the culmination of a movement

---

84   Linebaugh and Rediker 2000.

that developed in this fashion over two decades'.[85] There is a direct line connecting the 1877 and 1894 strikes.

This is where the ARU comes into the picture. Barely a year old, with one strike victory against the Great Northern Railway under its belt, the ARU was designed by its widely dispersed membership to exploit the standardisation of railroad work into an organisational strategy that would bring all railroad workers into one union. The ARU was an outgrowth of the lessons of its predecessor the Knights of Labor, which sought to organise all the workers in an industry rather than by job type, craft or even race. They had also taken advantage of the Industrial Armies' ability to leverage simultaneous, coordinated, and dispersed actions across the entire country only a few months before. The ARU provided the organisational backbone that formalised communications among these self-organised social networks.

Unfortunately, the ARU did not learn two key tactics of these two previous efforts. Unlike the KoL, internal racism doomed the union to a strategy of self-defeat by excluding black workers. While it has been widely reported[86] that the ARU included the requirement that members be 'white', at Debs's urging the original ARU constitution approved at the 20 June 1893 founding convention does not limit membership to whites or include any reference to race.[87] The colour bar was added at the June 1894 convention.[88] In the midst of Jim Crow segregation, railroad work was segregated, few ARU members were black, and many members were likely racial supremacists. The US Strike Commission reported blacks in Chicago supported the strike by tipping over railroad cars.[89] Considering the seizure of the ARU office and its records when the leadership was arrested and the apparent lack of a comprehensive ARU archive, the details of who advocated for the ban are unclear.

According to two clauses in the otherwise democratic constitution, at least ten reportedly white members were needed to form a local. At that time, its racism notwithstanding, the ARU was extremely democratic for a labour union. According to Section 54 of the ARU constitution, in order to strike each local formed a board of mediation which took up complaints forwarded by a majority vote of the local. The outcome of the vote then went to the chair of the

---

85   Kaufman 1991, p. 146.

86   See Horne and Young 2001, p. 52.

87   ARU 1893.

88   Zinn recounts that 'Debs wanted to include everyone, but blacks were kept out: at a convention in 1894, the provision in the constitution barring blacks was affirmed by a vote of 112 to 100'. (Zinn 2013, p. 279).

89   US Strike Commission 1895, p. 62.

general board of mediation and the president who conferred with the chair or chose a member of the board of directors to confer. This process can be contrasted to the process used by the brotherhoods which commonly required a two-thirds vote to strike and even then the grand master could still veto the decision.[90] As an illustration of its democratic decision-making process, during the Chicago convention the membership picked its own committee to pursue negotiations with Pullman. Although this delayed the strike vote, the convention still voted to strike over the opposition of both President Debs and Vice President Howard. When a body of the ARU called off the strike, the locals were still allowed to vote to continue striking, which a few locals did.

The second tactical lesson that the ARU did not learn was, unlike the Industrial Armies, the union concentrated the dispersed boycott into a single centralised leadership. Once Attorney General Olney backed the GMA's effort to break the strike, the federal court injunctions had the effect of severing Debs and other top leadership from the mass of strikers and supporters who could continue communication through their networks but not between them. Literally gagged, and then indicted and arrested, the dispersed strike lost its central coordination mechanism and fell apart. The failure to capitalise on the decentralised expanding strike and develop an organisational structure that facilitated and supported it raised the risk to the strikers. Repression at the central point of coordination wiped out the opportunity presented by decentralisation.

Shifting Balance of Power

Despite its defeat, a fundamental reconfiguration of the relationship between capital, labour, and the state emerged out of the defeated 1894 strike. The capacity of the workers to escalate their tactics drove capital to accept the unacceptable. Over the next two decades, states, the Civic Federation, individual capitalists, and the federal government would launch experimental mechanisms to de-escalate, negotiate, and institutionalise strikes. Using negotiations and collective bargaining would turn unions into an instrument of working-

---

90   The documentation of amendments to the ARU constitution is highly questionable. For example, the ARU constitution only has 48 sections and is 19 pages long. Despite that the 1895 *US v. Cassidy et al.* federal conspiracy case dealing with strike action in California introduces Section 54 as evidence. (*US v. Cassidy et al. April 1 and 2, 1895, N.D. California, No. 3059*). It is unclear if this 'evidence' was a forgery or if there was another version of the ARU constitution that has been lost.

class discipline, a role which unions would soon adopt as their own as ARU's leadership had offered to do. The strike forced capital to devise a new means to reimpose control over workers. With this in mind the US Strike Commission recommended a permanent commission modelled after the one established by Adams in Massachusetts that could ban strikes pending arbitration in exchange for the legal recognition of unions and the regulatory setting of wages.[91] As a result, the AFL found itself confronted by a new system it resisted as a result of the defeated efforts of militant workers. The initial official support for arbitration demonstrated that labour reform is driven by class struggle, not the other way around.

The 1894 strike demonstrated that the working-class was beginning to recompose its power after

> The panic of 1893 … had fostered an ominous restlessness among the underprivileged groups. The Coal Strike, the Commonweal [Industrial Armies] movement, countless labor difficulties, and a growing tendency toward lawlessness were but symptoms of this surging discontent. Never had labor been more vocal, and never had the 'have nots' been more willing to flaunt their misery before a dismayed public.[92]

Each of these events progressively contributed to the emerging recomposition of working-class power remembered as the 1894 strike. To understand the next insurgency it is necessary to study each factor in a similar way.

Despite its outcome, the fact that the 1894 strike happened at all hardly makes it a 'lost cause'. The outcome of the strike was secondary since the workers' act was an unmistakable assertion of their humanity, their will to power. Describing what Karl Marx called a 'class for itself', Pullman strike leader Thomas Heathcoate spoke to the strike as collective liberation in which people throw off the dehumanisation and alienation of work to embrace their collective humanity.

> We do not expect the company to concede our demands. We do not know what the outcome will be, and in fact we do not care much. We do know we are working for less wages than will maintain ourselves and families in the necessities of life, and on that proposition we absolutely refuse to work any longer.[93]

---

91   US Strike Commission 1895, pp. l, lii, and liv.
92   Lindsey 1942, p. 147.
93   Ibid., p. 126.

While the stated objectives of the strike exemplified the strivings of a 'class in itself', that is, to ameliorate the conditions of exploitation, the actions of countless strikers and supporters to go beyond mere negotiated compromises to literally stop everyone from working confirm Heathcoate's insights.

Hardly founded to realise the passion for human liberation, the ARU was rather an innovative organisational instrument to serve the strivings of a class for itself. The US Strike Commission acknowledged its attempt to replace the stifling strategy of craft unionism with industrial unionism.

> It should be noted that until the railroads set the example a general union of railroad employees was never attempted. ... The unions had not gone beyond enlisting the men upon different systems in separate trade organizations. These neutralize and check each other to some extent and have no such scope or capacity for good or evil as is possible under the universal combination idea inaugurated by the railroads and followed by the American Railway Union.[94]

The ARU emerged to meet the needs of workers to confront the new division of labour and organisation of the railroad companies. As a national industrial union the ARU used the secondary boycott as leverage to advance the interests of any part of its membership, just as the GMA was set up to share the burden of defending any members facing a strike. As ARU Vice President Howard confessed to the US Strike Commission,

> Yes, sir; in fact we had to do it or surrender; we were forced to do it because the general managers took the stand that they were going to stay by Pullman, which forced us to take the stand we did or else lay down.[95]

The ARU made it possible to circulate the strike to more companies across a wider geographical terrain in order to share the risks of escalating their tactics and thus increase the opportunity to realise their shared objectives.

Howard recognised that railroad workers had created the ARU as a tactical escalation to meet the threat of a better organised railroad capital. As capital combined, so must the workers. Combination allowed both capital and workers to strengthen themselves by sharing risks, and redistributing power and resources to any of its weakest links. Both the ARU and the GMA were set up

---

94   US Strike Commission 1895, p. xxxi.
95   Ibid., p. 14.

as an insurance policy to help any member company or group of workers targeted by their adversaries. However, the ARU had also devised a way to gain leverage by strategically deploying its resources where it would have the effect of disrupting the entire economy. Capital has no such leverage except to engage in a self-destructive capital strike. Even though the railroads avoided a capital strike, deploying the US Army had the same effect.

Because Pullman cars were ubiquitous throughout much of the highly dispersed national rail system, the potential gains for all the rail workers by boycotting Pullman cars engendered little initial cost. The system could not function without the several hundred thousand workers who struck in sympathy with the Pullman workers. The ARU likely expected that the companies would be quickly willing to make a modest concession to sever their link to Pullman and get the rail traffic flowing again. Getting the trains running again – without Pullmans attached – would put immense pressure on the company to also concede. Pullman served as a poster child for every insult and injury suffered by railroad workers and the rest of the population. It's likely that the ARU expected mass support to flock to help fight the reviled company and that Pullman would fight alone.

> The readiness to strike sympathetically was promoted by the disturbed and apprehensive condition of railroad employees resulting from wage reductions on different lines, blacklisting, etc., and from the recent growth and development of the General Managers' Association, which seemed to them a menace ... Hence the railroad employees were ripe to espouse the cause of the Pullman strikers.[96]

But it was not to be; the ARU's strategic targeting missed the mark. The companies exhibited a rare class solidarity by pooling their resources and coordinating their tactics and strategy through the GMA. The ARU was not prepared for the companies to rally around its most reviled member, the integrated anti-strike effort, or for the GMA to attack its potential negotiating partner, the ARU leader-

---

96　The US Strike Commission wavered in its assessment of the legitimacy of the boycott, later asserting that it was called for no apparent reason.

'No grievances against the railroads had been presented by their employees, nor did the American Railway Union declare any such grievances to be any cause whatever of the strike. To simply boycott Pullman cars would have been an incongruous step for the remedy of complaints of railroad employees'. (Ibid., pp. xxxix and xl).

The US Strike Commission was unable to see the cause of the strike in anything but specific grievances to be resolved, rather than the latest terrain of a class struggle for power.

ship. As a result, the strikers' weakest link turned out to be the ARU leadership and its centralised organisation.

One vulnerability the railroads faced was the unreliability of their Brotherhood partners, who faced rebellion in their ranks when their members joined the strike, wildcatting against their existing contract.

> In some instances they struck in disregard of existing contracts between their different organizations and the railroads, notably upon the Illinois Central. They evaded the responsibility of their organizations for this conduct by claiming to act as individuals. They justified themselves under the idea of balancing wrongs.[97]

Wildcat strikers strengthened doubt in the effectiveness of unions as a disciplinary force that could diffuse or deflect conflict and prevent disruptions.

One reason for doubt in the effectiveness of a union contract was that the wildcatting workers were striking against not merely the contract but their craft unions, which had become a partner with the railroad companies. To avoid arousing the organised workers, the 'Big Four' lines had begun to cut wages nationally by staggering the cuts for different classes of workers starting with unorganised labourers so as not to arouse opposition from members of the brotherhoods. Since the brotherhood leadership counselled inaction, many in the rank and file perceived them as complicit and ineffective organisations.

The new ARU shifted thinking about the appropriate tactics and strategy to fight the wage cuts. The brotherhood's unwillingness to break the contract and put their organisational prerogatives at risk stood in stark contrast to the ARU's strategy of industrial unionism. While it disavowed strikes, the unanimous vote for the boycott demonstrated that the rank and file recognised that a strategy of tension not collaboration brought about raises and better working conditions. Even Debs was forced to acknowledge that raises only happen by use of force.

> The railroad companies have never increased wages of their own accord. I would like to have that put upon record as one of the reasons for any unrest and lack of confidence in the ranks of railway employees, for every concession the railway companies have ever made has been wrung from them by the power of organised effort.[98]

---

97   Ibid., p. xl.
98   Ibid., p. 138.

The ARU leadership and rank and file agreed that force was unavoidable, even if the former found it undesirable and made many efforts to avoid it. That acknowledgement at the level of an organisation was unique because it placed the objectives of the struggle over that of the prerogatives of the union and its leadership. Deploying a strategy of tension was a dual threat because it threatened both capital but also the dominant ideas about unions.

Union Discipline

Pursuing a strategy of tension would be extremely hard to contain and channel into negotiations, concessions, and reform. It assessed a strike as a winner takes all strategy. When Debs explained why the ARU board voted unanimously to call off the strike, he said it was because he feared it could trigger a revolution.

> When we became satisfied that things were assuming too serious a phase, and that a point had been reached when, in the interest of peace and to prevent riot and trouble, we must declare the strike off, we advised with those committees. We gave it out as our opinion to the men, through the committees, that the strike had better be declared off, if we could do so honorably. The men agreed, without a dissenting voice that I heard, from every source and from every road that they were willing to declare the strike off, if they were allowed simply to go back to work. It was in the crisis when everything was at stake, where possibly it might have eventuated in a revolution.[99]

Debs was clearly cognisant of the ARU leadership having lost control of the strike. Although he held two very different positions during the 1877 and 1894 strikes, Debs remained consistently opposed to strikes for philosophical reasons, even though he led two. Reflecting his influence, the ARU constitution portrayed railroad boycotts and strikes as failures, 'disastrous to employer and employee', and 'hopeless struggles', and foreseeing their disappearance.[100] He explained that

---

99   Ibid., pp. 145–6.
100   ARU 1893, pp. 4, 6.

I am opposed to these strikes and always have been, and in twenty years of writing I can show I always tried to devise some way and means of overcoming a strike – never have been in favor of a strike; but there are times when a strike, in my judgment, is justifiable, no matter what the consequences may be.[101]

Paradoxically, Debs shared more in common with Pullman than he might have expected. In his testimony, Pullman recommended that the ARU 'take a position against all strikes, except as a last resort for unbearable grievances, and to seek the more rational methods of conciliation and arbitration'. Without a hint of irony, he also urged the union to offer

conservative leadership, legal status, and the education of members in governmental matters, with the principle in view that in this country nothing can accomplish permanent protection and final redress of wrongs for labor as an entirety except conservative progress, lawful conduct, and wise laws enacted and sustained by the public opinion of its rulers – the people.[102]

The AFL leadership's refusal to sanction the strike or call a general strike on 12 July impeded the strike from circulating to other industries where it was strong. Although the tide was turning by 12 July, making it appear as if the AFL made the right call, the federation had been dealing with wildcats and calls for a general strike for some time. With the federal government having already intervened, the AFL took the side of the Brotherhoods, capital and the state early in its history.

The AFL's refusal to join the strike reflected its role in disciplining insurgent disruptive workers. By refusing to call a general strike, the AFL forced the ARU to de-escalate.

The conference concluded that the strike was then lost; that a general sympathetic strike throughout the country would be unwise and inexpedient, and, at the time, against the best interests of labor. This conference issued a strong and temperate address to members, expressing sympathy with the purposes of the American Railway Union, advising those on strike to return to work, and urging that labor organise more gen-

---

101   US Strike Commission 1895, p. 161.
102   Ibid., p. xxviii.

erally, combine more closely, and seek the correction of industrial evils at the ballot box. To some extent the trade unions of Chicago had struck in sympathy, but this movement was checked by the action of the conference of the 12th and extended no further. This action indicates clearer views by labour as to its responsibilities, the futility of strikes, and the appropriate remedies in this country for labor wrongs.[103]

After 12 July, AFL President Gompers commanded its members to de-escalate their tactics. AFL members wildcatting in sympathy with the ARU members and supporters raised doubts as to the AFL's claim of the disciplinary role of either contract or a union. Wildcatters threatened the viability not only of their own AFL contracts but all union contracts and threatened to spread the disruption to additional sectors of the economy. In this open letter, Gompers told them to end their sympathy strike, go back to work, and vote for change. Gompers told the US Strike Commission

> While we may not have the power to order a strike of the working people of our country, we are fully aware that a recommendation from this conference to them to lay down their tools of labor would largely influence the members of our affiliated organizations; and appreciating the responsibility resting upon us and the duty we owe to all, we declare it to be the sense of this conference that a general strike at this time is inexpedient, unwise, and contrary to the best interests of the working people. We further recommend that all connected with the American Federation of Labor now out on sympathetic strike should return to work, and those who contemplate going out on sympathetic strike are advised to remain at their usual vocations.[104]

Although he sought to end the strike, Gompers told the US Strike Commission: 'I regard the strikes as the sign that the people are not yet willing to surrender every spark of their manhood and their honor and their independence'.[105]

Although it would be about another decade until Gompers himself embraced a role for the AFL in electoral politics to correct the 'industrial evils at the ballot box', he asserted that

---

103   Ibid., pp. xl–xli.
104   Ibid., p. 192.
105   Ibid., p. 195.

Against this array of armed force and brutal moneyed aristocracy would it not be worse than folly to call men out on a general or local strike in these days of stagnant trade and commercial depression? No; better let us organise more generally, combine more closely, unite our forces, educate and prepare ourselves to protect our interests, and that we may go to the ballot box and cast our votes as American freemen united and determined to redeem this country from its present political and industrial misrule, to take it from the hands of the plutocratic wreckers and place it in the hands of the common people.[106]

The ARU sought solidarity in the wrong place. The two models of working-class organisation, craft and industrial, were incompatible. Out of their shared interests with the companies, craft unions sought to diminish disruption not only by avoiding strikes but by keeping out potentially disruptive labourers who didn't share their skills and values. Gompers said as much when he assured the US Strike Commission that 'I believe in diminishing the number [of strikes] as much as possible, and I have worked and contributed, I think, as much as any other one living man to the diminution in the number of strikes ...'.[107]

The ARU's efforts to seek supporters wherever they could be found led them to court the hand of a recalcitrant AFL while it spurned the many supporters in the street who sought to turn the strike into an insurgency. The former would presumably give it leverage to de-escalate and settle while the latter gave it leverage to continue escalating.

The ARU needed AFL sanction for the Chicago Trades and Labor Assembly and Chicago Building and Trades Council to follow through on their commitments to strike in Chicago. Gompers wanted to keep the general strike from happening and break the sympathy wildcat strike, which included the very union he helped form, the Cigar Makers' International Union.

They [Cigar Makers' International Union] were on a sympathetic strike when the conference of which I spoke came to Chicago, and when we declared that it would be unwise and inexpedient to go on a strike and that we recommended members of the organizations affiliated with the Federation of Labor who were then out on sympathetic strike to return to their usual avocations, the cigar makers, the carpenters, and a number of other organizations that I can not just think of, all returned to work. The

---

106   Ibid., p. 193.
107   Ibid., p. 195.

building trades council of this city had decided to take affirmative action –
that is, to strike out of sympathy with the American Railway Union, and
deferred their action until after the conference decided what to do with
the matter, and when they learned the decision arrived at by the conference they concluded not to strike.[108]

The ARU placed too much emphasis on Gompers's support to decide the fate
of the strike. It was not because of Gompers's personal charisma or power.
Rather, the AFL, like the brotherhoods, played a disciplinary role in blocking
their members from acting in concert with workers in other related sectors and
expressing their shared power as a class. By aligning with employers to recruit
scabs, for example, which the brotherhoods were notorious for doing, the AFL
unions had the effect of preventing, slowing, or de-escalating the tactics of their
own members, even those on strike. As if to punctuate his effort to sabotage the
strike, Gompers recommended the AFL Executive Council donate the tiny sum
of $1,000 to Debs's defence fund, although it only approved $500.

The successful outcome of the strike depended on the ability of the ARU to
continue circulating it to other sectors, a strategy Gompers intended to prevent from being put into play. Responding to a question from one of the Commissioners, Gompers admitted that the strike could have spread even further
nationwide.

> (Commissioner WORTHINGTON). And that that strike would not only
> have existed in the city of Chicago, but would have spread to a greater
> or less extent over the whole country? – Ans. I think so, to a greater or less
> extent; yes, sir.[109]

Foreseeing the role of arbitration, bargaining and recognition, in managing
class conflict, the US Strike Commission praised the ARU and AFL's efforts to
de-escalate, although it failed to offer them anything for their effort, instead
vainly wishing for a post-class society.

> It is encouraging to find general concurrence, even among labor leaders,
> in condemning strikes, boycotts, and lockouts as barbarisms unfit for the
> intelligence of this age, and as, economically considered, very injurious
> and destructive forces. Whether they are won or lost is broadly imma-

---

108   Ibid., p. 199.
109   Ibid.

terial. They are war – internecine war – and call for progress to a higher plane of education and intelligence in adjusting the relations of capital and labor.[110]

About a week before the AFL meeting, the ARU had earlier written the GMA an offer to call the strike off without union recognition if there were no blacklist. In the letter Debs, Howard and Secretary Sylvester Keliher wrote defeatedly that

> The strike, small and comparatively unimportant in its inception, has extended in every direction until now it involves or threatens not only every public interest, but the peace, security, and prosperity of our common country. The contest has waged fiercely. It has extended far beyond the limits of interest originally involved, and has laid hold of a vast number of industries and enterprises in no wise responsible for the differences and disagreements that led to the trouble. Factory, mill, mine, and shop have been silenced. Widespread demoralization has sway. The interests of multiplied thousands of innocent people are suffering. The common welfare is seriously menaced. The public peace and tranquility are in peril.[111]

This was a curious letter, lamenting that the strike had far exceeded their original plans and shut down other industries. At the moment when the disruption had proven its most effective, the ARU leadership disassociated themselves from the leverage they held. Most importantly, they conceded that they had lost control over it and, unable to justify a compromise, offered to demobilise and de-escalate and take what they had before the strike. They offered to do what they could not do instead of taking advantage of what was immediately possible.

Offering to de-escalate when the GMA was escalating its tactics was a fatal miscalculation. The GMA returned the letter without a reply. It had no reason to parlay with the ARU; it had already escalated. US troops were on the field, strikers and supporters shot and arrested, and it expected the trains would be moved by force. But those plans were uncertain as scattered attacks and sabotage spread around the country.

ARU's letter may have come as little surprise. In addition to its repeated offers to negotiate rather than strike, the ARU leadership had even offered to punish strikers and supporters who engaged in attacks on railroad property. Because

110   Ibid., p. xlvi.
111   Ibid., p. 58.

it had good reason to be concerned about possible false flag attacks that could be blamed on the ARU, the union had employed detectives and told members to guard the railroad property. Howard turned in men to Mayor Hopkins for knocking over and burning cars. They were arrested and one of them was held by the grand jury. Cooperation with local authorities against its own members and supporters was not new. The ARU had advised members to shoot saboteurs, even fellow members, during the Great Northern Railway strike a few months earlier.[112]

By 13 July many of the GMA's tactics had come to fruition, effectively dismantling the strikers' forces and removing the sources of disruption.

> At this date, July 13, and for some days previous, the strikers had been virtually beaten. The action of the courts deprived the American Railway Union of leadership, ... enabled the General Managers Association to disintegrate its forces, and to make inroads into its ranks. The mobs had worn out their fury, or had succumbed to the combined forces of the police, the United States troops and marshals, and the State militia. The railroads were gradually repairing damages and resuming traffic with the aid of new men and with some of those strikers who had not been offensively active or whose action was laid to intimidation and fear.[113]

---

112 Ibid., pp. 19–20, 26, and 150.
113 Ibid., p. xlii.

CHAPTER 6

Managing the Class Struggle: A New Capital Composition

There is in every conflagration a time when a few pails of water would extinguish it; then there comes a time when the whole fire-department, with tons of water, can alone save what is left of the property; but sometimes a point is reached where even the boldest firemen are forced to recoil and give up the building to the devouring element. Two hundred years ago a little wise statesmanship might have averted the evils from which the world now suffers. One hundred years ago a gigantic effort, of all the good men of the world, might have saved society. Now the fire pours through every door, and window and crevice; the roof crackles; the walls totter; the heat of hell rages within the edifice; it is doomed; there is no power on earth that can save it; it must go down into ashes.

IGNATIUS DONNELLY, 1890[1]

∴

The use of the US military, militia, deputy sheriffs, and marshals, and local police to break the 1894 railroad strike demonstrated that capital had a new composition to meet the challenge of a newly recomposed working-class. Yet, the use of state force and violence to manage class struggle was approaching a turning point. The strike and its defeat encapsulate three important developments in the class struggle. It drove the deepening of the integrated relationship between capital and state power. A newly recomposed working-class had emerged, pursuing a new strategy of industrial organising in which all workers in a company or industry were organised together regardless of craft or skill. Finally, the 1894 strike was the forge in which a new composition of capital, which transformed management and work in the industry, was cast.

Perhaps one of the most intriguing reflections of these historical transformations was the life story of Dick Zepp. When Zepp first quit the B&O and then

---

1 Donnelly 1890, p. 175.

the militia in Martinsburg, West Virginia one hot summer day he helped light the spark that ignited the 1877 strike. When the strike was lost, the railroads blacklisted Zepp, forcing him and his family to hit the road as migrant workers. Nearly 17 years later, Dick somehow found his way back into a different kind of employment with a railroad. In the Spring of 1894 Zepp was hired by the B&O as an undercover detective posing as a tramp to keep Coxey's Army off the trains. Several months later he was killed by a freak gun accident in Chicago awaiting an assignment during the Pullman strike of 1894. Zepp's life had come full circle, from striker to deputy sheriff killed in the railroad strike.

Zepp's tragic arc from hero to senseless downfall is a metaphor for the workers who launched a strike that became an insurgency twice in about 17 years. The 1877 strike was a heroic missed opportunity to recompose working-class power and transform the railroads and maybe the country. The 1894 strike too became an insurgency that learned the lessons of organisation and coordination but was senselessly destroyed by the US courts and armed forces.

The new composition of capital that emerged after the 1877 strike was well organised and effective. The railroads unified around a single organisation and anti-strike strategy and successfully bypassed unreliable local and state officials to deploy the full force of the federal judicial and executive branches to defeat the 1894 strike. In the decades following the 1894 strike, the railroads consolidated ownership and introduced new technologies that altered railroad work and shifted power away from workers and to management.

In contrast, as we saw in Chapters 4 and 5, the recomposition of the workers' power was incomplete. The 1877 strike demonstrated the need for organisational capacity to coordinate a strike. However, the ARU's centralised organisational structure distanced the leadership from the strikers and their supporters and was an easy target for repression.

Above all, the 1877 and 1894 strikes fractured the elite consensus that class struggle should follow a winner takes all strategy. While the US Army and the federal court injunction delivered the final blows to both strikes, they could not win the class war. Despite the victory of repression, the elite coalition fragmented, welcoming into its ranks the reformers who found a new partner in arbitration, collective bargaining, and legalised unions. The American Federation of Labor (AFL) leadership now had a seat at the table.

The Curse of Success: From Insurgency to Organisation

Although the strike was defeated, that the GMA might have accepted the ARU leadership's offer to demobilise, de-escalate, and negotiate raised new possible complications for the strikers and their supporters. The effective combination of mobilisation and tactical escalation may result in the realisation of gains. But an insurgency that successfully uses disruption to obtain concessions through negotiations can bring with it 'the curse of success', robbing it of power and leverage.

Gurr argues that:

> By and large, dominant social groups have accommodated demands, but usually not without prolonged struggles ... Accommodations were made more often than not, some of them of broad benefit to the challenging groups, others designed to absorb or pacify their most able and vocal leaders.[2]

While accommodation may be common, it isn't the only response. Insurgents must contend with a combination of elite responses combining coercion and conformity in different variations. There is not necessarily a linear relationship between conflict, violence, and efforts to coopt and institutionalise insurgents.[3] There are three possible types of outcomes to insurgents' efforts to elicit a redress of grievances.

First, elites and insurgents may negotiate. If the concession is satisfactory, insurgents may demobilise and de-escalate, give up the use of disruption, and form a membership-based advocacy organisation to continue negotiations and monitor the implementation of agreements from within the polity. The advocacy process will allow insurgents to obtain and maintain tangible and intangible resources such as legitimacy, credibility, and financial support from the state, elites, existing established parties, organisations, or corporate foundations. The delivery and continuing flow of these resources to the membership or movement rank and file are necessary to maintain legitimacy and ensure the effectiveness of their efforts to prevent further disruption.

Second, if insurgents are unwilling to negotiate and compromise or see their struggle as lost, they may demobilise and de-escalate and discontinue their collective efforts. Although the insurgency is gone, individual insurgents or small isolated groups may continue their scattered attacks and sabotage against adversary targets or carry out terrorist attacks against the general population to generate the appearance of instability, fear, and disorder. Such continued escalation may become fleeting, irregular, and temporary as the lack of mass

---

2 Gurr 1989, p. 20.
3 Gurr 1972, p. 186.

support makes it impossible to sustain, especially as cell members are killed, captured, or incapacitated.

Lastly, the elite pairing of offering to negotiate while escalating tactics may amplify existing class and other divisions among insurgents and result in fragmentation. Factions may form differing on whether to pursue negotiations with or without de-mobilising or de-escalating. Negotiators and leaders may be invited to join the elite coalition, form or join a political party, run for office, form a union or advocacy organisation, serve in an official government position, and form coalitions with other advocacy organisations and corporations. Rubenstein explains that the tactic of elites is to offer

> symbolic inclusion of the group's members in the national 'consensus,' welfare programs for the group's lower class, and substantial benefits to the businesspeople and politicians that constitute the group's upper class. In short, elites use class divisions among insurgent movements by offering group leaders a place in the sun if they renounce anti-system goals and practices.[4]

Elite engagement with an insurgency creates a self-contradictory scenario. On the one hand, elites who are willing to negotiate with insurgents is taken as a sign that the insurgency 'got their attention'. On the other hand, engaging with elites detracts focus from rank and file self-organised efforts as the media and public spotlight shifts to the new high profile supporters. New attention and resources may result in new organisational formations to support it which have prerogatives of their own. Those engaging with elites change their style of dress, communication, and mannerisms while obtaining new complex specialised knowledge and information, thereby exacerbating the gulf between leaders and members. Elites and their allied organisations also seek to absorb insurgents into their sphere of influence both to build their own credibility and influence as a rising faction among elites or to deflect and dampen the insurgent threat. Negotiation and compromise are not neutral, but imperceptibly transform an insurgency into an organisation and disruption into collaboration. As Stanley Aronowitz put it, movements tied to specific demands for reform 'tend to dissolve in the wake of political integration'.[5]

There is an inverse relationship between elite support and mass support for an insurgency. The more insurgent leaders appear to be supported by elites, the

---

4   Rubenstein 1989, pp. 318–19.
5   Aronowitz 2015.

less support the insurgency will receive from its mass base. Existing supporters may perceive that with new better endowed supporters on their side their active participation and modest resources are no longer needed and withdraw. People power will be replaced by elite resources that fund the professionalisation of the movement. This will in turn attract new kinds of supporters, fellow travellers seeking paid employment, careers or notoriety. A volunteer, self-organised insurgency transforms itself into a paid staff-driven advocacy organisation purporting to represent and act on behalf of an absent base now referred to as a 'constituency'.[6] Members and supporters may also resent the arrival of outsiders who are seen as collaborators or opportunists and stop participating or split off to continue their mobilisation and escalation.

As insurgent leaders attract elite support and participation, they find themselves torn between the demands and interests of their members and supporters and altering their tactics and strategies to make them more acceptable to their new elite supporters, so that they can continue to participate in the 'rules of the game' of the polity from which they are no longer excluded. This dichotomous pull in two directions further feeds the loss of supporters which snowballs into greater dependence on elites for resources, legitimacy, and access. With more resources, leaders are paid salaries to do the work full-time, which further insulates them from the members and supporters who pay in dues and time to participate as they can beyond their paid work.

The now professional salaried and trained leaders increasingly place the interests of their own jobs, status and the survival of the organisation above the objectives and interests of their members and supporters, what McAdam calls 'oligarchization'.[7] McAdam's idea of oligarchisation originated in the anarchist and left critique of unions, the original professional membership-based organisational form. Errico Malatesta warned of oligarchisation nearly a century earlier when he observed 'the American labor movement seems to have been made more for the benefit of its leaders than for the workers'. Their salaries, Malatesta warned, not only separates them from the workers they represent

---

6 Replacing the rank and file with a 'constituency' is a remnant of pluralism's hegemonic rise to dominance in political science during the Cold War. As movements and insurgencies are transformed into dues paying 'members', political action is reshaped into a profit-making business venture that trades votes and public opinion for political influence, resources and services on behalf of a mostly anonymous passive constituency. Political science uses the demeaning term 'free riders' to describe those whose passivity is encouraged and yet benefit from such entrepreneurial advocacy on their behalf and are unable or unwilling to contribute their fair share.

7 McAdam 1999, p. 55.

but create an institutional imperative to pursue negotiations and peaceful settlements with government and capital to maintain their status, privileges, and
relationships with power.[8]

McAdam's focus on the institutional structure misses the point of the transition from disruption to accommodation the insurgency undergoes. For Piven
and Cloward, the oligarchical organisation becomes useless to elites once insurgents have been steered into normal politics, its constituency absorbed into the
elite coalition, and the threat of disruption dissipated.[9]

The irony is that an insurgency that once engaged in disruption to create
new forms of social organisation emulates the same model of organisation it
once challenged and sought to abolish. Today, this same critique can be applied
to membership-based non-governmental organisations (NGOs) that evaluate
their effectiveness based on the same principles of business management such
as quantifiable outcomes measured by new members, amount and number of
donations and grants, changes in regulations and laws, acres preserved, media
hits, and persons served, etc. In effect, social change has become modelled after
market-based mechanisms of the very system which created the very problems
that such NGOs were presumably created to solve.

The dynamic between the leadership and rank and file does not sufficiently
explain why an insurgency transforms itself into a non-threatening organisation. The combination of other factors including tactics, strategy, resources,
location, objectives, class composition, and the threat of disruption all play
a role. Insurgencies with a limited geographical range, such as local workplaces or individual employers, limited objectives such as raising wages or
obtaining union recognition, located away from strategically important locations, lacking resources important to elites, and engaged in actions that do not
present a threat of significant disruption to elite power may be more vulnerable
to absorption, diffusion, and deflection. For example, because the Industrial
Armies met these conditions, they may have generated extensive attention and
support but they could be ignored or scattered with minimal effort.

To counter the curse of success, insurgents have several options. First, they
can refuse any negotiations and fight the zero sum game to its ultimate conclusion, which raises its own costs and risks discussed in the introduction. Second,
they can de-mobilise after concessions have been made and prepare to fight
another day on the next terrain of struggle according to the changing class
composition. Lastly, they can rotate or prohibit leadership and self-finance.

---

8   Malatesta 2014 [1902], p. 324.
9   McAdam 1999, p. 55; and Piven and Cloward 1977, p. xxii.

Resources can be obtained from dues, setting up cooperatives, and illegal activities such as extortion, bank car robberies, kidnapping for ransom, smuggling, and drug sales.[10] For obvious reasons, many of these methods of self-financing are difficult to observe, let alone study, although there are documented court records in cases in which insurgents were arrested and prosecuted for such actions.

Insurgents using tactics of political violence are more likely to generate resources using difficult, dangerous, and unsavoury actions when they no longer depend on mass support or public opinion to conduct their struggle. Highly intense levels of tactical escalation will increasingly isolate insurgents from the very community from which they both emerged and on whose behalf they act. When elites retaliate in kind the rising costs of a strategy of tension scares away supporters and isolates insurgents. As a result, if insurgents find themselves unable to 'go public' to recruit new members and thereby regenerate themselves, their movement will soon wind down as members are jailed, killed, or leave the movement. What begins as an escalation of tactics in self-defence, or to hold existing strategic advantages soon becomes banditry and repression. Co-optation, legitimation, or institutionalisation of supporters further isolates militants who are forced to pursue unsavoury forms of self-financing. Like Gregory Peck's character Manuel Artiguez in *Behold a Pale Horse*, the Spanish Civil War guerrilla continues the struggle as a solitary bandit when his allies are captured, killed, or disappear.[11]

The threat posed by negotiations need not spell the finality of the insurgency. Insurgents may split from those that do become institutionalised and continue existing tactics that successfully extracted concessions from elites, escalate their tactics to avoid further co-optation, or demobilise. This was the model introduced by the ARU that would be attempted for decades to come by workers seeing their efforts to escalate sabotaged or suppressed by the AFL and elites. Workers continued to self-organise wildcat strikes, armed self-defence, sabotage, assassinations, and bombings.

Whatever the response, there is an all too common tendency to see accommodations as ends in themselves without assessing the political conditions which either brought them about or the different possible responses to it. Too often accommodations are perceived as temporary and fleeting, serving limited factional interests, or even the best possible outcomes at that time.

---

10   For example, the ARU collected dues, the Industrial Workers of the World (IWW) collected dues, sold newspapers, and set up shops, and the Black Liberation Army engaged in armed robberies during the 1970s.
11   *Behold a Pale Horse* 1964.

However, there is a range of possible outcomes that must be considered before deciding whether to accept concessions and de-escalate and demobilise, reject them and escalate and continue mobilising, or another variation of the two. First it is necessary to consider the intensity of the tactics currently being used. The further insurgents have implemented a strategy of tension the more likely it is that acceding to accommodation could undermine their credibility and ability to achieve their objectives. This is especially true when insurgents have broad mass support and costs of continued action are low. Settling for less than is promised by the existing opportunities is likely to be seen as capitulating by supporters and elites alike. When insurgents perceive that strikes, scattered attacks, street fighting, and sabotage are coalescing into a revolutionary situation, acceding to accommodations may be an unacceptable concession that legitimises the system they seek to discredit, destabilise, overthrow, and replace. To do otherwise would be what Piven and Cloward describe as the predicament of insurgents attempting to accomplish what is impossible by avoiding doing what is possible.

Second, insurgents may engage in negotiations during which they accept concessions while refusing to demobilise and de-escalate. Tilly calls this strategy 'pairing' and 'switching' in which insurgents choose among alternative tactics and the method and frequency of their use, whether simultaneously or consecutively with negotiations.[12] While this may reduce the threat of co-optation, diffusion, or deflection, it also makes insurgents an unreliable partner for elites willing to negotiate. These elites will lose credibility within their own coalition as they appear to be weak, sympathisers, or giving away something for nothing, losing influence and making concessions difficult. Further negotiations or concessions are unlikely and repression is possible if elites have sufficient resources and support. As long as insurgents have sufficient resources, continue expanding support, and hold critical resources such as factories or territory, elites may be forced to make continued concessions hoping they can retain power and control. This is what Rosa Luxemburg meant by using force to achieve reforms not for themselves but to expand the available political space so that they can be used as staging grounds for further reform *ad infinitum* until revolutionary conditions prevail to rupture capitalism.[13] Insurgents who can carry out tactical pairing and switching can also use the newly obtained resources to recruit and sustain more supporters until they are perceived as a viable alternative system to which people will flock, thereby destabilising the dominant system.

---

12   Tilly 1978, pp. 166 and 170.
13   Luxemburg 1900.

In order for an insurgency to continue opening and maintaining the existing political space it must avoid the perils of co-optation, deflection, diffusion, and institutionalisation by pursuing complete system overhaul. It must make apparent to all that the entire purpose is revolutionary and its tactics are dependent on the conditions in which they struggle, the strategy temporary and dynamic, and all gains are fleeting, precarious, and not intended to be institutionalised. An insurgency is undertaken as a precarious movement that contains a 'self-destruct' switch to be flipped at any level of success in order to avoid becoming transformed into instruments of discipline and social control. Survival is contingent on continually innovating with non-institutional disruptive tactics. Achieving concessions that spark runaway reforms is a strategy, reform is not the objective. The end game is revolutionary *crisis*, not reform. For Glaberman, wildcat strikes such as during 1877 and 1894 bypass the union as workers search for something entirely new.[14]

The process of recomposing working-class power that expressed itself in 1894 continued for another decade. Founded in 1905 with the participation of Eugene Debs, the Industrial Workers of the World (IWW), sought to provide an organisational vehicle to serve a strategy of crisis. It purposefully devised a self-destruct mechanism into every organising campaign at the turn of the twentieth century by rejecting all collective bargaining and contracts. The IWW centred its strategy of using class struggle on the shop floor to extract concessions and reform without making them the objective of class struggle. They saw, as Glaberman and Rawick assert, that 'life at the point of production is a constant struggle'.[15] By reading the emerging class composition, they recognised the strategic leverage provided by mass workers brought together by the intensified socialisation of capital could disrupt the accumulation process. As Tilly and Tilly observed,

> Workers who can easily disrupt production, impose large replacement costs by quitting, and put substantial capital at risk have great collection-action advantages over their fellows. So do those whose work, training, or nonwork connections give them more extensive internal communication.[16]

---

14   Glaberman 1975, p. 13.
15   Glaberman and Rawick 1977, p. 203.
16   Tilly and Tilly 1998, p. 243.

The IWW used disruption strategically to move towards worker self-control of the means of production in order to transform work to minimise neces-sary labour and free the full exploration of human existence. As a result, the IWW achieved a tactical innovation that eluded craft workers, for example, who sometimes used strikes to obtain recognition and negotiate contracts through collective bargaining. Such organisational success was soon turned into a defeat for the workers by transforming their union into a mechanism for restraining further mobilisation, intensification of tactics, and circulation of the struggle to more workers. These Pyrrhic victories of the brotherhoods were recognised by many railroad workers between the 1870s and 1890s, for example, who attempted to form shop federations to combine the crafts unions, uni-ons for un- and low-skilled shopmen, the Knights of Labor, and, eventually, the American Railway Union.

Although the Red Scare ultimately broke the IWW, its organising strategy shook the very foundations of American capitalism. The IWW's spiral stair-case strategy – using disruption to extract ever greater concessions to provoke revolutionary crisis rather than reform – was the spectre haunting capitalism. The IWW, combined with the wartime wildcat strikes (see Chapter 8) and the Seattle general strike (see Chapter 9) exposed the vulnerability of American capital and compelled the creation of a labour planning state that could har-ness class struggle as a driver of capital accumulation. What soon followed was the passage of the WWI National War Labor Board, 1933 National Recovery Act, and the 1935 National Labor Relations Act that absorbed unions into the elite coalition in order to regulate and manage the possibility of disruption.

The IWW made explicit what was implicit in the half century of cycles of class struggle. Its strategy of disruption made it clear how tactical innovations should inform organisational choices so that insurgencies can effect lasting fundamental change without being transformed into new mechanisms of con-trol and domination.

For Tilly the working-class is not an agent of revolutionary contestation because strikes are reactive tactics in the repertoire of contention used to defend existing gains and privileges. Demonstrating his Weberian influences, strikes become proactive once governments began to report, mediate, and reg-ulate them in the 1880–90s, and they became rules-based efforts to seek union recognition and collective bargaining between the 1910s and 1930s.[17]

---

17   Tilly 1978, p. 203.

These officials, employers, and organized workers hammered out standard definitions of strikes and lockouts. They worked out rules concerning the proper behavior of the parties to a strike. They developed means of registering and publicizing a strike's end and outcome. They, the courts, police, and other public officials were fixing the precise place of the strike in the day's repertoire of collective action. To be sure, the rules remained uncertain in important regards, the rules changed as the balance of power changed, and most of the rule making occurred as a by-product of bitter struggle. That is the way repertoires of collective action usually change.[18]

What Tilly overlooks is that once strikes meet the rules, they become institutionalised rituals of contestation by unions incorporated into the polity, not sources of revolutionary crisis and disruption. Such a functionalist explanation of strikes cannot explain the persistence of class struggle.

Part of the allure of insurgencies that take space such as buildings (squatters), factories (syndicalists), or territory (liberation movements) is the need to demonstrate not merely their ability to disrupt and survive but simultaneously take and sustain. When they acquire the resources necessary to keep people alive while giving them the space to govern themselves and the power to protect both, an insurgency will make the next transition to a revolution that carves what CLR James called 'the future in the present' within the shell of the old.[19]

Managing Class Struggle

The ARU leadership and rank and file defined success differently. For the leadership, because a negotiated settlement was the best that could be hoped for, it became the objective of the strike. Although negotiations never occurred – not for the lack of effort – they caught the imagination of the US Strike Commission, which made a startling endorsement of a process for resolving labour disputes in order to avoid strikes and disruption.

The focus on the US Strike Commission is illuminating. Although the testimony of key actors is missing, it provides a post-strike analysis from the different actors in the drama and federal officials considering a more elaborate role for government in regulating class relations. Strike leaders appear to dress

---

18   Ibid., p. 161.
19   James 1980.

themselves up under the threat of actual criminal prosecution, railroad company, and military officials avoided incriminating themselves, and local and state officials denounced everyone else's unruly behaviour to save their own credibility.

The most important, and as of yet unrecognised, revelation from the US Strike Commission is its endorsement of federal authority to establish labour relations policy that would manage and dampen the impact of class struggle. This came four decades before it could be fully realised under the 1933 NIRA and 1935 NLRA. This cannot be overemphasised. There is a near total consensus among historians that federal rights to organise, unionise, and collectively bargain came from above, an initiative of elite members of a fractured coalition trying to keep the country from chaos. Workers were then free to organise, we learn, once these reforms were in place. However, by pinpointing support for laws governing labour management in the immediate aftermath of the 1894 insurgency, a different picture comes into focus. Reform followed disruptive class conflict in an effort not to legalise organising, unions, and strikes but to control, manage, diffuse, dampen, deflect, and prevent them.

Hewing to the ideal of a neutral state that resolves conflicts, a key principle of what would later be called pluralism, the US Strike Commission draws a line from the social scientific investigation of the working-class begun after 1877 to well reasoned neutral policy solutions.

> We ought now to inaugurate a permanent system of investigation into the relations between railroads and employees in order to prepare to deal with them intelligently, and that we may conservatively adopt such remedies as are sustained by public opinion for defects or wrongs that may from time to time appear. In the long contest between shippers and railroads penal and specific legislation proved inadequate. The lessons of this period of legislation need to be well remembered by labor. Hasty, revengeful, and retaliatory legislation injures every interest, benefits nobody, and cannot long be enforced.[20]

The 'remedy' was to expand federal and state authority to manage class conflict by hampering and restraining efforts to escalate tactics, and channel and deflect tensions into negotiation and the polity. As Carroll Wright, chair of the 1894 US Strike Commission and later the first US Labor Commissioner, reminded recalcitrant capitalists resisting expanded federal authority, new

---

20   US Strike Commission 1895, pp. xlviii–xlix.

laws expand and enlarge the authority of the constitution and thus federal powers. Referring to the 1887 Interstate Commerce Act, which activated Congress's Article I inter-state commerce clause powers, Wright reminded them that Congress had asserted its authority to intervene in any strike action that threatened commerce that crossed state lines.[21]

While assuring his audience that he was opposed to socialism, Wright made a startling and pointed observation that business would want government ownership and operation of the railroads in the case it were threatened to ensure 'a small but reasonable rate of dividend'.[22] That so many bankrupt roads were already under the protection of the federal courts which allowed them to continue paying extraordinarily high returns in the midst of the depression underscored his argument.

But this was only a thought experiment because the US Strike Commission ultimately favoured recognition and regulation, not disruption. It pointed out, without acknowledging their shortcomings and limits for workers, that the federal government and 11 states had provided legal recognition of unions and arbitration existed in 15 states. Foreseeing the role labour law and collective bargaining would play to regularise unions on a level footing equivalent to the regulation of corporations, the US Strike Commission asked

> Is it not wise to fully recognize them by law; to admit their necessity as labor guides and protectors, to conserve their usefulness, increase their responsibility, and to prevent their follies and aggressions by conferring upon them the privileges enjoyed by corporations, with like proper restrictions and regulations?[23]

The US Strike Commission proposed that unions be legalised with all of the authority and responsibilities that comes with it and regulated as 'quasi-public servant ... in the interest of public welfare'.[24] One popular approach was to charter unions in order to dampen class conflict by making them subject them to civil and criminal liability for the consequences of their actions, creating a disincentive to strike, boycott, etc. For the Strike Commission legalisation would dampen escalation.

The rationale for federal regulation of unions was that since railroads were semi-public corporations under federal authority it was within the purview of

---

21   Wright 1894, p. 37.
22   Ibid., p. 39.
23   US Strike Commission 1895, p. xlvii.
24   Wright 1894, p. 40.

federal power to require the appointment of an investigatory body to arbitrate disputes between labour and capital and implement rules governing how
unions operated in these disputes. Wright pointed out that the US Strike Commission itself was authorised by the 1887 Interstate Commerce Act, which
empowered the President to create boards of arbitration to carry out investigations, conduct voluntary arbitration, and regulate wages.[25]

President Cleveland has already advocated for such arbitration boards, commissions, and a Commissioner of Labor as early as April 1886. Such institutions
were predicated on 'just and sensible recognition of the value of labor' and 'its
right to be represented in the departments of the Government'.[26] The labour
planning state had not yet arrived but it had been conceived.[27] The US Strike
Commission plowed the field for the National War Labor Board during WWI
(see Chapter 8) and the arbitration boards established under the 1920 Railroad
Labor Act.

Speaking to the regularisation of unions, Debs noted how the outcomes of a
negotiated process would be shaped by the fundamental character of the law
and power in society. Mandatory arbitration and legislative solutions would be
wielded by the class that holds the greatest power.

> If the laws we already have on the subject are enforced without merit
> against the employees and are ignored with reference to their application
> to the companies, what right have we to expect that the same discrimin-
> ation will not be carried into this matter of arbitration or any other law
> that may be enacted hereafter? If there was a disposition on the part of
> the authorities to impartially enforce the law against all violators of the
> law – that is a proposition to which I subscribe. I think men ought to be

---

25 Ibid., pp. 40–1.
26 Cleveland 1886, in Wright, p. 49. President Cleveland's Attorney General Richard Olney,
    who engineered the federal intervention to help crush the strike, later came to embrace
    Cleveland and Wright's position.
27 By labour planning state I mean an aspect of what CLR James, Raya Dunayevskaya and
    Grace Lee called 'state capitalism' in which the state plans, organises, and manages the
    capitalist economy. As the role of government in the economy expanded after 1877 to
    manage class struggle, the state and capital become not only more closely integrated
    but merged. A strategic response to socialism, the state has grown since the Civil War to
    assume responsibility for more and more of the capitalist economy from not only set-
    ting up, running and financing industry but disciplining and educating the working-class
    and managing class struggle, among other functions. As James, Dunayevskaya and Lee
    explained, state capitalism in both the Soviet Union and the West 'seeks desperately to
    remove the class struggle from the process of production'. (1986 [1950], p. 17)

punished that violate law, whether rich or poor, capitalist or tramp. If that were true in the administration of our law I would look for some relief, at least.[28]

Proposing that federal power should include imposing a negotiated settlement rather than exclusively judicial and military repression looked like de-escalation to some but to others the same balance of power promised a similar imbalanced outcome. Perhaps Gompers's opposition to mandatory arbitration was most succinct when he equated calls for a federal labour commissioner with an 'appointment of a coroner to hold an inquest'.[29] Requiring two classes unequal in power to put down their tactics to negotiate would have predictable outcomes when decided by members of the elite appointed to a government body.

The federal government's role in breaking the strike had normalised use of federal power on behalf of capital against the working-class and brought the law part of the way to mandatory arbitration but it did not make it any more popular among the labour movement and its allies. The role of the courts and US Army in the strike by the US government

> had established precedents considered dangerous for the future welfare of the workers. The 'unholy' alliance between the federal authorities and the railroads was viewed apprehensively. Was the government the servile tool of corporate interests? What rights did labor have?[30]

The regulation of labour was hardly a new concept. The abolition of slavery (except for prisoners) was codified in both the 13th amendment of the US Constitution and the freedom of contract principle wielded by the federal judicial and enshrined in the ideas of the ruling elite – of people such as Pullman, who thought that 'the labourer can work or quit on the terms offered; that is the limit of his rights'.[31]

The problem with this principle, Debs explained, is that it extended little actual freedom to workers who are compelled to work.

> We have men bidding and compelled to bid by their necessities, having families dependent upon them, and they have to work and they bid

---

28   US Strike Commission 1895, p. 167.
29   Ibid., p. 197.
30   Lindsey 1942, p. 350.
31   US Strike Commission 1895, p. xxvii.

against each other, and the man who bids the least gets the work, and the others are out of work. Now, I have said, I deny men have a right to do that; no matter what may be said about the freedom of contract under our Constitution, no man has a right to sell himself into slavery; no man has a right to do that; and yet that is what it amounts to if a man agrees to work at unliving wages, and that is precisely what they do – what the wage system compels them to do.[32]

The freedom of contract principle informed labour relations reform by assuming the existing relations of power at the same time it denied the social relations of production.

Another labour reform the US Strike Commission proposed was prohibiting strikes before mandatory arbitration could take place and prohibiting sympathy strikes for six months after an arbitration decision. A version of this proposal shaped the 1898 Erdman Act, in which the chairman of the Interstate Commerce Commission and the Commissioner of Labor could mediate a labour conflict, and various labour boards during their brief existence during WWI (see Chapter 8).[33] Under the 1935 NLRA, unions are prohibited from striking during a cooling off period, although workers without a union may strike at any time.

The US Strike Commission also recommended the formation of a permanent strike commission, granting power to the courts to compel railroads to obey its decisions (perhaps a welcome change from the courts being singularly focused on compelling unions to comply), require unions to incorporate and submit a written constitution, rules and by-laws, prohibit the use of blacklists, require unions kick out members who interfere with scabs and participate in the use of violence, and ban yellow dog contracts which require workers to exclusively join the company sponsored union. In this list of recommendations lie the programme of labour relations reform for the next four decades.

The objective of the call for reform was to regulate and harness class conflict for the purposes of accumulation not social transformation. Class struggle, the unions, corporations, and government officials agreed in 1877 and 1894, was disruptive. Since banning unions or strikes and repressing ones that persisted caused further disruption to the economy, an elite faction led by Strike Commissioner and US Labor Commissioner Wright proposed another approach.

---

32   Ibid., p. 170.

33   Other than the voluntary railroad arbitration mechanism set up under the Erdman Act all the existing state arbitration boards praised by the US Strike Commission were limited to their own states. (See US Strike Commission 1895 pp. l and lii; and Lindsey 1942, p. 350).

Despite its victory in the 1894 strike, the elite coalition pursuing a winner takes all intolerance to organised workers lost ground and fragmented. Corporations, elite-run organisations, and states and the federal government experimented with a range of reforms that became known as the Progressive Era that far exceeded the workplace and reached deep inside the working-class home. 'The ideological leaders of Progressivism', just like the later New Dealers, could turn class struggle into a winning majority coalition because, as Jeffreys-Jones observed, they 'wished to persuade the electorate to vote for reform from a fear of class conflagration'.[34]

Fragmentation among elites, the coming over to insurgents of an elite faction, and other conflicts that have displayed the lack of capacity or legitimacy of elites lowers the costs and increases the opportunity for insurgents. It opens new political space to continue provoking crises that result in further reforms, attract more mass support, and bring in new allies by overcoming existing barriers of race, gender, employer, and geography, which further recomposes working-class power. Most importantly, it also makes it possible to intensify tactics by shifting from scattered attacks to coordinated destruction or revolution. For this reason, Piven and Cloward observe, further conflict, disruption, struggle, and fragmentation of the elite coalition, drive concessions and reform, as elites attempt to restore control and legitimacy.

> We ordinarily think of major legislation as taking form only through established electoral processes. We tend to overlook the force of crisis in precipitating legislative reform, partly because we lack a theoretical framework by which to understand the impact of major disruptions. By crisis, we mean a publicly visible disruption in some institutional sphere. Crisis can occur spontaneously (e.g., riots) or as the intended result of tactics of demonstration and protest, which either generate institutional disruption or bring unrecognizable eruption to public attention. Public trouble is a political liability, it calls for action by political leaders to stabilize the situation. Because crisis usually creates or exposes conflict, it threatens to produce cleavages in a political consensus, which politicians would ordinarily act to avert. Whether political leaders then design solutions to reflect these terms depends on a two-fold calculation: first, the impact of the crisis and the issues it raises on existing alignments and, second, the gains or losses in support to be expected as a result of a proposed resolution.[35]

---

34   Jeffreys-Jones 1978, p. 6.

35   Piven and Cloward 1966, np.

The origin of the Progressive and New Deal reforms can be found in the US Strike Commission's framing of the 1894 strike as a Triton call for expanding the elite reform coalition. Its report listed a range of proposals but called them 'premature' and warned against government ownership as 'socialistic'. It drew the line at the wrong kind of reform, which can facilitate a shifting of class power which should be avoided. New regulations must be closely considered and those that further expectations of further reform should be discouraged. That the US Strike Commission was willing to even consider such ideas confirmed Debs's argument that reform can be driven by class struggle. Even more startling is that this came on the heels of the successful suppression of a national strike, which conventional reasoning would argue is a time when reform is least likely to occur. Apparently some elites recognised just how easy it might be for success to be turned into defeat.

Just like Pullman's hypothetical freedom of the individual worker in the labour market, reform would leave unaffected workers who have neither access nor power in the prevailing political system. Debs was an astute observer of the *dance macabre* by which contenders move in a political system closed to peaceful means for hearing and redressing grievances by applying the rules and procedures the same to everyone regardless of their position in the social hierarchy. With all the forces of the corporations and government arrayed against the ARU, Debs reasoned that tactical escalation should be expected.

> We have nothing to look forward to defend us in times of trouble. We have only got a number, and a limited number, of poorly paid men in our organization, and when their income ceases they are starving. We have no power of the Government behind us. We have no recognized influence in society on our side. We have absolutely nothing but the men who begin to starve when they quit work. On the other side the corporations are in perfect alliance; they have all of the things that money can command, and that means a subsidized press, that they are able to control the newspapers, and means a false or vitiated public opinion. The clergy almost steadily united in thundering their denunciations; then the courts, then the State militia, then the Federal troops; everything and all things on the side of corporations. When the authorities are called upon to intercede in troubles of this kind do they ever ask labor a question? Never. They always go to where capital sits in council and there receive their orders as I view it – do what they command shall be done.[36]

---

36   US Strike Commission 1895, p. 169.

Considering the existing conditions in which workers and capital meet either on the street or at the negotiating table, the outcome is determined by a struggle for power. When the political system is closed, the use of the courts, law, regulations, state police and military force can only serve the interests of capital.

> We have had a great many conflicts in this country between capital and labor. We know by experience and by the truth of history that in a great many of those conflicts the workingmen were right. We know that their wages were unjustly reduced and their rights trampled down. When and where did the militia ever come out and take its stand on the side of labor, to prevent the workingmen's being robbed and degraded? Never. Whenever and wherever they have been called out it was always to take their place on the side of the capitalist. They have gone into partnership with the oppressors of labor to crush labor. If there was a perfect sense of duty and justice prevailing at the proper places they would not have to exercise their powers as they now do, always with the one purpose of crushing the workingmen. They could enforce the demands of justice without any additional legislation on the subject, in my opinion; but the moneyed power, it seems to me, is potential enough to control all this machinery, and will be able to do it with the additional legislation that you propose, in my opinion.[37]

Ultimately, even reforms intended to reset the balance of power or dampen or prevent the kinds of leverage and opportunities that come from escalating tactics are subject to capture by the plutocratic elite.

Reform, Debs asserted, cannot be solicited but must be the product of a struggle for power. It must be the product of a shift in the balance of class power, not a means further to engrain it. Such conflict, he observed, is the telltale sign of progress.

> It seems to me if it were not for that resistance to degrading conditions, the tendency of our whole civilization would be downward; after awhile we would reach the point where there would be no resistance, and slavery would ensue.[38]

---

37   Ibid., p. 169.
38   Ibid., p. 162.

Eight years before the US Strike Commission advocated the regulation of labour unions, the US Supreme Court eviscerated the corporate charter, last remaining tool of state regulatory control of corporations, and went much further. The 1886 *Santa Clara County v. Southern Pacific Railroad Company* ruling indirectly found that corporations held 14th amendment equal protection rights as 'artificial persons'.[39] The defeat of the 1894 strike punctuated the conclusion of a transitional period. Corporations now had constitutional rights government was obligated to protect against trepidation by actual persons. While he didn't attempt to do so, President Cleveland had Supreme Court backing to define 'people' whose 'rights, privileges, or immunities' the federal government is obligated to protect under sections 5298 and 5299 of the Revised Statutes of the United States as including corporations. As corporations were being released from regulatory control by the charter, unions were becoming candidates for them.

A New Capital Composition

As with the aftermath of the 1877 railroad strike, the 1894 strike triggered the search for new technologies that could replace and deskill railroad workers who asserted tremendous power over the conditions, pace, and relations of work. As Glaberman and Rawick explained 'the working class always provides the impetus for a technological revolution: technological change is designed to cheapen or degrade or control or eliminate labor'.[40] Between 1870 and 1910, a number of transformative new technologies were introduced to the railroad industry. Steel rails replaced iron and were standardised in gauge, engines became more powerful, and freight cars could carry more weight. The automatic coupler and air brake were more widely deployed by the end of the 1890s.[41] If the new technologies required more workers, such as two firemen on larger locomotives, they also dramatically increased productivity per worker. Not by accident did the gains in productivity from the new technologies exceed those gained by geographic expansion after 1890, in which the continent was criss-crossed by railroad lines and vast new track mileage. The second widely disruptive strike in 1894 also provided an impetus to find a technological solution to managing class conflict. The outcomes of both strikes demonstrated

---

39   *Santa Clara County v. Southern Pacific R. Co.* 118 US 394 (1886).
40   Glaberman and Rawick 1977, p. 196.
41   Stromquist 1993, p. 101.

how David Noble argued the 'technology of production is ... determined by the "social relations of production" such that "its actual use in production is determined by the realities of the shop-floor struggles between classes"'.[42]

Each new innovation played a role in extracting the knowledge of an entire craft, partially automating it in a new device, and transferring power over more of the work process to management. The automatic coupler may have made switchmen's job safer but it also reduced the need for them to assemble the cars of a train. Similarly, the Westinghouse air brake eliminated the need for brakemen to ride dangerously on top of trains to set the hand brakes. The sub-contracting and standardisation of the manufacturing of locomotives and cars reduced the demand for shopmen.[43]

The reduction in reliance on switchmen from the introduction of the automatic coupler surely had an impact on organising. Since switchmen assembled cars from multiple rail yards they often interacted with many workers of different lines in the same geographical region. Stromquist insightfully identified the impact of the changes on railroad workers' ability to organise. 'In regular contact with men on other railroads, they were a natural bridge between workers employed on different roads. They were the quintessential sympathy strikers whose actions could quickly disrupt traffic over a wide territory'. As a result, they were organised in large numbers and increasingly struck over noneconomic control issues in the 1880s–90s.[44]

The automatic coupler is a revealing example of how new technology is introduced in order to alter the balance of class power. Because, as Panzieri explained, 'The capitalistic social relationship is concealed within the technical demands of machinery',[45] the introduction of the automatic coupler was predicated on the need to reduce the reliance on switchmen whose duties provided them with the capacity to circulate disruptive struggles among workers.

Organisational innovations were also motivated by the need to reduce wages, increase productivity, and assert greater control over the workers and the work process. The companies engaged in more recruitment, training, personnel policies to reduce turnover, amended work rules to allow more flexibility over which workers did which job, and other measures to increase the number of available workers in order to erode the leverage skilled workers maintained in controlling entry to their craft and thus the supply of workers

---

42   Noble 1979, p. 19.
43   Stromquist 1993, pp. 102 and 105.
44   Ibid., pp. 110–11.
45   Panzieri 1976, p. 9.

and their wages. Rather than cut wages overtly, these alterations eroded the authority and power of the craft workers over their labour, thereby deskilling and cheapening their labour while making them more interchangeable and as standardised as the equipment they worked with.[46]

Beginning in the 1880s, company management strategy increasingly concentrated power from local to system-wide departments in each geographic division. In the process they standardised management decisions over rates, purchasing, hiring, technology, wages, working conditions, and work rules. New centralised payroll, discharge lists, personnel records including work history and disciplinary procedures, corporate welfare, and standardising hiring and promotions across the company was coordinated between companies through industry organisations such as GMA. Doing so dampened the power workers could deploy to influence and shape local company policy because 'it also permitted the systematic manipulation of wage rates and work rules in ways that violated customary work practices and earning levels'.[47]

The companies were aware of their vulnerability to local organising from decentralised personnel policies. Northern Pacific general manager Kendrick complained that he was forced to spend half his time dealing with grievances that led to compromise, which encouraged the men to continue using the strategy each time they succeeded.[48] Standardising disciplinary policy weakened the power of local self-organisation by moving the decisions from local managers, who could be bent to pressure, to system-wide departments which made decisions from an impersonal and insulated distance. This in turn shaped the organising strategy of workers so that local organising circulated from one locale to another to shut down or disrupt an entire line, region, or the country. It is likely that such management changes spurred efforts to organise industrially across crafts, companies, and regions to overcome the loss of local leverage.

Personnel policies had a particularly caustic effect on workers' power over conditions, wages, and hiring. Using seniority to reduce turnover attacked the informal and formal networks in the crafts by which workers migrated from job to job. Centralised payroll was instituted at the Chicago, Burlington & Quincy railroad after the 1888 strike to screen for rising wages at the division level. Until they were banned by the 1898 Erdman Act, corporate welfare schemes served to dampen turnover and organising as workers risked losing their relief funds if they were fired or changed jobs.[49]

---

46   Stromquist 1993, pp. 101–3.
47   Ibid., pp. 108–9 and 230.
48   Ibid., p. 233.
49   Ibid., pp. 244–6.

Disciplinary records that recorded instances of 'disobedience', 'insolence', 'insubordination', and striking or union organising were used to fire workers and screen new applicants. Some lines required letters of reference and developed standardised forms for them. Employees were also sometimes required to file a tintype photograph.[50] Such policies were intended to take away the use of turnover and migration as a way for railroad workers not only to start over and find new jobs but also to spread organising campaigns and circulate strikes. In short, company policy was standardised as power over it was centralised.

Such 'discipline by record' policies became the basis for premium pay and bonus systems that were central to Taylorist productivity schemes. They also had a substantial impact on individualising and reinforcing the work relationship between an individual worker and the company despite the existence of a union contract.[51] The grievance procedure is a remnant of the disciplinary record, a midway point between workers and the prerogative of the employer to hire and fire. Because it assumes the premise of the work relationship it became a poor substitute for worker control over entry into their craft and hiring. The grievance procedure effectively normalised management prerogative over the individual workers and enshrined it in the union contract by giving the worker the right to complain about not control working conditions.

Personnel records were used a legal cousins of the blacklist to discipline and weed out troublesome workers or purge them from employment. They were also an early form of surveillance used in the class struggle that are extremely relevant today in the age of ubiquitous big data. William Pinkerton, who founded the infamous private police force bearing his name, confided that the companies use espionage and information-gathering systems that are 'interchangeable and unlimited in scope', so that details about workers are 'traced, tabulated, and in time arrayed against him'.[52] It appears that social media and the Internet have only vastly expanded Pinkerton's system, not invented it.

In this way, class struggle drove the standardisation of railroad work. Capital's innovation was a strategy in response to an insurgent working-class. As Stromquist observed 'Each major strike or wave of strikes created a more favorable climate within railroad management circles for the adoption of management reforms'.[53]

---

50   Ibid., pp. 238–9 and 240.
51   Ibid., p. 240.
52   Ibid.
53   Ibid., pp. 230–1.

The successful cooperation among the railroad companies through the GMA and its close alliance with the federal government to defeat the 1894 strike forged a new consensus over capital's strategy to discipline and manage class struggle. As Stromquist revealed, defeating the strike 'welded together a new consensus among railroad managers that systematic attention to the management of workers was needed'. As the industry continued to horizontally consolidate and vertically integrate with banking, mining, railroads, and steel until the penultimate formation of US Steel in 1902, the industry sought to put into place a new labour-planning state critical to state capitalism.

This strategy was centred around the 1898 Erdman Act, authored by Olney, which created the eight-hour day and collective bargaining in exchange for regulating strikes, arbitration, and management prerogative and control over technology, work, hiring and discipline. The labour-planning state recognised the brotherhoods, which 'could be enlisted to police a new era of industrial peace in return for a guarantee of their survival', but at great cost to the interests of railroad workers.[54]

Olney authored the original act, which was first introduced in 1895, because he had come to believe that there was an unavoidable role for the state to play in managing class conflict. 'If the combatants are left to fight out their own battles between themselves by the ordinary agencies', Olney warned, 'nothing is more certain that that each will inflict incalculable injury upon the other'.[55]

The labour-planning state for the single railroad industry would become a model extended to the entire war economy during WWI (examined in Chapter 8).[56] Stromquist found that the response to the strike

> brought about the broad application of federal authority in its suppression. None of the tools of federal intervention were new with this crisis ... But never before was the scale of federal intervention as great, and never before had it been as masterfully coordinated with a well-organised association of general managers.[57]

To meet the threat of railroad workers recomposing their power by leapfrogging the barriers imposed by their craft differences to organise industrially, the rationalisation and standardisation of railroad work accelerated the process of transforming them into indistinguishable industrial workers. Where as

---

54   Ibid., p. 263.
55   In Ibid., p. 260.
56   Ibid., p. 231.
57   Ibid., p. 256.

industrialism deployed by the workers was disruptive, industrialism deployed as a response by capital was a stabiliser, since it eroded the very leverage that precipitated disruption – it decomposed the basis of the workers' power. The counter-attacks following the 1877 and 1894 strikes demonstrated concretely and unambiguously that working-class struggle, the recomposition of workers' power, drives the composition of capital, not the inverse.

PART 3

Revolt of the Rank and File

∵

CHAPTER 7

The Dynamite Conspiracy: US Steel vs. the Iron Workers

> I see enough to convince me that the ramifications of your society are like a net-work of wires, all over the earth, penetrating everywhere, and at every point touching the most deadly explosives of human passions and hates; and that it needs but the pressure of your finger upon the pedal to blow up the world.
>
> IGNATIUS DONNELLY, 1890[1]

∴

Throughout the first decade or so of the twentieth century, capital began rationalising the work process, squeezing out excess surplus value, bottling up skilled craft workers with contracts, and incessantly deploying the repressive forces at its disposal. Workers persisted, appealing for recognition and negotiations, and lacking a response, escalating their tactics by wildcatting, disrupting, and carrying out street fights, sabotage, and scattered armed attacks. The list was long. Among them are the 1900–3 national miner's strike, 1903–4 Idaho Springs Colorado strike, 1904 meat packers strike, 1907 Nevada mining and mills conflicts, 1908 Great Lakes Seamen's strike, 1909 Philly streetcar strike, 1909 McKees Rocks Pressed Steel Car Co. strike, 1897–1911 West Virginia bituminous coal strikes, 1910 Columbus, Ohio street car strike, 1910 Bethlehem Steel strike, 1912 Brotherhood of Timber Workers (IWW) Louisiana strike, 1913–14 Calumet Michigan copper strike, and the epic 1911–15 railroad strike.

But no battle shook the ground more than the 1905–10 industrial war between US Steel and the International Association of Bridge and Structural Iron Workers (IABSIW) union. The extended bombing campaign orchestrated by both capital and workers would continue into the early 1920s, pausing only for an even larger bombing campaign that would begin in Europe, known as WWI. During these tumultuous years ironworkers demonstrated a willingness to run

---

1 Donnelly 1890, p. 174.

the gamut of tactics, eventually turning to a coordinated bombing campaign when the opportunity for achieving any objectives were lowest and the costs they could impose on capital rose. A relatively small and isolated craft union with only a modest presence in the iron industry, IABSIW rapidly escalated their tactics, lacking an effective strategy to counter the composition of capital, the opportunity to negotiate, and access to the polity. The union's decision to carry out clandestine scattered attacks on property without any mass support illustrates just how ineffective a bombing campaign can be when faced by a consolidated and well organised industry prepared to escalate its tactics as well.

Class Composition and Recomposition

Iron workers held the power over the industry by the skilled nature of the work. As a group they sought ways to make it difficult to rationalise their work according to the Taylorist principles taking place in the steel plants. From its founding in Pittsburgh on 4 February 1896, when few steel buildings had been built, the IABSIW proved adept at exploiting its tactical advantages in its struggle with the companies, controlling entry into the building trades, the conditions of work, and wages. According to a report of the Commission on Industrial Relations, the IABSIW used its power as an independent union as leverage to drive up wages in its industry, very rapidly becoming the envy of the labour movement. 'From the lowest paid trade on a building, the ironworkers through organization have advanced their wages in fifteen years well toward the top of the column of upwards of thirty unions in the building industry'.[2] This took place at the time when urban slums were spreading rapidly and the buildings trade generated tremendous profits in the rapidly urbanising America.

The work was among the most deadly and dangerous. Workers lived an average of 34 years. In 1911–12, for example, there were 124 deaths in the industry, 109 due to accidents, which came to an astonishing 1 percent of the IABSIW membership. During one period of this era an estimated 20 union members died per month.[3] The ironworkers had a lot to be fearful and angry about. Life was cheap and profits were high in their line of work.

The rapid rise in the union's fortunes came about through a rare but short-lived industry-wide contract. IABSIW's proposed 1902 tentative national agreement with the largest iron erector American Bridge Company (ABC), negotiated

---

2   Grant 1915b, pp. 5, 6, and 20.
3   Ibid., p. 8.

while Frank Buchanan was president, illustrated how powerful the union was at that time. The contract dictated that the company promise only to hire union members on US work and give them preference on foreign contracts, allowed sympathy strikes and arbitration, and required ABC subcontractors to abide by the contract. The 1902 tentative agreement was the template for contracts until 1915. It didn't limit work hours or the use of machines and tools and allowed a 12-hour day, effectively giving up control over the length of work (absolute surplus value) and the productivity of work (relative surplus value) that could be imposed on the ironworkers.

Despite its limitations, the agreement was an impressive acquisition of a closed shop in exchange for compromising hours and wages. It guaranteed work for its members and established some control by the union over the industry. However, local unions rejected the national contract in favour of local contracts and prevented its ratification. After the vote the union adopted a new strategy of coordinated national action rather than focusing strictly on local issues during the 1902 Philadelphia strike against ABC.[4] If it had been ratified, the agreement could have established a precedent of patterned bargaining replicated with the other companies in the industry.

After the local unions voted down the tentative national agreement, the IAB-SIW launched a national strike against ABC on 12 March 1903 resulting in its first national contract signed 12 April 1903, a few weeks after the employers reorganised their National Erectors' Association (NEA). After only seven years of existence, the national contract established uniform working conditions, hours, and wages. The settlement was a boon to the National Civic Federation (NCF), which helped settle the strike by bringing together Buchanan and J.P. Morgan, establishing its credentials as a labour conflict mediator.

The agreement was not as good as the earlier tentative agreement. It was an open shop agreement on paper that allowed the company to fire anyone, as long as it was not related to union membership, and protected scabs, prohibited strikes and sympathy strikes, lockouts or work stoppages, required local arbitration, set an 8- or 9-hour working day, and did not include a minimum wage rate.

Subcontractors were covered by the contract according to a verbal agreement. This soon become a flashpoint once the IABSIW realised how expansively US Steel was moving into the industry under the guise of sub-contracting out to ostensibly independent firms who were not parties to the contract, and in fact turned out to be wholly owned by US Steel.[5] This was the IABSIW's deadli-

---

4 Ibid., pp. 21–3.
5 Ibid., p. 41.

est mistake. In its hubris, it failed to adequately perceive US Steel's strategy to consolidate the industry and create a new composition of capital to meet the ironworkers' power.[6]

Although the contract was short-lived, the IABSIW's de-mobilisation and de-escalation for what it thought were long terms gains turned out to give capital several short-term strategic advantages. First, by de-escalating tactics the contract provided a momentary pause, giving the NEA time to organise and retaliate to meet the growing threat. The now empowered and confident NEA refused to renew the national contract, leaving only a few local contracts in place for the rest of the year.

The key to the shift of power to the companies was the resurgence of the NEA. The NEA 'has within the past twenty years undergone an evolution from a weak negotiatory organization in New York City to a strong belligerent national association'.[7] With 50 member companies, NEA member companies fabricated and erected about 75–80 percent of the structural steel and iron, giving it an exceptional monopoly over the national industry. It had no written constitution or by-laws and an annual budget of $30k which grew during the campaign to smash the IABSIW, with $50k spent in a two to three year period on its secret service alone.

The second advantage was that the contract transformed the union into a disciplinary mechanism to tamp down on recalcitrant locals and militant workers. When an employer locked out New York City Local 2, which was dominated by Italian-Jewish radicals, for refusing to accept the contract, Buchanan sided with employers and broke it up.[8]

The NEA borrowed from the strategy J.P. Morgan had used a few years earlier in the coal mines. In 1905, the NEA signed contracts with locals in large cities while refusing to do so in small cities in order to prevent the recomposition of workers in the industry. By doing so, the companies could assure a continued flow of steel in organised plants even if struck in the urban ones. Realising that it was being encircled, the IABSIW called a national strike on 10 August 1905 against ABC for subcontracting out work and then denying they had done so.

Despite escalating to a strike, the IABSIW's strategy was severely flawed in three ways. First, it failed to recognise that US Steel continued to subcontract to non-union firms that it already owned. Second, it failed to adapt its tactics

---

6 While US Steel was undertaking consolidation primarily in the US, Silver notes that the process of consolidation and workers' resistance to the new composition of capital was a global process. (Silver 2003, p. 132).

7 Bonnett 1922, pp. 137–9.

8 Grant 195b, pp. 11–12, 27–8, 29, and 31–2; and Montgomery 1974, p. 517.

to the new composition of capital once it had a better understanding of how J.P. Morgan was using US Steel to vertically integrate the industry. Lastly, it failed to realise the strategic importance of J.P. Morgan's horizontal integration across related industrial sectors.

The new composition of capital paralleled the reorganisation of the NEA to better serve the consolidated industry. The NEA consolidated its local members by replacing its confederated organisational structure with a unified central organisation.

> In anticipation of this movement, a commissioner [Walter Drew] had been secured in March and preparations made for the opening of employment bureaus and the taking of such steps as might become necessary. A working agreement for mutual assistance and co-operation was made with the Allied Iron Associations of New York City, which had also adopted the open-shop policy, and the affairs of all the associations were placed in the hands of one commissioner. Employment bureaus were conducted in New York, Pittsburgh, Cincinnati, Chicago, Cleveland, and temporary recruiting stations were established at other places at different times ... In order better to carry on its fight against the union, the Association has established and maintains District Offices and Labor Bureaus in New York City, Pittsburgh, Pa., Cleveland, O., Kansas City, Mo., Buffalo, N.Y., Milwaukee, Wis., and Philadelphia, Pa.[9]

Capital had put into place a new composition of power at both the point of production and policy to meet the power of the ironworkers to disrupt the industry.

The IABSIW was unusual among other AFL unions in its willingness to escalate its tactics to counter capital's tactical escalation. As the iron assembly industry was being reorganised on a national basis, the union attempted to do so as well. Due to insufficient progress in doing so, Buchanan was ousted by the insurgent membership at the September 1905 convention and replaced by Frank Ryan.[10] The IABSIW's tactics of consolidation were surprisingly similar to US Steel's. After affiliating with the AFL in 1903, in 1904 IABSIW began raiding the United Metal Workers International Union (UMWIU) which organised the

---

9   Bonnett 1922, p. 140.

10   Buchanan had been exposed for owning stock in the McCain Construction Company which was then fighting the union. Despite this duplicity, he was later elected to Congress in 1911, became the chief organiser of the New York Central Federated Union, and established the National Peace Council that opposed WWI and claimed 1 million members by July 1915. (Grant 1915b, pp. 35–7; and Foner 1987, pp. 51, 54).

unorganised along industrial lines through a city-wide metal workers' council. In 1904, the AFL planned to split up the UMWIU and distribute its members to the trades unions, but it withdrew and reformed in 1905 as part of the IWW.[11]

However unsavoury the IABSIW's strategy of taking over unions in plants they did not organise, it was an attempt to counter US Steel's strategy of preventing new plants from being organised.

> The policy of the U.S. Steel Corporation at the time of its formation and for several years thereafter, was to prevent the spread of organization among its employees, rather than to crush existing organizations. This policy, pursued to its logical conclusion, would in the end have the effect of crushing the unions, but the process would be gradual and attract less public attention than an open fight resulting in strikes or lockouts.[12]

US Steel did this by subcontracting out work to their subsidiaries whose ownership they had obscured. US Steel, as did other trusts, organised holding companies as means of the recomposing the power of capital by overcoming the problem of workers striking at choke points in the industry. With a single nationally integrated corporation controlling a large share of an industry, production could be more easily shifted around to outmanoeuvre local or even regional strikes. While much attention has been given to holding companies and trusts to consolidate market power, little has been said about it as a strategy to confront the threat of workers organising across industries and be able to use their leverage to disrupt the entire industry at various choke points.

Another obvious solution to avoiding such disruption was to sign an industry-wide contract with a union that could then be expected to prevent disruption at the risk of violating the contract. Although IABSIW offered just that, US Steel's strategy was moving along another entirely different track. The company sought to control enough of the industry that any strikes that did occur would be unable to create sufficient disruption. The rationalisation of the industry under the integrated national ownership of a single company would prevent the recomposition of workers in that industry and the formation of a single union that could circulate a strike nationally in order to open up multiple geographically separated choke points in order to create leverage by disrupting national production.

---

11   Ramirez 1978, pp. 112–13.
12   Grant 1915b, p. 46.

Using the contract to prevent the organising of workers at the supposedly independent contractors was central to this strategy.

> The negotiations before and during the strike of the steel workers show that the company was determined to prevent the spread of unionism, but was not opposed to making contracts for mills already organised. In defense of this policy, it is generally admitted that when the US Steel Corporation was formed, some of the subsidiary companies which had been non-union, made it a condition of their entering the combine, that the open shop policy would be continued in their plants.[13]

The IABSIW was unaware at the time that the US Steel policy executive committee had passed a resolution on 17 June 1901, six weeks after it was formed, instructing all subsidiaries not to allow unions where they didn't currently exist. The resolution read

> That we are unalterably opposed to any extension of union labor, and advise subsidiary companies to take firm position when these questions come up, and say that they are not going to recognize it – that is, any extension of unions in mills where they do not now exist – that great care should be used to prevent trouble, and that they promptly report and confer with this corporation.[14]

While the 1935 NLRA requires recognition and collective bargaining, a variation on this strategy used today is negotiating which class of workers at which shop are included in a fundamental bargaining unit.

US Steel was also motivated to avoid further unionisation and concessions for fear investors would question its ability to turn consolidation into a higher return on investment. The company was particular vulnerable as its stock, estimated to be watered by 50 percent, was being challenged by investors. US Steel's share price and return on investment had been declining steadily. Its poor rate of profit was coupled with a share price that had declined from its $55.00 high in 1901 to $9.00 in 1904. Its common dividend was cut in the fourth quarter of 1903 and in 1904 it earned only 7.6 percent on its investments, down from 15.9 percent in 1902. Its share of the steel market was shrinking rapidly,

---

13   Ibid., p. 47.
14   Gompers, 1 February 1913, p. 622.

dropping from 61.6 percent of the entire steel output in 1901 to 39.9 percent in 1920.[15] The long costly integration strategy to outmanoeuvre the coal, steel and ironworkers contributed to the decline of US Steel's dominant position in all three industries.

Once the company could purge its financial liabilities, and thereby insulate itself from anxious investors, the company would have more room to manoeuvre against the union. The IABSIW

> realised time was on the side of the employer, that if the union were unable to establish itself before the United States Steel had solidified its financial position by disposing of a large block of securities, it would be virtually banished from the industry.[16]

The merger creating US Steel was close to the tail end of the wave of mergers. Mergers were a crucial answer to a recomposed working-class, a 'fundamental change in ruling class strategies' that reduced the costs of damaging competition and created the managerial mechanisms to respond to the threat.[17] Yet, consolidation was costly and hard to maintain. US Steel's difficulty maintaining a high return on investment was hardly unique. As the concentration of capital slowed so did the return on investment, available investment capital, and output. Between 1907 and 1915, mergers dropped to about 25 percent what they were in the previous ten years. The total capital invested in manufacturing between 1909 and 1914 increased at half the rate of the previous decade and output declined by one-third compared to the previous five years.[18]

These developments, what Marx called the tendency of the rate of profit to fall, were a result of the changing composition of capital and human labour.[19] As Glaberman and Rawick elaborated Marx's idea,

> The more technologically advanced capitalism becomes, the greater the proportion of nonvalue-producing constant capital (means of production) required to put relatively lesser amounts of variable capital (labor) in motion. Since the rate of profit is determined by the ratio of profit

15   Kolko 1963, pp. 33–4 and 37.
16   Perlman and Taft 1935, p. 102.
17   Silver 2003, p. 136.
18   Ramirez 1978, p. 132.
19   Marx 1863–83, pp. 317–78.

TABLE 3   *Rate of return on capital in California, 1860–1900*

Capital	($m)	Rate of profit/return on capital (percent)
1860	22	58.1
1870	39.7	45.5
1880	61.2	36.8
1890	146.8	26.6
1900	205.4	24.9

SHOUP 2010, P. 389

(surplus value) to total investment (constant plus variable capital), as the proportion of constant capital continues to rise, so the rate of profit must tend to fall.[20]

Capital responds to disobedient and insurgent workers by increasing the composition of constant capital (technology) relative to variable capital (workers) which in turn further increases the productivity of the latter while reducing profits per unit of production. The key outcome, what has been called the 'zerowork paradox', is that as capitalism relies on fewer and fewer workers to produce more and more goods and services, the usefulness of it as a social system for keeping the population under control declines.[21] It is at this point that class struggle threatens to rupture capital's dialectic.[22]

The declining return on capital investment was not exclusive to J.P. Morgan but was endemic to the economy. In California, for example, despite a nearly ten-fold increase in invested capital, the rate of return on investment declined by more than one-half (see Table 3).[23]

Wages hardly kept pace with rising productivity. 'Output per worker has risen 471 percent from 1899 to 1966, while the average real purchasing power of the wages of these workers before taxes has risen only 345 percent in the same period of time'. Although money and real wages increased, relative wages declined because of the cheapening of commodities.[24] In the post-Fordist era

---

20   Glaberman and Rawick 1977, p. 214.

21   Caffentzis 2013, pp. 150–5.

22   Cleaver 2016.

23   Shoup 2010, p. 389.

24   The rate in which output eclipses wages reflects the weakened ability of workers to disrupt production resulting in a net inflow of capital into 'developed' economies. Heilbroner

today productivity continues to rise as wages fall due to the decomposition of working-class power.

US Steel was pursuing a costly strategy to consolidate its control across several integrated industries in order to counter the threat of disruption. It was a race against falling profits, falling dividends, and a plummeting return on investment that threatened to become undone.

The Strike

Without fully assessing the emerging composition of capital arrayed against them, the leadership of the national unions fell into the trap set by the companies to accept unions and contracts where they had existed before a merger. To achieve the low cost gains of negotiating a contract over a limited part of the industry, the leadership prevented the tactical escalation demanded by the rank and file, expecting a greater opportunity for an industry-wide contract later. By preventing further mobilisation and escalation they raised the costs of pursuing an industry-wide contract. The leadership's purposeful de-escalation to make partial gains eventually raised the costs of holding onto or extending them.

The climax to this duel was the strike against ABC for subcontracting with National Tube Company to build the tube mill at McKeesport. The IABSIW escalated its tactics by setting into motion a 'secondary boycott' of two supposedly unrelated companies in order to enforce the union's power over supposedly 'independent' subcontractors which were in fact US Steel subsidiaries.

However, the union mistakenly allowed members to work on subcontracted non-union jobs to earn wages, hoping it would sustain their commitment to the strike on the struck companies. The approach was not new; the New York local received approval to allow its members to work on non-union jobs in 1908 and it became national union policy until 1913. But it was controversial because the members saw it as a losing strategy. It weakened the union, as men left the union and sought non-union jobs since there was no longer any leverage from being a member. Allowing some members to work on non-union subcontrac-

---

noted a shift between 1897 and 1969 from US Foreign Direct Investment (FDI) moving opposite to expectations. During this time, US FDI was moving from primarily agriculture, mining, and railroads to manufacturing but also from the underdeveloped increasingly to the developed world. (Glaberman and Rawick 1977, pp. 200–1 and 224). Today this is being promoted as 'in-shoring' as productivity continues to rise and wages continue to fall in the US.

ted projects (the 'local option') undermined the union membership's effort to make 'a stand for all the work, or none'. If locals allowed their members to take non-union subcontracted work it would destroy the union's strategy of forcing a national contract on the companies.[25] But by working elsewhere during the strike, the strikers actually helped sustain production during the strike, thereby quarantining its impact to an isolated sector of industry. IABSIW's strategy horribly misfired and the strike was lost.

In response, the membership revolted once more at the Philadelphia convention. It banned all union officers from making a verbal contract for US Steel to hire union men on subcontracted work, effectively making them strikebreakers, in order to defend the local threatened by the subcontracting. The IABSIW rank and file clearly understood that 'Unless the union treated all of the mills of a combine as a single unit, there was nothing to prevent the combine from defeating the union by shifting work from union to non-union plants with no inconvenience to itself'.[26]

At a time when AFL officials would cut back-room deals and ignore the membership's demands, the IABSIW's rank and file's unwillingness to concede on the non-union contractor issue demonstrated that it was 'too democratic ... Successful prosecution of a war, or a strike, demands centralized authority'.[27]

> There were ways through which a single local could easily have been brought to time [sic] by the international. But Mr. Ryan was too conscientious to go against the expressed instructions of the convention and so committed a fatal blunder.[28]

While an assertive rank and file was undesirable to the Commission on Industrial Relations, it reflected the difficulty union leadership continued to have with unruly workers who preferred disruption rather than conciliation to achieve their goals.

When it became clear that the rank and file would prevent the IABSIW from being easily converted to an instrument to control and discipline the workers, the NEA declared open warfare on the union and escalated its tactics.

> The experience of the ironworkers in dealing with large corporations, may have taught them to hesitate before placing absolute power in the hands

---

25   Grant 1915b, pp. 65 and 68–71.

26   Perlman and Taft 1935, p. 101.

27   Grant 1915b, p. 51.

28   Ibid., p. 52.

of their officers, but there seems little doubt that the failure to do so, prevented a settlement of the strike in October, 1905, and brought on the
open shop warfare in the structural iron industry, which five years later
attracted the attention of the entire country.[29]

It became clear that any settlement between the industry and the IABSIW could
not be depended upon.

Capital's Counter-attack

The NEA's constitution called for an 'open shop' which it achieved by breaking the IABSIW's sympathy strike against ABC. NEA ratcheted up its tactics by
demanding a non-union clause in subcontractor contracts and even required
they pay a cash bond to make sure it remained an open shop.[30] Companies
that violated this rule were dropped from membership. In no time, few companies were under contract, mostly small independent companies that were
being rapidly squeezed by the larger US Steel. The NEA had found a way to use
the union contract against the workers.

Like the General Managers Association during the 1894 railroad strike, the
NEA designed new tactics and strategies that became a model for other industry
trade groups. The NEA was described as 'undoubtedly the most class-conscious
and belligerent national association in America today', seeking to not only
defend the interests of the industry but all capital by cooperating with the
National Association of Manufacturers and as a member of the Industrial Conference Board.[31] The NEA was adept at evaluating the situation and organising,
purchasing and deploying the necessary tactics, strategies and resources to
build an effective alliance to share employment bureaus to recruit strikebreakers, share resources, and coordinate their anti-union campaign. The NEA agilely
worked the polity, lobbying and testifying before Congress against any AFL
sponsored legislation, supported a ban on strikes in utilities, and opposed mandatory federal arbitration during WWI (see Chapter 8), although it never used
a court injunction during a strike.[32]

---

29   Ibid., p. 51.
30   Ibid., p. 73.
31   Bonnett 1922, p. 141.
32   In contrast to other industry organisations, the NEA publicly claimed to support man-
      datory arbitration, although there is no evidence it actually arbitrated any issue with the
      IABSIW. (Ibid., pp. 141–2, 144, and 149).

The NEA's campaign effectively allowed the companies to further shift power from the ironworkers in just a few short years. By 1913, NEA US Steel affiliated members controlled 75 percent of fabricated steel production in addition to iron structure assembly. ABC, the target of the 1903 strike, alone fabricated 35 percent of all structural steel.[33]

Compounding IABSIW's mistake in allowing members to take non-union jobs during a strike was the lack of solidarity from other building trades workers. Although this was partly caused by the lack of organised workers in some of the firms in smaller urban and rural areas, it was also a consequence of IABSI's notorious record of raiding another union.

The open shop firms controlled practically all the bridge work, where there are no other unions to assist the ironworkers by sympathetic strikes. The union, on the other hand, controlled practically all the building construction work in cities where the ironworkers are supported by other trades.[34] Even with allied unions, no strike rules in the building trades made solidarity strikes difficult to launch. In NYC, for example, building trades unions were not allowed to call strikes on any work being done by members of the Building Trades Employers' Association.

Part of the NEA's aggressive strategy was its willingness to unilaterally escalate its tactics. The NEA didn't merely mobilise a stronger coalition and manoeuvre to prevent the IABSIW from nationalising a strike. It further escalated its tactics to sabotage the union from within by hiring private police to work as informers and agent provocateurs that planted false evidence of a bombing campaign and then carried out their own manufactured conspiracies. Private police have an inherent conflict of interest that leads them to manufacture the very threats they are hired to uncover. As Luke Grant wrote in a Commission on Industrial Relations report,

> If they [private police] find that labor unions are not criminal organizations and that acts of lawlessness never are discussed in union meetings, they have nothing to report to those employing them. If they do not report matters which the detective agencies employing them can carry to corporations to frighten them, it follows that they cannot last long as spies, or 'operatives' as they are professionally known. The very nature of the business, therefore, makes it virtually necessary for the spy to do either of two things. Either he must make reports that are false, in which case

---

33   Grant 1915b, pp. 15–17, 53–4, and 75.
34   Ibid., pp. 17–18.

discovery would be inevitable sooner or later, or he must create a basis on which to furnish truthful reports. The latter plan is the better suited to his purposes, and he governs himself accordingly.[35]

Grant concluded that such spies are 'ready to go to almost any extreme to please those who employ them'. During the 1903 strike, IABSIW president Buchanan had eight spies on his staff who were paid by ABC. It is estimated that about 25 IABSIW members were on the company payroll as spies, some of them serving as local officers.[36]

The NEA soon escalated beyond using private police merely to collect information but to generate it by attempting to carry out a false flag bombing. According to Grant,

> In the spring of 1906, a man named Guthrie was admitted to the New Jersey local. A short time afterward, with two other members of the union he was arrested carrying dynamite into a building being erected by Post & McCord at Twenty-second street and Second avenue in New York City. He was released on bonds, said to have been furnished by a member of the Iron League Employers' Association. The other men pleaded guilty and were sent to prison. Guthrie disappeared.[37]

This was but 'a part of the espionage system to control the union and destroy its effectiveness'.[38]

The suspicion of spies in the union provoked a reciprocal tactical escalation by the Ryan leadership. Realising that the companies were both unwilling to negotiate while escalating their tactics to infiltrate, disrupt, and destroy the IABSIW, the leadership launched its own strategy of tension.

> It aroused in them a feeling of bitter antagonism against the firms opposing them, that made reprisals natural, if not inevitable. The ironworkers felt that the existence of their union was being threatened from without and within. That did not justify the resort to physical violence and the destruction of property which marked the fight against the open shop, but it suggests an explanation for the attitude of mind which made such acts possible.[39]

---

35   Ibid., pp. 99 and 100.
36   Ibid., p. 102.
37   Ibid., p. 101.
38   Ibid., p. 104.
39   Ibid.

With all avenues to either a peaceful resolution of grievances through negotiations or a limited strike blocked, the IABSIW planned a series of targeted
armed attacks coordinated by the brothers James and John McNamara and a
small cell of members. Unbeknown to them was that the cell was infiltrated
by paid agents of the NEA who prodded and facilitated the attacks. Without
mobilising mass support, the cost of escalating to the use of armed attacks dramatically raised the costs to the workers while the opportunity of making gains
from doing so fell in inverse ratio.

The McNamara Bombing Campaign

The IABSIW began targeting a non-union steel job in summer 1905. Over the
coming years the bombings targeted unfinished jobs, and destroyed material
non-union job sites, on rail cars, in storage yards, derricks, cranes and various
equipment, causing relatively little financial loss and damage and no loss of life
until the *Los Angeles Times* building bombing.[40]

The flash point that brought about the IABSIW's downfall was the 1 October
1910 explosion at the *Los Angeles Times* building in support of a monumental
attempt to expand the organising campaign to Southern California. The target
was Harrison Otis's *Los Angeles Times*, the point man for the open shop movement in the city which refused to negotiate with any union. San Francisco had
become a closed shop city run by the Labor Party which had a majority in the
city and county government. The McNamara's bombed the *Los Angeles Times*
building as part of campaign to end open shops in Los Angeles so that workers
in San Francisco and Los Angeles would no longer be pitted against each other.

Although the IABSIW claimed to have nothing to do with the *Los Angeles
Times* explosion, treasurer James McNamara's guilty plea appeared to have
implicated the union and allowed the companies to escalate its tactics by using
the government to further repress it. Although the explosion and fire killed 21
people and injured many, it did not actually wreck the building or stop the
presses. The bomb blew up barrels of printer's ink which caught fire because
they contained petroleum. Workers in the building had been warned that the
building was a firetrap. The fire spread quickly, suffocating or burning the vic-
tims to death.[41]

---

40   Fine 1991, pp. 6–7.
41   Grant 1915b, pp. 121–2.

For about three years, the majority of the bombings were carried out by paid private police agents who had infiltrated the union. The NEA Executive Council created a Committee on Dynamiting on 14 April 1908 and a secret service agency on 19 July 1909. The NEA placed spies in high level positions in the union and one as a janitor in the union's headquarters. As Walter Drew, the NEA's commissioner and legal counsel warned in a letter of 3 February 1911, the 'dynamiting habit', if not suppressed, would become 'thoroughly entrenched as an incident of labor troubles'. But rather than suppress it, they made it their own while giving the exclusive credit to the IABSIW as a classic false flag campaign. It's no wonder that Drew claimed to know who carried out nearly all the bombings.[42] Perhaps Drew intended to so discredit the IABSIW with the bombings that no union would dare risk being accused of following the same strategy.

During the Indianapolis dynamite conspiracy trials one of NEA's infiltrators H.S. Hockin made a shocking revelation about the dynamiters' activities. Hockin revealed that he had been informing L.L. Jewel, a manager at the McClintic-Marshall Construction Company, of the bombing campaign. Jewel had turned over this evidence to the US Secret Service and detective William Burns, who had been hired by the Los Angeles mayor to investigate the *Los Angeles Times* building bombing.

A member of the IABSIW Executive Board, Hockin was suspected of planning many of the bombings and pocketing funds for the campaign by short-changing dynamiter Ortie McManigal on his fee. After coordinating the dynamite campaign for three years Hockin reported McManigal and the McNamara brothers as the *Los Angeles Times* bombers. It must have been relatively simple to use McManigal as the fall guy because, according to a journalist who extensively covered the trials, McManigal actually put frozen dynamite on the radiator to thaw it out and once found his young daughter playing with it when he returned home.[43]

Yet, even after Hockin reported McManigal and McNamara, the NEA purposely let the bombings continue.[44] McManigal and the McNamaras carried out eight to ten more bombings until they were arrested on 11 April 1911. One reason for the delay was that the two private police agencies were not collabor-

---

42   Fine 1991, pp. 8 and 11.

43   Fitch 1913, p. 609.

44   According to Fine betrayal and deceit was layered upon betrayal and deceit. Hockin remained part of the union even through the trial until it ended in December 1912. During this time he was involved in at least one more bombing and went to work for Burns after the trial. (Fine 1991, pp. 9–10).

ating with one another because Burns did not share the information obtained by tracking McManigal and James McNamara with Drew. The operation of the covert infiltration campaign confirmed Grant's observation 'that it does not appear that it always is the work of detectives to prevent the commission of crime'.[45] Hockin took over as Secretary and Treasurer when McNamara was convicted, while still working as an informant.

The Burns Agency arrested the McNamara brothers, smuggling John Mc-Namara and McManigal out of Indiana in violation of Indiana's extradition law. Drew accompanied the Los Angeles Assistant District Attorney and Indianapolis Superintendent of Police when the extradition papers for John McNamara were delivered to Indiana Governor Marshall. The governor had John Mc-Namara arrested, arraigned at a brief hearing, and turned over to Los Angeles detective Hossick and Burns, who drove him to California in a car. The NEA effectively privatised the extradition with the cooperation of authorities from two states.[46] The events that followed the illegal extradition by a private police agent illustrated how the courts were closed to workers as an avenue to protect their Fourth, Fifth, Sixth, Eighth, and Tenth Amendment rights. Drew, Burns, and two others involved in the extradition, as well as NEA's staffer investigating the dynamiting cases, were arrested for kidnapping the suspects and held by the grand jury in Marion County, Indianapolis. City police court judge Collins fined Drew $1 for assault and battery on a police officer sent to arrest them and then dropped the fine. The grand jury refused to indict Drew and two others but returned indictments on Burns and the Los Angeles detective and then later dismissed the charges. Judge Collins wasn't through yet serving the NEA. He gave Drew a search warrant to search the IABSIW's Indianapolis headquarters in the American Central Life Building, where they seized records and found as many as 19 sticks of dynamite in addition to another 541 sticks at McManigal's fathers' farm.[47] McManigal, who was paid by both the McNamaras and employers, was called as the prime witness at the trial, convicted of perjury, and served a two-year sentence. James and John entered guilty pleas to avoid the death sentence for James. John served 15 years in prison and James served a life sentence, dying in San Quentin prison in 1941.

---

45   Grant 1915b, pp. 105–6.

46   This case mimicked the one a few years earlier in Colorado in which Western Federation of Miners officers Charles Moyer, William Haywood and L.J. Simpkins were similarly taken out of the state by secretly obtained extradition papers and without being able to file a *habeas* petition. (Witte 1932, pp. 162–3).

47   Fine 1991, pp. 15–16.

Not only did the NEA orchestrate the arrests and extradition – it also privately funded the investigation and prosecution. NEA paid for guards to secure the grand jury room and the evidence, secured witnesses, persuaded the US attorney in Indianapolis to take the case, and with a contribution from the Merchants' and Manufacturers' Association of Los Angeles paid the Los Angeles District Attorney John Fredericks at least $75,000 in 1911. Drew and the Los Angeles District Attorney, who consulted privately with the NEA on legal matters, pushed for a federal trial for carrying explosives on the railroads and a conspiracy charge. Along with the bombers, the Los Angeles grand jury also indicted San Francisco labour leaders reportedly involved in the *Los Angeles Times* bombing, but the charges were eventually dismissed.[48] All but two of those who were indicted, a carpenter and Olaf Tveitmoe, a cement worker and secretary of the San Francisco Building Trades Council, were members of IAB-SIW.

The NEA also aided the US Federal Attorney in Indianapolis in 1912 with legal training, staff, a potential witness, helped write the government's brief, had a dictograph placed in Ryan's office, and paid some of the government's expenses preparing for the grand jury. At the Indiana trial the defendants had 15 defence lawyers, including a then Indiana US Senator, former Special Assistant US Attorney and 1908 Democratic Party candidate for Vice President, former Philadelphia Assistant District Attorney, and a former Missouri US Attorney.[49] Despite the all-star defence team, the judge refused to allow any evidence concerning the manner in which the employers fought the unions or the conditions of life and work for the workers.

The NEA's state and federal legal campaign against the IABSIW hit pay dirt on 6 February 1912 when the federal grand jury in Indianapolis indicted 54 union members, 51 from the IABSIW, including all the top leadership and local officers, on 32 counts of conspiracy.[50] Of the 51, 46 were eventually arraigned and 45 went to trial on 1 October with bonds totalling $340,000. Of the 40 whose trials concluded, all but two were found guilty. Five received suspended sentences and the others received one to seven years. On 1 January 1913, 33

---

48   The journalist John Fitch was allowed into the document room in the Federal Building in
      which evidence turned over by the District Attorney was guarded and maintained by the
      NEA. (Fitch 1913, p. 616; and Fine 1991, pp. 18–26 and 29).

49   Fitch 1913, p. 613; and Fine 1991, pp. 33–4 and 301.

50   According to a journalist who covered the trials extensively at the time, 'The charge at
      Indianapolis was not murder nor the dynamiting of buildings; it was a charge of conspir-
      acy to transport explosives on passenger trains from one state into another, and aiding
      and abetting in accomplishing that end'. (Fitch 1913, p. 607).

arrived at Leavenworth prison and were released on bonds totalling $2.14 million. Of the 30 who appealed, the Court of Appeals for the 7th Circuit upheld the sentences for 24 men, including Ryan, and sent six back for retrials. After years of expense that drained the union of funds and mass support, only one of the six was later convicted in the retrial. The US Supreme Court refused a *writ of certiorari* leaving the sentences for the 24 standing. Two others who were on the run were captured in 1915 and convicted in 1916.

Drew also aided the state in prosecuting IABSIW's attorney Clarence Darrow twice for bribery, but he was acquitted in both jury trials. To drive in the stake further, Drew also pursued damage suits against the union. After the trial McManigal was paid a substantial sum of money by the NEA which also supported two other witnesses until or near their deaths in 1919 and 1924.[51]

Estimating the Costs

In all, prior to the deadly *Los Angeles Times* bombing, no one had been killed, and the average financial loss from all the explosions was about $1,000. Only a few attacks actually caused damage in the thousands of dollars. Because the larger firms had dynamite insurance there was little to no financial loss except for the need for more guards. From 1906 to the end of 1911, there were about 100 attempted or actual explosions.[52] By one estimate, of the approximately 70 explosions between February 1908 to April 1911, only 43 were on NEA member property. Of the 70, co-conspirator McManigal was involved in 20 and the McNamaras in 16. The question that has never been resolved is who carried out the other 34 explosions. One possible explanation is that they were set as false flag operations to discredit the IABSIW.[53]

In contrast, before the *Los Angeles Times* bombing the only mortalities in the struggle were caused by the NEA's open shop campaign. In its first few years, three guards were killed and about 100 non-union ironworkers and company guards were assaulted.[54] This doesn't include the many killed on the job. Commenting on the later trials Gompers asked:

51 Fine 1991, pp. 33–5 and 37–8.
52 Adamic gives a higher estimate that the IABSIW dynamited about 150 buildings and bridges in the US and Canada (Adamic 1931, p. 141).
53 Grant 1915b, pp. 122–3.
54 Ross and Taft 1969, np.

> Just what is the social interpretation of the alleged crimes, the trial, and the conviction? Whether or not there was a conspiracy to do violence by some labor men, is there any doubt that there was a conspiracy by 'big business' to disrupt organised labor?[55]

However, no one was ever held accountable for the loss in life, money, and other resources from the use of a bombing campaign by the companies and the NEA. The lack of legal and financial accountability demonstrated that the costs of tactical escalation of carrying out false flag bombings were low and the opportunity to use them for the ultimate objective to crush organised workers were extremely high.

The cost of the dynamite conspiracy to the IABSIW was not merely in appearance but was used as a financial weapon to bankrupt the union. The criminal prosecutions and civil suits that followed allowed the companies to shift the costs of their own campaign to the workers. According to Grant,

> The Dynamite Conspiracy Trials, as a result of which twenty-two former officials of the ironworkers' union, in addition to the McNamara brothers, are now serving sentences in a federal prison, cost the organization [IABSIW] at least $150,000 as shown by the records, independent of what the ironworkers contributed to the defense of the McNamara brothers. If to this sum is added the price paid to the actual agents who wrought the work of destruction, together with their expenses, it will be seen that the average cost to the union of each explosion was about $2,000, or twice the estimated cost to the employers. In addition the union is continuing to pay $25 a week to each of the men in prison ...[56]

The Strategy of Tension

The bombing campaign was embraced at the highest levels of the IABSIW leadership, as they believed it offered them a source of leverage against the companies, offsetting the declining opportunity to achieve their objectives by striking. The Commission's Grant explained their strategy in his report on the bombing campaign:

---

55   Gompers 1913, p. 622.
56   Grant 1915b, pp. 123–4.

it is the fear of possible assault that brings results; not moral suasion. The 'moral suasion' argument is good in the courtroom or on the public platform, but around the factory it counts for practically nothing. Every one with practical experience of conditions knows that.[57]

The IABSIW was locked out from the bargaining table, unable to expand mass support, impeded from expanding the strike, and under pressure from its militant members to escalate its tactics to match that of the companies that fought any attempt to improve working conditions, wages, or safety. Grant insightfully explained that locked out of the polity where they could seek redress for their grievances and facing an adversary unwilling to negotiate, the IABSIW was left with only one option: escalation.

There are some conditions, however, that cannot be improved by legislative enactment. The question of physical violence and violation of law, is therefore largely one of local conditions. As the laws are mainly designed to protect property rights, with little regard for human rights, it is inevitable that in fighting for the latter, the law will at times be violated.[58]

One of Grant's most insightful observations is that political change is the product of what could be called a working-class 'strategy of tension'.[59] Laws change in response to the seesaw struggle over power between capital and workers which drives progress and reform.

In the case of the lockout in the factory referred to, it might be possible for the workers to keep strictly within the law. They might submit to the conditions which the employer imposed, or they might quietly go about their business and find employment elsewhere, if they could. That is what the employer and what the law says they must do. But it is not human nature to do it. It is not the way of progress. Had the workers always taken the course which the letter of the law requires them to take, they would, in all probability still be working twelve or fourteen hours a day.[60]

---

57   Ibid., p. 110.

58   Ibid., pp. 111–12.

59   Although a 'strategy of tension' is associated with government counter-insurgency campaigns, such as in Italy against the autonomist movement and underground armed groups in the 1960–70s, I have adapted the term in reverse.

60   Grant 1915b, p. 112.

Force is written into the law as a hidden code that is rarely revealed except after the fact by historical investigation. According to Grant, force

> runs through our whole business and social life. Force is everywhere apparent, differing only in decree and method of application. The nature of the force is determined by the immediate environment, of the person applying it. It may be legitimate, that is, within the written law, or it may be otherwise according to circumstances. But it is there.[61]

Any claim that force is necessary to make lasting change must contend with what Rubenstein called 'the myth of peaceful progress' that change is made through pluralist coalitions, give and take, negotiations, compromise, and de-escalation.[62]

Because force on behalf of capital is obscured by the laws and norms of the time, only its use by workers ends up in the spotlight of public attention, abuse, denunciation and scorn. While the NEA resorted to several types of force only those used by the IABSIW have been remembered.

To recognise the role of force in making laws and norms is not enough. There is a different normative signifier depending on the context and the class which both inflicts and gains from it. Grant insightfully observed that

> The use of force may be a symptom of savagery or of strength and virility, according to the point of view and the object for which it is invoked. In legalized warfare the man who fights and maims his fellows, is hailed as a hero. In an industrial war the man who maims an opponent is termed a 'thug.' Monuments are erected to the memory of one and prison doors yawn open to receive the other. In both instances violence is committed. And the law of property rights makes the difference.[63]

With its use of force shielded by a system of law established to protect property, capital may escalate its tactics to the use of violence with little or no legal or normative cost for doing so.

---

61   Ibid., pp. 112–13.
62   Rubenstein 1970, pp. 7 and 13.
63   Grant 1915b, p. 113.

Dynamite was Tried: The Effectiveness of Escalation

The employers, through the NEA, escalated their tactics by deploying a campaign of false flag bombing attacks only one-third to one-half of which could be attributed to the IABSIW cell. Tactical escalation allowed the companies to exploit the opportunity to complete the reorganisation of the structural iron industry with little direct resistance from the ironworkers. According to Grant, as a result of the false flag bombing campaign

> the National Erectors' Association is today in a stronger position than it ever occupied ... Its membership controls a larger proportion of the steel erection work than it did when the fight began. Its force of open shop workers are more efficient due to their greater experience ... [and] some of its members were protected against financial loss through dynamite insurance ...[64]

The NEA could carry out the campaign with little cost to its credibility, as the media widely attributed it to anarchists, militants, and the labour movement, claims which only grew louder after the arrests. While lowering the costs for the industry, it dramatically raised them for the IABSIW. As the agent provocateurs were being directed by an informer sitting on the union board, it served to redirect and divert the union's efforts from mobilising and building mass support, deflecting it from engaging the companies where its strength and leverage lay. Because the target locations of the bombings were designed to cause minimal damage, they had little disruptive effect on industry. The greatest disruption was inflicted on the union, redirecting attention, resources, and personnel to carry out a futile and ineffective bombing campaign. Once the cell was captured and dozens more supporters and allies prosecuted, the costs of a campaign that returned little rose dramatically, costing the union credibility, financial resources, public support, allies, and leverage over the industry.

The bombing campaign opened a clear path for the NEA to achieve its objectives. It not only removed an impediment to industry consolidation and integration, the new composition of capital, but set back worker organisation in the iron and related sectors, especially among workers who had cooperated or publicly supported the IABSIW such as in San Francisco and Los Angeles.

---

64   Ibid., p. 124.

There was also a paradoxical outcome for the IABSIW, whose credibility lay in its apparent willingness to escalate tactics despite the declining opportunity to achieve its objectives through negotiations. Grant provided great insight into the process by which capital and workers travelled along the trajectory of violence. With all avenues for redress of their grievances closed, the ironworkers became willing to draw tactics from their repertoire, employing increasing levels of force and tension to achieve their goals. Describing the escalation from slugging to scattered attacks to sabotage in the course of the strike, Grant finds that

> As a rule in labor disputes where there is a resort to the destruction of property, it comes only after other methods to obtain the desired results have failed. The first form of violence comes in the shape of attacks on those who take the places vacated by strikers. When that proves ineffective; when the strikers find they cannot prevent the work being done, the next step is to seek to destroy that work.[65]

The ironworkers were already renowned for paying sluggers $150 to attack strikebreakers, and were unlikely to hesitate before further escalating. With the odds stacked heavily against them, the self-survival of its members and the fate of the union depended on it. Moving from slugging to dynamite became a means of not only protecting the well being of the workers but a survival strategy of a union on the brink of obliteration. Locked out and blacklisted men pressured the union to act, or at least appear to act, with force.

> Union men out of work daily see the open shop men at work. They complain to their business agent and at their union meetings. They declare they cannot find jobs while 'snakes' are steadily employed right under their noses. They demand to know what they are paying dues for. The business agent realises that a storm is brewing and he must do something ... The argument is logical and the union business agent knows it. If he does not make some effort to stop the non-union work, another firm, probably, will be lost to the union. He is pressed by the members of his union demanding protection from the unfair competition of the non-union man, and he is pressed by the union employer who demands protection against his unfair competitor. Neither suggests violence, but if the non-union firms will not meet the business agent or discuss conditions

---

65   Ibid., p. 132.

with him, he resorts to the only expedient which appears open to him. Either the non-union men are assaulted, or an attempt is made to destroy the work.[66]

Whether the bombing campaign was a widely held secret among the membership is unknown, but when it became public the rank and file rewarded the leadership even in costly defeat.

Unilateral escalation of tactics can easily become a self-fulfilling prophecy. The more the companies refused to make any concessions, the more the workers were left with the stark choice of either capitulating and returning in defeat or continue escalating with the expectation that it will eventually wring some concessions no matter how remote. They chose the latter. 'The main reason for the resort to dynamite is found in the uncompromising attitude of the open shop employers'.[67] Since ABC and US Steel refused to sign a contract covering shops not currently unionised, the union felt compelled to strike in 1905, and then escalate:

> Without a conference, no settlement of the strike was possible. For the union it meant either unconditional surrender or a fight to a finish. There was no middle course open while the employers refused to confer ... When the hopelessness of the situation became apparent to the union officials, resort was made to the destruction of property. Diplomacy was out of the question, so dynamite was tried. It proved to be a colossal blunder, as was the rejection of the peace terms offered in the beginning of the fight.[68]

But the 'colossal blunder' was really one-sided on behalf of the ironworkers who paid all the costs – or not.

The prosecution and conviction of the McNamaras actually bolstered their credibility. James reached a leadership position calling for escalation and, despite his deeds, he was true to his strategy, and the membership rewarded him and the other co-conspirators for it. Their convictions and prison sentences made them martyrs to their convictions that a strategy of tension, not capitulation, protects the workers, preserves the union, and gets the goods. Union leaders like the McNamaras were elected to their offices, Adamic asserted, because they

---

66   Ibid., pp. 135–7.

67   Ibid., p. 137.

68   Ibid., pp. 137–8.

believed in dynamite in the case of emergency. Behind their 'dynamite conspiracy,' as I have emphasized, was the desperation of big labor unions finding themselves face to face with brutal anti-union capitalist associations, behind their doings was the desperation of tens of thousands of workers to whom the union was the only hope of a better life.[69]

During the bombing campaign between 1905–6 and 1910–11 the IABSIW's membership grew about 30 percent, a few new locals were formed in small cites, and its budget grew nine-fold, despite the fact that it controlled a smaller fraction of the industry than before. Its organising efforts alongside the bombing campaign expanded its support and kept the leadership in office. Ryan was re-elected president, even in 1913, after he had been convicted and while awaiting appeal. James McNamara was re-elected as secretary-treasurer in 1911 while in prison in Los Angeles and two months after pleading guilty, an admission that sent shock waves around the country. He served in this position from 1905 until 1913. Ryan was re-elected as president after his release and remained a member of the AFL national executive committee in charge of organising ironworkers. By November 1919, 11 of those convicted in Indianapolis still held office in the union.[70]

The IABSIW indirectly achieved part of its objective to expand unionisation into new US Steel plants during WWI. To settle the wildcat strikes by 21,000 machinists, of which only 2,000 were International Association of Machinists members, the federal National War Labor Board imposed the eight-hour workday to workers under government contract and a limited collective bargaining over grievances at the Bethlehem Steel's Bethlehem, Pennsylvania plant.[71]

Against all odds the IABSIW delivered. Workers supported the union because it doubled their wages in its 15 years of existence. The

organization raised the wages of structural ironworkers almost 50 per cent in a period of fifteen years. It was natural that they should rally to the support of that union when they believed that its existence was threatened. It was natural that they should feel bitter toward the employers who were hiring secret spies to destroy that union.[72]

---

69   Adamic 1931, p. 180.

70   Grant 1915b, pp. 126 and 129; and Fine 1991, p. 41.

71   Although making the award only for workers doing government contract work was a classic example of divide and conquer, it ironically vindicated the IABSIW's long campaign. (See Conner 1983, pp. 122–3).

72   Grant 1915b, p. 147.

As Adamic explained, the ironworkers stuck by the IABSIW because the alternative was worse.

> Then, very likely, there comes a business depression – unemployment, wagecuts, lockouts, desperation. The union is their only hope, and they are willing to go to almost any length to preserve it. They elect leaders willing to use violence when violence is the only means of preserving it.[73]

Common sense assumes that a union that unsuccessfully escalates its tactics will lose support among the rank and file and supporters. But quite the opposite happened to the IABSIW. Although the campaign failed to accomplish its objective of organising the entire industry, support for the union actually widened even after the revelation of the leadership in the bombing campaign. According to Grant,

> While the dynamite campaign does not appear to have had much effect on the big open shop employers, except to intensify the feeling of bitterness toward the union, it does seem to have had a beneficial effect on the numerical strength and financial standing of the organization.[74]

Despite the relentless prosecutions and lawsuits, a Congressional investigation into the US Steel Trust found IABSIW was the only union it had not yet completely smashed and that it actually grew. During the more than five-year dynamite campaign, the union's membership grew from 5,000 to nearly 14,000 members, one-third of the increase during the nearly three years of trials. The union proved it could deliver by escalating its own tactics to meet the escalation of tactics by the industry. Their efforts reduced the 10-hour day to eight hours and doubled the wage scale to $4.30.[75] Journalist Fitch, who covered the dynamite campaign and trials, estimated

> that the McNamaras became convinced that no amount of pleading, no amount of argument, no amount of logic, no amount of Christianity, no amount of politics, would convince the steel trust that they could give eight hours and give them living wages. Labor would have to organise.[76]

---

73   Adamic 1931, p. 141.
74   Grant 1915b, p. 125.
75   Perlman and Taft 1935, p. 325; and Adamic 1931, p. 141.
76   Fitch 1913, pp. 615–16.

The IABSIW's escalation of tactics achieved its objectives at great human costs. Even without a national contract, the IABSIW achieved the broader objectives of the class struggle: to work less and be paid more. Its ability to achieve this is written in the slipping financial position of the world's first, largest and presumably most powerful billion dollar company. From this perspective, the dynamite campaign, whether strategy or manufactured plot, became leverage in itself that allowed the ironworkers to wring concessions from capital that would never have been possible at the negotiating table. The union was seen as sacrificing itself to protect the workers' interests, which deepened the commitment of its members, attracted the ironworkers to join, and provided the leverage to wring concessions from industry. Endeavouring to achieve what was impossible, they did what was possible to get it.

Writing about the McNamara brothers' confession, journalist Lincoln Steffens asked what can be done

> about conditions which are bringing up healthy, good tempered boys like these McNamara boys to really believe, as they most sincerely do – they and a growing group of labor – that the only recourse they have for improving the conditions of the wage-earner is to use dynamite against property and life.[77]

The dynamite campaign provided grist to progressive reformers like Steffens and the Commission on Industrial Relations staff's call for reforms. Providing access to the polity would diffuse class conflict and prevent disruption and political violence. But if Steffens was critical of the tactics remaining in the workers' repertoire he made it evident what happens when corporations proceed to make it impossible for any other recourse but a strategy of tension to succeed. Gompers echoed this sentiment when he asked his readers to

> ponder how it is said that among people professing to believe in the brotherhood of man and the gospel of love, men, American citizens, came to look upon violence, dynamite, terror, as the only defense left them against the grinding, conscienceless tyranny of those controlling hours, wages, and conditions of work. That is a terrible charge against society.[78]

---

77   See Kellogg, 30 December 1911, p. 1412.
78   Gompers, 1 February 1913, p. 621.

Gompers understood the need to escalate tactics but as in 1894 he wasn't about to allow AFL members to use them if he could help it. His denunciation cloaked his call for recognising the role of unions in managing class struggle in order to avoid what he warned was inevitable.

The outcome of the nearly decade-long struggle between the ironworkers and US Steel provides an exception to Tilly's axiom that low mass support, rising costs, and little opportunity to achieve gains drives insurgents to demobilise and de-escalate. Although the IABSIW's struggle faced both rising costs and dwindling promise of achieving their primary objective of organising the entire iron assembly industry, they continued to escalate their tactics, albeit driven in part by agent provocateurs, and gained support in union density rather than lost it.

It has long been assumed that public perception of insurgents' increasing militancy and use of political violence will result in a loss of mass support. But the ironworkers proved an exception to this rule. As Grant found,

> The remarkable increase in the treasury balance, however, cannot be explained on any other basis than that the membership approved of the campaign and willingly contributed to support it. The members believed that the open shop fight directed against the union, was, in fact a war of extermination and their loyalty was such that they were ready to meet every assessment levied without protest.[79]

The evidence for Adamic's provocative claim that 'dynamite was effective' is that the IABSIW was the lone union willing to deploy the tactics necessary to survive a relentless foe out to destroy the union.[80] Fitch recalled how a fellow reporter covering the conspiracy trials found that

> Most of them are the product of their environment. The danger of their work calls for red-blooded men – men of recklessness and courage. In their fight for union recognition they found themselves up against a bitter struggle with the Steel Corporation, and they actually believed, many of them, that the only way to avoid a loss of the eight hour day and complete subjugation was through the use of dynamite.[81]

---

79   Grant 1915b, p. 127.
80   Adamic 1931, p. 141.
81   Fitch 1913, p. 615.

354   CHAPTER 7

Thanks to the extensive historical record it is possible to argue that the iron-workers' escalation of tactics to use political violence increased mass support, although not the opportunity to achieve the objectives of the struggle, even while costs grew steeply. As we will see with the 1914–21 cycle of struggle in the coal mines of West Virginia, sometimes an increase in mass support is accompanied by a rising opportunity to achieve the objectives of the struggle (See Chapter 10). This is in contrast to the 1900–3 national miners' strike de-escalating tactics when mass support was strong, costs were high, and oppor-tunities were low, resulting in the evaporation of public support for insurgents and their eventual defeat. Common sense would seem to dictate that any-one not immediately involved in the struggle would avoid the risk of publicly supporting a 'lost cause'. But the ironworkers' struggle proved otherwise. Even when losing strategically, escalating tactics gave supporters the expectation that those with the most to risk, who were willing to take it despite the low chance of success, were worth supporting. That is the counter-calculus that attracts some people to the underdog.

One explanation for this possible outcome can be found in an examination of the larger cycle in which a particular struggle in situated. The ironworkers mobilised in the context of a working-class in the process of recomposing its power. As workers in other sectors organised according to the strategy of indus-trial unionism and syndicalism, their efforts found their way to the ironworkers. The IABSIW's dynamite campaign was but one peak of a much larger cycle of workers' escalation of tactics to disrupt the accumulation of capital in the years preceding WWI. This same cycle had swept US Steel into related sectors to escape the disruption caused in mining, railroads, and steel in the previous decade. As Fitch observed,

> this dynamite campaign has been part of a larger struggle. It is one of the most sinister manifestations of that struggle. Nevertheless it is a part of it, and we must not think that the matter is settled when we have the dynam-iters in jail.[82]

It was in the midst of a newly rising disruptive cycle that continued even as capital took up arms against itself in WWI.

---

82   Ibid., p. 616.

Blowing Up a Social Relationship

The lesson of the dynamite campaign illustrates Arendt's point that force can destroy power but it cannot create it.[83] There could be no starker lesson for the IABSIW dynamite campaign. While the union sought to destroy its enemy, its tactics offered no means by which to do so. Dynamite destroys but it cannot replace or reconstruct a new social relation of production.[84]

> Force may subjugate one side or the other in an industrial dispute, but it will not remove discontent. It will not establish justice. When one side is all-powerful and the other side is subservient, there is sure to be injustice. Where there is injustice, there will be discontent.[85]

While IABSIW members prospered, the bombing campaign destroyed the labour movement in Los Angeles. The city-wide strike in LA was lost by February 1912, metal trade workers failed to win the eight-hour day or a union wage, and the favoured labour-backed Socialist Party candidate for mayor lost the election in the final days after being tainted by the bombing.[86]

Only a few years later, the ironworkers miraculously re-emerged as a threat to industry's effort to push the US into WWI. In 1915, the ironworkers and the International Association of Machinists (IAM) organised successful strikes in the munitions industry around Bridgeport, Connecticut (see Chapter 8). By spreading the strikes throughout New England that summer they managed to reduce the average workday from 10 to 8 hours. The war provided a new vulnerability for capital that the ironworkers and their machinist allies were well placed to exploit. This is why both unions were targeted by industry, the Wilson administration, and the IAM national leadership. The National Civic Federation's Ralph Easley and J.P. Morgan's Henry Davidson contributed money to set up a unit to investigate and attack the anti-war union movement. As a result of the investigation, the grand jury indicted Rep. Buchanan, the former IABSIW president, and eight others associated with the National Peace Council (NPC) under the Sherman Anti-Trust Act, costing Buchanan re-election in 1916 while awaiting trial. Although Buchanan was acquitted, the 23-day trial

---

83   Arendt 1971, p. 53.
84   This is a crucial argument in the debate over whether the use of violence is a tactic or an ideology. (See Libertarian Socialist Organisation 1979).
85   Grant 1915b, p. 139.
86   G. Adams 1966, p. 11.

resulted in three convictions and one-year sentences in the federal prison on 20 May 1917 only one month after the US entered WWI and long after the NPC had imploded.[87]

Was it Terrorism?

Although it was described as terrorism, the structural ironworkers' bombing campaign seems more like coordinated sabotage. This is because, prior to the *Los Angeles Times* bombing, the attacks targeted symbolic company property with the intent to cause minor damage and compel the companies to negotiate. The attacks did not target the civilian population to cause death, fear and instability among the general population. It must also be kept in mind that, because the IABSIW's objective was a negotiated contract, not system change, it also paired the attacks with continued attempts to negotiate and strike. The IABSIW was coordinating both the above-ground effort to seek redress for their grievances with US Steel while also carrying out underground attacks to inflict mostly symbolic damage to the appearance of monolithic corporate power.

In addition to the ironworkers, elites also carried out scattered attacks and sabotage, this time of their own property. These were false flag attacks conducted with the intent to blame the IABSIW. The NEA knew the union was doing them because its unpaid informants planned many of the bombings, an unknown number were likely directly carried out by NEA agent provocateurs, the attacks continued even after the McNamara brothers and McManigal had been arrested, and only about 61 percent of the attacks targeted property owned by its member companies.

But was the dynamite campaign terrorism?

Because there is no consensus, the answer to this question is not as direct as it might appear, and is beyond the scope of this book. Not only do different governments and the United Nations define terrorism differently, but so too do agencies, departments, armed forces, police, and intelligence services within a single government. Definitions of terrorism are broad, overlapping, and contradictory. They are defined by an array of factors including threats or 'unlawful use of force or violence' or 'any activity' on government officials, armed and unarmed military personnel, forces and property, and civilians and non-combatants. Both people and property may be targeted including critical infrastructure, and private or public property. 'Attacks' can include threats,

---

87   Foner 1987, pp. 55, 57, and 61.

vandalism, and sabotage of a wide range of property such as the Internet, ski resorts, businesses, medical facilities, abortion clinics, logging companies, and car dealerships. Such actions are perceived to be motivated by the objectives to 'affect', intimidate or coerce society or government policy and action and inculcate fear to achieve 'goals that are generally political, religious, or ideological'. In 2003 the US State Department also reported that 'the line between insurgency and terrorism has become increasingly blurred as attacks on civilian targets have become more common'.[88]

Although the origin of the word terrorism (*terreur*) was used to describe the Jacobin government during the French Revolution, it is now primarily used to mean attacks by individuals or non-governmental groups. When states are associated with terrorism it is qualified as a 'state sponsor' or 'terrorist state'. Discussions about what terrorism is tend to replicate what Noam Chomsky calls the 'fallacy of the wrong agent'.[89] As Moore explains, 'part of what is radically wrong may be the prevailing conception of violence. It fails to draw the crucial moral and political distinctions between the violence of the oppressors and those who resist oppression'.[90]

Terrorism is defined to also include threats as well as planned and actual attacks, the intent to create fear, disorder, and instability, to make political change, to generate media publicity, to make a statement, and for philosophical and theological reasons. Sometimes the definitions include many or all of these characteristics. In other words, definitions of terrorism are a jumble of perpetrator, target, strategy, objective, theology, immorality, and ideas. They vacillate between people and the state, people and property, and planning, threats or actual attacks.

Rarely is the tactic of what is called terrorism ever considered; doing so would require a more nuanced definition that parses the use of political violence by the tactical use of violence. Directing coordinated violence at the target of a grievance in self-defence out of fear of pending attack or replying to one would be a scattered attack by a citizen's militia. But an attack which seeks to cause damage to property to inflict monetary costs or disrupt operations is sabotage. Coordinated attacks which target a specific person, rather than a group or institution, in order to kill them would be an assassination. These are tactical actions that serve a strategy to move a contender toward achieving

---

88   These definitions come from the US State Department, FBI, Department of Homeland Security, and the Department of Defense. (Hoffman 2006, pp. 30–41).

89   Chomsky 2004.

90   Moore 1969, p. 5.

their political objectives. As a result, these tactics are directly linked to a specific political objective that the contender has some expectation of achieving.
It does not matter who the perpetrator or target is, whether governmental or
non-governmental, because it is the tactic that matters. While people may be
killed or injured, except for assassinations, they are not targeted and serve no
objective interests. These are not yet terrorism.

In contrast, terrorism is a tactic that primarily targets the general population
and may target the object of the grievance. Its strategy is to create the fear or the
perception of disorder and instability by punishing the population for its perceived passive or active complicity with the target. The strategy is to push the
population to rise up against the target out of anger for failing to protect them.
While the perpetrator may have specific grievances and strategies to achieve
its ends, it does not have a specific objective or any expectation of achieving
it. Its objectives are mixed up with the strategy, because it seeks to punish the
population, expecting it to carry out the removal of the source of its grievances
because it lacks the power to do so itself.

Arendt makes the point that terrorism is relied upon when power has been
destroyed and because terrorism cannot produce power it looks elsewhere for
those with power to make the change its perpetrators desire. Terrorism is the
substitution of violence for power. 'Politically speaking, the point is that loss
of power becomes a temptation to substitute violence for power ... and that
violence itself results in impotence'.[91] A more nuanced definition of terrorism
would be that it is a tactic to instil fear, reduce the appearance of elite stability,
disrupt normal life, and provoke instability without the objective of achieving
specific gains such as seizing territory. The use of violence becomes tactical
when insurgents lack mass support and thus the necessary power to realise
their objectives alone. As Marcuse observed, 'As long as the opposition does
not have the social force of a new general interest, the problem of violence is
primarily a problem of tactics'.[92]

The tactic of terrorism, carrying out attacks that target adversaries and the
general population as part of a strategy to create disorder, fear, and instability, is several levels of intensity beyond the scattered attacks and sabotage on
the trajectory of political violence (see Figure 1) carried out by the IABSIW. For
scattered attacks and sabotage to escalate into terrorism the union would have
first needed to use their cell to seize territory (factories, cities or regions) to
establish a liberated area or base to which they could recruit members and from
which they could launch attacks. Since that stage, what is also known as guer-

91   Arendt 1971, p. 54.
92   Marcuse 1967.

rilla warfare, did not occur and was not part of the union's strategy, the bombing campaign was not yet terrorism (see Figure 1).

Scattered attacks, sabotage, and guerrilla warfare are most commonly paired
with other lower intensity tactics, whether or not they are coordinated with
above- and below-ground sections of the insurgency. Tactical forms of violence
may be used for self-protection in a conservative, defensive manoeuvre. This is
what D'Arcy calls the 'common view of violence' in which 'armed force should
be minimized, sometimes justified if there is no other way to protect yourself or
others, must never be indiscriminate or disproportionate'.[93] The self-defensive
use of violence takes the form of the 'citizen's militia model' in which the
'armed force of the militia is subordinated to higher-level social movement
organizations' and 'relies crucially on broad popular support from the wider
community outside its ranks, in the absence of which it could not carry out
its aims' and 'refrains from targeting noncombatants'. Moving seamlessly back
and forth between both, the militia 'members work and struggle in collaboration with justice-seeking social movements. There is no attempt to usurp the
agency of the wider movements, or to substitute the bravery and sacrifice of
tiny groups of people for the self-activity of thousands or millions'. Armed self-
defence does not displace, replace, or subsume non-military struggle because
it 'is in the first instance a popular struggle, not a military one'.[94]

The citizen's militia model stands in contrast with the 'clandestine cell
model' in which the armed insurgents drive the insurgency, claim to lead it,
and ultimately become isolated and alienated from it. As a result, it 'cannot
count on broad popular support, but must accept its own political isolation
from the wider community' and 'is often either indifferent to or at least suspicious of the notion of non-combatant immunity'.[95] The clandestine cell model
inescapably undermines the tactics, strategy, and objectives of class struggle.
'The autonomy of the people is not only the goal of anticapitalism; it must also
be its method'. D'Arcy argues,

> if militancy is conducted in a manner that usurps agency from the ag-
> grieved parties, placing leadership and decision-making about the strug-
> gle in the hands of a self-appointed counterelite, the effect will be to
> replicate, within the oppositional movement, the same dynamic of dis-
> empowerment and rule by others that constitutes the core of the problem
> to which militancy is supposed to be a solution.[96]

---

93   D'Arcy 2013, pp. 162–3.
94   Ibid., pp. 165, 179–80, and 182.
95   Ibid., pp. 179–80.
96   Ibid., pp. 181–4. D'Arcy assesses the use of militancy, including armed violence, according

It's unclear which of D'Arcy's models the IABSIW's bombing campaign would fall into. The IABSIW carried out the bombings in an opportunistic manner. Does it meet the citizen's militia self-defence criteria? While workers were being injured and killed on the job, the NEA and the companies weren't physically carrying out fatal attacks on workers. Yet neither was the cell claiming to lead or transpose the class struggle. In fact, not only were the bombers subordinate to the above-ground non-military leaders, they retained widespread support from the membership and other supporters, which was evidenced by the substantial growth in membership after the arrests. In some ways, the bombing campaign was an offensive citizen's militia.

Guerrilla warfare and citizen's militias raise substantial questions about the dominant view of tactical violence as terrorism. Hoffman argues for a more nuanced definition of terrorism, rightly arguing that

> terrorists, however, do not function in the open as armed units, generally do not attempt to seize or hold territory, deliberately avoid engaging enemy military forces in combat, are constrained both numerically and logistically from undertaking concerted mass political mobilization efforts, and exercise no direct control or governance over a populace at either the local or national level.[97]

For this reason, terrorism is not paired with low intensity tactics. Terrorism becomes the tactic when all other tactics are perceived to have failed, been defeated, repressed, co-opted, diffused, or deflected. Because the strategy of terrorism, punishing the population to coerce it to rid itself of the terrorists' adversary, cannot be achieved by the perpetrators, they are unwilling to de-escalate or demobilise to negotiate and compromise. There is no above-ground organisation other than to issue *communiques*. As a tactic, terrorism is zero sum, a winner takes all situation in which the perpetrators expect to die and even willingly send themselves to their own deaths in suicide attacks or attacks from which there is little chance of escape.

The blurring of scattered attacks, citizen's militias, sabotage, and guerrilla warfare with terrorism is often used to justify an elite's response to such tactics

---

to the criteria of whether they further democracy rather than class struggle. The clandestine model violates the democratic legitimacy of armed struggle because the vanguard cell prevents the most affected from taking the lead to get their grievances addressed and gain more autonomy, thereby undermining what he calls the agency and autonomy principles. (See Ibid., pp. 180–1).

97   Hoffman 2006, p. 35.

by deploying overwhelming asymmetrical counter-insurgency warfare. Elites will use the same tactics with the objective of decomposing insurgents' power by draining their financial resources and destroying the insurgents, the communities from which they operate, their facilities and bases, and their supporters. Supporters are brutally kept off the streets and repressed, liberated areas are targeted, parallel governing structures are attacked and dismantled, and insurgents are killed in battle, bombings and assassinations. Elites' attacks cause disproportionately more destruction and loss of life than can be inflicted by insurgents using any of these higher intensity tactics. With all political space closed, supporters destroyed or alienated, and elites controlling the disproportionate balance of power, scattered attacks, sabotage, and guerrilla warfare may become terrorist attacks not merely limited to symbolically important elite targets but even extended to former allies, groups of non-combatants, and unprotected groups scapegoated for lost opportunities and rising costs. In such a case, elites will expand their support as internal factions close ranks, the population turns to it for protection while blaming the insurgents for the violence, disorder, and instability, and former insurgents or their allies change sides.

At any stage along the trajectory between scattered attacks, sabotage, and guerrilla warfare, insurgents and elites may choose to de-escalate and negotiate. If new political space opens up for insurgents to present grievances with a reasonable expectation of redress, some insurgents will demobilise and de-escalate their tactics to take advantage of the existing opportunities to pursue some of their objectives through negotiations. In such cases insurgents may split so that some insurgents continue the high intensity tactics, or insurgents will form a parallel above-ground organisation to negotiate that is coordinated with the under-ground insurgents. Insurgents that continue to escalate their tactics may also find elites doing the same in order to raise the costs and force insurgents to the negotiating table. Failing to reciprocate may in turn provoke a spiral of escalation and a return to the *danse macabre* in which insurgents, allies, and supporters are killed and injured, property is destroyed, and suffering is inflicted.

The tactic of political violence should be seen as a range of tactical choices from a repertoire along a trajectory described in Figure 1 from which elites and insurgents choose their tactics, depending on the inter-relationship between their class composition, mass support, and the costs and opportunity for achieving their objectives. Political violence is not an A to B proposition, but rather the outcome of the complex interplay of these factors and the pairing and switching between tactics of differing levels of intensity. Contenders rarely begin their struggle by using tactical violence and commonly pair tactical violence with lower intensity tactics. To claim otherwise is to commit the origination fallacy (see Introduction).

As insurgents present demands for redress of grievances, they must take into consideration the factors of support, threats, gains, and the opportunities for gains. When the political system is closed because elites manoeuvre so as to block their access to the available political space, insurgents are forced to escalate their tactics if they wish to continue pursuing their objectives. The question is: what kind of tactics will they use to carry on their struggle? What causes political violence to take so many different forms?

These questions address what Tilly calls

> The problem of explaining variation in the character and social organization of violence ... The point is not to establish general laws for all sorts of violence but rather to identify crucial causal processes: those that operate similarly in the short run across a wide range of circumstances yet produce dramatically different forms of collective violence depending on their settings, combinations, and sequences.[98]

For Tilly, the form and frequency of political violence is a factor in the balance of power between elites and insurgents and the conditions under which they struggle.

To answer these two questions Tilly classifies political violence in several different groupings along a 'facilitation curve' distributed among types of individual (individual aggression, brawls, opportunism, and violent rituals) and collective violence (broken negotiations, scattered attacks, and coordinated destruction), revolution, and terrorism.[99] According to Tilly, the tactics are shaped by the conditions, balance of power, or expectations about options and outcomes.

---

98   Tilly 2003, pp. 13 and 23.

99   Tilly provides the first two groupings and I have added the last two. Sabotage is used here to refer to what Tilly calls 'coordinated destruction'. The types of scattered attacks used in the 1877 and 1894 strikes ranged from street clashes and gun fights, sniping, attacks on property, blockades, train derailments, and bombings. Forms of individual action Tilly attributes to aggression, opportunism, and violent rituals such as brawls, slugging, lynchings, shaming ceremonies, enslavement, mass rapes, looting, and hostage taking do not interest us here as they do not meet the conditions of collective action (Ibid., pp. 14–16, and 131). While Tilly leaves out revolution entirely from this book, a significant departure from his classic 1979 work *From Mobilization to Revolution*, it is included here as a type of collective violence. Similarly, Tilly does not identify terrorism as a category of collective violence as I have done.

The facilitation curve tells us that even relatively powerless groups receive incentives to carry out certain highly acceptable collective actions; the result of that circumstance is to squeeze the range of collective action on the part of slightly powerful groups which simply tolerated: either they can't do it or they must do it. As a result, relatively powerless groups find their world more totalitarian than do the powerful or the completely powerless.[100]

Insurgents move along this curve, or what I call a trajectory of political violence (see Introduction) which implies a rising intensity, from broken negotiations to scattered attacks when elites violate claims to rights, privileges, obligations, rules, and laws of the existing political relations of the social contract. Escalation back and forth along the trajectory does not proceed in sequential order, but is determined by the interplay of conditions elites and insurgents face, assessments of costs and opportunities, and levels of mass support. As Tilly explains, 'alterations in social relations produce not only surges and declines in collective violence but also the whole range of switching behavior'[101] in which insurgents pair or switch between tactics of differing tactical intensity.

Once perceiving the social contract is irrevocably broken (e.g. 'broken negotiations'), insurgents may begin carrying out scattered attacks and sabotage in a strategic war of manoeuvre to assess their level of mass support, the costs of escalation, elites' counter-escalation, and the effectiveness of the disruption. In class terms, scattered attacks and sabotage are initially used to assess the recomposition of working-class power and probe the strength of the composition of capital.

According to the strategy of Sun Tzu, scattered attacks can be used to probe for weaknesses and advantages. They may also feign a willingness to continue escalating even when insurgents are incapable or unwilling to continue doing so. Scattered attacks may also be an attempt to get elites to show their strength, overreact and waste resources.[102] Whatever the strategic value of scattered attacks, attacks on symbolically important places and people are a signalling device to elites that they are prepared to raise the costs of refusing to make concessions by escalating along the trajectory. These attacks also signal to supporters that their support provides new opportunities to achieve gains that are not possible through the polity, negotiations and other low intensity tactics.

---

100   Tilly 1978, p. 114.
101   Tilly 2003, p. 225.
102   Sun Tzu 512 BC.

Distinguishing between the four groupings of political violence is extremely difficult because of the fluid nature of the pairing and switching that occurs. Low intensity tactics, such as protests and attempts to negotiate, are paired or switched with a range of high intensity tactics along the trajectory including arson, sabotage, armed attacks on symbolically important property, and assaults on high status officials and institutions. 'Scattered attack stands out for the relatively low salience of violent interactions, damaging acts occur in the midst of mostly undamaging interactions'.[103] In this way, the bombing campaign is a model example of the interplay between these four groupings of political violence paired with lower intensity tactics.

All three of the strikes discussed in this book so far are case studies in the fluidity between broken negotiations, scattered attacks, and sabotage. Each cycle of struggle effectively followed an analogous process of development as groups of workers presented their grievances and attempted to parlay with the companies. Their grievances concerned breaks in the social contract: repression of their 1st amendment rights to assemble and petition capital and government long before these rights were tested in the courts in the 1919 *Schenk v. United States* espionage and sedition case during WWI. Elites' refusal to allow workers to engage in any political activity precluded negotiations until the elite consensus broke and elected officials intervened, except in the case of the ironworkers, to call in troops, impose a cooling off period, establish an arbitration process, and impanel commissions to carry out investigations that informed later reforms. Until the 1935 NLRA was passed, this process occurred on an impromptu basis that generated an unpredictable conflict engendering disruption, instability, and disruption.

As we have seen in 1877, 1894, and in the dynamite campaign, tactical violence can be deployed when costs are high and the opportunity for achieving gains are low as well as the inverse. While this seems counterintuitive, the complex interplay of factors may lead insurgents to utilise tactical violence under very different conditions in which they struggle and with differing compositions of their own and their adversary's power. There is no hard and fast rule for predicting or making a general theory about when insurgencies turn violent or resort to terrorism. This is part of the reason why wars on terrorism, whether anarchist, far left, far right, white supremacist, Zionist, national liberation, or Islamist, are mostly ineffective. Insurgents who resort to tactical violence draw from their tactical repertoire depending on the complex relationship of strategy, objectives, costs, opportunities, conditions, mass support, and class composition.

---

103   Tilly 2003, pp. 171–2.

It is possible that tactical forms of violence, such as scattered attacks, sabotage, and guerrilla warfare, can attract more mass support, thereby shifting the balance of power. This is why scattered attacks and sabotage often dissipate once insurgents and elites come to a settlement, or guerrilla armies disarm and enter the polity as factions, advocacy organisations or political parties. We have seen examples of insurgents entering the government in recent decades in Venezuela, Bolivia, Chile, Brazil, El Salvador, Nicaragua, Iraq, Lebanon and South Africa. Because tactical violence is used in such diverse, contradictory, and even opposed conditions, it is fallacious to suggest that the use of tactical violence is ideological, theological, or even ahistorical. It is similarly fallacious to assume that using tactical violence has reduced mass support for the insurgency. The use of violence in a political conflict is tactical. To argue otherwise is to provide a pre-emptive justification for the endless use of asymmetrical counter-insurgency warfare by elites to inflict their will where power has been lost and all forms of persuasion and coercion have been eviscerated.

The use of tactical violence can also have a conservative objective to protect and not to expand existing gains, when negotiations are blocked and an adversary is poised to unilaterally escalate. This is why Fitch and Grant both described the IABSIW's dynamite campaign as fundamentally a conservative use of higher intensity tactics. The strategy of the dynamite campaign was to keep the workers from losing what was gained in previous struggles and merely survive in a hostile industry where the union was encircled and outmanoeuvred by an unvanquishable US Steel. When the company used the NEA to unilaterally raise the intensity of its tactics, the IABSIW responded in kind by also escalating to protect its existing gains in order to continue using its leverage to negotiate an industry-wide contract.

There is a double standard at work in the way press, courts, and historians explain this dynamic interplay of tensions. This is not exclusive to just the dynamite campaign, but is ubiquitous in political, academic, and media accounts of international relations. The most obvious hypocrisy occurs when states deploy tactical violence against other states. In such events, the use of violence is rationally explained by the relative gains perspective as a tactic or criticised as worsening the security dilemma since it provokes a violent response. Yet when political violence is deployed by *non-state* insurgents against elites or a state, it suddenly and inexplicably ceases to be considered tactical and is suddenly transformed into a ahistorical, ideological or theological objective. While the agents differ, state vs. state in contrast to insurgents vs. elites and a state, the political violence remains a tactic.

To understand which tactics are non-violent and when and why they are used, one must understand which tactics are violent and when and why they

are used. 'A paradoxical lesson for researchers: to understand and explain violent actions, you must understand nonviolent actions'.[104] While there is no
agreement on what 'violence' is, most of what is called violence is rather a
use of force, directed at property rather than people, assumed by violent state
responses, and is framed by the observer's political perspective.[105] Understanding which tactics are used by an insurgency requires understanding the conditions in which the IOMO factors (interests, organisation, mobilisation, and
opportunity – see Chapter 10) intersect. Insurgents escalate from using non-
violent to violent tactics or pair and switch between them depending on their
assessment of IOMO.

What Chomsky has called the 'fallacy of the wrong agent' guided the decades-long 'war on anarchism', more than half-century 'war on communism'
and national liberation movements, and the current two-decade-long endless
'war on terrorism'. These are ostensibly wars against a tactic misportrayed,
intentionally or otherwise, as an ahistorical war on an ideology and theology
for extremely profitable financial and political purposes.[106] Since the 1990s, a
global cottage industry of anti-terrorism experts has managed to strip political
violence of the conditions and context in which it is used and has refashioned it
as an ideological objective deceptively applied to some theologies (e.g. 'radical
Islam') and not others (e.g. Judaism, Christianity, Hinduism and Buddhism),
and politically marginalised groups, especially when they are people of colour or ethnic and racial minorities. The same appellations are inconsistently
applied when identical tactics are deployed by elites, dominant or majority
groups, or the state. In effect, anti-terrorism theory and practice today follows
the dictum of 'different perpetrator, different tactic'. Just as the wheel of history
often spins us back around to analogous periods of our past. The obsession of
today's war on terrorism as a conflict almost exclusively with Islamist insurgents, and as the late comedian George Carlin excoriated, as a 'war on brown
people', has a parallel in the same mistake the fledgling FBI made in declaring
war on socialism, anarchism, syndicalism, and immigrants a century ago.

---

104   Tilly 1978, p. 182.
105   Ibid., p. 177.
106   Chomsky 2004, p. 195.

Give Someone an Inch and They'll Take a Mile

There is more at stake in the iron and railroad workers' struggles than the explanatory power of Tilly's theory of contention. This book is not about giving Sociology an effective explanatory power for when political violence is likely to be used as a tactic but explaining how unruly workers have sometimes used it to bring about lasting systemic transformation. The outcomes of each of these struggles call into question the entire presumption that change happens in America according to the 'myth of peaceful progress'. The central tenet of the myth is the pluralist doctrine in which contenders form organisations, build coalitions, advocate for their positions via established channels, negotiate with elites, and de-escalate to receive the rewards of short-term concessions and compromises.

The myth of peaceful progress has lingering, unaddressed questions obscured by faithful obedience to its doctrine. What is the source of the grievances? Does the power actually lie in the formal rules of the polity or somewhere else? And if it lies elsewhere, what are the necessary tactics to compel those with power to concede anything to insurgents? Nowhere does the myth allow for any power of disruption. Force in the application of leverage, it argues, makes concessions impossible because it creates a disincentive for elites to deliver, since they can no longer be sure where it will end. As the old adage goes, give someone an inch, and they'll take a mile.

The IABSIW actually gained credibility among the ironworkers by fighting to retain a grip on some of its previous gains. It did this by escalating its tactics, rather than negotiating and conceding, demobilising, and de-escalating.

> No union can stand still and hope to hold its membership. It must advance, either by peaceful methods, or by fighting. If it advances rapidly without much opposition, it is apt to develop a false notion of its own strength and importance, which frequently leads to abuse of power. For that reason the union that has had to fight for every concession gained is likely to be much more conservative and much more stable than the union that has had smooth sailing.[107]

A struggle that achieves gains when costs are low, such as through negotiations, is more likely to be crushed because it will later demobilise believing itself to be invincible. As the cost to mobilise rises, insurgents may not mobilise or escalate

---

107   Grant 1915b, p. 127.

their tactics because they fail to realise the conditions have changed, and they are no longer assured of the same outcome. Insurgents have been defeated by their own hubris. This is what underlies the long decline of unions since the 1970s. Not so for a struggle that achieves gains when the costs are high. Insurgents who mobilise and escalate tactics when facing high costs are unlikely to let down their guard during the next struggle.

For Fitch and Grant, the bombing campaign was a conservative reaction to maintain what they had rather than an attempt to expand their gains in the face of an ever more powerful adversary.

> Yet it is common psychology that men will go to greater lengths to hold what they have than to gain more. A $3 man strikes harder against a wage cut than a $2 man will strike for a raise. It is significant that nearly all discussion of this matter in labor circles turns sooner or later to the condition of the other workers in the steel industry – their twelve-hour day and seven-day week, their low wages and their unorganised helplessness.[108]

The organised ironworkers gained credibility by doing something the rest of the union movement was unable or unwilling to do: they rejected the ideology of shared interests that dominated the AFL and guided the so-called Progressive Era. The IABSIW rank and file did not associate the interests of ironworkers with that of capital and removed President Buchanan when they discovered that he did, replacing him with leadership willing to escalate their tactics.

> Society does not always ostracize the transgressor of moral or civil law. To expect a labor union to do so, especially when the transgressions committed were aimed at furthering the material interests of that union, is to expect something unreasonable. That is the view the average union man takes of a situation of the kind, whether he is an ironworker or some other mechanic. It may not be a moral view as some would look at it, but there is no cant or hypocrisy about it. The question here is not whether that view is the right one from a moral standpoint, but whether it is the correct one from the ironworkers' point of view.[109]

That is why dynamite lost the battle, but got the goods.

---

108   Fitch 1913, p. 615.
109   Grant 1915b, p. 130. Grant's ideas were apparently so controversial and unconventional that the Commission never listed or published his report.

CHAPTER 8

War in Europe, War on Capital: The WWI Wildcat Strike Wave

The common man has won the war and lost his livelihood.
THORSTEIN VEBLEN, 1921[1]

∴

War changes everything. Facing a rising tide of wildcat strikes, resistance to Taylorism, disruptive strikes by the Industrial Workers of the World (IWW) and the meteoric rise of the Socialist Party, the Wilson administration imposed mandatory arbitration from the top down, without negotiations or union recognition, in an attempt to impose a temporary ceasefire between capital and workers. New policies that extended state power to regulate class conflict and criminalised dissent and militant organising were designed to manage the conflict between capital and labour. At the centre of Wilson's wartime strategy was the short-lived National War Labor Board (NWLB), an improvised institutional mechanism for controlling and managing class struggle during the war that still exists today as the labour and welfare laws of the 1930s.

Although war is invaluable for channelling, diffusing, and redirecting anger and unresolved grievances away from the point of production, these policies never succeeded in leashing the unruly war industry workers. When Congress declared war on 6 April 1917, the entire economy became a choke point overnight. Industries from agriculture to weapon production became so critical to the war industries that disruption had to be prevented by any means necessary even if it meant making significant temporary concessions in response to strikes. Metals were also critical to the imperial rivalries that for several decades had repeatedly gone to war as they powers sought to carve up Africa and Asia. As a result, the wartime strike wave threatened not only the US and its allies' war effort but global imperialism.[2]

---

1   Thorstein Veblen 1921, p. 11.
2   Silver notes that the metal trades were also a centre of revolutionary struggles in Germany and Russia (Silver 2003, pp. 140–1).

The well-worn alternatives – judicial, police, and military repression – had a poor record over the past several decades in disciplining insubordinate workers for very long and promised to inflame the situation. Mobilised workers demanding immediate redress of pent up grievances threatened not only the war effort. They could fracture the new elite coalition that now included the American Federation of Labor (AFL) that had used decades of labour agitation to move into the polity. As Foner observed,

> Officials in Washington soon realised that there was a vital need to keep workers content up to a reasonable point, since widespread industrial unrest could seriously hamper the prosecution of the war. Consequently, the government had no choice but to use its influence to deal with the issues of wages, hours, and working conditions – especially in view of the insatiable rush for wartime profits by industrial concerns.[3]

By extending its authority into these conflicts during the war the Wilson administration did what is often misattributed to President Franklin Roosevelt's New Deal: 'the federal government authorized pervasive policies to govern working conditions in American industries'. The experience of the wartime planning state demonstrated that 'collective bargaining is the solution to bolshevism and socialism' and should continue in a time of peace.[4] The ideas of Section 7a and the National Labor Board of the 1933 National Industrial Recovery Act and the 1935 National Labor Relations Act were actually first proposed by the NWLB co-chairs. Former President and NWLB co-chair Howard Taft proposed legislation to protect workers' right to organise and collectively bargain in order to avoid the 'wasteful strife by strike and lockout'. His second co-chair Basil Manly proposed President Woodrow Wilson enshrine these rights under the authority of a National Labor Board to function as a 'supreme court of labor relations'.[5]

It would be a mistake to conclude that 'the advantage went mostly to labor' from the wartime labour-planning state.[6] As Conner observed, the NWLB 'did nothing revolutionary. Its policies were meant to keep workers on the job'.[7] Whatever workers' gains were delivered by government intervention, were forced upon the government by the threat of disruption. But even those gains,

---

3   Foner 1987, p. 156.
4   National Civic Federation founder Ralph Easley and president V. Everit Macy in Conner 1983, pp. 173–4.
5   Conner 1983, pp. 175–6.
6   Ibid., p. ix.
7   Ibid., p. 183.

shot through with exceptions, exclusions and contradictions, were tempered for fear of workers using them to engage in further disruption.

The labour-planning state, of which the NWLB was its centrepiece, was intended to manage what it could not prevent. Manley saw the labour board as critical to state industrial policy that would 'progress by orderly evolution rather than by strife and revolution' so as not to allow class conflict to 'threaten the entire industrial stability of the nation, if not the very existence of government itself'.[8] The impact of their efforts in the post-war era were immediately evident. President Wilson called for the first Industrial Conference which began meeting on 6 October 1919 in an unsuccessful attempt to delay and arbitrate the 1919 steel strike.[9] (See Chapter 9).

Foner's point speaks to the three dominant premises in labour and left histories of the wartime strike wave that will be reconsidered here. The first is that 'the wartime strikes presaged the industrial unionism of the 1930s CIO'. The second premise is that 'the NWLB anticipated the New Deal industrial relations system'. The final premise is that 'this was not a revolutionary moment in the United States'.[10]

While it was the last strike wave to precede the 1930s, it needs to be examined in the context of nearly four decades of efforts to recompose working-class power, beginning in the 1877 railroad strike. Although the labour-planning state assembled during WWI was an improvised effort to expand state power into managing class struggle, the process was already underway, beginning with the use of receivership and the reorganisation of local police, state militias and the US Army in the 1870s. What was new during the wartime incarnation was the integration of the AFL into the labour-planning state and government mandated arbitration, which presaged government mandated collective bargaining between capital and labour. It would be far too easy to dismiss the strike wave as un-revolutionary since it was ultimately repressed. That repression was required to counter what could not be quelled by the wartime labour-planning state illustrates that a recomposed working-class had inflicted such widespread disruption that not only the outcome of the war, but also the survival of capitalism, was in doubt.

---

8   Manly wrote the majority report with Frank Walsh for the Commission on Industrial Relations, on whose recommendations the NWLB was modelled. (See Ibid., p. 177).

9   The Industrial Conference was not only undermined by US Steel's chair Elbert Gary's refusal to arbitrate, but also by the steel workers who continued to pressure Gompers to allow them to proceed with the planned strike. (See Chapter 9).

10   Bucki 2009, p. 202; and Conner 1983, p. 15.

Borrowing from Canada

The Wilson administration's strategy was shaped by attempts to use government voluntary arbitration in coal and iron strikes over the previous two decades. According to the National Civic Federation (NCF) and the Commission on Industrial Relations (CIR), which had just wrapped up its three year long investigation in 1915, government intervention through arbitration could be used to diffuse class tension, de-escalate tactics, de-mobilise forces on both sides, restore the credibility of the political system, salvage the fragile elite coalition, and restart the accumulation of capital.[11] Although the NCF existed to offer private voluntary arbitration by its corporate and labour members, the CIR recommended such services be provided by government to address the growing class conflict growing out of the imbalance of power between capital and labour.

The issue of government mandated arbitration was a recurring theme for the CIR, which invited Mackenzie King, the author of the 1907 Canadian Industrial Disputes Investigation Act (CIDIA), to testify. Although the CIR split over whether arbitration should be mandatory (minority report) or voluntary (majority report) the system of arbitration Congress and the Wilson administration put into place during WWI was influenced by the CIDIA, which the US Bureau of Labor found to be 'the logical first step toward government intervention in labor disputes'. Unlike the CIDIA, neither collective bargaining nor strikes were sanctioned after an award was made, although that would change with the 1935 NLRA.[12] Ultimately, the minority report recommendations won out during WWI and CIR Chair Frank Walsh became a convert after he was appointed Co-Chair of the NWLB with former President Howard Taft.[13]

---

11   The NCF not only helped inform the recommendations of the Commission Industrial Relations (CIR) endorsing government intervention in class conflict by providing voluntary arbitration, it also shaped the Wilson administration's new labour planning strategy and staffed several of its agencies. The Department of Labor, approved by President Taft at the end of his term, included a Division of Conciliation that mimicked the services offered by the moribund NCF. Among the linkages between the three was former President Taft, who was a member of the NCF, requested that Congress establish the CIR, and co-chaired the NWLB. Even labour was included with James O'Connell on the NCF executive committee, the CIR, and a member of the Council of National Defense's Committee on Labor during WWI. His service in the NCF contributed to his ouster as IAM president.

12   Although several states considered legislation modelled after the CIDIA Colorado was the first to put it into law. (See Ramirez 1974, pp. 544–5 and 547).

13   In a curious connection to the aftermath of the 1894 railroad strike, in the 1894 case *In re Phelan* Taft sentenced Frank Phelan, an American Railway Union organiser, to six months

Compulsory arbitration was long opposed by unions which argued that it 'served primarily the interests of capital and that it worked against the interests of organised labour'.[14] Yet, that all changed during the war as labour leaders gained access to the polity in exchange for resisting rank and file demands to strike and steering them towards arbitration. The NWLB, which emerged from the Wilson administration's admiration for the CIDIA, became 'a ready solution to the impending industrial chaos' unleashed during the war by self-organised workers in the war industries.[15] It is here that a labour-planning state that could manage as well as repress class struggle was born.

Wartime Opportunities for Disruption

Workers recognised the extremely high cost of being portrayed as disrupting the war effort in order to exploit new opportunities to disrupt the accumulation process. Although Gompers had issued a wartime no strike pledge as the chair of the Council of National Defense (CND) Committee on Labor, disruption was far too tempting when the opportunities far exceeded the costs.[16] Workers learned that they could initiate their own 'counter-plan' by self-organising and bypass the union with little cost, in short, sharp strikes that triggered federal arbitration that quickly proved willing to impose significant hour and wage concessions and restart production to avoid further threats of disruption.[17] After a few months of successfully extracting concessions, workers realised that escalating and intensifying their tactics 'got the goods', to paraphrase the famous IWW slogan.

Guided by the new academic fields of human resources, public relations, social work and sociology, the energy of class conflict was channelled into exchanging temporarily arbitrated wage increases and shorter work hours for greater productivity through Taylorist rationalisation of work. Workers proceeded to turn the rationalisation of work into new opportunities to tactic-

---

in jail for violating a court injunction issued against the union. Although Taft is credited for endorsing the right of workers to unionise and strike, he convicted Phelan for pursuing the strategy of a secondary strike against Pullman. (See Burton 1998, pp. 46–7).

14   Ramirez 1974, p. 554.
15   Ibid., p. 557.
16   The AFL Executive Board refused to pass the pledge. (See Foner 1987, pp. 163, 166, and 168; and Bucki 2009, pp. 94–5).
17   Watson 1971.

ally disrupt production. Deskilling and the emerging assembly line had further integrated the workforce in two ways. First, the new division of labour made all workers interchangeable factors of production. As distinctions based on skills, status, and wages eroded, workers shared more and more connections with one another and less and less with management. Rationalisation further socialised the relations of production and sharpened the class antagonisms. Second, the rising technological composition of capital, in which machines became increasingly integral to the production process, also provided new choke points in which production could be disrupted by the actions of a few or even a minority of workers with or without union strike sanction.[18]

The dual vulnerability of the assembly line and war production made strikes more disruptive than ever. The government's immediate needs to prosecute the war became leverage to wring concessions that expanded the membership and power of organised workers with and without unions. WWI provided the conditions for workers to recompose their power, allowing them to undermine the new composition of capital.

The WWI wildcat strike wave was made possible by the recomposition of working-class power as a force of rupture.[19] Tactical escalation by self-organised workers prompted capital to further expand the role of government into the economy and reorganise production, which imposed a new composition of capital in the face of threats to its control. Expanded federal intervention initially restrained elite power in class conflicts and tilted the balance of power to self-organised workers. But intervention was hardly neutral. Wildcat strikes became a primary impetus for state planning from the shop floor to national industry in order to devise new mechanisms to manage class struggle. Although the US would only be in WWI for about 18 months, it became a trial run for responding to the next period of crisis wrought by a new global recomposition of working-class power that triggered the Great Depression and subsequently the New Deal.

The Decline of the Crafts

Before the Taylorist era, capital and the labour movement operated according to a 'gentleman's agreement' that promoted the perception of shared interests that exchanged concessions over productivity, wages, control, quality, and

---

18   Mathewson 1931, p. 68.
19   Bell and Cleaver 2002; and Holloway 2002.

hours for relative labour docility. The labour-capital consensus over the rigid racial division of labour made this possible. Racially segmented labour markets excluded black workers as potential competitors to white craft workers and preserved their racial status. Capital profited from the exclusion of black workers by exploiting the racism of craft workers to recruit strikebreakers. The power of skilled workers was fleeting, however, as employers began to see it as an impediment to expansion, raising productivity, and higher profits. The assembly line rationalised and standardised work, displaced the specialised knowledge of craft workers to a new middle level management, and made workers interchangeable inputs. Skilled craft workers found themselves rapidly declining in number and isolated in the production process which, according to Alquati, is 'controlled via decomposition and simplification of labour'. These new managers and technicians

> are for us, above all else, the mass of new professionals demanded by the new levels of automation and mechanization of the productive circuit: these are the new professions attaching to auxiliary functions, especially to overall programming, to applied research, etc. ...[20]

As work became timed and standardised and workers became interchangeable, race began to matter less to employers. Capital's use of race as a strategy of divide and conquer prompted skilled unions to impose racial bars, further isolating craft workers from mobilised industrial workers.[21]

While there had been a number of attempts to create regional and national labour federations, each failed during times of depression when rising unemployment decimated their membership, drove affiliates under, and propelled workers into migrating in the search for work elsewhere. In 1881, several craft unions joined together to form the American Federation of Labor (AFL) in order to coordinate their efforts across employers and sectors. Although it was founded with heavy participation by many members of the inclusive Knights of Labor (KoL), which sought to incorporate skilled and unskilled, and black and white workers in single unions, the AFL emphasised its own organisational interests in maintaining the privileged position of craft workers at the top of the

---

20   Alquati n.d.

21   Ironically, it was craft workers, along with farmers, and the gentry, to whom time first began to take on a new importance in work in the mid-eighteenth century. The need for regulating and synchronising work turned time against them as a weapon of their extinction. (Thompson 1967, pp. 67 and 69).

division of labour. Driven by the idea of shared interests between craft workers and employer, the AFL pursued friendly negotiated settlements with capital
that allowed them to maintain their class privileges in exchange for labour
peace.

Craft workers had emerged from the same British guilds that gave birth to the
first corporations. They worked in small shops, rented their tools and obtained
materials from an absentee owner, and controlled entry to a trade as a way
to control prices, productivity, wages, and profits by preventing competition.
Craft workers operated in some ways as subsidiary companies or subcontractors until the mid-nineteenth century, when employers began to take a more
active managerial role in the production process.

The AFL sought to preserve this relationship between skilled workers and
capital through 'business unionism' that sought to protect the power, privileges,
and status of its members. As the number of industrial workers grew, the AFL's
refusal to open itself up to semi- and unskilled black, women, and immigrant
workers strengthened the hand of employers who gladly channelled them into
low paying, deadly industrial and mining work, not only at far lower wages, but
with no control over their conditions of labour and repression of industry-wide
worker organising. The AFL's model of unionisation didn't just exacerbate the
class divisions among workers, but helped to institutionalise the gender and
racial divisions and disparities still prevalent in the labour market and society
today. The fragmentation of unionised workers by job type, wage and power
today so that a single workplace can have many different union locals under
different contracts is the continuing legacy of the AFL's failed model.

Taylorist rationalisation of work emerged in response to the recomposition
of worker power on the shop floor as a strategy to counteract the rigidities of
craft workers and decompose the new forms of organisation and disruption by
unskilled workers. 'If Taylorism and scientific organization of labour had political objectives, it was to put in crisis the level of political organization achieved
by these specific workers, the factor workers'.[22]

By the 1920s the steel, auto, electrical, petroleum, textile, and chemical sectors were highly rationalised.[23] The technological developments that followed
expressed the level of the threat posed by the recomposition of working-class
power. For example, the discovery of the internal combustion car engine drove
the expansion of transport shipping by the newly mass-produced truck after
WWI. This was not merely the result of neutral technological innovation, but

---

22   Alquati n.d.
23   Rawick 1969.

reflected a new composition of capital emerging in response to the vulnerability of the centralised railroad systems to disruption. The series of railroad strikes since 1877 demonstrated how easily railroad workers could disrupt not only the railroad lines but the entire economy by circulating their struggle to other vertically integrated industries such as coal and steel. The truck drove oil production and road building to facilitate it, in turn prompting workers to devise new tactics to counter the new composition of capital.

The apparent inability of the AFL in controlling unruly workers excluded from membership was also a driving force for rationalisation. The AFL was excluded from the elite coalition that ruled the polity because it had little to offer in controlling class conflict. At the same time, the AFL was also challenged by its own members, who had to be kept on a short leash lest they join wildcat strikes or new industrial unions such as the American Railway Union in 1893–4. With the exception of the Knights of Labor in the 1870s–1880s, each attempt to form a national federation of skilled and unskilled workers in specific industries and across industrial sectors were stillborn or outright repressed. The founding of the Industrial Workers of the World (IWW) in 1905 and its rapid rise over the next decade demonstrated that its tactics made it less susceptible to accommodation, co-optation, and institutionalisation. Although many of its organising campaigns began with legal and accepted forms of political action such as petitioning, advocacy and protests, it very rapidly escalated its tactics when those limited political spaces were shut down.

The wartime wildcat strikes demonstrated the fragility of the position of craft workers and the AFL in the rapidly industrialising economy. Workers excluded from AFL unions did not hesitate to organise their own informal shop floor organisations to coordinate resistance to hated work rules, low wages, and long hours. With little support and even active hostility from the AFL unions, these workers experimented with the strategy of industrial unionism and syndicalism and used disruption to provoke federal intervention and win immediate victories, even without establishing formal organisations to defend their gains.[24]

---

24   Syndicalism can be understood to mean the use of disruption, sabotage and strikes to shift power to the workers with the objective of taking over and running the economy. Rocker explains anarcho-syndicalism in a more limited manner as

'the taking over of the management of all plants by the producers themselves under such form that the separate groups, plants and branches of industry are independent members of the general economic organism and systematically carry on production and the distribution of the products in the interest of the community on the basis of free mutual agreements' (Rocker 2004 [1938], pp. 62–3)

Short Sharp Shocks

Despite the AFL's no strike pledge, the NWLB's efforts to curb strikes, and the Committee on Public Information's nationalist propaganda campaign to coerce workers and capital into joining hands to win the war, the exact opposite was happening. Although labour conflicts during the effort to supply the allies before the US entered the war were escalating, they were eclipsed by the nearly 3,000 strikes that occurred in the first six months following 6 April 1917. In the midst of the strike wave, the Wilson administration established the Mediation Commission and a number of mediation agencies for particular industries. As a result of their mostly futile efforts to suppress strikes most of their authority and precedent-setting rulings were consolidated into the NWLB, what Conner called the 'Supreme Court of Labor Relations'.[25] There were more than 2,000 work stoppages in the war industry during the approximately nine months that the NWLB operated as a 'hurried improvisation created by executive proclamation under stress of war' to resolve labour conflicts.[26] The strike wave continued despite the formation of several other similar agencies. In all, there were 6,205 strikes during the 18 months the US participated in the war.[27]

Strikes continued even after the NWLB was formed because workers were spurred to continue wildcat strikes due to the lower cost and improved opportunity to achieve significant gains by doing so. Of the 19,915 work stoppages between 1914–18, 7,414, or 56 percent, occurred during the 18-month period the US was at war. This was a dramatic increase since 1914 when there were about 1,300, 3,600 in 1916 and 4,359 in 1917.[28]

There was a nearly 25 percent decline in the number of wartime strikes in 1918, the year the NWLB was established, although the number of workers on strike was nearly the same. (See Table 4). In 1919, the year the NWLB stopped taking new complaints and was shut down, the number of strikes remained nearly the same, but the number of strikers more than tripled. These changes in the number of strikes and strikers seem to have been affected by the existence and discontinuance of the NWLB and other labour-planning agencies.

There are two possible lessons to be extracted from this data. First, the short wartime experiment demonstrated that expanding state power to regulate class struggle could reduce disruption by strikes. However, since the number of

---

25   Conner 1983, p. vii.

26   Gregg 1919–20, pp. 61–2.

27   McCartin 1992, p. 519; and Foner 1987, pp. 169, 342, and 345.

28   Foner 1987, pp. 169, 342, and 345.

TABLE 4   *Strikes and lockouts, 1914–18*

Year	No. strikes & lockouts	No. employees
1914	1,080	n.a.
1915	1,405	504,275
1916	3,786	1,599,610
1917	4,359	1,213,000
1918	3,285	1,235,459
1919	3,374	4,112,507

BUCKI 2009, P. 192

strikers remained the same while the number of strikes declined, strikes were getting larger. Second, the decline in the number of strikes may be an effect of credible strike threats. Workers threatened to strike and brought their complaint to the NWLB which issued a favourable award before the workers needed to strike to obtain the same gains. In effect, the costs of mobilising and threatening to strike had gone down since it could be expected that the government would intervene to award a concession. Therefore, the number of labour conflicts may have actually gone up if strike threats had also been recorded, since workers had an incentive to mobilise and act as the costs of doing so declined and the opportunity to gain from doing so went up.

The WWI strike wave took place at the tail end of a cycle of growing class struggle during which wildcat strikes were extraordinarily common, especially between 1881–1905. During this period the number of strikes gradually increased and the number of workers on strike grew dramatically. For example, in 1886 the number of strikes doubled from the previous year, 47 percent of them were wildcats, and 60 percent more workers were on strike.[29] Although the number of strikes remained flat in 1894, the year of the Pullman strike, the number on strike increased by 250 percent, 37 percent of the strikes were wildcats, and there was a doubling in the number of sympathy strikes. Overall, the

---

29   This was certainly due to the 1 May 1886 strike for the 8 hour day. Peterson estimated the number of strikes not called by a union as only increasing 2 percent from 1885 6 and the number of workers in them declining by 8.9 percent. However, these estimates are imprecise. A wildcat strike may take different forms such as unaffiliated workers going on strike, a strike losing its union sanction, and other reasons. However they are defined, after 1927, the federal Bureau of Labor Statistics stopped collecting any data about both wildcat strikes and those over work rules. (Peterson 1938, pp. 32 and 166).

number of strikes and workers grew as much as 500 percent, and the number of wildcat strikes remained between 18 to 52 percent.

After a short lull, the following period of 1915–22 compared not only to the earlier waves of 1886 and 1894, but also to the better-known 1934 and 1937 strike waves. For example, in 1915, only 43 of the 179 machinist strikes were union-sanctioned, meaning that 80 percent of all machinist strikes were wildcats. In 1916 alone, one in 12 workers had gone on strike.[30] Worldwide, the number of strikes during this period eclipsed both the period of the mid-1930s and following the end of WWII. While not the focus of this book, it is critical to observe that the strike wave in the US was part of a larger cycle of working-class struggle around the world.[31] Despite extremely low levels of unionisation, workers were self-organising and escalating their tactics to disruptive strikes.

The causes and objectives of the number of strikes and the number of workers involved in them were startling. Between 1896–1901, for example, the number of sympathy strikes experienced the greatest increase of about tenfold. The number of strikes over recognition and rules, and wages alone grew about threefold each, combined wage increase and hour decrease grew by about fivefold, and decrease in hours exploded by more than 16-fold.[32] While all causes became more frequent, the greatest increase was over 'recognition and rules'. A class analysis of 'recognition' could mean not only the most common assumption of attempting to force the employer to recognise the union as the workers' bargaining agent, but the ability to circulate the struggle to other shops, companies, sectors, or industries. 'Rules' could be interpreted to mean a struggle over who held power over work, productivity, and output. The next fastest rising cause, to increase wages and reduce hours, was an assertion of their humanity and their resistance to work.

The number of workers on strike between a slightly longer time period of 1896–1902 is also telling. The number of workers involved in sympathy strikes was explosive, rising nearly 37 times. The number on strike over recognition and rules grew by nearly tenfold, combined wage increase and hour decrease by more than fourfold, and decrease in hours by more than eightfold, even reach-

30   Montgomery 1979, p. 20; and Smith 2006, p. 157.
31   Silver also notes that the strike wave in the 'colonial and semi-colonial world' during this period was on par with the mid-1930s and the 1960s to 1980s, but lower than following WWII, a period of rapid successes of the anti-colonialism movement. (Silver 2003, pp. 125–6 and 128). In his comparison of strikes between 1890–1924, Tilly found that the US was the only one of six countries (Russia and four European) to not experience a drop in strikes during WWI. (Tilly 1989, p. 436).
32   See Table 8 in Peterson 1938, pp. 33.

ing more than 26 fold. By contrast, the number on strike for wages alone dropped by about one-third.[33]

What this data demonstrates is that striking workers were clearly not limited to realising narrow self-interests, but struck as leverage to assert their power to control the conditions of work, reduce the hours of labour, and increase their pay. In effect, workers were actively attempting to expand their non-work time and get paid to do it. Their success in getting paid more to work less would have reverberations throughout the economy. Most significantly, it gave them the power to circulate their strikes across the economy in disruptive sympathy strikes. Perhaps not accidentally, the AFL, formed in only 1886, began to gain recognition and legitimacy among factions of elites as a disciplinary stabilising force to manage this explosive class struggle.

Successful strikes attracted mass support, lowered the costs of mobilisation and escalation and increased the opportunity to achieve gains. This attracted workers in other shops, companies, and sectors to mobilise, triggering a new cycle of struggle launched by a recomposed working-class. The struggle circulated as each action signalled the ineffectiveness of repression. Each strike, whether successful or not, led to a signal spiral that informed other workers of the rising opportunity and declining costs from escalating tactics.

A key tactic to recomposing their power was the sympathy strike, in which workers walk out to disrupt production in one shop or company, whether under contract or not, with no immediate connection to a strike occurring elsewhere, to create leverage for the strikers. Not surprisingly, sympathy strikes were at the top of the list during 1885–1894. While smaller in total number, sympathy strikes increased by sixfold, even reaching tenfold during 1891. However, the number of workers involved in sympathy strikes exploded almost 24-fold.[34]

Sympathy strikes could be understood as an expression of what Karl Marx called a 'class for itself' which used the strike as a way to expand non-work time for the free expression of their own humanity and to develop alternatives to work.[35] This strike tactic allows workers to expand their base of support and circulate their struggle across and between sectors of the economy, regardless of contract, industry, or company. Banned by the 1947 Taft-Hartley Act, sympathy strikes were embarrassing to union leaders who celebrated the union contract as a means of ensuring control and stability of their members.

---

33   See Table 9 in Peterson 1938, p. 34.
34   Peterson 1938, p. 34.
35   Cleaver 1979, pp. 81–94.

The common causes of these strikes and how they spoke to power over production, less work and more pay was bookended by a strike wave in the three years preceding the US's formal entry into WWI. The number of strikes between 1914–17 quadrupled (see Table 4) and remained there until 1921, tamped down by the abrogation of wartime arbitration agreements, welfarism, and government political repression.[36]

WWI came at the tail end of one of the most turbulent periods of class conflict in American history and had the unintended effect of continuing to fuel it.

> These six years [1911–16] rank among the most violent in American history, except for the Civil War. Although the origins of violent encounters were not different from those in the past, they frequently attained a virulence seldom equaled in industrial warfare in any nation.[37]

Although it is common to see war as a great unifier that detracts attention from unresolved political and social conflicts, WWI appears to have provided an effective vehicle for workers to escalate their tactics to disrupt production as leverage to achieve their objectives.[38] Glaberman and Rawick's optimistic point that 'when workers are forced to choose between patriotism and class interest, they will usually choose class interest (and consider it patriotic)'[39] was the case during WWI despite the heavy-handed pro-war propaganda campaign coordinated by the Committee for Public Information.[40]

---

36   Bucki notes that companies began to expand corporate personnel and welfare strategies such as cafeterias, victory gardens, efforts to reduce turnover, Americanisation programmes, and war bond contests, to discipline 'recalcitrant' immigrant and skilled workers. (See Bucki 2009, pp. 199–200; as well as Ramirez 1978; and Peterson 1938, p. 35).

37   Ross and Taft 1969, p. 18.

38   This argument was most famously made by Howard Zinn about the Spanish-American War serving to deflect growing class conflict to the cause of nationalism. While this has some explanatory power, it glosses over the class contradictions that are exacerbated during wartime and cause them. (Zinn 2001, ch. 12).

39   Although nationalism has proven to be a dangerous ingredient in class conflict, often being manipulated and turned against subordinate groups such as immigrants, students, blacks, or 'radicals', it can sometimes be a tactic used by workers such as with the Amazon Army waving flags as they shut down the Kansas coal mines in the 1920s. (See Schofield 1984; and Goossen 2011). Similarly, the strike wave during the Vietnam War probably caused more disruption to the war effort than the anti-war protests, at least until after 1970.

40   Glaberman and Rawick 1977, p. 220.

WAR IN EUROPE, WAR ON CAPITAL: THE WWI WILDCAT STRIKE WAVE   383

During the US's brief formal participation in the war, from 6 April 1917 until 11 November 1918, the mostly short 6,205 strikes 'took on an outlaw quality' despite the AFL's no strike pledge.[41] Their mostly short duration was an extremely effective tactic because, as Tilly explains,

> lightning mobilization, if it occurs, does reduce the chances for the incremental challenging, testing, and coalition-formation which belong to the routine acquisition of power, and concentrates the attendant collective violence in a short period of time.[42]

Combined with a labour shortage and high turnover, short strikes were a successful tactic to drive up wages while shortening work hours. Because annual factory turnover was a stunning 1,600 to 2,000 percent, the costs to striking were extremely low because even if the strike was lost and the workers were fired other jobs were relatively easy to find.[43] Companies had difficulty finding sufficient workers, let alone strikebreakers, and were forced to concede in order to avoid having to stop production. There is an embedded class power obscured in the data about 'tight labour markets'. High turnover indicated that workers used individual 'exit strategies' to pit employers against one another by moving to jobs that presumably had better pay, lower hours, better working conditions, and were maybe organised and under contract. Being able to easily find another job made exiting low cost, high opportunity leverage to impose gains on employers. It also lowered the costs and increased the opportunities of organising and striking. As a result, strikes tended to become shorter as management found itself with a limited range of tactics in its repertoire to break the strike. Finding replacement workers and strikebreakers was difficult and introducing a technological solution took too long and had significant up front costs. The companies also feared the government might impose a settlement that gave the workers more than they might otherwise get or even nationalise the plant or industry to avoid disruption. During the last 12 months of the war, the NWLB contributed to the shortening of strikes by quickly imposing a settlement and sending the workers back to the shop floor.

Whether or not they had a union and contract, the WWI strike wave made the workers extremely successful in their efforts to work less (both absolutely and relatively) and get paid more. Not only did wages rise and work hours decline,

---

41   Montgomery 1979, p. 96.
42   Tilly 1978, pp. 201–2.
43   Montgomery 1979, p. 96.

but output per man hour declined. 'Output per hour was declining during the war years at the very same time that the number of hours regularly worked each week were falling'.[44] Although this period was brief, workers were able to achieve a rare ability to both reduce the length of time they worked (absolute surplus value) *and* the productivity of their work (relative surplus value). In cases where strikers' demands for higher pay and less work were not awarded by the NWLB, they would reduce their output to compensate (or as the IWW would say 'struck on the job') and lay the foundation for renewing the conflict with management. In this way, workers used their leverage to effectively win more pay for less work.

The workers' rare success was fleeting. More pay for less work 'not only injured the war effort, [employers] claimed, it also threatened their plans for the postwar world'.[45] In 1916, the president of the National Metal Trades Association warned that 'the current war of arms would be followed swiftly by a war of economic competition'.[46] Literally days after the ceasefire, employers began mass layoffs, further inflated consumer prices, slashed wages, abrogated NWLB arbitration rulings, and returned to the tactics of violently repressing organised workers and strikes in order to rapidly return the balance of power in their favour.[47]

Struggle for Control over Work

The wave of wartime wildcats was launched a few years earlier, primarily by self-organised women factory workers in Bridgeport, Connecticut, which produced two-thirds of the arms and armaments shipped to the allies in Europe. Building trades workers won a months-long strike for eight hours and recognition in the summer of 1915. Their success inspired organised and unorganised, mostly women workers to begin a series of wildcat strikes for the eight-hour workday (48-hour workweek), repeal of hated fines and work rules, and union recognition. Following capitulation to demands for eight hours and a wage increase at Remington Arms Company but not recognition, a walkout by 100 women at the nearby Union Metallic Cartridge Company arms plant won them eight hours but a smaller raise. Self-organised women garment workers followed, coordinating seven consecutive short, sharp strikes in seven plants over

44   Ibid., p. 121.
45   Ibid.
46   Ibid.
47   Ibid., p. 96.

the next four days starting with 1,600 corset workers at Warner Corset Company. The garment workers' wildcat spread and soon about 12–14,000 other garment, electric, graphaphone, textile, cable, arms, foundries, rubber, and laundry workers wildcatted including 5,000 women on the assembly line at Remington Arms. The women struck apart from International Association of Machinists (IAM) members also striking for the eight-hour day, who went back to work earlier. According to Bucki, these workers had little union involvement but self-organised their own elected shop committees. During the month of August an estimated 12,000 women won the eight-hour day and wage increase. Over a period of about 10 weeks the majority of the 55 strikes launched were settled with shorter workweeks, higher pay, and time and a half for overtime and double time for Sunday. What they didn't get was union recognition.[48]

Without a union, and despite an attempt by a woman organiser to get some workers to not strike simultaneously, mostly women industrial workers used the leverage of the growing demand for labour in the burgeoning war industries to successfully self-organise and escalate their tactics. The success of these self-organised workers soon attracted interest from both the IWW and the IAM. Organising expanded throughout the state and the Northeast and membership in the IAM grew after it abandoned its patriarchal hostility to organising women workers and elitism towards unskilled immigrant workers. By expanding the job categories which could belong to the union, the IAM was better positioned to call 128 strikes in 35 cities for the eight-hour day, no reduction in pay, and union recognition. On 1 May 1916, 600 strikes were called during a nationwide general strike. A gun battle with company police occurred when strikers attempted to shut down US Steel's Edgar Thompson works. Eventually troops were sent in and strikers and 30 strike leaders were arrested and charged with treason, many of whom were sentenced.[49]

The IAM was under pressure from the organising efforts of the IWW-affiliated American Industrial Union (AIU) at Westinghouse Electric which had struck in 1914. AIU organised all workers regardless of skill and gender to assert their power on the shopfloor to extract demands rather than negotiate contracts. The AIU contested management's prerogative to control the speed and productivity of work, demanded the abolition of piecework and incentive pay, rotation of layoffs, and the pace of work slowed. Led by socialists inspired by

---

48   New England Historical Society n.d.; and Bucki n.d.
49   To counteract the railroad brotherhoods' threat to also strike for eight hours in September 1916, Congress passed the Adamson Act on 3 September granting their demand and time and a half for overtime but only for interstate workers, which was upheld the following march by the Supreme Court.

IWW's organising strategies, the AIU strikers 'aimed straight at scientific man-agement's jugular vein'.[50] During the war the president of Westinghouse wrote to NWLB co-chair, former President Taft, that the company faced constant struggles with 'bad faith, restriction of output, violence, disregard of obligations and irresponsibility' of the workers organisation with which he had to deal.[51] Eventually, the AIU and IAM combined their efforts on the shop floor and the streets against Westinghouse, although they lost the strike in 1916.

The wartime strikes were not limited to the US. 'Winnipegitis', the tendency to launch general strikes such as in Winnipeg from 15 May to 25 June 1919, was born in nearby Hamilton, Ontario. IAM workers launched a series of wildcat strikes in the arms industry demanding a nine-hour day, more pay, time and a half for overtime and double time on Sundays and holidays.[52] Although there was not a formal no strike pledge, the Trades and Labor Congress of Canada had relied on the Imperial Munitions Board to impose a settlement through invest-igations of grievances, hearings, and negotiations. After IAM leaders admitted it had lost control of the workers the government formed the Snyder Com-mission, which eventually endorsed the workers' demands although not recog-nition. IAM's repeated attempts to delay demands for a strike in response to the companies' refusal to implement the ruling eventually receded. In June 1916, about 2,000 skilled and unskilled, unionised and non-unionised workers struck at about 30 city arms factories with wide public support and at least one sympathy strike. Machinists in Toronto then called for a general strike unless demands for the 50-hour workweek were granted. Fearing the spread of the strike in the area and to other cities, the government imposed press censorship of what had been broad sympathetic coverage of the strike but not advertising by the companies. Ultimately a combination of factors led to the strike's defeat after about a month. Among the causes of its defeat were workers leaving to find work elsewhere in a tight labour market and

> fierce employer resistance to the demands of organised labour; opportun-istic policy decisions by government and the Imperial Munitions Board which were geared not to secure social justice but to avert work disrup-tions; and embattled trade union leaders struggling to assert their own code of responsible union behaviour against a restive membership.[53]

---

50   Montgomery 1989, pp. 282–3.

51   Taft was just one of those who made the jump from the Nation Civic Federation to the new welfarist institutions of the Progressive Era. (See also Montgomery 1979, pp. 120–1 and 125).

52   Siemiatycki 1978, p. 141.

53   Ibid., p. 151.

But Siemiatycki placed the primary cause for the defeat of the strike at the feet of the IAM's persistent effort to negotiate in order to prevent and delay the strike, channel the workers' militancy through the commission, and finally help prevent the strike from circulating. As he explained, the IAM leadership

> gave public assurance that the union's leadership would do all in its power to prevent the strike from spreading. In the eyes of this leadership an overly militant strike – especially one which included the call for other union members to quit work in violation of their own agreements – would intensify employers' opposition to trade unionism. Since union officers attempted to portray their organizations as valuable allies of manage-ment in the pursuit of industrial productivity and stability, labour leaders found themselves increasingly compelled to control and moderate the radical impulses of their members.[54]

The union's disciplining of unruly workers had lasting negative effects on its Hamilton members, who were irreparably weakened. By 1919 their wages remained uncharacteristically lower than in 1914, although half of the workers who had struck in 1916 had realised the nine-hour day working somewhere else.

1917 began with railroad and shipbuilding strikes and protests against the rising cost of food and other necessities in working-class Jewish neighbour-hoods of Brooklyn which quickly spread to Philadelphia, Boston, and Chica-go.[55] By the time the US entered the war, strikes, especially 'control strikes', were widespread throughout the war industry, which was already up and run-ning on contracts for the allies. 'Control strikes' were appropriately named struggles over who controlled work and productivity levels, what Peterson called 'recognition, rules and others' during an earlier period. They were as frequent between 1916 and 1920 as they had been between 1901 and 1904 and would be again from 1934–1941.

Wartime control strikes also contested the role of the contract in enfor-cing management's control over work. To protect their new contracts the AFL 'induced their leaders to suppress sympathy strikes, which had been the main-spring of their growth in earlier decades'.[56] Wildcat strikes were a tool to bypass the union in order to continue asserting their power to determine the terms of work. Its use was an implicit refusal to abandon the very leverage that was used

---

54   Ibid., p. 147.

55   Foner 1987, p. 155; Frank 1985, pp. 255–85; Frieburger 1984, pp. 217–39; Marcy 1917, pp. 582 and 584.

56   Montgomery 1979, p. 92.

to force employers to recognise, negotiate, and concede the terms of the contract in the first place. The strikers also appeared to be keenly aware that such
escalation was more likely to succeed if they were able to expand their base of
support by circulating the strike to other shops, companies and sectors.

Workers were exceptionally unruly during this decade despite the contract.
As Montgomery explained,

> The direct, mass-involvement challenge to managerial authority and con-
> tempt for accepted AFL practice workers exhibited in 1909–1910 were to
> remain outstanding characteristics of American labor struggles, not epis-
> odically but continuously for the next dozen years. That most large strikes
> of the epoch ended in total defeat for the workers testifies both to the
> audacity of the strikers' pretensions and their willingness to act in defi-
> ance of warnings from experienced union leaders that chances of victory
> were slim.[57]

It is likely that the infrequency of success of these strikes can be better explained less by tangible objectives of control, hours, and wages and more as
an intangible expression of workers striking because there was little risk from
striking so as to enjoy some unplanned 'free time' from work.

If the workers' 'bad faith' in work wasn't already disruptive enough, all
remaining inhibitions about further action seemed to have ended with the
Allies' war orders and the end of business uncertainty. Strikes became increasingly common even in the unlikeliest places such as munitions plants where
nationalist war fever ran high and small towns where the employers' anti-union
'open shop' movement was strongest.[58]

Wartime strikes were not limited merely to control, wages, and hours issues,
but released pent up working-class discontent as city-wide general strikes,
coordinated shutdowns of production and the take-over of formal power across
an entire geographical area. Between September 1917 and April 1918 there
were five city-wide general strikes in Springfield, Illinois, Kansas City, Missouri,
Waco, Texas, and two in Billings, Montana.[59] The successful week-long March
1918 Kansas City general strike began when many workers in the city struck in
solidarity with female and male laundry workers on strike for higher wages and
better conditions. Strengthened by workers crossing the gender barrier, par-

---

57   Ibid., pp. 94–5.
58   Ibid.
59   Ibid., p. 98.

ticularly among the integrated street and railway workers, the general strike resulted in a NWLB settlement for higher wages, equal pay for women workers, and a right to organise.[60] It can only be imagined what might have been had these general strikes continued circulating to other key cities and industries.

The wartime strikes had a profound influence on class struggle, bringing to light the struggle between business and industrial unionism and the emerging tactics to confront and disrupt the new division of industrial work. Using mass mobilisation to shut down production by focusing on demands rather than bargaining a contract, these workers 'project[ed] an image of workers' control of modern industry'. They also provided a newfound credibility for both unions and the state in managing that class struggle to prevent the realisation of these objectives.[61]

But even these general strikes obscure everyday forms of resistance that are not directly recorded either by historians or by government strike data. It is possible to glean workers' resistance to work by reading through investment flows, return on investment and productivity data. Class struggle against work takes other forms besides strikes, what the IWW called 'striking on the job': absenteeism, machine breaking, strictly following rules ('book of rules' or 'work to rule'), purposeful inefficiency ('putting the machine on strike'), and tricking the Taylorist timers by working more slowly than normal. These types of everyday forms of resistance are common both when conditions make organising and unionising risky and where workers are organised. Sometimes they are resorted to when an overt strike is defeated.[62] These tactics are a form of workers' self-organisation that may be hinted at in the category of 'control strikes', where workers responded to rationalisation with overt actions when management attempts to punish and prevent further everyday forms of resistance.[63]

---

60 The general strike had been preceded by a short successful strike the previous August that was also settled by the NWLB. During that strike as many as 20,000 mass supporters blocked and sabotaged street cars and attacked about 1,000 strikebreakers, driving them out of town. It followed by another strike in December 1918. (Stilley 2017; and Onasch nd).

61 Montgomery 1989, pp. 286–7.

62 Flynn n.d.

63 While Silver suggests that the data on such forms of everyday forms of resistance are rare, an issue that is 'especially significant in situations where strikes are illegal and open confrontation difficult or impossible', it is possible to read through capital's efforts to control recalcitrant workers whose struggles are not immediately visible by analysing data, new technology, organization, rules, etc to tease out the details of class struggle. (Silver 2003, p. 35; see also Mathewson 1931; Glaberman 1965, 1973, and 1977; Bell and Cleaver 2002; and for peasant forms of everyday resistance, see Scott 1985).

The strategy proceeded from the IWW's approach of organising workers according to the workers' ethnic and racial diversity and the existing migratory and contingent conditions in which they worked. As Bologna observed,

> the merit of the IWW was that it attempted to organise the American proletariat in terms of its intrinsic characteristics. It was primarily an immigrant proletariat and, therefore, a mixture of ethnic groups which could only be organised in a certain way. Secondly, it was a mobile proletariat: thus, it was not only completely against identification with any specific task or skill but it was also against any link with individual factories (even if only to take them over). The IWW succeeded in concretely individuating the concept of social factory, and thus it sought to exploit the extraordinary level of communication and coordination allowed by a mobility-based struggle.[64]

The IWW strategy to capitalise on workers' mobility made negotiating contracts superfluous. Asserting their power to disrupt production had immediate consequences. Because the work was sporadic, seasonal, or impermanent, establishing contractual obligations for better pay and conditions would be of no consequence once the job ended and they moved on. The IWW was a potent threat because it turned contingency into a vector of mobilisation and deployed disruption as leverage to extract immediate concessions.[65]

As a result of ubiquitous striking on the job and other everyday forms of resistance, the rationalisation of work proceeded by fits and starts. Despite his legendary reputation, Taylor had reorganised fewer than 30 factories by 1917.[66] His reputation far exceeded his actual achievements, for reasons that aren't well understood. A close study of the strike waves during the Taylorist era demonstrates that the rationalisation of work was not only a response to unruly workers, but also faced resistance from informal groupings of unknown committees of workers on the shop floor, some craft unions, and the spread of the IWW. It was during WWI that these efforts exploded in a wave of wildcat strikes that threatened the war effort.

---

64   Bologna 1976, p. 72.
65   Ibid., pp. 86–7.
66   Montgomery 1979, p. 113.

Wartime Strikes

Immediately preceding and during the war, working-class insubordination reached new heights both on and off the shop floor. In response, the federal government set up several boards to address war production and to arbitrate grievances and conflicts between employers and workers and issued rulings to settle them. To counter the risk of disrupting wartime production, the hastily formed NWLB was set up to provide a mechanism through which workers could express their grievances and seek redress. The premise of the NWLB was that the workers were at last being heard and would demobilise and de-escalate their wildcat strikes in order to take advantage of this new access to the polity.

The threat of disruption triggered the NWLB's arbitration process. Workers with a grievance and threatening to strike, or already on strike, would petition the NWLB, which would quickly respond by holding an impromptu on-site hearing to hear testimony and issue a ruling. Because NWLB policy explicitly prevented the board from intervening during a strike, its involvement got the workers to de-escalate and return to the job.[67] But did forcing workers to de-escalate in order to carry out arbitration work to subdue class conflict?

Government intervention into war production conflicts had two unintended feedback effects on the unrest. A ruling that included concessions to the workers prompted the conflict to circulate to other locations and workers. This was soon followed by more wildcat strikes and disruption after which the NWLB process began again somewhere else. Workers who escalated the intensity of their tactics found that it triggered the federal government to intervene to impose concessions in exchange for de-escalation of both capital and labour. Government intervention made the costs of escalation extremely low while rapidly raising the opportunity for achieving desired gains. This had the effect of encouraging workers to quickly circulate their struggles to other shops, companies, and industrial sectors. Imposing concessions on industry was preferable to allowing any further disruption to war production, due to the exceptionally high costs to the war effort in Europe. This rapidly ignited the circulation of struggle as workers increasingly became aware that both capital and the state were unable and unwilling to repress strikes in key industries.

The NWLB of the First World War helped to feed rank-and-file militancy in at least two ways. First, in practice workers had to either strike or threaten a walkout in order to secure an investigation of their grievances

---

67   Conner 1983, p. 54.

by the NWLB. Thus, the national strike rate actually *increased* by 25 percent during the Board's first month of operation. Once such militancy was triggered, it was often difficult to contain. Second, the NWLB's pro-labor decisions served to both embolden workers and to raise their expectations.[68]

The NWLB may have had the unintended consequence of encouraging rank and file workers to defy their unions and call a strike in order to trigger NWLB involvement. Although the NWLB did not provide collective bargaining or union recognition, most rulings raised wages and/or lowered working hours. Workers were quick to take advantage of this pattern. While the number of strikes declined the number *on* strike remained steady between 1917–18.

The NWLB revived and expanded the earlier arbitration model of the 1902 Coal Commission in which government used voluntary arbitration to intervene in the class struggle. The Commission ultimately issued a ruling which settled the strike for the anthracite miners but excluded the bituminous miners, thus setting the stage for two more decades of conflict in the latter mines. A significant difference was that the NWLB crafted rulings in light of their powerlessness to prevent workers from disrupting the war economy. As a result, 'federal regulation in many ways strengthened the hands of rank-and-file workers, complicating the efforts of AFL leaders who sought to quell unrest'.[69]

Arbitration rulings were designed to grant concessions to both sides with the objective of de-escalating tactics of both capital and workers and restoring production. Rulings made concessions to capital by consistently denying union recognition and punting on work control issues in exchange for awarding substantial wage increases to wildcatting workers.

Despite the attempt to 'split it down the middle' by giving something to both sides, the process actually favoured the strikers. Rather than arbitration *preventing* a strike by awarding concessions, the workers' strike *triggered* the arbitration. And where the outcome of arbitration was likely to favour the company, NWLB rulings predictively awarded a substantial concession to the workers to get them back to work. Workers had learned to turn mandatory arbitration on its head by using both actual or threatened disruption to extract concessions without limits or constraints.

While workers demobilised to access the newly open space in the polity to address their concerns to the NWLB, the state was simultaneously escalating its

---

68   McCartin 1992, p. 521, italics in original.
69   Ibid.

use of police state powers to repress the militant wing of the labour movement. In effect, workers in East Coast arms plants were encouraged to de-escalate to negotiate, with the high probability of achieving their gains by doing so, in order to gain their acquiescence in the repression of more militant workers in the hinterlands. Arbitration lowered the short-term costs and raised the opportunity for short-term gains in wages. But it made it harder to maintain those gains beyond the end of the war by clamping down on those workers most capable of defending them.

The Labour-Planning State is Born

The NWLB kept war production going by using hearings, investigations, and rulings to smooth out potential disruptions in war production by managing working-class insubordination. Rather than openly suppress strikes, it sought to subtly smother them in complex layers of bureaucracy. The new arbitration mechanism required workers to demobilise and de-escalate in order to engage with a government organisation whose procedural complexity made it nearly inaccessible, if not incomprehensible, and utterly frustrating. Even its rulings required further bureaucratic procedures to set up a shop floor committee, hold elections, establish more procedures and hold meetings.

The NWLB also established the beginnings of an apparatus for elites to extend patronage to union leadership in the form of political access, higher wages, and other concessions in exchange for their obedience in implementing the prerogatives of capital. The AFL didn't merely sign onto the war, as many historians are keen to point out; it endorsed and actively collaborated on efforts to vastly expand government power to manage class conflict.

Arbitration was just one piece of the social control policy that included the AFL's subservience to the war effort, its declaration of its unofficial 'no strike' pledge, silence during government criminalisation of dissent, and the suppression of the IWW, anarchists, socialists, and radical labour organisers inside the AFL. Gompers had come full circle from his earlier denunciation of arbitration as a 'system of slavery' and adamant rejection of any role for the AFL in elections and lobbying.[70] But his reversal on mandatory arbitration cannot be

---

70   Gompers told the Commission:
       'As soon as the Government steps in and says to the workingman ...: you must work under such conditions as are here stipulated; if you do not work you will go to prison. At that moment slavery has been introduced ... call it by whatever name you please, compulsory arbitration or compulsory investigation, compulsory work pending the final

merely explained by 400,000 members of the railway brotherhoods gaining the eight-hour day under the 1916 Adamson Act.[71] It must also be examined in light of Gompers tempering his demands for closed union shops in War Department contracting. Rather, Gompers and much of the AFL came around to it as a factor in the integration of the union leadership into the polity. The NWLB was the most significant driving force wedging organised labour into the polity.

The NWLB was established following several other bodies with a similar mandate to manage class conflict in the railroad, shipping, and other war production sectors. The Council of National Defense (CND) was created on 29 August 1916 under Section 120 of National Defense Act of 3 June 1916 and Section 2 of Army Appropriations Act. President Wilson appointed the seven-member Advisory Commission to the CND and a Committee on Labor (CoL) which was chaired by AFL President Gompers.[72] The CoL had a 14-member executive committee that was an early model of stakeholder negotiations. It included employers, financiers, corporate directors, and union officials, including James O'Connell, President of the AFL's Metal Trades Department, and National Civic Federation (NCF) President W. Everitt Macy and staffer Ralph Easley. The CND eventually formed eight national committees to assist the executive committee.

One of these committees was the 75-member Committee on Mediation and Conciliation (CMC) that operated briefly from mid-1917 to January 1918. The committee helped arrange arbitrators for the parties in labour disputes. The CMC's second recommendation established a 'continuous administrative machinery for the orderly disposition of industrial problems and the avoidance of an atmosphere of conflict and the waste coming from work stoppages'.[73] While short-lived, the CMC created model government regulations that attempted to rationalise class conflict that were later enshrined in Section 7 of the 1933 NIRA and the 1935 NLRA. The NIRA's controversial price controls were earlier put into place on 28 July 1917, when the War Industries Board (WIB) was established to set prices for government purchasing agencies, made purchases for

---

determination of that investigation ... establishes the System of slavery ...' (see US Commission on Industrial Relations 1916, p. 721).

He was echoed by former UMWA President John Mitchell, who called it 'a species of involuntary servitude'. (See Ramirez 1974, p. 548).

71   This is Bucki's explanation. (See Bucki 2009, p. 194).

72   That no black members were appointed at any level of these committees is not surprising considering the explicit policy excluding blacks from AFL unions. The few that belonged were literally segregated into Jim Crow locals. (Foner 1987, pp. 156–7).

73   Ibid., pp. 156–7.

the Allies, and set priorities for industrial production and distribution.[74] It also paved the way for the creation of the military planning apparatus that integrated the economy during WWII and laid the foundation for what President Eisenhower later famously called the Military-Industrial-Complex.

To dissuade workers from entertaining expectations that these governmental agencies would institute permanent changes in industry, on 6 April 1917 the executive committee of Gompers's CND Committee on Labor (CoL) issued a declaration approved by the Advisory Commission that advised 'neither employers nor employees shall endeavor to take advantage of the country's necessities to change existing standards'. Gompers's surprising announcement provoked numerous protests from union leaders, state federations, and city central labour councils from all over the country. But the committee wasn't finished yet. A second 'amplifying statement' issued by the CoL insisted that no strikes or lockouts take place before all mediation and arbitration efforts had been pursued first to give 'an opportunity to adjust the difficulties without a stoppage of work occurring'. Gompers argued that 'a strike during the war is not justified'.[75] He didn't just accede to a no strike pledge, he authored it. Since the 1917 AFL convention and executive board refused to endorse the ban or alter its opposition to the 'open shop', Gompers turned to the government to enforce it.[76] Because the NWLB would not impose a union contract where none currently existed, Gompers's pledge effectively endorsed the open shop on government war contracts.[77] Gompers's attempt to put a brake on class struggle as labour's contribution to the war effort would cement its legacy as a useful mechanism for decomposing working-class power.

If there was any doubt about his roundabout endorsement of the open shop, several months later Gompers made it official. Gompers's NDAC committee recommended the CND support government sanctioning of existing conditions. He used this position to negotiate an agreement with Secretary of War Newton Baker that allowed 16 army cantonments to be built, guaranteeing union wages and hours without recognising the union. The resulting Cantonment Adjustment Commission became not only the first labour board but established a precedent later enforced by the NWLB.[78] The Baker-Gompers memorandum allowed 'open shops' with union wage and hour scales

74   Ibid., p. 150.
75   Ibid., p. 168.
76   In an attempt to join its class and national interests, the same convention endorsed the pro-war Alliance for Labor and Democracy. (See Conner 1983, p. 27).
77   Foner 1987, pp. 163, 166, and 168.
78   Conner 1983, pp. 22–3.

for the construction of training camps. Gompers signed the agreement without approval from the AFL's Executive Council, effectively endorsing the employers' post-war open shop counter-attack that decimated the AFL rank and file.[79]

Gompers's Faustian bargain allowed the union to deliver higher wages to the membership at the cost of further alienating it from its own rank and file and the rest of the working-class. The absorption of the AFL leadership into the war effort and the labour-planning state is an illustrative example of how negotiations are used to split the leadership from the rank and file, obscuring how concessions are obtained. When leaders advocate for de-mobilisation and de-escalation to negotiate, it is because they expect to be able to deliver a modicum of resources to members by aligning their interests to elites. In the meantime, insurgents who refuse to exclusively use negotiations continue to escalate their tactics to contest this newfound alliance between the leadership and elites. The intensity of escalation may continue when leaders are able to deliver some gains because there is confusion about whether these were made possible by negotiations or tactical escalation. As a result of the split, divided insurgents appear to be using pairing or switching when in actuality their efforts are not coordinated, especially when the leadership governs without democratic input from the rank and file. The split may even become irrevocable when the leadership takes elite positions that undermine the interests of the membership.

In January 1918 the CMC was eclipsed by the establishment of the War Labor Conference Board (WLCB) as an advisory council to Secretary of Labor William B. Wilson. The WLCB consisted of five employer and five labour representatives nominated by the AFL. One of its first actions was to declare that employers could not prevent workers from joining a trade union. Weeks later, on 21 February 1918, the US Railroad Administration, the agency administering the newly nationalised railroad system, banned strikes, and issued General Order No. 8, which gave the right of all railroad workers to organise into trade unions and is still in effect today.[80] With these directives the AFL had found its home inside the newly expanded Democratic Party's big tent.

In 1917, the Shipbuilding Labor Adjustment Board (SLAB) was created as a result of an agreement between the government and all the AFL shipbuilding unions except for the carpenters. The SLAB included members from the Navy, Shipping Board Emergency Fleet Corporation, and the AFL. SLAB was incapable of preventing strikes on the Pacific Coast where the board granted

---

79   Foner 1987, p. 150.
80   The newly established Railroad Administration's Wage Commission conceded to the systems federation of railroad unions' wage demands in 1917. (See Bucki 2009, p. 195; and Foner 1987, p. 174).

a 31 percent wage increase over their June 1916 wage level. Another agreement was made on 8 May 1917 for the Atlantic Coast and the International Seamen's Union, with a 50 percent bonus for serving through the war.[81] Although the national unions were intent on getting their members back to work, they could not stem the wildcat strikes. On the West Coast the Iron Trades Councils stirred the insurgencies inside the unions by organising skilled and unskilled together and demanding an industry-wide contract that raised wages for the lowest paid workers.[82] Much like IAM District 55, it sought to strengthen the recomposition of working-class power by overcoming barriers of status and wages.

NWLB: Supreme Court for Labour

The array of labour planning agencies was uncoordinated and incapable of stemming the tide of strikes or establishing consistent rules or satisfactory settlements for workers and employers.[83] In light of the disarray, the industry National Industrial Conference Board (NICB), the AFL leadership, and the WLCB called for the establishment of a single labour-planning board for all war industry sectors. On 9 April 1918, nearly a year to the day after the US declared war, President Wilson issued an Executive Order that effectively turned the WLCB into the National War Labor Board (NWLB). The board had five employer and five labour members proposed by the NICB and the AFL, and two public representatives who became the co-chairs. Former President Taft and Commission on Industrial Relations Chair Walsh served as the co-chairs. During the 16 months that it existed, a little less than half the time during the war, the NWLB held investigations, conducted hearings, and issued awards, findings, recommendations, and orders concerning 490 cases.

Although the NWLB initially consolidated the ad hoc Cantonment Adjustment Commission and the President's Mediation Commission, it began to operate in practice as the national board if no other agency had jurisdiction as

---

81   Another layer of the labour planning bureaucracy was the Committee on Women in Industry chaired by J. Borden Harriman (whose wife Florence J. Harriman had just served on the Commission on Industrial Relations). (Perlman and Taft 1935, p. 404).

82   Bucki 2009, pp. 195–6.

83   The Byzantine array of interlocking wartime labour-planning agencies was incomprehensible then as it is now. Wilson created yet another coordinating board, the War Labor Policies Board headed by future Supreme Court Justice Felix Frankfurter, that lost its struggle to have authority over the NWLB. (See Conner 1983, pp. 33–4; Foner 1987, pp. 175 and 340; and McCartin 1992, p. 519).

a board of appeal from another agency. The NWLB's task was to maintain conditions of labour as existed before the war but generally lacked legal authority to impose its own rulings on either capital or workers. Both parties to a dispute had to agree to arbitration by the board and board rulings had to be unanimous. If the board could not reach unanimity an umpire would issue a binding ruling.

Because the NWLB was not created by statute or funded by an act of Congress, it lacked all legal power to impose its settlements and relied on moral suasion backed by the force of the Wilson administration. Since it was not funded by Congress, but rather a war-time fund at the discretion of the President, the NWLB lacked the permanence it would need once the war ended and industry began to defy its claim of authority to settle labour disputes. The lack of statutory authority didn't just make the NWLB 'lack real power', as several historians have observed. Instead, it had two contradictory effects: it both encouraged self-organised workers to continually defy the NWLB's own rules to extract concessions, and employers to run the clock out to prevent it issuing rulings or avoid implementing rulings they didn't like, especially knowing the concessions and truce would end with the war.[84]

Although it was hurriedly formed and began to operate on an ad hoc basis to address the wave of wildcat strikes, the NWLB quickly assembled its own principles and rules of procedure. As it walked the razor's edge of appearing to balance the demands and interests of the war, industry and the unions, it had the self-contradictory objective 'to protect the status quo and to undermine it'.[85]

Its core principles included the following:

1.   No strikes or lockouts during the war.

Workers had the right to organise in associations, groups, or trade unions and bargain collectively. Employers were prohibited from interfering with this right or firing workers for exercising it. The right did not imply that workers could use leverage to impose their advantage by force. 'The workers in the exercise of their right to organise should not use coercive measures of any kind to induce persons to join their organizations nor to induce employers to bargain or deal therewith'.[86]

---

84   Gregg 1919–20, p. 40; and Conner 1983, p. 31.

85   Conner 1983, p. 30. See also Foner 1987, pp. 176 and 341; and Kenyon 1921, pp. 13–14.

86   See 'Principles and Policies to Govern Relations Between Workers and Employers in War Industries for the Duration of the War' in Trachtenberg 1920, p. 46.

2.   Workers and employers have a right to organise a union and bargain col-
     lectively.

Workers could organise and have their grievances presented to the NWLB but
they were expected to abandon tactics such as strikes that attempted to force
employers to negotiate or prevent the use of strikebreakers. Employers could
not be compelled to negotiate and were prohibited from locking out striking
workers. Workers were effectively prohibited from striking. These rules explicitly required workers to de-mobilise and de-escalate if they were to be allowed
at the negotiating table or face rising costs and declining opportunities if they
continued escalating their tactics. Since the bargaining agent was not exclusively required to be a union, employers attempted to negotiate with company
unions. One reason this did not stem the wildcat strikes was that workers soon
discovered that they had more opportunity to achieve their objectives by not
seeking negotiations or formal recognition.

The caveat to these first two principles was that workers had a right to
organise but not to strike over a demand for recognition. Employers, on the
other hand, were compelled to recognise and negotiate with a 'shop committee'
whether or not it was dominated by a union. In effect, a shop that was unionised
before the dispute could remain unionised but one that was non-union could
not be unionised.[87] This clearly disadvantaged workers more than employers. If workers self-organised and struck, they were prevented from forming
a formal union with a permanent presence in the shop as a result of their
strike. The NWLB would impose a shop committee on them after the settlement that could become a 'company union'. Workers were therefore forced to
organise informally. Bucki appears ambivalent about the impact of shop committees. While shop committee elections 'solved the competing demands by
giving workers a voice but not union representation', the denial of a formal
voice did little to impede workers from trying to dominate them as they continued self-organising.[88]

Although self-organisation has a number of advantages, such as exempting
strikers from legal consequences of disruptive strikes, it requires that workers 'reinvent' their organisation every time they have a grievance while the
employer is free to maintain their organisation. Whatever the advantages and
disadvantages, such a prohibition did little to discourage workers from self-

---

87   Gregg 1919–1920, pp. 59–60.
88   The assertion that the NWLB gave labour a 'voice' is an oft-repeated refrain in histories of
     the agency. (See Bucki 2009, p. 201; and Conner 1983, p. 18).

organising and striking. This was the case at Bethlehem Steel in Bethlehem, Pennsylvania where 21,000 machinists, only 2,000 of whom were IAM members, struck in April 1917 and again in May, even after federal and state arbiters had brought about a temporary settlement. Another July settlement was never implemented by the time the war ended.[89]

3. Union-organised shops and existing conditions and standards, whether unionised or not, should be maintained.

Rulings were intended to maintain existing local conditions and standards. Because the bargaining agent was not required to be a union and employers were prohibited from interfering where a union existed, union shops essentially remained union and non-union shops remained non-union. The NWLB cleverly let it cut both ways. It granted a right to unionise but did not require employers to recognise or negotiate with them unless they had done so before. In effect, the 'open shop' was the law of the land.[90] As it asserted,

> The declaration, however, is not intended in any manner to deny the right or discourage the practice of the formation of labor unions or the joining of the same by the workers in said establishments, as guaranteed in the preceding section, nor to prevent the War Labor Board from urging or any umpire from granting, under the machinery herein provided, improvement of their situation in the matter of wages, hours of labor, or other conditions, as shall be found desirable from time to time.

Employers could not relax occupational health and safety rules or alter the division of labour as it currently existed by geography, job classification, wages, hours, and other conditions of work. By not allowing employers to recognise newly unionised shops, the NWLB rules were an attempt to prevent workers from circulating their struggle to new shops and sectors. It also banned control strikes to effect a change in the division of labour.

4. Maximum productivity should be maintained and no delays or limits on production are allowed; existing wages, hours, and conditions should be maintained.

---

89 The company refused to implement the pay increases or allow a shop committee to be elected. Although Taft declared it in 'contempt' the NWLB was powerless to force it to implement its ruling. (See Conner 1983, pp. 11–114 and 159).

90 Ibid., p. vi.

The NWLB prohibited employers from using productivity schemes (raising relative surplus value) that exceeded the current maximum production in all war industries. This inexplicably contradicted its arbitration rulings that traded higher wages for increased productivity. Workers were likewise also prohibited from resisting Taylorism with 'methods of work and operation ... which operate to delay or limit production, or which have a tendency to artificially increase the cost thereof'. This rule clearly addressed the IWW inspired tactic of 'striking on the job', sabotaging the implementation of Taylorism on the shop floor.

5.   Women workers should receive 'equal pay for equal work'.

The board established that women workers 'must be allowed equal pay for equal work and must not be allotted tasks disproportionate to their strength'. This mandate was self-contradictory and inconsistently applied. Not only did it allow employers to continue banning women from 'men's work' based on patriarchal conceptions of fitness, hazard, and strength, it sometimes set women's wages lower than men's. Although the board awarded equal pay in 48 cases, it established lower wages for women in 14 of them.[91]

Ironically, women were treated as unfit to work for the NWLB, as Wilson refused to appoint any women to the board despite a prominent campaign to pressure him to do so. Wilson also abolished the Division of Women Administrative Examiners. In a rank display of hypocrisy, women were also denied equal pay in the Wilson administration's own Committee on Public Information, the propaganda agency that provoked support for the war and repressed dissenters.[92] As the NWLB never embraced equality of women, the principle could be interpreted to mean it would only apply in cases where there were no other men available.

6.   Basic eight-hour day is established.

The Board recognised the recently hard won eight-hour day (absolute surplus value) but limited its application to 'all cases in which existing law requires it', again an attempt to keep the popular demand from spreading.[93] But spread it did. Between the start of 1915 and June 1918 the government reported that 1,440,532 workers had their workday reduced to eight hours. Among these workers were 180,00 anthracite miners in 1916, about 600,000 shipyard, packing-

91   Ibid., p. 156.
92   Ibid., pp. 143, 145, 147, and 148–9.
93   Kenyon January 25, 1922, p. 8

house, lumber mill and other factory workers between June 1917 to July 1918, and about 116,000 machinists by 1918. In all, the NWLB granted the eight-hour day in 151 cases (29 percent of its rulings and awards) either with or without overtime.[94]

The eight-hour workday didn't mean the same thing for everyone. Workers accompanied it with demands for higher wages and keeping productivity level as a demand for less work for more pay. The AFL opposed them if time and a half or double time were excluded. Industry opposed them because they effectively increased wages 50 percent after eight hours. Government temporarily conceded it only if it meant that production would not be disrupted.

The NWLB principle limited all other demands concerning hours by 'due regard to governmental necessities and the welfare, health, and proper comfort of the workers'. This was echoed by Congress, which authorised the president in 1917 to suspend the existing weak federal eight-hour law in case of emergency. In effect, NWLB eight-hour rulings reducing hours to eight were moot since workers under federal contract could now be required to work overtime at time and a half pay.[95]

7.   Workers have a right to 'the living wage'.

Awards were guided by the principle of awarding a 'living wage' which will insure the subsistence of the worker and his family in health and reasonable comfort.[96] Conner attributes this principle to Walsh, who sought to use the NWLB to set a national wage policy in order to stop employers from shifting the cost of their low wages onto the community. While the NWLB was unsuccessful in standardising wages, they did significantly increase wages for unskilled labourers, in effect creating a wartime minimum wage.[97]

8.   The Department of Labor should keep data on workers' skills for the purpose of war industry.

---

94   Conner 1983, p. 107.

95   Ibid., pp. 90–1.

96   While this has more recently become a common demand by unions, its origin actually lies in a pronouncement advocating a 'just payment' by Pope Leo XIII in 1891. This idea, also known as the 'family wage', became a way to justify keeping women from working for wages so they could focus on their unwaged domestic responsibilities. (See Ibid., p. 50).

97   Only 12 states passed minimum wage laws after 1912 but none required equal pay for equal work for women workers. (See Ibid., pp. 57, 66–7, and 143).

Lastly, the Department of Labor was mandated to develop and maintain employment data and a blacklist for all war industry workers to aid in the provision of needed labour.

The NWLB was established to act as a federal mediator and conciliator. It had a busy schedule. From 9 April 1918 to 31 May 1919 when it was shut down, the board received 1,245 complaints and received 193 joint requests from both employers and workers to arbitrate a dispute. About 20 percent, 269 of 1,245, of the complaints received by the NWLB came from workers who did not belong to a union. That so many complaints were received by non-unionised workers demonstrates a high level of self-organisation among war industry workers and their use of both disruption and arbitration to assert their power on the shop-floor. Awards or findings and supplemental decisions were made in about 42 percent of the complaints (520) and about 57 percent of the complaints were either passed to another agency (315) or dismissed (391). Collective bargaining was established in 18 percent (226) of the awards.[98]

Protect the Status Quo by Undermining It

While the NWLB struggled to consistently apply its own code in its rulings, its intentions were clear. The board would avoid rulings that altered the unequal wages, working conditions, productivity, division of labour, and unionisation status of a shop. The NWLB's intervention was made palatable to employers as a temporary wartime emergency measure because it was explicitly committed to maintaining the balance of power between employers and workers as it currently existed.

But its claim to neutrality obscured how adhering to 'existing local conditions' actually strengthened the hand of employers who established yellow dog company unions, which was allowed as one type of 'associations, groups, or trade unions'. If no union currently existed the NWLB allowed 'employee representation schemes' modelled after Rockefeller's 'Social Plan' which he presented in testimony to the Commission on Industrial Relations. In effect, by not requiring that employers recognise self-organised workers as a 'union', the NWLB opened the door for the companies to put forward their own fabrications as legitimate collective bargaining agents.

After June 1918 the NWLB mandated time and a half after eight hours but because it rarely awarded an eight-hour day this decision was moot. The eight-

---

98   Gregg 1919–20, pp. 46, 48, and 61.

hour award granted in October 1918 in the steel industry only lasted for the last six weeks of the war. As Foner succinctly concluded, such procedures and rulings ensured that, despite the AFL leadership's highest hopes, 'no lasting precedents were established by the war policies'.[99] In addition, its wage awards were significant but hardly radical; rather they were intended to slow turnover by workers who sought higher pay and better conditions during a labour shortage.[100]

There were several reasons why no lasting precedents were established. First, the NWLB rules attempted to prevent newly organised workers from forming an officially recognised bargaining agent where none had yet existed. In effect, the workers' self-organisation was prevented from becoming more than an ad hoc group that presented its grievances but would be supplanted by the shop floor committee. This, of course, was in the interest of the AFL, as it might drain away members dissatisfied with it.

Second, the NWLB bottled up organised workers in shops where they were already in a union. Although workers struck frequently in both unionised and non-unionised plants, the arbitration concessions did not establish a contractual basis for either. Once the war ended, neither were better off than before it began and non-unionised workers were self-organised but still unrecognised.

The last reason is that the NWLB was intentionally designed 'wholly devoid of real power', lacking enforcement power short of the threat of presidential intervention.[101] After President Wilson nationalised the railroads on 26 December 1917,[102] the Board relied on the fear of more extreme federal intervention to ensure compliance from both capital and workers. The presence of the NWLB merely recognised the workers' leverage and made concessions for them to withdraw it to get them back to work. By doing so, the unions were being subtly integrated into the labour-planning state, 'transforming their organizations from independent trade unions to a government department and surrendering the labor movement to the employers'.[103]

Although it lacked the power to impose its decisions on both parties, it agilely deployed the authority of the president to both establish its authority and ensure two of its rulings were followed by both recalcitrant capitalists and

---

99   Foner 1987, pp. 176 and 341.

100   Conner 1983, p. 67.

101   Ibid., p. x.

102   Proclamation 1419 – Government Assumption of Control of Transportation Systems, December 26, 1917, By the President of the United States of America, A Proclamation. Available at: http://www.presidency.ucsb.edu/ws/?pid=24412.

103   Foner 1987, pp. 176 and 341.

workers. This became necessary as its workload grew and the board stopped arbitrating disputes directly and passed them to a combination of investigators, umpires, and administrators. After the armistice, however, many companies began to defy the board and after 5 December 1918 the NWLB only intervened in cases in which both workers and the company jointly petitioned for arbitration. It only managed to intervene in a few cases before the President asked the board to shut down on 25 June 1919, which it did on 12 August 1919.

The Western Union Telegraph Cases

A study of several high profile NWLB arbitration rulings illustrates why employer recalcitrance prevented the establishment of lasting precedents. One of its first cases was the 1 June 1918 *Employees v. Western Union Telegraph Co.* in which the company refused to abide by the NWLB's finding. The board found that the company had denied workers the right to join the AFL Commercial Telegraphers' Union of America (CTUA), formed its own company union, and fired about 800 members. Taft engaged in a long contentious exchange with the company, eventually issuing a ruling ordering the company to rehire the fired employees. The ruling did not require the company to recognise the CTUA but only to deal with the elected shop floor committee. In exchange for rehiring the fired workers the CTUA pledged not to strike and to submit their grievances to the NWLB. However, the company refused to accept the ruling and even dismissed President Wilson's entreaties to accept the decision, saying it would prefer 'government control'. In the meantime, the CTUA temporarily renewed its threat to strike in 400 cities until Secretary Wilson was able to assure them presidential intervention was expected. On 31 July 1918, both the company and union got their wish when the government took control of the telegraph and telephone system under the 26 December 1917 Presidential Proclamation. It was put under the management of Post Master General Albert Burleson and the authority of the Wire Control Board. Despite the government take-over, workers struck between April and July 1919, although they lost the strike due to some workers settling and the union being unwilling to continue expanding the strike. Ironically, the company union joined the CTUA to petition the NWLB to intervene against Burleson, who lowered telegraphers' wages beginning in 1919, and continued to lock out workers in Seattle and rehire many elsewhere, just as he had threatened.[104] Nationalisation of the telegraph turned out to be a great service to the absentee owners.

---

104   Conner 1983, pp. 164–6; Foner 1987, pp. 342–3; and Brenner et al. 2015, pp. 503–4.

The *Western Union* decision was controversial, as it effectively nullified the December 1917 Supreme Court ruling in *Hitchman Coal & Coke Company v. Mitchell* that banned unions from attempting to organise or communicate with workers who had signed a yellow dog contract. As Conner explained, 'Taft ... had resolved the potential conflict between the principles and the *Hitchman* case by ignoring it'. However, the NWLB had no statutory authority and could not overturn a Supreme Court ruling. Such actions were improvised wartime policies that neither established an obligation or right to engage in collective bargaining with either the company or the state, nor altered the balance of power between capital, the state, and workers. If *Hitchman* ignored that there is 'no liberty of contract where there is no equality of bargaining', as Justice Louis Brandeis wrote in his dissent, acting as if the precedent could be ignored without reshuffling the balance of power was illusory. Ironically, the company was placed under Burleson's authority, who opposed the right of government employees to unionise if they abrogated the right to strike. Nationalisation may have actually aided the company in its efforts to keep labour costs down since it expected control to revert to it when the war ended.[105]

The lack of enforcement power was also centre stage in the 12 July 1918 IAM[106] strike at the Smith and Wesson Arms Company in Springfield, Massachusetts. On 21 August 1918, the NWLB again bypassed the *Hitchman* precedent when it prohibited the yellow dog contract and ordered the company to rehire all the fired strikers, pay back wages, and enter into collective bargaining. When the company fired union members and refused to accede to the NWLB President Wilson ordered Secretary of War Baker to take over the company, which he did on 13 September.

The intent of the NWLB's rules was to put a brake on the escalation of tactics and block the circulation of struggle to new shops and sectors. While the lack of formal organisation may have hindered efforts to spread the struggle, it hardly impeded it. Although it prevented strikes or lockouts in at least 138 instances many still took place, were begun, or occurred even after a finding or award. What the rules accomplished was to make it more difficult to sustain the gains that self-organised workers managed to wring from the NWLB. As workers redirected their struggle against the companies toward the NWLB hearings and then the shop floor committees, momentum was lost. Gains had no contractual or legal basis and existed with a wink and a nod from employers, the NWLB, and

---

105   Conner 1983, pp. 42, 46, and 48; Foner 1987, pp. 343–4; Gregg 1919–20, p. 50; and Green 2015, pp. 204–5.

106   Foner refers to the union as the 'Machinist Union' but appears to have meant the IAM.

the AFL for the length of the emergency. The repression that followed the end of the war made it possible to reverse the gains.

The Remington Arms Company Case

The NWLB also faced difficulties when machinists struck in sympathy with the metal polishers at the Remington Arms Company in Bridgeport, Connecticut who had been on strike since July 1917. The Remington strike was the epicentre of strikes in the area for the eight-hour day. They also demanded wage increases, standard pay rates, abolition of premiums, overtime, time-and-a-half for Good Friday and other holidays, equal pay for women where they were used in place of craftsmen, no discrimination against strikers and union members, draft deferments, union recognition, and the right to fraternise and cooperate (e.g. assert their control over work time).

The Government Ordnance Department issued an award that established new job classifications and a minimum wage for workers in all the arms plants in the city.[107] The award had created fewer new wage classes for the skilled but ignored the less skilled. The ruling was opposed by IAM District 55, the Remington Arms workers' union, Remington, and one other smaller company although it was accepted by the remaining companies. As a result, the Secretary of War withdrew the award and forwarded the dispute to the NWLB in June 1918.

NWLB umpire Otto Eidlitz granted the eight-hour day not only for the company but all 54 factories in the city. The award also included a minimum wage for unskilled workers, large wage increases for low skilled workers, banned discrimination against union workers, ordered shop committee elections, and rejected the new classifications proposed by the union.[108] District 55 machinists opposed the award because they thought the increases were too low and variable. They struck again in September 1918, demanding both the eight-hour workday and standardised job classifications in defiance of the IAM which required 75 percent of the members voting to strike. The shop committee elec-

---

107 Although the issue concerned two arms manufacturers, the case is named after the larger Remington Arms Company which manufactured about 90 percent of all the cartridges. (See Gregg 1919–20, p. 54; and Conner 1983, p. 130).

108 45 of the companies were already working on the eight-hour day so Eidlitz just extended it city-wide. This was no great victory by a friend of labour. Eidlitz was a well-connected New York developer, member of the NCF, a housing official in the Department of Labor, and president of the US Housing Corporation. He was acting to avoid potential disruption and raise productivity. (Conner 1983, p. 104).

tions were interrupted by the 5,000 striking workers who demanded President Wilson seize the factories and enforce the earlier Ordnance Department ruling that established the six wage classes for skilled workers. A national IAM officer threatened to revoke District 55's charter if the members didn't go back to work.[109]

The military was becoming anxious about the potential disruption of war production and sent military intelligence to monitor the situation. In late August the NWLB refused to change the method of payment but changed 2,000 women piece workers over to a minimum wage, granted wage increases on a sliding scale, established the eight-hour day, and called for a government supervised election of shop committees and the formation of a city-wide committee of six union representatives and six employers to hear disputes from any factory.

Whether intentionally or not, the Remington ruling was received as an attempt to divide the skilled and less skilled workers by granting large increases to non-union unskilled workers and changing how women workers were paid. As in the Western Union case, it also established government supervised shop committees rather than require the company recognise the union, which would dilute the craft workers' influence who dominated the IAM local. By maintaining and even inflaming internal divisions among the workers, the proposed settlements were intended to inhibit the workers' ability to maintain unity in their shop, continue building their mass support, and continue circulating and escalating the struggle elsewhere.

The strikers used the impasse to rapidly expand the strike to most war contractors in the area by holding large rallies that closed all the metal factories in the city. A week into the strike they wrote President Wilson requesting he take over the company.[110]

The union got what it asked for, but not what they expected – the second wildcat strike went too far for President Wilson. On 13 September 1918, the same day he seized Smith and Wesson, Wilson threatened to withdraw strikers' draft

---

109   It may be the only recorded strike against a NWLB award before the war ended, but not the only one against an award by a labour-planning agency. After the war ended, the Seattle general strike (see Chapter 9) was precipitated by the walkout of 16,000 harbour workers with the Marine Workers Affiliation opposed to a SLAB award. (Ibid., pp. 129–30, and 168–71).

110   The strategy behind District 55's call for the government to take over the company was revealed in its 1919 petition to the NWLB in which it saw the shop committee as a means for achieving 'collective participation of the workers in the control of the industry'. (See Montgomery 1974, pp. 520–2).

exemptions and bar them from working in the war industry for one year if they didn't return to work.[111] The workers soon voted to return to work but didn't get their jobs back until President Wilson intervened a second time. Although the NWLB examiner imposed an elected 'mediation commission', the Remington strike ended without a formal settlement since the war ended about two months later.

District 55 combined control issues with wage and hour demands as a result of its leadership by IWW member Samuel Lavit, who led actions against layoffs calling for cooperative ownership and democratic management of industry. District 55 was formed as three lodges, one a plant-wide rather than craft based lodge and another for women workers. It also encouraged and supported wildcat sympathy strikes. These strategies demonstrated how the Bridgeport IAM organised all the workers in the arms plants regardless of their skill.

Like IWW and Iron Trades Councils on the West Coast, IAM District 55's organising strategy strengthened working-class recomposition by overcoming barriers of craft, status, wage, and gender. This strategy made District 55 a target of not only the AFL, with which it was affiliated, but also President Wilson, who threatened to take over the plant and then used the President's Mediation Commission and the NWLB to prevent more locals from deploying District 55's organising strategies. The repression proved relentless. Once the war had ended, Lavit and his core group were literally run out of town on the rails.

After the workers called off the strike and returned to work, they soon experienced an escalation of what Tilly calls 'counter class repertoire' wielded by capital and the government that would become commonplace once the war ended.[112] The city Board of Education, Committee on Public Information, and President Wilson's daughter launched a virulent propaganda campaign to promote industrial peace spiced with anti-German propaganda that was a thinly veiled attempt to taint District 55 as unpatriotic German sympathisers. Although Lavit and two other strike leaders were chosen for the city-wide arbitration panel, the employers ignored them. Government war contracts were cancelled in December 1918 after the Armistice and unemployment rose as war production workers were laid off in droves. The combination of overt and subtle repression transformed the IAM, which turned its focus to campaigning for national labour agencies to regulate collective bargaining and initiate public works programmes. In August 1919, 22,000 workers again struck in other firms.

---

111   Wilson's letter was written by Taft and Walsh. (See Lambert 2005, p. 78; Montgomery 1979, pp. 103–4 and 129–33; and Conner 1983, pp. 133–4).

112   Isaac 2002, p. 396.

District 55 had gone too far for the IAM, which suspended Lavit, refused to pay strike funds to support the members, and revoked the local's charter causing the strike to be lost.[113]

Gompers's No Strike Pledge

The strike wave during the war was not supposed to happen; the AFL traded its loyalty for an expectation of a post-war pay off. The pledge transformed the AFL 'from an independent trade union center to a government department which assumed the duty of preventing strikes and if necessary breaking them'.[114] The era of modern labour relations, in which granting recognition denotes not merely legitimacy but institutionalisation and social control, had arrived.

The ability to prevent workers from escalating their tactics further enshrined the AFL leadership's legitimacy and credibility to capital and the state. Gompers's no strike pledge demonstrated its loyalty, opening doors to the polity which further alienated the leadership from the rank and file while carving out a space for unions in the Democratic Party coalition of elites that remains to this day. The AFL leadership's attempt to aid the suppression of wartime strikes illustrates the low capacity of the federal government during the war. To prosecute the war effort, elites were willing to make temporary concessions by allowing limited participation in the polity by marginalised groups such as unions. The state came to rely on the compliance of the AFL leadership with elite interests in order to maintain its stability. In turn, the AFL acquired status and resources in the form of limited gains on wages and hours that it could use to protect the shrinking number of skilled workers, in order to prevent them from escalating their tactics and even force them to de-escalate to obtain them.

In his unpublished, groundbreaking 1915 Commission on Industrial Relations study of the use of violence in strikes, Grant observed that workers who are spurned by employers from negotiating to resolve their grievances were more likely to escalate to using violence, especially when they were not organised into a union.[115] As Grant rightly warned,

---

113   Montgomery 1979, pp. 103–4 and 129–33.

114   See Steuben in McCartin 1992, p. 520.

115   Grant's report is extremely well buried in the historical record. It took me several years to locate what may be the only remaining copy of the report. Although it was listed as an official Commission on Industrial Relations report, no copy was filed with the Library of Congress along with its other reports and it was never published. I am eternally grateful for the assistance of the Library of Congress and San Francisco State Labor Archives

Repressive measures adopted by employers to prevent their employes [sic] from organizing, usually lead sooner to later to a revolt. In recent years some of the most violent outbreaks in the industrial field have occurred where there was no previous organization among the employes [sic]. Such outbreaks invariably are followed by more violence than is the case where the employes [sic] are organised in an established labor union.[116]

But Grant only had part of the story. Workers' efforts to be recognised and negotiate were not merely blocked; they were also regularly confronted by the integrated forces of capital and the state including agent provocateurs, spies, private police, court injunctions, and police and military forces. As capital escalated its tactics, workers were more likely to resort to a strategy of tension to achieve their objectives.

Note that Grant identifies 'revolt' and 'violent outbreaks' as more likely to be associated with workers not organised into unions than those who are. While he must have appeared to elites as partisan in favour of unions at the time, which perhaps may explain the disappearance of his report, he made the case for the disciplinary role of unions. Workers under a contract are less likely to escalate for the leadership's fear of losing the tangible and intangible assets obtained both by recognition by elites but also the resources they are expected to deliver to the rank and file. Grant's argument underpinned the Wilson administration's labour planning policy during the war.

The wildcat strikes undermined Grant's analysis. Despite being allowed a limited right to organise, the wildcat strikes discredited the AFL as a reliable partner in disciplining the rank and file as hoped, and as a result arbitration was quickly abandoned after the war, dashing the AFL leadership's expectation of a further post-war alliance. The no strike pledge became another short-lived exploratory model that few elites fully expected unions to be able to live up to, short of a catastrophic crisis.

On the flip-side, the absorption of the AFL into both the arbitration mechanism and the electoral arena it had only a few years earlier vehemently resisted, discredited the AFL not only among its own members but among many workers. As a result of its collaboration in attempting to suppress wartime strikes and its complicity in the Red Scare after the war, membership in the AFL declined precipitously.

---

and Research Center staff that helped me obtain locate a copy of the original from the Wisconsin Historical Library. (Grant 1915a).

116   Ibid., p. 11.

While abandoned immediately at the end of the war, the NWLB model would later be resurrected in Section 7(a) of the 1933 National Industrial Recovery Act and later the 1935 National Labor Relations Act during the New Deal. These policies transformed ad hoc NWLB arbitration rulings into collective bargaining by establishing a process that draws out, slows down, and diffuses collective bargaining with complex bureaucratic petitions, signatures, elections, mediation, fact finding, arbitration, cooling off periods, etc.

Welcome to the Democratic Party

Although the AFL began to selectively inject itself into elections in 1908 it wasn't until the Wilson administration that it found access to the state. The entry of the AFL into the Democratic Party as a loyal member of the coalition was probably most clearly stated by President Wilson in his speech at the AFL's 1917 annual convention in Buffalo when he praised Gompers for knowing how to 'pull in harness', warning that 'the horses that kick over the traces will have to be put in the corral'.[117] 'Pulling' as a team enabled the AFL to obtain new material gains it could deliver to its members from what was called 'industrial democracy', a state-managed 'cease fire' between capital and labour.[118] These gains were the fruits obtained in exchange for demonstrating its value in disciplining its sometimes militant locals and members. The AFL's new institutional power was contingent upon its alliance with reformers that made it a member of the polity where grievances can be addressed through executive, judicial and legislative policy:

> At any point in time, some (and only some) of the contenders have achieved recognition of their collective rights to wield power over the government, and have developed routine ways of exercising those rights. They are members of the polity. All other contenders are challengers. They contend without routine or recognition.[119]

Reform-oriented members of the polity seek non-member allies to acquire assets to help them overcome their own internal marginalisation. 'Coalitions between members and nonmembers often occur when the members are seek-

---

117   Conner 1983, pp. 26–7.
118   Ibid., pp. ix and 25–6.
119   Tilly 1978, p. 125.

ing ends for which there are not enough coalition partners within the polity, and/or for which the resources being mobilized by the nonmembers would be useful'.[120] Such coalitions can be mutually beneficial for the member and non-member.

> The challenger is likely to accept a coalition where it offers a defense against repression or devaluation of its resources and the member is likely to accept it when the polity is closely divided, or when no coalition partners are available within the polity, or when its own membership is in jeopardy for want of resources.[121]

The AFL gained access to the polity when elites found it necessary to use arbitration, a modified form of negotiations in which the decision resolving a dispute is made by a supposedly outside third party rather than the parties in conflict, in order to dampen the effects of escalation and prevent its further occurrence.

The AFL leadership's participation as a member of the dominant coalition in the polity was predicated on its ability to deliver resources to its members in order to justify its participation and discredit demands to further mobilise and escalate.

> Membership in the polity gives important advantages to a group. In the most general sense, its power rises: ... polity membership produces a rise in the curve of returns from collective action. Departure from the polity produces a drop in the curve. Concretely, recognition pays off in collective access to jobs, exemptions from taxation, availability of privileged information, and so on.[122]

For the AFL leadership, the NWLB and other wartime labour agencies provided dual advantages. It allowed it to deliver wage increases, maintain or reduce work hours, and reverse onerous work rules for the rank and file while preventing it from attempting to use further disruption to get even more. When NWLB rulings sent workers back to the shop floor and restored production, the AFL leadership proved its value to capital as a mechanism for managing class conflict. As Gompers told the Commission on Industrial Relations, organised workers are disciplined workers.

---

120   Ibid., p. 126.
121   Ibid., p. 213.
122   Ibid., p. 125.

Always bear this in mind, that strikes, in the largest number of cases, consist of those unorganised or the newly organised. As workmen and workwomen remain organised for any considerable time, strikes diminish. They establish for themselves and with their employers means and methods of conciliation, of arbitration, and it is only when those absolutely fail that there is a stoppage and break in their relations.[123]

As long as it remained a part of the elite coalition, the AFL could have the best of both worlds of capital and the working-class, or so it thought.

Rupture and Reform

Fragmentation of the elite coalition is not only a means for absorbing the insurgent leadership. If the coalition continues to fracture while elites and insurgents are enmeshed in conflict, it may result in a total breakdown among the elite that will prevent it from exercising its power, creating crisis conditions necessary for a revolutionary situation. If the state collapses, insurgents will face higher costs but rapidly growing opportunities to achieve gains as elites resort to brutal state terror to hold onto power or one elite faction seizes power by force in a coup. Alternatively, the costs would fall dramatically if workers begin seizing the means of production and communities establish the means for their own self-governance through workers councils and general strikes.

The revolutionary strike wave at the close of WWI could be attributed to the lower costs of mobilisation and intensification of tactics as losing governments lost legitimacy and collapsed, making them vulnerable to demands by insurgents.[124] Although elites were no longer able to either make concessions or impose their will by force, insurgencies quickly escalated into a revolutionary crisis. Syndicalists took over factories throughout Europe, socialists came to power in Vienna, revolutions took place in Mexico and Russia, a revolutionary government came to power in Hungary and nearly in Germany, insurgencies spread throughout the collapsed Ottoman Empire, and general strikes erupted in Canada and the US.

The new cycle of class struggle had the effect of splitting elites and giving the strategic advantage to reformist members of the polity who had established ties to the labour movement. Such coalitions were attractive to the AFL leader-

---

123   See US Commission on Industrial Relations Apr. 9, 1914.
124   Tilly 1989, p. 444.

ship because they provided an opportunity to resolve conflicts while preventing the strikes that it so disliked. The wildcat strikes provided an opportunity for the AFL and its elite allies to act on long-festering grievances by changing policy. These outcomes were made possible, according to Tilly, by the pairing of different tactics. 'A proper explanation of strike activity must include an account both of the choice among alternative forms of collective action and of the process of negotiation'.[125] The ties between elite reformers in the polity and union leaders became crucial to the success of inside/outside strategy. 'The forms, frequencies and personnel of collective action depend intimately on the existing structure of government and politics'.[126] Because reformers were receptive to the AFL the disruptive role of the wildcat strikes strengthened their hand inside the elite coalition.

Inversely, that elites were sufficiently fractured that reformers sought an alliance with the AFL – an indicator of the level of effectively recomposed working-class power and the depth of the crisis. The AFL's position inside the polity made it possible to move institutional reforms forward over long existing blockages. Elites were out of options to restore control, restart production, and fight the war. Circulating the struggle beyond the specific waged workplace transformed the struggle from one of wages, hours, control over work, or recognition into an insurgency that threatened to disrupt not just wartime production but continue escalating to transform the entire organisation of life, governance, and the economy. If it manages to avoid being harnessed, at such times insurgencies can have the effect of challenging, shifting, or replacing norms and values, transplanting or overthrowing the existing order of things or putting it into a deep crisis from which a new society or societies emerge flowering out of the humus of the decaying system. The ability of strikers to accurately read the existing level of mass support can provide them with the necessary base from which to escalate their tactics both offensively and defensively to provoke a crisis of transformational proportions.

Since the AFL membership was almost exclusively for skilled white male workers, access to the polity could be expected to result in what sociology calls 'opportunity hoarding' by the upper tier of privileged workers. This has two outcomes. First, it served the interests of capital by reproducing the internal divisions among workers inherent in the division of labour. AFL members could be given gains from arbitration and used to discipline the rest of the working-

---

125   Tilly 1978, p. 166.
126   Ibid., p. 170.

class. During WWI, this did not work. AFL members ignored the no strike pledge and benefits of arbitration awards and struck anyway, often with workers who weren't AFL members. Given the opportunity to mobilise and escalate with little costs and high opportunity of gains from doing so, these workers used their privileged position not merely to strike for themselves but to organise all the workers in their shop and circulate their struggle throughout the company, city, and industry in order to share in what the AFL had made available by its access to the polity. By demanding more than it was allowed, the AFL's own rank and file ruptured the class deal it had made on its behalf.

WWI was the first test of the hypothesis that insurgents can pursue an 'inside/outside strategy' to achieve structural change by using the rules of the system without further escalation. For this to happen, elite reformers inside the existing coalition partner with non-member insurgents as leverage to move their reforms forward. Reformers gain credibility for their proposals when insurgent participation in the political process through negotiations and concession-making turns down the level of tension, and disruption ceases when insurgents de-escalate. Rising credibility and additional supporters are translated into votes and institutional power for the reformers who use their new majority status to change the rules of the political and presumably economic systems.

Progressive reformers pursued the inside/outside strategy by partnering with the AFL at the turn of the twentieth century while also allying with conservatives to change the rules of the system to slow the rise of the Socialist Party through the ranks of local and state elections.[127] Reformers in the elite coalition parlayed the wildcat strikes during WWI to strengthen their position within the Democratic Party, leading to their rise to dominance, a position from which they could implement their policies during the war and then again later during the New Deal.

As a new member of the polity, the AFL leadership allied with elites to fight this threat to its institutional power within the Democratic Party coalition and dominance in the labour movement. As Tilly explains,

---

127 Among the rules changed were: making local elections non-partisan, changing many cities from having a directly elected 'strong mayor' to a powerful appointed city manager and 'weak mayor', using investigative commissions to deflect tensions, ratifying the 17th amendment for the direct election of senators in order to prevent socialists from being appointed to the US Senate, and civil service reforms to prevent patronage services from being exchanged for working-class votes.

> The asymmetry ... produces a deep conservatism in every polity. Members
> of the polity resist changes which would threaten their current realization
> of their interests even more than they seek changes which would enhance
> their interests. They fight tenaciously against loss of power, and especially
> against expulsion from the polity. They work against admission to the
> polity of groups whose interests conflict significantly with their own.[128]

The AFL unions not only refused to help organise the strikes, but it refused to
provide organisers and other assets to help them. With members of the leadership serving as appointees in the panoply of wartime labour-planning agencies,
it worked contrary to the interests of its own members who appeared before its
hearings with grievances, having been absorbed into the instruments of state
power. Once it became apparent that arbitration would be sufficient to stem
the wave of wildcat strikes, the AFL waited out the war to identify, isolate and
purge leaders of the rank and file revolt such as District 55 President Lavit, and
stayed mute as the Red Scare was unleashed.

Putting the Wildcat Back in the Bag

The wildcat strikes successfully resisted rationalisation. According to Montgomery,

> output per hour was declining during the war years at the very same time
> that the number of hours regularly worked each week were falling. This
> trend not only injured the war effort, they claimed, it also threatened their
> plans for the postwar world.[129]

Capital was quite aware of the setback and set out to make it temporary. In 1916,
the National Metal Trades Association president warned the 'the current war
of arms would be followed swiftly by a war of economic competition'.[130]

The NWLB arbitration model routinely failed to adequately manage class
struggle. Strike after strike elicited the board's investigation and ruling but the
pace of strikes continued nearly unabated. As the US Bureau of Labor Statistics made apparent, 'the influence of wartime demand for labor, the dislocations

---

128   Tilly 1978, p. 135.
129   Montgomery 1979, p. 121.
130   Ibid.

which accompany wartime economic activity, the sharp rise in union membership, and reduced unemployment all exercised an influence on the potential for labour violence'.[131]

One typical example of the feedback effect created by the NWLB's attempt to de-escalate a wildcat strike was what happened at General Electric (GE). When the workers threatened to strike the Schenectady, New York plant on 1 May 1918 for a 25 percent raise, 44-hour workweek, eight-hour day, and equal pay for equal work for women workers, the NWLB board co-chairs Taft and Walsh quickly arrived in town to investigate. Schenectady was on the verge of a general strike with locomotive factory and streetcar workers also threatening to strike. The rapidity with which the Board intervened demonstrated to workers elsewhere in the company that striking had lower costs and a higher likelihood of success than before the war, prompting them to also strike.

Taft and Walsh also sent two mediators to Westinghouse and the International Association of Machinists (IAM) to Pittsfield to settle a strike there. When the NWLB didn't act quickly enough Pittsfield workers sent a delegation (whose names were not recorded in the minutes or transcript) to Washington D.C. on 28 June 1918. The delegation carried out a sit-down protest in the hallway of the NWLB offices and refused to leave until they were heard. The occupation worked; they got their hearing at which the workers pressed Taft to act quickly or face another strike. Their threat didn't amuse the former President Taft who apparently wasn't accustomed to being challenged so discourteously. At one point in the hearing, Taft replied to a worker who was berating him that 'it is a little trying, a little trying to have a gun put at your head when you are trying to do justice' to which 'the Witness' replied that 'I am not trying to use the gun act on anybody or any committee. I am trying to explain the situation'.[132] The NWLB ordered General Electric to stop using yellow dog contracts and to establish shop committees that could negotiate grievances. The workers returned home promising not to strike.[133]

This was an extraordinary exchange between anonymous workers and a powerful former president and future Supreme Court Chief Justice. The arbitration process allowed workers, unmediated by union officials or lawyers, to directly engage with and challenge a former President without any risk of retaliation. It was a rare moment in which not only the bounds of class status had broken down, but also worker militancy became unhinged, unmanageable,

---

131   Ross and Taft 1969, p. 23.
132   See McCartin 1992, p. 526.
133   Conner 1983, pp. 118 and 123.

threatening. When government mandated arbitration and collective bargaining re-emerged in the 1930s it was a rationalised process that slowed down, channelled and bureaucratised disruptive class conflict. It was only then that unions managed to become adequately institutionalised as a mechanism for disciplining workers in order to manage class conflict.

The workers' apparent ability to arbitrate a labour conflict unmediated by union leadership didn't lead to a de-escalation of tactics. Rather, the workers began to deploy tactical pairing and switching techniques by simultaneously participating in the NWLB hearings in DC while meeting up in the capital to coordinate sympathy strikes between their plants back home.[134] The fragmentation between the union leadership working close to the halls of power far from the rank and file simply did not exist.

Despite the NWLB's reluctance to address work control grievances, workers continued to launch strikes challenging management's control over work, particularly the rationalisation and intensity of output. Although the awards made by the NWLB rulings were limited to addressing wage complaints due to rising wartime prices, the strikes were launched to resist the increasing of absolute (by lengthening the workday) and relative (by intensifying the work) surplus value. For example, the earlier 1914 and 1916 Westinghouse strikes demanded the abolition of 'premium pay', which used productivity bonuses to pit workers against each other to produce more, and slow the pace of work.

The NWLB was also backed into the position of having to democratise the shop floor. The GE arbitration ruling finalised one month after the DC hearing prohibited the use of a yellow dog contract that prohibited workers from joining an independent union and ordered the election of shop committees as well as mandating retroactive wage increases. Although the NWLB ruled for the workers in the 1918 GE strike, the company refused the NWLB's order to abolish bonus payments and institute minimum wages for different classes of work.[135] This didn't discourage the GE workers who used the newly opened political space to also organise GE plants in Lynn, Erie, and Fort Wayne. By the end of the war, all of GE's major plants were organised into the new Electrical Manufacturing Industry Labor Federation (EMILF) according to the principles of industrial unionism.[136]

Mandating the election of shop committees was a common award for the NWLB for several reasons.[137] Although it initially appeared to be a victory for

---

134   Montgomery 1979, p. 124.
135   Ibid., pp. 121 and 124.
136   McCartin 1992, p. 527.
137   Bucki argues that the NWLB borrowed shop committees from John D. Rockefeller Jr.'s com-

workers, it was embraced by the companies because it did not require that they recognise a union. Both the board and the companies rightly expected the strikers to transform their self-organised strike coordinating committees into a militant local un-beholden to or relatively independent of any existing AFL union, which they frequently did. Requiring the election of shop committees forced the workers to de-escalate to prepare for an election. It also shifted the advantage back to the company to gain time to regroup and field their own candidates who often dominated the committees and log-rolled the deliberations. As the strikers redirected their energy and focus away from disruption to sitting at the table, they abandoned the very leverage that got them there. Here again workers gave up what was possible, immediate concessions through disruption, by de-escalating to get what was impossible, power through negotiations. Mandating the establishment of shop floor committees might have successfully de-escalated and demobilised wildcat strikers in individual plants but it did not stem the copycat wildcat strikes elsewhere and may have actually encouraged them.

NWLB rulings became an explicit tool for disciplining worker militancy by sanctioning acceptable tactics and prohibiting others. In the *Employees v. Corn Products Refining Company* case the NWLB upheld a shop committee's authority to fire strikers who refused to grant the committee authority to negotiate for them.[138] In its October 1918 award ordering that 11 of 16 men who had been fired for striking be rehired, the NWLB also sanctioned the firing of two strikers at GE's Lynn, Massachusetts plant because they had organised sit down strikes, a tactic Taft opposed.[139] As this was the third case concerning GE the NWLB's earlier interventions were not immune to workers circulating the struggle to new sites elsewhere in the company.

Although the NWLB made it possible for strikes to quickly achieve dramatic gains it cannot be overemphasised that they were extracted by applying

---

pany union strategy after the 1914 slaughter at Ludlow, Colorado (Bucki 2009, p. 201). Bologna traces the shop committee to being mandated by capital in 1905 and endorsed by the social democrats once they entered the government to counter the workers' council movement.

'In Germany, the interests of collective capital were protected by the state or, in 1918, by social democracy. In 1905 the initiative of introducing labour representation in the factory came from capital. It was a far cry from anything like co-management: they were merely organisms meant to deal with local disputes to prevent them from erupting in overt struggles which may have eventually led to a general struggle.' (Bologna 1976, p. 74).

138   Gregg 1919–20, pp. 57–8.
139   Conner 1983, p. 135.

leverage to a temporary opening necessitated by wartime urgency. This is best reflected in the data which shows while union membership rose significantly between 1916 and 1920 from 2.8 to 4.8 million along with the number of strikes between 1917 and 1922, both dropped precipitously once the war ended.

The Claw Back

Once the wartime conditions were gone, the gains proved to be pyrrhic victories. When the war ended, employers and Taft refused to allow the NWLB to continue to function and it hobbled on in name only until mid-1919. 'The threat of government takeover in the interest of war production had passed. With it had gone the NWLB's ability to impose its awards upon unwilling employers'.[140] Almost immediately upon the cessation of the war, GE locked out its workers in December 1918, broke the EMILF, and blacklisted many of Pittsfield's activists. A new campaign of political and economic repression was underway.

One of the most effective means of repression was the Red Scare that targeted anarchists, socialists, and Wobblies during the war and arrived on the shopfloors with the armistice. The key agency in carrying out the assault was the Federal Bureau of Investigations (FBI) focused on anti-radicalism and draft resisters. It created the American Protective League with 200,000 trained volunteers with badges authorised to spy on neighbours and provide manpower for mass raids.[141] IWW strikers in agriculture, copper, and timber faced a range of brutal repression, persecution, prosecution, execution, lynching, and mass deportation.[142] The 1917 Espionage and 1918 Sedition Acts criminalised dissent and radical and revolutionary political action. The 1918 Immigration Act, or the Dillingham-Hardwick Act, amended the 1903 Immigration Act, e.g. the 'Anarchist Exclusion Act', which prohibited entry by anarchists and other radicals, to

---

140   It could also be added that the NWLB lost its ability to impose its awards on unwilling self-organised workers as well (see Conner 1983, p. 141).

141   Gage 2009, p. 127. Originally named the Bureau of Investigations, it went through several name changes since its founding in 1908, eventually renamed the FBI (which is used here) in 1935.

142   In addition to the federal government deporting hundreds of militant immigrants, local elites also violently persecuted IWW strikers in the West. In July 1917 vigilantes imprisoned and then force-marched about 1,800 striking copper miners, their families, and local supporters from Bisbee Arizona over the state line into New Mexico. The strike had been organised by an IWW affiliate. (See Foner 1987, pp. 265–80; and Ross and Taft 1969, pp. 24–5).

allow the deportation of militant and socialist workers. About half the states and colonies passed criminal syndicalism and sedition laws that criminalised challenges to capitalism as well.[143] In September 1918, 166 IWW officials and organisers were indicted by the federal government under the Sedition Act.

The campaign of repression was propelled by a new bombing campaign in 1920–2 targeting prominent capitalists and politicians. On 1 May 1920, 36 mail bombs were sent to financiers, industrialists, and politicians. On 2 June bombs exploded in eight cities including on the doorstep of Attorney General A. Mitchell Palmer's home. In Chicago alone there were 50 bombings in 1920 and more than 60 bombings in each 1921 and 1922.[144] The targets of the Chicago bombings included buildings under construction, and homes of unfriendly builders and contractors among other sites of intense labour struggles. Adamic estimated that more than half were associated with labour. Some of the labour related bombings, like those of the ironworkers a decade earlier, may have been set as false flag operations to pin the blame on the unions and their members.

These wartime laws not only emboldened the formation of a paramilitary right such as the American Legion to target militant workers, but empowered the FBI to carry out their legal persecution. Attorney General Palmer's 17 June 1919 formation of the new Department of Justice Radical Division under the direction of the FBI's Flynn coordinated the counter-attack. It collected files on 200,000 radicals in its first year, growing to 450,00 by late 1921 under the direction of the young agent J. Edgar Hoover. The Radical Division was formed to dismantle the Socialist Party, two new communist parties, and the IWW.

On 2 January 1920, simultaneous raids in 33 cities led to the arrest of about 2,500 radicals and immigrant workers. The Bureau of Immigration issued about 5,000 deportation warrants of which about 3,000 were served and 556 were ordered deported.[145] Former AFL official and Secretary of Labor Wilson ruled that membership in the Communist Party was a deportable offence. As Gage observed, these measures were pushed because 'nothing in the peacetime federal statutes forbade the expression of revolutionary ideas. Palmer's solution to this problem was a peacetime sedition law modeled on the wartime speech restrictions, combined with aggressive surveillance by the Radical Division and a program of mass deportation'.[146]

---

143   White 2006, p. 652.

144   Adamic 1931, p. 237.

145   Between June 1920 and June 1921 an estimated 446 'alien anarchists' were deported, exceeding the 314 deported in the previous year. (Gage 2009, p. 273).

146   Ibid., p. 179.

Of particular focus was the IWW. While it had earlier raised the concerns of the Commission on Industrial Relations as a source of active unrest and revolt, ultimately it was the post-war campaign of repression that put these fears to rest.[147]

Whether the aim of the bombers was intended to serve as what Johann Most called 'action as propaganda', they provided the pretext to escalate not merely the persecution of the left but of labour as well.[148] The tenuous acceptance of mandatory arbitration during WWI was dismissed in favour of a return to expulsions, armed vigilante groups of elites, use of the US Army and National Guard, blacklisting, martial law and the range of other tactical escalations in capital's repertoire. In early 1920, five New York City Socialist Party state assemblymen were expelled from office by their colleagues. Their constituents resisted, re-electing all five during the 16 September election arranged with the intention of replacing them. The expulsions weren't unique. Wisconsin Socialist Party Congressman Victor Berger had been expelled from Congress during WWI only to be returned by his constituents.[149] This treatment of the non-violent Socialist Party that pursued democratic socialism through the ballot box only confirmed just how inaccessible any legal change was.

One of the most notorious events of 1920 illustrated how far capital would be willing to use the courts to rid itself of militant workers who openly advocated or supported the use of political violence as a part of the tactical repertoire. Among those were the Italian immigrants Nicola Sacco and Bartolomeo Vanzetti, who were indicted on 11 September 1920 for reportedly carrying out a robbery and murder of a shoe factory employee making a money delivery. Although the evidence raised significant doubt as to their guilt, Sacco and Vanzetti were closely allied with several well known Italian militants who carried out bombings in Italy and were wanted by authorities there. While the full details of their plight is thoroughly recounted elsewhere, Sacco and Vanzetti were sentenced to death and after years of appeals and an international movement that called for commuting their sentences, they were executed in 1927. Their executions went further than any other use of judicial persecution had gone before from Debs's 1894 contempt and 1918 sedition convictions to the treason trials for the 1920–1 Miners' Army insurgency in West Virginia (see Chapter 10) that coloured about two decades of class conflict. But unlike these

---

147   Commission on Industrial Relations 1916, pp. 29–30.

148   Although commonly attributed to Most, it is unclear who invented the most commonly known version of the concept, 'propaganda by the deed' (Most 1885).

149   Gage 2009, pp. 191–3.

strike leaders before them, Sacco and Vanzetti had not organised any workers, led any strikes or even overtly interfered in any way with capital. They had
only publicly supported workers' causes by sympathetically writing about and
materially supporting them. Above all, they were working-class immigrants
who entered American society at the basement level of the social hierarchy
and espoused hated ideas at a time of venomous nativism and racist violence.

Sacco and Vanzetti were transformed into necessary scapegoats for the wave
of bombings that were hitting close to home, albeit creating more smoke than
heat. Their persecution represented the nativist and racist fear of disruption of
capital accumulation rather than actual disruptions. These two men became
avatars for the perpetrators who could not be identified and held accountable.

The 16 September 1920 Wall Street bombing that followed Sacco and Vanzetti's indictment five days later caused both physical and symbolic damage at
the heart of the emerging global financial system of capital centred in New York
City. The bombing happened the day before Constitution Day when the Sons
of the American Revolution had planned to gather at noon for a ceremony at
Wall and Broad. It was just one of a series of bombings that rocked the country.

It was almost precisely 81 years before the most recent attack on American capitalism on 11 September 2001. As Gage suggested, the bombing 'was an
alarming sign of vulnerability, proof that a horse-drawn wagonload of explosives could halt the nation's capitalist machine'.[150] Indeed, the primitive forensic
analysis concluded that the bomb had been literally delivered by horse-drawn
wagon to the doorsteps of the building that housed both the US subtreasury
and J.P. Morgan.

Although the owner of the horse and wagon was later identified, the plotter
who rented them has never been identified. The attack struck at the hubris and
self-confidence of decades of unrelenting growth in the power to suppress and
co-opt the class struggle. It was a hubris that had not yet entirely discovered
how to harness and transform it for the purposes of capital accumulation. The
bomb had a devastating impact. Not only did it damage the front façade of a
building otherwise considered impregnable, but it also killed 38 and seriously
wounded 143 people. The tragedy of the bombing was that the damage to capital was symbolic, but the loss to the working-class was real. Most of those killed
and injured by the blast were workers, two-thirds were under 30 years old, four
were teenagers, five were women, and six were recently returned veterans of
WWI.[151]

---

150   Ibid., p. 153.
151   Ibid., p. 161.

Its mark would be felt in American politics for decades. A 32-year-old specu-
lator named Joseph Kennedy was knocked down by the bomb. He later went on
to become a titan of junk bonds and speculative financial capitalism. Kennedy
also became an indispensable financier of Democratic Party political campaigns, appointed by President Franklin Delano Roosevelt to head the new
Securities and Exchange Commission (SEC), and of course father of a future
American President, three US Senators, and grandfather of several Congressmen.

The reverberations of the 16 September bombing were not merely symbolic
or personal. They provided a pretext for retroactively rationalising the permanent use of state police powers to intervene in, repress if necessary, and arbitrate
if unavoidable, labour conflicts. The state's new permanent role would be to
provide the process by which those who would escalate their tactics to engage
in such propaganda by the deed would need to be separated and practically
isolated from those who, like it or not, asked for redress of their grievances over
work, hours, conditions, and wages. Kennedy's role as victim in the bombing
would not fully unfold into his role as facilitator of cross class compromise until
his controversial appointment as SEC chairman in 1937. Capital would be given
the reigns to self-regulate itself with the tacit promise that labour could do the
same if it agreed to permanently remove certain kinds of tactics from its repertoire. This overlooked concession could be called the 'New Tactical Legitimacy
Deal' that, while explored briefly and haphazardly during the Progressive Era
and WWI, was raised to the level of statutory authority and judicial precedent by
the New Deal's 1935 NLRA. Kennedy played a central if indirect role in connecting these two phases in the attempt to regulate and rationalise class struggle
so as to not only remove its potential to disrupt capital accumulation but also
normalise and integrate it.

The bombings legitimised Hoover's massive domestic surveillance programme and quickly transformed the relatively new agency. Expanded during
WWI to root out saboteurs and spies, the Bureau soon began to focus on both
organised crime and organised labour, one and the same for some in government. Its newfound mission was shaped by the August 1921 appointment of William J. Burns, one of the private corporate agents hired to break the earlier IAB-
SIW's dynamite campaign, to the position of director.[152] Much like the massive

---

152   One of the most prominent private police agents investigating the bombings was Wil-
      liam J. Burns who, as a result of his work on the McNamara case several years earlier, had
      been consulted to help identify the perpetrator of the Wall Street bombing. A skilled self-
      promoter, Burns managed to mislead the public and the government into thinking that
      he was on the way to solving the case when in fact he didn't have a clue. The publicity and

reorganisation of customs, immigration, the US Coast Guard and other domestic security agencies into the newly created behemoth Department of Homeland Security soon after 11 September 2001, Burns used the bombings to propose merging all federal detective agencies, Secret Service, Post Office inspectors, and even military intelligence, into a single agency under his direction. He never lasted long enough in the position to realise his plan because he proved too inept to break the bombing conspiracy, much as he failed to singularly break the ironworkers' dynamite campaign a decade earlier.

The bombing campaign was the most publicly recognised aspect of class conflict in the 1920s. However, it has never been demonstrated that it was in any way connected to the many little heralded struggles taking place on the shop floor to contest for control over work. Those who publicly advocated for bombings and sabotage as 'propaganda by the deed' were minuscule groups with likely little to no demonstrable connection to either formal or informal groupings of workers. In typical strategies of armed struggle, many of the bombings were infrequently timed to correspond to specific labour conflicts. Certainly more research is needed to tease out whether any material connections existed. The lack of material linkages to struggles on the shop floor taking place at the same time may raise doubt as to the thesis of this book that tactical violence was part of a repertoire of tactics deployed in class struggle. Nevertheless, the conditions of the time encouraged groups that eschewed the hard work of organising, striking and disrupting the accumulation process in favour of supposed shortcuts. Carrying out bombings during this time of hysteria and repression strengthens the argument that many workers perceived that the political space between peaceful petitioning of grievances and scattered attacks was entirely closed. But after nearly a century of elapsed time since the wave of bombings and the secretive nature of the actions, it has become apparent that while they provided a symbolic threat to the appearance of economic and political stability they hardly disrupted the actual accumulation of capital.

As the number of union members, strikes, and other tactics of class struggle appeared to be on a steady decline, workers withdrew to anonymity by organising fluid informal groupings to contest the new composition of capital on the shop floor. These forms of what variously became known as everyday forms of resistance, soldiering, striking on the job or featherbedding, sidestepped the AFL to contest the control and power of management to drive down wages and increase work productivity and profits. Out of these everyday forms of

notoriety catapulted him into a brief appointment as director of the Bureau of Investigations (later renamed the FBI) in August 1921. (See Ibid., pp. 261–3 and 271–3).

resistance at the level of production exploded the sit down strikes, general strikes and running street battles of the 1930s. The 1930s uprisings cannot be understood without examining counter-planning on the shop floor among 'unorganised' workers.

Post-war repression was lauded for having broken the self-organised workers in the midst of the longest sustained cycle of struggle over the past decade in US history. It also succeeded in significantly raising the costs of the strategy of tension that had made these struggles so successful. One measure of the effort was that by the mid-1920s there was 'a sudden lull in bombings and assassinations, a pronounced decline in terrorism as a weapon of class warfare'.[153]

The short history of the NWLB resulted in awards that mostly ranged from wages and hours and elected shop committees that required management negotiate with workers over grievances.[154] The short sharp strike during wartime lost its tactical effectiveness once the war ended as the NWLB lost the support and political will to continue imposing arbitration awards. With the end of the war, employers took advantage of the removal of government prohibitions on tactical escalation and clawed back what it had lost over the previous year and a half. Capital once again had access to its entire tactical repertoire and used it. The first tactic it deployed was unemployment, which it used to shift power back in its favour. With wartime contracts ended, unemployment rose rapidly from 2.4 percent in 1918 to 8.6 percent in 1920 and 19.5 percent in 1921.

Unemployment combined with hyper-nationalism, a remnant of wartime hysteria, became a potent disciplinary weapon to defeat the wartime strike wave.

> with the ending of hostilities the country experienced severe tension in the labor market. Several factors accounted for heightened labor discontent … Considerable dissatisfaction existed as a result of rises in the cost of living during wartime and the general malaise that war normally generates. Many employers who had accepted union organization as a wartime necessity or as a result of government fiat were now anxious to rid themselves of labor organizations. This is evident from the power of the campaign by antiunion employers who espoused the American Plan

---

153 Ibid., p. 310.

154 Conner's reference to workers' grievance issues with management in elected shop committees as 'shar[ing] power with employees' and 'collective bargaining' is incorrect since the NWLB did not require recognition of either self-organised workers' groups or unions. (See Conner 1983, p. 127).

of Employment, a program designed to support employers opposing the presence of unions in industry.[155]

Between 1919–21, both the number and percentage of workers who struck or were locked out declined by 75 percent. The number of control strikes declined by about 47 percent.[156] The end of the war, rising unemployment, a strengthened elite coalition, deactivation of the NWLB, and lingering nationalism combined to unleash the Red Scare, quickly raising the cost of mobilisation and tactical escalation for workers while reducing the opportunities for defending existing gains, let alone expanding them.

While mostly described in political terms, the Red Scare characterised the new composition of capital unleashed to break self-organised groups of workers, seize back the ground gained by industrial unions, and scare off the supporters that workers had gained over the previous decade. Although scattered organising continued to transform their unions and promote more aggressive tactics, the cycle of struggle came to an end. Despite the 1919 Seattle and Winnipeg general strikes and the railroad strikes and armed insurgencies by West Virginia and Kansas miners and their families, workers were unable to sustain their efforts and de-escalated to carry out everyday forms of resistance against work at the level of the shop floor.

Repression was so successful that by the mid-1920s capitalism was being celebrated for roaring profits and exuberance. Such a triumph was predicated on substantially raising the costs of mobilisation and tactical escalation to prohibitively high levels that destroyed the insurgency of the past decade. As Gage rightly surmised,

> beneath the advertisers' sheen was the darker legacy of the 'weighty and compelling' conflicts of the wartime and postwar years. If Americans were less inclined toward agitation than consumption, it was partly because the range of political opportunities had been drastically condensed, and because the cost of political involvement had grown so high. The galloping success of American capitalism in the 1920s rested to some extent on the successful repression of available alternatives that had taken place in the preceding years.[157]

---

155   Ross and Taft 1969, p. 333.
156   Montgomery 1979, p. 96.
157   Gage 2009, pp. 314–15 and 317.

Dilemma of Success

An insurgency that pursues an inside/outside strategy can either ally with existing reformers in the elite coalition, form its own 'above-ground' body to engage with reformers or enter the polity as its own distinct organisation. Once the above-ground body enters 'inside' the polity by becoming an organisation, obtaining recognition, merging with reformers, and beginning negotiations it faces a range of new risks.

Some of the above-ground leadership become influenced by the newly available attention, resources, and status regardless of their personal ambition or psychology. In this case they are slowly transformed so as to internalise the language, norms, and actions of their adversaries. Recognition creates new boundaries, limits, and rules for adversarial action, conflict, contestation, and mobilisation that begin to harness the insurgents into what Tilly and Tilly call regularised 'performances'.[158] It establishes or narrows the rules of when workers can strike, who can be designated to represent workers, and what is a justifiable strike demand; outlaws certain tactics such as beating up scabs; and establishes strict rules concerning picketing, entering the workplace, arbitration, the process for ratification of settlements, and the orderly return to work. According to Tilly and Tilly, these

> pushed the entire process toward an orderly, nonviolent withdrawal of one firm's wageworkers (or some recognized subset of them) from the employer's premises ... and establish the strike as a highly recognizable, increasingly standardized set of routines engaging workers and employers with each other.[159]

As they become individually co-opted and their organisation institutionalised as legitimate members of the polity, this isolates them from the remaining insurgents who remain underground and outside the polity and cut off from the specialised knowledge obtained through formal politics and negotiations.

The interaction with elites subtly transforms the insurgent leaders. While they arrived as representatives chosen by the rank and file, they become transformed into leaders by elites. If these leaders can enter the polity and obtain

---

158   'Performances' is defined by Tilly and Tilly as 'a continuous sequence of actions by which an actor makes a claim' and those performances compose the 'repertoire of contention'. However, performance is a euphemism that obscures what are otherwise called tactics or actions. (Tilly and Tilly 1998, pp. 239 and 240).

159   Ibid.

compromises and concessions to deliver to the rank and file they can obtain status, benefits, and power from both elites and insurgent rank and file.

> At any point in time, some (and only some) of the contenders have achieved recognition of their collective rights to wield power over the government, and have developed routine ways of exercising those rights. They are members of the polity. All other contenders are challengers. They contend without routine or recognition.[160]

As leaders adapt to the routine of normal politics, such as union leaders serving as appointed officials, intervening to stop threatened strikes, and lobbying on public policies, they achieve recognition as a recognised legitimate negotiating partner. But their credibility as a negotiating partner depends on their ability to deliver compromises that restore profitable conditions of production. As a consequence, their interests imperceptibly become more closely aligned with the elites which dominant the polity, and against whom the rank and file had originally launched their insurgency. Leaders walk the razor sharp edge of delivering just enough concessions to the membership so that they will demobilise and de-escalate to return to work, while not demanding more than elites are willing to part with so as to not cut too deeply into their advantageous position. Slowly but surely the insurgent leadership aligns their interests more with elites than the rank and file. To the former they are allies. To the later they begin to appear as an auxiliary to the ruling powers on the shop floor and in society.

The credibility of insurgent leaders also hinges upon the credibility of the polity to obtain not only a commitment to compromise, but also the delivery and maintenance of concessions reached by negotiations. Tilly quantifies the ability to deliver by the formula of 'asset value x probability of delivery' (or availability).[161]

> If the resources are free of competing claims, if the action clearly defends the interests of every member, and if the group is an all-embracing moral community, the probability of delivery is close to 100 percent. Loyalty is

---

160   Tilly 1978, p. 125.
161   The 'asset value' can refer to the intangible mechanism of negotiation or a tangible concession from it. 'Probability of delivery' means whether members are willing to follow the rules of negotiations, actually deliver the available resources, demonstrate necessary loyalty (e.g. lack competing claims) to deliver resources, and face a high cost of exit. (Ibid., p. 69).

then at its maximum, the probability of departure or contestation – exit or voice – is at its minimum.[162]

For Tilly, leaders can deliver on the terms of their compromise when they have exclusive disciplinary control of the rank and file. The insurgents' ability to deliver also applies to elites whose concessions are more valuable if insurgent leaders are able to de-escalate members' tactics and restore production. The ability to enforce and impose the union contract accomplishes this for elites.

Negotiations must not be merely style but substance if the leadership are to sell concessions to the rank and file. Both sides must not merely appear to be getting something of importance by giving up something of value; they must actually get it. Employers and elites must have prior conditions of production restored at a minimum. If they are unable to deliver concessions from both employers and insurgents, reformers' credibility will be damaged and they will lose influence inside the polity. In such a case, insurgent leaders would also lose their credibility and mandate and will likely be deposed. If workers, for example, make concessions but the employers refuse to meet their commitments, the cost of de-escalating to negotiate will rise, the opportunity to gain from doing so will fall, and tactical escalation will follow. If the leadership has been co-opted into the polity and institutionalised as a disciplinary force we may then observe them collaborating in efforts to repress their own rank and file. This was the case at the end of the war when the AFL leadership became an integral part of the Red Scare.

This is what has been called the dilemma of success. While success can be understood as the outcome of successfully obtaining tangible concessions that need to be defended, success may also mean intangible access to the polity and elite coalition. Either way, tangible and intangible success creates new sets of interests to defend which gives rise to new organisations with their own prerogatives which 'often conflict with the interests around which the group organised and mobilized in the first place'.[163] As Glaberman and Rawick and Malatesta warned, the interests of the union leadership soon diverges from that of the rank and file.

Tilly and Tilly attribute this meshing of insurgent leadership and elites to how 'repertoires both limit and facilitate contentious action because the actors involved have learned their parts in established performances'. In short,

---

162   Ibid., p. 71.
163   Ibid., p. 57.

'struggle generates its own means'.[164] But those parts are closely tied to how interests subtly shift to align with the available possible outcomes. If actions are incapable of delivering certain outcomes according to the established rules leaders will avoid them to maintain their legitimacy and recognition. It is struggle, not theatre. By 1998, Tilly had left far behind the materialism that led him to observe two decades earlier that

> The repertoire of collective actions therefore evolves in two different ways: the set of means available to people changes as a function of social, economic and political transformations, while each individual means of action adapts to new interests and opportunities for action.[165]

During WWI, the AFL was a textbook case of the dilemma of success. It played off the threat of unorganised workers' disruptive wildcat strikes as leverage to prompt federal intervention to settle strikes. Once arbitration rulings were issued it attempted to coerce the membership to demobilise and de-escalate in order to protect the newly obtained gains and its new collaborative relationship with the state even past the point at which the gains were rescinded and the rank and file were repressed.

Despite its rapid growth from wartime strikes, in 1921 IAM's general secretary called for eliminating the 'economic waste' of strikes. The union even partnered with the Taylor Society in 1922 to launch the Baltimore and Ohio Plan to reorganise the railroads.[166] The IAM leadership so internalised its shared interests with employers that it began operating businesses such as a bank and international trading firm.[167]

Mother Jones captured how the dilemma of success turns the leadership into the enemies of the workers.

> In those days labor's representatives did not sit on velvet chairs in conference with labor's oppressors; they did not dine in fashionable hotels with the representatives of the top capitalists, such as the Civic Federation. They did not ride in Pullmans nor make trips to Europe.
> The rank and file have let their servants become their masters and dictators. The workers have now to fight not alone their exploiters but

---

164 Tilly and Tilly 1998, p. 241.
165 Tilly 1977, p. 493.
166 Montgomery 1989, pp. 287–8.
167 Ibid. The IAM continues in banking as the owner of the IAM Community Federal Credit Union in Alabama. (See http://www.iamcfcu.com/).

likewise their own leaders, who often betray them, who sell them out, who put their own advancement ahead of that of the working masses, who make of the rank and file political pawns.[168]

While federal intervention provided credibility to liberal reformers' regulatory proposals and nationalisation gave hope to social democrats of an emerging mixed state capitalist economy, expanded federal authority was the last tool in the tactical repertoire for managing class struggle. It came after workers self-organised on the shop floor to launch wildcat strikes repudiating the AFL's no strike pledge and federal arbitration. Workers' direct action where they held leverage elicited relatively quick concessions by the NWLB and other federal labour arbitration bodies. These concessions indicated to other workers the low costs and extremely high opportunity of success from launching their own actions creating a signal spiral that launched a new cycle of struggle. Reform became not an end in itself but an expression of workers' ability to disrupt production and threaten the war effort by asserting their power.

NWLB rulings had three major impacts on the recomposition of worker power. First, NWLB awards mandated an election of workers to choose their representatives to engage in informal shop floor committees. Although they could be usurped by management, shop floor committees could be used to further grow membership in the informal groups that provoked federal intervention as the low costs of mobilising became apparent to the workers.[169]

Second, despite the NWLB's policy of maintaining local conditions and prohibiting the spread of union or non-union shops, the rulings unintentionally encouraged workers to continue self-organising. The informal groups continued circulating the struggle to other shops, geographical areas, and industries even without union support. The relatively low costs and rising opportunity to achieve gains by encouraging NWLB intervention encouraged these workers elsewhere to escalate tactics in order to threaten or actually disrupt war production. Its relatively rapidly intervention and rulings encouraged the perception that elites were incapable of repressing organised workers due to the high costs to the war effort of doing so.

Lastly, the cycle of struggle fed the rapid growth in union membership despite the NWLB's refusal to require union recognition. Union membership nearly doubled by the end of the war. Even in 1923, when employers had launched their counter-attack, union membership was still nearly a third higher than

168   Mother Jones 1925, p. 149.
169   Foner 1987, p. 342.

TABLE 5   *Union membership by number and*
            percentage, 1910–23

1910	8.6 percent	1914	2.7 million
1920	17.5 percent	1920	5 million
		1923	3.6 million

Note: While the Commissioner of Labor collected strike
statistics between 1881 to 1905 and the US Bureau of Labor
Statistics resumed collecting them in 1914, their methods
changed, measuring the number rather than the percentage which is why both appear in Table 2. (Peterson 1938,
p. 35; Foner 1987, p. 339; and Ross and Taft, 1969, p. 23).

in 1914 (see Table 5). While the AFL leadership could attribute the growth to
its ability to deliver benefits to the membership from participating in the elite
coalition, workers used the strikes to build the unions in order to lock in some
of their gains.

There was an important caveat to the increase. The growth in union membership was extremely concentrated in limited sectors of the economy.[170] Between 1915–20, 75 percent of the increase was limited to the building, transportation, metal, machinery, shipbuilding, and clothing sectors. 'In most of
these cases, moreover, unionism was expanding where it had already made
inroads before the war; in few industries did increases take place where there
had been no prior organization before the war'.[171] In effect, the wartime arbitration awards allowed union membership to grow as long as it was bottled up in
shops and sectors that were already unionised before the war. Unions in these
sectors limited their focus to where they were strongest and neglected further
mobilisation where they were not leaving the field open to independent unions like the IWW. These were also industries subject to federal intervention and
would not cause frictions with their allies in the Wilson administration.

Underplaying the reactive role of federal intervention, Perlman and Taft
attribute the growth in union membership during the war to how

> the government … opened the doors to unionization in industries hereto-
> fore closed – not that unionism forced the doors open by its own strength.

---

170   There is some reason to believe that this may be a result of the methodological flaws and
       the gap in the data collection between 1905 and 1914.
171   Foner 1987, p. 339.

The government, by virtue of its war-time power and prestige, gave the unions the all-important right to organise against a temporarily confounded and half rebellious employing group.[172]

While it is true that the government opened the door, wildcat strikes wedged it open in the first place by threatening to disrupt production for the war effort. Because repression further exacerbates disruption, the AFL and NCF advocated the mostly unused strategy of arbitration to manage and channel the rupture and gain the upper hand. 'Organised labor was strategically placed not only for giving support to the government's decision to make war but also to prevent chaos on the labor market'.[173] During the wartime machinists strikes the government cultivated the IAM through the arbitration process as a 'counterweight' to the more radical AIU that favoured disruption and challenged Taylorism.[174] Just as the strike made the union, the threat of the strike made the government institutions to prevent and harness the class conflict that provoked them.

The AFL leadership gained access to the polity as a useful new ally to respond to the threat of class struggle. It gave the reformers in a fractured elite coalition the necessary weight to counter the resistance of industrial elites who refused to comply with urgent wartime emergency measures. In return for its loyalty, the AFL leadership gained newfound political credibility and legitimacy and became a stakeholder in the Democratic Party, long before historians have attributed it to the later Roosevelt administration. The AFL's ability to achieve redress for its grievances was conditional on its ability to deliver a disciplined workforce to the war effort. While it never fully succeeded, the AFL cooperated with federal administrators to tamp down disruptions so that they did not threaten anything worse. In turn, the leadership could justify its collaboration by delivering higher wages and shorter workdays to the membership through arbitration rather than general strikes. That the rank and file demobilised and de-escalated to accede to arbitration rather than collective bargaining was contingent on the leadership's ability to deliver these material gains.

In order to serve both masters, the AFL leadership hitched its fortunes to the war effort. The leadership recognised that its ability to deliver on both sets of conflicting obligations depended on the fortunes of its new ally, the Democratic Party, both during and after the war. Once the war ended, its new allies

172   Perlman and Taft 1935, p. 524.

173   Ibid., p. 403.

174   Montgomery 1989, p. 286.

quickly abrogated its obligations by rewarding its friends (the AFL leadership) and punishing its enemies (the working-class).

Saving Capitalism

The failure of the NWLB's byzantine system of arbitration was quickly evident. Employers refused to abide by its rulings and workers continued striking. The intransigence led the Wilson Administration to nationalise or impose strict regulatory oversight of several companies and industries in which disciplined production could not be restored because recalcitrant employers and workers would not de-escalate their tactics and abide by NWLB rulings.

Having run to the right of the Socialist Party's platform of national ownership of the economy, the Wilson administration now extensively resorted to nationalisation as a wartime contingency to save capitalism.

> Within a year after the declaration of war, the government took over the nation's communications network, assumed direct control of most of its railroad lines, completely dominated the shipbuilding industry through the establishment of the Emergency Fleet Corporation, and under the authority of the Food and Fuel Control Act, regulated the production, distribution, and conservation of foodstuffs and fuel supplies across the land.[175]

In an effort to manage class conflict, the US economy was becoming increasingly centrally planned, much like the Bolsheviks were doing in the new Soviet Union. US state capitalism had become, if for a brief time, socialism for the corporations and the military. Nationalisation became a critical stop-gap measure to overcome the split among elites and the failure to discipline and manage the working-class, which weakened the state's capacity to both fight a war in Europe and a class war on the shop floor.

What happened first with the railroads would become the model for nationalisation. The Wilson administration assumed control over the railroads in December 1917 to counter the growing mobilisation and strike threats of railroad workers who were experimenting with industrial forms of organisation. During the war the AFL and railroad brotherhood enrolled hundreds of thousands of new members, with some unions even tripling in size, although few

---

175   Foner 1987, pp. 149–50.

members were black.[176] Recognising the growing power of the railroad workers, President Wilson used his authority under the Army Appropriations Act of 1916 to seize control of the railroad systems including the telegraph and telephones and water transport lines.

The railroads were put under the management of the US Railroad Administration which set wages, hours and working conditions for two million workers. To ensure union cooperation, the Director-General of the US Railroad Administration prohibited discrimination against union members. W.S. Carter, leader of the employer-friendly Brotherhood of Locomotive Firemen, was appointed head of the Division of Labor. In February 1918, Congress voted to limit the President's control to 21 months after peace is declared. To sweeten the bitter medicine, it also guaranteed an average rate of return on the railroad's investment based on the three years prior to 30 June 1917. Congress ignored the railroad brotherhood's Plumb Plan to pass the 1920 Transportation Act which established the Railroad Labor Board to arbitrate labour disputes and returned the railroads to private ownership. The railroad unions had proposed the Plumb Plan for the federal government to retain ownership of the railroads, transform them into a public utility, and operate it in partnership with the employees and management in order to achieve 'industrial peace' by removing the profit motive.[177]

Short of nationalisation, federal intervention also took place in the meat-packing industry. The Chicago packers attempted to organise everyone in the stockyards through an informal national federation of stockyards unions in 1917. This model was envisioned by the tactical genius of the Secretary of the Chicago Federation of Labor (CFL) William Z. Foster. Foster translated the industrial organising strategy he learned as a member of the IWW into the AFL. The new stockyards federation was planning a meat workers' strike against the big five Chicago packers until it was prevented by the Wilson administration, which coerced the CFL and the packers to sign a Christmas Day pledge of no strikes or lockouts for the rest of the war. The CFL's prohibition on blacks joining weakened the mobilisation because many were recruited to sign up with company unions. It appeared that Foster had only learned part of the IWW's strategy of interracial industrial organisation.[178]

---

176   Ibid., p. 221.

177   *The Nation*, 27 September 1919, p. 425; Foner 1987, p. 159; Perlman and Taft 1935, pp. 407–8; and Montgomery 1979, p. 99.

178   NWLB Co-Chair Walsh was a volunteer attorney representing the packinghouse workers, successfully arguing their case in arbitration for a higher minimum wage and reduction from a ten to an eight-hour day without a reduction in pay. After Walsh resigned as co-

Coal strikes similarly provoked federal intervention and mandatory arbitration. After Secretary of Labor Wilson prevented coal strikes in Central Pennsylvania and Alabama, he formed the US Fuel Administration on 23 August 1917 to arbitrate disputes to prevent interruption in production. The Fuel Administration imposed the Washington Agreement on the Central Competitive Field which expired on 1 April 1920. Further blurring the boundaries between union leadership and government, UMWA's President White resigned to work in the Fuel Administration's Bureau of Labor.[179]

Counter-Planning on the Shop Floor

One of the most important developments of the WWI wildcat strike wave was the capacity of workers to self-organise not merely to resist Taylorism but to impose their own 'counter-plan' on the shop floor. It wasn't the fledgling labour-planning state that spurred the rapid growth of union membership during the war as Perlman and Taft assert but the self-organised struggles of the workers. If the wildcat strikes made the union, it was the 'unknown committees' of self-organised workers who made the wildcat strikes to impose their own plans for work.

A small informal group of craft workers could function as a beachhead against management prerogatives. 'The resistance of [of labourers and operatives] to speed-up and management's authority tended to take the form of continuous, covert, self-organization by small informal groups at work'.[180] Sometimes these obstacles were motivated by individualism or the need to preserve privileges and sometimes by worker solidarity.[181] At other times these beachheads were caused by everyday forms of resistance, sabotage, and strikes. Either way they were seen as a threat to management prerogatives.

The disruptive power of such small informal groups grew alongside the concentration of capital. The integration and concentration of production created choke points because 'the new forms of production are more integrated, not less, and as a result smaller groups of workers now have greater power than ever before'.[182] This was evident during the 1902 coal strike which threatened to shut

---

chair he returned before the board as an attorney for several other unions. (See Conner 1983, pp. 52–3; and Foner 1987, p. 236).

179   Perlman and Taft 1935, p. 469.
180   Montgomery 1974, p. 520; and Montgomery 1979, pp. 101–2 and 106.
181   Mathewson 1931.
182   Glaberman and Rawick 1977, p. 215.

down the economy when the reserves the company had built up in advance of the strike began to run out. Similarly, even the limited WWI strikes in the war industries threatened to block the flow of raw materials or parts crucial to the war economy. Concentrating and integrating production can allow even small-scale disruption at a strategically vital location of the production process to bring an entire industry or the economy to a stop.

These small self-organised groups engaged in a hit and run type of guerrilla war, or what Watson called 'counter-planning on the shopfloor', that mucked up management's plan for speed, productivity and organisation.[183] Their *modus operandi* was

> defiance of the management's will and instructions, as sabotage. The small informal work group persisted, not as an agency of explicit control, as it had been under craft unionism, but as a submerged, impenetrable obstacle to management's sovereignty.[184]

The study of the rationalisation of work can provide insight into the emergence of new forms of class struggle out of the small, informal, self-organised groups of workers who use the various tactics of 'striking on the job' to undermine management prerogatives. The IWW called such everyday forms of underground struggle 'sabotage'.[185] IWW member Walker Smith provocatively portrays sabotage as having a 'revolutionary, economic end', while organizer Elizabeth Gurley Flynn explains it as simply an ever-changing tactic used to shift the balance of power on the shop floor. 'Sabotage is to this class struggle what the guerrilla warfare is to the battle. The strike is the open battle of the class struggle, sabotage is the guerrilla warfare, the day-by-day warfare between two opposing classes.' According to Flynn, sabotage is a non-violent 'means of strik-

---

183 Watson 1971.

184 Montgomery 1980, p. 518.

185 Smith has a more elaborate definition, defining sabotage as:

> 'the destruction of profits to gain a definite, revolutionary, economic end. It has many forms. It may mean the damaging of raw materials destined for a scab factory or shop. It may mean the spoiling of a finished product. It may mean the displacement of parts of machinery or the disarrangement of a whole machine where that machine is the one upon which the other machines are dependent for material. It may mean working slow. It may mean poor work. It may mean mis-sending packages, giving overweight to customers, pointing out defects in goods, using the best of materials where the employer desires adulteration, and also the telling of trade secrets. In fact, it has as many variations as there are different lines of work'. (Smith 1913).

ing at the employer's profit for the purpose of forcing him into granting certain conditions, even as workingmen strike for the same purpose of coercing him. It is simply another form of coercion.'[186]

Sabotage may take a variety of tactical forms. Affecting the quality, quantity and service, sabotage may entail 'losing' forms or parts, misassembling or omitting parts, cracking machines, or wrongly machining parts causing a backlog of unusable parts. Workers may also use what Flynn called 'open mouth sabotage' by being honest about the poor quality of goods or services to customers and adulterating or refusing to adulterate products with the intent of eating into profits.[187] By gumming up the production process, workers use sabotage to also create breaks that allow them to temporarily halt production in order to give themselves them time to rest, socialise and organise across internal class divisions including race.[188]

While some workers may resort to sabotage after losing the above-ground struggle, it may also proceed open class warfare. According to Mike Davis, 'these struggles marked the entry of the "submerged" majority of industrial workers into open class conflict'.[189] In his classic treatise Emile Pouget described sabotage as 'The most important part of a strike, ... precedes the strike itself and consists in reducing to a powerless condition the working instruments'. He found that it is the preferred weapon of the working-class, the 'dark, invincible, terrible Damocles' Sword that hangs over the head of the master class, [that] will replace all the confiscated weapons and ammunition of the army of the toilers'. The increasing prevalence of sabotage may inversely correspond to the closing of access to the polity to address and resolve grievances.

For Flynn, Smith, and Pouget sabotage is the ideal tactic because it is difficult to identify and suppress. For Pouget it is nearly impossible to counter or defeat because

---

186   Flynn n.d.
187   Flynn n.d. For Flynn sabotage is a non-violent weapon in workers' tactical repertoire that provides leverage and power.
188   Auto workers used many of the IWW sabotage tactics including placing faulty parts in an engine. This caused a backlog of useless engines that forced the assembly line to be shut down while they were dealt with by management. Workers would take turns causing the shutdowns to spread around the down time and rest. Most of these actions were carried out by the most unlikely groups of workers, black and newly arrived Southern whites who made up 50 to 75 percent of the workers in the plant. 'In both the case of the "6s" and the V-8s, there was an organised struggle for control over the planning of the product of labour; its manifestation through sabotage was only secondarily important' (Watson 1971).
189   Davis 1975, p. 356.

In vain may they invoke old laws and make new ones against it – they will never discover it, never track it to its lair, never run it to the ground, for no laws will ever make a crime of the 'clumsiness and lack of skill' of a 'scab' who bungles his work or 'puts on the bum' a machine he 'does not know how to run'. There can be no injunction against it. No policeman's club. No rifle diet. No prison bars. It cannot be starved into submission. It cannot be discharged. It cannot be blacklisted. It is present everywhere and everywhere invisible.[190]

While some labour historians have documented the resistance to rationalisation, few have seen within these tactics the germ of new types of worker self-organisation with which workers directly confront the source of their grievances and see an immediate impact to their efforts without union intervention, collective bargaining, or grievances. But the dividing line between ad hoc self-organisation and new organisational strategies is blurry. 'It is difficult to judge just when working-class practice at the point of production learned to bypass the union structure in dealing with its problems, and to substitute (in bits and pieces) a new organizational form'.[191] Because sabotage is subterranean and opaque it is difficult to asses the organisational capacity of the workers who use it.

Nevertheless, the prevalence of sabotage has corresponded to periods of new forms of worker self-organisation at the point of production outside of and beyond the existing union structures. This was the case for both the period preceding the WWI wartime wildcat strikes, the 1930s, and the 1960s. Writing about auto workers between the 1930s and 1960s, League of Revolutionary Black Workers organiser Bill Watson saw counter-planning as 'the building of a new form of organization today by workers'. These were 'the outcome of attempts, here and there, to seize control of various aspects of production. These forms are beyond unionism ...'.[192] Counter-planning is most pronounced in the absence of organised unions because it violates the assumption of management's total control over the production process. Counter-planning creates what Holloway calls 'counter-power' wielded by insubordinate workers using covert forms of organisation.[193]

---

190   Pouget 1913, pp. 35–6 and 93–4.
191   Watson 1971.
192   Ibid.
193   Holloway 2002.

As Watson and Davis would later argue, Flynn observed that 'sabotage' is merely a tactic which workers come to from their immediate knowledge and experience in the class struggle. A good organiser would

> see what the workers are doing, and then try to understand why they do it; not tell them its [sic] right or its [sic] wrong, but analyze the condition and see if possibly they do not best understand their need and if, out of the condition, there may not develop a theory that will be of general utility. Industrial unionism, sabotage are theories born of such facts and experiences.[194]

For this reason such tactics are not fixed. As she argued,

> sabotage is in the process of making. Sabotage itself is not clearly defined. Sabotage is as broad and changing as industry, as flexible as the imagination and passions of humanity. Every day workingmen and women are discovering new forms of sabotage, and the stronger their rebellious imagination is the more sabotage they are going to invent, the more sabotage they are going to develop. Sabotage is not, however, a permanent weapon.[195]

Although there is little historical documentation of such covert forms of organisation, management's persistent efforts to reorganise work would not have taken place if resistance were absent. The level of repression, automation, displacement, deskilling and outsourcing can be read as indicators of the level of threats to the prerogatives of capital.

Stanley Mathewson's unique study of so-called 'unorganised' workers demonstrates that the continuing need to innovate and remain vigilant in the implementation of Taylorist rationalisation was driven by the persistent resistance on the shop floor even in the absence of a formal union. Interviewing 65 managers of companies employing more than 500,000 workers, Mathewson found counter-planning to be widespread and practised by workers and low level 'straw' bosses, former workers promoted to foremen, alike. He showed that workers were resisting more than just low wages. They also took action to set wages, assert power over production, protect other workers, undermine management's authority, and to stretch out work to avoid unemployment.[196]

---

194   Flynn n.d.
195   Ibid.
196   Mathewson 1932, p. 131.

In his analysis of Mathewson's findings, Leiserson even went so far as to suggest that Taylorism was defeated by unorganised workers using everyday forms of resistance to capital's plan.

> In spite of the widespread adoption of more scientific methods in industry since the war, the evils of restriction, which was the starting point of Taylor's activity, continues unabated. Management has not been able to abolish the conditions which bring it about.[197]

Mathewson's work illustrates that workers were already self-organised, even if they lacked formal organisation, and had the capacity to pursue a strategy of tension. Non-violent sabotage might emerge above ground in various forms of tactical violence as their attempts to organise openly are repressed and their access to the polity is blocked. As Grant observed in his unpublished report for the Commission on Industrial Relations on the ironworkers' dynamite campaign,

> Repressive measures adopted by employers to prevent their employes [sic] from organizing, usually lead sooner to later to a revolt. In recent years some of the most violent outbreaks in the industrial field have occurred where there was no previous organization among the employes [sic]. Such outbreaks invariably are followed by more violence than is the case where the employes [sic] are organised in an established labor union.[198]

Grant's study of the dynamite campaign not only confirmed Mathewson's findings, but warned of further escalation by unorganised workers that threatened the system of production. In this way, the prevalence of sabotage and other forms of tactical violence corresponded more to the political conditions and class composition than ideology or forms of organisation. Grant's observation was intended to strengthen the argument for normalising unions as a means to manage and regulate class conflict. As others like Gompers argued at the time, unions can serve to tamp down the ability of self-organised workers to escalate their tactics and disrupt production.

One union, however, provided an organisational vehicle for unorganised workers to deploy a strategy of tension. The IWW gained a reputation in part

---

197   Leiserson 1931, pp. 174–5.
198   Grant 1915a, p. 11.

for articulating a strategy by which workers could use sabotage to counter-plan on the shop floor. Flynn and Smith demonstrated how apparently unorganised workers could engage in the kinds of tactics found by Mathewson.

The IWW's embrace of sabotage was preceded by many other tactics along the trajectory. Many IWW organising campaigns began with and were limited to presumably accepted forms of First Amendment-protected free speech campaigns which were soon tested in the courts. In Tacoma and San Diego, for example, the IWW protested against the combined repressive power of local owners of capital and government using marches and parades, open air meetings, publishing newspapers, pamphlets and flyers, organising strikes, and establishing local offices and stores. The IWW didn't start with sabotage but it was a key tactic in their repertoire.

To dismiss Flynn and Smith's essays on sabotage as criminal, violent, or hyperbole would be to under-appreciate how deeply the IWW validated the existing tactics and strategies of self-organised workers. As a sometimes late-comer to strikes already self-organised by the workers, the IWW could articulate and circulate submerged everyday forms of class struggle that often escaped the public spotlight, capital's control, and union support. As Flynn and Smith described it, sabotage merely meant the actions of fluid informal groups of workers contending for relief from the daily oppressive exploitation of work by contesting and undermining management's plan. Too weak to strike openly, they covertly struck on the job. As Smith observed, '... Sabotage is coined from the slang term that means "putting the boots" to the employers by striking directly at their profits without leaving the job'.[199]

Sabotage is used by workers to assert counter-power to confront the arbitrary power of a foreman, to stretch out a nearly completed job when other work was not forthcoming, or simply to compensate for low wages.[200] According to Smith,

> The labor power of the workers is a commodity. In selling their merchandise the workers must sell themselves along with it. Therefore they are slaves – wage slaves. In purchasing goods from a merchant one receives an inferior quality for a low price. For a low price – poor products. If this applies to hats and shoes, why not equally to the commodity sold by the laborer? It is from this reasoning that there arises the idea: For poor wages – bad work.[201]

---

199   Smith 1913.
200   Leiserson 1932, pp. 165 and 167.
201   Smith 1913.

For the IWW, class power begins on the shop floor. Tactics that have an immediate impact on efficiency, productivity, sales, and profits provide what Flynn called the necessary 'coercion' to extract concessions not otherwise obtainable through open tactics.[202] What made the IWW most threatening was not its public advocacy of sabotage but its ability to read the everyday forms of resistance in a workplace, region or industry, teach these tactics to other already self-organised workers, and facilitate the circulation of their struggles for more control over their work, lives, and ultimately society.

As a strategy for recomposing working-class power sabotage is woefully inadequate. Absent a recomposed working-class, sabotage can only soften exploitation by slowing or stalling it on isolated shop floors. It does not dismantle or seize power as an objective but wields it to tilt the balance of power as a strategy of counter-power. As Flynn noted, sabotage is not a strategy for getting beyond capitalism.

> Sabotage is not, however, a permanent weapon. Sabotage is not going to be necessary, once a free society has been established. Sabotage is simply a war measure and it will go out of existence with the war, just as the strike, the lockout, the policeman, the machine gun, the judge with his injunction, and all the various weapons in the arsenals of capital and labor will go out of existence with the advent of a free society.[203]

During WWI, the IWW managed to successfully carry out this strategy in key wartime industries such as mining and spruce timber. By refusing to negotiate contracts, they taught workers how to strike at key weak links in a wartime economy, apply leverage to achieve their objectives, and use counter-power to retain them. For the IWW, disruption was a tactic that moved them towards their revolutionary goal of worker self-control of the economy. 'The main concern to revolutionists is whether the use of sabotage destroy [stet] the power of the masters in such a manner as to give the workers a greater measure of industrial control'.[204] Disruption was virtually costless because it was covert and nearly anonymous. It avoided the need for bargaining by directly reducing the intensity of work exploitation and imposing concessions workers wanted.

As a tactic of disruption sabotage was a vehicle for a longer-term objective of reconstituting the power of the working-class and imposing it on the means of

---

202   Flynn n.d.
203   Ibid.
204   Ibid.

production. Sabotage tactically served to create disruption at key chokepoints but these needed to be replicated and generalised to shift power to the working-class. As Smith explained,

> sabotage is simply one of the many weapons in labour's arsenal. It is by no means the greatest one. Solidarity action is mightier than the courageous acts of a few. Industrial class formation gives a strength not to be obtained by mere tactics.[205]

Foreseeing the Italian autonomists of nearly a half-century later, Smith asserted that 'No analysis of the labor movement is complete where sabotage is not accepted as a weapon'.[206]

But the tactic of sabotage is insufficient for recomposing working-class power. Smith's strategy was control of work as the terrain of struggle. 'Armed with a knowledge of sabotage the workers return to their task, more terrible in defeat than in victory'.[207] Since alienation and exploitation were experienced by millions of workers in their everyday lives, the struggle to assert their own humanity as something more than just a reified appendage was likely to assert itself again and again. While it might be hard to identify from the outside, the statistical output, earnings, staffing, and profit reports by employers and the state provided sufficient coded evidence of the give and take struggle over and against work that awaits class analysis.[208] Such contention was endemic, continuous, corrosive, directionless and potentially explosive, disruptive, and transformative. Even in the absence of overt organisation or action, workers still managed to express wilful disobedience. 'Sabotage is a direct application of the idea that property has no rights that its creators are bound to respect'.[209]

Smith's whimsical, if not explosive, essay offered employers and the state sufficient ammunition to justify not only the passage of the Espionage and Sedition Acts but to use local and state police, the new FBI, and the federal courts to suppress and shatter the IWW as an organised movement.[210] Attention was given to some of his most provocative passages.

---

205 Ibid.
206 Ibid.
207 Ibid.
208 Cleaver developed a methodology for reading the class content of such data and reports as what he calls the 'inversion of class perspective' (Cleaver 1992).
209 Smith 1913.
210 For example, according to the University of Arizona exhibit on the Bisbee Deportation

What is more civilized than for the workers to create powder that refuses to explode? What is more civilized than to work slow and thus force employers to give a living to more of the unemployed? What is more civilized than to spike the guns when they are trained on our working class brothers in other countries? ... Sabotage will put a stop to war when resolutions, parliamentary appeals and even a call for general refusal to serve are impotent. But, as stated before sabotage is but one phase of the question. Anti-military and anti-patriotic agitation must also [stet] carried on.[211]

Whether intended literally to advocate active resistance to the prosecution of the war, these passages were widely cited to justify the relentless assault on the IWW.

The IWW drew from what non-IWW and unionised and non-unionised workers were already doing in active resistance to Taylorism. The target of workers' counter-planning illustrated the objectives of their soldiering. Time itself became a terrain of contention. Mathewson also described how lumber workers changed the way they picked up wood to undermine the time study.[212] Machine workers banked excess production, did not turn in completed work tickets, and then drew from the 'bank' in order to set the pace of production.[213] Sometimes resistance to Taylorism escalated into a strike or direct action. When the Starrett Tool company attempted to install clocks in the shop in 1910, machinists struck pledging to treat them as part of the furniture. Another strike occurred at the Norfolk Navy Yard in 1915 with the appearance of time clocks and work tickets.[214] Many of the war industry strikes during WWI included among their demands an end to Taylorist premium pay schemes.

During the long decade of the 1920s, when most labour historians wrote an obituary for the organised working-class, pervasive small informal struggles on the shop floor attempted to recompose working-class power. Workers learned how to turn Taylorist techniques into a means to restrict work output.

---

of 1917, Flynn's *Sabotage* pamphlet was 'originally used in the trial of the United States vs. William D. Haywood, et al. This exhibit was introduced into the trial of Michael Simmons vs. the El Paso and Southwestern Railroad Company through the deposition of John W. Hughes.' (Flynn n.d.).

211   Ibid.
212   Mathewson 1932, p. 25.
213   Ibid., pp. 78 and 80.
214   Montgomery 1979, p. 115.

Mathewson found that unorganised workers cleverly turned the very logic of rationalisation in on itself, covertly restricting output. 'Payment plans, designed as incentives to increase production ... turn out to be incentives to restriction'. Montgomery recounted how the 'mere intimation that the time-study man is to make his appearance will often slow up a worker, a group or a whole department' in order to shift the baseline measurement.[215] The union craft worker's control of the pace of production was defeated, dismantled, and went underground to re-emerge as what the IWW called 'striking on the job'. IAM International Vice President Conlon confirmed this in his testimony to the Commission on Industrial Relations,

> ... we believe that it (scientific management) builds up in the industrial world the principle of sabotage, syndicalism, passive resistance, based on economic determinism. We did not hear of any of these things until we heard of scientific management and new methods of production ... we find that when men can not help themselves, nor can they get any redress of grievances, and are forced to accept that which is thrust upon them, that they are going to find within themselves a means of redress that can find expression in no other way than passive resistance or in syndicalism.[216]

Unknown Committees

The presence of counter-planning on the shop floor illustrates the workers' dual system of power in which, regardless of the presence of a union, workers, and management contend for control of production. Planning and counter-planning in the plant creates contending dual power. A regular phenomenon in the daily reality of the plant is the substitution of entirely different plans for carrying out particular jobs in place of the rational plans organised by management.[217] The IWW successfully identified locations where dual power existed and provided its expertise to parlay it into above-ground struggle.

The IWW built upon existing informal ethnic and shop floor networks and groupings already engaging in counter-planning to form the core of a strike group. The eruption of resistance to rationalisation into overt class warfare was

---

215   Ibid., p. 116.
216   Commission on Industrial Relations 1916, pp. 874–7; and Montgomery 1974, p. 518.
217   Watson 1971.

evident in several of the most high profile strikes of the time such as McK-ees Rocks. As Davis noted, 'It is particularly significant that the storm centers of these strikes were located in the industries being rationalized by scientific management and the introduction of new mass-assembly technologies'. The Pressed Car Company had used a piece wage system to engineer a deadly speed up in which an estimated one worker a day was killed on the job. Workers were paid by a pool in which all the workers were collectively punished for the worker with the lowest productivity. Worker was pitted against worker in an effort to use them to discipline one another. The system backfired when the workers rejected the system and struck in 1909.[218]

The nucleus of the strike emerged out of a small informal self-organised group of immigrant workers, the 'Unknown Committee', which asserted leadership over the strike from the weak union of exclusively native skilled workers.[219] The Unknown Committee included experienced agitators from at least nine countries, some of whom were reportedly involved in the failed 1905 Russian Revolution.[220]

Several years later, rationalisation again prompted workers to self-organise and call in the IWW for help to fight the premium system, speed-up, and a wage cut in Paterson, New Jersey. Davis explained that Taylorism had the opposite effect than was intended since 'the silkworkers were driven to desperate rebellion by the introduction of the multiple-loom system, an especially fatiguing variety of speed-up which made weavers responsible for twice as many looms as before'.[221]

The IWW's organisational tactics at McKees Rocks and Paterson was an outgrowth of its highly developed ability to closely study the current composition of capital and devise a strategy to recompose working-class power by using direct democracy by all ethnic groups to generalise the tactics they were already using in isolation.

> The Wobblies were particularly adept at turning the weaknesses of immigrant strikers into sources of strength. Ethnic cohesiveness, traditionally so divisive, became a wellspring of unity when strikes were organised on a radically democratic basis with strictly representative commit-

---

218   Davis 1975; and Ingham 1909, p. 356.
219   Foner wrote that, to German workers, the committee was known as the 'Kerntruppen', a term derived from the military system of Germany where it referred to a 'choice group of fearless and trained men who may be trusted on any occasion' (Foner 1965, pp. 287–8).
220   Ingham 1909, pp. 363–77.
221   Davis 1975.

tees that could be recalled. Leaflets, speeches, and songs were presented in every language, while in each strike every conceivable parallel was found with the historic struggles of various European nationalities.[222]

At McKees Rocks and Patterson, the IWW helped the workers transform their ethnic communities into integrated forms of counter-power. This created a system of 'dual power' in which 'two distinct sets of relations, two modes of work, and two power structures in the plant ... is the object of constant turmoil and strife'.[223]

The focus on the recomposition of working-class power at the centre of the IWW's organising strategy led to its rapid growth. The success at McKees Rocks led the IWW to organise locals in Hammond, Woods Run, Pullman, Hegewisch, and Lyndera which helped spark a strike wave throughout key railroad car assembly plants. At the 1911 convention the IWW had grown to 21 voting locals in addition to the national textile union, two-thirds of which were based in the western mining states. At the convention two years later, there were 89 voting locals along with the textile union. 38 of the locals, most of the biggest in membership, were based in the east, proving that the IWW was growing rapidly into new areas of the country.[224]

Dual or counter power is a threat to the disciplinary role of unions as well. The unions became the object of derision by workers in a system of dual power, who flaunt the limits and controls set by the contract. Soldiering and wildcat strikes are instances by which workers are 'experimenting with new forms of organization to bypass the restraining force of the union'.[225]

By shifting actual decision-making over work and pay to themselves, counter-power lessens the drudgery of work by allowing workers to assert their humanity.

---

222 Ibid.

223 Watson 1971, pp. 77 and 82–5.

224 See St. John 1911 and 1913. Although the number of locals was growing and its geographic presence was spreading, it is unclear how substantially the IWW's overall membership was growing.

   Between April and August of 1911, for example, even as 70 new locals were being organised, the disbanding of 48 old locals for reasons such as 'lack of interest' was registered. But it has to be remembered that the AFL was also in deep crisis.

225 Glaberman and Rawick 1977, p. 208.

A distinct feature of this struggle is that its focus is not on negotiating a higher price at which wage labor is to be bought, but rather on making the working day more palatable. The use of sabotage ... is a means of reaching out for control over one's own work. ... we can see it extended as a means of controlling one's working 'time.'[226]

The point of identifying counter-power is not merely to organise and insti-tutionalise it, but to circulate its transformatory power, perhaps the greatest threat posed by this strategy. Watson stressed counter-power as a

new social form of working-class struggle. ... Within these new independ-ent forms of workers' organization lies a foundation of social relations at the point of production which can potentially come forward to seize power in a crisis situation and give new direction to the society. I would urge, in closing, that our attention and work be focused on the investig-ating and reporting of the gradual emergence of this new mode of pro-duction out of the old. 'Like a thief in the night' it advances relatively unnoticed.[227]

Counter-power points to another vision of life beyond work. The focus of counter-planning tactics is to disrupt the production process to reduce or escape work and thus the reduction of the people to being merely workers.

The 'sabotage of the rationalization of time' is not some foolery of men. In its own context it appears as nothing more than the forcing of more free time into existence; any worker would tell you as much. Yet as an activ-ity which counteracts capital's prerogative of ordering labor's time, it is a profound organised effort by labour to undermine its own existence as 'abstract labor power'.[228]

Counter-power contests management's plan in the form of a cooperative game, the workers' playfulness as an indicator of their resilient vision and passion for life – the direct antithesis of rationalisation which is predicated upon deleting human will and subordinating the person to the machine.

---

226   Watson 1971.
227   Ibid.
228   Ibid.

Not only does it demonstrate the feeling that much of the time should be organised by the workers themselves, but it also demonstrates an existing animosity toward the practice of constantly postponing all of one's desires and inclinations so the rational process of production can go on uninterrupted. The frequency of planned shutdowns in production increases as more opposition exists toward such rationalization of the workers' time.[229]

The assertion of humanity on the shop floor grows in inverse relation to the growth of the accumulation of capital. Such counter-power exists, though it is difficult to observe and comprehend.

Understanding the contestation between management and workers suggests that we see the strike waves of this period as not triggered spontaneously by frustrated workers, as relative deprivation theory suggests. Rather, they may be understood as persistent efforts originating in small informally self-organised groups circulating resistance to management's plans that periodically erupt into publicly visible organised class struggle. Taylor was well aware of workers' use of everyday forms of resistance to counter capital's control on the shop floor, calling it 'soldiering' to refer to the conscious 'restriction of output'. 'The natural laziness of men is serious but by far the greatest evil from which both workmen and employers are suffering is the systematic soldiering which is almost universal ...'.[230] Soldiering was targeted because of its potential to become a much more disruptive organised threat.

In vivid contrast, the response to Taylorism by the craft unions was to retain their power to control the work process by banning piecework by their members. In July 1901, the IAM banned members from accepting piecework, though the leadership considered revoking this in 1904. This strategy illustrated the ways which

> craft unions stood as a rigid barrier to the full utilization of the labor market. The dramatic expansion and recomposition of the workforce – enhanced by the high rate of immigration and internal migration of those years – made it imperative for employers to enjoy a free hand so they could mold the expanding work force according to the technical requirements of production. Craft unions, however, undermined this possibility.[231]

---

229   Ibid.
230   United States House of Representatives 1912, p. 1430.
231   Ramirez 1978, p. 91.

As long as the craft unions used their leverage to inject rigidity over hours, productivity, etc. they threatened the process of capital accumulation. Their opposition to industrial unionism as a capitulation to mechanisation and an increase in relative surplus value turned out to be self-defeating. Once the craft unions negotiated contracts to protect their own narrow sphere of control within the production process, they had relinquished such leverage over the rapidly expanding industrialised sphere and relegated themselves to irrelevancy. Bans on piecework by skilled workers meant less and less as they became an increasingly smaller proportion of the workforce. The tactic of holding onto their rapidly shrinking sphere of control evaporated in their hands as their skills became rationalised and made obsolete by a new division of labour.

This was undergoing a vast challenge from the rank and file. In 1911, 16,000 workers on the Illinois Central Railroad (Chicago to Kentucky) and Harriman lines (linking Chicago to New Orleans) line struck in reaction to the introduction of a Taylorist time-motion study in the repair shop. Harriman was in the spotlight at the time, especially with Florence Harriman as a member of the Commission of Industrial Relations. Crossing craft lines, shopmen met unofficially in Memphis where they formed a 'system federation' which spoke for a range of skilled and unskilled clerks. The system federation demanded the end of premium pay, time-motion studies, and even the keeping of personnel records – an insightful demand that reflected their awareness of the danger of human relations to workers. The railroads would only negotiate with each craft union separately, which the system federation wisely refused to agree to. The strike lasted four years, gunfights were common, 553 people were jailed, and 1,069 lost their homes before the union called it off.

Although the strike was defeated, everyday forms of resistance began to happen openly. Engaging in white-collar sabotage, clerks hid records and swapped and removed cards from railroad cars to create chaos on the lines. The workers had studied the new composition of capital in the railroad sector and devised new tactics to disrupt the accumulation process at its weakest links with the least cost. 'The strike had revealed a readiness among some craft unionists of long standing to fuse all grades of workers in open confrontation with scientific management'.[232] Out of this a Federation of Federations was created that laid the foundation of the general railroad strikes in the 1920s.

---

232   Montgomery 1979, pp. 107–8; and Montgomery 1974, pp. 523–4.

A Temporary Solution

Many of the WWI strikes weren't just over wages, but also challenged management's control over work, particularly the rationalisation and the speeding up of the pace of work.[233] The 1914 and 1916 Westinghouse strikes demanded the abolition of premium pay and slowing the pace of work. The wartime emergency provided an opportunity of greater gain with lower costs for workers who were able to escalate their tactics. This leverage allowed some strikers to push back against the rationalisation of work, shorten their work hours (absolute surplus value) and slow the pace of production (relative surplus value) although as we've seen their gains were short-lived once the war ended.[234] By attacking both hours and productivity simultaneously, the workers exhibited an understanding of the relationship of the two in their struggle, a lesson lost today in union tradeoffs between higher wages and higher productivity. Their strategy countered what Marx had observed decades earlier:

> So soon as the shortening [of the working day] becomes compulsory, machinery becomes in the hands of capital the objective means, systematically employed for squeezing out more labour in a given time. This is effected in two ways: by increasing the speed of the machinery, and by giving the workman more machinery to tend.[235]

By doing so, counter-planning and strikes put the struggle over work at the centre of their objectives, an objective the temporary emergency of WWI could neither manage nor defeat with the labour-planning state. As Conner concluded, 'the war had neither solved the problem of labor relations nor left organised labor in a position to deal equally with management, even though labor had greatly increased in numbers'.[236] What it had done was tamp down on disruption, expand government authority into managing class struggle, and bring the unions deeply into the Democratic Party coalition and harness them to the state.

---

233 Bucki argues that these strikes transcended industrial unionism to embrace workers' control. In reality, the answer to their demands was watered down 'industrial democracy', promoted by the Commission on Industrial Relations' majority report that underpinned progressive-era labour law reforms (Bucki 2009, pp. 200–1).

234 Montgomery 1979, pp. 120–1.

235 Marx 1867b, p. 450.

236 Conner 1983, p. 180.

CHAPTER 9

Revolt of the Rank and File: The Steel and Seattle General Strikes

The end of WWI in 1919 was a critical turning point, bringing both danger and opportunity. A coordinated multi-pronged roll-back of the gains achieved by the wartime strike wave was paired with the persecution of militant workers, the Industrial Workers of the World (IWW), socialists, anarchists, and other dissidents. But in some places the wartime mobilisation, escalation, and resulting gains became the new baseline to continue the struggle. Revolutions swept Mexico and Russia, an uprising nearly succeeded in Germany, a revolutionary government came to power in Hungary, socialists took over Vienna, insurgencies spread throughout the collapsed Ottoman Empire, independence movements were in the ascent in many colonies, and general strikes erupted in Canada and the US. In the US, the wartime wildcat strikes provided workers the capacity to further expand newfound gains by continuing to mobilise, intensifying their tactics, expanding mass support, and circulating their struggles into general strikes in the steel industry and a general strike that took over and ran the city of Seattle. *The Nation* called the year 1919 the 'revolt of the rank and file', a time in which 'authority cannot [sic] longer be imposed from above; it comes automatically from below. This is the revolution'.[1]

Despite the repression, the outcomes from continued tactical escalation to preserve and even expand on wartime gains were mixed. Steel workers who continued to mobilise and escalate were defeated primarily by their own unions, which functioned as breaks on their ability to intensify their tactics. In Seattle, however, for a period of just a few days, the general strike defied the countervailing conditions and demonstrated that workers would tactically escalate to establish a vibrant, living demonstration of what CLR James called a post-capitalist 'future in the present'.[2]

---

1 *The Nation*, 25 October 1919, p. 540.
2 James 1980.

More Pay for Less Work

Rather than disciplining workers, tamping down on strikes, and preventing disruption from spreading, arbitration and nationalisation only encouraged further mobilisation and escalation. (See Chapter 8). The reduced cost of further tactical escalation encouraged the circulation of class struggle to other sectors and unorganised workers, threatening to transform the strike wave into a general strike. In a few places the strike circulated out of the war industry and spread so thoroughly in an entire geographic area to other shops and industries that the local economy came to a standstill. In the Seattle general strike, workers didn't merely withdraw their labour, but joined with their supporters to take over and run the city themselves.

There were more general strikes in the US between 1917 and 1919 than during any previous period of American history. This strike wave was not limited to key war industries but became endemic throughout the economy. 'The industrial unrest was not confined to any one section of the country or any single industrial group, but rather it characterized almost every industry in every section of the country'.[3] The wave of general strikes didn't stop at the border. It was not merely a national strike wave but a global cycle of revolutionary struggle not seen since the 1780–1820s that crossed the border from Mexico, proceeded into Canada, traversed the Atlantic, and swept across Europe into Russia. The general strike was a sign of an emboldened recomposed global working-class that had managed to end a world war and take over in Mexico, Hungary, Vienna, Russia, and Seattle.

A sampling of some of the city-wide general strikes that took place during the war confirms the extensive reach of the general strike. Street car workers striking for union recognition in Springfield, Illinois, Lincoln's hometown sparked a general strike in September 1917. There was a general strike in Billings, Montana in 1917. Two other general strikes took place in March 1918, one in Waco, Texas again sparked by street car workers and a week-long general strike in St. Louis, Missouri in sympathy with a laundry drivers' strike that had begun in July 1917. In Winnipeg, Canada the second and larger general strike in about a year lasted from 15 May 1919 until it was crushed on 26 June.

The 1919 Seattle general strike demonstrated that there was something fundamentally different about these types of strikes. These were not merely strikes over conditions, wages, and recognition by waged unionised craft workers. Rather, they were social insurgencies that used their power to shut down the

---

3   Foner 1987, pp. 170 and 172.

economy of an entire local geographic area. In Seattle they went even further, governing the city, redirecting resources and providing services to the needs of the local working population. The wartime wildcat strikes illustrated that the recomposed working-class was continuing to escalate the intensity of its tactics by shutting down entire cities and attempting to reorganise them to serve working-class needs. In Seattle the general strike did not merely shut down production, but restarted it under workers' direct democratic control. Workers' short, sharp wildcat strikes during the war provided them invaluable experience in recomposing their power, circulating their struggles, and achieving modest gains by escalating their tactics. This changed their awareness of what more was possible.

The wartime strikes delivered further success in the struggle against work by reducing both the length of work (absolute surplus value) and the productivity of work (relative surplus value). Demands for an eight-hour workday with a rise in pay and no productivity increase were widely achieved. Working hours decreased during the war, expanding the time and space for workers to explore other ways of organising life beyond work. In 1914, 11.8 percent worked 48-hour six-day workweeks or less in manufacturing. In 1919, 48.7 percent did.[4]

Wage increases for skilled and unskilled workers were also common if uneven. Increases ranged from 50 to 100 percent for iron, steel, shipbuilding and munitions workers, 31 percent and a 50 percent signing bonus for seamen if they served for the entire war, 30 percent for shoe workers, and 6.4–10 percent for book, newspaper and printing workers. While wages for unskilled packing workers rose 42.5 percent and the unskilled iron and steel workers obtained 80–87 percent increases, the wages of office workers in manufacturing and railroads actually fell 10–14 percent.[5] With the exception of office and railroad workers, the wartime strike wave successfully resulted in more pay for less work.

Although organised disruption posed the most significant threat to war production, individual acts of everyday resistance were widespread and on the rise, particularly by the 1920s as organised workers were on retreat after a decade of repression. The labour shortage encouraged both collective and individual forms of resistance such as high turnover in the labour force, an endemic problem for employers. Turnover increased tenfold during the war from 300 to 3,000 percent, throwing war production into turmoil. Workers frequently left their job to find a better one as a low-risk way to increase their pay and reduce work hours and productivity short of organising and striking. To address the

---

4   Ibid., p. 342.
5   Ibid., p. 154; and Perlman and Taft 1935, p. 404.

problem, employers hired more women to do the same work as men, and the
NWLB mandated equal pay for equal work to keep the women from also leaving. While more women workers and the equal pay rule might at first appear to
be an effort to address gender inequality, it was a tactic to undercut individual
worker mobility and prepare a pool for non-unionised replacement workers for
strikes.[6]

The United States of Steel

According to William Z. Foster, in 1919 about 75 percent of steel workers were
immigrants from about 40 different ethnicities, most of whom were low-paid
unskilled and semi-skilled labourers. Not only were previous attempts to organise and strike complicated by the vast ethnic and linguistic diversity, cultural
norms, and prejudices of steel workers not to mention the distinctions between
the majority of non-white unskilled workers and minority of white skilled
workers. These class divisions were intentionally stoked by the steel industry
attempting to undermine organising attempts, prevent the workers from consolidating their power across the industry, and keep wages low and profits
high.[7] The complex issues of ethnicity were also accompanied by threats posed
by the use of blacklists, labour spies, informers, and deportations against union
members and organisers. Employer exploitation of these intra-class divisions
served to keep wages low. The 1920 Interchurch World Movement Commission
of Inquiry reported that the pay of semi-skilled and unskilled workers fell below
the minimum level of subsistence.

Two previous strikes organised by the Amalgamated Association of Iron,
Steel and Tin Workers (AAISTW) in 1901 and 1909 ended in dreadful defeats
that nearly wiped out the union. The 1909 strike began when American Sheet
and Tin Plate Company declared it would move to an open shop, refusing to
negotiate or sign any more union contracts. The company obtained injunctions
against picketing in three towns but no restraining orders were granted in two
others where the workers were on strike. After its 1901 defeat, the union went
into the 1909 strike with virtually no influence among local officials. The Executive Board ended the strike after 14 months in August 1910. The defeat gave US
Steel hegemonic control of the industry, which Perlman and Taft described as
'an absolute government so far as labor was concerned'. As we saw in the case of

---

6   Mathewson 1931; and Foner 1987, p. 155.
7   Keeran 1989, pp. 387–8.

the International Association of Bridge and Structural Iron Workers (IABSIW) in Chapter 7, US Steel consolidated its power both within and across industrial sectors while the craft unions retained their narrow focus on skilled workers in each separate sector.[8]

By 1919, the AAISTW was a shadow of its former self. Its refusal to organise the growing number of unskilled workers in the steel plants led its membership of skilled workers to rapidly dwindle. The union leadership was more concerned with maintaining its haemorrhaging membership than risking further tactical escalation to mobilise and organise new unskilled and semi-skilled workers both in the steel and other related sectors. In fact, after 1901 the AAISTW resisted efforts to organise workers in the large mills, focusing primarily on its 10,000 members who mostly worked in small firms. This played a crucial role in the union's abandonment of its commitment to the 1919 general steel strike as it peeled away to unsuccessfully try to negotiate a separate peace with the smaller companies that saw a union contract as the means to hold off threats from the corporate behemoths.[9]

The developments in the steel industry mirrored that occurring simultaneously in the bridge and iron industry described in Chapter 7. The 1901 formation of US Steel fused together the steel industry by shifting production from primarily an assortment of small companies in 1890 to consolidated control under a single company. By 1910 US Steel controlled about one-half of the industry and six other companies shared the other half.[10] Consolidation of the industry ushered in a new composition of capital in the industry intended to stabilise production and prevent disruption by strikes at the plant level by decomposing skilled workers' control over production. With so much of the industry under the control of a single trust it could respond to disruptions in some plants by quarantining them while ramping up production in undisturbed plants. For this reason, US Steel had made it company policy to allow collective bargaining and sign contracts only in plants where a union already existed. It used this policy in an early media campaign to refute claims the company was anti-union since, Morgan was fond of reminding journalists, it was a party to contracts with unions in some of its plants. As Morgan reminded government officials and the media, this meant the company had no philosophical hostility to unions per se.

---

8   Perlman and Taft 1935, pp. 141 and 143.

9   Haydu 1999, p. 318.

10   Foner 1973, p. 190.

US Steel received extensive media coverage praising it for embracing social welfarism. In 1902, US Steel claimed it allowed lower paid workers to purchase company stock and in 1906 it also publicised programmes that offered voluntary accident relief, company housing, and vocational, social and medical facilities.[11] However, these claims were later disputed by the union and the 1920 Interchurch World Movement Commission of Inquiry, which found they had little effect on the poverty level wages and long hours of steel workers.

US Steel employed 268,000 of the 600,000 US steelworkers in 145 different mills.[12] As the largest single employer in the industry, the cost of taking action against US Steel was extremely high. Known union members and organisers were placed on its unacknowledged blacklist and anyone interested in joining the union or striking ran the risk of joining them on it. With the cost of failure so high an effective organising campaign in steel meant escalating tactics in such a way as to raise the opportunity to achieve gains that would offset them.

The rationalisation of management in the back offices was integrally connected to the rationalisation of steel work at the plant level. The use of Taylor's time motion studies allowed experts to break down each minuscule task of steel work and rationalise, standardise, and transfer the knowledge of how to make steel to a shop foreman and mid-level manager. Deskilling of steel work reduced steel workers to performing simple repetitive tasks that could be taught to anyone at any plant. Knowledge of the steel-working process, a fundamental source of power for skilled steel workers, was expropriated and transformed into the means of control and discipline. That expropriation of workers' knowledge and control was a prerequisite to the integration and reorganisation of the industry under US Steel.

While rationalisation consolidated power over the steel industry, it also broke down intra-class divisions among workers brought together in the new division of labour. The rationalisation of the production process further socialised production and raised the possibility of cooperation among workers by eroding the hierarchy of labour between skilled and unskilled workers and closing the gap between the two. Unskilled workers' sense of powerlessness over their work and low wages provoked them to action at the same time as skilled workers whose control over their work was under attack and eroding rapidly. Because nearly one-half of all steel workers had US Steel as their employer, fewer workers were faced with the hurdle of relating their grievances to workers in mills and plants run by a different employer. And because of US Steel's

---

11   Perlman and Taft 1935, pp. 138–9.
12   Painter 1987, p. 370.

dominant position in the industry, workers in its competitors' shops stood to gain from the struggles of US Steel workers. Consolidation of the industry from above removed barriers to circulating the strike from below. US Steel provided the workers with a clearly identifiable 'shared enemy'. Its integration of one-half of the industry, as well as fusing it with other sectors such as the railroads, iron, coal, and banking, illustrated Karl Marx's observation that as capitalism further socialises the means of production, it brings closer together the workers who can rupture it. This is what the AFL's National Committee for Organizing the Iron and Steel Workers was counting on.

The 1919 Steel Strike

With much of the steel industry centrally coordinated by US Steel, plant level strikes could be blunted and defeated by either ramping up production and stockpiling product before the strike began or by shifting production to unaffected plants. Using strikes in individual plants to disrupt the entire industry at its weakest link was no longer possible. Consolidation made it possible to contain and cordon off a local strike and dampen its disruptive impact. The reorganisation and rationalisation of the entire industry made it possible to keep production unaffected industry-wide even if individual plants had been shut down.

In preparation for the 1919 strike, Foster developed his strategy by closely studying the new composition of capital in the steel industry. He realised that steel workers needed to take these new conditions created by the rationalisation of the industry into account if they were to successfully recompose their strength. A successful strike was only possible if it were general, capable of shutting down the entire industry at once while circulating the strike to other industries that were horizontally integrated with the steel industry. That meant circulating the struggle to the coal mines to deplete the supply of fuel to power the mills, the railroads to block the movement of steel and coal, and the bridge and iron industry which needed the steel to assemble bridges and buildings. Just as capital had consolidated across and within industrial sectors, so must the working-class.

Foster attempted to carry over some of his experience as a former IWW organiser and syndicalist. His new plan for the steel industry was modelled after his 1917 campaign to organise all the packinghouse workers into neighbourhood-based locals coordinated by a single systems federation, the Chicago Stockyards Labor Council (CSLC), like what had been done with the railroad unions. The president's Mediation Commission eventually headed off a strike by issuing a settlement and mandating elected shop committees, an award that became a model of the soon to be formed National War Labor Board (see Chapter 8). The recomposition of workers in the packinghouse industry ran aground on the AFL's racist ban on blacks which discouraged many black workers from joining CSLC locals the following year.[13]

Turning the AFL ship of state and its many affiliates in the steel industry to embrace the industrial organising model took nearly a decade. After the disastrous 1909 AAISTW strike, the November 1909 AFL convention called a meeting on 13 December to organise the steel workers. The meeting was attended by 50 of the 87 international unions operating in the industry. Delegates to the meeting instructed their unions to send organisers to cities where steel mills operated, prepare a strike fund, and write lists of grievances. Most importantly, the delegates urged 20 of the unions, including the International Association of Bridge and Structural Iron Workers (IABSIW; see Chapter 7), to amalgamate into one union. Unfortunately, only five of the unions sent organisers. When Gompers made a second request to send organisers, he was ignored. Gompers then called President P.J. McCardle to tell him to call off the new organising campaign, which he did in February 1910. One of McCardle's organisers told him that having 20 different unions to fight the 'Steel King ... instead of bringing all of these workers directly into one union is to enter a combat with a mighty giant, its detectives and paid hirelings, with one arm tied around ones back'.[14]

The unions' refusal to revise their strategy and escalate their tactics in light of the new composition of capital had devastating consequences for the steel workers. The 1920 Interchurch World Movement's Industrial Relations Department's Commission of Inquiry into the steel industry reported many startling findings about the conditions of steel workers. It found that three-quarters of US Steel workers worked up to 12 hours per day and 72 hours per week, some with 18–24 hour shifts every two weeks.[15]

The AFL leadership was unable to resist continued agitation from its rank and file membership in light of these horrendous conditions. In June 1918 the membership passed a resolution to renew steel worker organising. The National Committee for Organizing the Iron and Steel Workers was established

---

13   It also didn't help that race riots in 1917 in East St. Louis and other cities in 1919, particularly the segregated Chicago stockyards, stoked further hatred and white violence against blacks who were moving north and west out of the south to escape white terrorism. That the stockyards were the site of one of the most deadly riots illustrated how entrenched racism, promoted by the AFL unions, sabotaged Foster's organising strategy.

14   Foner 1973, p. 191.

15   Yolen 1936, p. 373.

in August, the day after the NWLB issued its rulings for the Bethlehem and Pittsfield strikes (see Chapter 8), and the AFL Secretary-Treasurer Foster was put in charge of organising. However, the commitment by the unions in the industry was meagre since only 24 member unions contributed a total of $2,400 in funds and restricted organising to the Chicago area only.

When the campaign got off the ground on a shoestring budget, steel workers signed up in droves, overwhelming the skeletal National Committee, and gave impetus to Foster's push for nationwide general strike. The National Committee used the IWW tactic of sending out flying squadrons of ten organisers into the field, moving from town to town challenging bans on public meetings that were passed by local governments in the pockets of the steel industry. By June 1919, 100,000 signed up.

What workers were signing up for wasn't what they had expected. The AFL leadership couldn't ignore the popularity of the industrial model of organisation to counter the new composition of capital and the momentum for a general strike but pulled out all the stops to derail it. Workers were prohibited from organising by shop and had to mimic existing craft designations and union jurisdiction for each category. Although membership was growing they were split up among the 24 existing craft unions. A factional fight emerged inside the National Committee over the craft model being imposed on it. Immigrant semi- and unskilled workers wanted to organise a general strike while the leadership of the craft unions just wanted new members to fill up their long depleted coffers.[16]

The initial spark of enthusiasm soon waned. Members began making ultimatums that the National Committee plan a national strike and then began dropping out when it hesitated because the craft unions insisted that only they, and not the workers, could call a strike. In the meantime, the AFL and affiliate leadership delayed every effort to call a strike vote for several months and called for arbitration in an attempt to redirect the demands to escalate tactics.

On 15 May 1919, AAISTW President Tighe asked US Steel for a conference without consulting with the National Committee but was ignored.[17] Tighe was immediately denounced for betraying the National Committee of which AAISTW was a member. But Tighe wasn't alone. Gompers was working alongside him to unilaterally de-escalate National Committee tactics. On 25 May the National Committee made an effort to keep the Pittsburgh meeting from calling a strike. Two days later, on 27 May, the National Committee formed a nego-

---

16   Interchurch World Movement Commission of Inquiry, 1920; and Brecher 1972, pp. 136–7.
17   Perlman and Taft 1935, p. 463.

tiating committee which included Gompers, another AAISTW officer, Foster, John Fitzpatrick, and one other. On 20 June Gompers wrote US Steel Chairman Elbert Gary a letter offering to 'sit down around a table' in order to 'enter into an agreement for collective bargaining'. Gompers's offer to de-escalate and nego- tiate caught Gary's attention but not the kind he wanted. The firings of union members soon followed, as Gompers awaited a reply that never came.

The several historical accounts of the strike cited here are unable to explain this apparent equivocation by the National Committee. The AFL leadership was attempting to de-escalate even though mass support for the strike was growing fast. The circulation of struggle throughout the steel industry was accelerating and transforming the steel workers into an ungovernable force that threatened to exceed the bounds of both capital and the unions. Preparations for the strike was taking off despite the AFL's management of the organising campaign and attempt to immunise the industry from this threat by demonstrating the value of arbitration and a union contract to manage class struggle.

A month later, the AFL lost control of the workers they had invited to organ- ise. At the 20 July conference of the cooperating unions, the delegates voted to send a strike ballot to the membership. The membership unequivocally sup- ported the strike with 98 percent of the 100,000 voting members voting for it. They spoke for 250,000 more unorganised steel workers who joined them on the opening day of the strike.

Despite the vote, Gompers immediately requested a meeting with US Steel within ten days but again received no reply to his letter. Either Gary wanted the strike or was convinced that the AFL was powerless to stop it.

On 4 September the National Committee was still hesitating to call the strike and requested Gompers ask President Wilson to intervene and call a confer- ence of the parties, but Wilson declined. Less than a year after the war had ended, the AFL leadership had little to show for its access to the polity and loy- alty to the Democratic Party. Desperate to avoid the inevitable, the 24 union presidents sent yet another telegram to Wilson but he was still non-committal.

Unable to demobilise and de-escalate to negotiate, the National Commit- tee was out of options. It soon set the strike date for 22 September. The threat to escalate, not polite requests, ultimately prompted Wilson to intervene. The President sent a telegram asking for the strike to be postponed until after 6 October so an Industrial Conference could begin meeting on that day to address the strike.[18] As the National Committee deliberated over Wilson's re- quest telegrams poured in from organisers and locals protesting postpone- ment and demanding the strike begin as planned. Recognising that the workers

---

18   The Industrial Conference was modelled after the National War Labor Board which had

would move with or without the AFL, Foster later recounted that 'it would have been folly to have the steel workers abandon their strike preparations even if it could have been done'.[19] Ultimately Wilson's request to postpone the strike was refused because the cooperating unions saw 'the danger of losing control of the movement, resulting in an epidemic of sporadic and unauthorized strikes'.[20] Gompers refused to give in, again attempting to delay the strike to allow the 6 October conference to arbitrate the dispute. He offered a resolution that workers would postpone the strike pending the decision of an arbitration committee but it was not voted on due to the rules of the conference. On 17 September Gary again refused to negotiate for what was now the fourth and final time. The workers were fortunate he did so because Gompers's proposal offered to give up the demand for recognition and implicitly allowed company unions to continue.[21]

Wilson yet again asked the AFL to postpone the 22 September strike date without success. In a final last ditch effort, National Committee head John Fitzpatrick appealed to employers to concede to President Wilson's request to arbitrate. Fitzpatrick offered to end the strike in exchange for agreeing to allow the Interchurch World Movement Commission of Inquiry to arbitrate, but his proposal was rejected by Gary.[22]

Despite Wilson's interventions and the AFL leadership's many offers to demobilise and de-escalate to arbitrate, on 22 September about 275,000 steel workers struck as planned, with the number walking out increasing to 350,000 by the end of the month. Although only 100,000 were union members the strike was immensely popular despite the many efforts to constrain and prevent it. It struck a nerve among non-union members, office workers, and unskilled European immigrant workers who had been excluded by the craft unions.

Unfortunately, the massively popular strike was undermined by two key factors. First, the strikers were sabotaged by the National Committee unions that contributed little to organising the strike, insisted on controlling the planning and coordination, limited organising to Chicago, and attempted to delay, diffuse, and de-escalate the strike. Secondly, the strikers met widespread repression by local elites, local, state, and federal authorities, and capital. While the AFL leadership was equivocating, delaying, and deflecting elites had been

---

shut down only seven weeks earlier. Among those at the meeting were John D. Rockefeller, Jr. and US Steel Corporation chair Elbert Gary. (Conner 1983, p. 177).

19 Yolen, 1936, p. 268.
20 Perlman and Taft 1935, p. 465.
21 Ibid., p. 465; and Conner 1983, pp. 178–9.
22 Perlman and Taft 1935, p. 466.

organising in preparation to escalate their repressive tactics. By threatening to
strike without actually intending to, and causing a long delay until the strike
began, the AFL leadership allowed capital to ready its own tactics. The delay and
equivocation gave elites time to regroup and prepare. Because the AFL leadership didn't want to move forward with the strike, even though it could no longer
avoid doing so, elites had the advantage.

Any hope that President Wilson would remain neutral in the strike, which
would have given the strikers an important advantage, was dashed when he
sent in US troops to Gary, Indiana. The steel companies used the AFL's racial bar
as a tactic against it by bringing in 30,000–40,000 black workers as strikebreakers. On 4 October strikers fought with black strikebreakers in Gary giving Governor Goodrich an excuse to send the National Guard to Gary. When the strikers
proceeded with their planned parade the governor used it as a provocation to
request federal troops. Martial law was declared, picketing was limited, and
2,000 US troops under Major General Wood, seasoned by the recent invasion
of Mexico to pursue Pancho Villa's forces, soon patrolled the streets in Gary.[23]
Supported by the National Guard, the US troops suppressed the parade of veterans and strikers, arrested strikers, and broke up picket lines. Troops arrested
union officers for threatening to call a strike. The military repression forced the
strike to be called off. Facing the combined military force of the state and federal governments, workers 'became bitter and disillusioned, convinced that the
federal government was on the side of the companies'.[24]

While the use of military force in Gary, Indiana displayed the willingness of
elites to escalate repressive measures, local governments attacked the strikers'
efforts to continue mobilising mass support. Many counties, towns, and cities suppressed civil liberties. For example, Allegheny County Sheriff Haddock
banned outdoor meetings and rallies and deputised 5,000 strikebreaking employees of US Steel to join police to enforce the ban, clubbing, arresting, and
fining strikers and their supporters. Immigrant strikers were particularly targeted for arrest and charged with being 'suspicious persons' and given high
bail to keep them off the streets.[25] Strikers were arrested without warrants,
imprisoned without charge, and had their homes invaded and meetings
banned. Arrested strikers were routinely offered release from jail only if they
went back to work.

---

23   Ibid., p. 467; and Painter 1987, p. 372.
24   Brecher 1972, p. 140.
25   Ibid., pp. 138–9.

The courts were deaf to the widespread violations of civil liberties. The Pittsburgh City Council and Common Pleas Court refused to hear petitions about the repression of civil liberties. Two later federal investigations into the suppression of civil liberties in the area for the US Secretary of Labor and the National War Labor Board were suppressed. Pennsylvania became a model throughout the areas of the country effected by the strike. Local, state, and federal governments entered the strike on the side of the steel companies and there was no recourse for workers to hold them accountable.

In many locations police, the National Guard, US troops, and deputy marshals were aided by a new mercenary organisation. After decades of local elites forming so-called citizen, safety, and vigilance committees and linking them together nationwide, a new organisation came about in preparation for the steel strike. The para-military American Legion was formed as a federally chartered corporation by an act of Congress on 16 September 1919 and held its first convention on 11 November 1919.[26] It was an innovative new type of paramilitary organisation unseen since the remnants of the Confederate Army reorganised itself into the precursors of the Ku Klux Klan under the leadership of former General Nathan Bedford Forrest, who brought his guerrilla fighting tactics to the fields of the Reconstruction-era South. The Legion was explicitly formed to only enrol veterans as members and to organise them into a paramilitary fighting force that was both outside the formal command structure of the US military and interwoven with it.

There were a few exceptions to the use of the state at the service of capital. The Illinois State's Attorney raided the offices of the Sherman Service private detective agency. He had indicted one of the company's directors for incitement to riot and intent to kill and murder large numbers of persons for its role in strikebreaking. However, after one and a half years of delays the company was not brought to trial. Because 1,500 workers were on strike in Wheeling, West Virginia the sheriff deputised strikers and 33 delegates to the Wheeling Trades Assembly to keep the peace and prevent violence by strikebreakers. Strikers were allowed to hold meetings in public. A similar tolerance existed in Ohio. These exceptions, while encouraging, were insufficient to offset the widespread use of local police working in coordination with elites to suppress the strike.[27] With limited support of local and state officials, the strike faced

---

26   The Legion continues to be federally chartered and is required to issue an annual report
     to Congress. (See Painter 1987, p. 376; and United States Code Annotated, Title 36, Chapter
     21701–21708).

27   Perlman and Taft 1935, p. 466.

overwhelming forces of repression aided in their efforts to mobilise by the incessant delays by the AFL leadership.

The steel strike was hampered by efforts to keep it from circulating to other related industries in order to transform it into a nationwide general strike. Coal miners were already on strike. Railroad workers were still dissatisfied by the outcome of their recent strike and wanted to strike but were opposed by national leadership. Of the nine states where the strike had spread, Pennsylvania was a particular hotbed of strike activity. On 1–2 November, the Pennsylvania Federation of Labor threatened to call a state-wide general strike but was opposed by Foster. The Pittsburgh railway locals voted to strike but the Brotherhoods would not support them. Elsewhere in the state other rail workers struck but their unions gave them no benefits and allowed other members to scab their jobs.

Once again, the craft form of organisation, centralised strike coordination, and the separate prerogatives of the leadership and organisations served to impede workers' efforts to circulate their struggles and recompose their power within and across industries. The triple opposition to the steel strikers from their own leadership, capital, and the state prevented them from making the necessary tactical escalation that would have allowed them to take advantage of the widespread public support to lower the costs of escalation and raise the opportunities to achieve some of their objectives. While capital had recomposed itself by integrating the majority of the steel industry and consolidating the railroad, coal, iron, and banking sectors under a centralised corporate management, the workers in these industries were blocked by their own unions from recomposing their power to meet this challenge. By blocking each separate effort to join the strike, the union leadership doomed the strike to defeat. If the workers were to overcome the rapidly organised forces of repression, the strike would need to build more mass support and be circulated to other related sectors to be able to create sufficient disruption of the economy to extract the concessions they sought.

Even while facing defeat, some of the unions attempted to discipline their own members for working to make the strike a success. After Tighe's failure to arrange a separate concession with US Steel in May, many AAISTW locals under contract struck anyway. Their actions defied not only the steel companies, but also their union, and even the sacred contract. Six weeks after the strike began Tighe used their contracts as a disciplinary tool to force the wildcatting locals back to work. The AAISTW fired a strike organiser and revoked the charter of several Cleveland locals that refused to go back to work. On 19 November, Tighe again tried to propose a separate settlement with the Bethlehem Steel Corporation but was rejected.

The National Committee ended the strike on 8 January 1920. If the AFL leadership couldn't prevent the strike from starting, it made sure it failed as quickly as possible. The lack of financial, organisational, and logistical support took its toll on the strikers. The number on strike eventually fell from 365,000 to 110,000. With public meetings banned, strikers in fear of being arrested for visiting one another's homes, and misinformation and poor communications about the progress of the strike, workers trickled back to work. The misinformation was intentional. The National Committee actually published false reports that the strike was waning and workers were returning to work. Strike organisers only published a weekly strike bulletin and didn't issue clear statements of objectives and facts about the progress of the strike. The 24 member unions contributed little money, few organisers, little resources, and almost no leadership. Ironically, most of the money supporting the strikers came from outside unions because the 24 unions provided no strike benefits. Strikers had little to sustain themselves and their families. There were only 45 local commissaries set up, giving out twice weekly rations to all strikers. Worst of all, later investigations uncovered that some officers of the 24 unions and the National Committee were on the payroll of the detective agency Corporations Auxiliary, hired by the steel companies to sabotage the strike from within.

The strikers didn't win a single concession. In fact, the workers' own unions made it an utterly bloody and costly defeat. Twenty workers were killed, 18 of them strikers, and workers lost between $87–112 million in wages.[28]

The 1919 steel strike demonstrated that working-class power was being decomposed. Workers were willing to escalate their tactics but their ability to circulate their strikes through an entire industry and into multiple related sectors at once was impeded their own unions. By helping defeat the steelworkers' strike, the AFL demonstrated what had evaded it during WWI: its effectiveness in controlling its own membership. To join the polity the AFL leadership had embraced de-mobilisation and de-escalation in favour of federally mandated arbitration, serving on regulatory bodies, and participation in the Democratic Party. Once the balance of power in the elite coalition shifted back to the faction favouring repression over conciliation, the workers were left facing a triumvirate of capital, the state, and their own union leadership, which asserted a new power on the shop floor. Because the threat of disrupting wartime production was no longer present there was no longer any pressing need for elites to resort to arbitration or make concessions to restore production. The short-lived experiment with the labour-planning state had definitively waned.

---

28   Ibid., p. 467.

The defeat of the 1919 steel general strike ushered in the triumph of the new composition of capital. Just as victorious Roman generals would insist on their right to a 'triumph' upon their return to Rome and assume their position as pro-consul and possibly later emperor, so too did capital insist on its triumph by calling upon the police and military powers of the state to reassert power, control and discipline.

The AFL leadership's co-optation into the elite coalition was complete. But as the balance of power swung back away from the reform faction of elites, the AFL could offer little to its allies or the membership. It offered few votes and resources to its allies or tangible and intangible benefits to its members. The long decade of defeat for the working-class had begun.

The Seattle General Strike: From Disruption to Transcendence

At the beginning of 1919 workers in Seattle managed to do what the steel workers would later be prevented from doing: they launched an effective general strike. Unlike the intention to shut down the steel industry and perhaps the national economy, Seattle workers shut down the city so they could re-open it under worker self-management.

On 21 January 1919, two weeks after the armistice, 35,000 skilled shipbuilding and other shipyard workers refused to accept a pay increase for only themselves and walked out together with other dockworkers. The workers were protesting against continuing wartime wage controls by which the international unions, Navy, and US Emergency Fleet Corporation collaborated to set wages under the authority of the Shipbuilding Labor Adjustment Board (SLAB), often awarding the highest wage increases to skilled workers. Although the war was over, SLAB continued to assert control over wages and issued an award without a raise.[29] (See Chapter 8). On 2 February, the shipyard workers voted to begin the strike on 6 February. Soon a proposal before the Seattle Central Labor Coun-

---

29   16,000 of the strikers were members of the Marine Workers Affiliation which struck   ·
      against the SLAB award on 9 January 1919. The SLAB award was decided by its chair V. Everit
      Macy who was not only a banker but also chair of the National Civic Federation after which
      much of the labour-planning state was modelled (see Chapter 8). Everit then became the
      NWLB umpire whose award triggered the second strike on 4 March. The award included
      no wage increases and the eight-hour day for about 4 percent of the workers. After three
      weeks the strike was won with large pay increases. That there had just been a general strike
      must have helped. Workers had resisted the labour-planning state and won. (See Conner
      1983, pp. 168–71).

cil for workers to take over the shipping industry was expanded into taking over control of the entire city.[30]

With some of the leadership out of town to plan a national action on behalf of jailed San Francisco labour leaders Tom Mooney and Warren K. Billings, the Central Labor Council asked its affiliate locals to poll members as to whether they would join a general strike to support the shipyard strike. Over the next two weeks 110 locals voted to join the general strike by wide margins. Among those who voted to support the strike were the longshoremen, defying the president of their International Longshoreman's Association who had threatened to rescind their charter if they struck.

The general strike that took place over the next several days was the fruition of years of organising by both workers and supporters throughout the area. The quadrupling of union membership between 1915–18 had made Seattle a strong union town where even the IWW and AFL Metal Trades Council worked together.

Unlike the later general strike in the steel industry, the intention of the Seattle general strike was more than a show of workers' power to disrupt production. Nor was it focused on production alone. It was a demonstration of the power of workers to take over and reorganise both production and reproduction to lessen the exploitation of labour by subordinating production to social needs rather than profit-making.

The Central Labor Council formed a General Strike Committee (GSC) composed of three elected representatives from each striking local which set up and ran the city for the entire five days of the strike. The GSC became a parallel system of worker self-governance, running wet garbage collection, homes for the destitute, fire, public safety, and publicity. Its operations were effective and efficient. Milk delivery drivers organised distribution to 35 neighbourhood milk stations and purchased milk from small dairies. Food workers served 30,000 meals per day to the community and strikers in 21 cafeterias. Critical services such as hospitals were kept in operation and continued to be supplied with linen and fuel. There was a semblance of cross-racial alliances, illustrated when the Japanese Labor Association of hotel and restaurant workers voted to join the strike.[31]

The GSC organised 300 volunteers for a Labor War Veterans Guard which operated a watch that used persuasion rather than force, police power, or weapons. The watch successfully kept the Skid Row bars closed, which reduced

---

30   O'Connor 1964, pp. 126 and 134.
31   Ibid., p. 139.

the opportunity for troubles to brew which could discredit the strike. The watch force grew out of the Private Soldiers and Sailor Legion formed by workers under the Central Labor Council as a rank and file counterweight to elite vigilante groups. The Labor War Veterans Guard was so effective that during the general strike the redundant chief of police said no further police were needed because the unions were providing their own security. No arrests related to the strike were made during the strike. The chief of police and Major General Morrison, who was sent from Camp Lewis to Seattle, both attested to the peacefulness and orderliness of the city. In the criminal syndicalism prosecutions after the strike, the prosecutors were unable to charge even one person with either a seditious speech or act.[32]

Unlike all the other city-wide general strikes of the past few years, the workers literally ran the city. The strike turned the world upside-down with employers and government officials, including the King County Commissioners, the Mayor, and the Port of Seattle approaching the GSC to obtain permission to resume limited services or business operations. The *Seattle Union Record*, the General Strike Committee's daily newspaper that provided a conduit of information to the strikers, their supporters, and other residents of the city, explained the tactics and strategy of the general strike: 'They are singularly alike in nature. Quiet mass action, the tying up of industry, the granting of exemptions, until gradually the main activities of the city are being handled by the strike committee'.[33]

The *Seattle Union Record* summed up the qualitative difference between a strike, which applies leverage to shut down production, and the general strike they had launched, which took over production to reorganise and subordinate it to social needs.

> NOT THE WITHDRAWAL OF LABOR POWER, BUT THE POWER OF THE STRIKERS TO MANAGE WILL WIN THIS STRIKE ... Labor will not only SHUT DOWN the industries but Labor will REOPEN, under the management of the appropriate trades, such activities as are needed to preserve public health and public peace. If the strike continues, Labor may feel led to avoid public suffering by reopening more and more activities, UNDER ITS OWN MANAGEMENT.[34]

---

32   Ibid., pp. 121 and 135; and Perlman and Taft 1935, pp. 440–3.
33   *Seattle Union Record* 1919.
34   Ibid., caps in original.

The *Seattle Union Record* served an invaluable function that was absent in the other strikes covered in this book. The paper provided a daily multi-directional source of information that flowed outward from the GSC to the strikers and their supporters and back again with news and information to the GSC. Strikers produced and distributed the newspaper. Although its production was centrally organised and subject to possible disruption, it was less vulnerable than the telegraph or telephone which were both owned by corporations. As a means of communication about the coordination of the strike originating from but still apart from the GSC, the newspaper resolved another weakness of previous strikes, such as during the 1894 railroad strike, in which the coordination of the strike and communication between the leadership and the rank and file were one and the same. By operating the paper relatively apart from the GSC with its own distribution and information collection systems the strikers added a second separate target if elites attempted to suppress the strike.

Diffusing the leadership of the strike among 110 local unions also reduced the vulnerability of the general strike to the threat of repression. In fact, it is inaccurate to refer to the GSC as the leadership. Rather, because of its size and disparate participation it functioned to coordinate rather than run the strike. The absence of the CLC's leadership certainly played a role in this unique characteristic of the strike. The centralised horizontal organisation of the GSC and the use of a newspaper to establish two way communication between the strike coordinators and the rank and file demonstrated the lessons the strikers had learned about coordinating a workers' insurgency from decades of efforts.

The Seattle strikers escalated their tactics bypassing disruption to assume control over a distinct geographical area, replacing the established elite dominated elected government with one run by the workers who did the work and community that shared the fruits of their labour. The GSC coordinated the supplanting of the dominant system of organising life in the city and replaced it with a new system of self-governance and production for need. Rather than exerting power to ask for changes or contend for more power the strikers took over and ran their workplaces and communities deciding what they needed, how much work was required to provide it and with whom they would share both the work and output of their labour.

Their general strike was qualitatively different from any other strike, general or otherwise. They did not shut down production and allow elites to make sufficient concessions to get the workers to restart production. That would have left the dominant ruling order in place. Rather, the workers explored another way of organising life by making the decisions themselves. In that way, the intensification of their tactics moved beyond a strike that *disrupts* to a strike that *transcends*, carving out a short-lived autonomous space where they could exer-

cise their multiple visions of what life could be like. And because the general
strike had little use for armed self-defence it also transcended the need to establish liberated territory, which would become more common in the national
liberation struggles of the next half century. Rather than reorganising territory it reorganised the relations of production and power. Absent the need to
ensure their security by force of arms the Seattle workers protected themselves
by placing their hands on the means of production rather than their finger on
the trigger of a gun.

The Seattle strikers provided perhaps the most self-conscious effort to take
over and reorganise social life, institutions, and services since the Workingmen's Party takeover of St. Louis and East St. Louis in 1877. The similarities
end there. The St. Louis Workingmen's Party had no intention and made little
effort to facilitate workers assuming control over the city. It organised few services other than to protect certain properties, made no governance decisions
other than those concerning internal party matters, and even stopped communicating with strikers and supporters when it was called upon to organise a
self-defence. In this way, the Seattle General Strike is totally unique in American history. Perhaps more analogous to the 1871 Paris Commune or the seizure
of vast estates by the Mexican revolutionaries over the previous decade, the
Seattle general strike shows what is possible when workers put down the gun
and pick up self-control over all of life.

The storm clouds of repression began forming over Seattle almost immediately. The state Attorney General and University of Washington President
Suzzallo, also the Chairman of the State Council of Defense, called upon Secretary of War Baker to send in troops. 950 sailors and marines soon arrived
and deployed around the city. They were joined by US Army troops from Camp
Lewis who set up machine guns, although it was unclear exactly at whom they
were pointed. Suzzallo used university Reserve Officer Training Corps students
as paid uniformed guards.[35] The Kiwanis Club advised its members to stock
up on arms in preparation for a fight. Seattle Mayor Hanson added 600 more
police, deputised 2,400 special deputies, and requested that Governor Lister
send in the National Guard.[36] With his forces aligned the Mayor issued an ultimatum for the GSC to end the strike by 8 February.[37]

As the strikers considered the Mayor's ultimatum, the old order reappeared
at gun point. The newspaper of business, *The Star*, began to distribute its paper

---

35   O'Connor 1964, p. 137.
36   Mayor Hanson left office soon after the strike ended and hit the road on a nationwide
      speaking tour giving lectures about how he supposedly beat the 'Bolsheviks' in Seattle.
37   O'Connor 1964, p. 134.

again guarded by police mounted on trucks with machine guns. At first the GSC blinked, voting 13 to 1 to end the strike, and the strike appeared to be heading in the same direction as St. Louis in 1877. But after a dinner break the GSC returned and reversed itself, voting to continue the strike.

At this point the AFL got into the act by demanding that workers of its affiliated locals return to work, which some did. The AFL leadership clearly understood that the Seattle strike was made by local unions defying their own international unions and violating contracts with employers. Rather than serving the larger class interests of their fellow workers, the AFL unions had their contracts, and organisational prerogatives, at stake. For the Electrical Workers' union business agent Leon Green, who had taken a $3,000 bribe from the Retail Merchants Association while negotiating a contract, the risks were even more personal. The streetcar workers returned to work but offered to go back out if requested to do so by the GSC. Although the teamsters returned to work as well they were expected to vote to strike again. When the GSC voted to end the strike on 11 February the shipyard workers were still continuing their strike.[38] In the meantime, the labour printing plant and the offices of the local Socialist Party and IWW hall were all raided and 39 Wobblies were arrested. The general strike was broken by the combined force of capital, the state, and the AFL.

The Seattle General Strike demonstrated that counter-planning on the shop floor by informal groups of workers could escalate from disrupting production to democratically reorganising and redirecting it to serve human needs. The process of transforming disruption into transcendence need not involve any political violence. In Seattle workers demonstrated that political violence is unnecessary if the recomposition of their class power provides them with the power to take over both production and their communities, subordinating the economy to democratic worker control. Although modest about its objectives, the *Seattle Union Record* explained the reason for the absence of violence:

> Apparently in all cases there is the same singular lack of violence which we noticed here. The violence comes, not with the shifting of power, but when the 'counter-revolutionaries' try to regain the power which inevitably and almost without their knowing it passed from their grasp. Violence would have come in Seattle, if it had come, not from the workers, but from attempts by armed opponents of the strike to break down the

---

38 The longshoremen were never broken. In October 1919 longshoremen in Seattle refused to load a shipment of 50 freight cars containing arms manufactured by Remington Arms for the counter-revolutionary White Russians. (Ibid., pp. ix and 142).

authority of the strike committee over its own members. We had no violence in Seattle and no revolution. That fact should prove that neither
the strike committee nor the rank and file of the workers ever intended
revolution.[39]

As the *Seattle Union Record* documented in its reporting, elites were the only
ones prepared and willing to use violence as a tactic. When the GSC called off
the general strike elites had aligned forces composed of police, National Guard,
military, and vigilante forces against the worker controlled free city.

The Seattle general strike extended workers' counter-power throughout the
entire social factory. Self-organised workers shifted control almost imperceptibly by reappropriating the existing resources and wealth for the self-valorising
purposes of existence.[40] The success of its tactical escalation was in avoiding
the direct contestation over power because such a conflict would have inevitably meant the asymmetrical use of force and violence that the workers could
not expect to win in one city alone.

> Our experience ... will help us understand the way in which events are
> occurring in other communities all over the world, where a general strike,
> not being called off, slips gradually into the direction of more and more
> affairs by the strike committee, until the business group, feeling their old
> prestige slipping, turns suddenly to violence, and there comes the test of
> force.[41]

From Coordinated Insurgency to General Strike

The intensification of tactics from what Tilly calls scattered attacks to 'coordinated destruction' (sabotage) or armed self-defence does not occur in a linear
sequential order but as the outcome of a complex interrelationship between
class composition, mobilisation of mass support, circulation of struggle, costs,
and opportunities. With sufficient mass support insurgents will use scattered

39   *Seattle Union Record* 1919.
40   Harry Cleaver defines Toni Negri's concept of 'self-valorization' as 'not merely the self-
      activity of workers, but those aspects of struggle which went beyond mere resistance or
      negation to the creation of new ways of being'. The central idea is that self-valorisation
      in class struggle transforms society from being centred around work to the autonomously
      self-determined multiplicities of existence. (See Cleaver 1992; and Negri 1991)
41   History Committee of the General Strike Committee March 1919.

attacks to demonstrate their capacity and willingness to contest elite power. Scattered attacks might take the form of street clashes and armed self-defence while being paired with the formation of autonomous or liberated zones, setting up parallel governance structures, the seizure of control of production and/or local communities in general strikes, and set piece battles. Such escalation may amplify a signalling spiral in which insurgents and elites each reciprocate the other's escalation of tactics with their own.[42]

The category of coordinated destruction is problematic in several ways. Tilly explains that it occurs when coercive means are used to inflict damage to people or objects through war, terrorism, and genocide.[43] But these examples are troubling because the examples he provides seem more apt to be carried out by states rather than worker insurgencies which lack the capacity to inflict such large scale destruction. Furthermore, using the word 'destruction' is misleading because while property may be destroyed, in workers' attacks the objective is to produce disruption and not destruction for its own sake.

The term 'scattered' also raises questions because it implies uncoordinated, disconnected, and even disorganised. While they may appear disconnected it may just mean that attacks are planned and carried out by disparate local groups lacking a means by which to coordinate their efforts. Where such coordination exists, scattered attacks might be better called 'coordinated attacks', although they are extremely rare in the strikes analysed here. However, because coordinating attacks carries with it high costs if caught, the coordinating efforts are often obscured by secrecy and thus difficult to pinpoint with precision. One way to tell if coordination exists is if attacks drop in frequency or become less purposeful after key leadership are arrested or eliminated.

As we have seen in the strikes discussed so far in this book, coordinated attacks happened during the ironworkers' dynamite campaign, although many attacks were false flag operations by the employers' group. (See Chapter 7). As we will see in Chapter 10, coordinated attacks escalated further into set piece battles between miners and elite forces during the nearly decade-long mine wars in West Virginia when miners organised themselves into the 'Redneck Army' (or Miners' Army). Although each phase of these struggles only lasted for a few days, in each case they showed a high level of coordination that confronted capital and the state in overt above-ground military attacks. What distinguishes them from examples of scattered attacks is that although short-lived

---

42   Tilly 2003, p. 205.

43   Ibid., pp. 14–16.

they were coordinated in the open in military formation with a red bandana around their necks and arms to identify the members of the Miners' Army.

There is quite a bit of difference between an insurgency with scattered attacks and a coordinated insurgency that moves beyond disruption to self-control. When coordinated insurgency is generalised throughout society and elites are no longer able to impose their domination, elites fragment and a faction or some officials go over to the side of the insurgents, attempt to remain neutral in the conflict, or even appeal to insurgents for permission to continue limited operations or services such as security. If the local economy or all operations by an entire industry have been interrupted and prevented by workers and their supporters from continuing, a general strike is taking place.

When insurgents' above-ground parallel system of self-governance acquires recognition or authority during a general strike it begins displacing the systems of government and the economy by seizing and running the means of production and reorganising society. When this happens it could be said that a general strike is becoming a revolutionary crisis in which elites no longer wield power and the population has taken over direct control themselves. Although not revolutions, the general strike in St. Louis in 1877 and the six city-wide general strikes between September 1917 and April 1918 had some of these characteristics although the January 1919 Seattle general strike went much further along the trajectory than the others.

The possibility of de-mobilisation and de-escalation is ever present as coordinated insurgency becomes a general strike. Insurgents are constantly presented with the tension between further intensification of tactics into the unknown world in which 'a general strike, not being called off, slips gradually into the direction of more and more affairs by the strike committee'[44] or de-escalating to extract concessions and place the insurgency at risk of co-optation, deflection, or dissipation. This creates an unavoidable dilemma for insurgents whose tactical escalation is sufficient to force elites to concede but also promises to achieve even more by further intensification. At this crossroad to reform or revolution

> There lies the eternal dilemma of the militant group which finds a protective cleft in the legal system: solidary resistance with a chance of destruction, or adaptation with a chance of absorption or dissolution.[45]

---

44   History Committee of the General Strike Committee March 1919.

45   Tilly 1978, p. 168.

A careful study of the composition of forces is necessary but may be complicated by the 'fog of class war' that makes an accurate assessment impossible.

It may be impossible to definitively know the opportunity and costs of continued escalation. Once the spark of insurrection is in the air and the insurgency continues to escalate the outcome becomes exceptionally simple: complete annihilation or victory. Anything in between appears to inevitably threaten co-optation and defanging.

If insurgents choose to not fully de-escalate and integrate but rather merely threaten further escalation to raise the costs to elites of attacking or eroding previous gains (reforms) a stalemate may occur which will likely provide an advantage to elites to survive the long contestation. A stalemate gives elites valuable time to regroup, recruit new allies, obtain new resources, and assess new possibilities of counter-attack.

Alternatively, insurgents may attempt to go above-ground to strategically use concessions as a staging ground to expand the scope and depth of the reforms by further escalation of underground insurgent tactics. If challengers retain a well coordinated above-ground/underground organisational symbiosis they may attempt to continue escalating tactics to rack up more reforms *ad infinitum*, in order to avoid reform becoming the end in itself. Here the strategy evokes the old saying that 'if you give an inch, they'll take a mile'.

German revolutionary Rosa Luxemburg described this as a tension between reform as an end in itself and revolution.[46] For her, no reforms were acceptable in and of themselves because the entire system must be overthrown and replaced in a catastrophic transition beyond capitalism. Yet reform and concessions open up political space for which insurgents can further mobilise and intensify their tactics with less risk of doing so. Tilly alludes to this dual outcome of de-escalation:

> the current combination of interest, mobilization, power, and opportunity/threat leads us to expect the contender to engage in two kinds and levels of collective action: a low intensity of action to counter threats of loss, a higher intensity of action to take advantage of opportunities for gain in the area of the group's interest.[47]

In their study of militant movements of the 1930s and 1960s, Piven and Cloward suggested that deploying disruption may make a movement short-lived once

---

46 Luxemburg 1900.
47 Tilly 1978, p. 140.

elites concede. However, they fail to recognise that concessions may provide the launching pad for further escalation as insurgents see increasing opportunity and declining costs from further confronting vulnerable elites until workers and their supporters spark a new crisis.

The WWI strike wave reflected self-organised workers' ability to transform concessions from federally mandated arbitration into a tactic to be built upon for further low cost runaway reforms. The unwillingness to grant recognition by both capital and the state actually prevented absorption and co-optation from taking place and gave impetus for strikers to continue escalating tactically with little or no costs and rising opportunities for further gains. The Seattle general strike was the next level of escalation made possible by reforms extracted during the wartime strike wave that were not ends in themselves but set the stage for the next higher level of struggle. While this led to the scenario of runaway reforms once the war ended, they were quickly met by repression and a reversal in fortunes.

By 1935, the next strike wave resulted in the institutional sanction of union recognition, collective bargaining, and a complex process for managing class conflict enshrined in the NLRA. Union recognition, collective bargaining, and the contract became the coercive institutions that pushed reform back into being an objective in itself, precluding its continued use as a tactic for further escalation. As unions continue to shrink, contracts become uncommon, and recognition is banned under state so-called 'right to work' laws, the use of reform as a tactic rather than the objective is re-emerging, particularly in the mostly un-unionised low waged service, retail, and home care sectors.

Another possible outcome of runaway reforms is that costs of mobilisation continue falling as mass support grows, leading to the collapse of elite authority and power and stimulating a revolutionary crisis.[48] Turning reform from an objective into a tactic demonstrates to mass supporters the politics of what is possible, building further mass support that reduces threats and costs and continues to raise the potential gain by circulating the struggle to new sectors of the economy and society.

Revolution

The concept and practice of revolution have been elusive for centuries. But what does it really mean and how does it occur? To answer these questions is to

---

48   Moore uses Trotsky's idea of the 'crisis in the affairs of the ruling order' to describe when the elite coalition splits. (Moore 1969, p. 9).

delve into the depths of the meaning of power and locate it in the functioning of institutions and the relationships between people.

For Tilly, revolutionary situations emerge when the following conditions are at play:

– Mobilized challengers make a competing claim to control the government
– Challengers are becoming increasingly popular
– Challengers have the active mass support of the population that defies the commands and sanctions of the government
– The government unsuccessfully attempts to forcibly de-mobilise the challengers
– Sectors of the government are unable or unwilling to suppress the challengers or actively take their side
– Challengers have formed an 'alternative coalition' that has, and is continuing to expand, control over part of the government or territory, or that has the active allegiance of government officials ('multiple sovereignty'); and
– New governmental control is imposed either under challengers, a faction from the fragmented challengers, or the coalition[49]

For Tilly, political violence is most likely to be used once existing 'multiple sovereignty' declines and insurgents consolidate power.[50] This process assumes that challengers must absorb and control significant portions of the existing resources of government including weapons, police and military forces, in order to take power.[51] Seizure of control raises questions about the new state's capacity to deliver resources to the population and whether it can meet expectations, which raises the paradox of post-revolutionary instability caused when the population fights the new government composed of former revolutionaries after the revolution. This occurs, Tilly argues, because 'The victorious polity still faces the problem of reimposing routine governmental control over the subject population even after multiple sovereignty has ended'.[52] What Tilly perceives as revolutionary could be better described as a coup or civil war that changes the polity not the relations of production. It tells us who controls the existing or reconstituted instruments of government while leaving the economic system unchanged.

---

49   Tilly 1978, pp. 200–17.
50   Ibid., p. 216.
51   Ibid., p. 217.
52   Ibid., p. 219.

While Tilly finds that 'in theory, a group can mobilize without contending for power' he doesn't give it much credence.[53] Rather, the continued growth and proliferation of mass support for insurgents across different sectors of a population continually raises the opportunity for continuing to escalate tactics to achieve unlimited gains with little to no cost. When these factors coexist it may be said to be a revolutionary situation. The elite coalition fragments and power shifts to the insurgents. 'Where the effect of coalition is to split the polity into factions making exclusive and incompatible claims on the government, however, a high degree of collective violence is likely to follow. That is, in fact, a revolutionary situation'.[54]

But not all revolutionary situations will escalate to the use of political violence. Elites may no longer be willing to absorb the costs inflicted by the insurgency, split among themselves, or be overwhelmed by the size of the population joining the insurgency.

Gene Sharp explains that insurgents may still escalate from 'non-cooperation', which prevents the system from operating, to 'non-violent intervention' when these conditions are met. 'If the opponents are emotionally unmoved by nonviolent resistance in the face of violent resistance and therefore unwilling to agree to the objectives of the nonviolent struggle group, the resisters may apply coercive nonviolent measures. Difficult enforcement problems, economic losses, and political paralysis do not require the opponents' agreement to be felt'.[55]

Whatever the outcome, violence may be beyond the capacity of elites who not only lack authority but the capacity and willingness to wield it. As Arendt reminds us, violence may substitute for power but it cannot create it.[56] Recognising this axiom, elites may relinquish power without attempting to deploy violence in order to continue imposing its will. With no light between insurgents and supporters the population control the streets, seizes control of the means of production, and creates the means by which it puts into place its own system of self-governance. At that moment the insurgency has transformed from a general strike into a revolutionary crisis.

The outcome of runaway reform inevitably leads to an explosive revolutionary crisis in which the collapse of elite authority and power is quickly replaced by insurgents becoming revolutionary authorities. This is the Leninist concept of revolution: an identifiable catastrophic and explosive transition in which

53   Ibid., p. 125.
54   Ibid., p. 126.
55   Sharp 2005, pp. 21–2.
56   Arendt 1971, p. 53.

power transfers from elites to the insurgent leadership to erect new norms, values, institutions, and relationships – in short, power.

In contrast, the Seattle general strike offered us a glimpse into a kind of counter-power in which power is not destroyed and replaced by another, but rather in which affairs gradually, almost imperceptibly, slip in the direction of the self-determination of life and the means of existence. Here is the autonomist marxist concept of the autonomous self-organisation of the working-class that ruptures the dialectic of capital without taking it over and replacing it with another. The power of capital rests just outside the city walls but is powerless to enter as there is no longer anyone to work, since everyone has begun to play with determining how life should be lived beyond work. Power slips like vapour from the grip of elites; the only means of re-imposing itself is to annihilate that which it is. No workers, only tools, worthless buttons and levers that sit silently, unmoving, akin to Philip K. Dick's post-capitalist world in his short story 'The Last of the Masters'.[57]

The imperceptible slipping of power, what Thorstein Veblen described as 'the visible drift of things into the calculable future', may occur in conditions where fractures among elites are widened causing instability, evaporating their power, and preventing them from effectively deploying force to re-impose compliance. If insurgents are able to maintain the coordination between above-ground and underground efforts, they may be able to continue amplifying elite fragmentation so as to allow the dominated to take control and reorganise everyday life according to self-valorising desires and projects.[58]

At this moment the above-ground side of the insurgents loses relevance except to merely provide necessary information to the underground about lingering threats from elites to transformational self-organising projects in order to carry out necessary self-defence operations. In Dick's story the Anarchist League become the self-defence league on the look out for any signs of the re-emergence of the state two centuries after the revolution.[59] The above-ground insurgents gradually lose the characteristics of insurgents and turn themselves into facilitators of communications, cooperations, and coordination between the countless self-organised projects coordinated by what Mikhail Bakunin called 'free federation of worker association', so that they make themselves obsolete.[60]

---

57   Dick 1980 [1954].

58   Veblen 1921.

59   Dick 1980 [1954].

60   Bakunin 2005 [1869].

Tactical violence is but one tactic along a range of options of varying intensity insurgents draw from as they pair and switch between tactics to achieve or protect gains, avoid co-optation, defend against repression, or conduct coordinated attacks to provoke a revolutionary crisis. In none of these is tactical violence inevitable or even necessary. If elites are overwhelmed by counterpower, its control over production and society disintegrates, and they do not use violence to reassert control, as in the Seattle general strike, workers may not need to deploy tactical violence at all.

Violence is but one of the tactics available in insurgents' repertoire, deployed in particular existing political conditions and class composition in order to realise their strategy and achieve their objectives. Whether violence is used is not a question of ideology or theology but the outcome of the complex interplay of tactics, strategy, objectives, mobilisation, political conditions, and class composition. These factors do not interact in a linear manner but as a dance among the acceptable costs to realise the available opportunities for gain under the existing rules of legal political action along a trajectory of increasing conflict, force, intensity, and tension that may or may not include political violence.

We are still far from undoing the self-contradictory dominant assumption that insurgents only resort to political violence in desperation when they are losing, that it exacerbates alienation of insurgents from their supporters, that its use undermines the credibility and sustainability of their struggle, and that it is an unavoidable step towards a revolutionary crisis. The landscape of writings and studies of twentieth century liberation struggles are littered with such notions.

At the moment when insurgents parlay runaway reforms into instability and the breakdown of elite power, new spaces may widen in which a new society begins to grow within the old. It is these events that may be called revolutionary moments, during which the cohesion of existing economic and political arrangements erodes and breaks down, allowing a multiplicity of open ended possibilities of transcendence to make themselves known. In the historical cases examined in this book, tactical violence has taken the form of self-defence of these new spaces of autonomy from counter-attacks. The voluminous histories of capitalist crises are replete with examples of new arrangements in which many hands are constructing the new while one grips the gun to hold off the forces of repression that seek to encircle it. When to pick it up and put it down was a salient question for workers during these decades of insurgency.

CHAPTER 10

The Redneck Army: West Virginia Mine War

'You remember, boys,' Ermel said, 'anything will bend if you put enough
fire to it. You remember that'.

DENISE GIARDINA, *Storming Heaven: A Novel*, 1987[1]

• • •

They call Keeney a radical. Who made him a radical? I've seen the time
when I didn't have the right to eat in this State. I've seen the time when I
was refused a job. I've been served with eviction papers and thrown out
of my house. I've seen women and children brutally treated in mining
camps. I've seen hell turned loose.

FRANK KEENEY, UMWA District 17 President, 1921[2]

• •
•

This cycle of the class war ended in the same state where it had begun 40 years
earlier. The 1877 railroad strike began on the Baltimore & Ohio railroad line
between Baltimore and Martinsburg, West Virginia where Dick Zepp walked
off his engine, sparking the nationwide strike that nearly shut down the country. This time West Virginia miners attempted to take advantage of decades of
efforts to recompose working-class power to launch their own armed insurgency but were eventually suppressed by a recomposed capital now solidly
integrated with government into state capitalism. The consolidation of capital within and between sectors could now dependably rely on the reorganised and expanded state and federal government police and military powers in
times of class warfare. Augmenting the US Army fresh from the battlefields of
Europe were armed paramilitary organisations such as the American Legion
and private police such as the Baldwin-Felts and Pinkertons. The new balance

---

1 Giardina 1987.
2 In Lane 1921, p. 87.

of power finally brought to a close more than four decades of class struggle when workers shot back.

The several years of pitched battles between the Miners' Army and elite forces have only recently been rediscovered by historians. The captivating final episode of the West Virginia miners' war on Blair Mountain, what journalist Winthrop Lane called 'a state of civil war', had the makings of headlines but is not easily explained.[3] Why did thousands of miners repeatedly take up arms and march into battle in military formation against the coal companies and the state? How did the miners organise their army, and did it have a 'general'? Was one of the few organised armed struggles in American history an act of irrational anger and desperation, senseless violence, or neither?

The miners' war demonstrates how insurgents deployed tactical violence to create leverage when the optimal mix of mass support, costs, threats, and opportunities are present. Sometimes the conditions may not be apparent without expanding the boundaries of the time frame to look at the cycle of struggle rather than particular instances of peaks and valleys in a strike wave. What may appear as unilateral tactical escalation by insurgents may actually be a war of manoeuvre informed by the conditions inherited from previous cycles of struggle.

Tactics are rarely chosen by present conditions alone, but informed by previous use of repression by elites; by available political space to present grievances or co-opt insurgent leadership; and by broken negotiations and unenforced prior settlements. The choice of either defensive or offensive tactics depends on the success of lower intensity tactics, mass support, and class composition.

Offensive tactics must appear to correspond to their widely supported strategy and objectives. The target of their tactic must correspond to supporters' perception of the righteousness of their cause. Tactics must be escalated in such a way that maintains or expands the existing level of mass support. They must not be perceived as moving too fast too soon. To do so means controlling the ability communicate effectively, clearly, and widely about the details of their tactics. Workers must control the framing and filtering of the message. The Miners' Army used scattered attacks and dynamite against recalcitrant mine companies and deadly local officials. Such offensive tactics gained mass support because they were carried out under the direction and in the service of the above-ground organisation of strikers rather than subordinating the strike to its military tactics and command.

---

3   Ibid., p. 15.

Defensive tactics must appear to be justified in light of capital's unilateral escalation of tactics. Whether they initiate and are responding to capital's initial reply or escalating in response to capital's unilateral escalation, workers' tactics must be perceived by supporters as 'the right thing to do' for the circumstances. The West Virginia miners skilfully read the conditions of their defensive tactical escalation and launched their Miners' Army military invasion of neighbouring counties where the miners were being brutally repressed. Using what D'Arcy calls a 'citizen's militia' in self-defence attracted increasing mass support along their line of march even when they faced off against the US Army and local police and a sheriff which bombed their lines in one of the first aerial bombing raids in the world.[4]

The miners' use of tactical violence was informed by the outcome of previous mobilisation and repression. The outcomes of previous cycles of struggle will change the tactics currently available and spur innovation to create new ones. As Tilly observed 'the successes and failures of contention for power produce changes in the repertoire of collective action ...'.[5] The notion that there is a static set of tactics to be applied in sequential order is not supported by the historical evidence. Tactics change along with strategy and objectives in the cauldron of struggle. In the strikes explored in this book we have seen how workers have drawn on, adapted, disposed of, and fashioned new tactics for use at different times in their insurgency as the conditions warranted.

It is necessary to understand how past and present conditions shape insurgents' willingness to intensify tactics to achieve their objectives. In this way, rather than being irrational, the use of violence is a tactic that serves a larger strategy. For the miners of West Virginia, forming the Miners' Army was the appropriate tactic for the conditions in which they struggled.

Capital Composition

West Virginia was the closing chapter in the struggle to recompose working-class power to confront the new composition of capital. 'Coal was the center of some of the bloodiest labor disputes after World War I around the efforts of the UMWA to organise the non-union counties of McDowell, Mingo, and Logan Counties in West Virginia'.[6] Hardly impoverished, marginal, and backwards, the

---

4 D'Arcy 2014, pp. 179–81.
5 Tilly 1978, p. 158.
6 Ross and Taft 1969, p. 25.

TABLE 6   *Bituminous coal production in West Virginia, 1880–1920*

Year	No. short tons	Percentage of national production
1880	1.8 m	2
1900	22.6 m	8.4
1912	66.8 m	12.5
1920	87.5 m	25

PERLMAN AND TAFT 1935, P. 329; *COAL REVIEW* 1921, P. 6; AND
GREEN 2015, P. 221

state had one of the richest deposits of coal and was the site of growing investment in the industry. The miners and their communities were poor, not the
state or coal industry.

After the emergency of the war had passed, the miners saw the tactical
advantage of continuing to escalate the struggle. The low costs and increased
opportunity to make gains during the war encouraged the miners to deploy a
strategy of tension. On 9 September 1919 the UMWA convention passed resolutions calling on the US Fuel Administration to permanently nationalise the
coal industry, increase wages by 60 percent, and impose a six-hour, five-day
workweek.[7] The miners were demanding more pay for less work. The union
cancelled all contracts on 1 November and announced that it would meet on
15 October 1919 to declare a general strike if no new national contract was signed
by that date. But with the war winding down, the Wilson Administration had
other plans. The administration planned to return full control to the operators
and intervene on their behalf to suppress any threat to production by organised
miners.

Although the 1912–13 Paint Creek and Cabin Creek strikes were defeated the
miners had intensified their tactics by taking up arms in self-defence, earning
them the name 'redneck army' (or Miners' Army).[8] The redneck label is attributed to the red bandanas they wore around their necks or on their arms to
distinguish themselves from the agents hired by the mine operators to repress

---

7   The 1920 US Bituminous Coal Commission Minority Report by the union representative pro-
    posed the shortened workday and week, modelled after mine work in the UK, as a way to
    spread out the work in a seasonal industry with too much capacity. (US Bituminous Coal
    Commission 1920, pp. 83–4 and 86).

8   West 1913, pp. 37–50. During those strikes, local and state police and deputies were aided by
    300 Baldwin-Felts agents hired by the coal companies. (See Lane 1921, p. 20).

their mobilisation and strikes. Despite their efforts few mines were organised and no contract was signed until 1918.

The miner strikes nevertheless drove the operators to ramp up the search for a way to produce more coal with fewer miners. Coal production in West Virginia was growing fast, nearly quadrupling tonnage in the past 20 years and almost tripling its share of national coal production. (See Table 6).

The introduction of energy efficiency and productivity measures in other sectors in response to their own unruly workers simultaneously reduced their need for coal.

> New boiler technologies that efficiently burned small sizes of coal following World War I stimulated demand for 'run of mine' coal which was shipped without screening or sizing. In addition, new combustion technology also improved efficiency, netting several key industries considerable savings and reductions in fuel requirements during the 1920s. Railroads reduced fuel consumption for freight service 18 percent and for passenger service 13 percent from 1920 to 1925. Electric utilities reduced the amount of coal needed to generate a kilowatt-hour by 34 percent during the same period. While increased efficiency by itself reduced demand at least 11 percent through the 1920s, oil and natural gas consumption accelerated, making inroads into coal's traditional markets. Automobiles fueled with gasoline began to supplant rail travel, and fuel oil and natural gas furnaces reduced domestic demand for coal.[9,10]

New technologies such as the shift from rail to trucks for shipping drove the changing composition of capital which reverberated in the coal fields. It would be misleading to conclude that the 1912–13 strikes were failures without examining the changing composition of capital in the coal fields themselves. The miners had lost the strikes, but the impact of their armed insurgency was told by introduction of new labour-saving technologies.

> Mechanization's first wave came in the form of coal-cutting machines, which functioned like huge electric chainsaws to undercut the coal seam. These devices were first used in the Fairmont field in J.N. Camden's Monongah Coal and Coke mines as early as 1890. Samuel Brady's Osage

---

9   In 1920 the railroads consumed 30 percent of the coal supply. They are followed by the public utilities and steel industry as the 2nd and 3rd largest consumers. (US Bituminous Coal Commission 1920, p. 27).

10   Ross 1994, p. 5.

mine opened in 1918 with two cutting machines, and its entire production of 19,701 tons that year was produced with machine undercutting. These devices quickly became ubiquitous, and no mine that survived the mid-1920s operated without them. By 1927, Chaplin used seven cutting machines in its Louise mine and Continental's Brock mine used ten. The coal, once undercut and blasted, was then loaded by hand and hauled to the tipple. The early Scotts Run mines used mules for this task, but replaced them with a variety of electrically powered main-haulage and gathering locomotives. The earlier locomotives received power through a trolley pole, and by the mid-1920s, some were powered by storage batteries. Again, the Osage Coal Company was the technological leader in this area, installing an electric haulage locomotive in 1918 with the mines opening.[11]

By 1920, 57 percent of bituminous coal was mined by machines. This certainly drove productivity, which increased by 50 percent between 1910 and 1920 from about 6.4 tons to 10 tons per miner.[12] By 1920, profits were $198 million for the 1,287 mines worked by 87,000 miners.[13]

The year 1919 was a turning point in the investment in bituminous mining. From 1880 to 1919, the investment of fixed capital rose about 4 percent annually per worker followed by an annual drop of about 2 percent annually between 1919–39. The changing attraction to invest in bituminous mining corresponds to the levels of class conflict in the industry. The rising investment could be attributed to the defeat of successive attempts to organise bituminous miners in contrast to the more successful attempts in the anthracite mines. Greater profits could be extracted from weaker organised workers. While the second decade of the period of decline in investment could be explained by the Great Depression, the first decade followed a period of 'runaway prices' directly attributed to the Miners' Army strikes after 1919.[14]

1919–20 National Coal Strike

When the mine operators refused to concede to their demands, UMWA President John L. Lewis called for a national strike to begin 31 October. After a failed

---

11   Ibid., p. 10.

12   US Bituminous Coal Commission 1920, p. 48; and Green 2015, p. 221.

13   Green 2015, p. 221.

14   US Department of Labor 1961, p. 12; and Emmet 1924, p. 1.

attempt by Secretary of Labor Wilson to mediate about 400,000 miners struck on 1 November. About half of the 95,000 miners in West Virginia, 53,000, were members of the UMWA. However, the strike was weakened by the continual supply of coal coming from West Virginia and Kentucky where the miners were weakest.[15]

On 8 November US Attorney General A. Mitchell Palmer obtained a federal court injunction against the strike under the 1917 Lever Food Control Act, which gave the president emergency wartime authority to regulate fuel and other commodities. The US Fuel Administration had been established to set prices and arbitrate miners' grievances and strikes. So many miners had struck that they tied up 71 percent of national coal production as the strike spread into other states with bituminous coal mining. Although the UMWA leadership soon after called off the strike, many remained on strike, including in West Virginia. On 3 December, 84 international and district union officers named in the injunction were cited for contempt. Every union official in Indiana was arrested, martial law was declared in Wyoming, and US troops were sent in.

President Wilson intervened to extend the ban on strikes long past the end of the war, nearly a year after the Armistice had been signed. On 6 December 1919, with a steel general strike looming, he stepped into the fray, declared the planned strike unlawful, and ordered the miners to return to work.

With the government lined up against it, the union leadership rejected the US Fuel Administration's 26 November award of a 14 percent wage increase above 1913 levels. Instead they approved President Wilson's offer to establish the three-member Bituminous Coal Commission which would include one mine operator and union representative each in exchange for calling off the strike on 10 December.

In 1920, during the ongoing contempt proceedings, part of the 1917 Lever Act was declared an unconstitutional extension of wartime emergency power into peacetime by the US Supreme Court.[16] The ruling put into doubt the legality of the President's effort to break the strike using either the law or the courts. But the Wilson Administration had another strategy to apply its leverage. In January 1920 Attorney General Palmer launched raids in 23 states, rounding up thousands of radicals and labour organisers and deporting hundreds of immigrant radicals. The intent was to break the back of the labour movement and remove its radical allies from the picture.

---

15   Lane 1921, p. 20; and Savage 1990, p. 14.
16   *United States v. L. Cohen Grocery Company*, 255 US 81 (1921).

The most significant part of the 10 March 1920 Bituminous Coal Commission's ruling, approved by two of its three members, increased the US Fuel Administration's 14 percent wage raise to 27 percent, created an unpopular three-tiered raise for machine miners (48.5 percent) and pick miners (35.5 percent), paid by tonnage, and miners paid by the day (76.1 percent), one in the Central Competitive Field and the other in the bituminous mines.[17]

The ruling was unsatisfactory for many of the rank and file miners. The Commission's award came in at under half of the UMWA's demand for a 60 percent increase for all classifications, rejected the six-hour, five-day workweek, and never addressed nationalising the mines. Shortening the workday to six days was not just a demand or a strategy; it was enshrined in the UMWA constitution as a matter of principle. The Commission refused the demand to shorten the workday and workweek, calling it an 'economic crime', and never addressed demands to rein in 'company towns'.[18] The Commission also warned the workers that the issue of technology was beyond the pale: 'the right of the operator to introduce and operate any such new device or machinery shall not be questioned'.[19] It even proposed further study of ending the UMWA's ability to check off dues.[20]

The miners had reason to issue the Minority Report rejecting much of the Commission's Majority ruling. The industry was immensely profitable. According to the Commission, the average net return on investment was nearly 19 percent and profits were almost 10 percent after taxes. The average net income of 31 companies producing 14 percent of the bituminous coal doubled during the war. In 1917, the Department of Treasury reported return on investment among 400 companies to be 38 to 45 percent before taxes and 24.5 to 31.5 percent after taxes. The Pittsburgh Coal Co., for example, with $68

---

17   US Bituminous Coal Commission 1920, pp. 37–9.

18   Ibid., p. 45. The UMWA had joined the railroad brotherhoods' Plumb Plan in calling on the federal government to nationalise both industries. (See Chapter 8).

19   The Minority Report gave the position of the UMWA on this point to be that the union has 'always been favorable to and have never opposed the introduction of machinery or labour-saving machinery in the operation of the mines'. It does appear to be the case as the number of machines grew by 450 percent and the percentage of the total mined by machines more than doubled between 1900–18. The union's position was that the savings in labour costs from rising productivity should be passed along to workers. (US Bituminous Coal Commission 1920, pp. 48, 105, and 107–8).

20   Eliminating dues check off has remained a centrepiece of so-called open shop 'right to work' laws intended to drain unions of revenues and weaken their capacity to act.

million in capitalisation, earned a 40 percent return on investment in 1917 and 20 percent in 1918.[21]

The unions made their argument clear in the Minority Report, proposing an award that compensates the union for crushing the strike. Their proposed award mostly differed with the operators and government on the size of the wage increases and the lack of a cut in work hours. Reiterating their commitment to arbitration and conciliation in the UMWA constitution, they argued that the award should be based on the 'substantial consideration in the claims that they are making if our commission is to be instrumental in rendering an award that will stabilize the coal industry'.[22] The UMWA had no expectation of carrying out this threat of disruption; rather they expected their rank and file to do so.

The Minority Report appealed to the assumption of shared interests between capital and labour, which could be served by recognising the union as a force of stability. Some elites, including Presidents Woodrow Wilson and Warren Harding, shared this assumption. The experience of government serving as a neutral arbiter between capital and labour had become bipartisan. Referring to the Coal Commission settlement, President Harding appealed to engaging with unions as one of many factions to be regulated by law.

> Finally, just as we are earnestly seeking for procedures whereby to adjust and settle political differences between nations without resort to war, so we may well look about for means to settle the differences between organised capital and organised labor without resort to those forms of warfare which we recognize under the name of strikes, lockouts, boycotts, and the like. As we have great bodies of law carefully regulating the organization and operations of industrial and financial corporations, as we have treaties and compacts among nations which look to the settlement of differences without the necessity of conflict in arms, so we might well have plans of conference, of common counsel, of mediation, arbitration, and judicial determination in controversies between labor and capital ... Indeed, we have come to recognize that the limited liability of the citizen as a member of a labor organization closely parallels the limitation of liability of the citizen as a stockholder in a corporation for profit.[23]

---

21 US Bituminous Coal Commission 1920, pp. 40 and 99–100.

22 Ibid., p. 109.

23 Harding 1921, p. 11.

Making an analogy to the use of diplomacy to regulate wars between states, President Harding spoke to the role of the labour-planning state in regulating class struggle for the purposes of stabilising capital accumulation. This became the kernel of what would later be known as Fordism, in which class struggle is harnessed to the accumulation process.

During the 1921 US Senate Committee on Education and Labor hearings on the West Virginia strike, Committee Chair Senator William Kenyon took up the mantle of the Commission on Industrial Relations. He argued for expanding the role of the state to regulate the relations between capital and labour.[24] The strike was not only an opportunity to make the case for the country's short-lived experience with voluntary government arbitration during WWI. Kenyon used it to further craft what would become a core assumption of the plural-ist perspective – the principle of the public interest. Avoiding disruption to a critical utility made it the prerogative of government to regulate class struggle as a matter of public policy. 'Coal is a public utility, and in its production and distribution the public interest is predominant', he wrote.[25] As a result,

> The granting of this right to the workers is in the interest of sound public policy. A large industry, such as the coal industry, is vested with a pub-lic interest hardly second in importance to railroad transportation. The public therefore cannot be indifferent to the relations between employer and employee in that industry when conditions arise which threaten or interrupt the supply of one of the commodities most essential to life and industry. If direct and uncontrolled relations between operators and labor are no longer capable of maintaining peace and insuring a coal supply at a fair price, the State must intervene even to the extent, if necessary, of infringing upon private rights.[26]

This underlined the dominant rationale for the labour-planning state. Here is the germ of the idea of the state as the neutral arbiter of class interests working on behalf of a mythical public shorn of any competing interests and overlook-ing the mismatch of class power.

New York Evening Post journalist Winthrop Lane, who reported on and wrote a book about the Miners' Army, equated legal recognition of corporations with legal standing for unions based on Congress's inter-state commerce clause

---

24   The committee was established by a resolution proposed by Republican California Sen-ator Hiram Johnson following the Three Days Battle in May 1921.

25   US Senate 1921, p. 25.

26   Ibid., p. 23.

power in Article I, Sect. 8, Clause 3 and due process for property in the Fifth and Fourteenth Amendments.

> It is a great convenience to treat a corporation as an individual, and to hold that a contract between a subsidiary of the Steel Corporation and an employee of that subsidiary is an individual contract, to be protected by 'natural and constitutional right' ... If so, the court should investigate the artificial being which it has created, and inquire whether another artificial being, the labor organization, is not just as natural and constitutional. It would seem that if financiers have obtained a natural right to join a powerful corporation and thus give up their right to make individual contracts in that respect, so workers might be protected in a similar natural right to join an organization powerful enough to deal with that corporation. The natural right to contract is not always a natural right to give up the right to contract.[27]

What President Harding, Kenyon, Lane, and others advocated was the mutual legal recognition of corporations and labour unions not as a matter of justice or to rectify the imbalance of power between capital and labour but as a means to manage class conflict by holding unions legally accountable for the actions of its members. Legalising unions would create a disincentive to engage in disruptive actions for fear of suffering financial costs and the survival of the organisation. To do that required the extension of the fiction of corporations as 'artificial persons' established by the 1886 *Santa Clara County v. Southern Pacific R. Co.* Supreme Court precedent to labour unions.

The argument to extend legal recognition to unions as a matter of constitutionally protected property rights was premised on the fallacy of equivalency. It presumed that workers' labour was like any other property to be bought and sold, not extracted and exploited, as it actually is in capitalism.

Drawing further upon the experience of the National War Labor Board and other wartime labour boards, Senator Kenyon also argued that state regulation of the relations between capital and labour served the interests of capital accumulation.

> During the war period the development of an industrial code received a great impetus. The government found it necessary to deal directly with employers and trade-union representatives as a means not only of main-

---

27   Lane 1921, p. 9.

taining the continuity of production but also for accelerating production to its maximum proportions.[28]

The brief experience of WWI proved to be an effective laboratory of regulating and normalising class conflict and channelling it into a force for driving the accumulation process.

Shook the Steep Mountain

Although the Bituminous Coal Commission award was intended to resolve grievances through 31 March 1922, the same basic conditions for miners remained around the country. This was sure to give the industry and federal government reason to be worried. Even after the 1900–3 coal strikes were defeated class struggle in the mines continued. According to the US Fuel Administrator, labour shortage and strikes disrupted 23 percent of the mining season in 1918 and 25 percent in 1919, although the union minority report disputed the figure citing the US Geological Survey's estimate of 10.6 percent.[29] Considering that the 'mining season' averaged only 93 days per years over the previous 30 years, the willingness of the miners to engage in that level of disruption demonstrated how unruly they still were.

This formal cessation of the conflict did not stop some miners from restarting the wildcat strike over the terms of the pay increase.[30] While the UMWA leadership attempted to wield the Commission ruling like a club to end the strikes and block any further tactical escalation, neither the West Virginia miners nor the mine operators were willing to abide by it.

After the national spotlight of the Senate committee hearings, the UMWA had little expectation of access to the polity. As Green observed, Frank Keeney, Fred Mooney, Chief Sid Hatfield, and others who attended and testified 'had now exhausted all avenues citizens normally used to redress their grievances'.[31] Conditions of the coal miners in West Virginia were little different in 1920 than in 1897. As Blizzard recounted, 'the coal operator held the position of the feudal lord, and he kept plenty of armed men in his demesne to enforce his mandates'.[32] The miners continued to have no political space in which to negotiate

---

28   US Senate 1921, p. 12.

29   US Bituminous Coal Commission 1920, pp. 25 and 82.

30   Ross 1994, p. 6; and Blizzard 2005, pp. 113–14.

31   Green 2015, p. 243.

32   As one of the District 17 leadership William Blizzard has provided an extraordinarily rare

over their grievances short of looking down the barrel of a gun. The strike and
the Miners' Army to enforce it were the only weapons the miners had in a state
under absolute plutocratic rule of the mine owners backed by the federal government and the acquiescence of the UMWA. In West Virginia, William Blizzard
wrote, 'The coal miners were treated as less than citizens of a free republic, they
had no redress from any governmental body, and, like brave men, they preferred
armed revolt to abject slavery'.[33]

The Commission award failed to bring stability to the coal mines. In addition to living under a corporate police state, West Virginia miners lived lives of
deprivation, hunger, underemployment, low wages, and inflated prices, especially those who resided in Pullman-like company towns.

The labour peace was extremely short. On 1 May 1920 some miners wildcatted and met with District President Keeney, told him they were on strike, and
asked for District 17's support. Keeney refused to support them until they went
back to work. The UMWA had covertly almost completely organised the mines
in Mingo County into 25 new locals by June in preparation for a strike called
for 1 July. The coal operators launched an offensive against the newly organised
miners, fired about 2,800 men, and evicted them from their homes. Now about
10,000 miners and their wives and children were living in camps on land rented by and fed by the UMWA. In order to meet this threat of rapidly organising
miners in March 1919 Governor Cornwell passed a bill through the legislature
to establish a new state police to replace the National Guard demobilised after
the war.[34] But not all the mine companies resisted because four signed a con-

---

source of historical documentation of the strike from eye level view. While originally published in a series of articles entitled 'Struggle and Lose ... Struggle and Win!' for *Labor's
Daily* about three decades later between late 1952 to early 1953, they are one of the defin-
itive sources for this period and this chapter. (Blizzard 2005, p. 123). Although written
decades after the events, they confirm much of the earlier published firsthand accounts
by reporters such as Winthrop Lane and court records. However, it should be emphasised
that due to military censorship of reporters under martial law and coercion used by state
and corporate attorneys who prosecuted the case during the insurgency, both of which
are discussed below, these sources are also plagued by credibility and validity flaws.

33   Ibid., p. 173.

34   The bill was widely opposed in the state. A petition with about 80,000–100,000 signatures
     was delivered to the legislature and protests stalled the bill which passed by narrow votes
     in both houses. One of the most prominent opponents of the bill was labour organiser
     Mother Jones who explained: 'Officials of state and nation squawk about the dangers of
     bolshevism and they tolerate and promote a system which turns out bolsheviks by the
     thousands. A bunch of hypocrites create a constabulary supposedly to stamp out danger-
     ous "reds" but in truth the constabulary is to safeguard the interests of the exploiters of
     labor' (Mother Jones 1925, p. 126).

tract with District 17 for periods as short as two and a half months and mostly resulted in increased wages, although three soon closed because of a lack of customers.[35]

Around 1 September, about 6,000 miners began organising themselves into a second Redneck Army (or Miners' Army) in preparation to march to Logan County in Southern West Virginia through counties not yet organised by District 17. They assembled at Lens Creek near Marmet armed with high-powered rifles. This Miners' Army would prove to be a determined self-organised insurgency that would be difficult for the combined efforts of the UMWA, the state or the federal government to intimidate, demobilise, and disarm.

In fear of the miner army, Governor Cornwell sent a telegram to UMWA District 17 President Keeney ordering him to stop the miners from marching. Keeney told the miners that the governor promised to launch an investigation of conditions in Logan County. Later, Keeney described the scene as 'Dante's inferno ... with the moonlight shining on the rifles' held by the miners which included among them 'Negroes, Italians, and Hungarians'. The miners refused to demobilise.[36]

Governor Cornwell then went to speak to the miners himself. Standing on an ice cream wagon, the governor was surrounded by thousands of armed miners illuminated by the light of their campfires. Governor Cornwell asked them to withdraw and return home and promised to investigate. What he didn't tell them was that he was ready to call out federal troops stationed in Chillicothe, Ohio a few hours away. Although many demobilised, about 1,500 miners ignored him and marched another 32 miles the next day, continuing spreading the strike. Keeney made another attempt to stop them, this time successfully. Although the miners reluctantly lived up to their end of the temporary truce, Cornwell never launched the investigation.[37] It's no wonder he backtracked. Governor Cornwell later became attorney for the Baltimore & Ohio Railroad, one of the largest mine operators in the state.[38]

It may never be conclusively known what role Keeney and Mooney played in mobilising the Miners' Army, although local elites and the coal operators attempted to tag them as the plotters. *Daily Gazette* reporter Jack Spivak, who

---

35   Lane 1921, pp. 115–17; and Savage 1990, pp. 18 and 35.

36   Green 2015, p. 188.

37   Although Lane says Governor Cornwell established a commission to investigate conditions in Logan County following the truce, Lane conflates it with the investigative committee he set up in 1919 that did not publish its report. (See Lane 1921, p. 108).

38   Ibid., pp. 106–7; Blizzard 2005, pp. 113–14; and Ross and Taft 1969, p. 25.

was also volunteering for District 17 to investigate civil rights violations and repression in the miners' camps, was with Keeney and Mooney when they went to the armed miners' camp. After wondering out loud to Keeney and Mooney how the miners could spontaneously appear in the same spot, Spivak concluded that they had called for the march on Logan County as a war of man-oeuvre. In any event, UMWA President Lewis defended Keeney and Mooney against Governor Cornwell's claim that they had planned the invasion.[39]

Assuming they had called for it, Keeney and Mooney almost immediately lost the ability to control or steer it. A *Nation* reporter who covered the miners' march called it an 'unprecedented revolt of the rank and file' that was happening around the country in Seattle and in the steel strike which rebelled against the local and national AFL leadership. 'The common man, forgetting old sanctions, and losing faith in the old leadership, has experienced a new access of self-confidence, or at least a new recklessness, a readiness to take chances ...'.[40]

West Virginia was one of the states with the fewest organised coal mines in the nearly 20 states with mining. Unionisation came rather late to the state with the first locals formed in 1894. After 1917 the number of union miners grew nearly sixfold from 6,000 to about 53,000. Since nearly half of the non-unionised bituminous miners in the country worked in West Virginia, the outcome of the strike offered the miners significant leverage over the entire industry.[41]

The 1920–1 strike was atypical, what Blizzard called 'an economic, trade union battle, not a political demonstration'.[42] The threat of battle reverberated all the way to the White House. In July 1920, President Wilson sent two Labor Department mediators who proposed collective bargaining, ending the black-listing of union miners, reversing the evictions, and removing private police from the mines.

However, without the threat of nationalisation hanging over the heads of the operators, the President's intervention was insufficient to settle the strike. The owners wouldn't negotiate and Wilson gave up the effort to mediate. The cost of fragmenting the Democratic Party coalition by continuing to push for a resolution of the conflict was too great. Instead, Wilson changed tack and wrote a letter to the UMWA warning that its strike in Mingo and another underway in Illinois were a violation of the Bituminous Coal Commission agreement. The

---

39   Green 2015, pp. 189 and 191.
40   *The Nation*, 'The Revolt of the Rank and File', 25 October 1919 in Green 2015, p. 189.
41   Lane 1921, pp. 42–3.
42   Blizzard 2005, p. 173.

threat was real because about 400,000 steel workers had just lost their general strike in January and the Red Scare was underway (see Chapter 9).[43]

Elites began organising militarily and recruited about 780 armed American Legion members in Mingo. They were joined by the new state police force. If the level of repression is an expression of the level of the threat, as Eduardo Galeano has suggested, the mobilisation of the forces of soldiers and armed vigilantes demonstrated the strikers' tactical strength and their decades long track record of putting their threats into action.

The miners faced several difficulties to sufficiently recompose their power. As a divide and conquer strategy, the operators purposefully recruited a wide variety of ethnic and racial groups to work in the mines, more than 30 nationalities. An indicative example was the Fairmont Coal Field whose workforce included at least 28 different ethnicities, with whites making up 54 percent and blacks 12.5 percent. To win the next miners' war the miners would need to overcome the divisions of ethnicity, race, and language to maintain their organisational cohesion in the face of threats by the operators and the state.[44]

Mingo County was again a front in the mine war. The miners escalated their tactics anew after union men were fired and evicted from their homes. On 12 May 1920 strikers fought guards and deputies in several locations.[45] On 19 May 1920, 13 Baldwin-Felts agents led by Albert and his brother Lee Felts arrived in Matewan to evict strikers from the Stone Mountain Coal Company houses. They were confronted by Mayor Testerman, Chief Hatfield, and some of a hundred miners deputised by Hatfield and Sheriff Blankenship for having an invalid authorisation to do so and left town.[46] In the meantime, Mingo County Sheriff Blankenship offered to send Chief Hatfield warrants to arrest Felts and his posse. The agents returned with a forged warrant from a Bluefield judge to the mayor permitting them to arrest Hatfield. A battle broke out when they opened fire on Chief Hatfield, his deputies and the Mayor, killing three,

---

43   Ibid., p. 167.

44   Emmet 1924, p. 3; and Lane in Corbin 1997, p. 5. Although the remaining third were classified as other races it is likely that whites made up a larger percentage due to the common practice of classifying white ethnicities as separate races at the time.

45   Perlman and Taft 1935, p. 480.

46   Albert Felts and one of his employees also played a central role in the deadly repression of the Ludlow strike years earlier. He had rigged a machine gun to an armoured car which was used to fire on a miner's camp several times in 1914 during the Ludlow strike. In all, 21 strikers, two women, and 11 children were killed in his assaults with the 'death special'. (See Green 2015, p. 207).

including Mayor Testerman. In return fire, seven Baldwin-Felts men, including Albert and Lee Felts, and two unarmed miners were killed and four others were wounded.

Chief Hatfield and his Deputy Ed Chambers were charged with murder, but released on bond by Williamson Judge Damron, who was sympathetic to the Chief and his men and empaneled a grand jury to investigate the causes of the shootout.[47] Such shows of sympathy or even impartiality to either the miners or the coal companies were rare. Sheriff Blankenship, who also refused to deputise private guards to be put at the disposal of the Red Jacket Consolidated Coal and Coke Company, and Chief Hatfield were rare examples. Even these rare examples were too much for the coal companies, who complained that the law and their property were not being enforced.[48]

In reality the coal companies didn't have much to complain about. Hatfield and his deputies faced District Attorney Avis in his 1920 trial for the killing of Albert and Lee Felts. Avis had been hired by Felts and the coal companies, not the county.[49] The jury selection process provided a preview of the contentiousness of the pending trial when a motion to exclude blacks failed but another to exclude women was accepted. About 1,000 potential jurors were called and more than 400 questioned before the jury was seated.[50] Ultimately, despite one defendant turning state's evidence and miner C.E. Lively disclosing his identity as a paid agent, the jury voted not to convict on any of the eight murder charges and Hatfield and 16 co-defendants returned home to a heroes' welcome.

Soon after the state legislature passed a bill to prevent a repeat acquittal by allowing a jury to be drawn from out of county residents. The bill was sponsored by Senator Sanders, the former state supreme court justice who worked for the coal companies on the prosecution team in the Matewan case. It also doubled the size of the state police, and re-established the National Guard.[51]

---

47 Judge Damron eventually resigned from the circuit court to take a job with the coal companies working to convict Chief Hatfield and his deputies. (See Savage 1990, p. 42).

48 Green 2015, pp. 212–13 and 216.

49 Ibid., p. 223. Avis, who was also hired to prosecute Chief Hatfield by Felts and the coal companies, was a lawyer for the Williamson Coal Operators. In his new capacity he participated in the cross examination of witness Chief Hatfield during the 16 July 1921 US Senate Committee of Education and Labor hearing on conditions in the West Virginia mines and the strike. His seat at the table illustrates just how deeply the coal companies' political power extended beyond West Virginia reaching deeply into the halls of Congress.

50 Savage 1990, p. 44.

51 Ibid., pp. 42, 48, and 51.

Despite support from local officials, the events in Matewan proved to be a turning point that convinced the miners that sufficient political space to achieve redress of their grievances was closed to them and that they would need to escalate tactics from their repertoire. This street fight, reproduced in John Sayles's 1987 film by the same name, convinced the miners that even support from sympathetic local elected officials was not enough to either help them achieve redress to their grievances or shield them from violent repression.

The state and coal companies were now prepared to even further escalate their tactics, setting the *danse macabre* into motion. A few months later on 21 August 1920 another battle took place in Mingo County between strikers and guards that lasted three hours and resulted in six killed. More battles broke out after Governor Cornwell sent in National Guard troops and received about 500 more US troops to protect strikebreakers on 29 August, reversing his earlier refusal to send for them on 1 July. The troops were armed with a machine gun and a one-pound cannon. The local sheriff also assembled a force of 1,600 deputies and declared martial law. When US troops left on 4 November strikers carried out scattered attacks on scab miners, a tipple in Thacker was dynamited, and arson attacks on two mine company buildings occurred until the troops returned again on 27 November. Although President Wilson had not granted a declaration of martial law, Colonel Herman Hall directed his 500 men of the 19th Infantry Regiment to ban assemblies, parades, and demonstrations, effectively imposing it without authorisation. His men patrolled with fixed bayonets and went door to door coercing residents to hand over their arms. The Governor again soon imposed martial law, although the state Supreme Court later ruled it enforceable only by state militia not local police, of which there were few available.[52]

When the US troops left yet again on 16 February 1921, a group of armed volunteers was put under control of the head of the state police and used to suppress the miners. Soon after taking office on 4 March 1921, Governor Morgan requested federal troops. The Mingo District Attorney indicted 23 people for the 1st degree murder of 16 people killed during the strike.[53]

'In the first months of 1921 it appeared that peace had been restored, but by May each side was arming for renewed warfare'.[54] A power plant was dynamited in nearby Merrimac and then on 11 May telephone and telegraph wires were cut

---

52   Ibid., pp. 38–9; Cole 1998; and Cole 2003.
53   Blizzard 2005, p. 177; and Perlman and Taft 1935, p. 480.
54   Taft and Ross 1969, p. 25.

and armed miners stormed the mine from the hills above. The state police were sent into Mingo County but Colonel Jackson Arnold refused to take over local authority from Sheriff Blankenship. The governor then transferred command to Captain Brockus whose forces disarmed Chief Hatfield, dismissed his men and usurped power over the entire county.[55] Brockus and his men soon found themselves ambushed by gunfire while patrolling in the Tug River Valley. At about the same time, six more mines were assaulted in Mingo County and at the Mohawk mine in McDowell where the tipple was dynamited. About 200 miners also fired on a mine from the Kentucky side of the Tug River where the strike also included the Pond Creek Coal field. On 16 May the Big Splint mine was attacked.

During the Three Days Battle, between 12–14 May 1921, guards, assisted by a Kentucky militia company, used machine guns to attack four miner tent colonies. Although it is unknown how many miners were killed, four guards were killed in self-defence. On 19 May Governor Morgan implemented the state emergency public safety law by declaring 'a state of war, riot, and insurrection' existed in Mingo County. This allowed him to remove the locally elected sheriff and police chief, impose martial law, and request that President Harding send in troops. The Governor banned all meetings, parades, flyers and publications critical of the government, and the possession of guns by miners, and threatened to arrest journalists. The ban was not enforced against the coal companies and their hired agents.

This posse had been first assembled by Captain Brockus at a meeting of local elites assembled by a hyper-patriotic call to arms soon after the Three Days Battle. It took place in the Williamson County Courthouse, where the Hatfield trial had recently taken place.[56] The next day Governor Morgan declared martial law, putting acting State Adjutant General Major Davis in charge of a force of 100 state police joined by about 800 special police including American Legion vigilantes, 250 deputised members of a 'citizens' committee', and 650 mine employees paid by the operators. Davis, nicknamed Emperor of the Tug, was a vigilant enforcer of military rule which banned all public activities, arms, and publications of any sort under the governor's decree. He prevented the cir-

55   Savage 1990, p. 26. After his acquittal and being forced out as police chief, Hatfield became a constable and with his new wife Jessie, the widow of Mayor Testerman, sold arms and ammunition to the miners in her store. (See Ibid., p. 50).

56   Ibid., pp. 55–6; Warner in Corbin 1997, pp. 114–16; and Cole 2003, pp. 4–5. Davis had a similar job during WWI when he also commanded the state police, 800 special police and 250 vigilante force established by the State Council for Defense to guard private property. (See Green 2015, p. 230).

culation of the union *West Virginia Federationist* for criticising the governor and arrested men found reading it as well as the *United Mine Workers Journal*. His threat to continue doing so limited the union to handing out the papers in the miners' camps. The ban only applied to the miners and the UMWA but not to groups such as the American Legion and Salvation Army that held marches to recruit more men to the posse.[57]

On 14 June the state constabulary and sheriff's deputies attacked the Lick Creek tent colony of the Mingo strikers which housed 10,179 men, women and children. Responding to sniping at passing cars from guards in the tent colonies, Captain Brockus and Davis's forces twice attacked the camps armed with a machine gun, slashed tents, destroyed food supplies, arrested 43, including family members, and shot and killed one miner. One of their own was paralysed in the arm when the miners fought back. No one was convicted for killing the miner. None of the state police were bonded even though bonding was required by the State Treasurer.[58]

The same day the state Supreme Court struck down Governor Morgan's declaration of martial law in response to two *habeas corpus* appeals by jailed union organisers who were released. The Court disputed claims of military occupation.

> The justices held that while Mingo County was officially declared to be in a state of war, no actual military forces were in occupation. The only military man present was, in fact, Major Davis. The governor's attempt to inaugurate martial law through civil agencies 'constituted no more than mere military color'. Morgan could not 'by a mere order convert the civil officers into an army and clothe them with military powers'. There being no troops in the field martial law did not exist in Mingo County and the arrests were invalid. Accordingly, the petitioners were ordered released from custody.[59]

Since nearly all of Davis's men were vigilantes the Supreme Court effectively prevented the governor from placing the county under a private military occupation. To get around the ruling the governor issued a new declaration on

---

57   Davis had participated in the prosecution of strikers in the first military commission in
      Pratt and commanded the raid on the *Labor Star* newspaper during the 1913 strike when
      martial law had also been declared. (Savage 1990, p. 57; and Green 2015, pp. 229–31).
58   Warner in Corbin 1997, pp. 114–16; Cole 2003, pp. 5–6; and Green 2015, pp. 237–9.
59   Savage 1990, p. 58; and Cole 2003, p. 6.

27 June 1921, calling up 130 men to serve in the newly established re-activated National Guard, then called the West Virginia Enrolled Militia. Major Davis then immediately used the reorganised state force to raid the UMWA office in Williamson.[60] Twelve UMWA organisers who were feeding the miners and their families living in the camps were arrested in the raid and charged with unlawful assembly and jailed without bail. The West Virginia Supreme Court heard another *habeas corpus* hearing on 14–15 July 1921 but ruled to keep the men in jail. The cumulative effect of the governor's actions 'had the effect of suspending the state and federal constitutions in the affected area'.[61]

Despite martial law and the armed attacks on the strikers and their families, the miners remained on the offensive, dynamiting the War Eagle Coal Company and burning the Stone Mountain Coal Company head houses, looting and burning a company store in Lynn, and battling with Kentucky militia and West Virginia state police.

New reports and rumours of the raid on Lick Creek soon enraged miners all over the state who began assembling for another Miners' Army. On 8 July, Major Thomas and Captain Brockus led a raid on the UMWA office in Charleston, arresting all twelve people found there, and jailed them in McDowell County. The continued insurgency kept coal production at about 50 percent below normal levels.[62]

Martial law was a key to tactical escalation by elites and the coal companies to dampen public support for the strikers. It was one tactic in their broad repertoire of repression. As Lane, a reporter covering the strike wrote, the industry waged war on the strikers 'in the courts, through the power to withhold jobs, through ownership of men's homes, through the control of government'. The coal companies also used the US Supreme Court in the 1917 *Hitchman Coal & Coke Co. v. Mitchell* case which enjoined workers from organising workers who had signed yellow dog contracts. As Green made clear, 'the jurists had in effect made nonviolent attempts at persuasion by a labor union as illegal as violent methods of coercion'.[63] With the forces of repression arrayed against them, the miners' use of tactical violence was to be expected.

---

60   By the time the workers conceded in September four state police had been killed in addition to the one wounded. (See Cole 2003, p. 7).

61   Blizzard 2005, p. 189. Warner says five were arrested and Green puts the number at 12. (See Warner in Corbin 1997, pp. 114–16).

62   Savage 1990, pp. 58–60; Warner in Corbin 1997, pp. 114–16; and Green 2015, p. 240.

63   Green 2015, p. 242.

On 1 August 1921, a few weeks after testifying before Congress, Chief Hatfield and Deputy Chambers were brought to the McDowell County courthouse in Welch on charges of conspiracy. They were accused of plotting to dynamite a coal tipple at the Mohawk mine which Hatfield had only became aware of when questioned by Avis at the US Senate hearing. Hatfield and Chambers were murdered by C.E. Lively and other Baldwin-Felts agents on the steps of the courthouse. At their funeral, as rain fell on 3,000 people who had gathered to remember Hatfield and Chambers, Samuel Montgomery concluded his eulogy by saying that 'even the heavens weep with the grief-stricken relatives bereaved friends of these two boys'. Local elites paid the bonds for the killers who were soon back out on the street.[64]

Lively had grown up with Mooney and joined the UMWA in 1902 but later became a double agent. He was both a paid organiser for the Western Federation of Miners and a paid agent of the Pinkertons in Colorado. Now Lively was being paid between $75 and $225 plus expenses per month by the Baldwin-Felts Detective Agency. Lively ran a restaurant in Matewan below the union's office in a building owned by the union. After the murder Lively was let out on bail, although 100 miners remained in jail without charge under martial law.

The murder of Chief Hatfield struck a genuine blow to the miners who otherwise lacked the support of elected officials in a state under the plutocratic rule of the coal industry. He was a rare example of a local elected official who actively used the power of his office on behalf of the strikers which made him a mortal enemy of the coal companies. Hatfield was extraordinarily young, 28 years old, when he was murdered. He was a former miner but not a UMWA member, although his Deputy Chambers was.

According to Mother Jones, Keeney and Mooney organised a mass meeting of miners and supporters at the state capitol on 7 August to express their outrage over the assassinations. They listed their grievances and demands, many of which they thought they had won during WWI and from the US Bituminous Coal Commission that had been ignored. The miners asked for:

- An end to martial law
- No blacklisting of union miners
- An eight-hour day (which existed on paper elsewhere in the industry)
- The abolition of the company store
- The right of the miners to elect their own checkweighmen
- A 2,000 pound ton

---

64   Savage 1990, p. 73; and Green 2015, p. 248.

- The creation of the long promised joint commission to set wage rates and resolve grievances, and
- A joint Board of Arbitration to resolve commission disputes.[65]

Many of these demands were familiar because even though they had been widely mandated during WWI by several federal wartime labour-planning agencies, little progress had been made to achieve them.

Ten days later they had their answer: Governor Morgan refused to end martial law, would not prosecute the Baldwin-Felts agents, refused to set up a joint commission and absolved all actions by the mine owners, their agents, and the state police against the strikers and their supporters.[66] The coal operators refused to negotiate and Governor Morgan refused to call a special session of the legislature to respond to demands that the privately financed mine guard system be outlawed.

Miners Come Creeping

Hatfield's assassination precipitated the workers to give up on negotiations and take up arms in self-defence to protect workers in Mingo and neighbouring counties. The *dance macabre* was on. While UMWA District 17 threatened to call a general strike, miners began to carry out attacks and clashed with state police in Clothier at Blair Mountain near the Boone County line. Armed miners began assembling to patrol the roads into their mining towns. Savoy Brown, a miner from Cabin Creek, travelled from town to town in the Kanawha Valley reading what he claimed was a letter from Keeney calling miners to assemble with arms to march on Mingo County. What compelled many to respond to his and others' call to arms was that Lively and other Baldwin-Felts assassins were out on bail while miners were jailed under martial law.

In no time, about 4–5,000 miners, joined by uniformed nurses, began forming themselves into another Miners' Army. In Lens Creek Hollow, ten miles from the state capitol, 600 armed miners assembled, soon followed by thousands more.[67] Each union local mobilised their members and organised them into their own camp with their own passwords including 'I come creeping'. One company called roll using numbers assigned to its members in place of their

---

65   The last two demands were addressed nearly two years before by the US Bituminous Coal Commission which included references to it in its report.
66   Green 2015, pp. 250–1 and 253–4.
67   Ibid., p. 256.

names. They set up mess halls and commissaries, commandeered trains, and established a corps of about six nurses wearing white headdresses emblazoned with UMW. Miners rounded up cars to move troops, supplies, and supporters into position. As the Miners' Army moved toward Logan County supporters from Boone County showed up with food and fed them along the way. The Miners' Army became known as the 'Redneck Army' for the red bandanas they wore around their necks and on their arms along with their signature blue bib overalls. The army was organised into military squads, platoons, companies, and battalions and instructed on military strategy by veterans of the Spanish-American War and WWI dressed in their old uniforms and helmets all without a designated leader. Miners were instructed in how to fight machine guns and take out snipers. Such organisation was hardly spontaneous but appeared to be self-organised and expertly coordinated.[68]

Was the Miners' Army self-organised, or directed from above and commanded by a general? This question is by no means settled by the historical record. Green argues that Blizzard was the 'general' of the Miners' Army.[69] While Blizzard played a central role in the Miners' Army his contributions to its coordination should not be confused with him conducting and directing it. Journalist Boyden Sparkes, who reported from the Blair Mountain during the three days of intense battles, is one of the primary sources for the claim that Blizzard was the 'generalissimo' of the Miners' Army. Blizzard was a charismatic organiser who played into reporters' hands by bragging about how the men would listen to him if he asked them to withdraw. There have also been claims that Keeney and Mooney functioned as 'generals', playing the miners like puppets on a string, and even running the battle operations, although they were in hiding in Ohio at the time.[70]

However, the assumption that the miners initially responded to Keeney's call to assemble for the march from afar indicates that the army was formed in part by self-organisation of the miners themselves from below rather than in response to dictated orders from above. Lane found no conclusive evidence of how the march began or who called it and Savage observed that 'no one seemed in charge' and the Miners' Army moved out of its original staging area 'without control or direction'. Although some point to Keeney's 29 August letter responding to the reports of miners being beaten and jailed in Logan County

---

68   Savage 1990, pp. 80, 88, and 132; and Green 2015, pp. 260–1.

69   Blizzard was certainly no stranger to tactical escalation. His mother Sara led women who tore up C&O train tracks near Eskdale after the 'Bull Moose Special' driven by Baldwin-Felts agents shot at a miners' camp during the 1913 coal strike. (See Green 2015, p. 261).

70   Savage 1990, p. 150; and Green 2015, p. 281.

as the spark, the letter merely insists they will not be deterred from continuing to organise there. The claim by some mine operators that they were informed a day before the march that workers would not show up to work is not conclusive evidence that it was planned from above.[71] Savage asserts that Keeney and his staff 'unquestionably had helped to organise the rebellion, [and] he acted as if he had nothing to do with it', although the supporting evidence is slim.[72]

If there was a general then it should be expected that he helped arm his troops. Savage asserts Blizzard and four other District 17 leaders, including its attorney Walter Allen, met men at the camp and 'handed out rations and guns, answered questions, and sent men forward' but he provided no evidence.[73] Savage is hardly exceptional among historians who have almost universally glossed over or ignored how the miners got their weapons in a state where one must be permitted and bonded to carry a gun. Although it is widely believed that the miners used their own guns in the Miners' Army, they also acquired them by pooling their money to buy them or by taking them from the coal companies' armouries.[74] Because union local leaders raised funds for their own contributions to the Miners' Army, it is possible that some union funds were used to purchase them. But considering the ambivalent and inconsistent support for the Miners' Army from District 17 and UMWA national leadership it is most likely that the miners organised much, if not all, of their acquisitions from below.

The miners' refusal to entirely or immediately disperse despite Keeney's repeated directions to do so is evidence that the miners were not commanded from above. They were certainly loyal to District 17, but only up to a point. If the leadership accurately read the needs and desires of the membership, the Miners' Army supported its decisions, a correlation that could be easily misread as complying with a command. But when the leadership acted in a way that did not resonate with the widespread sentiments of the membership, they were ignored or countermanded. This may be the reason for Keeney wavering between escalation and de-escalation as he took a misstep, then course corrected to come back in alignment with the membership as an effective leader should do. Rather than commanding, Keeney appeared to follow.

We could rather look toward named and unnamed charismatic members who stepped into positions as leaders and organisers. Among them were unnamed black miners who publicly called for other black miners to join the fight

---

71 Lane 1921, pp. 107–8; and Savage 1990, pp. 6 and 86.
72 Savage 1990, p. 9.
73 Ibid., p. 77.
74 Lane 1921, p. 99.

despite the risks, leaders in the locals who coordinated companies, and WWI and Spanish-American War veterans who trained their fellow miners in combat tactics and strategy. We should also consider miners who raided armouries and commandeered trains and cars, guarded the safety of the miners and their families living in the camps from attacks by state police and Baldwin-Felts agents, and planned attacks on the mines, as well as female family members who coordinated a brigade of nurses and medical supplies. Among the miners whose names were never recorded in the history books were those who constructed 'miners' specials' out of commandeered engines, freight cars, and coaches to move miners up to Blair Mountain.[75]

There were also known militants such as Ed Reynolds who commanded a company of 300 men and reported that President Keeney had no intention of stopping the Miners' Army. Or the lay Baptist minister and miner John Wilburn who proclaimed 'the time has come for me to lay down my Bible and pick up my rifle and fight for my rights', and organised a company of 70 black and white miners in Blair to join the army. There was also 'Red Thompson', a black miner from Blair, who formed a company of 75 men wearing khaki riding pants, leggings, and a white hat with a wide brim. Two doctors, W.F. Harliss of Clothier and L.F. Milliken of Blair, treated the wounded and evacuated them to requisitioned school buildings where they were treated by nurses. The unheralded 'Bad Lewis' White, reportedly wearing two revolvers, protected the army from sneak attacks, punished collaborators and defectors, guarded prisoners on Blair mountain, and helped commandeer a train to move the army to Logan and roused miners in towns along the line of march to join the army.[76]

There is evidence that Keeney was already facing an internal insurgency among the membership prior to the start of the second miners' war. Wildcat strikes, or what Lane called 'many petty strikes', appear to have been common. A common collective bargaining agreement for the approximately 53,000 unionised miners actually imposed a $1 per day penalty on all miners who wildcatted. A miner who did not follow the grievance procedure and refused to work could be fired. According to Lane, 'many stoppages of work have undoubtedly occurred at individual mines in violation of the above agreement'. He reported 63 wildcats in an 11-month period in the area of a single unnamed coal operators' association, about six per month, 25 to 30 of which were confirmed by Keeney and Blizzard.[77]

---

75   Savage 1990, pp. 92, 95–6, and 127.
76   Ibid., pp. 92, 95–6, 122–3, 127, 133, and 141. Bad Lewis White was the brother of Sheriff Chafin's jailer.
77   Lane 1921, pp. 94–6.

Keeney's apparently contradictory encouragement of the Miners' Army and his orders that it disband may not have been contradictory after all. Rather, they were the actions of a union leader caught between the irreconcilable demands of the UMWA upper leadership, workers, and capital, a product of his having to both appease an increasingly insurgent membership and the UMWA and the coal companies' demands that he rein in the workers if he hoped to negotiate a new contract.

Confronted by these irreconcilable demands, Keeney responded by leaning heavily towards one side – the coal companies – by suppressing far more wild-cat strikes than calling official strikes. Keeney recounted a day when there were 17 wildcat strikes happening simultaneously, 13 of which he shut down by dir-ectives sent by telegraph and four of which he shut down in person. In his four years as District 17 president, Keeney had only started one strike while cancel-ling 12 local charters for apparently engaging in wildcat strikes. One other strike was called by an International Board member.[78]

To argue that the leadership commanded the Miners' Army like a general is to overlook that the workers' movement is fundamentally a struggle for demo-cratic control of the economy by the workers. The Miners' Army is but one means by which workers practised democracy to pursue that objective. To assert that they were commanded from above is to denigrate the immense effort and capacity of workers to organise themselves, identify the necessary tactics, strategy, and objectives, and put them into action. If the District 17 lead-ership made a call for them to assemble, the workers responded and made it happen because it resonated with what they already knew to be true: their grievances would not be redressed by appealing to the coal companies or state and local government for peaceful negotiations.

After Secretary of War John Weeks refused Governor Morgan's request to send in US troops, Morgan asked Logan County Sheriff Don Chafin to set up a posse. Within a few days the sheriff had assembled 3,000 armed men composed of local businessmen, elites, and miners coerced to join or lose their jobs.[79]

Mother Jones also visited the governor and departed assured he would inter-vene. The legendary Mother Jones opposed the armed march, appeared on the line of march and told them to go home. In her hand she claimed to have a telegram from President Harding offering to work to end the private police in West Virginia if they returned home. When Keeney demanded to see the telegram and Mother Jones refused, he denounced her as a 'fake'. Because she

---

78   Ibid., pp. 96–7.
79   Green 2015, pp. 257–8.

refused to show anyone the telegram she was suspected of having fabricated the story. Mother Jones not only refused to allow anyone to read the document, the President's secretary denied ever having sent one. After she fled the camp she reportedly suffered a nervous breakdown.[80]

Mother Jones was joined by President Keeney and other UMWA officials who were also pressuring the miners to go home. Although Mother Jones organised for decades on behalf of the UMWA in West Virginia and even denounced the state as medieval, the chapter of the same name in her autobiography, she mostly praises Governor Morgan for defending the 1st amendment freedom of the labour weekly *The Federationist* to publish. His refusal to consent to the mine owners' request that he ban the paper demonstrated to Mother Jones that he 'refused to comply with the requests of the dominant money interests. To a man of that type I wish to pay my respects'.[81]

Mother Jones's praise for Governor Morgan was not only misinformed and misguided humiliation or self-delusion as has been claimed. It was a maternalistic attempt to use a lie in order to defuse, diffuse, and de-escalate the miners' decision to reject further futile efforts to negotiate with elites who answered with the gun. The legend of Mother Jones is somewhat deflated once this episode – one widely excluded from popular accounts of her contributions to the labour movement – is known.

Jones's actions hardly stood out as exceptional. She was only doing what many union leaders, including Keeney, Mooney, and Lewis, had been doing for years: provoking miners to escalate as leverage to return to negotiations, obtain just enough concessions to justify de-escalation and marginal access to the polity in the expectation that future conflict could be pre-empted.[82] But the UMWA leadership was powerless to stop the miners. In addition to expected resistance from the combined forces of capital and the state, the miners also faced resistance from their own union.

The Miners' Army reportedly stretched for 20 miles as it moved through Boone County towards Logan County. Upon learning of its movement Sheriff Chafin sounded the Logan fire siren and with his 44 deputies opened up his armoury of ten machine guns, 1,000 rifles, and 67,000 rounds of ammunition. The courthouse was converted into a commissary in order to distribute these supplies and local women opened a food distribution point in a hotel. Chafin

---

80   Savage 1990, pp. 78–9; and Green 2015, pp. 258–9.

81   Apparently Jones didn't know or overlooked that Morgan had received about $1 million in campaign donations from industrialists in the 1920 election. (See Mother Jones 1925, pp. 144 and 232–5; and Green 2015, p. 218).

82   Green 2015, pp. 258–9.

threatened to defend Logan with 'every engine of modern warfare'. He sent for private cars to move men and supplies and three biplanes to be dispatched to conduct surveillance flights of the Miners' Army. One of those planes hit a tree and crashed onto a house. The local press showed its support by excluding details of Chafin's preparation while deputy miners pressed non-union miners into the posse to fight or be fired or go to jail. Men were plied with moonshine whiskey and children as young as 14 and 15 years old were enrolled.[83]

The governor established eight National Guard companies in the area and transferred command of Chafin's 2,800 men to newly appointed National Guard Colonel William Eubanks at Login, who reportedly drank heavily while on duty.[84] The forces were created in haste and confusion, lacked a clear chain of command and training. It wasn't long until the first fatality in the second march occurred, not in battle, but rather from an accidentally discharged rifle that killed a state policeman.

Lacking the manpower to stop the Miners' Army, local elites' fear of the invading workers' army came out coloured by their racism. One mine company executive tellingly warned that 'at any turn you were liable to butt into a colored man with a high powered rifle', a fear that illustrated the growing power of two groups in the state who were not to be kept down any longer.[85]

Ignoring President Harding's order to disperse, on 24 August the Miners' Army began marching up Lens Creek into Boone County over Blair Mountain. They were accompanied by wives and daughters singing 'John Brown's Body', an apt reference to a favourite song of Union soldiers marching into battle during the Civil War. Most particularly relevant to the miners was the last stanza of one version which began:

> Oh, soldiers of freedom, then strike while strike you may
> The deathblow of oppression in a better time and way ...

The town of Logan held symbolic importance to the Miners' Army, the dividing line between union and non-union mines, between autocracy and working-class power. It was here that US troops, Keeney and other UMWA officials tried to stop their line of march. About 2,000 US troops, 106 officers, and a number of military intelligence officers arrived from Fort Dix on 26 August under the command of US Army General Bandholtz. The general called in Keeney

---

83   Savage 1990, pp. 82–3 and 116; and Green 2015, p. 263.
84   Ibid.
85   Ibid.

and two other UMWA officials and told them to order the miners to turn back. General Bandholtz was especially worried about the miners' armed insurgency inspiring other workers around the country. According to Mooney, General Bandholtz told them 'there are several million unemployed in this country now and this thing might assume proportions that would be difficult to handle'.[86]

On 27 August, Keeney called a meeting at a baseball field to tell the Miners' Army to turn back or face the US Army. Concerned he might lose control of the meeting and the vote, he called for a voice vote which favoured disbanding. General Bandholtz, UMWA Sub-district No. 2 President William Blizzard, and two other military officials drove to Boone County to confirm they had turned back as reported. Satisfied that they had, the general and his troops returned to Washington DC the next day.

But not all the miners had retreated. Blizzard and others led about 300 more miners out of Madison towards Logan County, claiming that Keeney had only held the vote to mislead General Bandholtz and that he was encouraging them to continue their march.[87] It's unclear whether Keeney was engaged in 'deception' or was caught in a tenuous position. He was certainly trapped between the US government's demand to demobilise or have their union destroyed and the thousands of members who preferred to push on despite the resistance or risk abandoning the union. That Keeney was either unwilling or unable to defy the membership is further evidence of the self-organised direction of the Miners' Army from below.

The departure of General Bandholtz and his troops did not, however, end the siege in Mingo County which remained under martial law. Soon after, Captain Brockus, 200 of Sheriff Chafin's men, and about another 100 state police marched to Clothier to arrest the miners who had humiliated his deputies two weeks earlier. After arresting ten miners they marched them at gunpoint as human shields until they came under fire from armed miners in Shaples that killed two of the captive miners. In the chaos of the firefight five of Brockus's hostages escaped. Along their overnight retreat four of the deputies were taken captive and offered in exchange for the remaining five miners held in Logan.[88]

On 28 August 1921 reports of Brockus's attack almost immediately provoked the Miners' Army to continue the temporarily delayed march.[89] Word of the attack prompted as many as 8,000 armed miners to stop their retreat and return

---

86   In Green 2015, p. 266.
87   Savage 1990, p. 91; and Green 2015, p. 268.
88   Savage 1990, pp. 103–5; and Green 2015, pp. 269–70.
89   Although Green dismissed these reports as 'lurid and inaccurate' he doesn't give any evidence. (See Green 2015, p. 270).

a few days later and others to join up. The miners again marched into battle against the state and local police, the Baldwin-Felts agents, and the coal companies. 'Sid Hatfield's death now was fast receding into history, what seemed at stake was full-fledged civil war'.[90]

They now headed toward the foot of Blair Mountain with the plan to move into Logan County. To speed their advance, about 500 miners took control of a train to transport supplies and reinforcements while others followed in cars and trucks and on horses and wagons. Hundreds more were marching accompanied by women who cared for and fed the miners along with several doctors. Within a day, the Miners' Army captured machine guns and food from coal company stores and swelled to a force of at least 5,000.[91] Along Cabin Creek communication lines were cut and miners seized a machine gun from a company store near Holly Grove. This one was added to an arsenal that included a machine gun that had been stolen a year earlier from Baldwin-Felts agents. This time volunteers also began rolling in from the neighbouring states of Ohio, Indiana, and Illinois.

Within a day the military reported that miners had control of a 500-mile area from the Kanawha River to Logan County.[92] 'All government, law, and industry in the area now rested in the hands of armed miners'.[93] In that area,

> they took automobiles and trucks from citizens at will; they operated the c&o trains and controlled the railway tracks, stations, and railyards; they patrolled the highways and regulated automobile and pedestrian traffic and issued passes to authorize citizen movements within the battle area; they refused to allow mines to operate; they commandeered school buildings and used them as mess halls, and sleeping quarters. Sheriffs, judges, and other public officials in the area looked on helplessly.

---

90 Savage 1990, p. 114. The Miners' Army should more accurately be considered an insurgency rather than a civil war, because civil war implies a war between two factions of elites, which this was not.

91 Estimates of the size of the force range widely between 4,000 to 20,000 (Bailey 2013). Most estimate around 5,000 with Perlman and Taft offering a low of 4,000 men and women. (Perlman and Taft 1935, p. 481). The documentary film *Even the Heavens Weep* puts the number of people in the redneck army at about 10,000 (*Even the Heavens Weep* 1985). The *Mine Wars* documentary puts the number at 8,000. (*The Mine Wars* 2016). Savage quotes Keeney estimating the Miners' Army at 10,000 and gives a wide range of between 5,000 to 13,000 men and women. (Savage 1990, pp. 6 and 87).

92 Savage 1990, p. 8; and Green 2015, p. 271.

93 Savage 1990, p. 92.

In short, the Miners' Army had not only mobilised a workers' self-defence militia and seized complete control of the area and the economy, but it ran it themselves for several days, without a centralised authority or government. Without any apparent ideology to guide them, the Miners' Army had put the ideas of syndicalism into practice. On Blair Mountain the Miners' Army leapfrogged the factory council syndicalists who were seizing and running factories in Italy, Germany, Russia, and elsewhere. It was a repeat of the Seattle general strike in which the miners took over and ran all of society and had the means to defend it. Although they controlled the mines, the miners did not take over and run them. They controlled the territory and roads, ran some trains, and organised medical care, the food supply, and security. The miners developed a language to communicate with one another using passwords and passes to allow non-fighters such as doctors to move in the combat zone.

Despite the attempts to imagine one, the miners occupied and ran Blair Mountain without any centralised authority. Asking who the 'general' of the Miners' Army was, the *Charleston Gazette* assumed one was needed 'for everything is done with system. Every man is accounted for. Every little detail is worked out in advance'.[94] But Savage disagreed, insightfully explaining that

> actually, little was done with system [stet]; every man was not accounted for; the details were not worked out in advance. Leaders, indeed, emerged and they served as corporals, sergeants, lieutenants, and captains ... all were leaders of the rebellion, and there were more. But they were not generals. No one of them commanded the miners' army. They assumed leadership by their own personalities and abilities, not by official recognition ... In the more than half century since the rebellion, many have discussed the fabled 'general' of the miners' army, but no such person has emerged. It is inconceivable that the commander of such an enterprise could have remained hidden. The answer, of course, is that there was no general.[95]

Without a 'leader', Savage recognised the Miners' Army as a new society composed of a ménage of the existing forms of organisation as black and white workers, members of families and local communities, and people self-organised in these particular subterranean groups.

---

94   Ibid., p. 135.
95   Ibid., pp. 135–6.

The miners' army was a singular example of a working anarchy, held together for a time by a common drive, a common understanding, a set of common emotions, added to a touch of muscle, a bit of mob rule, and occasional terror attacks. The men knew where they wanted to go and how to get there, and they were united in this knowledge. They moved in groups, comparable to platoons or companies, because they ran in groups from their own mining camps and union locals. In most groups, leaders already existed; where there were none, leaders emerged, as they always do.[96]

The workers drew on their own interpersonal connections, skills, and experiences with institutions and self-organisation to mobilise themselves to provide for their recognised needs. Their extensive local familial relationships and shared cultural norms were critical to their ability to self-organise. Savage expertly continues:

The rest came naturally. They brought guns and food because they needed guns and food, they organised their supplies because supplies moved more quickly that way. No 'general' was needed to tell them all this, or that they needed cars, trucks, trains, and guns, or how to get them. By the law of averages and by varying interests and judgments of miners, hundreds of uncoordinated separate decisions somehow resulted in a collective harmony, a leaderless army that was incredibly efficient.[97]

One could only speculate what might have followed having achieved these 'hundreds of uncoordinated separate decisions' of which anarchists, autonomist marxists, and syndicalists have found in the rare moments of revolutionary self-organisation. Had the miners halted their advance and retained control of the area, they might have carved out an autonomous workers' state or further circulated their struggle to construct a society that functioned without a centralised authority that would sit alongside the Paris Commune, early soviets, anarchist Spain during the Civil War, the squats of Europe and Mexico, Rojava Kurdistan, El Alto Bolivia, Zapatista autonomous municipalities in Chiapas Mexico, and the occupied farms of the Brazilian landless workers' movement. Unfortunately, their patriotism got in the way.

---

96   Ibid., p. 136.
97   Ibid.

President Harding again refused Governor Morgan's plea to immediately send more troops. Instead the president issued an order for the miners to disperse by 1 September and sent General Bandholtz to make sure they obeyed with orders to bring in his troops to put down the insurrection if they refused.[98] Two regiments were put on alert at Fort Dix, New Jersey, and Camp Sherman, Ohio. General Bandholtz soon returned and met with Governor Morgan. UMWA President Lewis sent UMWA Vice President Philip Murray to pressure the miners to return home. Seeing that he would neither be able to persuade the Miners' Army to turn back, nor be safe in attempting to do so, Murray fled to Charleston.[99] After two of Bandholtz's officers also failed to persuade the Miners' Army to disband, he called for the US Army troops on alert to be sent in.

These attempts by the UMWA district and national leadership, the president, governor, and the general all failed because the miners were no longer willing to unilaterally de-escalate, leaving their fellow miners in Logan and Mingo counties to be violently repressed and thereby raising the costs to their mobilisation and reducing the opportunities to achieve their objectives state-wide. The advantage of leverage now lay with the miners and that would not be given up unless they perceived the costs of their tactical escalation to rise too high. The miners governed their insurgency themselves now.

The Miners' Army established their lines on Blair Mountain, preparing to confront a force of about 2,800 sheriff deputies, private police, and deputised company employees under the command of the West Virginia National Guard spread out along a 15- to 18-mile long battle line.[100] Governor Morgan told the Law and Order League that 'moonshine liquor, pistol-toting, and automobiles' were the three greatest sources of lawlessness. The miners, he said, were assembled at Marmet 'for the sole purpose of terrorizing the government of the State'.[101]

Expecting the miners to further escalate their tactics into a full-scale military style invasion of Logan County, Keeney and Governor Morgan again personally tried to stop them. This time the attempt to demobilise the Miners' Army didn't work. Only about 600 workers initially surrendered, disarmed and returned home and the remaining force continued the march, preparing to engage in battle.

---

98   President Harding signed a second declaration of martial law in West Virginia but never issued it. (Ibid., p. 156).

99   Ibid., p. 131; and Green 2015, p. 279.

100   Ross and Taft 1969, p. 25.

101   *Independent* in Corbin 1997, p. 109.

The battles began on 31 August and continued for three days. The fighting in five major skirmishes on the forks of three creeks in the watershed was fierce with each side firing an estimated 500,000 shots from a wide range of weapons including Thompson submachine guns or 'Tommy guns' purchased by the sheriff, coal companies, and local vigilantes from local gun stores. Three anti-union men and at least one miner Eli Kemp, who was a black member of Wilburn's unit, were killed, although the total number of miners killed or injured is still unknown.[102] Sheriff Chafin managed to find an excuse to use his biplanes to drop pipe bombs filled with gas, TNT and shrapnel. Two journalists were reportedly shot and temporarily arrested by the state police as spies until they showed signed military passes. One of those shot in the battles on Blair Mountain was Maine Island Creek Coal Company President Jack Dalton, the largest coal operator in the state with 27 mines on 27,000 acres in Logan and other counties, who was hit in the leg and scalp.[103]

Once the battles began, neither the UMWA national nor District 17 leadership could convince the Miners' Army to back down. On the night of 1 September a car of miners pulled up to Mooney's house and told him and Keeney that there was no longer anything they could do and to leave town. 'They had set the miners' march in motion, but now rank-and-file leaders had taken command'. That night both District 17 leaders went into hiding in Ohio after learning they had been indicted by a grand jury in Mingo County for the firefights from the previous summer.[104]

On 2 September, 2,100 US troops arrived in West Virginia on General Bandholtz's command. Troops were sent from Kentucky, Indiana and Ohio. Among them were machine gun and howitzer companies belonging to the 26th Infantry at Fort Dix and the 40th Infantry at Camp Knox armed with machine

---

102 Ross and Taft estimated that at least 21 people were killed in the three days of battle. Savage concludes the final fatality count was lower, putting the figure at about 16, 12 of which were members of the Miners' Army, although no bodies were found on Blair Mountain. Because of scarce details, fatality reports were 'casual, incomplete, and unsubstantiated' and no later effort was made to verify the total deaths. 'The precise number would never be known' because with extended families and doctors and nurses marching with the Miners' Army it may be that the army took care of the wounded and buried the dead without taking the risk that could likely accompany disclosing that they did. One of those who died was Mr. Comiskey, an IWW member, had only been in Logan 36 hours before he was executed in the Huntington jail. State police fired at four journalists and their three miner guides wounding *New York Tribune* war reporter Boyden Sparkes. (See Ross and Taft 1969, p. 25; Savage 1990, pp. 133–4, 140, 154–5, and 161; and Smith-Christmas 2014).

103 Savage 1990, pp. 125–6; Sparkes in Corbin 1997, p. 127; and Blizzard 2005, pp. 312–22.

104 Green 2015, p. 276.

guns, trench mortars, and 37 millimetre guns.[105] This was reportedly the largest deployment of US troops inside the US since 6,000 troops were deployed against the Lakota Sioux Ghost Dancers on the Pine Ridge Reservation in 1890 resulting in the slaughter of 146 Indians at Wounded Knee. Once more, the link between genocide, slavery, and repression of working-class struggle came full circle.

The last gap in the circle was closed during the battle of Blair Mountain when the most advanced weapons of WWI were used against the nation's own citizens in an escalation of tactics by the government. The US troops included a small air force of 17 DeHavilland fighter-bomber biplanes and four Martin bombers under the command of General Billy Mitchell. General Mitchell, who formed the first US air force during WWI, called out the 88th Air Squadron from Langley Field. General Mitchell arrived from Bolling Field ahead of his squadron dressed with a pistol, spurs, and four rows of ribbons. The planes were armed with machine guns and bombs, carried a flight surgeon and communications and photographic teams.

Insisting airplanes could be used against a domestic insurrection, he threatened to drop gas first and then artillery if the miners didn't disperse, although the skirmishes ended before he could do so. When reporters asked Mitchell how he would confront the well dug in Miners' Army, he told them 'You understand we wouldn't try to kill these people first. We'd drop tear gas all over the place. If they refused to disperse then we'd open up, with artillery ... and everything'. After landing in Roanoke to refuel, they were guarded by members of the American Legion.[106]

It soon became clear that Mitchell oversold the capabilities of not only air power to put down a domestic insurrection from the sky but to even take off and reach the intended destination. In Roanoke, one plane crashed on take off in a corn field, two others were stranded due to engine trouble, and a fourth plane had trouble over West Virginia and made an emergency crash landing in a field. Two more planes lost their way in fog and ended up in Tennessee. After taking off one plane crashed trying to escape from a storm and a second crashed into a fence. The 9 remaining biplanes managed to make it to Charleston, West Virginia but only three of the Martin bombers joined them since one also hit a fence and crashed. In all, only 12 of the 21 planes made it to West Virginia. The remaining three Martin bombers mostly sat on display in a field in Kanawha City although two of them were severely damaged. While return-

---

105   Savage 1990, pp. 148–9 and 153.
106   Ibid., pp. 142–3; and in Green 2015, p. 266.

ing to Langley Field one of the three remaining Martin bombers crashed killing four of the five crew members and a second was stranded until the crew could figure out how to take off again in a field that was too small.[107]

Despite his claim that the mission offered 'an excellent example of the potentialities of air power, that can go wherever there is air' Mitchell's plans to deploy this new weapon in counter-insurgency were not to be. Although the 88th Squadron served under General Bandholz's command, carrying out several surveillance flights, the miners fired at and damaged several of the planes. They never did 'drop tear gas all over the place' or 'open up, with artillery ... and everything' on the Miners' Army. The principle that counter-insurgency cannot be fought from the air likely originated in Mitchell's ill fated mission.

Sheriff Chafin and National Guard Colonel Eubanks both used the airplanes to drop four to six inch wide pipes filled with black powder, and nuts and bolts, and bombs containing tear gas designed to cause nausea and vomiting, an early form of cluster bombs. Four bombs were dropped on the Crooked Creek miners' camp particularly targeting a school being used as a hospital and sleeping quarters. Luckily it missed its target but it sent a shock that 'virtually shook the steep mountain'. This too may also have been the first time in which US troops deployed aerial weaponry against, and local police and National Guard dropped bombs on, the US population.[108] Colonel Eubanks's gas bombs caused vomiting and injured one of Chafin's men when he spilled the contents, burned his leg, and had to be hospitalised. No miner was reported to be injured by the bombs.[109]

On 3 September, General Bandholtz moved his troops into position. When the Miners' Army retreated and saw the US troops they greeted them with relief. The firing slowly began to dissipate and eventually fell silent by Sunday evening. Although the newspapers had reported that 50 miners had been killed and another 50 wounded the troops found no wounded miners. There were some killed but not in the battles. On 8 September 1921 a plane flying over the miners

---

107   Savage 1990, pp. 143–6. General Mitchell's career ended in 1925 after first being demoted to colonel and court martialed and suspended for five years. Ironically, he was court martialed for criticising his commanding officers for two deadly air crashes. (Maksel 2009).

108   Green is incorrect when he suggested that 'for the first and only time, American citizens were subjected to aerial bombardment on their own soil'. The Philadelphia police dropped bombs on the MOVE house in 1985 burning it and the entire block to the ground. (See Stevens 1985; *Let the Fire Burn* 2013; and Green 2015, p. 278).

109   In addition to Sheriff Chafin and General Mitchell's airplanes, the coal companies also hired planes for their Baldwin-Felts agents to drop tear gas and bombs on the miners. (See *Even the Heavens Weep*, 1985; Savage 1990, pp. 126, 139–40, and 150).

CHAPTER 10

dropping copies of President Harding's 30 August 1921 proclamation ordering the miners to return home crashed near Poe in Nicholas County, killing four of its five crew members.[110]

Four days later on 7 September General Bandholz pulled out the troops without even firing a shot, dropping a bomb, making an arrest, or incurring an injury.[111] He wired the War Department that his troops reported not even a single act of hostility from the Miners' Army. The Miners' Army's retreat was a guerrilla war tactic right out of Sun Tzu's *The Art of War*, appearing to follow the principle 'So in war, the way is to avoid what is strong and to strike at what is weak'.[112]

The Miners' Army de-escalated in the face of the far stronger force of the US government. Because of their overwhelming patriotism and the fact that their insurgency was against the mine companies, the Baldwin-Felts agents, and repressive local county and state forces, they never had intended to overthrow, let alone engage in battle with, the federal government. Since many were veterans themselves, they had a loyalty to the government that overwhelmed their loyalty to their class and their fellow miners under the gun in Mingo and Logan counties. Once they faced the US Army troops, the objective for forming the Miners' Army went out of focus. Despite the brutality and violence – even bombs and gas dropped from the air – that had been thrown against them in the past two years, it 'all paled into insignificance when compared with shooting at soldiers of the United States Army ... There was no decision, no judgment to make. They would not, could not, make war against their own country'.[113] While the local and state governments had lost legitimacy, the US government had not.

Faced with the US Army, the miners 'had accomplished nothing they set out to do'.[114] Although it didn't succeed in invading Mingo County and freeing the miners imprisoned there, ending martial law, overthrowing Sheriff Chafin, or punishing the Baldwin-Felts assassins, they had demonstrated how far workers would organise to confront corporate and government oppression with the force of arms. Sadly, if any miners saw, as Green did, 'the arrival of federal forces as a victory, one that would pave the way for a new era in which coal miners would enjoy the rights and liberties the Constitution guaranteed to all American citizens', they and their children, and grandchildren, would be sorely

---

110   Corbin 1997, pp. 106 and 133.
111   Savage 1990, p. 163; and Colonel Ford in Corbin 1997, pp. 120–5.
112   Sun Tzu 2009.
113   Savage 1990, pp. 147–8.
114   Ibid., p. 164.

disappointed.[115] By intervening militarily, the US government actually prevented the Miners' Army from tilting the balance of power away from the coal companies and their elite allies. The use of the military was hardly neutral but rather helped to lock in corporate domination of the state to this very day.

In the end about 600 miners surrendered but very few guns were turned in, about 300 in all. The US troops, National Guard, Baldwin-Felts agents and volunteers marched the defeated miners along a 60-mile stretch of the Chesapeake & Ohio railroad starting 15 miles outside Charleston south into Logan and Boone counties.[116]

So ended the last, and perhaps the largest since the Civil War, armed worker insurgency in American history. The Battle of Blair Mountain was perhaps the only other recorded time in US history when an organised army of workers engaged in hand to hand combat with police, vigilantes, and National Guard troops. Although strikers and their supporters engaged in street fighting with troops during the 1877 railroad strike, there is not yet any evidence that they coordinated, organised, and trained as the Miners' Army did.[117] Green highlighted just how significant the Miners' Army was:

> The nation had never witnessed such a large body of workingmen undertaking a militant action on such a massive scale. The miners' march that summer was a huge general strike as well as a massive political protest against the abuse of civil liberties by private employers and government officials. But this movement of nearly ten thousand armed miners amounted to something more: By August 25, it had become the largest civil insurrection the country had ever experienced since the Civil War.[118]

The miners and their supporters resorted to insurrection by rapidly escalating their tactics when all attempts to peacefully address their grievances and demands to the coal operators, local and state officials, state courts, and the federal government had been repulsed. As Green observed, 'for more than a year,

---

115 Green 2015, pp. 282–3.

116 Blizzard 2005, pp. 310–11 and 317.

117 Armed slave rebellions should be added to this list as many were apparently very well organised and the insurgents trained themselves (Aptheker 1983). There have been other battles with troops from the centuries long war of resistance by Native Americans, and battles between people and troops have occurred on a number of occasions in American history from the brief battle at the start of Shay's Rebellion in 1787 and the urban rebellions of the 1960s.

118 Green 2015, p. 262.

union miners had waged their battles in a variety of ways: guerrilla tactics in the field, legal appeals in the courts, petitions to governors, publicity efforts in the press, and lobbying efforts on Capitol Hill'.[119] Merely attempting to organise, march, and defend themselves in the courts had brought down unilateral repression by forces of capital and the state, martial law imposed, organisers jailed or killed, tent encampments sniped, journalists censored, and police, troops, and armed vigilantes sent to occupy mining towns.[120] The only remaining option that had given the miners leverage in past organising campaigns was armed insurrection to raise the costs to capital for refusing to concede to the workers' demands for modest reforms.

The redneck army was defeated not merely by the injection of the US Army on the side of the coal operators, but also efforts by the UMWA's district leadership to demobilise and de-escalate them. Perhaps intimidated by the authoritarian forces of the coal companies and their state allies, the UMWA continued trying to discipline and manage the rank and file by attempting to prevent them from circulating and escalating the struggle. Although 350 miners were later indicted for treason, none were ever convicted. Nor was anyone ever prosecuted, let alone convicted, for murdering Chief Hatfield, including Lively, who was acquitted in 1922.[121]

The miners had made numerous attempts to unilaterally de-escalate their tactics in order to seek redress through access to the polity and negotiations. Both governors refused to respond to their de-escalation, making apparent what had miners had instinctively known: access to legal forms of political action were still sealed tight. No access to the polity in order to advocate for state intervention to seek a mediated solution to the class struggle was going to be made available to them. Blizzard clearly explained their sense of utter frustration and isolation.

> The miners of West Virginia had by this time exhausted every possible avenue of 'law and order' in their appeals to the governor, to the legislature, to county officials and to federal investigators ... By late August, 1921, the miners had exhausted every legal means of redress.[122]

---

119   Ibid., p. 273.
120   Several of the journalists reporting on the fighting on Blair Mountain were subject to military censorship. (See Savage 1990, pp. 157–9).
121   Ross and Taft 1969, p. 25; Brecher, 1972 pp. 153–5; and Savage 1990, pp. 166–7.
122   Blizzard 2005, pp. 250–1.

The elite coalition controlling the state was engaged in total warfare of winner takes all. Using absolute gains to pursue cooperation and negotiations would mean utter defeat against an adversary pursuing a relative gains 'winner takes all' zero sum strategy. The miners were left with only the options of complete capitulation, defeat, and subjugation or to continue mobilising and escalating their tactics by taking up arms.

Although the presence of the US troops, several thousand deputies, most of which were private Baldwin-Felt gunmen and employees of the operators, American Legion vigilantes, and the imposition of martial law enraged communities throughout the state, the defeat of the 1919 national miners' strike prevented the miners from organising critically needed mass support outside West Virginia. Because the UMWA demobilised and de-escalated in order to participate in the US Bituminous Coal Commission and begrudgingly accepted the concessions imposed by it, the union had committed to meeting the terms of the agreement until its expiration date. With the arbitration award in place, the role of the union shifted to enforcing it by attempting to control and discipline dissatisfied rank and file members, especially in West Virginia.

From the Mountain to the Courtroom

'The suppression of the West Virginia miners' rebellion did not end with the surrender of the miners', observed Savage. By demobilising, disarming, and de-escalating the miners became vulnerable to the inevitable legal prosecutions that followed as well as continued rampant exploitation in the mines. After the second march ended, special and grand juries issued 1,217 indictments, including 325 for murder, and 24 were tried for treason against the state. The Logan County grand jury alone issued about 550 indictments for treason and 200 others for sedition, conspiracy, and carrying weapons.[123] Among those indicted and jailed was District 17 organiser Blizzard. District 17 President Keeney and Secretary-Treasurer Mooney were indicted for the murder of a deputy sheriff in Mingo County and the battle in Matewan. The mine company lawyers did double duty as prosecutors and the companies paid the costs of the trials.

If the federal government was missing from the legal onslaught unleashed against the miners, their leaders, and the UMWA it was well intended. Des-

---

123   Savage 1990, p. 165. Blizzard says the statewide total was 543 men (Blizzard 2005, p. 334) and Corbin reported 550 miners (Corbin 1997, p. 135). The figures for Logan do not appear to be included.

pite the Justice Department recommending a criminal indictment of Keeney, Blizzard, and others, President Harding quashed it for fear of implicating prominent Republicans in bed with the coal companies.[124]

As an irony of history, miners who had taken up arms to free themselves from waged slavery by coal capital were tried in the same courthouse in Charles Town where John Brown had been tried and hanged for treason in 1859 for attempting to spark a slave uprising at Harper's Ferry. It may never be known if the Miners' Army, marching into battle singing 'John Brown's Body', as did Union troops about 50 years earlier, understood the parallels.

The miners did miss a vital lesson that tied armed abolitionists to the Miners' Army. W.E.B. DuBois's argument that Reconstruction was defeated by the racism of white industrial workers who refused to connect their struggle with that of freedmen and women, was confirmed in the mines of West Virginia. Although about 12.5 percent of miners in Fairmont were black, for example, most historical and press reports made only anecdotal references to black members of the Miners' Army.

Savage provides the most detail of multi-racial cooperation among the Miners' Army. In describing its racial composition Savage says 'many were black', although he doesn't provide a specific number. However, he identified numerous instances of black miners actively recruiting men, raising money, serving as Chief Hatfield's deputies, giving speeches supporting the insurgency, being shot and killed, and filling the jails. In 1919, District 17 Vice President Bill Petry even shot Logan Sheriff Chafin when the sheriff had chased a black miner to the Charleston headquarters.[125] The Logan UMWA local had a black Vice President, George Echols, despite there only being about 150 black people in the area. A black preacher was a prominent speaker in Matewan at a rally in 1920 during which a miner addressed the shared bondage of black and white miners.[126] But these were the exception, not the rule. The effort to incorporate these workers was insufficient to fully recompose their power and overcome the mine companies.

Ultimately, 24 miners, UMWA officials, and the editor of the labour paper *The Federationist*, were selected to be tried for treason beginning in May 1922. The legal rationale for the prosecution was undermined by the near total capture of the state government and its subordination to the interests of the coal companies. At the trial, perhaps acknowledging his past mistakes in turning against

---

124   Green 2015, p. 284.

125   Savage 1990, pp. 4, 7–8, 35, 38, and 82. For example, he identified Ben Page as the only black miner jailed with Hatfield and the others after the Matewan battle.

126   Green 2015, p. 206.

the majority of his state's population, Governor Morgan testified that a private government with an army of mine guards existed but that he couldn't stop it. Laying the blame not only on the coal operators but, by implication, on himself, he said that

> If this condition exists it would seem that the treason prosecution should be against the organisers and maintainers of this private government rather than against the citizens of the state who went on the warpath to suppress it.[127]

Of course it was the Governor and his predecessor who had created the conditions for private government by imposing martial law, forming a new state police and re-activating the National Guard to enforce it, failing to prosecute crimes by police, troops, and vigilantes, and refusing to ban private police.

Morgan's assessment of the legitimacy of the miners' tactic of taking up arms was repeated by the Washington DC *Daily News* which wrote

> It looks as if the entire machinery of government in the state of West Virginia had been turned over to the coal operators, to be used as the operators see fit to use it, in their private war on the coal miners of that benighted state. West Virginia may earn the title of The Outlaw State.[128]

During the US Senate committee investigation into the strike, West Virginia Attorney General England testified that

> Now, so far as Logan County is concerned, I feel that the mine-guard system, as maintained there, is one, if not the greatest source of trouble in that particular county. That is on account more of possibly the excesses they commit.[129]

The state Attorney General and the final Senate committee report both confirmed Luke Grant's 1915 warning in his report to the Commission on Industrial Relations that the use of private guards is one of the factors that lead workers to escalate their tactics to defend themselves from violent repression.[130]

---

127 Blizzard 2005, p. 334.
128 See Blizzard 2005, pp. 335–6.
129 See England in US Senate 1922, p. 7.
130 Grant 1915a.

The treason trials appeared to be intended less to punish the guilty than redirect the efforts and resources of the miners and their union into a costly and exhausting legal proceeding that would hamper ongoing organising efforts, discourage them from considering further efforts at insurgency, and bring retaliation from the national UMWA leadership against District 17. A federal civil lawsuit asking for $1 million in damages for the 1919 strike was also filed against the UMWA and an attempt was made to attach the union's properties in Charleston and Beckley. The criminal prosecution and civil lawsuit not only tied up the resources and attention of the miners but fragmented their forces.

The media widely reported that the charges against Blizzard were predictably hypocritical. The *New York Evening World* observed that 'Attorneys for Blizzard might have claimed that crime charged was impossible, because no Government existed in West Virginia against which treason was possible'. *The New York Herald* agreed that 'In fact, Government in West Virginia had broken down, and its power had passed in part to the mine operators'. The *New York Times* also similarly observed that the miners' actions hardly necessitated the use of martial law enforced by US troops under Article IV, Section 4 of the US Constitution because 'Logan County can scarcely be said to have been under the rule of law or to have had a republican form of government. Private war was answered by private war'. The *New York World* joined in noting that 'It cannot be treason by any definition to rebel against a denial of constitutional guaranties'.[131]

The 'complete industrial autocracy' sucked the air out of any political space the miners might occupy to ply their grievances. Blizzard makes it clear that

> Striking coal miners had no rights. They were subject to the military. It was a SELECTIVE martial law, which applied only to one class of people: strikers and their representatives. The close tie between the coal operators and the state, county and municipal governments was now a naked thing, unclothed by democratic platitudes.[132]

The miners had no access to the polls, press, courts, legislature, or streets.

> They had for many years appealed to their elected representatives for some sort of justice. And they had seen these same representatives give aid and comfort to their enemies after the most demagogic of pre-election

---

131   See *The Literary Digest* 1922.
132   Blizzard 2005, p. 230, caps in original.

promises. The miners of West Virginia, after these years of neglect and oppression, had lost faith in the ability or willingness of any governing body to aid them in their fight for a decent life.[133]

Faced with these conditions, the miners opted to continue organising and build extensive mass support. Such support encouraged them to escalate their tactics despite the little promise of gains and the fatally high costs of doing so. As a writer for the *Independent* observed, 'These people took the law into their own hands because they believe that that is precisely what "the other side" has been doing for a long time'.[134] Any attempt to equate the use of violence by both capital and labour either ignores or distorts the reality that the war was between two highly mismatched forces engaged in asymmetrical warfare with the local, state, and federal governments solidly in the service of capital.

Blizzard remained the prime target of the prosecution and the coal companies despite his efforts to get the Miners' Army to de-escalate, de-mobilise, and retreat. In total, 1,600 witnesses were called as the treason trial continued throughout May 1922, costing the union $1,000 to $2,000 per day. The UMWA was on trial alongside the men. UMWA Vice President Philip Murray testified that the UMWA officially opposed the march.[135] At one point in the criminal proceeding the judge removed the jury from the room and did not enter into the record that the president of the Logan County Coal Operators Association had admitted it had spent $15,000 to finance the treason trial against Blizzard.

Two days after the trial ended, on 27 May 1922 the jury reported that it was deadlocked and acquitted Blizzard. Walter Allen was convicted of treason on 16 September 1922, sentenced to 10 years, appealed to the Supreme Court, and then disappeared while out on bail.

Blizzard and Keeney were also tried for murder in June 1923 and acquitted after a month long trial. Two miners convicted of killing a deputy in one of the Blair Mountain battles and sentenced to 11 years had their sentences commuted to five years by Governor Morgan in exchange for testifying against Blizzard and Keeney in their murder trial. The jury deadlocked on Blizzard and Keeney's trial was moved to another county and then dropped. The miners were eventually pardoned by Governor Gore.[136] It wasn't yet over for Blizzard who was tried yet

---

133   Blizzard 2005, p. 244.
134   *Independent*, 17 September 1921 in Corbin 1997, p. 110.
135   Murray rose through the ranks of the labour movement from UMWA Vice President to President of the United Steelworkers of America and the President of the CIO from 1942–52.
136   Blizzard 2005, p. 351.

a third time in August 1923 for attempting to bribe jurors in the first trial.[137] Once again, in March 1924, he was eventually acquitted.

The total number of indictments and prosecutions between 1920–4 were staggering, intended not only to destroy the union, but also to suffocate any thoughts of another miners' insurgency. Despite the legal deluge, few of those indicted were ever tried and of those who were convicted many had their sentences reduced or were pardoned. More than 20 union members were tried for murder for the killing of Baldwin-Felts agents in Matewan in 1920. Two tried in Pocahontas County for murder were freed when a hung jury resulted in a mistrial and the charges against the rest were eventually dropped after a time. 300 were indicted in Boone County and about 550 were indicted in Logan County for the Miners' Army war in 1921. Yet another 230 were indicted for the attack on the Cliftonville mine in Northern West Virginia in early 1922 and tried for treason, murder, inciting to murder, assault and other offences. Of all of those brought to trial, the majority were acquitted but about 41 pled guilty and were convicted. According to an October 1922 Associated Press report, at least 631 UMWA members were indicted for serious felonies including 411 for murder during the 1922 coal strike.[138] The miners finally got their day in court but it was not for redress of their grievances. It was to punish them for forcefully pursuing redress where none was available or offered.

Press accounts of the political conditions in West Virginia made the case for the Miners' Army insurgency. The state of West Virginia was under the plutocratic control of the coal companies whose elite coalition controlled nearly all local government, dominated the state legislature, and held the grip of executive police and military power. Although it sometimes lost court cases, such as the Supreme Court ruling on martial law, the coal operators had near total hegemonic control of the courts, even financing the treason trials and providing their attorneys as prosecutors.

Although the years of nearly endless trials wrecked District 17 of the UMWA, the miners won the supermajority of the cases in the courts if not the armed battles. It was a pyrrhic victory, however. The strategy of using the courts to prosecute insurgent workers originated during the 1877 national railroad strike when injunctions were used to break the leadership, tie up the union's financial resources, and deflect its focus to costly judicial proceedings.

In the face of the legal persecution, District 17 saw its treasury emptied, members flee in droves and its independence yanked by the UMWA. The strike

---

137   Perlman and Taft wrote that Blizzard was tried in May 1922. (Perlman and Taft 1935, p. 481).

138   Brown and Rice 1985, p. 232; and Witte 1932, p. 169.

was called off in 1922 by the UMWA executive committee after costing it $2 million. The $1.3 million spent on expenses was paid by a $1 increase in dues paid by the members to fund it.[139] District 17 has been bankrupted, many of its leaders resigned, more than 20 people had been killed, and many miners and their families continued living in the camps until jobs could be found for them in union coalfields.

As their troubles in the courts wound down, District 17's rank and file friendly leadership came into the sights of the UMWA's national leadership. In 1923, District 17 helped launched the Farmer-Labor Party in West Virginia that ran in opposition to the UMWA and AFL's alliance with the Democratic Party consummated during WWI. Their rank and file driven policies, tactical militancy, and attempt at political independence didn't sit well with the UMWA's national leadership. On 15 January 1923, UMWA President Lewis sent an assistant to assume control of District 17. It was apparently difficult but not impossible to do. On 17 June 1924, the UMWA revoked the District 17's autonomy and transferred power over the District to the national leadership. Two weeks later, on 30 June 1924, Keeney was removed as President. Blizzard was also removed from his position but kept on as a district organiser.

The combined military repression, criminal prosecutions, and internal UMWA disciplinary procedures decimated the UMWA in West Virginia. Membership in District 17 dropped from 42,000 in 1920–2 to about 1,000 between 1924–7, and to 512 by 1930. At the 23 June 1933 UMWA Charleston, West Virginia convention, there were 2,579 delegates from four states representing 160,000 miners in 728 locals with members in nearly every non-union coal mine. But as the result of UMWA's policy of suppressing District 17's independence, only 150 delegates came from Logan County. District 17 president Van Bittner, installed by the national UMWA, still advocated a policy of cooperation with management and opposed wildcat strikes.[140]

Outgunned by Industrial Autocracy

The miners did not merely lack political space for redress; it was completely out of the question. Plutocratic control at all levels raised the costs of both escalation and de-escalation as both promised total defeat. Despite the costs the miners persisted for decades to mobilise and deploy a strategy of tension not

---

139   Green 2015, p. 222.
140   *UMWA Journal*, 1 August 1933.

merely for self-defence but to disrupt the industry, raise the costs of autocratic control, and attempt to tip the balance of power back in their favour.[141]

In the face of capital's counter escalation, demobilising and disarming the miners came at dangerously high costs, the threat of total annihilation, and the elimination of all opportunities to achieve their gains in any way. Denied the promise of an arbitration commission, no opportunity to negotiate, unable to successfully advocate for their interests in the state legislature, and subject to martial law that made it illegal to advocate, assemble, and organise, the miners lived under an authoritarian state. After Matewan Mayor Testerman and Chief Hatfield were assassinated, the miners were left with virtually no local support in the counties where the strike was centred. To make matters worse, despite the strike the NWMA leadership provided them with minimal support and the District 17 leadership publicly did all it could to avoid confrontation.

The situation faced by the West Virginia miners was not new. The 1900–1903 national miners' strike put into place an internal division among miners that paralleled the industry. President Roosevelt's Interstate Disputes Commission 1903 ruling didn't recognise the UMWA and put into place a multi-tiered wage scale that purposefully benefitted anthracite miners while excluding much of the West Virginia fields. As a result, the UMWA was primarily focused on defending gains in the anthracite sector, thereby exacerbating the divisions among the miners. This was exemplified by UMWA President Mitchell's successful attempt to block the 1 April 1906 bituminous miners' strike from turning into a national strike and its capitulation the following month. Mitchell's disastrous leadership and the divisions among the rank and file he helped put into place made it difficult for the West Virginia miners not merely to obtain UMWA support for the strike in their own state but assistance and resources to circulate their strike to other states throughout the industry. The miners were on their own.

With District 17 decimated and the Miners' Army defeated, the coal operators were no longer confronted by militant workers. Between 1922–5, 50,000 miners were kicked out of company housing. As Blizzard succinctly concluded,

> The coal operators had won a complete victory in West Virginia. Through injunction, through supine and active government accomplices, through far-reaching court-action, through pistol and blackjack, the coal owners in the 1922–32 period virtually extirpated the United Mine Workers from West Virginia ...[142]

---

141   See *The Literary Digest* 1922, p. 14.
142   Blizzard 2005, p. 377.

After years of self-organising, the miners had little to show for their efforts, finding themselves in virtually the same position as when their last cycle of struggle had begun. They faced both a hostile union and authoritarian repression from the combined forces of the mine companies and local, state, and federal power. The same two tiered agreement the West Virginia miners rebelled against was still in place. On 16 February 1924 the UMWA and Central Competitive Field coal operators of Ohio, Indiana, Illinois, and only Western Pennsylvania signed the concessionary Jacksonville Florida agreement to extend the 1920 wage scale another three years – once again excluding the miners of West Virginia from the agreement.[143]

The West Virginia miners' defeat had unmistakable causes. They escalated their tactics without being able to adequately recompose their power by circulating their struggle throughout the entire state, to the the mines outside their state, and into other sectors. Isolated geographically, opposed by the combined forces of the state, capital, local political elites, and their own national and local union leadership, the miners escalated to armed warfare when the costs were extremely high and the opportunity to achieve any gains were low.

Despite the near total control of the coal industry by the absentee US Steel trust, the Senate Committee report predictably blamed both sides for the violence. But the blame could not be applied equally when the mine owners had the balance of power of most of the local government officials, the state, federal government, US troops, and the courts behind them. Living under martial law the miners had only mass support and their willingness to escalate their tactics to assert their demands. But the Senate Committee report also surprisingly concurred with the newspapers and the miners' claim that they lacked a reasonable expectation for successfully achieving any redress of their grievances in the current state political conditions. Putting it bluntly, committee chair Senator Kenyon concluded that 'There is complete industrial autocracy in this country' and among the worst examples was the state of West Virginia.[144]

Among the evidence Kenyon cited to establish his claim of autocracy was evidence from a 1919 investigative committee appointed by Governor Cornwell. The committee found that the Logan County Coal Operator Association paid Logan County Sheriff Chafin $32,700 to station 500 reserve deputy sheriffs on coal company property to prevent union members from entering the county, protect private property, collect rents, and other duties.[145] Chafin received one-third to one-half a cent on every ton of coal mined on the Guyan River and later

---

143   Ibid., p. 368.

144   US Senate 1922, p. 7.

145   These figures came from a 1919 investigative committee appointed by Governor John

disclosed his wealth to be more than $300,000.[146] Such schemes were an 'exercise of public power under private pay which is one of the fundamental causes and is the most lively occasion of the bad blood between owners and workers'.[147]

Despite the committee condemnation 'on the ground that no officer should receive money or remuneration from any source other than the state or county', Governor Cornwell assured journalist Lane that he lacked the authority to stop it. Lane found that despite a state law explicitly prohibiting public law enforcement officers from working for and being paid by private companies, there was no penalty for doing so. While prosecution was still possible the political will to do so was missing.[148]

Ultimately, the private use of state armed power to its own advantage provided ample evidence that access to the polity was not only closed, but that it was being wielded against the miners. Lane captures this precisely when he concludes that 'the mine workers of West Virginia regard the payment of the salaries of these deputies by the operators as an attempt to use the agencies of government against them'.[149]

As Savage succinctly observes, 'the mine war was fought not only with gunfire in the mountains; it was also fought with lawsuits and injunctions'.[150] With a few exceptions, the state courts were also at the disposal of the coal companies. After 32 coal companies in McDowell County and 14 in Mercer County were denied an injunction by Mercer County Circuit Court Judge I.C. Herndon

---

Cornwell to investigate the mining industry in Logan County. The committee issued a reportedly unpublished report more than 600 pages long of which there appears to be only one remaining copy in the archives of the Logan County Operators Association. (See Lane 1921, pp. 52–3; and Special Investigation by the State of West Virginia, Hearings at Charleston, West Va. Sept. 30 and Oct. 1, 2, 1919) Lane also published excerpts of unverified notes from Albert Felts after he was killed in the May 1920 gun battle in Matewan given to him by Chief Hatfield. These notes document an effort to similarly put Chief Hatfield, Mayor Testerman, and Sheriff Blankenship on the payroll of the coal companies. The notes propose creating a dispute between these officials and the miners and order to divide them and pit them against one another. (Lane 1921, pp. 74–9).

146   Green reported the figure as $30,000. The figure is likely much higher due to the percentage paid to Chafin for each ton mined and that two years later the Logan County Coal Operator Association's treasurer reported still paying Chafin the same amount. (See Lane 1921, pp. 53–4; Savage 1990, p. 82; Corbin 1997, pp. 97–8; and Green 2015, p. 183).
147   See Gleason in Corbin 1997, p. 97.
148   Lane 1921, pp. 54–5.
149   Ibid., p. 56.
150   Savage 1990, p. 36.

they successfully appealed the state supreme court which granted them and awarded legal costs to the companies to be paid by the UMWA.

The basis for their injunction was the Supreme Court precedent set by the 1917 *Hitchman Coal & Coke Co. v. Mitchell* case barring unions from communicating with or attempting to organise workers who had signed yellow dog contracts such as the one used by the Pocahontas Operators Association which covered McDowell and Mercer Counties. It should be remembered that US Steel was the absentee owner of the largest coal companies in the Pocahontas field through its interlocking directorships as well as the largest producer of coal in the state. Similar injunctions were granted in the fall by federal courts to the Red Jacket Consolidated Coal and Coke Company in Mingo County and the Pond Creek Coal Company in Williamson. In the latter case Federal District Judge Edmund Waddill banned the union from even posting flyers or posters anywhere in the state or elsewhere announcing a strike in the Pond Creek field. The *Hitchman* case, stemming from a case against UMWA President Mitchell, continued to pay dividends to the industry for years.[151]

In 1903 UMWA Vice President T.L. Lewis pointed out that the strategic value of the injunction for the companies is that it shifts the costs of fighting the class struggle to government, a struggle paradoxically funded by tax dollars paid by workers. The injunction, Lewis warned, is

> the most dangerous weapon ever brought into existence because of its sweeping character; the most effective in its application because it is used in the name of the law; the most destructive to labor's interests because there seems to be no appeal from the decisions of the individual judges who issue the injunction; the least expensive to the employers of labor because the official representatives of the Government enforce the provisions of the injunction.[152]

The mine operators also used the courts to attack the union's support for striking miners. One case was resolved in April 1922 when the US Court of Appeals stayed an earlier ruling by US District Judge McLintock who had ordered the

---

151   Lane 1921, pp. 65–70 and 72; and Savage 1990, pp. 36–7. Savage set the number of companies at 47.

152   In Lane 1921, p. 73. After serving as UMWA president for four years, Lewis went to work for the coal companies becoming Secretary of the New River Coal Operator's Association in West Virginia. (See Lane 1921, pp. 97 and 102).

union to stop relief payments to the striking miners and disband their tent camps in 30 days.[153]

Unchecked private power wasn't just limited to local law enforcement. It was woven into every aspect of life in the company towns. What some called welfarism Lane called a 'paternalistic, semi-feudal, regime' that ran the state. Lane observed corporate domination analogous to the Pullman town outside Chicago described in Chapter 4 in which

> the operators are not only the miner's employer; they are his landlord, his merchant, the provider of his amusements, the sanitary officer of his town, sometimes the source of his police protection and the patron of his physician, his minister, and his school teacher.[154]

For example, the Logan County Superintendent of Schools allowed the coal companies to pay part of the teachers' salaries and build schoolhouses by providing an advance that was repaid by the school districts, and loaned out their company doctors for services in the schools. The Island Creek Coal Company superintendent paid for teachers, play structures, and school milk. It also funded the YMCA, constructed and financed all the churches for blacks and whites, and paid the salaries of five deputies.[155] Because the miners were not paid in all cash, as required by law, but company script, the companies 'checked off' the goods and services from miners' pay, often leaving them hopelessly indebted as the price of the goods rose faster than their pay.[156]

Since the courts had upheld the property rights of the coal companies which allowed them to evict miners as soon as they stopped working for them, in effect, 'one-fourth of the adult males in West Virginia, comprising a labor force of a basic industry, have no security of residence' and do not own their own homes. The houses are built upon precarious spots between the mines throughout the mountains, are monotonous in design and linearly arranged, lack running water, and set on unpaved muddy roads.[157]

Lane rightly questioned whether these could be called 'towns' at all since the people who lived in them

---

153   Brecher 1972, p. 153; and Perlman and Taft 1935, p. 481.
154   Lane 1921, pp. 17, 22, and 31.
155   Ibid., p. 22; and Gleason in Corbin 1997, p. 11.
156   An 1891 state law amended an earlier 1887 law to allow script as 'a promise to pay' in lawful money although a state official condemned its continued use as illegal. The penalty was also made a misdemeanour. (See Lane 1921, pp. 27–8).
157   Ibid., pp. 17, 22, and 31–2.

live here to work. The communities exist for the coal mines. They are the adjuncts and necessary conveniences of an industry. They are not independent groups of people. They are not even called towns in the language of the locality. They are called 'camps'.[158]

As such, the people who live in them have no political space to speak of. Because they own no property, run no businesses, or have any wealth they have no influence on the local elected officials and no possibility of exercising their civil liberties and rights. The companies not only controlled security but free assembly, association, and movement:

> it takes care of the roads, provides the lighting ... it can exercise supervision over persons coming into the town and events there. It can keep undesirable people out. It can, if it wants to, even censor the mail, since the Post Office is usually located in its general store and one of its employees is Postmaster.

In this way, the coal companies functioned as private government by subjecting the state to a corporate totalitarianism in which, as Hannah Arendt defined such systems, the companies functioned as 'parties above parties'.[159]

The ubiquitous presence of the coal companies in all aspects of life raises several questions. Was the companies' embrace of welfarism a response to the unruly mine workers and their willingness to use armed struggle to disrupt the industry and the state? What role did welfarism play in supplementing low wages as a means to control, discipline, and socialise the miners and their communities? How much did the companies profit by replacing higher wages for charity? Such patronage certainly bought the acquiescence of local leaders who otherwise feared the loss of needed resources if they spoke up, costing the miners a potentially influential ally in their struggle.

Union Misleadership

Although the Miners' Army had widespread mass support in the counties where the strike was underway, which helped them recruit allies and resources to the redneck army, they were far too isolated not only geographically in

---

158   Ibid., pp. 21–2.
159   Arendt 1958, p. 38.

the mountainous terrain but also the perilous political and class terrain. The UMWA did not serve as a conduit to help mobilise mass support both inside and outside the state, circulate the struggle throughout the industry and into the related industrial iron, steel, railroad, and banking sectors. Rather, the union leadership served to block, dampen, deflect, and diffuse their attempts to intensify their tactics in order to build a firewall around the rest of the UMWA membership in the anthracite fields. While the union was invaluable during the later criminal prosecutions its efforts to demobilise and de-escalate the West Virginia miners only made the judicial counter-attack and corporate totalitarian domination of the state worse. The UMWA leadership is one of the main reasons the miners were defeated in West Virginia.

Like the International Association of Bridge and Structural Iron Workers (IABSIW) more than a decade earlier, the UMWA was unwilling to allow the workers to recompose their power to confront the conditions of struggle posed by the new composition of capital. Despite the available evidence, the union was either unaware or did not address how many of the supposedly isolated coal fields had already been consolidated under the control of US Steel.

The existing organisation of capitalist forces had them out-strategised and out-gunned. The linkage between the IABSIW and the UMWA was even more tangible. The 1921 US Senate Committee on Education and Labor report on the West Virginia coal mine strikes thoroughly documented 'the domination of the West Virginia scene in 1921 by United States Steel' which was extracting the wealth of the state as an absentee owner. Samuel Untermyer, former counsel for the 1912–13 Congressional Pujo Sub-Committee of the House Committee on Banking and Currency, testified that US Steel's 'fingerprints ... are all over' West Virginia.[160]

By 1920 US Steel had become the absentee owner of 380,000 acres of coal fields in Logan and Mingo Counties and leased land in McDowell County indirectly through its interlocking directorates and subsidiaries. Morgan controlled the Girard Trust Company and the Norfolk & Western Railroad (owned through interlocking directorates and stocks holdings by the Pennsylvania Railroad) which owned nearly the entire Pocahontas Coal & Coke Company, which itself owned about 295,000 acres, or about four-fifths, of that field, and produced 5 million tons per year. By 1918, the Pocahontas field, primarily located in McDowell and Mercer Counties in West Virginia, was the largest coal supplier in the state, producing 4.7 million tons. But the Pocahontas Coal & Coke Company didn't mine the coal directly but rather leased the lands to more than 25

---

160   US Senate 1921, p. 705.

coal mining companies and collected royalties on the lands. Many of the lessees were fellow subsidiaries of US Steel.[161]

Lane also identified an additional 256,496 acres owned by US Steel in 1919 in these and nearby counties and states. He documented US Steel owning 53,736 acres of coking coal land and 32,648 acres of surface land in Logan and Mingo Counties, and 74,344 acres of coking land and 32,002 acres of surface coal land in nearby Letcher and Harlan Counties in Kentucky. It also leased 63,766 acres through its Illinois Steel Company subsidiary in the Pocahontas field in McDowell and Wyoming Counties and Tazewell County, Virginia. Its United States Coal Company subsidiary employed 3,888 miners in 11 mines on the 50,000 acres it leased in McDowell, making it the largest coal company in West Virginia. US Steel disclosed its control of the McDowell County coal lands at its first annual meeting on 17 February 1902.[162]

Whatever the total acreage US Steel controlled in Logan, Mingo, McDowell and nearby counties and states, it was clear that US Steel controlled the coal industry in West Virginia. If there was a general directing its troops from a distant command centre, it was US Steel. 46 companies in the Pocahontas field cooperated in order to obtain an injunction under the Hitchman precedent to ban UMWA organisers from their mines. Logan County Sheriff Chafin was a paid agent of the coal companies, commanding a repressive badge wearing paramilitary force against the miners. The state deployed a new state police and National Guard and was backed up by the US Army. The companies mobilised and obtained local, state, and federal force to support them under the auspices of US Steel. Although the story of the role US Steel played in coordinating this strategic response has yet to be written, it was always there.

The UMWA was quite aware of the dominant, if absentee, role played by US Steel, which had been well-documented by several investigative journalists and the Senate Kenyon committee. Jett Lauck, an economist who consulted for the UMWA, noted the impact of US Steel's dominance of the state:

> It is also apparent that this colossus, while extending its holdings and control of coal lands in and around this district, is at the same time, extending to this district its labor policy of crushing labor unions. This is the guiding hand behind the effort to crush out the mine workers' organization in Mingo County. These interests are refusing the mine worker the right of collective bargaining.[163]

---

161   US Senate 1921, pp. 706–7; Lane in Corbin 1997, p. 6; and Blizzard 2005, pp. 252–6.
162   Lane 1921, pp. 119–21.
163   In Ibid., p. 122.

The failure or refusal of the UMWA to effectively respond to this extensive consolidation of the industry under the control of US Steel left the West Virginia miners strategically out-manoeuvred. The miners could not hope to win without circulating their struggle to miners elsewhere in the coal and other industries to match or exceed capital's efforts to do the same. Because US Steel was capital's new strategic organising model the miners and other workers needed to counter with a new strategy of their own that circulated the struggle throughout the vertically integrated coal and into the steel, bridge, railroads, and banking industries in order to check the company.

The UMWA did cooperate with the railroad brotherhoods a few years earlier in 1919 but it wasn't to coordinate disruption. The UMWA had formed a committee to meet with them to figure out how to help them achieve nationalisation of the railroad in the Plumb plan and then later piggybacked it by advocating that the federal government also nationalise the coal industry. The unions were under the impression that removing the profit motive would bring about 'industrial peace' through collective bargaining.[164] These plans were predicated on the assumption that the unions could achieve their objectives without a class struggle that would transform class relations. But without the leverage of class struggle to impose them, these legislative shortcuts were never on the agendas of the federal government and the industries.

Escalating their tactics in one region of the bituminous coal sector alone was insufficient. The miners were carrying out their struggle without the participation of the rest of the coal miners in other states who were covered by the US Bituminous Coal Commission award and received little initial support from the UMWA leadership. The strike was called for Mingo County and the struggle limited to only three counties in West Virginia and one county in Kentucky, because about half of the miners in West Virginia were already working under contracts. The insurgency took place in the aftermath of the post-war Red Scare and absorption of the AFL as a disciplinary weapon (as described in Chapters 8 and 9) that had severely decomposed the working-class's power everywhere else. The Miners' Army was alone.

In contrast, the coal companies were well organised. One indicator of the level of coordination and cooperation among the coal companies were the county level coal operators associations. For example, the Williamson Operators' Association assessed its members ten cents per ton to pay the costs of the anti-strike campaign. As discussed below, other operators' associations also financed the salary and costs of a local sheriff, prosecutions of UMWA dis-

---

164   *The Nation*, 27 September 1919, p. 425.

trict officials and members, and the legal costs of obtaining court injunctions. Ultimately, this corporate 'mutual aid' funded the components of an offensive strategy that did more than merely fight the miners to a 'standstill' but injected the US Army into the struggle that defeated the insurgency.[165]

Whether the UMWA didn't know or knew and refused to act on this raises questions as to its catastrophic misleadership of the own rank and file. By continuing to accept separate deals for the anthracite and bituminous sub-sectors of the industry under the pretext of protecting gains in the former, the UMWA was undermining the interests of all its members. The UMWA had been making a series of tactical and strategic blunders that not only caused defeats for striking miners but decades of destitution, legal and political persecution, and loss of life. It is no wonder that the West Virginia miners continued to self-organise as long as they did. What is even more startling is that they survived to relaunch their struggle again and again for decades.

Full of Sound and Fury

And all our yesterdays have lighted fools
The way to dusty death. Out, out, brief candle!
Life's but a walking shadow, a poor player
That struts and frets his hour upon the stage
And then is heard no more: it is a tale
Told by an idiot, full of sound and fury,
Signifying nothing.
SHAKESPEARE, *MacBeth*[166]

The outcome of the miners' war can be understood by the dynamic interplay between the four factors based on Tilly's 'facilitation curve' I call IOMO (see Chapters 2 and 7):

I: interests
O: organisation
M: mobilisation
O: opportunity

---

165   Lane 1921, pp. 126–7.
166   Shakespeare 1606.

Tilly uses these four factors to identify how elites and insurgents will deploy the appropriate tactics (what he refers to as 'mobilisation'), and build mass support ('organisation') in order to take advantage of opportunities to realise ('facilitate') their objectives ('interests'). These options exist along the facilitation curve by which contenders move along the continuum in relation to one another depending on conditions, responses, evaluation of previous organisation and mobilisation, and their effectiveness.

For Tilly, there is a dynamic interplay between the presence and level of mass support and the potential for tactical escalation. The question of whether a tactic is appropriate depends on where insurgents feature on what Tilly calls the 'repression curve'.[167] Insurgents with little power are more likely to face repression because they are a greater threat than those with no power. However, the more powerful insurgents are, the slower elites will escalate their tactics and the more likely they will be to make concessions.

A weak insurgency presents little to no risk to the elite coalition that it will escalate its tactics to achieve workers' objectives. Insurgents will fail to obtain sufficient mass support and an opportunity to gain by escalating their tactics because of the overwhelming perception of inevitable defeat and will de-escalate. Inversely, a strong insurgency with widespread mass support is more likely to escalate its tactics.

However, the West Virginia miners' strike presented another possible variation on the interplay between mass support and escalation. The Miners' Army had widespread mass support in the counties where it was best organised, obtained the necessary resources, and included WWI war veterans to provide the necessary military training and strategy.

Herein lies the problem. The character of its widespread mass support was also its weakness. The miners' mass support originated from an extremely limited geographical space and as such they were subjected to the same kind of forces of repression as the miners. Supporters from outside the area were scarce because the miners' geographical isolation and the lack of support from from the UMWA leadership prevented them from mobilising outside their region of the state and the state itself, not to mention the rest of the coal industry. The Miners' Army had wide mass support but in itself was insufficient to lower the costs and increase the opportunity for achieving gains by intensifying their tactics.

Although the strike spread outward through other parts of the state and the nation, the West Virginia Miners' Army simply lacked the organisational

---

167   See Fig. 4.6 in Tilly 1978, p. 113.

capacity to facilitate further mobilisation and circulate the struggle sufficiently to make the armed struggle successful. For example, in Brooke County, West Virginia, strikers launched attacks on the mine, killed several including the sheriff, and closed the mine for two months. Their efforts failed when it was reopened as a non-union mine guarded by private agents, the sheriff, and a squad of deputies. Nonunion miners also struck in Pennsylvania and Indiana and carried out dynamiting, bombings, and derailed coal trains. In Scofield, Utah strikers blocked trains carrying strikebreakers, set an engine house and company houses on fire, and carried out sniper attacks on private agents and strikebreakers. The miners in these states were repressed by a combination of the National Guard, martial law, and suppression of civil liberties necessary to continue mobilising. Ultimately, these efforts were too scattered, fragmented, and disconnected to adequately circulate the West Virginia miners' insurgency nationwide.

If all of Tilly's facilitation curve factors that would have made the miners' armed struggle promising were insufficient, why did they escalate along the trajectory? Did they merely take up arms out of anger or fear as a last resort? Were they prompted to use guns because everyone already had guns and community restorative 'vigilante justice' was common in the rural, nearly stateless areas?

We need to look elsewhere to understand why the miners escalated despite lacking the necessary organisational capacity, dispersed mass support, and opportunity to gain from doing so. McAdam suggests a weak insurgency may be forced to escalate because it lacks the necessary leverage to force elites to negotiate. It may be, as McAdam explains, that a 'fundamental powerlessness *within* institutionalized channels that led insurgents to abandon "proper channels" in the first place'.[168] This certainly describes the miners' predicament. Since they lacked access to the polity and any possibility to arbitrate, compromise, and negotiate, they bypassed normal politics. Relying on extra-institutionalised forms of politics allowed the miners to intensify their tactics to make the insurgency a more effective threat of disruption in order to destabilise the extremely valuable bituminous mine fields and overturn the existing balance of power in the state.

However, escalating tactics without a sufficient mass base of supporters to dampen the threat of repression raised its costs. When elites escalated, the miners lacked sufficient mass support to further escalate nationwide.

---

168   McAdam 1999, p. 58.

The miners were politically marginalised from the elite coalition both inside and outside the state. As a result there was no risk of elites losing resources or allies by repressing them or outside intervention by the federal government or prominent supporters. Tactical escalation did not result in any compromise, concessions, or reform because force alone proved to be a sufficient low cost response to the insurgency. Even after the media denunciations of the deluge of treason trials and the US Senate committee investigation, there was little cost to maintaining plutocratic domination. In fact, the coal operators and their elite allies gained from the repression by nearly wiping out the UMWA in the state for a decade, keeping wages low and profits high.

With no local allies, few sympathetic local officials, and the balance of power overwhelmingly aligned against them there was no possibility of compromise and concessions through negotiations. Such autocratic conditions of life in the state made change impossible because it created 'the situation of an irresistible force meeting an immovable body', wrote Senator Kenyon in his own concluding remarks, published with the committee report.[169]

The union confirmed Kenyon's denunciation of conditions in the state. According to the UMWA brief submitted to the committee, the problem was less economic warfare than the absence of political space for the miners to exercise their right to free speech and assembly.

> The problem in West Virginia is not a question of unionism versus non-unionism, but is a question of the establishment, acceptance, and observance of fundamental principles and practices which are essential to peace and orderly progress in all industry.[170]

Drawing on the assumption of shared interests, the union noted that such conditions ran counter not only to the interests of the miners but of the industry itself.

> Conditions in the non-union fields of West Virginia and the controversy there constitute a menace to the public welfare, prevent the stabilization and orderly development of the entire bituminous coal industry, and tend to foment discord and unrest in all industry.[171]

---

169   US Senate 1921, pp. 4 and 7.
170   See UMWA in US Senate 1921, p. 4.
171   Ibid.

With the union on both sides, the miners could not have expected it to act exclusively in their interests. The conditions for achieving any gains from demobilising and de-escalating did not exist. If there was little expectation of gaining from tactical escalation, there was a certainty of continued losses by de-escalating.

The previous chapters examined why insurgents demobilised and de-escalated in order to arbitrate and negotiate, resulting in the splitting of the insurgent rank and file from a newly formed leadership that is co-opted, institutionalised, and legitimised into the existing dominant relations of power. When insurgents have sufficient mass support to become disruptive they not only become tolerated but 'as the power of a particular group rises – as, for example, it actually becomes identical with the government – the range of collective actions denied to it eventually dwindles to nothingness'.[172] Once at the table, the interests of insurgent leaders become intertwined with elites and their opportunity to achieve their previous objectives decline. In order to deliver both to their new allies and the rank and file, insurgent leaders must allow the interests of elites to take precedence over their previous objectives, because their ability to achieve any gains is harnessed to the fortunes of the dominant group. As we saw in Chapter 8, this is what the AFL experienced during WWI. As it was absorbed into the big tent of the Democratic Party and harnessed to the labour planning state, the AFL leadership found its objectives shift and the range of possible collective action shrink.

Such is the paradoxical axiom of insurgency: the ability to use a strategy of tension to cause disruption leads to insurgents being invited to demobilise and de-escalate to achieve some of their objectives. To achieve reform a successful insurgency must abandon the insurgency. Yet, the paradox only applies for objectives short of overthrowing the existing state of things and replacing it with a new system.

Insurgents must evaluate the IOMO factors to assess the returns on their continued mobilisation and escalation. At what point will the opportunity to take advantage of their mass support to achieve their objectives peak and continued escalation become more costly? Tilly illustrates how insurgents can de-escalate in the face of the threat of escalating repression to defend existing gains or continue to escalate at some point when the returns begin to decline.[173]

But what if there are no gains to defend?

172   Tilly 1978, pp. 113–14.
173   See Fig. 4.6 in Ibid., p. 113.

There is also the possibility that insurgents escalate even when lacking sufficient mass support and without an apparent opportunity to achieve gains, such as in West Virginia. Insurgents may instead be seeking to preserve something intangible they already possess or assert something intangible that they lack. Because the Miners' Army was the armed citizen's militia of the strikers and their families who had been evicted from their homes, taking up arms was necessary to assure their own safety from vigilantes, private police, and deputies shooting at their tent camps. Deploying their arms was a show of strength that supported their strike action. Lacking sufficient local allies and indifference and even interference from their union, making an organised public display of their fire power was more than a mere symbolic expression of their strength. Because they put to work the experience of WWI combat to repeatedly go on the defensive, they transformed the strike into a workers' armed uprising to disrupt and push back the plutocratic powers that terrorised that part of the state. The killings of despised local sheriffs and deputies in self-defence represented a parallel system of class justice in the absence of a legitimate local judiciary dispensing the law consistently. Because it was rooted in and defending a specific territory the redneck army transcended its status as a citizen's militia to become a guerrilla army playing a similar self-defence role as a national liberation struggle. They were not merely asserting an abstract notion of dignity or humanity, as Fanon described the motive for the Algerian insurgents, but pursued the tangible objectives of security for the strikers and their communities and a deterrent that raised the costs of further repression by elites.

It is worth exploring this last point in more detail. The cost of repression was not cheap. Deputy sheriffs and elected officials were injured and killed along with strikers. Local governments and counties were so short of money the prosecutions had to be funded by loans from the coal operators and staffed by their attorneys. Production was severely disrupted, pushing down revenues and profits. Mining equipment, housing, and other capital assets were damaged or destroyed. While no estimate of the total costs to the state from years of class warfare has been published, it was likely substantial. The US Bituminous Coal Commission reported that the price of coal was rising fast partly due to the strikes since 1916, which may have been driven by declining supply and rising costs inflicted by the miners.[174] The costs of repression are rarely born by the insurgents when disruption, sabotage, coordinating attacks, and armed struggle are used by insurgents.

---

174   Emmet 1924, p. 1.

While escalation may bring increasing gains, there is a break-even line after which the return on the costs of escalation (opportunity) begin to decline as the threat increases. In this case insurgents must decide whether to continue escalating for potentially more gains or demobilise to protect existing gains. As the level of threat grows, Tilly argues, escalation becomes less intense and lasts for a shorter duration.[175] Higher threat of repression and costs may lead challengers to not escalate as intensely or for very long and begin to de-escalate earlier and quicker. Inversely, when the threat of repression and costs are lower challengers may escalate more intensely and for longer in the expectation of increased gains.

Here again, the Miners' Army presents another scenario in which the rising level of the threat, expectation of rising costs, and no expectation of making tangible gains didn't shorten the duration of mobilisation and escalation but actually lengthened it. With no alternative source of security from either local, state, and the federal governments or their own union the Miners' Army became a working-class security force in reserve to be re-deployed as the threat and costs rose.

The Miners' Army again defies Tilly's attempt to use his general theory of contention to explain the relationship between escalation and outcomes and between escalation, threat, and expected costs. Without a detailed analysis of the class composition of elites and workers and the conditions in which workers launch their insurgency, it may not be possible to explain why insurgents will rapidly intensify their tactics to armed struggle even when it seems hopeless.

Without an examination of the conditions in which insurgents struggle, it becomes difficult to assess the relationship between escalation, the level of threat, outcomes, or the IOMO factors on Tilly's facilitation curve. It is unclear why the gains of continued escalation would necessarily decline. It could be argued that the Miners' Army continued its escalation even as the threat level rose in order to obtain more security than they otherwise had. Security is hard to measure since it is a combination of perception, feelings, well-being, and other tangible and intangible factors.

Why would insurgents postpone escalation when the returns are rising? Here Tilly appears to assume that insurgents seek concessions that will allow them to demobilise and de-escalate rather than continue escalating to achieve gains that would provoke elite breakdown and a revolutionary crisis. For example, in Seattle the shipyard workers escalated their strike into a general strike

---

175   See Fig. 5.1 in Tilly 1978, p. 150.

until the threat level rose from elites assembling their forces. It is likely they realised that without circulating the general strike throughout the country they would be crushed. Taking over the city and running it themselves was their objective. They tasted what a post-capitalist society might be like by doing it – even if only for a brief moment.

By portraying de-escalation as bottoming out on the other side of the 'bell' shaped curve, Tilly's facilitation curve assumes that continued escalation will never lead to an indefinite continuing increase in returns. In effect, the assumption is that the only rational decision is *when* to de-escalate, not *whether*. The facilitation curve is a dead end; it assumes no way out of the existing relations of power, i.e. a revolution, despite the title of his book *From Mobilization to Revolution*. Rupturing the dialectic of the existing system of capital's power relations is not possible in Tilly's theory of contention.

This means Tilly doesn't consider what happens when insurgents escalate when costs are high and de-escalate later or not at all. A group may be very popular because it is providing effective armed self-defence against forces of repression and is able to attract more mass support and recruits and resources even when the threat of repression and costs are high. This was certainly the case during the several rounds of strikes in West Virginia when, despite overt repression and continued rising threat of escalated repression, miners continued to both build mass support and escalate their tactics. It is also a common outcome in countries under repressive plutocracies such as Colombia and Sri Lanka, military juntas such as El Salvador and Guatemala in the 1970s to the present, and foreign military occupations such as Afghanistan, Iraq, and Palestine.

Making system change the objective of an insurgency arrays all the forces of the dominant order against it. As AFL President Gompers suggested while observing the 1913 coal strikes, system change raises fundamental questions about the threat of blurred economic and political and public and private power to representative democracy. He asked us to consider a future of corporate totalitarianism, a question even more relevant to us today:

> In short, the coal operators who own this section of the state arrogate to themselves all rights of government except such as must be conceded to the county. To make the situation more vivid and forcible, take another illustration. Suppose the United States Steel Corporation had been in existence in 1800 and had realised the value of the Louisiana Territory. The purchase price the United States paid for that territory would have presented no difficulties to the United States Steel Corporation. After purchasing that immense tract of land, approximately nine hundred thou-

sand square miles in extent, what would have been the property rights of the corporation? Would the Steel Corporation have been permitted the absolute unrestricted right of government over that vast territory, controlling municipal affairs, sanitation, police, locomotion, the privilege of assemblage, the erection of churches and school-houses, and the control of doctrines and theories taught by schools and churches? The difference in the size of the two territories does not affect the underlying principle.[176]

The Senate committee report still blamed the union for 'indefensible' treasonable actions despite the autocratic political conditions Gompers warned about, in which the reins of government at all levels were in the hands of the coal operators and all forms of political action and participation were denied to the miners. As Senator Kenyon pointed out,

> That members of the United Mine Workers have done acts of violence in this Mingo controversy cannot be disputed. Many of their acts are absolutely indefensible. Men have been killed, property had been destroyed, telephone wires cut, trains commandeered and misused, and a march of some thousands of men organised and policies carried out which bordered close on insurrection against government, and other things that are entitled to the most emphatic condemnation.[177]

Here Kenyon follows the same line of thinking that led the General Managers Association to deflect and reframe the 1894 railroad strike from an insurgency against the railroads into an insurrection against the US government. By reframing the war against capital into a war on the US government itself, the committee provided a rationale to justify the US government coming to the defence of the autocratic coal operators while trying to avoid actually doing so. It was indisputable that

> The intensity of the violence in Southern West Virginia can be traced to the oppressive, exploitative nature of life and work in the coal fields there. The heart of that authoritarian system was the company town.[178]

---

176   See Gompers in Corbin 1997, p. 18.
177   See Kenyon in US Senate, 1921, p. 7.
178   Corbin 1997, p. 1.

Gompers had insightfully identified the fundamental danger to democracy that has existed since the founding of a country with an economic system based on the ownership of people as commodities, its constitution written so as to give slaveowners disproportionate power and a minority veto. We continue to grapple with the fundamental dilemma of corporations becoming more powerful than the government and the people who presumably provide the consent to be governed. Today, we are faced with new variations on the plutocratic autocracy the Miners' Army sought to destroy, which appear as corporate rule over specific geographical spaces such as 'free trade zones', 'charter cities', 'charter schools', gated communities, and multinational corporations with civil and international rights of personhood unchecked by the democratic self-government of the people. Today, we all risk living in West Virginia of 1921.

Armed Struggle in a Democracy

The Battle of Blair Mountain has attracted growing interest in the past decade, as we approach the 100-year anniversary of the Miners' Army insurgency. It appears startling to observers of American history that anyone would be compelled to take up arms in a functioning representative democracy. It not only seems extreme but counter-productive in a system in which the myth of peaceful progress shapes tactics, strategy, and objectives of elites and insurgents alike, creating the same set of rules and expectations by which groups and classes with a vast disparity of power must operate.

Tilly suggests that weak insurgents are more likely to achieve their gains in what he calls 'high capacity' democratic regimes because they are more likely to make concessionary overtures to them.[179] But such overtures are coercive because insurgents are too weak to either continue mobilising and escalating or de-mobilising and de-escalating.

> The facilitation curve tells us that even relatively powerless groups receive incentives to carry out certain highly acceptable collective actions; the result of that circumstance is to squeeze the range of collective action on the part of slightly powerful groups which is simply tolerated: either they can't do it or they must do it. As a result, relatively powerless groups find their world more totalitarian than do the powerful or the completely powerless.[180]

---

179   Tilly 2003, pp. 47–54.
180   Tilly 1978, p. 114.

In other words, such regimes have little to lose by acceding to some concessions to remove the low cost threat from weak insurgents.

But Tilly's observation is unsatisfactory because it fails to explain two other
issues. First, why do high capacity democratic regimes (the term is plagued
by an unacknowledged 'democracy exceptionalism') resort to repressing even
weak insurgencies? There is no shortage of examples of the US or European
democratic governments, systems Tilly assigns to this category, repressing
movements of women, students, minorities, and workers. Tilly's observation
is also insufficient in explaining why weak insurgencies with little or no mass
support escalate rather than negotiate and compromise. Here again, there are
many examples of militant groups engaged in armed struggle in these same
high capacity democratic regimes. Armed struggle seems incompatible with
democracy, but it still happens; Tilly's facilitation curve is silent on the reasons.

According to Tilly, how elites respond is shaped by the type of state under
which they function. 'Low capacity' regimes are incapable of preventing dissidents from mobilising publicly while also being unwilling or incapable of
engaging in co-optation through negotiations.[181] As a result, such regimes are
likely to escalate rapidly and deploy violence against nonviolent protests and
other claim-making groups. In such regimes insurgents will rapidly escalate to
tactical violence once they see all political space closed to them.[182] The contestation of claims by insurgents and counterclaims by elites results in collective
violence:

> one group undertakes a large action which directly or indirectly states a
> claim; a second group challenges that claim; they struggle. The group stat-

---

181   Tilly 2003, p. 106.
182   Tilly's distinction between low and high capacity regimes is far from clear and runs
       counter to fundamental principles of governance. For Tilly,

   'Low-capacity regimes, especially undemocratic ones, live with greater vulnerability to
   coordinated destruction within their domestic politics because they allow greater scope
   for dissidents and rivals to organise their own violent specialists on a large scale' (Ibid.,
   p. 106).

   The problem with this distinction is that Tilly is unclear about what he means by 'capacity' which in this context appears to mean the capacity of elites to control access to the
   polity and thus secure their dominance. If so, the only difference between a repressive
   and democratic low capacity regime is that the former is quicker to deploy violence and
   less likely to pursue co-optation through negotiations. However, confusion arises because
   the same strategy was used by elites in the US's supposedly high capacity representative
   democracy during the time period examined here. In this case, the exception makes the
   rule.

ing the counterclaim is often a specialized repressive force-police, troops, posse, vigilante-acting on behalf of the dominant classes.[183]

A low capacity regime might be better used to describe a regime vulnerable to a coup, a civil war in which a competing elite faction forces out the ruling faction, or a revolutionary crisis in which elites can no longer impose their authority through passive compliance or coercion. In such cases the regime may realise their power is gone and resort to brute force and terrorism to maintain their dominance. Here Tilly presumes low capacity regimes to be characterised primarily as non-western systems of governance. A more contemporary term for such a regime is a 'failed state'.

Tilly finds tactical escalation more likely to occur in low capacity regimes because they lack the capacity or assets to make concessions that bring insurgents into the elite coalition. But tactical escalation is also common among what Tilly refers to as high capacity democratic regimes, which are more likely to engage in pairing and switching from among from what Isaac called a 'class counter repertoire'.[184] Elites may deploy repressive force by using vigilante Committees of Safety, paramilitaries, militias, state police, court injunctions, private police, deputies, and carrying out false flag terrorist attacks blamed on insurgents, all recognisable examples from the struggles studied in this book.[185] The widespread use of private police and the military was identified as one of the primary causes of violence in strikes.[186] The origin of these models of elite mobilisation and escalation lay in the eighteenth to nineteenth century slave patrols that became the militias, local police, the Confederate Army during the Civil War, and the Ku Klux Klan and other similar terrorist groups after the war. High capacity democratic regimes are hardly missing institutions by which elites impose their will by force and violence.

Elites may pair or switch between these repressive tactics and offers to negotiate, settle, reform, and provide access to the polity. When insurgents are invited into the polity but co-optation, concessions, reform, or recognition are not forthcoming, there may be a willingness to escalate as the gulf between promise and expectation grows.

---

183   Tilly 1978, p. 174.

184   Isaac 2002, p. 396.

185   Lane 1921, p. 101. An example of a 'false flag' attack was provided by Lane. He reported an attack on buildings at a mine in Mingo County, West Virginia that was traced by bloodhounds to the home of an official of the mine. (See Lane 1921, p. 101).

186   Grant 1915a, pp. 28–47.

The likelihood that a new contender will accept and employ the means of acquisition of power the members of the polity prescribe (e.g., gathering enough votes to elect a party, sacrificing enough people in war, bringing in enough food from the hunt, buying enough government officials) depends on the congruence of the conceptions of justice which prevail within it to those built into the operation of the polity. Where they diverge widely, the challenger is likely to employ irregular means – which means applying resources to the government and to members of the polity which are rarely used in those relationships.[187]

In short, where the rules appear to be, or are actually rigged against insurgents, they will escalate the intensity of their tactics even to violence. The pairing of access to the polity and the promise of resources may be accompanied by the velvet glove of repression that pushes insurgents to demobilise, de-escalate, and fragment as the leadership is absorbed into the elite coalition and remaining insurgents continue the struggle. For this reason tactical escalation is as likely to happen in high capacity democratic regimes as in low capacity undemocratic regimes depending on the conditions and composition of elites and insurgents.

For Tilly, the relationship between the scale of action and acceptability differs according to four types of governments: weak (low repression, high tolerance, and minuscule facilitation); tolerant (modest repression, tolerance, and facilitation); repressive (high repression, low tolerance, and low facilitation); and totalitarian (modest repression, minuscule tolerance, and extremely high facilitation).[188]

But these categories of state types are ahistorical and inflexible, ignore non-state actors such as classes, and are unable to adapt to changing conditions in which elites and insurgents struggle. It could be described as idealistic, since at what point does a 'tolerant' state's toleration of insurgents' gains through absorption and co-optation blur with a 'totalitarian' state's facilitation of insurgents by transforming them into institutions of control? Insurgents mobilising in a tolerant state will have a hard time distinguishing its use of police, National Guard, private police, the courts, martial law, and the media from a totalitarian state's use of the same. All police sticks swing the same way in democratic and totalitarian regimes. After all, totalitarian West Virginia was part of the democratic US.

---

187   Tilly 1978, p. 132.
188   Ibid., pp. 114 and 117.

These models may be better used to explain how states (or rather elites) respond at different stages of an insurgency rather than distinct static types of states. A state can initially be tolerant towards an insurgency only to escalate to repression when it proves unable to absorb, co-opt, deflect, diffuse, or institutionalise it. It may also be simultaneously tolerant of the above-ground leadership while repressing the underground rank and file.

These other possible outcomes raise questions about Tilly's ahistorical attempt to generate a grand theory of contention. Not all states and elites respond to insurgents in the same way because the conditions in which elites and insurgents struggle are not constant. Elites in high capacity democratic regimes may be weak and have fragmented coalitions, and the composition of capital is vulnerable to disruption. The composition of both capital and the working-class at each stage of an insurgency determines the tactical and strategic response of the state, not just the formal system of governance it presumes to be. Tilly's theory of contention does not make sense without an analysis of the class composition of both elites and insurgents.

Conclusion

The threat of violence and some actual violence on a minor scale remain in the background, helping mainly to dramatize the issues. In the form of political blackmail it helps to get the dirty work done.

BARRINGTON MOORE JR., 1969[1]

• • •

The terrorist and the policeman both come from the same basket. Revolution, legality – counter moves in the same game; forms of idleness at bottom identical. He plays his little game – so do you propagandists.

JOSEPH CONRAD, *The Secret Agent*, 1907[2]

• • •

A strong man makes a weak people. Strong people don't need a strong man.

EMILIANO ZAPATA, *Viva Zapata!*, 1952[3]

• •
•

From the 1877 strike to the Miners' Army, workers fought back, taking up arms if necessary, against the combined onslaught of capital and the state. Were these mobs, riots, insurrections, insurgencies, armed struggle, guerrilla warfare, or terrorism? There seems to be little agreement. Perhaps they were a little of each. Perhaps they were each an example of what John Holloway calls the scream of 'No!'. For about four decades, the working-class proved to be unruly, unpredictable, and insubordinate. With each rupture of the 'volcano under the sidewalk' a new path, a new leash, and a new solution was introduced to manage the permanent crisis that is class struggle.

In the lessons of the past, we find the story of a future being born in the present. The return to an ever widening gap of wealth between the rich and

---

1 Moore 1969, p. 6.
2 Conrad 1907, p. 56.
3 *Viva Zapata!*, 1952.

everyone else, and the yawning gulf of power between capital and workers is an
eerie reverberation to the time when capital had at its disposal the full means
of the organised violence of the state and workers were ready and willing to
shoot back when all else proved impossible or ineffective.

While workers lost every strike and insurgency portrayed in this book, and
hundreds of workers and strikers were killed and countless more injured, they
actually won victories – sometimes weeks, months or decades later.[4] In the
next cycle of struggle, workers tried what tactics they may to discover their
new power to face the new conditions, escalating as mass support allowed and
as opportunities of success promised. Wage cuts were rescinded, productivity enhancing measures withdrawn, wages increased, unions recognised, contracts signed, collective bargaining conceded, and laws changed. But these were
fleeting victories that were transformed into the basis of a new defeat. The ebb
and flow of class struggle showed itself in capital regrouping to lay out a new
composition, transforming work, introducing a new division of labour, replacing skilled with unskilled workers, reworking the responsibility of the state.
Workers mobilised yet again, made the necessary linkages, brought production
and life to a standstill, and disrupted the order of things. The cycle of struggle
began again at a new level of composition, intensity, and dreams. Capital conceded a little to buy time while it manoeuvred in the shadows, reworking the
shop floor yet again until the workers found themselves divided and weak.

This is the story of the ever-unfolding story of class composition, the war
of manoeuvre between capital and workers that shaped the relations of production. As workers seek to escape the confines of work and domination of
capitalism, capital seeks to escape its vulnerability to the workers that it cannot do without.

Today, the decline in unionisation to record-low numbers hardly means the
disappearance of class struggle. Evading the bounds of labour law, collective
bargaining and other methods of managing class conflict that followed the
cycles of struggles in this book, capital and workers continue this dance just
below the surface. While the loss of union density has generated great con-

---

4   Harring estimated over 300 people were killed during strikes by the turn of the twentieth
    century. An estimated 35 people were killed by police on the last day of the 1877 strike in
    Chicago and as many as 100 in total by police and militia in Pittsburgh alone. He disputes
    Jeffreys-Jones's lower estimate of deaths for not counting railroad strike deaths caused by
    mis-operation by scabs and for undercounting street railway deaths by about 20. Many work-
    ers' deaths and injuries also likely went unreported due to the lack of adequate medical care
    and local government record keeping, as well as to avoid apprehension by police. (See Harring
    1983, pp. 190 and 270; and Jeffreys-Jones 1978, pp. 27 and 199–201).

cern, there is a shining opportunity that is evoked through the cracks. Fewer and fewer workers are subject to the rules put into place following these decades of class struggle to manage it. No union, no rules. As in 1877, so in 2017. 140 years later, a lot looks very similar.

A lot looks very different too. Why did workers organise and intensify their tactics from attempting to negotiate to strikes, scattered attacks, sabotage, dynamite, and armed invasion? Locked out of a two-party elite coalition, workers time and again disrupted the national economy and between 1913 and 1921 joined a cycle of struggle that exploded into international revolutionary crisis.

If there is one lesson from 1877 for us in 2017 it is that reform is impossible without what Moore, writing about the urban insurgencies of the 1960s, called a 'form of political blackmail [which] helps to get the dirty work done'. Violence sharpened the argument for reform to keep the system from bursting at its seams. Thomas Jefferson made this clear when he wrote 'the tree of liberty must be refreshed from time to time with the blood of patriots & tyrants. it is it's natural manure'.[5] And as long as we continue to live in a capitalist system, it will be the waged and unwaged workers that choose to either keep those seams in place or remove them. The periods of populist and progressive-era reform didn't occur during these decades preceding the New Deal by accident. There was no other choice. Disruption and a strategy of tension held the system hostage. Reform bought precious time, putting off the revolutionary crisis until an unknown future. There is no way of knowing if reform will be sufficient to resolve the crisis next time.

While explaining about my book to curious questioners over the years, I have frequently been asked why I have delved back nearly a century and a half to explore the question of tactics, strategy, and objectives of class struggle. My original reasons for doing so are still the same years later. The US faces a startling repetition of conditions today that mirror those during the era of the late nineteenth century Gilded Age, in which a rising plutocratic elite ruled the country, dominated the halls of government, and vacuumed up nearly all the fruits of the capitalist economy. Using deskilling, automation, and mass surveillance, all types of work from unskilled to professional have become increasingly insecure, unstable, and contingent. The final report of the 1913–15 Commission on Industrial Relations, for example, could have been describing the present when it warned that the wealthiest 2 percent of the population owned 60 percent of the wealth, while the bottom 65 percent only owned 5 percent.[6]

---

5 Jefferson 1787.
6 The findings of the Commission concerning the inequitable distribution of the products of the capitalist economy then have an eerie correspondence to the widely reported income and

If the income and wealth gap today is returning to the similarly yawning gulf as that era, it is not merely because of the rising power of the plutocratic elites. It is a result of the utter defeat of the working-class in the class struggle. By the 1970s, with unions well anchored to the elite Democratic Party's big tent, organising and strikes have dropped precipitously. It is not merely that union density has surprisingly returned to the levels of just prior to WWI, but little is being done even with the unions we have.

The way out of these conditions is unclear because it is not well understood how we got to the New Deal labour law reforms. The myth of peaceful progress tells us that union recognition and collective bargaining were outcomes of access to the political system. What has been left out of the story is the role of more than four decades of disruptive class struggle that used a strategy of tension, sometimes escalating into the use of tactical violence, to extract concessions. As Cleaver observed, albeit beginning several decades too late,

> The growth in workers' struggles and power during the 1920s and 1930s … prevent[ed] any substantial fall in wages … by increasing demands on the state as collective capitalist for jobs and more social services. In order to survive that crisis capitalism required a new strategy and a new ideology to replace 'laissez faire'. The solution which emerged was the ideology of growth and full employment based on a strategy of harnessing workers' struggles for higher wages through productivity deals negotiated in collective bargaining. That wages and thus consumer demand would not rise faster than productivity would be guaranteed by state intervention with monetary and fiscal policy. In other words, the American answer to the last crisis of capitalism was Keynesianism as a strategy and thus an ideology.[7]

---

wealth and income gaps today. Then, as for the past 40 years, the evidence that capital was winning the class war was reflected in the disproportional distribution of profits and wages:

'The wealth of the country between 1890 and 1912 increased from sixty-five to one hundred and eighty-seven billions, or 188 per cent, whereas the aggregate income of wage earners in manufacturing, mining, and transportation has risen between 1889 and 1909 only 95 per cent, from two thousand five hundred and sixteen millions in 1889 to four thousand nine hundred and sixteen millions in 1909. Furthermore, the wage earners' share of the net product of industry in the case of manufactures was only 40.2 per cent in 1909, as compared with 44.9 per cent in 1889' (Commission on Industrial Relations 1916, pp. 21, and 23–79).

7   Cleaver 1979, p. 8.

Over time, the working-class's success in extracting concessions through a disruptive strategy of tension was transformed into defeat. The concessions became reforms that provided the means of harnessing, managing, and suppressing working-class insurgency. We are trapped in our own myths. These myths present great peril if tactical violence returns as part of the repertoire of contention and the plutocracy is unprepared and unwilling to respond with concessions and reform.

To look forward it is inescapable to look back and ask why the railroad workers of 1877 and 1894, the ironworkers of the 1910s, and West Virginia miners of the 1910s–21 resorted to tactical violence. A group locked out of power will launch an insurgency and participate in the polity to give it the leverage to negotiate for its demands. When access to the polity is blocked, what William Gamson calls 'stable unrepresentation' that 'operates to prevent incipient competitors from achieving full entry into the political arena' is sure to be followed by tactical escalation.[8] To overcome this lack of access, leverage, and power, 'insurgents must bypass routine decision-making channels and seek, through use of non-institutional tactics, to force their opponents to deal with them outside of established arenas in which the latter derive so much of their power'.[9] An insurgency that successfully destabilises and disrupts existing power relations is more likely to force redress of grievances. In such cases a strategy of tension gets the goods.

The myth of peaceful progress has left out a key part of the story of how collective action made social change happen. Umoja's study of the civil rights movement found that insurgents commonly bypassed institutional channels not just by deploying non-violent direct action but also tactical violence, most notably portrayed by the efforts of Robert Williams's self-defence group in North Carolina.[10] This newly recovered history of the civil rights movement demonstrates that insurgents paired and switched between non-violent civil disobedience, boycotts, and lawsuits, and armed self-defence, patrols, retaliation, and armed struggle before the Black Panthers even formed in 1966. What is unique about these armed groups is that they didn't dictate the direction or the non-military character of the larger civil rights movement, but rather functioned as what D'Arcy calls a 'citizen's militia' that was subordinated to the movement.[11]

---

8   Gamson 2009.
9   McAdam 1983, p. 735.
10   Umoja 2013; and Williams 1964 and 1965.
11   D'Arcy 2013, pp. 179–81.

Escalating to use tactical violence prompted federal intervention to abolish segregation, prosecution against armed racist violence, federal spending to reduce poverty, and other reforms. The strategy of tension also provided further leverage when the civil rights leadership was absorbed into the elite Democratic Party coalition and could no longer deliver adequate gains by negotiations. Insurgents continued to arm until the late 1970s, even after the passage of the swath of civil rights legislation when activists 'had little confidence in federal intervention to ensure their security'.[12] Tactical pairing and switching fills out the missing history of the civil rights movement. It is becoming evident again today during the Black Lives Matter protests against police and racist killings of black men and women. The pairing and switching between non-violence and tactical violence raises doubts about the myth of peaceful progress that obscures the history of the civil rights and labour movements.

Political violence is but one tactic in a strategy of tension. The tension between reform and insurgency looms over the tension between capital and workers that sometimes explodes into a *dance macabre*. Workers' ability to recompose their power and launch a new cycle of struggle is met with an attempt by capital to reorder the relations of production and define a new expanded role of the state to manage class struggle and impose a new balance of power. As reformers jockey for influence and power within the elite coalition, the call for investigations and hearings to get to the bottom of the disruptive insurgency become ever louder. What the oft-formed investigative commissions often report is that disruptive class struggle signalled the coming insurgency much as Triton blew his conch shell to enrage the seas and announce the coming of Poseidon. The waters are not calm today.

When all forms of acceptable legal political action were blocked, repressed, or ineffective, workers escalated the intensity of their tactics to insurgency. This didn't escape the observation of the Commission on Industrial Relations, formed in the midst of the rise of the Socialist Party at the ballot box, the Industrial Workers of the World, and the ironworkers' dynamite campaign. As it presciently warned in its Final Report,

> Violence is seldom, if ever, spontaneous, but arises from a conviction that fundamental rights are denied and that peaceful methods of adjustment can not be used ... Throughout history where a people or a group have been arbitrarily denied rights which they conceived to be theirs, reac-

---

12   Umoja 2013, p. 258.

tion has been inevitable. Violence is a natural form of protest against injustice.[13]

In his close study of the Commission on Industrial Relations and much of the period explored in this book, Graham Adams found that the more prevalent tactical uses of violence raised a fundamental doubt about the claims to pluralism, shared interests, absolute gains, and peaceful progress.

> As in previous Commission studies, the evidence revealed a disposition on the part of a significant number of Americans to disregard the usual agencies of organised society and to resort to violence. This testimony lent little comfort to those who envisioned their nation as a community of harmonious classes.[14]

Nearly half a century later, the nation again found itself in the midst of a long decade of urban insurgencies for which calls for investigations and reforms were renewed. After President Johnson appointed the Kerner National Advisory Commission on Civil Disorders on 27 July 1967 to study the causes of political violence during the 1960s urban uprisings, Student Nonviolent Coordinating Committee Chair H. Rap Brown retorted that 'Violence is necessary. Violence is part of America's culture. It is as American as cherry pie. America taught black people to use violence. We will use that violence to rid ourselves of oppression if necessary'.[15] Although these rebellions and the guerrilla warfare that followed unleashed a virtual cottage industry of academic research and think tank reports into political violence in the 1960s and 1970s, the consensus explanation was that violence was anything but a tactic of class struggle. This insurrectionary era appeared to be reduced in such a way that Marcuse warned 'the problem of violence is primarily a problem of tactics'.[16]

Moore contested the myth of the marginal role of violence: 'it is untrue that violence settles nothing. It would be closer to the mark to assert that violence has settled all historical issues so far, and most of them in the wrong way'.[17] The violence inherent in capitalism is not always one-sided. Between 1877 and 1921 the violence of capitalism was met by the violence of the class struggle – when workers shot back.

---

13   Commission on Industrial Relations 1916, p. 92.
14   Adams 1966, p. 203. Adams appears to be unaware of Grant's missing report (Grant 1915a) since he does not cite it among the list of Commission on Industrial Relations reports.
15   Brown 1967. H. Rap Brown later changed his name to Imam Jamil Al-Amin.
16   Marcuse 1967.
17   Moore 1969, p. 13.

Bibliography

Adamic, Louis 2008 [1931], *Dynamite: The Story of Class Violence in America*, Oakland: AK Press.

Adams, Charles Francis, Jr. 1877, 'The Brotherhood of Locomotive Engineers', *The Nation*, 22 March, 24: 173.

Adams, Jr., Graham 1966, *Age of Industrial Violence, 1910–1915: The Activities and Findings of the United States Commission on Industrial Relations*, New York: Columbia University Press.

Alexander, Michelle 2012, *The New Jim Crow: Mass Incarceration in the Age of Colorblindness*, New York: New Press.

Alquati, Romano n.d., 'Networks of Struggles in Italy'. Available at: https://la.utexas.edu/users/hcleaver/networka.html.

American Postal Worker 2010, '1913 Silk Strike United Diverse Workforce', November/December, available at: https://www.apwu.org/labor-history-articles/1913-silk-strike-united-diverse-workforce.

American Railway Union 1893, *Constitution of the American Railway Union*, 20 June, Chicago.

Anthracite Coal Strike Commission 1903, *Report to the President on the Anthracite Coal Strike*, May–October, Washington DC.

Aptheker, Herbert 1983, *American Negro Slave Revolts*, New York: International Publishers.

Arendt, Hannah 1958, *The Origins of Totalitarianism*, Cleveland: Meridian.

Arendt, Hannah 1971, *On Violence*, New York: Harvest.

Aronoff, Kate 2015, 'Unveiling the Prophets of Profit in St. Louis', *Waging Nonviolence*, 10 July, available at: http://wagingnonviolence.org/2015/07/unveiling-prophets-profit-st-louis/

Aronowitz, Stanley 2015, 'Power Outage: Why Left Governments Falter Once in Office' *The Indypendent*, 5 August, 2008, available at: https://www.indypendent.org/2015/08/05/power-outage-why-left-governments-falter-once-office

Altgeld, John March 1915, 'The Governor's Second Protest: July 6, 1894', *Machinists' Monthly Journal*, Washington, DC: International Association of Machinists, XXVII, 3: 230.

Bailey, Kenneth R. 2013, 'Battle of Blair Mountain', *e-WV: The West Virginia Encyclopedia*, available at: http://www.wvencyclopedia.org/articles/532

Bakunin, Mikhail 2005 [1869]. 'On Cooperation', in *No Gods No Masters*, edited by Daniel Guérin, Oakland: AK Press.

Battle of Algiers, The 1966, directed by: Gillo Pontecorvo.

Baum, Frank L. 1907, *Ozma of Oz*, New York: Scholastic Book Services.

Behold a Pale Horse 1964, directed by Fred Zinnemann.

Bell, Peter and Harry Cleaver Autumn 2002, 'Marx's Theory of Crisis as a Theory of Class Struggle', *The Commoner*, 5: 1–61, available at: https://libcom.org/files/cleaver05.pdf

Bellesiles, Michael 2010, *1877: America's Year of Living Violently*, New York: The New Press.

Berman, Edward March 1928, 'The Supreme Court and Compulsory Arbitration: An Analysis Based on the Kansas Cases. The Present Status of the Kansas System of Compulsory Arbitration', *American Economic Review*, 18(1): 19–45.

Bernstein, Irving 1960, *The Lean Years: A History of the American Workers 1920–1933*, Boston: Houghton Mifflin Co.

Bimba, Anthony 1950, *The Molly Maguires: The True Story of Labor's Martyred Pioneers in the Coalfields*, New York: International Publishers.

Blizzard, William C. 2010 (2005), *When Miners March*, edited by Wes Harris. Oakland: PM Press.

Bologna, Sergio 1976, 'Class Composition and the Theory of the Party at the Origin of the Workers Councils Movement', *The Labour Process & Class Strategies*, CSE Pamphlet no. 1, London: Conference of Socialist Economists: 68–91.

Bonnett, Clarence 1922, *Employers' Associations in the United States: A Study of Typical Associations*, New York: Macmillan Co.

Bowers, John Hugh 1922, *The Kansas Court of Industrial Relations: The Philosophy and History of the Court*, Chicago: A.C. McClurg & Co.

Bowman, John B. [1832–85], available at: http://politicalgraveyard.com/bio/bowman.html

Boyd, John R. 2005 [1986], *Patterns of Conflict*, Powerpoint, edited by Chet Richards and Chuck Spinney, produced and designed by Ginger Richards, powerpoint, Atlanta, GA: Defense and the National Interest, available at: http://www.dnipogo.org/boyd/patterns.ppt

Boyd, John R. 2005 [1987], *The Strategic Game of ? And ?*, edited by Chet Richards and Chuck Spinney, produced and designed by Ginger Richards, powerpoint, Atlanta, GA: Defense and the National Interest, available at: http://www.dnipogo.org/boyd/strategic_game.pdf

Boyer, Richard and Herbert Morais 1977 [1955], *Labor's Untold Story: The Adventure Story of the Battles, Betrayals, and Victories of American Working Men and Women*, New York: United Electrical, Radio and Machine Workers of America.

Brecher, Jeremy 1999 [1972], *Strike!*, revised and updated edition, Boston: South End Press.

Brenner, Aaron, Benjamin Day and Immanuel Ness 2015, *The Encyclopedia of Strikes in American History*, London: Routledge.

Brown, H. Rap 1967, SNCC press conference, July 27, available at: https://www.youtube.com/watch?v=4jNfaSeZwlk

Brown, Stephen and Otis Rice 1985, *West Virginia: A History*, 2nd edn, Lexington: The University Press of Kentucky.

Bruce, Robert 1987 [1959] *1877: Year of Violence*, Chicago: Ivan R. Dee.

Bucki, Cecelia 2009, 'World War I Era Strikes', in *The Encyclopedia of Strikes in American History*, edited by A. Brenner, B. Day and I. Ness, Armonk, NY: M.E. Sharpe.

Bucki, Cecelia n.d., 'Strikes for the Eight-Hour Day in Summer 1915 Bridgeport', available at: http://bportlibrary.org/hc/bridgeport-at-war/strikes-for-the-eight-hour-day-in-summer-1915-bridgeport/

Burbank, David 1966, *Reign of the Rabble: The St. Louis General Strike of 1877*, New York: Augustus M. Kelley.

Bureau of Labor Statistics of California 1891–2, 'Investigation: Labor and Capital', *Fifth Biennial Report of the Bureau of Labor Statistics of California*.

Burns, Joe 2014, *Strike Back: Using the Militant Tactics of Labor's Past to Reignite Public Sector Unionism Today*, New York: IG Publishing.

Burton, David 1998, *Taft, Holmes, and the 1920s Court: An Appraisal*, Plainsboro, NJ: Associated University Presses.

Caffentzis, George 2013, *In Letters of Blood and Fire: Work, Machines, and the Crisis of Capitalism*, Oakland: PM Press.

Carlin, George nd, 'Bombing Brown People', available at: https://www.youtube.com/watch?v=dDw-zFFhFgc

Carlsson, Chris 1995, 'The Workingmen's Party & Denis Kearny Agitation', *Found SF*, available at: http://www.foundsf.org/index.php?title=The_Workingmen%E2%80%99s_Party_%26_The_Denis_Kearney_Agitation

Case, Theresa Ann, 2015, 'Labor Upheaval on the Nation's Railroads, 1877–1922', in *The Encyclopedia of Strikes in American History*, edited by A. Brenner, B. Day and I. Ness, London: Routledge.

Chaplin, Ralph May 1985 [1933], *The General Strike*, The Industrial Workers of the World, available at: http://www.iww.org/history/library/Chaplin/TheGeneralStrike

Chomsky, Noam 2004, *Hegemony or Survival: America's Quest for Global Dominance*, New York: Holt.

Clark, Peter H. 1877, 'Socialism: The Remedy for the Evils of Society', *The Cincinnati Commercial*, 23 July, available at: http://www.blackpast.org/1877-peter-h-clark-socialism-remedy-evils-society#sthash.LzxQHADs.dpuf

Cleaver, Harry 1979, *Reading Capital Politically*, Austin: University of Texas Press.

Cleaver, Harry 1989, 'Work, Value and Domination: On the Continuing Relevance of the Marxian Labor Theory of Value in the Crisis of the Keynesian Planner State', paper and lecture to Annual Meetings of the Conference of Socialist Economists (UK), July, Sheffield.

Cleaver, Harry 1992, 'Kropotkin, Self-valorization and the Crisis of Marxism', available at: https://la.utexas.edu/users/hcleaver/kropotkin.html#13

Cleaver, Harry 1992, 'The Inversion of Class Perspective in Marxian Theory: From Valorization to Self-Valorization', in *Essays on Open Marxism*, edited by W. Bonefeld, R. Gunn and K. Psychopedis, London: Pluto Press, available at: https://la.utexas.edu/users/hcleaver/Inversion.pdf

Cleaver, Harry 1997, 'Nature, Neoliberalism and Sustainable Development: Between Charybdis & Scylla?', paper was prepared for the 4th Ecology Meeting on "Economy and Ecology" held by the Instituto Piaget, Viseu, Portugal, April 17–19, 1997 available at: https://la.utexas.edu/users/hcleaver/port.html

Cleaver, Harry 2016, *Rupturing the Dialectic: The Struggle Against Work*, Chico, CA: AK Press.

Cleveland, President Grover 1886, 'National Board of Arbitration', Senate Executive Document No. 130, 49th Congress, first session, Message from the President to the United States Relative to the Disputes Between Laboring Men and Employers, April 22, 1896, in Carroll Wright 1894, 'The Chicago Strike, Paper read at the Seventh Annual Meeting of the American Economic Association, Columbia College, December 27, 1894', Publications of the American Economic Association, Vol. IX, Rejoinder.

Cloward, Richard and Frances F. Piven 1984, 'Disruption and Organization: a Rejoinder [to William A. Gamson and Emilie Schmeidler]', *Theory and Society*, 13(4): 590–1.

Coal Review 1921, 'Salient Points of Bituminous Coal Industry', Vol. III, 12, 21 September.

Cole, Merle T. 1998, 'A Comprehensive History of the West Virginia State Police, 1919–1979', available at: http://www.wvsp.gov/about/Pages/History.aspx

Cole, Merle T. 2003, 'Mere Military Color: The State Police and Martial Law', *West Virginia Historical Society Quarterly*, XVII(3), available at: http://www.wvculture.org/history/wvhs/wvhs1731.html

Commission of Inquiry 1920, *Report on the Steel Strike of 1919*, Interchurch World Movement, New York. New York, Harcourt, Brace and Howe.

Conner, Valerie Jean 1983, *The National War Labor Board: Stability, Social Justice, and the Voluntary State in World War I*, Chapel Hill, NC: University of North Carolina Press.

Conrad, Joseph 2007 [1907], *The Secret Agent: A Simple Tale*, New York: Penguin.

Cooper, Jerry M. 1977, 'The Army as Strikebreaker – The Railroad Strikes of 1877 and 1894', *Labor History*, 18(2): 179–96.

Corbin, David Alan 1997, *The West Virginia Mine Wars: An Anthology*, Martinsburg: Appalachian Editions.

D'Arcy, Stephen 2013, *Languages of the Unheard: Why Militant Protest is Good for Democracy*, London: Zed Press.

Darrow, Clarence 1894, 'Brief and Argument for Petitioners *Ex Parte Eugene V. Debs et al.*', Supreme Court of the United States, October Term, available at: http://darrow.law.umn.edu/documents/Pullman_strike_BRIEF_Supreme_Court.pdf (last retrieved May 9, 2018).

Davies, James 1970, *When Men Revolt – and Why: A Reader in Political Violence and Revolution*, New York: The New Press.

Davis, Colin J. 1992, 'Bitter Conflict: The 1922 Railroad Shopmen's Strike', *Labor History*, 33(4): 433–55.

Davis, Mike 1975, 'The Stopwatch and the Wooden Shoe: Scientific Management and the Industrial Workers of the World', *Radical America*, 9(1): 69–96, available at: https://dl.lib.brown.edu/pdfs/1125403651398134.pdf

Dick, Philip K. 1980 [1954], 'The Last of the Masters', in *The Golden Man*, New York: Berkeley Books.

Divine, E.T. 1909, *Misery and its Causes*, New York: MacMillan Co.

Donnelly, Ignatius 2003 [1890], *Caesar's Column*, Middletown: Wesleyan University Press.

Doree, E.F. 1916, *Shop Control and the Contract: How They Affect the IWW*, reported in the Stenographic Minutes of the Tenth Convention.

Douglass, Frederick 1857, 'If There Is No Struggle, There Is No Progress', West India Emancipation speech, 3 August, Canandaigua, New York, available at: http://rbscp.lib.rochester.edu/4398

Dubofsky, Melvyn 1967, 'Review of Graham Adams, Jr., *Age of Industrial Violence, 1910–1915: The Activities and Findings of the United States Commission on Industrial Relations*', *Labor History*, 8(1): 87–109.

DuBois, W.E.B. 1935, *Black Reconstruction in America: An Essay Toward a History of the Part Which Black Folk Played in the Attempt to Reconstruct Democracy in America, 1860–1880*, Cleveland: Meridian Books.

Eggert, Gerald G. 1966, 'A Missed Alternative: Federal Courts as Arbiters of Railway Labor Disputes, 1877–1895', *Labor History*, 7(3): 287–306.

Emmet, Boris July 1924, *Labor Relations in the Fairmont, West Virginia Bituminous Coal Field*, United States Department of Labor Bulletin of the United States Bureau of Labor Statistics, No. 361, Washington: US Government Printing Office.

Engels, Friedrich 2004 [1884], *The Origin of Family, Private Property and State*, Australia: Resistance Books.

Ernst, Daniel Spring 1989, 'The Yellow Dog Contract and Liberal Reform, 1917–1932', *Labor History*, 30(2): 251–74.

Even the Heavens Weep 1985, directed by Lou Buttino, Danny L. McGuire, and Mike Connors.

Fanon, Frantz 2005 [1963], *The Wretched of the Earth*, New York: Grove Press.

Filipelli, Ronald L. Spring 1972, 'The Railroad Strike of 1877 in Reading', *Historical Review of Berks County*, available at: http://www.berkshistory.org/multimedia/articles/the-railroad-strike-of-1877-in-reading/

Fine, Sidney Winter 1991, 'The National Erectors' Association and the Dynamiters', *Labor History*, 32(1): 5–41.

Fishback, Price 1995, 'An Alternative View of Violence in Disputes in the Early 1900s: The Bituminous Coal Industry, 1890–1930', *Labor History*, 36(3): 426–56.

Fisher, Will 1910, 'Industrial Unionism, Tactics and Principles', *Industrial Worker*, 19 March.

Fitch, John 1913, 'The Dynamite Case', *The Survey*, 1 February, 607–17.

Flynn, Elizabeth Gurley n.d., *Sabotage*, Chicago: IWW.

Fogelson, Robert 1971, *Violence as Protest: A Study of Riots and Ghettos*, NY: Anchor Books.

Folsom, Franklin 1991, *Impatient Armies of the Poor: The Story of Collective Action of the Unemployed 1808–1942*, Niwot: University Press of Colorado.

Foner, Eric 1990, *A Short History of Reconstruction*, New York: Harper.

Foner, Philip S. 1978 [1947], *History of the Labor Movement in the United States: From Colonial Times to the Founding of the American Federation of Labour*, Volume 1, New York: International Publishers.

Foner, Philip S. 1973 [1965], *The Industrial Workers of the World, 1905–1917*, New York: International Publishers.

Foner, Philip S. 1973, *History of the Labor Movement in the United States: The Policies and Practices of the American Federation of Labor 1900–1909*, Volume 3, New York: International Publishers.

Foner, Philip S. 1977, *The Great Labor Uprising of 1877*, New York: Monad Press.

Foner, Philip S. 1987, *History of the Labor Movement in the United States: Labor and World War I, 1914–1918*, Volume 7, New York: International Publishers.

Fones-Wolf, Elizabeth and Ken Fones-Wolf 1994, *Labor History*, 35(2): 237–59.

Forbath, William E. 1989, 'The Shaping of the American Labor Movement', *Harvard Law Review*, 102(6): 1249–56.

Fraina, Louis 1913, 'The Call of the Steel Worker', *International Socialist Review*, 83 (July).

Frank Dana 1985, 'Housewives, Socialists, and the Politics of Food: The 1917 New York Cost-of-Living Protests', *Feminist Studies*, 11(2): 255–85.

Free State of Jones 2016, directed by Gary Ross.

Freedman, Lawrence 2013, *Strategy: A History*, New York: Oxford University Press.

Frey, John P. May 1916, 'Modern Industry and Craft Skills', *American Federationist*, 365–6.

Frieburger, William Spring 1984, 'War Prosperity and Hunger: The New York Food Riots of 1917', *Labor History*, 25(2): 217–39.

Gage, Beverly 2009, *The Day Wall Street Exploded: A Story of America in its First Age of Terror*, New York: Oxford University Press.

Gailbraith, John Kenneth 1961, *The Great Crash of 1929*, New York: Time.

Galeano, Eduardo 1971, *Open Veins of Latin America: Five Centuries of the Pillage of a Continent*, New York: Monthly Review.

Gamson, William 1975, *The Strategy of Social Protest*, Homewood, IL: Dorsey Press.

Gamson, William 2009, 'The Success of the Unruly', in *Readings on Social Movements: Origins, Dynamics, and Outcomes*, 2nd edn, edited by Doug McAdam and David Snow, London: Oxford University Press.

Giardina, Denise 1987, *Storming Heaven: A Novel*, New York: Ivy Books.

Glaberman, Martin 1965, 'Be His Payment High or Low: The American Working Class in the Sixties', *International Socialism* (1st series), 21(Summer): 18–23.

Glaberman, Martin 1973, 'The American Working Class in Historical Perspective', *Radical America*, 7(6): 81–90.

Glaberman, Martin 1975, ' "Be His Payment High or Low": The American Working Class of the Sixties', reprinted from *International Socialism*, 21, 1965, in *'Be His Payment High or Low': The American Working Class of the Sixties*, Detroit: Bewick Editions.

Glaberman, Martin 1984, 'Review of Trade Unions Under Capitalism', *Labor History*, 25(4): 629–31.

Glaberman, Martin 1991, 'Review of The Right to Be Lazy', *Labor History*, 32(1): 143–4.

Glaberman, Martin and George Rawick 1977, 'The American Economy', *Work and Society*, edited by Mary Robischon, Bruce Levine, and Martin Glaberman, Detroit: Wayne State University.

Gleason, Arthur 1920, 'Company-Owned Americans', *The Nation*, 12 June.

Gleason, Arthur 1920, 'Private Ownership of Public Officials', *The Nation*, 29 May.

Gompers, Samuel 1913, 'AF of L and the Iron Workers', *The Survey*, 1 February, 621–3.

Gompers, Samuel 1913, 'Russianized West Virginia: Corporate Perversion of American Concepts of Liberty and Human Justice – Organised Labor to the Rescue', *The Federationist*, XX (October): 10.

Goossen, Benjamin Autumn 2011, ' "Like a Brilliant Thread": Gender and Vigilante Democracy in the Kansas Coalfield, 1921–1922', *Kansas History: A Journal of the Central Plains*, 34: 206–23.

Gowaskie, Joe Winter 1985/86, 'John Mitchell and the Anthracite Mine Workers: Leadership Conservatism and Rank-and-File Militancy', *Labor History*, 27(1): 54–83.

Gowen, Franklin B. 1876, *Argument of Franklin B. Gowen, esq*, no publisher.

Grant II, Don S. and Michael Wallace 1991, 'Why Do Strikes Turn Violent?', *American Journal of Sociology*, 96: 1117–50.

Grant, Luke 1915a, *Violence in Labor Disputes and Methods of Policing Industry*, Unpublished report, Washington DC: Commission on Industrial Relations.

Grant, Luke 1915b, *The National Erectors Association and the International Association of Bridge and Structural Ironworkers*, Washington DC: Commission on Industrial Relations.

Grant, US 1877, speech, 15 June, London: Guild Hall.

Grant, US 1877, 'Regarding keeping U.S. Army soldiers stationed in southern U.S. states to protect the safety and civil rights of freed slaves' [26 August], *The Papers of Ulysses S. Grant: November 1, 1876–September 30, 1878*, Volume 28, Carbondale: Southern Illinois University Press.

Green, James 2015, *The Devil is Here in These Hills: West Virginia's Coal Miners and Their Battle for Freedom*, New York: Atlantic Monthly Press.

Gregg, Richard B. 1919–20, 'The National War Labor Board', *Harvard Law Review*, 33(1): 39–63.

Grossman, Jonathan 1975, 'The Coal Strike of 1902 – Turning Point in U.S. Policy', *Monthly Labor Review*, US Department of Labor, available at: http://www.dol.gov/oasam/programs/history/coalstrike.htm#3

Gurr, Ted Robert 1972, 'A Causal Model of Civil Strife: A Comparative Analysis using New Indices', in *Anger, Violence, and Politics: Theories and Research*, edited by Ivo K. Feierabend, Rosalind L. Feierabend and Ted Robert Gurr, New Jersey: Prentice Hall.

Gurr, Ted Robert 1989, *Violence in America: Protest, Rebellion, Reform: Volume 2*, Newbury Park: Sage.

Gutman, Herbert George 1959, *Social and Economic Structure and Depression: American labor in 1873 and 1874*, PhD dissertation.

Gutman, Herbert George 1976, *Work, Culture and Society in Industrializing America*, New York: Knopf.

Hannon, Michael n.d., '*The Pullman Strike of 1894*', University of Minnesota Clarence Darrow Digital Collection, available at: http://darrow.law.umn.edu/trialpdfs/Pullman_Strike.pdf (last retrieved May 9, 2018).

Harding, Warren 1921, First Annual State of the Union December 7, 1921, available at: http://www.presidency.ucsb.edu/ws/?pid=29562

Harring, Sidney 1983, *Policing a Class Society: The Experience of American Cities, 1865–1915*, New Brunswick, NJ: Rutgers University Press.

Harvey, David 2007, *A Brief History of Neoliberalism*, Oxford: Oxford University Press.

Hay, John 1905, 'To Amasa Stone Room I, Cushing's Block, Cleveland, O., July 24, 1877', *The Life and Letters of John Hay In Two Volumes*, Volume II, Boston: Houghton Mifflin Co.

Haydu, Jeffrey 1999, 'Counter Action Frames: Employer Repertoires and the Union Menace in the Late Nineteenth Century', *Social Problems*, 46(3): 313–31.

Hayes, Rutherford Birchard 1924, *Diary and Letters of Rutherford Birchard Hayes*, edited by Charles R. Williams, Volume 4.

Hearing of Subcommittee of House Committee on Appropriations 1922, Federal Troops in West Virginia Coal Disturbances, Rep. Martin Madden, Chairman, 67th Congress, 2nd Session, 21 February, Washington DC: Government Printing Office, 493–4.

Helfand, Barry F. 1977, 'Labor and the Courts: The Common-Law Doctrine of Criminal Conspiracy and its Application in the Buck's Stove Case', *Labor History*, 18(1): 91–114.

Higgens-Evenson, R. 1998, 'From Industrial Police to Workmen's Compensation: Public Policy and Industrial Accidents in New York, 1880–1910', *Labor History*, 39(4): 365–80.

Hill, Joe 1914, 'How to Make Work for the Unemployed', *International Socialist Review*, XV(6): 335–6.

History Committee of the General Strike Committee 1919, March, available at: http://struggle.ws/hist_texts/seattle1919_p2.html

Hoffman, Bruce 2006, *Inside Terrorism*, New York: Columbia University Press.

Holloway, John 2005 [2002], *Change the World Without Taking Power*, London: Pluto Press.

Horne, Gerald and Mary Young (eds) 2001, *W.E.B. DuBois Encyclopedia*, Westport, CT: Greenwood Press.

Howling Mob Society, available at: http://www.howlingmobsociety.org

Independent 1921, 'War in West Virginia', 17 September, 121–2.

Ingham, John N. 1909, 'A Strike in the Progressive Era-McKees Rocks', *The Pennsylvania Magazine of History and Biography*, 90(3): 353–77.

Isaac, Larry 2002, 'To Counter "The Very Devil" and More: The Making of Independent Capitalist Militia in the Gilded Age', *American Journal of Sociology*, 108(2): 353–405.

James, C.L.R., Raya Dunayevskaya and Grace Lee 1986 [1950], *State Capitalism & World Revolution*, Chicago: Charles H. Kerr Publishing Company.

James, C.L.R. 1963, *The Black Jacobins: Toussaint Louverture and the San Domingo Revolution*, 2nd revised edition, New York: Vintage.

James, C.L.R. 1980, *Future in the Present: Selected Writings of C.L.R. James*, Westport, CT: Lawrence Hill & Co.

Jefferson, Thomas 1787, 'Extract from Thomas Jefferson to William Stephens Smith Paris Nov. 13. 1787', available at: http://tjrs.monticello.org/letter/100

Jeffrey-Jones, Rhodri 1978, *Violence and Reform in American History*, New York: New Viewpoints.

Johnson, Bruce 1976, 'Taking Care of Labour: The Police in American Politics', *Theory and Society*, 3(1): 89–117.

NLRB v. Jones & Laughlin Steel Corp. 301 US 1 (1937).

Josephson, Matthew 1934, *The Robber Barons: The Great American Capitalists, 1861–1901*, New York: Harvest Book.

Kaufman, Stuart 1991, 'Review of Sheldon Stromquist, *Generation of Boomers: The Pattern of Railroad Labor Conflicts in Nineteenth Century America*', *Labor History*, 32(1): 145–7.

Kautilya 2000, *Arthashastra*, New Delhi: Penguin.

Kazin, Michael 2008, *The Great Strikes of 1877*, edited by David Stowell, Urbana: University of Illinois Press.

Keeran, Roger 1989, 'The International Workers Order and the Origins of the CIO', *Labor History*, 30(3): 385–408.

Kellogg, Paul 1911, 'Conservation and Industrial War', *Survey*, 30 December, 1412.

Kennedy, John F. 1962, Address on the first Anniversary of the Alliance for Progress, 13 March, available at: http://www.presidency.ucsb.edu/ws/?pid=9100

Kenyon, William, 1922, United States Senate, January 25, 1922, West Virginia Coal Fields,

Committee on Education and Labor, 67th Congress, 2nd Session, Report No. 457, Personal Views to accompany S. Res. 80 in *Senate Reports*, December 5, 1921-September 22, 1922, Vol. 1, Washington DC: Government Printing Office, 1922.

Kerner Commission 1968, Report of the National Advisory Commission on Civil Disorders, 1 March, Washington DC: National Institute of Justice.

Kipling, Rudyard 1914, 'The Workingman's Answer to the Capitalist Class', *International Socialist Review*, XIV(8): 453.

Kolko, Gabriel 1963, *The Triumph of Conservatism: A Reinterpretation of American History, 1900–1916*, Chicago: Quadrangle Books.

Lambert, Josiah B. 2005, *'If the Workers Took a Notion': The Right to Strike and American Political Development*, Ithaca: Cornell University Press.

Lane, Winthrop 1921, *Civil War in West Virginia: A Story of the Industrial Conflict in the Coal Mines*, New York: B.W. Huebsch, Inc.

Lane, Winthrop 1922, 'Black Avalanche', *Survey*, 25 March, 1002–5.

Lawrence, Thomas E. 1929, 'The Lessons of Arabia', *Encyclopedia Britannica*, 14th edition.

Le Bon, Gustav 2001 [1896], *The Crowd: A Study of the Popular Mind*, Kitchener: Batoche Books, available at: https://socserv2.socsci.mcmaster.ca/~econ/ugcm/3ll3/lebon/Crowds.pdf

Leach, Eugene E. 1994, 'Chaining the Tiger: The Mob Stigma and the Working Class, 1863–1894', *Labor History*, 35(2): 187–215.

Lebergott, Stanley 1964, *Manpower in Economic Growth*, New York: McGraw Hill.

Lens, Sidney 1973, *The Labor Wars: From the Molly Maguires to the Sitdowns*, New York: Doubleday & Co.

Lenin. V.I. 1964 [1902], 'Revolutionary Adventurism', *Iskra*, 23, 1 August and 24, 1 September, in *Collected Works*, Moscow: Progress Publishers, Volume 6, available at: https://www.marxists.org/archive/lenin/works/1902/sep/01.htm

Lenin. V.I. 1962 [1905], 'A Militant Agreement for the Uprising', *Vperyod*, 7, 21 February, in *Collected Works*, Moscow: Foreign Languages Publishing House, Volume 8, available at: https://www.marxists.org/archive/lenin/works/1905/feb/21.htm

Lenin. V.I. 1964 [1920], '"Left-Wing" Communism: An Infantile Disorder', Moscow: Progress Publishers.

Levine, Bruce 1977, 'US Labor, 1836 to 1936: A Century of Change and Struggle', *Work and Society*, edited by Mary Robischon, Bruce Levine, and Martin Glaberman, Detroit: Wayne State University.

Leiserson, William 1969 [1931], 'The Economics of Restriction of Output', *Restriction of Output Among Unorganised Workers*, edited by Stanley Mathewson, Carbondale: Southern Illinois University Press.

Let the Fire Burn 2013, directed by Jason Oder.

Libertarian Socialist Organisation 1979, *You Can't Blow Up a Social Relationship*, Mel-

bourne: Australia, available at: https://theanarchistlibrary.org/library/libertarian
-socialist-organisation-you-can-t-blow-up-a-social-relationship

Lindsey, Almont 1942, *The Pullman Strike: The Story of a Unique Experiment and of a Great Labor Upheaval*, Chicago: University of Chicago Press.

Linebaugh, Peter 1982, 'Labor History without the Labor Process: A Note on John Gast and His Times', *Social History*, 7(3): 319–28.

Linebaugh, Peter and Marcus Rediker 2000, *The Many Headed Hydra: Sailors, Slaves, Commoners, and the Hidden History of the Revolutionary Atlantic*, Boston: Beacon Press.

Lipold, Paul and Larry Isaac August 2009, 'Striking Deaths: Lethal Contestation and the "Exceptional" Character of the American Labor Movement, 1870–1970', *International Review of Social History*, 54(2): 167–205.

Literary Digest, The 1922, ' "Treason" and "Reason" ', 17 June, LXXIII, 1678, 14.

Lloyd, John 2009, 'The Strike Wave of 1877', in *The Encyclopedia of Strikes in American History*, edited by Aaron Brenner, Benjamin Day and Immanuel Ness, London: Routledge.

Loewen, James 2007, *Lies My Teacher Told Me: Everything Your American History Textbook Got Wrong*, New York: Touchstone.

London, Jack and Robert Fish 2005 [1907], *The Road*, New York: MacMillan.

London, Jack and Robert Fish 1963 [1916], *The Assassination Bureau, Ltd.*, New York: Penguin.

Luxemburg, Rosa 1974 [1900], *Reform or Revolution*, New York: Pathfinder.

McAdam, Doug 1983, 'Tactical Innovation and the Pace of Insurgency', *American Sociological Review*, 48(December): 735–54.

McAdam, Doug 1999, *Political Process and the Development of Black Insurgency, 1930–1970*, 2nd edn, Chicago: University of Chicago Press.

McCartin, Joseph A. 1992, 'Using "The Gun Act": Federal Regulation and the Politics of the Strike Threat during World War I', *Labor History*, 33(4): 519–28.

Maksel, Rebecca 2009, 'The Billy Mitchell Court-Martial: Courtroom Sketches from Aviation's Trial of the Century', *Air & Space Magazine*.

Malatesta, Errico 2014 [1902], 'In Relation to Strikes', in *The Method of Freedom*, edited by Davide Turcato, Oakland: AK Press.

Manning, Thomas 1960, *The Chicago Strike of 1894: Industrial Labor in the Nineteenth Century*, Part 4 of the Revised Version of *Government and the American Economy: 1870 to the Present*, originally prepared by Thomas G. Manning and David M. Potter, New York: Holt, Rinehart and Winston.

Marcuse, Herbert 1967, 'The Problem of Violence and the Radical Opposition', 'Psychoanalyse und Politik' lecture delivered at the Free University of West Berlin in July 1967, available at: https://www.marxists.org/reference/archive/marcuse/works/1967/violence.htm

Marcy, Leslie 1917, 'Food Riots in America', *International Socialist Review*, XVII(10): 582–
97.

Markham, Edwin 1899, 'The Man with the Hoe', available at: https://www.poets.org/
poetsorg/poem/man-hoe

Marx, Karl 1887 [1867], *Capital*, Volume I, edited by Frederick Engels, Moscow: Progress
Publishers, available at: https://www.marxists.org/archive/marx/works/download/
pdf/Capital-Volume-I.pdf

Marx, Karl 1973 [1858], *Grundrisse: Foundations of the Critique of Political Economy*, London: Penguin.

Marx, Karl 1992 [1867a], *Capital*, Volume 1, New York: Penguin.

Marx, Karl 1906 [1867b], *Capital*, Volume 1, Chicago: Charles H. Kerr & Company.

Marx, Karl 1991 [1863–83], *Capital*, Volume III, edited by Friedrich Engels, London: Penguin Publishers.

Marx, Karl 1970 [1875], 'Critique of the Gotha Programme', in *Marx/Engels Selected
Works*, Moscow: Progress Publishers, Volume 3, 13–30.

Marx, Karl and Frederick Engels 1969 [1848], 'Communist Manifesto', in *Marx/Engels
Selected Works*, Volume 1, Moscow: Progress Publishers, 98–137.

Marx, Karl and Frederick Engels 1987, *Marx and Engels on the Trade Unions*, New York:
International Publishers.

Matewan 1987, directed by John Sayles.

Mathewson, Stanley 1969 [1931], *Restriction of Output Among Unorganised Workers*, Carbondale: Southern Illinois University Press.

Metallica 1988, '... And Justice for All', Burbank: Warner Records.

Miller, David 2008, *The Great Strikes of 1877*, edited by David Stowell, Urbana: University
of Illinois Press.

Mitchell, John 1973 [1903], *Organised Labor: Its Problems, Purposes, and Ideals and the
Present and Future of American Wage Earners*, Philadelphia: American Book and
Bible House.

Molly Maguires 1970, directed by Martin Ritt.

Montgomery, David 1974, 'The "New Unionism" and the Transformation of Workers'
Consciousness in America, 1909–22', *Journal of Social History*, 7(4): 509–29.

Montgomery, David 1977, 'Immigrant Workers and Scientific Management', *Work and
Society*, edited by Mary Robischon, Bruce Levine, and Martin Glaberman, Detroit:
Wayne State University.

Montgomery, David 1979, *Workers' Control in America: Studies in the History of Work,
Technology, and Labor Struggles*, New York: Cambridge University Press.

Montgomery, David 1980, 'Strikes in Nineteenth-Century America', *Social Science History*, 4(1): 81–104.

Montgomery, David 1989, 'Strikes of Machinists in the United States, 1870–1922', *Strikes,
Wars, and Revolutions in International Perspective*, edited by Leopold Haimson and
Charles Tilly, Cambridge: Cambridge University Press.

Moore, Barrington Jr. 1969, 'Thoughts on Violence and Democracy', in *Urban Riots: Violence and Social Change*, edited by Robert Connery, New York: Vintage.

Morris, James O. 1979, 'The Acquisitive Spirit of John Mitchell, President UMW President (1899–1908)', *Labor History*, 20(1): 5–44.

Most, Johann 1885, 'Action as Propaganda', *Freiheit*, 25 July, available at: http://dwardmac.pitzer.edu/Anarchist_Archives/bright/most/actionprop.html

Mother Jones 1997 [15 August 1912], 'Proceedings Held at Front Steps of Capitol in Charleston', edited by David Alan Corbin, *The West Virginia Mine Wars: An Anthology*, Martinsburg: Appalachian Editions.

Mother Jones 2004 [1925], *The Autobiography of Mother Jones*, Chicago: Charles Kerr.

Negri, Antonio 1991, *Marx Beyond Marx: Lessons on the Grundrisse*, Brooklyn: Autonomedia.

Nelson, Daniel 1970, 'While Waiting for the Government: The Needle Trades Unemployment Insurance Plans, 1919–28', *Labor History*, 11(4): 482–99.

New England Historical Society n.d., 'Bridgeport Women Workers and the Birth of the Eight Hour Day', available at: http://www.newenglandhistoricalsociety.com/eight-hour-day/

New York Times 1885, 'Ex-Mayor Bowman Killed', 22 November, available at: http://query.nytimes.com/gst/abstract.html?res=F70A11FF395B10738DDDAB0A94D9415B8584F0D3

New York Times 1912, 'Taft for an Inquiry Into Cost of Living', 2 February.

New York Times 1913, 'Senator in a Row with Mining Man: Martine Withdraws from Conduct of Coal Strike Inquiry in Consequence', 18 June.

New York Times 1913, '"Mother" Jones: Mild-mannered, Talks Sociology', 1 June.

Nietzsche, Friedrich, 1909, *Thus Spoke Zarathustra*, Edinburgh: T.N. Foulis.

Noble, David 1979, 'Social Choice in Machine Design: The Case of the Automatically Controlled Machine Tools' in *Case Studies on the Labor Process*, edited by Andrew Zimbalist, NY: Monthly Review Press.

O'Connor, Harvey 1964, *Revolution in Seattle: A Memoir*, New York: Monthly Review Press.

Onasch, Bill nd, 'The Streetcar Strikes of 1917–18', *KC Labor*, http://www.kclabor.org/streetcar_strikes_of_1917.htm

Painter, Nell 1987, *Standing at Armageddon, The United States 1877–1919*, New York: W.W. Norton.

Panzieri, Raniero 1976, 'Surplus Value and Planning: Notes on the Reading of Capital', *The Labour Process & Class Strategies*, CSE Pamphlet no. 1, London: Conference of Socialist Economists, 4–25.

Papke, David Ray 2008, 'The *Debs* Case: Labour, Capital, and the Federal Courts of the 1890s', in *Federal Trials and Great Debates in United States History*, Federal Judicial Center Federal Judicial History Office, available at: https://www.fjc.gov/history/

famous-federal-trials/re-eugene-v-debs-pullman-strike-and-american-railway
-union-boycott

Parkman, Francis 1879, 'The Woman Question', *The North American Review*, 129(275): 303–21.

Perlman, Selig and Philip Taft 1935, *History of Labor in the United States, 1896–1932, Volume IV: Labor Movements*, New York: MacMillan.

Peterson, Florence 1971 [1938], *Strikes in the United States: 1880–1936*, Bureau of Labor Statistics, Bulletin No. 651, US Government Printing Office, Michigan: Scholarly Press.

Piven, Frances Fox and Richard Cloward May 2, 1966, 'The Weight of the Poor: A Strategy to End Poverty', *The Nation*, available at: https://www.thenation.com/article/weight -poor-strategy-end-poverty/

Piven, Frances Fox and Richard Cloward 1978, *Poor People's Movements: Why They Succeed, How They Fail*, New York: Vintage.

Politicalgraveyard.com, Index to Politicians, available at: http://politicalgraveyard.com/ bio/bowman.html#291.93.52

Porter, Glenn 1992, *The Rise of Big Business: 1860–1920*, Wheeling, IL: Harlan Davidson.

Pollock v. Farmers' Loan & Trust Company, 157 U.S. 429 [1895].

Pouget, Emile 1913, *Sabotage*, Chicago: Charles H. Kerr & Company.

President Harding, Warren G. 1921, 'Address of the President of the United States', *Journal of the Senate of the United States*, 67th Congress, 2nd Session, 8–12.

President Wilson, Woodrow 1917, 'Proclamation 1419 – Government Assumption of Control of Transportation Systems, By the President of the United States of America, A Proclamation', 26 December available at: http://www.presidency.ucsb.edu/ws/ ?pid=24412

Ramirez, Bruno 1974, 'US Responses to the Canadian Industrial Disputes Investigation Act', *Relations industrielles/Industrial Relations*, 29(3): 541–59.

Ramirez, Bruno 1978, *When Workers Fight: The Politics of Industrial Relations in the Progressive Era, 1898–1916*, Connecticut: Greenwood.

Rawick, George 1969, 'Working Class Self-Activity', *Radical America*, III(2): 23–31.

Ray, Gerda 1995, '"We Can Stay Until Hell Freezes Over": Strike Control and the State Police in New York, 1919–1923', *Labor History*, 36(3): 403–25.

Rocker, Rudolf 2004 [1938], *Anarcho-Syndicalism: Theory and Practice*, Oakland: AK Press.

Roediger, David 1994, *Toward the Abolition of Whiteness: Essays on Race, Politics, and Working Class History*, London: Verso.

Ross, Philip and Philip Taft 1969, 'American Labor Violence: Its Causes, Character, and Outcome', *The History of Violence in America: A Report to the National Commission on the Causes and Prevention of Violence*, edited by Hugh Davis Graham and Ted Robert Gurr, New York: F.A. Praeger.

Ross, Phil 1994, 'The Scotts Run Coalfield from the Great War to the Great Depression: A Study in Overdevelopment', *West Virginia History*, 53: 21–42.

Rubenstein, Richard E. 1970, *Rebels in Eden: Mass Political Violence in the United States*, Boston: Brown & Co.

Rubenstein, Richard E. 1989, 'Rebellion in America: The Fire Next Time?', in *Violence in America: Protest, Rebellion, Reform: Volume 2*, edited by Ted Robert Gurr, Newbury Park: Sage, 307–28.

Rubenstein, Richard E. n.d., 'Group Violence in America', Center for Conflict Analysis and Resolution, George Mason University, Working Paper 2.

Salvatore, Nick 1980, 'Railroad Workers and the Great Strike of 1877: A View from a Small Midwest City', *Labor History*, 21(4): 522–46.

Sandine, Al 2009, *The Taming of the American Crowd: From Stamp Riots to Shopping Sprees*, New York: Monthly Review Press.

Santa Clara County v. Southern Pacific R. Co. 118 US 394 [1886].

Savage, Lon 1990 [1985], *Thunder in the Mountains: The West Virginia Mine War 1920–21*, Pittsburgh: University of Pittsburgh Press.

Schenck v. United States 249 US 47 [1919].

Schneider, Nathan 2011, 'What "Diversity of Tactics" Really Means for Occupy Wall Street', 19 October, *Waging Non-violence*, available at: http://wagingnonviolence.org/ feature/what-diversity-of-tactics-really-means-for-occupy-wall-street/

Schofield, Ann 1984, 'The Women's March: Miners, Family, and Community in Pittsburg, Kansas, 1921–1922', *Kansas History: A Journal of the Central Plains*, 7(2): 159–68.

Scott, James, C. 1985, *Weapons of the Weak: Everyday Forms of Peasant Resistance*, New Haven: Yale.

Seattle Union Record 1919, 1–13 February, available at: https://depts.washington.edu/ labhist/strike/news.shtml

Self Negation n.d., 'Class Conflict and Workers' Self Activity on the Railroads: 1874–1895', *Libcom*, available at: https://libcom.org/history/class-conflict-workers-self-activity -railroads-1874-1895

Shakespeare, William 1606, *MacBeth*, available at: http://shakespeare.mit.edu/ macbeth/full.html

Sharp, Gene 2003, *There are Realistic Alternatives*, Boston: The Albert Einstein Institution.

Sharp, Gene 2005, *Waging Nonviolent Struggle: 20th Century Practice and 21st Century Potential*, Boston: Extending Horizons Books.

Shoup, Laurence 2010, *Rulers & Rebels: A People's History of Early California, 1769–1901*, New York: iUniverse.

Siemiatycki, Myer 1978, 'Munitions and Labour Militancy: The 1916 Hamilton Machinists' Strike', *Labour/Le Travail, Journal of Canadian Labour Studies/Revue d'Études*

Ouvrières Canadiennes, 3: 131–51, available at: http://www.lltjournal.ca/index.php/llt/article/view/2384

Silver, Beverly 2003, *Forces of Labor: Workers' Movements and Globalization Since 1870*, New York: Cambridge University Press.

Sims, Robert C. 1974, 'Idaho's Criminal Syndicalism Act: One State's Response to Radical Labor', *Labor History*, 15(4): 511–27.

Skolnick, Jerome 1969, *Politics of Protest: A Task Force Report Submitted to the National Commission on the Cause and Prevention of Violence under the Direction of Jerome H. Skolnick*, New York: Simon & Schuster.

Smith-Christmas, Kenneth 2014, 'Guns of the Battle of Blair Mountain', NRA *American Rifleman*, 13 March, available at: https://www.americanrifleman.org/articles/2014/3/13/guns-of-the-battle-of-blair-mountain/

Smith, Adam 1904 [1776], *An Inquiry into the Nature and Causes of the Wealth of Nations*, Chicago: University of Chicago Press.

Smith, Goldwin 1877, 'The Labor War in the United States', *The Contemporary Review*, xxx(June–November): 529–41.

Smith, Sharon 2006, *Subterranean Fire: A History of Working-Class Radicalism in the United States*, Chicago: Haymarket.

Smith, Walker C. n.d., *The Everett Massacre: A History of the Class Struggle in the Lumber Industry*, Chicago: IWW Publishing Bureau.

Smith, Walker C. 1917 [1913], *Sabotage: Its History, Philosophy & Function*, available at: http://www.iww.org/history/library/WCSmith/sabotage

Sparkes, Boyden n.d., 'Jack Dalton vs. Bill Blizzard: In These Two Leaders are Personified Conflicting Ideals', *Leslie's Weekly*, in 1997, *The West Virginia Mine Wars: An Anthology*, by David Alan Corbin, Martinsburg: Appalachian Editions, 127–32.

Special Investigation by the State of West Virginia, Hearings at Charleston, West Va. Sept. 30 and Oct. 1, 2, 1919, West Virginia State Archives, Logan Coal Operators Association Collection Ms90–82.

St. John, Vincent 1911, *Report of General Secretary-Treasurer Vincent St. John, Stenographic Report of the Sixth Convention of the IWW.*

St. John, Vincent 1913, *Report of General Secretary-Treasurer Vincent St. John, Stenographic Report of the Eighth Convention of the IWW.*

St. John, Vincent 1916, 'Testimony of Mr. Vincent St. John', *Final Report and Testimony Submitted to Congress by the Commission on Industrial Relations*, Volume 11, Washington DC: Government Printing Office, 1445–62.

Senate and House of Representatives of the Commonwealth of Pennsylvania 1878, *Report of the Committee Appointed to Investigate the Railroad Riots in July, 1877*, May 23, 1878, Leg. Doc. No. 29, Harrisburg: Lane S. Hart, State Printer.

Stephens, Glenn June 1995, 'Remodeling Collective Violence: James Tong's Rational Choice Model and the Great Strikes of 1877', *Political Research Quarterly*, 48(2): 345–69.

Stevens, William 1985, 'Police Drop Bomb on Radicals' Home in Philadelphia', *New York Times*, 14 May, available at: http://www.nytimes.com/1985/05/14/us/police-drop -bomb-on-radicals-home-in-philadelphia.html?pagewanted=all?

Stilley, Jeff 2017. 'August 11–12, 1917: when thousands of Kansas City citizens spent their weekend deporting professional strikebreakers', August 16, available at: https:// libcom.org/history/august-11-12-1917-when-thousands-kansas-city-citizens-spent -their-weekend-deporting-prof

Stone, Katherine 1973, 'The Origin of Job Structures in the Steel Industry', *Radical America*, 7(6): 19–66.

Stromquist, Shelton 1993, *A Generation of Boomers*, Urbana: University of Illinois Press.

Suggs, George 1972, *Colorado's War on Militant Unionism: James H. Peabody and the Western Federation of Miners*, Detroit: Wayne State University Press.

Sun Tzu 2009 [512 BC], *The Art of War*, Boston: Shambhala.

Swidowrski, Carl 2004, 'The Courts, the Labor Movement and the Struggle for Freedom of Expression an Association, 1919–1940', *Labor History*, 45(1): 61–84.

Taft, Philip 1966, 'Violence in American Labor Disputes', *The Annals of the American Academy of Political and Social Science*, 364(1): 127–40.

Taylor, Frederick W. 1911, *Principles of Scientific Management*, New York: Harper & Brothers Publishers.

The Last Pullman 1983, written by Jerry Blumenthal, Greg LeRoy, Gordon Quinn and Jenny Rohrer.

The Mine Wars 2016, directed by Randall MacLowry.

The Molly Maguires 1970, directed by Martin Ritt.

The Nation 1919, 'The Quest of Industrial Peace', 27 September, 109(2830): 425.

The Nation 1919, 'The Revolt of the Rank and File', 25 October, 109(2834): 540.

Thomas, Norman 1932, *As I See It*, New York: Macmillan Co.

Thompson, E.P. 1967, 'Time, Work-Discipline, and Industrial Capitalism', *Past and Present*, 38: 56–97.

Tilly, Charles 1977, 'Getting it together in Burgundy, 1675–1975', *Theory and Society*, 4(4): 479–504.

Tilly, Charles 1978, *From Mobilization to Revolution*, New York: McGraw Hill.

Tilly, Charles 1989, *Strikes, Wars, and Revolutions in International Perspective*, edited by Leopold Haimson and Charles Tilly, Cambridge: Cambridge University Press.

Tilly, Charles 2003, *Politics of Collective Violence*, New York: Cambridge University Press.

Tilly, Chris and Charles Tilly 1998, *Work Under Capitalism*, Boulder, CO: Westview.

Top Cat 1961–2, directed by William Hanna and Joseph Barbera.

Topeka State Journal 1921, 14 December.

Trachtenberg, Alexander 1920, *The American Labor Yearbook 1919–1920*, New York: Rand School of Social Science, 3.

Tronti, Mario 1962. 'La fabbrica e la società', *Quaderni Rossi*, 2: 1–31.

UE News 2002, 'The Great Strike of 1877: Remembering a Workers Rebellion', June available at: http://www.ranknfile-ue.org/uen_1877.html

Umoja, Akinyele Omowale 2013, *We Shoot Back: Armed Resistance in the Mississippi Freedom Movement*, New York: NYU Press.

Unionist.com, 'Today in Labor History, the Week of August 20th', available at: http://www.unionist.com/big-labour/today-in-labour-history. Accessed 19 December 2017.

United Mine Workers Journal 1933, 'Historic Convention Held by Miners of Four Southern States', 1 August.

United Mine Workers of America 1922, brief submitted to the Senate Committee on Education and Labor.

US v. Cassidy et al April 1 and 2, 1895, N.D. California, No. 3059, Federal Reporter, 67: 698–783.

United States Army Center of Military History 2006, 'Nelson Appleton Miles', 24 February, available at: http://www.history.army.mil/books/CG&CSA/Miles-NA.htm (last retrieved July 23, 2018).

United States Bituminous Coal Commission 1920, Majority and Minority Reports to the President, Washington DC: US Government Printing Office.

United States Department of Homeland Security 2011, 'Special Coverage: Occupy Wall Street', October, US Department of Homeland Security Information Network Critical Sectors, National Protection and Programs Directorate, Office of Infrastructure Protection.

United States Department of Labor 1961, 'Technological Change and Productivity in the Bituminous Coal Industry, Bulletin 1305', November, Washington DC: US Government Printing Office.

United States Commission on Industrial Relations 1916, *Final Report and Testimony Submitted to Congress by the Commission on Industrial Relations, Created by the Act of August 23, 1912,* Washington: Government Printing Office.

United States Code Annotated, Title 36, Chapter 21701–21708, The American Legion, Created by Act of Congress, Washington DC, on 16 September 1919.

United States Senate 2 March 1903, Federal Aid in Domestic Disturbances 1787–1903, Prepared under the direction of Major-General Henry Corbin, Adjutant-General, US Army, 57th Congress, 2nd Session, Document No. 209, Washington DC: Government Printing Office.

United States House of Representatives 27 January 1912, Special Committee of the House of Representatives to Investigate the Taylor and Other Systems of Shop Management. Hearings Testimony, 3: 1265–1938.

United State Senate 1921, West Virginia Coal Fields, Hearings Before the Committee of Education and Labor, July 14 to October 29, 1921, Senator William Kenyon, Chairman, 67th Congress, 1st Session, Washington DC: Government Printing Office, Volumes 1 and 2, available at: http://catalog.hathitrust.org/Record/008610716

United States Senate 1974, Committee on the Judiciary, Terroristic Activity: Hearings Before the Subcommittee to Investigate the Administration of the Internal Security Act and Other Internal Security Laws, of the Committee on the Judiciary, United States Senate, 93rd Congress, 2nd session, 94th Congress, 2nd session, Washington DC: US Government Printing Office, available at: http://catalog.hathitrust.org/Record/003217864

United States Strike Commission 1972 [1895], Report on the Chicago Strike of June–July 1894, Washington DC: Government Printing Office, Clifton, NJ: Augustus M. Kelly.

United States v. L. Cohen Grocery Company, 255 US 81 [1921].

Veblen, Thorstein 1921, The Engineers and the Price System, Kitchener: Batoche Books.

Viva Zapata! 1952, directed by Elia Kazan.

Walling, William English 1914, Progressivism and After, New York: Macmillan.

Walts, George W. 1893, Fifth Biennial Report of the Bureau of Labor Statistics of the State of California for the Years 1891–1892, Sacramento: State Office.

Warner, Arthur 1921, 'Fighting Unionism with Martial Law', The Nation, 12 October.

Watson, Bill 1971, 'Counter-Planning on the Shop Floor', Radical America: 77–85, available at: https://dl.lib.brown.edu/pdfs/112497585582936.pdf

West, Harold 1913, 'Civil War in the West Virginia Coal Mines', The Survey, 5 April, 37–50.

White, Ahmed 2006, 'The Crime of Economic Radicalism: Criminal Syndicalism Laws and the Industrial Workers of the World, 1917–1927', Oregon Law Review, 85(3): 649–761.

White, Richard n.d., 'The Rise of Industrial America, 1877–1900', Gilder Lehrman Institute of American History, available at: http://www.gilderlehrman.org/history-by-era/essays/rise-industrial-america-1877-1900

Williams, Robert F. 1964, 'USA: The Potential of a Minority Revolution', The Crusader, 5(4).

Williams, Robert F. 1965, 'USA: The Potential of a Minority Revolution, Part II', The Crusader, 7(1).

Wills, Garry 2010, Bomb Power: The Modern Presidency and the National Security State, New York: Penguin.

Winthrop, Col. W. 1901, A Digest of Opinions of the Judge-Advocates General of the Army, Revised edition, War Department, Document 137, Washington DC: Government Printing Office.

Witte, Edwin Emil 1969 [1932], The Government in Labor Disputes, New York: Arno & The New York Times.

Wright, Carroll 1894, 'The Chicago Strike, Paper read at the Seventh Annual Meeting of the American Economic Association, Columbia College, December 27, 1894', Publications of the American Economic Association, IX.

Yellowitz, Irwin Fall 1968, 'The Origins of Unemployment Reform in the United States', Labor History, 9(3): 338–60.

Yolen, Samuel 1980 [1936], *American Labor Struggles: 1877–1934*, New York: Pathfinder Press.

Zerzan, John 1999, 'Organized Labor vs. "the Revolt Against Work"', in *Elements of Refusal*, Columbia: C.A.L. Press: 185–198.

Zibechi, Raúl 2010, *Dispersing Power: Social Movements as Anti-State Forces*, Oakland: AK Press.

Zinn, Howard 2013 [2001], *A People's History of the United States: 1492 to the Present*, 3rd edn, New York: Routledge.

Index